The Minister's Manual

SEVENTY-NINTH ANNUAL ISSUE

THE MINISTER'S MANUAL
2004

Edited by

JAMES W. COX

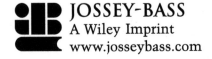

JOSSEY-BASS
A Wiley Imprint
www.josseybass.com

Editors of THE MINISTER'S MANUAL
G. B. F. Hallock, D.D., 1926–1958
M. K. W. Heicher, Ph.D., 1943–1968
Charles L. Wallis, M.A., M.Div., 1969–1983
James W. Cox, M.Div., Ph.D.

Translations of the Bible referred to and quoted from in this book may be indicated by their standard abbreviations, such as NRSV (New Revised Standard Version) and NIV (New International Version). In addition, some contributors have made their own translations and others have used a mixed text.

THE MINISTER'S MANUAL FOR 2004. Copyright © 2003 by James W. Cox.

Published by Jossey-Bass
A Wiley Imprint
989 Market Street, San Francisco, CA 94103-1741   www.josseybass.com

Jossey-Bass books and products are available through most bookstores. To contact Jossey-Bass directly call our Customer Care Department within the U.S. at 800-956-7739, outside the U.S. at 317-572-3986 or fax 317-572-4002.

Jossey-Bass also publishes its books in a variety of electronic formats. Some content that appears in print may not be available in electronic books.

Library of Congress Cataloging Card Number

25-21658
ISSN 0738-5323
ISBN 0-7879-6734-3

Printed in the United States of America
FIRST EDITION
HB Printing
10 9 8 7 6 5 4 3 2 1

CONTENTS

PREFACE

As I have indicated in previous volumes, *The Minister's Manual* presents sermonic contributions from a wide range of preachers, teachers, and writers, who come from many geographical, denominational, and theological backgrounds. Although the contributors do not always agree on every issue, they speak responsibly and their thoughts merit careful consideration. They share our common faith and enrich our personal understanding and devotion. Nevertheless, the contributors speak for themselves, and their views do not necessarily represent those of the publisher, the editor, or the Southern Baptist Theological Seminary.

To many individuals, I owe thanks for contributions, but one deserves my special gratitude. Professor Hugh T. McElrath, my longtime fellow student, friend, and colleague, began with me in producing *The Minister's Manual* in 1984 and continued annually through the 2003 edition with his articles on music and hymnody. His valuable influence continues through Paul A. Richardson, whom he recommended to succeed him in this 2004 edition.

I am grateful to the seminary, where I have taught since 1959, for providing valuable secretarial assistance in producing the manuscript. Again I wish to thank Linda Durkin for her faithful and efficient assistance and, for their aid in preparing this volume, Jessica Bates, Leah Finn, and Amy Whitfield. I also wish to thank the authors and publishers from whose works I have quoted. It is hoped that the rights and wishes of no one have been overlooked. Again, I am deeply grateful.

James W. Cox
The Southern Baptist Theological Seminary

SECTION I

GENERAL AIDS AND RESOURCES

CIVIL YEAR CALENDARS FOR 2004 AND 2005

2004

January
S M T W T F S
1 2 3
4 5 6 7 8 9 10
11 12 13 14 15 16 17
18 19 20 21 22 23 24
25 26 27 28 29 30 31

February
S M T W T F S
1 2 3 4 5 6 7
8 9 10 11 12 13 14
15 16 17 18 19 20 21
22 23 24 25 26 27 28
29

March
S M T W T F S
1 2 3 4 5 6
7 8 9 10 11 12 13
14 15 16 17 18 19 20
21 22 23 24 25 26 27
28 29 30 31

April
S M T W T F S
1 2 3
4 5 6 7 8 9 10
11 12 13 14 15 16 17
18 19 20 21 22 23 24
25 26 27 28 29 30

May
S M T W T F S
1
2 3 4 5 6 7 8
9 10 11 12 13 14 15
16 17 18 19 20 21 22
23 24 25 26 27 28 29
30 31

June
S M T W T F S
1 2 3 4 5
6 7 8 9 10 11 12
13 14 15 16 17 18 19
20 21 22 23 24 25 26
27 28 29 30

July
S M T W T F S
1 2 3
4 5 6 7 8 9 10
11 12 13 14 15 16 17
18 19 20 21 22 23 24
25 26 27 28 29 30 31

August
S M T W T F S
1 2 3 4 5 6 7
8 9 10 11 12 13 14
15 16 17 18 19 20 21
22 23 24 25 26 27 28
29 30 31

September
S M T W T F S
1 2 3 4
5 6 7 8 9 10 11
12 13 14 15 16 17 18
19 20 21 22 23 24 25
26 27 28 29 30

October
S M T W T F S
1 2
3 4 5 6 7 8 9
10 11 12 13 14 15 16
17 18 19 20 21 22 23
24 25 26 27 28 29 30
31

November
S M T W T F S
1 2 3 4 5 6
7 8 9 10 11 12 13
14 15 16 17 18 19 20
21 22 23 24 25 26 27
28 29 30

December
S M T W T F S
1 2 3 4
5 6 7 8 9 10 11
12 13 14 15 16 17 18
19 20 21 22 23 24 25
26 27 28 29 30 31

2005

January
S M T W T F S
1
2 3 4 5 6 7 8
9 10 11 12 13 14 15
16 17 18 19 20 21 22
23 24 25 26 27 28 29
30 31

February
S M T W T F S
1 2 3 4 5
6 7 8 9 10 11 12
13 14 15 16 17 18 19
20 21 22 23 24 25 26
27 28

March
S M T W T F S
1 2 3 4 5
6 7 8 9 10 11 12
13 14 15 16 17 18 19
20 21 22 23 24 25 26
27 28 29 30 31

April
S M T W T F S
1 2
3 4 5 6 7 8 9
10 11 12 13 14 15 16
17 18 19 20 21 22 23
24 25 26 27 28 29 30

May
S M T W T F S
1 2 3 4 5 6 7
8 9 10 11 12 13 14
15 16 17 18 19 20 21
22 23 24 25 26 27 28
29 30 31

June
S M T W T F S
1 2 3 4
5 6 7 8 9 10 11
12 13 14 15 16 17 18
19 20 21 22 23 24 25
26 27 28 29 30

July
S M T W T F S
1 2
3 4 5 6 7 8 9
10 11 12 13 14 15 16
17 18 19 20 21 22 23
24 25 26 27 28 29 30
31

August
S M T W T F S
1 2 3 4 5 6
7 8 9 10 11 12 13
14 15 16 17 18 19 20
21 22 23 24 25 26 27
28 29 30 31

September
S M T W T F S
1 2 3
4 5 6 7 8 9 10
11 12 13 14 15 16 17
18 19 20 21 22 23 24
25 26 27 28 29 30

October
S M T W T F S
1
2 3 4 5 6 7 8
9 10 11 12 13 14 15
16 17 18 19 20 21 22
23 24 25 26 27 28 29
30 31

November
S M T W T F S
1 2 3 4 5
6 7 8 9 10 11 12
13 14 15 16 17 18 19
20 21 22 23 24 25 26
27 28 29 30

December
S M T W T F S
1 2 3
4 5 6 7 8 9 10
11 12 13 14 15 16 17
18 19 20 21 22 23 24
25 26 27 28 29 30 31

Church and Civic Calendar for 2004

January

1	New Year's Day
5	Twelfth Night
6	Epiphany
10	League of Nations anniversary
11	Baptism of the Lord
17	St. Anthony's Day
19	Martin Luther King Jr.'s birthday, observed
25	Conversion of St. Paul

February

1	National Freedom Day
2	Presentation of Jesus in the Temple
12	Lincoln's Birthday
14	Race Relations Day St. Valentine's Day
16	President's Day
22	Washington's Birthday
24	St. Matthias, Apostle Shrove Tuesday
25	Ash Wednesday
29	First Sunday in Lent

March

7	Second Sunday in Lent Purim
14	Third Sunday in Lent
17	St. Patrick's Day
21	Fourth Sunday in Lent
25	The Annunciation
28	Fifth Sunday in Lent

April

4	Palm Sunday/Passion Sunday
4–10	Holy Week
6	Passover (Pesach)
8	Maundy Thursday
9	Good Friday
11	Easter
25	St. Mark, Evangelist

May

1	May Day Law Day Loyalty Day St. Philip and St. James, Apostles
1–5	Cinco de Mayo celebration
2–9	National Family Week
9	Mother's Day
20	Ascension Day
26	Shavuot
30	Pentecost
31	Memorial Day, observed

June

6	Trinity Sunday
11	St. Barnabas, Apostle
13	Children's Sunday Corpus Christi
20	Father's Day
24	St. John the Baptist
29	St. Peter and St. Paul, Apostles

July

1	Canada Day
4	Independence Day
22	St. Mary Magdalene
25	St. James, the Elder, Apostle

August

2	Civic Holiday (Canada)
14	Atlantic Charter Day
15	Mary, Mother of Jesus
24	St. Bartholomew, Apostle
26	Women's Equality Day

September

6	Labor Day
16	Rosh Hashanah (Jewish New Year)
21	St. Matthew, Evangelist and Apostle

25	Yom Kippur (Day of Atonement)	11	Armistice Day
			Veterans Day
29	St. Michael and All Angels		Remembrance Day (Canada)
30	First Day of Sukkot	14	Stewardship Day
		21	Bible Sunday
October		25	Thanksgiving Day
3	World Communion Sunday	28	First Sunday of Advent
		30	St. Andrew, Apostle
7	Shmini Atzeret		
11	Columbus Day observed	*December*	
15	First Day of Ramadan	5	Second Sunday of Advent
18	St. Luke, Evangelist	8	First Day of Hanukkah
23	St. James, Brother of Jesus	12	Third Sunday of Advent
24	United Nations Day	19	Fourth Sunday of Advent
28	St. Simon and St. Jude, Apostles	25	Christmas
		26	Boxing Day (Canada)
31	Reformation Day		St. Stephen, Deacon and Martyr
	National UNICEF Day	27	St. John, Evangelist and Apostle
November		28	The Holy Innocents, Martyrs
1	All Saints' Day	31	New Year's Eve
2	All Souls' Day		Watch Night

The Revised Common Lectionary for 2004

The following Scripture lessons are commended for use by various Protestant churches and the Roman Catholic Church and include first, second, and Gospel readings, and Psalms, according to Cycle C from January 4 to November 21 and according to Cycle A from November 28 to December 26.[1]

Jan. 4: Jer. 31:7–14; Ps. 147:12–20; Eph. 1:3–14; John 1:(1–9) 10–18

Epiphany Season

Jan. 6 (Epiphany): Isa. 60:1–6; Ps. 72:1–7, 10–14; Eph. 3:1–12; Matt. 2:1–12

Jan. 1–11 (Baptism of the Lord): Isa. 43:1–7; Ps. 29; Acts 8:14–17; Luke 3:15–17, 21–22

Jan. 18: Isa. 62:1–5; Ps. 36:5–10; 1 Cor. 12:1–11; John 2:1–11

Jan. 25: Neh. 8:1–3, 5–6, 8–10; Ps. 19; 1 Cor. 12:12–31a; Luke 4:14–21

Feb. 1: Jer. 1:4–10; Ps. 71:1–6; 1 Cor. 13:1–13; Luke 4:21–30

Feb. 8: Isa. 6:1–8 (9–13); Ps. 138; 1 Cor. 15:1–11; Luke 5:1–11

Feb. 15: Jer. 17:5–10; Ps. 1; 1 Cor. 15:12–20; Luke 6:17–26

Feb. 22 (Transfiguration Sunday): Gen. 45:3–11, 15; Ps. 37:1–11, 39–40; 1 Cor. 15:35–38, 42–50; Luke 6:27–38 or Exod. 34:29–35; Ps. 99; 2 Cor. 3:12–4:2; Luke 9:28–36 (37–43a)

---

[1]Copyright 1992, *Consultation on Common Texts.*

Lenten Season

Feb. 25 (Ash Wednesday): Joel 2:1–2, 12–17; Ps. 51:1–17; 2 Cor. 5:20b–6:10; Matt. 6:1–6, 16–21

Feb. 29: Deut. 26:1–11; Ps. 91:1–2, 9–16; Rom. 10:8b–13; Luke 4:1–13

Mar. 7: Gen. 15:1–12, 17–18; Ps. 27; Phil. 3:17–4:1; Luke 13:31–35

Mar. 14: Isa. 55:1–9; Ps. 63:1–8; 1 Cor. 10:1–13; Luke 13:1–9

Mar. 21: Josh. 5:9–12; Ps. 32; 2 Cor. 5:16–21; Luke 15:1–3, 11b–32

Mar. 28: Isa. 43:16–21; Ps. 126; Phil. 3:4b–14; John 12:1–8

Holy Week and Easter Season

Apr. 4 (Palm/Passion Sunday): Liturgy of the Palms—Luke 19:28–40; Ps. 118:1–2, 19–29; Liturgy of the Passion—Isa. 50:4–9a; Ps. 31:9–16; Phil. 2:5–11; Luke 22:14–23:56

Apr. 5 (Monday): Isa. 42:1–9; Ps. 36:5–11; Heb. 9:11–15; John 12:1–11

Apr. 6 (Tuesday): Isa. 49:1–7; Ps. 71:1–14; 1 Cor. 1:18–31; John 12:20–36

Apr. 7 (Wednesday): Isa. 50:4–9a; Ps. 70; Heb. 12:1–3; John 13:21–32

Apr. 8 (Holy Thursday): Exod. 12:1–4 (5–10), 11–14; Ps. 116:1–2, 12–19; 1 Cor. 11:23–26; John 13:1–7, 31b–35

Apr. 9 (Good Friday): Isa. 52:13–53:12; Ps. 22; Heb. 16–25; John 18:1–19:42

Apr. 10 (Holy Saturday): Job 14:1–14; Ps. 31:1–4, 15–16; 1 Pet. 4:1–8; Matt. 27:57–66

Apr. 10 (Easter Vigil): Gen. 1:1–2:4a; Ps. 136:1–9, 23–26; Gen. 7:1–5, 11–18; 8:6–18; 9:8–13; Ps. 46; Gen. 22:1–18; Ps. 16; Exod. 14:10–31; 15:20–21; Exod. 15:1b–13, 17–18 (resp.); Isa. 55:1–11; Isa. 12:2–6 (resp.); Prov. 8:1–8, 19–21, 9:4b–6 (alt.); Ps. 19; Ezek. 36:24–28; Ps. 42–43; Ezek. 37:1–14; Ps. 143; Zeph. 3:14–20; Ps. 98; Rom. 6:3–11; Ps. 114; Matt. 28:1–10

Apr. 11 (Easter): Isa. 65:17–25; Ps. 118:1–2, 14–24; Acts 10:34–43 or 1 Cor. 15:19–26; John 20:1–18

Apr. 18: Acts 5:27–32; Ps. 118:14–29; Rev. 1:4–8; John 20:19–31

Apr. 25: Acts 9:1–6 (7–20); Ps. 30; Rev. 5:11–14; John 21:1–19

May 2: Acts 9:36–43; Ps. 23; Rev. 7:9–17; John 10:22–30

May 9: Acts 11:1–18; Ps. 148; Rev. 21:1–6; John 13:31–35

May 16: Acts 16:9–15; Ps. 67; Rev. 21:10, 22–22:5; John 14:23–29

May 23: Acts 16:16–34; Ps. 97; Rev. 22:12–14, 16–17, 20–21; John 17:20–26

Season of Pentecost

May 30 (Pentecost): Acts 2:1–21 or Gen. 11:1–9; Ps. 104:24–34, 35b; Rom. 8:14–17; John 14:8–17 (25–27)

June 6 (Trinity): Prov. 8:1–4, 22–31; Ps. 8; Rom. 5:1–5; John 16:12–15

June 13: 1 Kings 21:1–10 (11–14), 15–21a; Ps. 5:1–8; Gal. 2:15–21; Luke 7:36–8:3

June 20: 1 Kings 19:1–4 (5–7), 8–15a; Ps. 42; Gal. 3:23–29; Luke 8:26–39

June 27: 2 Kings 2:1–2, 6–14; Ps. 77:1–2, 11–20; Gal. 5:1, 13–25; Luke 9:51–62

July 4: 2 Kings 5:1–14; Ps. 30; Gal. 6:(1–6) 7–16; Luke 10:1–11, 16–20

July 11: Amos 7:7–17; Ps. 82; Col. 1:1–14; Luke 10:25–37

July 18: Amos 8:1–12; Ps. 52; Col. 1:15–28; Luke 10:38–42

July 25: Hos. 1:2–10; Ps. 85; Col. 2:6–15 (16–19); Luke 11:1–13

Aug. 1: Hos. 11:1–11; Ps. 107:1–9, 43; Col. 3:1–11 (12–17); Luke 12:13–21
Aug. 8: Isa. 1:1, 10–20; Ps. 50:1–8, 22–23; Heb. 11:1–3, 8–16; Luke 12:32–40
Aug. 15: Isa. 5:1–7; Ps. 80:1–2, 8–19; Heb. 11:29–12:2; Luke 12:49–56
Aug. 22: Jer. 1:4–10; Ps. 71:1–6; Heb. 12:18–29; Luke 13:10–17
Aug. 29: Jer. 2:4–13; Ps. 81:1, 10–16; Heb. 13:1–8, 15–16; Luke 14:1, 7–14
Sept. 5: Jer. 18:1–11; Ps. 139:1–6, 13–18; Philem. 1–21; Luke 14:25–33
Sept. 12: Jer. 4:11–12, 22–28; Ps. 14; 1 Tim. 1:12–17; Luke 15:1–10
Sept. 19: Jer. 8:18–9:1; Ps. 79:1–9; 1 Tim. 2:1–7; Luke 16:1–13
Sept. 26: Jer. 32:1–3a, 6–15; Ps. 91:1–6, 14–16; 1 Tim. 6:6–19; Luke 16:19–31
Oct. 3: Lam. 1:1–6; Ps. 137; 2 Tim. 1:1–14; Luke 17:5–10
Oct. 10: Jer. 29:1, 4–7; Ps. 66:1–12; 2 Tim. 2:8–15; Luke 17:11–19
Oct. 17: Jer. 31:27–34; Ps. 119:97–104; 2 Tim. 3:14–4:5; Luke 18:1–8
Oct. 24: Joel 2:23–32; Ps. 65; 2 Tim. 4:6–8, 16–18; Luke 18:9–14
Oct. 31: Hab. 1:1–4, 2:1–4; Ps. 119:137–144; 2 Thess. 1:1–4, 11–12; Luke 19:1–10
Nov. 7: Hag. 1:15b–2:9; Ps. 145:1–5, 17–21; 2 Thess. 2:1–5, 13–17; Luke 20:27–38
Nov. 14: Isa. 65:17–25; Isa. 12; 2 Thess. 3:6–13; Luke 21:5–19
Nov. 21 (Christ the King): Jer. 23:1–6; Luke 1:68–79; Col. 1:11–20; Luke 23:33–43

Advent and Christmas Season

Nov. 28: Isa. 2:1–5; Ps. 122; Rom. 13:11–14; Matt. 24:36–44
Dec. 5: Isa. 11:1–10; Ps. 72:1–7, 18–19; Rom. 15:4–13; Matt. 3:1–12
Dec. 12: Isa. 35:1–10; Luke 1:47–55; James 5:7–10; Matt. 11:2–11
Dec. 19: Isa. 7:10–16; Ps. 80:1–7, 17–19; Rom. 1:1–7; Matt. 1:18–25
Dec. 25 (Christmas Day): Isa. 9:2–7; Ps. 96; Titus 2:11–14; Luke 2:1–14 (15–20)
Dec. 26: Isa. 63:7–9; Ps. 148; Heb. 2:10–18; Matt. 2:13–23

Four-Year Church Calendar

	2004	2005	2006	2007
Ash Wednesday	February 25	February 9	March 1	February 21
Palm Sunday	April 4	March 20	April 9	April 1
Good Friday	April 9	March 25	April 14	April 6
Easter	April 11	March 27	April 16	April 8
Ascension Day	May 20	May 5	May 25	May 17
Pentecost	May 30	May 15	June 4	May 27
Trinity Sunday	June 6	May 22	June 11	June 3
Thanksgiving	November 25	November 24	November 23	November 22
Advent Sunday	November 28	November 27	December 3	December 2

Forty-Year Easter Calendar

2004 April 11	2014 April 20	2024 March 31	2034 April 9
2005 March 27	2015 April 5	2025 April 20	2035 March 25
2006 April 16	2016 March 27	2026 April 5	2036 April 13
2007 April 8	2017 April 16	2027 March 28	2037 April 5
2008 March 23	2018 April 1	2028 April 16	2038 April 25
2009 April 12	2019 April 21	2029 April 1	2039 April 10

2010 April 4	2020 April 12	2030 April 21	2040 April 1
2011 April 24	2021 April 4	2031 April 13	2041 April 2
2012 April 8	2022 April 17	2032 March 28	2042 April 6
2013 March 31	2023 April 9	2033 April 17	2043 March 29

Traditional Wedding Anniversary Identifications

1 Paper	7 Wool	13 Lace	35 Coral
2 Cotton	8 Bronze	14 Ivory	40 Ruby
3 Leather	9 Pottery	15 Crystal	45 Sapphire
4 Linen	10 Tin	20 China	50 Gold
5 Wood	11 Steel	25 Silver	55 Emerald
6 Iron	12 Silk	30 Pearl	60 Diamond

Colors Appropriate for Days and Seasons

White. Symbolizes purity, perfection, and joy and identifies festivals marking events in the life of Jesus, except Good Friday: Christmas, Epiphany, Easter, Eastertide, Ascension Day; also Trinity Sunday, All Saints' Day, weddings, funerals. Gold may also be used.

Red. Symbolizes the Holy Spirit, martyrdom, and the love of God: Good Friday, Pentecost, and Sundays following.

Violet. Symbolizes penitence: Advent, Lent.

Green. Symbolizes mission to the world, hope, regeneration, nurture, and growth: Epiphany season, Kingdomtide, Rural Life Sunday, Labor Sunday, Thanksgiving Sunday.

Blue. Advent, in some churches.

Flowers in Season Appropriate for Church Use

January: carnation or snowdrop	July: larkspur or water lily
February: violet or primrose	August: gladiolus or poppy
March: jonquil or daffodil	September: aster or morning star
April: lily, sweet pea, or daisy	October: calendula or cosmos
May: lily of the valley or hawthorn	November: chrysanthemum
June: rose or honeysuckle	December: narcissus, holly, or poinsettia

Quotable Quotations

1. Although the world is full of suffering, it is also full of the overcoming of it. —Helen Keller
2. Love your neighbor, yet pull not down your hedge.—George Herbert
3. Christ has turned all our sunsets into dawn.—Clement of Alexandria (c. 150–215).
4. We first make our habits, and then our habits make us.—John Dryden
5. We don't go to church, we *are* the church.—Ernest Southcott
6. Is prayer your steering wheel or your spare tire?—Corrie Ten Boom
7. It is nearly always easier to make $1,000,000 honestly than to dispose of it wisely.—Julius Rosenwald

8. Patience is power; with time and patience the mulberry leaf becomes silk.
   —Chinese proverb

9. Religion is a way of walking, not a way of talking.—William R. Inge

10. God draws, but he draws the willing.—John Chrysostom (c. 347–407)

11. It is remarkable with what Christian fortitude and resignation we can bear the suffering of other folks.—Jonathan Swift

12. Opporchunity knocks at ivry man's dure wanst. On some men's dures it hammers till it breaks down th' dure an' thin it goes in an' wakes him up if he's asleep, an' iver aftherward it wurruks f'r him as a night-watchman.—Finley Peter Dunne, *Mr. Dooley's Opinions* (1901)

13. We steal if we touch tomorrow. It is God's.—Henry Ward Beecher

14. Baloney is the unvarnished lie laid on so thick you hate it. Blarney is flattery laid on so thin you love it.—Bishop Fulton J. Sheen

15. There are two kinds of people: those who say to God, "Thy will be done," and those to whom God says, "All right, then, have it your way."—C. S. Lewis

16. The most pleasant and useful persons are those who have some of the problems of the universe for God to worry about.—Don Marquis

17. Keep your eyes wide open before marriage, half shut afterwards.—Benjamin Franklin

18. Success in marriage is more than finding the right person: it is a matter of being the right person.—Rabbi B. R. Brickner

19. God does not die on the day when we cease to believe in a personal deity; but we die on the day when our lives cease to be illuminated by the steady radiance renewed daily, of a wonder, the source of which is beyond all reason.
    —Dag Hammarskjöld

20. Nothing is good for him for whom nothing is bad.—Baltasar Gracián

21. No one is rich enough to do without a neighbor.—Danish Proverb

22. Faith is to believe what you do not yet see; the reward for this faith is to see what you believe.—Augustine of Hippo (354–430)

23. To conquer oneself is a greater task than conquering others.—Buddha

24. Make the best use of what is in your power, and take the rest as it happens.
    —Epictetus

25. Christianity promises to make men free; it never promises to make them independent.—William R. Inge

26. Wherever we see the Word of God purely preached and heard, there a church of God exists, even if it swarms with many faults.—John Calvin (1509–1564)

27. There are a thousand hacking at the branches of evil to one who is striking at the root.—Henry David Thoreau

28. The measure of any man's virtue is what he would do if he had neither the law nor public opinion, nor even his own prejudices to control him.—William Hazlitt

29. We do better to adore the mysteries of deity than to investigate them.—Philip Melanchthon (1497–1560)

30. The Christian should resemble a fruit tree! For the gaudy decorations of a Christmas tree are only tied on, whereas fruit grows on a fruit tree.—John Stott

31. People who fight fire with fire usually end up with ashes.—Abigail Van Buren

32. Character consists of what you do on the third and fourth tries.—James A. Michener
33. Suddenly I heard the words of Christ and understood them, and life and death ceased to seem to me evil, and instead of despair I experienced happiness and the joy of life undisturbed by death.—Leo Tolstoy, *What I Believe*
34. I have come to the conclusion that politics are too serious a matter to be left to the politicians.—Charles de Gaulle, President of France
35. Whoever is spared personal pain must feel himself called to help in diminishing the pain of others.—Dr. Albert Schweitzer
36. I now perceive one immense omission in my psychology—the deepest principle of human nature is the *craving to be appreciated.*—William James
37. Courage is as often the outcome of despair as of hope; in the one case we have nothing to lose; in the other, everything to gain.—Diane de Poitiers
38. The first casualty when war comes is truth.—Hiram Johnson
39. The only time people dislike gossip is when you gossip about them.—Will Rogers
40. When one door of happiness closes, another opens; but often we look so long at the closed door that we do not see the one which has been opened for us. —Helen Keller
41. People who think that once they are converted all will be happy, have forgotten Satan.—Martin Lloyd Jones
42. If the creator had a purpose in equipping us with a neck, he surely meant us to stick it out.—Arthur Koestler
43. Those who never retract their opinions love themselves more than they love the truth.—Joseph Joubert
44. In war, there are no unwounded soldiers.—José Narosky
45. Half the misery in the world comes of want of courage to speak and to hear the truth plainly, and in a spirit of love.—Harriet Beecher Stowe
46. However just your words, you spoil everything when you speak them with anger. —John Chrysostom (c. 347–407)
47. Hope is necessary in every condition. The miseries of poverty, sickness, of captivity, would, without this comfort, be insupportable.—Samuel Johnson
48. I can see, and that is why I can be so happy, in what you call the dark, but which to me is golden. I can see a God-made world, not a man-made world.—Helen Keller
49. Art is the stored honey of the human soul, gathered on wings of misery and travail.—Theodore Dreiser
50. A man may go to Heaven with half the pains which it costs him to purchase Hell. —Henry Fielding
51. One can believe in God with a very complete set of arguments, yet not have any faith that makes a difference in living.—Georgia Harkness
52. When the well is dry, we know the worth of water.—Benjamin Franklin

Questions of Life and Religion

1. What are some logical and practical reasons for omitting certain things from our everyday living?
2. How do we get our convictions about right and wrong?

3. In what ways is adolescence a critical time in life?
4. What did Jesus say and do about adultery?
5. Is affirmation important in the building of character?
6. What role can adversity play in the building of character?
7. Does the word *love* need better definition today?
8. How can our doubts about God and religion be solved?
9. Is anger ever appropriate?
10. Is absolute atheism really possible?
11. What and where are the sources of authority for the way we live?
12. Why is baptism important in our Christian experience and practice?
13. Does art contribute to our religious experience?
14. Can belief be coerced?
15. How can one find strength and comfort in a time of bereavement?
16. Why does the Bible have a unique place in personal and corporate life?
17. How can the human body be called the temple of God?
18. What are some creative cures for boredom?
19. How does the call to Christian service happen?
20. Is burden-bearing a virtue?
21. What is the difference between certainty and certitude?
22. How is character formed?
23. How is our practice of charity related to the biblical teaching of *agape* (love)?
24. In what ways can children teach us important lessons about our relationship to God?
25. Do we have a real choice about our relationship to God?
26. Has Christianity as a part of history ever made bad decisions and moves?
27. What can we do to make Christmas more reflective of our faith?
28. What is the Church?
29. How can church and state remain separate and yet each contribute appropriately to the other?
30. What are the possible religious duties of good citizenship?
31. Is religion a vital element in civilization?
32. Are class distinctions possible or allowable in a true Christian community?
33. In what ways do we need and can we get comfort from our religion?
34. How are the Ten Commandments relevant to life today?
35. What valuable purposes does Holy Communion serve?
36. Why does the individual believer need the community of fellow believers?
37. How can we embody more of the compassion of Jesus Christ in our daily living?
38. What are the sources of guidance for our conduct in Christian living?
39. In what various ways can we confess our faith?
40. When we are timid and anxious, how can we build our confidence?
41. What are the truly Christian ways of resolving conflict?
42. Is it sometimes necessary to break out of the mold of conformity in order to do what is right?
43. What are the ingredients of a creatively functioning congregation?
44. Is conscience always a safe guide? If not, why not?

45. What consolation can we find for our losses in life?
46. How can dedicated contemplation help us to deal with the everyday mundane challenges of living?
47. Can we ever settle down to contentment?
48. What makes conversion possible and lasting?
49. Where do we get our convictions?
50. When does cooperation become difficult, if not impossible?
51. What are the sources of courage to face all kinds of conditions?
52. How can covetousness be a disturber of harmonious living?

Biblical Benedictions and Blessings

The Lord watch between me and thee when we are absent from one another.—Gen. 31:49

The Lord our God be with us, as he was with our fathers; let him not leave us nor forsake us; that he may incline our hearts unto him, to walk in all his ways and to keep his commandments and his statutes and his judgments, which he commanded our fathers.—1 Kings 8:57–58

Let the words of my mouth and the meditation of my heart be acceptable in thy sight, O Lord, my strength and my redeemer.—Ps. 19:14

Now the God of patience and consolation grant you to be like-minded one toward another according to Christ Jesus; that ye may with one mind and one mouth glorify God, even the Father of our Lord Jesus Christ. Now the God of hope fill you with all joy and peace in believing, that ye may abound in hope, through the power of the Holy Ghost. Now the God of peace be with you.—Rom. 15:5–6, 13, 33

Now to him that is of power to establish you according to my Gospel and the teaching of Jesus Christ, according to the revelation of the mystery, which was kept secret since the world began but now is manifest, and by the Scriptures of the prophets, according to the commandments of the everlasting God, made known to all nations for the glory through Jesus Christ forever.—Rom. 16:25–27

Grace be unto you, and peace, from God our Father, and from the Lord Jesus Christ.—1 Cor. 1:3

The grace of the Lord Jesus Christ and the love of God and the communion of the Holy Ghost be with you all.—2 Cor. 13:14

Peace be to the brethren, and love with faith, from God the Father and the Lord Jesus Christ. Grace be with all them that love our Lord Jesus Christ in sincerity.—Eph. 6:23–24

And the peace of God, which passeth all understanding, shall keep your hearts and minds through Christ Jesus. Finally, brethren, whatsoever things are true, whatsoever things are honest, whatsoever things are just, whatsoever things are pure, whatsoever things are lovely, whatsoever things are of good report; if there be any virtue, and if there be any praise, think on these things. Those things which ye have both learned and received, and heard and seen in me, do; and the God of peace shall be with you.—Phil. 4:7–9

Wherefore also we pray always for you, that our God would count you worthy of this calling and fulfill all the good pleasure of this goodness, and the work of faith with power; that the name of our Lord Jesus Christ may be glorified in you, and ye in him, according to the grace of our God and the Lord Jesus Christ.—2 Thess. 1:11–12

Now the Lord of peace himself give you peace always by all means. The Lord be with you all. The grace of our Lord Jesus Christ be with you all.—2 Thess. 3:16–18

Grace, mercy, and peace, from God our Father and Jesus Christ our Lord.—1 Tim. 1:2

Now the God of peace, that brought again from the dead our Lord Jesus, that great shepherd of the sheep, through the blood of the everlasting covenant, make you perfect in every good work to do his will, working in you that which is well-pleasing in his sight, through Jesus Christ, to whom be glory for ever and ever.—Heb. 13:20–21

The God of all grace, who hath called us unto his eternal glory by Christ Jesus, after that ye have suffered a while, make you perfect, establish, strengthen, settle you. To him be glory and dominion for ever and ever. Greet ye one another with a kiss of charity. Peace be with you all that are in Christ Jesus.—1 Pet. 3:10–14

Grace be with you, mercy, and peace from God the Father, and from the Lord Jesus Christ, the Son of the Father, in truth and love.—2 John 3

Now unto him that is able to keep you from falling, and to present you faultless before the presence of his glory with exceeding joy, to the only wise God our Savior, be glory and majesty, dominion and power, both now and ever.—Jude 24:25

Grace be unto you, and peace, from him which was, and which is to come; and from the seven Spirits which are before his throne; and from Jesus Christ, who is the faithful witness, and the first begotten of the dead, and the prince of the kings of the earth. Unto him that loved us, and washed us from our sins in his own blood, and hath made us kings and priests unto God and his Father, to him be glory and dominion for ever and ever.—Rev. 1:4–6

SECTION II

SERMONS AND HOMILETIC AND WORSHIP AIDS FOR FIFTY-TWO SUNDAYS

SUNDAY, JANUARY 4, 2004
Lectionary Message

Topic: In the Fullness of Time

TEXT: Eph. 1:3–14

Other Readings: Jer. 31:7–14; Ps. 147:12–20; John 1:(1–9) 10–18

I. *We all want to be part of something important.*

(a) People rise before dawn to stand outside the windows of the New York studios where the early morning network programs are broadcast. Just being there, a few feet and a plate glass window away from the movie stars and the global leaders who are being interviewed live on national television, or standing a few feet away from the celebrity anchorman as he works the crowd, gives a bystander a sense of importance.

(b) Tom Brokaw called his book *The Greatest Generation* because everyone alive during World War II had a part in something significant. From the GI on the beaches of Normandy to Rosie who riveted together the tanks to the schoolgirl who saved her nickels to buy war bonds, all were caught up in something greater than themselves that determined the course of history.

II. *The human spirit needs to be part of something important, something bigger than itself.*

(a) One of the most debilitating things that can happen to a person is to think his or her life does not mean much. We have heard about the abuses of the welfare system. We have heard tales of welfare queens and deadbeat dads. But statistics prove that most welfare recipients do not like being on the dole. They do their best to get off it as soon as they can because all of us have a basic need to feel like we're making a contribution.

(b) One of the greatest challenges of aging is to find purpose in life even as your capacities slow down. One of the saddest things you hear if you spend much time in nursing homes is the lament, "I'm no good to anybody anymore."

III. *The wonderful news of the gospel is that in Jesus Christ every one of us is part of something that has cosmic significance.*

(a) Listen to how the book of Ephesians opens. Listen to what you are part of in Jesus (Eph. 1:3–5):

> The God and Father of our Lord Jesus Christ . . . chose us in Christ before the foundations of the world to be holy and blameless before him in love. . . . He has made known to us the mystery of his will . . . as a plan for the fullness of time, to gather up all things in him, things in heaven and things on earth . . . having been destined according to the purpose of him who accomplishes all things according to his counsel and will.

12

(b) What we are part of in Christ is nothing less than his work of putting the whole creation back together. Heaven and earth, with all their brokenness, their failures, their pains, their disappointments, are healed, restored, given a new start. The prophet Isaiah in the Old Testament describes the goal toward which we're pressing as that time when everything we consider inevitable will be reversed, when even the most basic enmities will be abolished. "The wolf shall live with the lamb, the leopard shall lie down with the kid, the calf and the lion and the fatling together."

(c) When Jesus was born in Bethlehem, God began to restore creation to the way God intended it to be. Listen to how the book of Revelation describes the work of which we're a part (Rev. 21:1–4):

> Then I saw a new heaven and a new earth; for the first heaven and the first earth had passed away, and the sea was no more. And I saw the holy city, the new Jerusalem, coming down out of heaven from God, prepared as a bride adorned for her husband. And I heard a loud voice from the throne saying, "See, the home of God is among mortals. He will dwell with them as their God; they will be his people, and God himself will be with them; he will wipe every tear from their eyes. Death will be no more; mourning and crying and pain will be no more, for the first things have passed away."

IV. *We participate in Christ's cosmic work as we practice our faith.*

(a) That is an overwhelming task to be given. Of course it is not something God expects you or me to do by the end of next week. We are no more expected to bring in the Kingdom of God by ourselves than the members of the so-called Greatest Generation were expected to defeat Hitler and turn back Tojo single-handedly. But you and I, each one of us, is part of that great endeavor.

(b) You and I bear witness to that work, and we carry it out every time we do as Christ commanded us.

1. When we gather to worship, we get insights into what it will be like when heaven and earth are reunited. On those Sunday mornings when the music leaves you speechless, when you hear words that comfort and inspire, when your prayers draw you into the very heart of God—these are glimpses of what awaits us when our work here is done.

2. When we care for others in the name of Christ, when we spend time with an elderly friend in a nursing home, when we tutor a child at the settlement house, when instead of indulging ourselves we give to help flood victims in Venezuela or build a church in Taiwan—these are ways we show the world that something great is going on all around us.

3. There are times you may not be able to see it because of the greed and selfishness and violence that permeate this life. But every time we worship or teach a child or care for one in need, we take one step toward that day when the redemption of creation will be complete—Stephens G. Lytch

ILLUSTRATIONS

RESTORING CREATION.   Richard Mouw, president of Fuller Theological Seminary, describes how even sheep, those lowliest of creatures, have a stake in what we're about as part of Christ's work to restore the creation to its original glory:

Ever since the Garden of Eden, [lambs] have had a fairly miserable existence. Right around the time when Adam and Eve ate the forbidden fruit, I expect that there was a lamb, not too far away in the Garden, who was cuddled up against a wolf. All was going well, as was usual in that pre-fallen state, between the lamb and the wolf, and the lamb was feeling very secure. Then suddenly the wolf stirred like it had never stirred before and the lamb noticed a strange look in the wolf's eye. For the first time in its life, the lamb felt a primal fear fill its whole being. And then the lamb gave in to a strange new instinct: terrorized, it began to run away. Quickly, the wolf growled and began to chase the lamb. And ever since that moment, wolves have been chasing lambs.[1]

CHRISTIANITY'S BALANCE SHEET.   Martin Marty, professor emeritus of church history at the University of Chicago, recently wrote a millennial balance sheet on Christianity:

From a handful of followers who first heard the teachings of Jesus to the 2.2 billion members of various denominations alive today, Christians were to be a force to heal and transform the world. And after 2,000 years of believing, Christians comprise 33.1 percent of the world's population.

But beyond numbers, exactly how successful has this faith been? . . . If Jesus were to return to Earth today, would he recognize his teachings as preached and practiced by his followers through the ages? To answer such questions, friends or foes of Christianity would say, "Let's look at the record." What would a balance sheet turn up?

Any individual who has been lifted from despair to hope, moved from hate to love, or vaulted from doubt to faith is likely to judge the twenty centuries of Christianity as worthwhile. So would any company of believers who have been sustained in slavery, oppressed because of race or gender or class, and then . . . experienced liberation.

Anyone who has experienced healing, received solace when the candle burns low or the life of a dear one ebbs, or . . . been inspired or intellectually moved when the faith elicits art or makes sense will use that experience to do the measuring.[2]

SERMON SUGGESTIONS

Topic: When God Restores His People
TEXT: Jer. 31:7–14

Homecoming is not only for ancient Israel but also for God's people in any age. (1) As a loving Father and as a shepherd, God will lead his people. (2) God's providence is more significant than the strength of his people's enemies. (3) God's people will at least rejoice in the abundance of God's goodness.

Topic: Special Destiny
TEXT: Eph. 1:3–6, 15–18

God chose us (1) to be holy and blameless in his sight (v. 4); (2) to be his sons and daughters (v. 5); and (3) to know his purpose for us (vv. 17–18).

---

[1]Richard Mouw, "The Sheep in Bethlehem," *Perspectives*, Dec. 1999, p. 24.
[2]"A Millennial Balance Sheet on Christianity," distributed by Religion News Service, Copyright 1999 MSNBC.com.

WORSHIP AIDS

CALL TO WORSHIP.   "Praise ye the Lord. Praise the Lord, O my soul. While I live will I praise the Lord: I will sing praises unto my God while I have any being" (Ps. 146:1–2).

INVOCATION.   Lord of the ages, let this be the year when we open ourselves to God as never before, when we feed on the Word, walk in ways of righteousness, and serve the Lord with unhindered gladness.—E. Lee Phillips

OFFERTORY SENTENCE.   "And whatsoever ye do in word or deed, do all in the name of the Lord Jesus, giving thanks to God and the Father by him" (Col. 3:17).

OFFERTORY PRAYER.   Lord, let our giving this year match our faith, so that risk joins belief in an epiphany of praise.—E. Lee Phillips

PRAYER.   God, our Father, as the New Year looms before us, we know that we shall be faced with both routines and surprises. Our faithfulness in doing our duties and our courage in taking on new tasks will challenge us all along the way.

You have promised that you will never leave us or forsake us. But we know that things happen that sometimes seem to cast doubt on that promise. Help us in such circumstances to trust when we cannot understand, and to continue to sing your praises even in the darkest hours.

This very hour could be for some of us a time of life-changing decisions that will open doors to new ventures and to new successes measured by your standards of achievement. May your Holy Spirit strengthen even our faintest inclinations to serve you, and help us daily to do your will. Through Jesus Christ our Lord, who loved us and gave himself for us. —James W. Cox

SERMON
Topic: Our God—Known, Loved, and Served
TEXT: Acts 17:16–30

For those of us living in this age and in this culture, the possibility of hearing the good news for the first time simply isn't possible.

But what is interesting—and very important—to remember is that no matter when knowledge of Christ was shared, it was always in an environment of partiality and judgment.

This is exactly what we witness in the passage from the Book of Acts. We watch a group of people take in the truth of the gospel for the very first time in a very guarded way.

Just as Jerusalem served as the heart of the Church and a symbol of salvation history, and just as Rome represented the center of imperial power, Athens was held up as the axis of pagan thought and Hellenistic religiosity. It was the place to be if you were anyone of intellectual importance in the Gentile world.

"Athenians," Paul states with great care and deference, "I see how extremely religious you are in every way. I see that your idols are everywhere . . . but," and here we watch him move from a spirit of respectful flattery to that of Christian teaching, ". . . I found among them an altar with the inscription, 'to an unknown god.'"

Seeing those Athenians surrounded by so many self-created idols troubled Paul greatly, not simply because he wanted their faith to mirror his own but rather because he knew such efforts resulted in only futile waste and worry. Yes, to know God is possible, Paul is telling those pagans, for it is "in God we live and move and have our being."

Demonstrating that it is through creation, the Word, and the person of Jesus Christ that we come to know the reality of God's presence in this world, Paul shows that in Christianity there is no such thing as an "unknown God." On the contrary, there is a God to be known, to be loved, and to be served.

Paul's Jewish background makes the knowledge of God an intimately transforming process, as in the phrase "to know in the biblical sense," requiring not only belief in God but also engagement with God, as one learns from the revelation in Christ and applies the knowledge to daily living. A god who is known is not just a solitary intellectual concept. It is a creative, dynamic relationship that influences all of life.

Christians understand that, as described in Paul's Letter to the Ephesians (5.2), they are to "live a life of love, just as Christ loved us," following the command of Jesus himself that we are to "love one another" (John 13:34).

The same can certainly be said about the meaning of service. The frequent appearance of the words *serve, servant,* and *service* in both the Old and New Testaments shows that knowledge of God requires the devotion of our hands as well as our hearts and minds.

Integrating belief with action, the truth of the gospel requires one to be subservient to God, making it impossible for one's own ideas and idols to be gods themselves. With these teachings, with this so-called "good news," Paul was treading a fine line.

"Athenians, I see how religious you are in every way," he says to that crowd gathered in front of the Areopagus. "I see your idols and self-serving spirituality everywhere I turn. Let me set you free from these futile efforts through true faith in God. Let me help you know and love and serve the one who created the world and all of us in it."

Yet no matter where we go to try to understand God's message, no matter where we turn to seek God's ultimate truth, we must trust that Christ is there, that Christ is here, waiting to reveal the grace and mercy and loving nature of God.—Lael P. Murphy

SUNDAY, JANUARY 11, 2004
Lectionary Message

Topic: Caught Up in the Spirit
TEXT: Acts 8:14–17
Other Readings: Isa. 43:1–7; Ps. 29; Luke 3:15–17, 21–22

I. *The Spirit gives us power to do Christ's work.* If you know anything about sports, you know how important spirit is. Whenever archrivals play each other in basketball, records, predictions, and even National Collegiate Athletic Association injunctions go out the window. It's the spirit that rules the game.

But there's an even more powerful Spirit. Without it a church is like a car without a motor. It might look good, but it's not much use. This is the Holy Spirit that God gives us to do the work of Christ.

II. *There is something mysterious, unknown, and sometimes threatening about the Holy Spirit.* Maybe it is because we have so little control over the Holy Spirit that from time to time there is controversy about the Spirit in the Church. There are some who believe that you are not truly a Christian unless you have the gift of the Holy Spirit, and that you do not have the gift of the Holy Spirit unless you utter ecstatic sounds in worship, a practice called speaking in tongues. We all know of churches that have split because some had the gift and others did not. Those who spoke in tongues did not want to worship with those who did not, and vice versa.

More common than churches that get overwhelmed by the Spirit are those that know hardly a thing about the Holy Spirit. A man was visiting a church and was so moved by the sermon and the music that he stood up in the middle of the service and started shouting, "Amen! Alleluia!" One of the ushers came over and told him to sit down and be quiet. "We don't do that in this church," the usher said. The visitor said, "But I've got the Spirit." The usher replied, "Well, you didn't get it here. So be quiet."

III. *When someone is baptized in the name of the Father and the Son and the Holy Spirit, God pours out the Holy Spirit on that person.* Many of us have never given much thought to the fact that the Holy Spirit dwells within us. We know we love Jesus. We trust in him and try to do his will. But we never really think that the Holy Spirit is in us. Yet Romans 8:9 says this about those who belong to Christ: "You are in the Spirit since the Spirit of God dwells in you. Anyone who does not have the Spirit of Christ does not belong to him."

So if you belong to Christ, you have the Spirit. The way you know someone has the Spirit is by the way he or she relates to God and others. Galatians 5:22 says that the fruit of the Spirit is love, joy, peace, patience, kindness, generosity, faithfulness, gentleness, and self-control. There are times when we feel the Spirit more strongly than others, but the Bible assures us that when we belong to Christ, the Spirit is in us, whether we feel very emotional about it or not.

IV. *The Holy Spirit may or may not give us an emotional high.* Some have had moments that were obviously turning points, when they felt God's power flowing through them in a way they had never felt before and have never felt since. Sometimes they wonder why they don't have those mountaintop experiences more often. They wonder if there is something wrong with their faith because they don't feel that rush of the Spirit every Sunday when they come to church.

Sometimes those times of intense emotion, those spiritual highs, come after a period of spiritual dryness. They are like finally getting air after being under water for a long time. After holding your breath for a few minutes, you experience breathing in a totally different way. You have an appreciation for air that you don't have when you're breathing normally. But you can't live like that all the time. Ordinarily, you breathe constantly, in and out, in and out, so breathing is such a part of your life you hardly notice it. That is what we want our spiritual lives to be like, constantly filled with the Holy Spirit and always growing in the capacity to do the Spirit's work. We are thankful for moments of intense spiritual emotion when they come, but they are not the standard by which we judge whether the Spirit is at work within us.

V. *The Holy Spirit unites us with the community of believers, the Church.* Our baptism is a sign that we belong to God and are members of the family of Christ. That is why Peter and

John went to Samaria to see what Phillip had done by preaching to the Samaritans. Samaritans were the ultimate outsiders. Israelites looked down on them more than they looked down on anyone else. The story of the Samaritans' baptism is a story of how far God reaches to bring the outsiders in. No matter how far we stray from God, the Spirit is always pursuing us, reaching out to us, reminding us who we are.

When a friend wrote Martin Luther, the great Reformer of the sixteenth century, that he just couldn't make it anymore, that all his troubles had gotten him so down he felt he was totally defeated by life, Luther's advice to him was, "Remember your baptism." When you are at the end of your rope and do not know which way to turn, remember your baptism. When you want so badly to do something you know is not right, remember your baptism. When everything is going your way and the future is bright and you are on top of the world, remember your baptism. You have been redeemed through Jesus Christ. The Spirit that moved on the face of the waters at creation is in you. Remember your baptism.—Stephens G. Lytch

ILLUSTRATION

SPIRIT CAPACITY.   Spirit capacity is like lung capacity. All people have lungs and everyone needs air to live. Children have small lungs and take in a smaller amount of air. As we grow, our lung capacity increases, and we breathe in more air. But you can reduce your lung capacity. You can cause harm to your lungs by smoking. If you don't get enough exercise, your lungs lose capacity to hold air.

Some people reduce their Spirit capacity by going against what the Spirit wants them to do. Cheating, lying, and greed reduce their capacity to be enlivened by the Spirit. But most people reduce their Spirit capacity by lack of use, by ignoring or resisting it, by being too busy for God. And so their spiritual capacity becomes like the lungs of someone whose only exercise is going to the refrigerator during halftime of the football game. They are not capable of holding the Spirit in all its power.

SERMON SUGGESTIONS

Topic: A Preacher's Main Business
TEXT: Isa. 61:1–4
Like the ideal prophet, especially Jesus Christ, the faithful preacher (1) receives anointing for service (v. 1a) and (2) brings good news to all classes of the disadvantaged (vv. 1b–3a), (3) who in turn make their own constructive contributions to the work of God (vv. 3b–4).

Topic: The Gift of the Holy Spirit
TEXT: Acts 8:14–17
(1) Promised to all believers (see Acts 3:38–39). (2) Received in relationship to the Church.

WORSHIP AIDS
CALL TO WORSHIP.   "Give unto the Lord the glory due unto his name; worship the Lord in the beauty of holiness" (Ps. 29:2).

INVOCATION.   Almighty God, loving Lord, as we come to worship you, we confess our unworthiness, yet through your grace we are special to you and you make our worship acceptable in your sight. Teach us today how what we do here and elsewhere can glorify you.

OFFERTORY SENTENCE.   "Blessed be the God and Father of our Lord Jesus Christ, who has blessed us with every spiritual blessing in the heavenly places in Christ" (Eph. 1:3 NKJV).

OFFERTORY PRAYER.   Eternal God, sinners that we are, accept our gratitude as we share this offering to increase the kingdom of joy immeasurable through Christ our Lord.—E. Lee Phillips

PRAYER.   Each of us is a mixed bag, Father. We like to think that we are single-minded and of single purpose. But when we look closely at ourselves, we see that such is not the case. The demands of this world creep into our lives and destroy the single-minded purpose that we desire to follow. Because of those demands, we find ourselves giving partial energy to the eternal things of life. We do not meditate and pray as we ought. Consequently, we do not understand your will in matters we have to manage. We do not study your word as we should. Therefore we are not fortified to withstand many of the temptations that overtake us. We do not engage in answering the cries of those about us as we should; thus many miss the wonders of life that we could share. We fail to take seriously the crises that confront our society; therefore they grow more serious because of lack of management on our part. In so many ways we miss the one way by which the struggles and needs of life could be handled. Forgive us for trying to handle them in our own strength and for leaving you out of the equation, Father. Open our hearts this morning so that we may allow you in, so that you may become the true Lord of life. Then we will be able to do wondrous things as we are met by the world because we will gain your purpose, your peace, and your love to help us manage day by day.

Here today we intercede for the youth who is dealing with making decisions, asking you to give guidance that will strengthen and sustain him or her in the right choices. We pray for the family struggling with pains and problems that are about to tear it apart. Give stability to each family member and wisdom sufficient to help them manage, so they can indeed find harmony and peace. Be with those who grieve. Wipe away their tears and give them hope as they face life in the absence of one who is dearly loved. Bring salvation to the lost, so that new life may be a reality and eternity may be an assurance in their lives. Use us all to lift the fallen, love the unlovely, and bring joy to the world because we are indeed followers of the Lord Jesus, in whose name we pray.—Henry Fields

SERMON
Topic: What Troubles You?
TEXT: Matt. 2:3

Once the Wise Men from the East had arrived in the Holy City and inquired as to the birth of the king of the Jews, we are told that "when Herod the king heard this, he was troubled, and all Jerusalem with him" (Matt. 2:3). The word *troubled* is strong enough to cover our many moods, for it can mean "to be disturbed, startled, unsettled, worried" or even "to be dismayed, intimidated, terrified, confounded."

I. The cause of all this consternation is attributed directly to the question asked by the Wise Men, but we wonder why their investigation should bother the most powerful man in Palestine. Herod had reigned over Judea with the backing of Rome for more than thirty years, during which time he had ruthlessly thwarted every plot to seize his throne.[3] Moreover, in the final months of his life, he was now an aging tyrant, so what threat could a newborn baby pose for either him or his successors? "Wise Men from the East" would be Babylonian astrologers who had no influence among the Jews or Romans—hardly the kind to foment an insurrection on behalf of an infant whom they had never seen. They did not even know where the child was to be found, and their only purpose was to pay him homage and then go home—what harm in that? The superstitious might embark upon a seemingly quixotic quest because of some aberrational star in the sky, but Herod had whole battalions to do his bidding and a string of fortresses to protect his crown.

It may seem as if Herod badly overreacted to such an inconsequential query, until we realize how insanely suspicious he was of any real or imagined intrigue that might compromise his absolute authority. For years the royal court had been the center of endless rumor, plotting, blackmail, torture, and purges. Just a year or two before the birth of Jesus, Herod had ordered two of his sons, Alexander and Aristobulus, to be strangled to death, and even closer to Jesus' birth he had ordered the murder of Antipater just five days before his own death. During this time, the king was frequently rewriting his will, four drafts in all, determined to eliminate from succession any heir who was not subservient to his every whim until the bitter end. When Caesar Augustus heard of the death of Antipater, who all supposed would soon become king, he remarked that it was safer to be Herod's swine than his son.

To be sure, Herod lived in an age when human life was cheap. It was a time "when even the cultivated Greeks could regard as 'a mathematical axiom' a king's murder of his brothers, when crucifixions were ordered by the score as a commonplace sentence of a court of justice, where torture was a recognized legal process, when the destruction of man by man in the arena was a popular amusement."[4] But the Wise Men were up against an even greater problem, for during the last decade of his life Herod was not only brutally cruel but also mentally incompetent. By the time of his murderous rampage against his sons, even Augustus in Rome knew that Herod suffered dementia from acute arteriosclerosis. Added to mental insanity was awful physical decay, described by the Jewish historian Josephus:[5] internal swelling from acute dropsy (edema); intolerable itching over the surface of his body; ulcerated mouth, stomach, and colon resulting in putrid breath; abdominal pain that burned like fire; constant diarrhea; and gangrenous genitals with lesions infested by maggots. A modern medical evaluation of this ancient description concludes that the Herod encountered by the Wise Men was a dying wretch, "increasingly prone to mood changes, delusions of persecution, uncontrolled outbursts of hypertensive cerebral attacks, even attempted suicide."[6]

So why was Herod troubled? Because he worshiped power, and the only power that mattered to him was the power he could control. Now, near the end of his life, he had accumulated more power than any Jewish ruler in history. With this power he had brought peace and prosperity to Palestine, dotting the landscape with truly impressive buildings. But all of this power proved useless to accomplish what really mattered most. Herod lacked the power

---

[3]On the final years of Herod, see Stewart Perowne, *The Life and Times of Herod the Great* (London: Hodder and Stoughton, 1956), pp. 158–186.

[4]Perowne, *Life and Times of Herod the Great,* p. 179.

[5]Josephus, *The Jewish War,* Book I, Chapter xxxiii, Section 5; and *Jewish Antiquities,* Book XVII, Chapter vi, Section 5.

[6]Norman Manson, cited by Perowne, *Life and Times of Herod the Great,* p. 186.

to love and be loved by any of his ten wives, to build loyalty and character into his fifteen children, to inspire trust and integrity in his court. He could destroy enemies with a wave of his hand, but he could not root out the jealousy, envy, and hatred that plagued his daily life. He could compel peace in the nation with a sword, but he could find no peace of mind for himself. His treasury was filled with gold, but he could not buy a moment's freedom from pain at any price. At a time when his power was almost unlimited, Herod had never felt so utterly weak and helpless.

Imagine, therefore, his frustration upon hearing of the Wise Men's visit. He thought he had eliminated every possible rival, but here was the report of yet another competitor king. No sooner did Herod think he was in control of the future than a baby was born to awaken new hopes. Where would it ever stop?

So, what troubles you? Are you troubled because a reckless kind of evil has invaded our land that all of our preeminent global power was helpless to prevent? Are you troubled because rampant greed has wrecked the stock market, jeopardizing your investment plans for retirement? Are you troubled because you feel lonely and unloved, more feared than befriended by those around you? Are you troubled because so many sweeping changes are taking place in the world today that your future seems uncertain? Are you troubled because disease rather than health is steadily gaining the upper hand in your body? In short, are you troubled because you seem to be losing control of the course of your life and of the legacy that you will leave behind? If so, then yours are the same troubles that enraged Herod when the Christmas message first reached his ears, for Christmas always disturbs those whose security lies in maintaining the status quo.

What is God's remedy for such troubles? It lies in the report of the Wise Men, who announced three things to a startled city (v. 2):

(1) A baby "has been born." There is a new factor in our seemingly hopeless situation, for his is a life that has never been lived before.

(2) Though only an infant, he is already "king of the Jews." His royalty has been conferred by God, not earned from Caesar by endless power struggles. As the fulfillment of divine promises, his birth ushers in a new age of fulfillment.

(3) Because of what he will do to redeem the world, we "have come to worship him." This worship is not groveling submission to a tyrant who coerces our response by force, but glad adoration of a savior who seeks only the free response of faith.

The issue is now clear: choose the way of Herod and Christmas is troubling at best, but choose the way of the Wise Men and it becomes nothing less than a journey in hope.

II. Significantly, our text adds that Herod's response to the Wise Men was contagious: not only he was troubled, but so was "all Jerusalem with him" (v. 3b). Again we wonder why the citizenry should share their ruler's alarm. After all, their status as a conquered people was not threatened by a rival king. If anything, they should have rejoiced at the report of the Wise Men. For the populace had never accepted Herod as one of their own, because he was at best a half-breed born to an Idumean family and hence of a race that had long been hereditary enemies of the Jews. His reign was now characterized by chaos and cruelty, which made him universally hated, especially in the capital city, with its concentration of Jewish leaders. Why would they not welcome the announcement, especially from these visiting dignitaries, that they had come all this way to worship one who was by birth "king of the *Jews*" (v. 2)?

The clue to our answer is found in the construction of the text. By emphasizing the word *all*, and by putting the word for the residents of Jerusalem in the singular, Matthew is saying that the whole city responded as a single, collective entity, that everyone fell into lockstep conformity with Herod, that no one dared to deviate from the attitude of their leader. Here, in other words, was panic by proxy.

How often do we let somebody else's troubles determine our own mood? It is still amazing how the whole nation of Germany suddenly became alarmed about "the Jewish question," not because the Jews were bothering anyone but because a delusional Adolf Hitler was "troubled" about such a threat. Closer to home, the South became deeply distressed about desegregation, not because blacks were causing any major problems, but because the Ku Klux Klan and the White Citizens' Councils and officials such as George Wallace and Bull Conner were "troubled" about them gaining a political power base. Why do we so quickly borrow such senseless fears? Because somebody might knock on our door in the night, or burn a cross in our yard, or slash our tires in the parking lot, or report us to the review committee for investigation.

Few if any of us will ever face the temptation that destroyed Herod, which, in the words of Lord Acton, is to let absolute power corrupt us absolutely.[7] But when the text says "and all Jerusalem with him," *that's us!*

III. Here, then, is the little story of how the first Christmas set off false alarms when it should have brought tidings of great joy. Neither Herod nor the Jerusalemites would have had any reason to be troubled if their lives had been open to the surprises of God's salvation.

They should have been troubled that they hadn't seen the star. After all, it was shining just overhead. But they were not accustomed to looking up and searching the heavens for surprises. They should have been troubled that none of them went with the Wise Men to Bethlehem. After all, the Magi had already traveled fifteen hundred miles, whereas Bethlehem was only six more miles down the road from Jerusalem. They should have been troubled that the Wise Men never came back to Jerusalem. After all, Herod himself had issued them a special invitation to return and had offered to lend his prestige to their act of homage (v. 8).

Questions such as these would never be answered, because they never troubled Herod or those whom he controlled. After all, the hardest question to answer is the one that is never asked. The Wise Men, even though viewed as pagan foreigners, were at least willing to ask and seek and knock (Matt. 7:7), while the keepers of the Holy City would not even bestir themselves to satisfy their own curiosity. Their problem was not a lack of answers, for they now knew where they needed to go, how to get there, and what they needed to find. No, it was fear that immobilized their footsteps, a fear that refused to believe in the power of God to do a new thing.

Are you worried, as were Herod and his followers, about the incessant power struggles of life, afraid that you may not gain the upper hand and end up on the winning side? Reconsider your priorities and let a different set of questions trouble you instead: Will I live my whole life and never see the star, never experience anything truly transcendent? Will I cling to the securities of the status quo and never venture forth to test the thrill of a new discov-

---

[7]Lord Acton (John Emerich Edward Dalberg) in an 1887 letter to Bishop Mandell Creighton said, "Power tends to corrupt; absolute power corrupts absolutely."

ery, never know the dimension of depth disclosed only to those with faith? Will I never, like the Wise Men, learn to go home "by another way" (v. 12), escaping the clutches of conformity because I have met the King of kings and Lord of lords? The answers to such questions, my friend, await you in Bethlehem. Will you go now to find them there?—William E. Hull

SUNDAY, JANUARY 18, 2004
Lectionary Message

Topic: Believing Is Seeing
Text: John 2:1–11
Other Readings: Isa. 62:1–5; Ps. 36:5–10; 1 Cor. 12:1–11

I. *If we know what to look for, we will be able to see miracles taking place in our own lives.*

(a) One thing it is important to know about miracles is that they are often very subtle, and they are often not recognized for what they are. Jesus' first miracle was like that. Most of the people who benefited from it did not know a miracle had happened.

(b) Jesus and Mary were at a wedding that was such a roaring good time the wine ran out. Mary came to Jesus and said, "Jesus, they have no wine." Jesus knew his mother well enough to know exactly what she was asking him to do, yet he replied, "What business is that of mine? It is not time for me to do that yet." And Mary, who must have given him that look that only a mother can give, that look that overrules all filial objections, turned to the servants and said, "Do whatever he tells you."

(c) So Jesus quietly told the servants to fill the jars with water, then draw some out and take it to the master of ceremonies. When the master of ceremonies tasted the wine, he praised the host, not Jesus. "What a generous thing you have done," he told the bridegroom. "Instead of holding the cheap wine until last when the guests have drunk so much they can't tell the difference, you've saved the best till now. What an outstanding host you are!"

(d) But Jesus did not say a word. He did not say, "Excuse me, you missed it. I'm the Son of God and I've just turned water into wine. It was a miracle to make you believe. Watch closely while I do it again." The only people who knew what happened were Mary, the servants, and Jesus' disciples, who had already committed their lives to Jesus.

(e) There were other times that Jesus actually refused to perform miracles. The scribes and the Pharisees asked him to do miracles to prove to them that he was the Son of God, and Jesus refused. Jesus knew how quickly we tire of the spectacular, how easily the extraordinary becomes routine.

II. *Many people have problems with miracles because they expect them to be something they were never intended to be, either rewards for the faithful or tricks to convince the unbelieving.*

(a) One of the biggest problems people have with miracles is the way they defy the laws of nature. Today we know more about the way the world works than they knew in ancient times. We know that there are certain laws that govern the universe. According to the laws of nature, it is impossible to do some of the things Jesus is reported to have done. Our modern minds want to know how someone could turn water into wine, or what physical laws were at work when Jesus walked on water. People have come up with all kinds of scientific explanations for how different miracles might have happened. But we miss the point when we try to explain Jesus' miracles. Before we can understand what a miracle is, before we can see one before our very eyes, we have to believe that the same God who set up the laws of nature can also set them aside.

(b) Another thing about miracles that causes problems for some people is the idea that they are rewards for the faithful, favors that Jesus hands out to those who believe in him. Many people think that miracles are ours for the asking. They think that Christians have a right to ask God to do what they want, when they want it. They think that in exchange for believing we are entitled to service, the way you can call up AAA for a rescue when you are stranded by the side of the road as long as you are a member in good standing. If God does not come through, then they have a right to stop believing. But God never guarantees that miracles will happen in just the way we want them to happen every time we ask for them. Miracles are not rewards that God gives us for believing the right things.

III. *The Gospel according to John describes miracles as signs that Jesus is who he claims to be.* And as we see time and again throughout the Gospels, it takes more than miracles to make people believe in Jesus.

(a) It helps us understand Jesus' miracles if we don't see them as tricks we are supposed to believe without evidence. Instead, we should see them as assurance of God's presence among us. God does not have to prove to us that God can manipulate logic and science. God has better things to do than that. When Jesus performs miracles, he assures us that he is who he claims to be and that he is with us.

Jesus performs miracles every day. He gives us signs that we can recognize when we see them through the eyes of faith. Maybe it is a simple word heard in a Sunday morning prayer. Maybe it is a miraculous recovery from illness. Maybe it is the miracle of surviving a great tragedy and continuing to function. Maybe it is a miracle of the love you know from someone who is close to you. The way to see miracles is not to search for them in order to prove to yourself that Jesus is who he claims to be. The way to see miracles is to believe. When you believe in Jesus, you will see the signs he gives.—Stephens G. Lytch

ILLUSTRATIONS

SAYING GRACE.   George Braswell, a professor at Southeastern Baptist Seminary, tells about a dream he once had. In the dream a lion was chasing him at full speed. The faster he ran, the closer the lion pawed at his heels. He couldn't outrun the lion, so he prayed for assistance. "God, grant me a miracle; please convert this lion into a Christian." He stopped running, glanced back, and the lion was lying prostrate at his heels. In his dream he heard the lion praying, "God, I thank thee for this bountiful provision which I am about to eat."

TAKEN FOR GRANTED.   In 1962 the hero of every schoolboy was John Glenn, the first American to orbit the Earth. The entire country gathered around the TV set to watch the blastoff and landing. We followed his mission minute by minute. Upon his return, New York gave him a ticker-tape parade. He rode down Pennsylvania Avenue in Washington accompanied by the vice president and marching bands and throngs of admiring citizens. Nowadays, space travel is so routine, a launch is barely noticed. How many of us could name even three of the astronauts who were on the last shuttle mission? Jesus knew that if our faith in him were based only on miracles, we would eventually start to take his miracles for granted. Miracles would be for us like astronauts orbiting the Earth. We are impressed for a while, but then we take them for granted and want something else.

MIRACLES.   The writer Frederick Buechner once observed, "Faith in God is less apt to proceed from miracles than miracles from faith in God."

SERMON SUGGESTIONS

Topic: Will God Do Us Right?
TEXT: Isa. 62:1–5

(1) *Then:* God Promised vindication to his apparently abandoned people Israel. (2) *Always:* God either here or hereafter (sometimes both) gives justice to his suffering people. (3) *Now:* Regardless of present circumstances, we can dare be confident of God's gracious purpose for us.

Topic: Evidence of the Spirit
TEXT: 1 Cor. 12:1–11

(1) Confession of Jesus as Lord. (2) Working for the common good.

WORSHIP AIDS

CALL TO WORSHIP.   "Your love, O Lord, reaches to the heavens, your faithfulness to the skies. Your righteousness is like the mighty mountains, your justice like the great deep" (Ps. 36:5–6 NIV).

INVOCATION.   As we come to you, O Lord, continue to clarify our vision of you in your love and faithfulness. We thank you for the Christ, who opens the eyes of our hearts as we worship you.

OFFERTORY SENTENCE.   "There are different kinds of spiritual gifts, but they all come from the same Spirit. There are different ways to serve the same Lord, and we can each do different things. Yet the same God works in all of us and helps us in everything we do" (1 Cor. 12:4–6 CEV).

OFFERTORY PRAYER.   We acknowledge, O Father, that there are many things beyond our ability to do when we would like to help others, yet we now come to serve you through tithes and offerings that will bless untold numbers as the gospel is proclaimed at home and through-out the world. Receive these gifts, we pray, and use them to your glory.

PRAYER.   O God, we remember with sadness our want of faith in thee. What might have been a garden we have turned into a desert by our sins and willfulness. This beautiful life which thou hast given us we have wasted in futile worries and vain regrets and empty fears. Instead of opening our eyes to the joy of life, the joy that shines in the leaf, the flower, the face of an innocent child, and rejoicing in it as in a sacrament, we have sunk back into the complainings of our narrow and blinded souls. Deliver us from the bondage of unchastened desires and unwholesome thoughts. Help us to conquer hopeless brooding and faithless reflection and the impatience of irritable weakness. To this end, increase our faith, O Lord. Fill us with a more complete trust in thee, and the desire for a more wholehearted surrender to thy will. Then every sorrow will become a joy. Then shall we say to the mountains that lie heavy on our souls, "Remove and be cast hence," and they shall remove, and nothing shall be impossible unto us. Then shall we renew our strength, and mount up with wings as eagles; we shall run and not be weary; we shall walk and not faint.—Samuel McComb

SERMON
Topic: Good News for You
TEXT: Mark 1:1–11

Mark is a tremendously exciting Gospel in so many respects. It is the earliest of the four Gospels. It is the shortest of the Gospels. The way to read Mark is to sit down with a modern translation and read it starting with chapter 1 and through chapter 16. It can easily be read in less than an hour.

Now open your Bible with me to chapter 1, verse 1. "The beginning of the gospel of Jesus Christ, the Son of God." I get excited when I realize that I am reading the opening verse in the earliest Gospel ever written. This is not only the first Gospel about Jesus; it is also the first time any writing anywhere has ever called itself "gospel," which literally means "good news."

The writer of Ecclesiastes actually ends his ancient document with these gloomy words: "Of making many books there is no end, and much study is a weariness of the flesh" (Eccles. 12:12). This verse represents the despair of boredom and the emptiness of a great deal of ancient wisdom.

Notice the title of the book, "The Gospel According to Mark." It doesn't say, "More, more of the same old empty, boring, vanity of vanities rhetoric." This is not a book about ritual or philosophy or doctrine, or a collection of slogans that will help make you rich and famous. This is good news about the possibility of a whole new existence! It is, in fact, good news for you.

I. *Mark the writer.* What do we know about the Mark identified by the title as the author of this book? There is a very interesting passage toward the end of the Gospel of Mark. Turn with me now to chapter 14, verse 46. The scene is the garden of Gethsemane. Jesus has just been arrested. All of the disciples have forsaken him and fled into the darkness. In verse 51 we read, "And a young man followed him, with nothing but a linen cloth about his body, and they seized him, but he left the linen cloth and ran away naked." A number of scholars suggest that this is Mark's signature. Mark didn't really hear the teachings of Jesus. He did not observe the miracles. But this is the one time when he was in close touch with a dramatic event in Jesus' life.

The first time we see Mark he is running away in absolute terror. We meet Mark again in chapter 13 of the book of Acts. He accompanied Paul and Barnabas on the very first missionary journey of the Church. When things got rough, however, and there were persecution and difficulty, Mark really couldn't take it; he left Barnabas and Paul and returned home.

In fact, Mark contributed to the break-up of the first great missionary team. In Acts 14:36 we read, "After some days Paul said to Barnabas, 'Come let us return and visit the brethren in every city where we proclaimed the Word of the Lord and see how they are.' And Barnabas wanted to take with them John called Mark. But Paul thought best not to take with them one who had withdrawn from them in Pamphylia and not gone with them to the work. And there arose a sharp contention so that they separated from each other; Barnabas took Mark with him and sailed away to Cyprus, but Paul chose Silas and . . . he went through Syria and Cilicia, strengthening the churches" (Acts 15:36–41).

I want to talk to people who are being put down, whose self-esteem is under attack and who are struggling to maintain a sense of self-worth. I have a word for those who have been told there is no second chance and that they are forever banned, finished. This is what I want to say to you: When I read the earliest record of Jesus' life, I do not see the name of Luke, the beloved physician, or of John, the beloved disciple, or of Paul, the great missionary apostle. or even of Matthew, who had been a tax collector; I read instead the Gospel according to Mark, the scared kid who fled into the darkness of the night in the garden of Gethsemane. Mark, the young man who couldn't even finish the first missionary journey. The Gospel according to Mark. That is right! Something happened to Mark. He met the Risen Lord, and his life was dramatically changed so that even Paul wrote to Timothy from prison, "Get Mark and bring him with you." Hear Paul's cry from prison: "Luke alone is with me; get Mark and bring him with you." Isn't that exciting?

What if Barnabas hadn't seen the possibilities in Mark? What if Paul's harsh verdict had prevailed? Barnabas somehow saw the possibilities of a young man who looked to all the world like a total failure and a cowardly quitter. Barnabas believed in Paul as well. It was Barnabas who brought Paul into the Jerusalem church to introduce him. It was Barnabas who went to Tarsus and finally found Paul and told him that his help was needed at Antioch for the first missionary journey. Paul was an encourager. Barnabas gives us the model of the kind of ministry that is needed in our world today. It is a ministry that affirms confidence in unlikely people.

Mark was later associated with Peter in Rome. When Peter was crucified head downward in the year 64 A.D., in Nero's terrible persecution, Mark knew that the message Peter had preached had to be written. Finally, the day came when he took pen in hand and began to write, "The beginning of the gospel of Jesus Christ, the Son of God."

Mark never claimed to tell the whole story. He said, This is just "the beginning"—the introduction of the "Evangelion." Because Jesus Christ is the living Lord, there is *more* good news coming! There is *more* hope ahead! There is *more* forgiveness and grace to be received. There is *more* power and healing to be experienced.

II. *The anticipated Messiah.* Mark wants us to understand, first of all, that the good news had been anticipated for a long time. That is why Mark reminds us of the prophecy of Isaiah, "Behold, I send my messenger before thy face who shall prepare thy way. The voice of the one crying in the wilderness: prepare the way of the Lord. Make his path straight." John the Baptizer got excited about the good news. His appearance was like Elijah of old. He wore a garment of camel's hair and ate locusts and wild honey. It was widely anticipated that Elijah would return just before the Messiah came. His message was to call for repentance and for the forgiveness of sins.

John the Baptist had some good news. It didn't all depend on John the Baptist—"After me there comes one who is mightier than I, the thong of whose sandals I am not worthy to stoop down and untie. . . . I baptized you with water but he will baptize you with the Holy Spirit." That's the good news! Too often we associate the presence of the Holy Spirit with a particular dynamic, well-known leader. I have been trying for some years now to get a well-known speaker into our own church. He just sent a letter the other day saying that he will not be able to come. Does that mean we will not receive the Holy Spirit this year in our congregation? Of course not! Jesus is the one who baptizes in the Holy Spirit. He is the source of God's grace and power. That's good news!—Joe A. Harding

SUNDAY, JANUARY 25, 2004
Lectionary Message

Topic: But I Gave at the Office . . .

TEXT: Luke 4:14–21

Other Readings: Neh. 8:1–3, 5–6, 8–10; Ps. 19; 1 Cor. 12:12–31a

I. *Those words Jesus read from the prophet Isaiah have inspired millions of Christians to bring the good news they hear in church out into the streets.*

(a) But it is not just the Church that has been inspired by these first recorded public words of Jesus to relieve suffering and oppression. As Christians have become involved in the rest of society, Jesus' vision of a world where no one is hungry or oppressed or physically afflicted has inspired leaders in every walk of life.

(b) In fact, there are so many organizations that help the needy and improve the quality of life, from the United Nations to the United Way, that people sometimes ask why they should give their money to and volunteer their time for the Church. It is all going to a good cause.

II. *From the outside it is often hard to tell the difference between the good works the church does and the good works others do.*

(a) When you itemize your charitable deductions on your Form 1040 Schedule A, the IRS does not distinguish between the Church and any other charity. So many organizations are asking for our involvement in good things, it is easy to lose sight of what makes Jesus' mission distinctive. When the Church asks us to give, why not just say, "But I gave at the office"?

(b) There is something fundamentally different about our gifts to the Church. When we give our time, talent, and money to the Church, we give it overtly in the name of Jesus Christ. That does not mean that Jesus is not involved in the many of the good things we are involved in outside the Church, but there is no one else who does those things in the name of Jesus Christ.

III. *Jesus' vision for serving those in need is fundamentally different from anyone else's vision.*

Jesus did not come just to make the world a better place. He came to transform the world. He came not just to alleviate human suffering, but to do away with suffering altogether. That is something no human organization can ever do.

The forces behind hunger and sickness and war and tyranny are more powerful than anything in this world. We can treat the symptoms, but only Jesus can provide the cure. Jesus began his work by reading those powerful words from Isaiah. He ended his work on the cross. Without the power of the cross, everything we do to help those in need is like treading water. The final answer to human suffering is not in the good things we do. It is in Jesus Christ, who has promised that one day he will make everything right.

When we feed the hungry and care for the sick in the name of Jesus, we do it in the confidence that those deeds point to the one who is the true healer, the bread of life.

People notice when the Church is involved with those in need. Our service in Jesus' name points beyond the Church to the head of the Church, Jesus Christ.

We who claim Jesus Christ as our Lord and Savior and have dedicated our lives to him need to be clear about why we serve the poor, the oppressed, and the sick. It is not just because we are people of goodwill and compassion who want to see suffering relieved and justice done. We serve because Jesus has promised that there will be a time when there will be no more suffering.

IV. *So what is in it for us? What do we get out of giving Christ's Church our time and our efforts, besides a tax deduction and maybe a thank you—things we can get in other places? When we serve others in the name of Christ, we find deeper joy that lets us do even more.*

(a) There is a common misperception that when you give to others you have less for yourself. God's economy does not work that way. When we ration our generosity, we find ourselves living out of our human limitations. When we give abundantly out of our love for Christ, we find ourselves living out of God's unbounded generosity. Ask anyone whose life has been changed by going on a mission trip. Ask anyone who tutors a child. Ask anyone who tithes. They will all tell you that what Jesus says is true: It is in losing our life for the sake of the gospel that we find it. It is in holding on to it tightly that we lose it. Jesus came to bring release to the captives, and he releases us from our captivity to all those things we hold on to so tightly—our opinions, our needs, our passions, our possessions. He shows how much joy there is in giving as freely as he gave himself for us.

(b) So give generously at the office and at the civic club and to the arts organizations that enrich our lives so much. Give generously of your time and your money to anyone who is improving the quality of human life on Earth. But the good works of all our great civic and charitable organizations are not substitutes for what the Church does in the name of Jesus Christ. There is no substitute for what Jesus has to offer the poor, the oppressed, and the sick, those held captive by addiction or lack of education or unjust social systems. Jesus has inspired presidents, civic leaders, and people of goodwill through the ages. But only Jesus offers the cross, the resurrection to eternal life, and the promise that one day he will bring an end to human suffering. That is why what we give at the office, as good as it is, can never substitute for what we give in the name of Christ. Nothing we give can ever match what Christ has already given.—Stephens G. Lytch

ILLUSTRATION

IT ALL SUPPORTS MISSION.   Some of us hold back from giving of our time, talents, and money to the Church because not everything we do directly feeds the poor, heals the sick, or fights oppression. We worship, we study Scripture, we care for one another, we have fun together, and we educate our children and our youth. Occasionally someone will say, "I don't give so much to the Church because I can see more direct results by giving to this or that charity."

There are many things we can do for Christ's Church beside serving directly those who are poor and oppressed, but everything we do is directed toward Jesus' vision of transforming the world into a better place. Think of the U.S. Army. The Army's mission is to fight our country's enemies. In order to fight our enemies well, the Army has to do many other things well, things that have little to do with combat. The quartermaster corps has to develop a complex system of purchasing, storing, cooking, and serving food for thousands of people. There are schools to provide education for the children of soldiers who live on bases. There are gymnasiums and playing fields where soldiers stay in shape, doing conditioning exercises that are a lot like what your more ambitious friends do at the local fitness center. Computer experts design and maintain systems that might look a lot like the ones you use in your business. In fact, one of the Army's big recruiting pitches is that young people can join and learn skills they can carry with them into the civilian world. But no matter how nutritious its meals, how distinguished its schools, how fit its soldiers, and how sophisticated its computers are, or how well it prepares soldiers for civilian life, the Army can never forget that the reason it exists is to fight our enemies. Ultimately, everything it does has to serve that goal.

Jesus identified the Church's goal in his address to the synagogue that Sabbath day in Nazareth. It is to carry out his mission of bringing good news to the poor, freeing the oppressed, healing the sick, and releasing the captives. That is not all we do, but everything we do serves that goal.—Stephens G. Lytch

SERMON SUGGESTIONS

Topic: Glory and Goodness
TEXT: Ps. 19
(1) The majesty of God's creation (vv. 1–6). (2) The comparable truth of God's law (vv. 7–11). (3) The personal requirements of these realities (vv. 12–14).

Topic: Destiny Defined
TEXT: Luke 4:14–21
(1) Jesus' historic call (vv. 14–17a). (2) Jesus' timeless message (vv. 17b–19). (3) Jesus' timely application (v. 20).

WORSHIP AIDS

CALL TO WORSHIP.   "May my spoken words and unspoken thoughts be pleasing even to you, O Lord my Rock and my Redeemer" (Ps. 13:14 *The Living Bible*).

INVOCATION.   Holy God, empower our worship with praise and our prayers with insight so that as we listen and sing we will grasp anew the will of God for our lives.

OFFERTORY SENTENCE.   "Now you are the body of Christ, and each one of you is a part of it" (1 Cor. 12:27 NIV).

OFFERTORY PRAYER.   Lord, bless these gifts, the work of our hands and the dedication of our hearts, as together they point to the unending love of God.—E. Lee Phillips

PRAYER.   O God, we beseech thee to save us this day from the distractions of vanity and the false lure of inordinate desires. Grant us the grace of a quiet and humble mind, and may we learn from Jesus to be meek and lowly of heart. May we not join the throng of those who seek after things that never satisfy and who draw others after them in the fever of covetousness. Save us from adding our influence to the drag of temptation. If the fierce tide of greed beats against the breakwaters of our soul, may we rest at peace in thy higher contentment. In the press of life may we pass from duty to duty in tranquility of heart and spread thy quietness to all who come near.—Walter Rauschenbusch

SERMON
Topic: Listen
TEXT: Mark 4:1–20

Listen! We are bombarded with words on every hand. At the coffee shop, beside the radio and before the television set, in the lecture room, and at the department store, where salespeople are hawking products, quite often without bothering to know if we hear or not. Jesus wants to say something to us, and obviously it is not an indifferent matter to him whether we hear him or not. The unfortunate farmer in the story he tells us is doubtless a remarkably ordinary one—a sower of seed. There, some earthy, well-trodden paths across the fields, and the birds gobble up every grain. Here some shoulders stretch out where the earth scarcely covers up the rock, and nothing is expected to grow there. There, the thornbushes abound, and it is not hard to predict that the wheat has no chance. No miracle happens: the birds eat the seed, the sun withers the first shoots, and the thorns choke the little green sprouts. So that is how it happens. No doubt this is not the situation of the well-to-do farmer on the quiet, rich land, but of the little growers on the mountain who work themselves to death planting their plots of ground. Then what is there to hear in this? "He who has ears to hear, let him hear," says Jesus.

The parables of Jesus always orbit around the same theme: the reign of God. It is related to what we are indeed hearing this morning: what happens to this plot of ground belonging to a Palestinian farmer happens also with the reign of God. Rocks, birds, thornbushes—and that is about all that one can see. Do we see very much more than that with respect to Jesus himself? He narrates his parables, he heals a few sick people, he eats at the table of some tax collectors. Then powerful men calculate how they will be able to combat him; they laugh about him among themselves in the streets at the close of day, mentioning a preacher who is half-cracked, if not completely out of his mind; and already even those whom he has helped have amiably dismissed him because they see in him one of these innumerable idealistic benefactors who invade the world to proclaim their religious or humanitarian theories. So it is that the Kingdom of God comes: some combat it, others laugh it out of court, still others push it amiably aside. So comes the Kingdom of God: we see only the birds, stones, and thorns, and we think that absolutely nothing happens. Chance and death, which demolish everything, are in charge—not God. And Jesus confirms this for us: so it is with the Kingdom of God in our world. So it is in his own life, in which the Kingdom of God wants to penetrate to us. It comes to us in this strange, incomprehensible, and difficult way. No cramp paralyzes the open mouth of the birds when they sweep down to devour the grains. No trembling of the earth dislocates the rocks in order that the roots might be able to take hold. No fire consumes the bushes and spares the tender straws of wheat. How naturally it all happens where the reign of God wants to come over man.

But Jesus adds: You have, then, only one aspect of the truth. "And other seeds fell into good soil and brought forth grain, growing up and increasing and yielding thirtyfold and sixtyfold and a hundredfold." The seed is in the soil. It sprouts; nothing will stop it. The harvest is as excessive as was the failure of the farmer depicted at the beginning of the parable. The yield reaches sixty, even one hundred grains for one. And once more the summons of Jesus comes to us: "He who has ears to hear, let him hear." Something happens, something grows where God begins to reign. Perhaps it is still completely hidden, so we doubters see only stones, birds, and bushes. They are there, visible and big as life, although the green shoots of wheat can hardly be seen. But they will bear the sixty or one hundred grains, while the enormous strata of rocks and the billows of bushes head high and the noisy birds will bear no fruit. So it is with the reign of God. Jesus says nothing more. Is it surprising, then, if so few men have had ears to hear it?

And those who have no religion have shrugged their shoulders: What proof do you give us? they have asked him. Nothing but this, Jesus answers them: Let me take you with me on your way; follow me, place yourself with me under this astonishing reign of God which so often leads us from failure to failure and becomes, nevertheless, for whomever accepts it, always more real and powerful and an ever greater source of help. And those who have religion have shrugged their shoulders and explained that they have known it already for a long time. Of course, the victory of God comes only in the future. For them, Jesus has not spoken of what is really important: the defeat of the enemies of God, who will be brought low and thrown into hell. He has not recounted, therefore, the story of the massacre of the birds, the burning of the thorns, the shaking of the rocks; and he has said nothing about the faithful, who will receive their deserved reward. At the same time, he has not indicated that the various grains that pierced the rocks, overcame the thorns, and suffocated the birds will receive a decoration for distinguished service. No, Jesus has recounted nothing about all that. For him, everything happens so much more naturally and quite differently. Clearly, he thinks it ought to suffice to understand that the reign of God goes on toward its fullness; and we ought to know that just when we care only for his coming reign, God cares for us in a far better and far more glorious way than we could ever imagine, without having all the details described and spoon-fed to us in advance. Isn't this why neither the atheist nor religious people have wanted to hear Jesus, why they have gone on to crucify him or let him be crucified without raising serious protest, so that it happened to him exactly as his parable tells us of the reign of God?

The early Church added to the parable its explanation. That is what we have here; there is no doubt that these are the words of the early Church, terms that Jesus never used himself and that belong to the current language of the Epistles. But what is more significant, the explanation does not harmonize with the parable. The seed is at first the Word of God, then the man who hears it, then once more the Word, and finally man. What then did the Church have in mind when it added on its own interpretation in this way? First of all, it gave this explanation to others: Jesus was right and what he recounted is true—we have experienced it! Easter truly happened. God gave them eyes to see and ears to hear. They received courage to make an experiment with Jesus and to enter with him into his life. They discovered that the reign of God is reality. What happened with such power is a mystery that came in a way that we cannot simply account for or even describe: some disciples who were completely confused and in total rout became a group whose trust in and knowledge of the reality of God conquered the world. Though we cannot, of course, elucidate this mystery, we can listen to them when they repeat the parable of Jesus to us, and also when they add their own interpretation to it. They wish to tell us: no longer can we content ourselves with considering the parable as a story that Jesus told in another time, for Jesus continues to speak to us today. And the opponents of the reign of God—those who hide it, mask it, bury it, and destroy it before men—did not disappear into the past along with the Pharisees of Palestine, centuries and centuries ago. The adversaries are among us; they are not distinguished from ourselves; we too are involved. Perhaps we conceal Jesus from many men and women of today, even more than did the Pharisees of those times or the Romans who crucified him. We are going to return to our homes, perhaps as we return from the theater after a film that did not move us one bit: Jesus did not get through to us at all; he did not provoke anything, not even doubt or protest. Or we return home terribly shaken up, but nothing at all will come of it in our daily life. Or we were carried away and perhaps even said to others, This was terrific! This Jesus was quite right. Then everything stops there. The lectures, the theater on Thursday evening, vacation plans for which it is already quite late, and the garden that takes hard work for a long time, and a hundred other things get the upper hand for us. How then could the reign of God penetrate to others? How could they see anything else but stones, birds, and thorns, even if they had some suspicion that a truly living seed had been hurled to earth? The birds and the stones and the thorns truly need no one to point them out; they are visible enough by themselves.

This parable of Jesus is revealed to be true over and over again, and people see the reality of the birds and stones and thorns exactly. Only in this way can they or can we see it. But we as the Church find ourselves there, precisely where in the parable the birds, the stones, and the thorns are situated. . . .

"But those that were sown upon the good soil are the ones who hear the word and accept it and bear fruit, thirtyfold and sixtyfold and a hundredfold." In the same text we note something quite remarkable. It is said of those who have been mentioned up to that point that they are sown with seed over and over again, but they hear only one time and then are finished with it, because everything else possible is more important to them. It is said now of the last that they receive the seed only one time and that they hear and bear fruit over and over again. The Church that interprets the parable in this way remains in the school of Jesus. Unquestionably, it awaits the miracle of God. It does not anticipate it of itself; it expects everything from the parable of Jesus that it recounts. It expects that the power of the reign of God may also come upon us today, upon those of us who are listening to it at this very moment. But this miracle is not realized in the twinkling of an eye, so we, returning home from church, are not changed forever, like a scoundrel transformed into an angel. Perhaps nothing will happen but this: we shall wish to hear again, again, and again, simply because Jesus will have put an end to the way in which we rid ourselves so easily of him; simply because we shall have discovered behind the words a living reality; simply because it will be necessary for us now to put it to the test with him and attempt to hear him over and over again. It will be precisely there that the miracle happens; the fruit will increase and be multiplied—sixty times, one hundred times!—Eduard Schweizer, translated by James W. Cox

SUNDAY, FEBRUARY 1, 2004
Lectionary Message

Topic: Keeping It in the Family
TEXT: Luke 4:21–30
Other Readings: Jer. 1:4–10; Ps. 71:1–6; 1 Cor. 13:1–13

It is inevitable that members of a church ask the clergy for their prayers. Despite generations of good Reformation teaching about the "priesthood of all believers," something remains of the aura of the shaman or the cultic priest that subconsciously suggests to people that ordination brings with it a direct linkage to the Divine. This can involve as serious a matter as a gravely sick child or a crisis of faith. It can also be trivial. When asked to do something about the weather, for example, I usually use the line, "I'm in sales, not management."

I. *The dangers of being "special."*

(a) *You can never go home.* It is a similar scene that today's Gospel reading presents to us. The people of Nazareth have listened politely to the Lord's sermon during synagogue worship, but they now expect special favors from Jesus, the "local boy who made good." His response is exasperation, expressed by quoting two old sayings and turning them on his old neighbors: "Heal thyself," and "No prophet is accepted in his own country." This is an experience shared by anyone who has ever dared to "come home" and share the gospel, or any other new experience, for that matter. For every successful "favorite son" returning to general admiration, there are many more disappointments as the presumptions of long ago must be corrected in the light of how the child has become an adult. For Nazareth, this meant the lesson that Jesus wasn't just "their" wonderworker, but the Savior of the world.

(b) *Special deals.* The Nazareth community expected special favors, and often we do, too. Faithful members of our congregations who are regular worshipers, loyal to our parishes, and especially, generous contributors toward church finances, often expect a special deal. It is as if God truly does play favorites, despite what Peter says about that in his Pentecost address.

(c) *An attitude with a history.* This attitude doesn't even have to involve special prayers or influence; it can also involve our ideas about God's purpose for the world. Jeremiah's calling to be a prophet is described in today's first reading as being not only from before his birth but, equally surprising for the Chosen People to hear, "to the nations" as well. As the Old Testament weaves its story of the spiritual growth of Israel, Israel's God seems to grow in strength and power to become not only the personal protector of the tribe, but also a universal God truly worthy of the name.

Our Lord's words to his oldest neighbors may bring us today a certain righteous satisfaction that Jesus "told them off" for their demands for special treatment. However, Luke's story was written not for the Jews to read first, but for the first generation of Christians, who were still dealing with an equally painful issue concerning non-Jewish converts to the Christian faith. Their feeling seems to have been that they, as sons and daughters of the First Covenant, were first class compared to Gentile newcomers, who were expected to be satisfied traveling coach. Jesus' examples were meant to hit his listeners right between the eyes, but Luke's editing of the story packed a punch for the early Christians, too.

(d) *Is it I, Lord?* What does God say to us in today's readings? Are there those whom we would like to consider "also rans" in the race of the Christian life? Is our sense of our personal salvation so sure that we can look back with scorn on others who don't seem to come up to our standards or belong to our special group? Do we cringe at the suggestion that we share the gospel and life of our local congregation with other races and nationalities? What is our attitude toward our fellow Christians of differing traditions—Roman Catholics, Pentecostals, Eastern Orthodox, Protestants? Our danger is that we may think we are willing to share the gift of salvation, but only in restricted doses, and only with our friends and neighbors. There may be more of Nazareth in our local communities than we might wish to believe.

II. *Sharing the grace.*

(a) *The Hymn to Love.* The antidote to such thinking is found in today's second reading, one of the most beautiful passages of all Scripture and worthy of any number of sermons in its own right. Today, Paul's "Hymn to Love" acts as a foil to both those who would claim either faith ("understanding the mysteries") or works ("giving away all") as the ultimate means to salvation. It says that both of these are transcended by the compassion and self-emptying that is personified in our Lord Jesus Christ and meant to be copied in the lives of those who have joined themselves to him.

(b) *Sharing the grace.* This is the same kind of love that, when perfect, "casts out fear." In the case of today's theme, that fear might be that someone gets more than we do, or gets it first. All such greed, even for "spiritual" things, counteracts the liberating nature of the gospel. As Paul says in this passage, "I used to talk like a child and think like a child." Part of our spiritual growth involves "playing well with other children" in sharing the grace of God as we develop to full maturity in the Christian faith and life.

III. *Conclusion.* Today's readings from Scripture conspire to make us feel comfortable before sneaking in a powerful message. It is a message of open welcome to the whole world, which needs to hear the message of Christ every bit as much as our family and friends do. It is a message that tells us that the Church must become the biggest of all families, incorporating men and women from all backgrounds into a new and transcendent identity as Christ's brothers and sisters. Does God play favorites? Yes. He loves his Son best, because through him God has redeemed the whole world.—Tyler A. Strand

ILLUSTRATIONS

FREE TO LOVE.   What the thunders of Mount Sinai could not accomplish—the liberating of my heart to make it free to love, to be a child, and to feel at home in the Father's house—this is accomplished by the one who comes to me as my brother.

Coming down to the depths to fetch me, he says to the Father, "Look, here I bring him; I have bought him at a great price." And because and on account of my brother, Jesus Christ, I *can* come.

So now when we hear the words, "We love, because he first loved us," we know that this is not a "command" or a "law." We know that this answering love is only an echo that wells up overwhelmingly in my heart, an echo of an exultant certainty: I am loved, I am loved, I can come to God!—Helmut Thielicke[1]

OUR REFUGE.   It's clear that Luther, who helped redefine modern, faith-based Christianity, carried a high opinion of the place of music in worship. And which hymn was most central to the Reformation? That one's easy—"A Mighty Fortress Is Our God," a song Luther wrote based on Psalm 46. This hymn became the battle cry of God's people during the Reformation, a great source of strength and inspiration, especially among those who were martyred for their convictions. This hymn has been translated into almost every language, and there are more than sixty different English translations of the text itself.

When difficulty or discouragement came upon Martin Luther and his friend Philipp Melanchthon, the two key architects of the Reformation, sometimes Luther would say, "Philipp, come, let us sing the forty-sixth psalm." The two of them would bring out the metric version Luther had written, and they'd sing the words together. If you travel to Germany and visit the place where Luther is buried, you'll find the first line of the psalm engraved on the great man's tomb.

A mighty and awesome refuge is our God—for our time, for Luther's time, for any time. —David Jeremiah[2]

---

[1]*Life Can Begin Again* (Cambridge: James Clark, 1966).
[2]*A Bend in the Road* (Nashville: Word, 2000), pp. 234–235.

SERMON SUGGESTIONS

Topic: Prophet Making

TEXT: Jer. 1:4–10

(1) God's purpose. (2) God's promise. (3) God's program.

Topic: Love's Profile

TEXT: 1 Cor. 13:1–13

(1) Love counterfeited. (2) Love characterized. (3) Love consummated.

WORSHIP AIDS

CALL TO WORSHIP.   "I will praise you with the harp. I trust you, my God. I will sing to you with the lyre. You are the Holy One of Israel. I will shout for joy when I sing praises to you. You have saved me" (Ps. 71:22–23 NCV).

INVOCATION.   Still us, Lord, with holy quiet, the silence that emanates from the heart of God, which speaks in still, small ways, illuminating the mind, bringing the soul to proclaim the greatness of God.—E. Lee Phillips

OFFERTORY SENTENCE.   "I may be able to speak the languages of men and even of angels, but if I have no love, my speech is no more than a noisy gong or a clanging bell" (1 Cor. 13:1 TEV).

OFFERTORY PRAYER.   Lord, we know that our giving often defines our love. Trusting that our offerings today can be tokens of authentic love, help us to follow these gifts with other expressions of love in situations of immediate and urgent need that we see about us day by day.

PRAYER.   It is easy to get lost in the busyness of the world, with its demands and passing fancies, Father. This morning we come to this quiet place to find ourselves, to assess our lives, and to make commitments to the Lord of life and his Church. We need these moments, for in the vigor of life we too often turn from the truth that we are your children, by creation and through grace, and follow the more base instincts of selfishness, greed, possessiveness, and lust for the things we can see, touch, grasp, and claim for a brief moment with pleasure. So many times the higher values of life are clouded over. It is only in moments of silence and meditation that we come to value the things of God, the eternal dimension of life. Meet us here today, we pray, and open our eyes, minds, and souls to your truth, your grace, your directing spirit. Grant us the ability to see clearly that which matters most in life, and to forsake that which is passing and so often corrupting. We pray in Jesus' name.—Henry Fields

SERMON
Topic: Owning and Disowning

TEXT: Ps. 51

The issue is truth. When a witness rises to take the stand in the American court of law, a swearing-in ritual takes place. Traditionally the Bible was the icon of this rite as the witness was asked to place one hand on the Bible while swearing to tell the truth, the whole truth, and nothing but the truth, "so help me God." That just about covers the waterfront. Some witnesses tell the truth but stop short of telling parts of the truth that are embarrassing or intimidating to themselves or to the person they desire to protect. Some witnesses tell the truth but embellish the facts and put a spin on the story to mislead the court to a totally different conclusion than the real picture would support. Legally, for the truth to be the truth, it must include the whole story known to the witness, without any extraneous or added material. Of course, courtroom rules of perjury and truthfulness also apply to testimony given in a congressional investigation.

The biblical picture of truth still reaches to the depths that no investigative reporter can fathom. The light of God on our lives reveals the truth, the whole truth, and nothing but the truth. Original sin that has infected the whole world emerges in our lives in personal sin for which each of us bears a singular responsibility before God. The biblical right of confession establishes truth at the soul level of our link to God. Confession is not just "good for the soul" in the sense of a vitamin to keep one psychologically fit. Confession as a right of dealing with personal sin and a requisite to forgiveness from God is biblical. The psalmist hits the nail: God desires "truth in the inward being." All of us need to pray for "wisdom in my secret heart."

I. *Sin gets personal.* The traditional story behind Psalm 51 is about the abuse of authority, but it has all of the seductive qualities of an afternoon soap. David was king of Israel. He could have anything he wanted, and one might add, anyone he wanted. He already had eight wives, who had borne nineteen children. He also possessed a considerable harem of concubines. All of this was actually permitted by the morality of David's time and place. But David did not have the wife of Uriah the Hittite, Bathsheba. One lazy afternoon he observed her bathing on her housetop. He inquired about her identity. She was the wife of Uriah the Hittite, but David was the king, and monarchs have a way of believing that they are morally above the rules that apply to everyone else. David did not just seduce Bathsheba. He "sent for" her. She came to him and joined in his adultery by regal order. When she reported the ensuing pregnancy to the king, he began a series of actions to keep his affair secret. He exercised royal privilege to have her husband Uriah come home from battle. The strategy was to allow Uriah to spend an evening at home with his wife leaving no question as to the paternity of Bathsheba's child, thus covering the indiscretion of the king. But Uriah's loyalty to the king got in the way. He slept at the king's door and would not go home even when David succeeded in getting him drunk. What is a monarch to do? Everyone should understand that kings have human needs, and when they step over the line, they need to protect not only themselves but their royal posterity and the royal posterior as well.

David had Uriah sent to the front lines, where Bathsheba's husband was killed by the enemy. On hearing of Uriah's death, the king sent back word to his general, "Do not let this matter trouble you." Brueggeman notes the literal translation: "Do not let this appear as evil to you." The king was already working on the scenario of self-deception. David then added Bathsheba to his community of wives, and all was well on the home front. Then comes the prophet Nathan to confront the king with a parable on his abuse of power. David is judged by his own words as the final condemnation from Nathan rings down the corridors of time: "You are the man!" And now, finally, David repents, but not soon enough to save Uriah's life or that of the unborn child, to keep Bathsheba's fidelity, to bring peace into the king's house, or to preserve the memory of King David's virtue.

The psalm is set as the prayer of David in confession and repentance for his sin against Uriah, against his children, against his calling, against Bathsheba, but ultimately and finally, as is the way of all sin, against Yahweh. Finally all sin is personal and theological. It comes out of the heart and behavior of a person, and its power affects the lives of particular persons and destroys the tie that binds us to God. The psalm is often read on Ash Wednesday as a confession that applies to all of us. The confessional is not a joke. James admonishes Christians, "Confess your sins to one another, and pray for one another, so that you may be healed."

II. *Only the truth will set us free.* A few years ago an article in the publication *Psychology Today* attempted to define human nature as an onion. The psychologist suggested that we are our masks of deception. We go through life playacting our roles of faithful husband, loving father, and devoted employee, while the truth is always something besides all of this. The writer suggested that there is no soul, no real person at the core, just the onion. The anthropology of the Bible views a core of truth, the soul at the center of every person.

Following the September 11 crisis, the news reported research and development of an infrared lie detector that measures variations of temperature in the human face. Hypothetically, this simple device, by detecting the lie, could weed out the terrorist in the security check at the airport. The imagination runs wild at the applications in police investigation, on the job, or in the home. One might even keep a monitor on the face of the pastor during a sermon to detect ministerial exaggerations.

The truth is bigger than our technology. The light of God's holiness has been cast on all of God's children from the beginning. That holy light breaks through our walls of deceit and exposes our secret thoughts. The truth is already known. Paul does not long just to know in his hymn to love (1 Cor. 13), he longs to know as we are known. He assumes that God already knows me "Just As I Am Without One Plea."

Confession is not to inform God of something unknown to the Creator and Lord of life. Confession is an act of ownership of our thoughts and behavior, baring our souls before God that we might stand outside ourselves and listen and perhaps discover who we really are. Such honesty is possible only with the God of grace and forgiveness, who can hear with mercy and create in us a clean heart and a new spirit.—Larry Dipboye

SUNDAY, FEBRUARY 8, 2004
Lectionary Message
Topic: Reclaiming Christian Practices of Traditioning
TEXT: 1 Cor. 15:1–11
Other Readings: Isa. 6:1–8 (9–13); Ps. 138; Luke 5:1–11

I. The language of tradition often evokes negative responses in our contemporary context. Connotations of the archaic, dead, or irrelevant may be attributed to the language of "tradition" and stand in opposition to the more favorable ideals of the fresh, vital, and improved. American society, shaped by the subtexts of technology and capitalism, seems to have little interest in the traditional. Similarly, American Protestant Christianity sometimes lacks interest in tradition. American Protestant Christianity has experienced steady membership decline since the 1960s. In recent years, strong support has emerged for the development of new strategies and techniques to reverse this trend. Shaped by American society and its disinterest in tradition, Protestant denominational leaders at times seem unaware of or unwilling to learn about traditional Christian foundations such as canonical texts and doctrinal standards. This disinterest tends to relate to ill-informed presuppositions that Christian tradition lacks the capacity to provide effective responses to the current situation of decline. However, when appropriately acknowledged, tradition may be embodied in vital practices within Christian communities of faith formed by the narrative of salvation history through Jesus Christ for reconciliation with God through the Holy Spirit. Christian tradition, when consistent with canonical Scriptures, can perpetuate its vitality by informing constructive and faithful responses to contemporary issues.

II. *Tradition.* A contributing tendency toward the negative connotation of *tradition* is its prevalent use as a noun, or as an adjective, *traditional.* In light of the Scripture text from 1 Corinthians 15:1–11, such a narrow use of the term truncates the richness of the concept. In verse 3, Paul describes the practice of "traditioning": "For I handed on to you as of first importance what I in turn had received: that Christ died for our sins in accordance with the Scriptures." Paul continues in this pericope, elaborating on the confession that is implied as an aspect of the action of the verb *traditioning.* The Greek term for "handing on what has been received" translates most directly into the English term *traditioning.* Paul reminds the congregation at Corinth that he handed on to them what he had received—traditioning them into the confessional faith. The traditioning to which Paul referred demonstrates the significance of confessional beliefs for the forming of Christian practices among disciples within communities of faith.

Although verbal confession is an important witness to one's faith, that confessed faith must also be embodied in gestures and practices that ideally constitute the lifestyles of individuals living in community. The embodiment of our faith in practices enables Christian communities to remember the acts of faith of our forebears for the purpose of receiving encouragement, nurture, and even reproof for our current lives of faith. In remembering the narrative of salvation history, Christian communities not only intellectually comprehend the tradition of faith, but may also participate in that narrative as individuals and communities are integrated, similar to Paul in this Scripture text (vv. 8–11). Paul tells the Corinthians that, after appearing to numerous brothers and sisters, including the apostles, though he had persecuted the Church of God, Jesus appeared also to him (vv. 8–9). Paul explains that through the grace of God his proclamation of faith in Jesus Christ resulted in the Corinthians' belief (vv. 10–11). Likewise, through the grace of God the proclamation of contemporary Christians continues the traditioning process, inviting and integrating others into communities of faith. However, Paul's reference to the practice of traditioning implies more than a verbal proclamation of faith in Jesus Christ; it represents the embodiment of faith within the practices of Christian communities.

III. *Traditioning as evangelistic ministry.* The Pauline concept of traditioning is evangelistic because its central purpose is "handing on the faith" and thereby integrating individuals into Christian communities. Reflection on traditioning from this pericope can help communities of faith understand their Christian practices as evangelistic witness. The language of evangelism has fallen into disfavor throughout much of contemporary American Protestantism. During the last two centuries, the use of language related to evangelism has grown synonymous with preaching, narrowing the connotation of evangelism to verbal proclamation. However, the biblical exegetical foundations of evangelism, and its use throughout most of Christian tradition, reveals a more complicated notion of proclaiming the good news that is inclusive of verbal witness as well as communal practices related to traditioning. Canonical Scripture, particularly Pauline Scripture, is clear that faith is essential to salvation, while practices are conditional. However, as many have recognized, faith may occur instantaneously, but is seldom sustained without participation in Christian practices. Such practices in Christian tradition are often referred to as means of grace. They are usually organized into two groups (the following categories are taken from the writing of John Wesley, organizer of the eighteenth-century Methodist movement): *instituted* (by Jesus Christ) and *prudential* (those that Wesley considered prudent). Instituted means of grace correspond to traditional Christian understandings of works of piety and include prayer, searching the Scriptures, the Lord's Supper, fasting, and Christian conferencing. Prudential means of grace correspond to traditional Christian understandings of works of mercy or charity and include feeding the hungry, clothing the naked, entertaining the stranger, and visiting those who are in prison, sick, or variously afflicted. These Christian practices, among others, constitute the Pauline concept of traditioning and contribute to a communal witness that proclaims the salvation narrative to the world. Such a proclamation through words and actions invites persons to receive the salvation narrative as their own. Individuals are then initiated into Christian communities that will nurture their faith in Jesus Christ and facilitate their participation in Christian practices, including the initiation of additional disciples, thus continuing the process of traditioning. Although traditioning may not result in rapid quantitative development of membership, it will contribute to the integration of disciples within Christian communities, and to the cultivation of deeply grounded faith.—Laceye Warner

ILLUSTRATIONS
TRADITIONALISM.   "Traditionalism is the living faith of the dead, traditionalism is the dead faith of the living."—Jaroslav Pelikan[3]

TRADITION.   Scripture is considered the primary source, particularly for Protestant Christian beliefs and practices. Additionally, tradition, reason, and experience are considered means to assist in the interpretation of Scripture. For Protestants in particular, reason and experience may also be seen as secondary sources for Christian beliefs and practices, while tradition is more often overlooked or underestimated as such. This perspective largely grows out of the Protestant Reformation's suspicion of tradition. Tradition, particularly of the patristic period, offers a rich secondary resource for Christian beliefs and practices.—Laceye Warner

SERMON SUGGESTIONS
Topic: Cleansing for Service
TEXT: Isa. 6:1–8 (9–13)
(1) A vision of God produces a consciousness of sin. (2) The action of God conveys forgiveness of sin. (3) The call of God prepares prophets for warfare against sin.

---

[3]*The Vindication of Tradition* (New Haven: Yale University Press, 1984), p. 65.

Topic: This Is the Gospel Truth
TEXT: 1 Cor. 15:1–11
(1) The fact of Christ's death for our sins. (2) The reality of Christ's Resurrection. (3) The certainty of Christ's salvation. (4) The necessity of the believer's determined faith.

WORSHIP AIDS
CALL TO WORSHIP.   "The Lord will accomplish his purpose for me. Your love endures for ever, Lord; do not abandon what you have made" (Ps. 138:8 REB).

INVOCATION.   Father God, as we sing the great hymns of faith; pray the prayers of petition, thanksgiving, and intercession; and listen for the eternal voice that compels us to action in your name, we pray that you will come to us in all power and love and change us inside, that we might live worthily in your fashion on the outside, thus giving mighty witness to your continuing presence among us, even as earlier followers found you ever present and learned to pray: [Lord's Prayer].—Henry Fields

OFFERTORY SENTENCE.   "You are saved by the gospel if you hold firmly to it—unless it was for nothing that you believed" (1 Cor. 15:2b TEV).

OFFERTORY PRAYER.   Your word, O God, tells us that faith without words is dead, but every day in many ways our faith is strengthened and proven, as true love and caring have their way in acts of compassion and giving. We give of our time and our tears, of our skills and our energy, and of our very selves, and we are blessed. Now grant that our offerings will not only bless us as we give, but bless others whose lives are enriched through the gospel of Christ.

PRAYER.   O God, there is an awful danger in that hearing a sermon about the poor and the needy, the homeless and the rejected, becomes a kind of catharsis for our soul, and we are subtly duped into believing that we have done our duty when we have not even begun.

We pray that this church may be a launching pad for catapulting us into the world with its crying and desperate needs—this world for which you die a thousand deaths every day. We are so reluctant to die that you may live in and through us. Christ emptied himself—may we empty ourselves that we may be filled with the fullness of your grace and love in him toward *all* persons. So often we pick and choose those to whom we are going to show love.

O Father, this morning we have received our marching orders—we have heard the gospel, the goodness of your coming to the lowliest, the neediest, the weakest—in the flesh and blood of unconditional love, which alone redeems. Now send us forth to be your reconcilers—your healers—in all the brokenness of this world for which you died and are still dying to heal and make whole.

In our saner moments we know that to whom much is given much is required. We pray through the one who is here praying and working for our peace and the peace of the world, as God's perennial Word is teaching us to pray and work together.—Adapted from John Thompson

SERMON
Topic: God and Our Choices
TEXT: Luke 6:12–13

Choices are like legs. They give us movement and help us to get on with life—on our own terms. They are also like doors; through them we enter into new areas—although we are then shut off from where we previously came. Choosing has to do with making a selection between alternatives, deciding about a matter, giving preference to one alternative over another on the basis of some plan or criterion or end that is envisioned. Choices are necessary and inevitable. They are awesomely personal and decisive. We often need help in making them. Our text reports a decision time in the life of Jesus, that time when he had to choose and appoint leaders to extend his ministry to the masses. It is an account of how Jesus handled crucial decision making. This account also grants insight into how God can relate to us when we need help to make wise choices.

Jesus was concerned about the future of his work. He saw and felt the need to train a small group to expand his strategic ministry of preaching, teaching, and healing. There were needs among the people—many, many unmet needs—and other hands would be required for the work necessary to help people in need.

Jesus knew that he had made an impact on a growing group of followers, and the sight of a thronging mass of listeners as he preached and taught here and there must have encouraged him. But Jesus also knew that not everyone in the throng was listening to him for the right reasons, and that not everyone would give his words full freedom in their lives. I can believe that Jesus looked with ever-deepening interest at certain faces in the crowd, sensitive to those who seemed most alert, open, eager, and responsive to his presence and message.

The time finally came, the text states, when Jesus decided to single out certain persons from within the listening crowds. It was a special time for choosing. A crucial decision was in the making. A vision of human possibilities had taken shape in his heart and mind, and the pressure of choosing wisely was upon him. The text tells us what Jesus did as he reached that point of concern.

1. *Under pressure to decide, Jesus withdrew to pray about the action he needed to take:* "*He went out to the mountain to pray.*" Decision making is best handled when steeped in the flavor of prayer. Prayer to God about what we feel or know is necessary: it focuses the human spirit and heightens the consciousness; it lights up the mind and exposes any dark corners of thought. Prayer lets dialogue with God happen. "He went out to the mountain to pray."

2. *Jesus honored the gravity of the concern by setting himself to "pray through." He spent the entire night in prayer to God.* Decisions of a major nature call for unceasing and unhurried prayer, a time with God that is uninterrupted, an extended time when our thoughts and impressions and concerns can be corrected or confirmed, and our options can be explored in the spirit of reverence and illumined thought.

3. *Having "prayed through," Jesus seized the moment and acted on his decision. "And when the day came, he called his disciples and chose twelve of them."* The fact that Jesus prayed when making decisions reminds us that his commitment to God was always the framework for his planning. Small wonder, then, that he received such steady praise from God as he went about handling the tasks of his life. What strength he must have received from this unexpected commendation from God: "You are my Son, the Beloved; with you I am

well pleased" (Luke 3:22b). Right choices, responsibly followed, are always blessed by God. When we wisely use our freedom in a commitment that honors God, we too receive the praise of God. Our deepest character shows itself in our choices and how we make them.

No human, not even Jesus, has escaped the demand to choose between paths to follow, the doors to enter, and the possibilities to entertain. He too had to choose his path, his friends, his style of ministry, his approach to handling the issues of life. Yes, Jesus was like us in having to invest his freedom. He chose to keep himself in the plan God had announced as willed for him, and he used his freedom to serve God's bidding, assured that God would help him rightly shape his end.

All of us who are serious about God and life want to be able to look back over our years with some satisfaction about the choices we made as we lived. We all want to rejoice at some future time that our decisions worked meaningfully and fruitfully for us. We all want to be confident that our lives are not shaped by accident or mere chance but by a God-approved design, and that God is actually at work with us as we live and make our choices.

The account about Jesus suggests that this can indeed be the case when we invite God into dialogue with us about the details of our living. Our decisions can be God-guided. They need to be, because we invest all of our past in each act of choice, and we need divine wisdom in risking so much.

We can make God-approved decisions if we are willing to study the issues prayerfully. Wisdom from Scripture can be trusted to illumine the issue before us, while a firm commitment to God can grant us needed perspective. In all major decisions we need an adequate set of facts and a clear focus. Clarity and focus usually result sooner if we release our fears and feelings of insecurity to God as we pray, and as we stay open to fresh impressions and any last-minute cautions or reinforcement God might give.

We can expect God-governed results when we make our decisions and act on our choices in a timely way. If a decision is not made on time, or if it is not acted on with timeliness, the delay itself can render the decision ineffective.

When we act on what we have decided, we must trust God to oversee the results of our actions. We humans must make our decisions, but the full results of any decision involve many factors beyond our control. We must think, decide, and work as if everything depends on us, and yet trust as though everything depends on God. Jesus had to do that. Interestingly, Jesus chose Judas along with the other eleven after praying all night to God. Was Judas part of God's answer to Jesus' prayers? Yes, he was; but we must understand that Jesus chose all twelve apostles on the basis of their possibilities in grace. Judas began as did the other eleven, as a trusted disciple, but somewhere along the way after Jesus chose him, his choices turned sinister. He did not continue to match trust with honor, or to match the cause with his commitment, an offered career with sound character. Judas was not a traitor when he was first chosen; it was by his own wrong choice that he became a traitor, which is what the narrative distinctly tells us (Luke 6:16). Jesus took a risk in choosing every one of the twelve. Judas Iscariot failed the trust Jesus placed in him, and became an agent of ill, yet God still controlled the "fallout" from that ill-fated selfish choice when he used Judas's dreaded betrayal to effect the divine rescue of a fallen humanity through the death of Jesus on a cross.

Be serious about the decisions you must make. Bathe the decision-making process in prayer and reexamine all known factors under the searching, illumining light of Scripture. Yield all anxieties and fears about your plans to God. Make your decision, then act on it with timeliness, trusting our wise and sovereign God to oversee the results and any fallout from them. Jesus made his decision this way, and his way holds wisdom and promise for us as well.—James Earl Massey[4]

SUNDAY, FEBRUARY 15, 2004
Lectionary Message

Topic: The Ground Zero of Our Hope

TEXT: 1 Cor. 15:12–20

Other Readings: Jer. 17:5–10; Ps. 1; Luke 6:17–26

I. What is the ground of our hope in times of tragedy? Millions of people around the world, but especially in the United States, had to confront that question after terrorist attacks on September 11, 2001. In news coverage and in televised memorial services, people revealed what they believed about death and resurrection. People to whom the idea of "giving a testimony" is utterly foreign nevertheless bore witness to the beliefs that kept them going in that terrible time. At a rally hosted by Oprah Winfrey in Yankee Stadium, a prominent theme was that "the spirit of America lives on." This sentiment was made visible by the number of American flags waved at intervals throughout the service. Others proclaimed that the firefighters, police, and emergency workers who lost their lives that day would "live in our hearts," which suggests that immortality consists of being remembered by others. Occasionally, a relative or friend of someone who died would declare, "we'll be together again in heaven," or they would speak of friends or coworkers who died together now having a wonderful time with one another in some glorified version of their earthly lifestyle.

I wish that in the midst of these professions of faith someone had gently asked people *why* they believed what they did. My guess is that, living in a culture that is suspicious if not hostile toward religious claims of ultimate truth, they have sought refuge in myths, civil religion, and wishful thinking. The Christian faith has more to offer than any of these, as Paul proclaims in today's passage from 1 Corinthians.

II. *The ground of our hope.* The fifteenth chapter of 1 Corinthians is a summary of Paul's Gospel, particularly the first eleven verses. The sine qua non of his beliefs appears here: "Christ died for our sins in accordance with the Scriptures. . . . He was buried. . . . He was raised on the third day in accordance with the Scriptures. . . . He appeared to Cephas, then to the twelve. . . ." The physical death and bodily Resurrection of Jesus Christ are the cornerstones of Christian life and hope. Even in the first generation after the Resurrection, however, there were some who debated whether Christ had indeed risen, and whether resurrection of the dead was possible for anyone else. Paul draws on a number of sources to answer questions we may have as to *why* he believes what he does. First, he reminds his listeners that Jesus' death and Resurrection were the fulfillment of the Scriptures. Second, he points to eyewitnesses to the Risen Christ, some of whom were still alive to testify to what they had seen. Third, he appeals to logic; in verses 12 to 13 he demonstrates the absurdity

---

[4]*Sundays in the Tuskegee Chapel* (Nashville: Abingdon Press, 2000), pp. 125–129.

of claiming that there is no resurrection of the dead when Christ was raised. Finally, he points out the futility of their faith if Christ is not risen.

Later in this chapter we are offered a variety of images to evoke a sense of what resurrection life will be like. Our present, earthly bodies will return to the dust, but we will be clothed with imperishable resurrection bodies. We will be transformed in the twinkling of an eye and put on immortality. The sting of death will be no more. A contemporary Swedish hymn writer presents another evocative and orthodox image of what heaven will be like:

> They shall see him, their living Redeemer,
> Whom they knew once by faith, now by sight.
> They shall praise him, their hope and salvation,
> They shall be transformed in his holy light,
> They'll be singing, singing, yes, singing
> A new, jubilant song.[5]

III. *Holding our ground.* Old Testament theologian Elizabeth Achtemeier once made the wry statement that we should beware any sentence that begins, "Well, I like to think of God as . . ." because such a statement is the projection of the speaker's wishes rather than backed up with something substantial. As Christians, we have substantial reason for believing in the Resurrection of Jesus Christ, the first fruits of those who have fallen asleep. We can rejoice that we have more than a national *esprit de corps* or fairy tales to sustain us in a day of sorrow and every other day. Like Jesus' followers of the first century, we are called to bear witness to what we believe, and to why we believe it.

One martyr—for martyr is another word for witness—on September 11, 2001, was an airline passenger named Todd Beamer. While great capital has been made of "Let's roll," the last words he was heard to say before his flight crashed in a Pennsylvania field, he can be called a martyr because before he said those words he asked the telephone operator with whom he was talking to say the Lord's Prayer and other Scripture with him. Todd Beamer bore witness to the ground of his hope: the Lord of life. And in the midst of grief, his widow did more than pay her respects; she praised his Risen Savior.

The Church of Jesus Christ has purpose and power when it proclaims that because Christ is risen, we too shall be raised. We can offer a troubled and sometimes terrifying world both solace and a glorious future when we remember the Ground Zero of our hope. It's not a place in New York City or Washington, D.C., but rather Calvary and the empty tomb.—Carol M. Norén

ILLUSTRATIONS

THE LAST WORD.   In recent years, death has been rehabilitated by popular culture. Death is now interpreted as just another experience of life, a natural part of the rhythm of the cosmos. Death is one point along the so-called circle of life that moves from birth to maturity to death to rebirth. As fall turns into winter and then winter into spring, our bodies will wither

---

[5]O. Ahlén, verse 4 of Britt G. Hallqvist, "De Skall Gå till den Heliga Staden," in *Psalmer och Sånger* (the Swedish Hymnbook) (Stockholm: Verbum förlag AB, 1987), p. 172. English translation by Carol M. Norén.

and age, then die, then pass into the soil. where they will give birth to new life forms like flowers and trees. I don't know about you, but this explanation hardly strikes me as tidings of comfort and joy. I've visited my father's grave. In the summer his old friend Nick plants beautiful red and white geraniums on it. Somehow, I am not filled with gratitude and fulfillment that the body of my father, rotting away in the soil, is providing nutrients for the local flora and fauna. My father was worth more than that. But the Bible does not teach anything about the circle of life. The Bible teaches that death, far from being a natural part of life, was never intended to be part of God's good creation. It came about as a result of sin. The whole story of the Bible is the story of how God entered human history to deal with that sin, so that death would not have the last word.—Joy J. Hoffman[6]

EARNEST MONEY.   When a person buys a house, it is normal to present "earnest money" to the seller along with the written offer. The earnest money demonstrates the buyer's serious intent to go through with the sale. It is a pledge of what is to come. And if the offer is later withdrawn, the buyer usually forfeits this money. In the Resurrection of Jesus from the dead, God offers us "earnest money" on the inheritance awaiting us. We can trust this pledge, for God gave his own Son in promise.

SERMON SUGGESTIONS

Topic: Toward True Success
TEXT: Jer. 17:5–10
(1) It is easy but tragic to trust and worship our natural desires and go the way of human pride and presumption. (2) But it is wise and blessed to fix our faith and affection on the Lord, who gives us strength, security, and a fruitful life.

Topic: If There Is No Resurrection
TEXT: 1 Cor. 15:12–20
(1) Is the preaching of the gospel in vain? Often it is, for various reasons, but it would be definitely so if Christ had not been raised. (2) Is our faith in vain? Many of our expectations of God may come to disappointment, but our faith in God would amount to nothing if Christ had not been raised. (3) Are our sins forgiven? Acknowledgment of our wrongdoing may bring relief to our conscience, but our guilt remains if Christ has not been raised.

WORSHIP AIDS
CALL TO WORSHIP.   "Blessed is the man who does not walk in the counsel of the wicked or stand in the way of sinners or sit in the seat of mockers. But his delight is in the law of the Lord, and on his law he meditates day and night" (Ps. 1:1–2 NIV).

INVOCATION.   O Lord, you are calling us along the ways that build us up in the most hold faith, that strengthen our resolve to be a blessing to family, friends, and others whom it is

---

[6]Joy J. Hoffman, "Ain't No Grave Gonna Hold This Body Down," in Carol M. Norén, *In Times of Crisis and Sorrow: A Minister's Manual Resource Guide* (San Francisco: Jossey-Bass, 2001), p. 157.

our privilege to meet. In our heart of hearts we know that your way is the best way, and we pray that this service of worship will increase our joy in you.

OFFERTORY SENTENCE.   "The same Lord is the Lord of all, and his generosity is offered to all who appeal to him, for all who call on the name of the Lord will be saved" (Rom. 10:12–13 NJB).

OFFERTORY PRAYER.   Our gracious Father, your generosity has made us witnesses to the whole world, to tell of your love poured out in Jesus Christ for our salvation. Grant now that what we bring in tithes and offerings may be used to give our faith and love a voice.

PRAYER.

1. Give thanks for the gift of life.
2. Give thanks for the privilege of work.
3. Give thanks for the gift of hope, family, and church.
4. Pray for those who suffer, those who sorrow, those who struggle with life-involving issues.
5. Give thanks for those who have experienced joy, felt happiness, known success.
6. Ask forgiveness for known personal sins, for the sins others commit against you, for the sins of the country.
7. Ask that this hour be the hour of redemption for us all, that the Spirit of the Lord move among us, calling each of us to renewed faith and commitment.—Henry Fields

SERMON
Topic: The Spirituality of Dr. Carver
TEXT: Job 12:7–10 (RSV)

Across almost the whole of forty-seven years, from 1896, when he answered the call of Principal Washington to come and teach here, to 1943, when he died, "old and full of years," George Washington Carver was the living center of public imagination and discussion. He was a uniquely gifted person, both a genius and an achiever. We honor his life and work by remembering his accomplishments as a chemist, artist, naturalist, agriculturalist, ecologist, educator, and humanitarian.

But Dr. Carver was more. He was also a believer, a person who openly honored God and God's ways with us. I have talked with many persons who knew Dr. Carver, and I have read the serious studies about his life and thought, and they all rightly called attention to a spirituality that marked his living. As he went about the business of his life, there was a vital faith and infectious attitude of reverence that influenced how Dr. Carver viewed and responded to the natural world around him, the stirring currents of life within him, and the unmet needs of the people he met. All of this is in my view as I speak here about Dr. Carver's "spirituality."

The word *spirituality* is a relational term; it has to do with one's development and deportment when there is a vital and reciprocal tie between God and the self. There is a steady emphasis in our culture on what aids "healthiness" of the body, by which we mean the harmonious functioning of all its parts; but there is also a harmony in life for us called "godliness" or "spirituality," which is gained and maintained when the self rightly relates to God and life. George Washington Carver understood and taught this, and his life shows this clearly at several points that are important for us to notice.

First, Carver's spirituality was aided by his view that *the natural world is an organic unity.* Aware, as Psalm 8 forthrightly tells us, that God has placed the natural world at our disposal, and left it vulnerable to our control, Carver was one of the most vocal scientists in reminding us that our human welfare is tied up with the right understanding, proper use, and preservation of the created order.

Carver listened to the voice of living things, and because he openly regarded each living thing as precious and meaningful, with something to say on its own, those living things betrayed their secrets to him as he took time with them. It can be readily said that to George Washington Carver, living things were points of entry for discussions with God; they expanded his awareness of the mystery of life.

Like Job, whose admonition about this is poetically stated in my text, the beasts of the field, the birds of the air, the fish of the sea, and the plants of the earth all declare something about our Creator. Carver often quoted Tennyson's incisive poem:

> Flower in the crannied wall,
> I pluck you out of the crannies,
> I hold you here, root and all, in my hand;
> Little flower—but if I could understand
> What you are, root and all, and all in all,
> I should know what God and man is.

A practical spirituality includes an openness to living things, an avid listening to life, and an interest in learning what this natural world has to tell us about itself and about its Creator.

Second, Dr. Carver's spirituality involved *a deep humility before the mystery of life that was balanced against a persistence to solve the problems life presents.*

It is important to understand that a vast difference exists between what constitutes a "problem" and what is essential "mystery." Gabriel Marcel has ably explained that a problem is something that can be solved; it is out there in front of the self, and once a solution to it is found, one can move beyond it. But a mystery is not something external; a mystery involves us existentially as something the utter strangeness and stubbornness of which is part of us, and it resists any and all attempts on our part to domesticate, dominate, or even define it. A problem can be solved and dismissed, but a mystery cannot be dismissed because it cannot be isolated from our own being. Dr. Carver understood this, and he stood reverently before the mystery of life as he engaged in the business of living.

There is a story he used to tell that helps to show how his love for God and reverence for life kept him both humble before mystery and persistent in dealing with problems. There was that day, he reported, when he had been meditating on life and nature. He moved from his thought to prayer and asked God, "Mr. Creator [his way of addressing the Almighty], why did you make the universe?" God responded to Carver's query, but it was an admonition to ask for something more in keeping with what his mind might more readily grasp. So Carver revised his question, scaled it down, and asked God why he had made humans. He was told inwardly that he still wanted to know too much. Praying there with his eyes open, Carver was aware of some peanuts drying on a nearby shelf, and he asked God to tell him the purpose they were created to serve. The Almighty seemed pleased and told Carver that if he would busy himself to separate the peanut into its many elements, then he would learn much about its uses.

So, using what he knew of chemistry and physics, Carver worked and separated the oils, gums, resins, sugars, starches, and acids found in the peanut. In separating the constituent elements of the peanut that way, Carver was working on a problem, and over time his solution to the problem posed by the peanut uncovered or discovered or invented new uses for the peanut—three hundred new uses, actually—but the mystery of humans and the universe continued to haunt Carver's mind and spirit across the rest of his life.

We humans can indeed solve problems, which happens when we rightly use our minds, but we are vastly and inevitably limited mentally when we confront mystery. Dr. Carver wisely embraced the mystery in life, aware that it embraced him. Practical spirituality helps any human to do so.

Third, Dr. Carver's spirituality helped him *to deal creatively with the hard times of life, even the harsh limitations imposed on him by racism because he was black.* Given his long life in a then-racist South, much could be reported about this, but perhaps this one illustration will suffice.

In January 1921, Carver went to Washington, D.C., to speak to a congressional committee about the possibilities of the peanut as a commercial product. He appeared before the House Ways and Means Committee, the group responsible for deciding whether to impose a higher tariff on imported peanuts. Carver was there before the committee at the request of the United Peanut Association of America, a group seeking to protect their then-infant business from the lower-cost peanuts imported from the Far East—peanuts grown in China, processed in Japan, and then sent here for sale.

Expecting such a high-level committee to do its business with dignity and decorum, Carver was shocked when, as he made his way to the front when his turn approached to speak, he overheard one of the committee members yelp out, "I suppose if you have plenty of peanuts and watermelons you're perfectly happy!" Being wise, he ignored the jibe; but being black, his spirit felt the intended sting. He was further shocked when one of the committee members sitting at the table made this surly comment to the committee chair: "Down where I come from we don't accept any nigger's testimony, and I don't see what this fellow can say that will have any bearing on this meeting." Carver had not even spoken yet but was being thus prejudged. He was strongly tempted at that point to withdraw from the room, but a higher thought held him steady. Carver reasoned that the opportunity before him was greater than the insults he had just received, so he offered a quick, silent prayer to God for grace to carry out his reason for being there.

Given only ten minutes to present his statement, Carver felt as if he were racing against time. He opened the case he had brought with him and began talking about the peanut and some of his findings from the many experiments he had conducted on its properties. The disclosures were so engagingly reported that as the ten minutes allotted were about to end, one of the committee members offered a motion, which passed, extending Carver's time. And even more time was granted afterward. According to the record, the ensuing report from Carver lasted one hour and forty minutes longer, including a display of some of the 165 products Carver had made from the peanut. When he concluded, the Committee stood and applauded him. What followed from all this is a part of the history of how the economy of the South changed for the better. Carver's gifted work and counsel made much of that change possible.

If he had not been saved from selfishness, bitterness, and hate by a deep and steadying tie with God, George Washington Carver might never have given to the world the many contributions he shaped and shared as a creative scientist who happened to be black. Carver understood well that selfishness short-circuits gifts and abilities, that it ruins one for a right handling of choice opportunities. A true spirituality always works against what discredits, demeans, and limits us. "No matter what the circumstances," Carver once stated to a friend, "hatred and resentment must never have a place in our hearts." This is a wisdom that spirituality teaches, an understanding reached by any and all who take Jesus as a model for their life. Carver openly confessed that he took Jesus seriously and sought always to follow him.

Fourth, Dr. Carver's spirituality was *steadied and sustained by a disciplined openness to God.* He took time daily for devotional study of the Scriptures, and for meditational thought about God—in the presence of God through prayer. He also cherished occasions for regular worship with others. Carver had known persons shaped by such disciplines, persons whose lives had intersected meaningfully with his. He set his mind and heart toward the goal of *being what he should* in order to *do what he should.* This is what a true spirituality is all about.

Until his death, Dr. Carver treasured the memory of Mrs. Moriah Watkins. She was that black washerwoman-midwife who had opened her heart and home to Carver when he, a young homeless waif, had drifted into Neosho, Missouri, seeking a school to enter so he could learn. Moriah Watkins found the lost boy sitting beside the fence of her yard as he waited impatiently for the nearby school to open for the day. The homeless boy was a stray creature to others, but Moriah Watkins looked at him with eyes of concern; the opening of her heart and home to him blessed the young boy's life and met his need for love.

It was Moriah Watkins who gave Carver that Bible that was so dear to him, the Bible that always companioned him, positioned for ready reading across his knees as he sat in the old chapel, that leather-covered volume almost tattered by wear from regular use across his youth and later life. Moriah Watkins was to Carver like a mature shade tree to its setting, and he said so; he lauded her as having been "a great shady oak tree, strong and cool and full of comfort." This fitting image describes Carver's life also, since he used his mind and strength to provide comforting service to this institution, this region, this nation, and innumerable persons here and elsewhere who sought and needed his help. This is the proper end of spirituality, and Dr. George Washington Carver's life illustrates this in graphic "living color."—James Earl Massey[7]

---

[7]*Sundays in the Tuskegee Chapel* (Nashville: Abingdon Press, 2000), pp. 159–165.

SUNDAY, FEBRUARY 22, 2004
Lectionary Message

Transfiguration Sunday
Topic: This Is My Son, My Chosen; Listen to Him!
TEXT: Luke 9:28–36 (37–43a)
Other Readings: Exod. 34:29–35; Ps. 99; 2 Cor. 3:12–4:2

What is the mystery of a mountaintop experience that is so present throughout Scripture? Perhaps they word *mystery* answers the question. What we do know is that mountaintop experiences have led to change. We know that something very powerful occurred in each of the biblical mountaintop experiences. It is clear that the hand of God was and is at work. They are times that belong to the soul, times that we must accept without question. They are times when God has entered our lives and spoken. Perhaps he is asking us to *listen*—and listen we must. There are times in all our lives when we have experiences that must not be captured, must not be held back. The word *transfiguration* is the word for our metamorphosis. It is a change from the inside out.

A common thread that I have noted in each of the mountaintop experiences is prayer. Prayer forms the central context of salvation in the Gospel of Luke. Jesus prays before he chooses the Twelve (Luke 6:12). He is in prayer in today's text, as he is about to be transfigured (Luke 9:29). We find him in prayer once again when his disciples ask him to teach them to pray. Jesus revealed the Lord's Prayer. The disciples may have missed the point on other well-known occasions, but they were bright enough to understand that the right relationship with God the Father involves prayer. I propose that prayer is a direct connection to change. Our quiet moments spent alone with God can be our own mountaintop experiences that "only thee and we" may know the meaning of, and they may be moments of transfiguration. Prayer is the intimate action of lifting up our spirit to meet with God's will. It is that time in which the unseen and mysterious God can be experienced. It is a time when we can be at one with the sacred. In Scripture, as we have seen, being on the mountain was about experiencing some revelation, some word from the Lord, some assurance that God was with his people.

Let us move this experience of prayer to the public arena. We now call this act of prayer *worship*. We gather in community to give thanks to God. It is on this unseen and mysterious God that our attention is focused as we give thanks. It is at this time that we are shaped into God's people. It is here that we are compelled by that voice from heaven, "This is my Son, listen to him!" It is here, in a community of worship and prayer, that we can begin to know the mind of Jesus Christ. It is here that we can experience change. It is here, in prayer, that we are given a new opportunity to effect change in the lives of others. It is here that we may understand our mission of ministry in our world. These fleeting moments of connection are awesome. They are not meant to be hoarded. They are meant to have life breathed into them. They take shape and have greater meaning when they are put into the action of ministry to others.

We are warned, however, that this time of discovery must not take too long. Jesus demonstrates this to us as he hustles the disciples back down the mountain. Just about now, they, and we, want to settle into this newfound knowledge and bask in its glory. The danger lies in missing the connections we have made in our newfound experience. Our new connection to the mind and heart of Jesus is no longer a singular experience. We are now wholly members of the body of God. When we entered the mind of Christ, we entered his ministry. We will no longer be able to leave our community of worship and prayer in the same way again. As did Jesus, when we leave the mountaintop experience and the solemnity of the sanctuary, we must go out into the world to carry on the work of ministering. It is too tempting to keep our sanctified moments safe. Where our newfound truths really belong are in the homeless shelters, the battered women's shelters, the food pantries, and the countless addiction centers. The list is entirely too long. The greater sin here is *not* recognizing that what happens in our community worship and prayer must go with each of us into the balance of the week. We must put God's words to work. We need to be tending to the needs of the poor, the forgotten, and the lonely. We need to be about healing. We need to be about being among all people: *all* people.

Let us be clear about this message. This is not about gathering in community to worship and hear a few moralistic lessons once a week. In prayer and worship together, we express our love to God, and in turn we experience that love being returned to us, shaping us into new people. As we long to have our prayers heard by God, so too we are drawn to those in our community who need to be heard by us. When we leave worship, we go out into the world fuller. We can better understand that praying, worshiping, and living in a world embraced by the love and peace of God can mean only that we are better equipped to welcome all people into this fold. Something happens when we pray that evokes a response in us, and that response is lived out when we enter into the mind of Jesus Christ. When we transform our newfound hope and energy into fulfilling the cares and concerns of the world, we too become equipped to bring light into an often too dark world.

The call of Jesus is to go up to the mountain, to experience a holy presence, and to see the world as God wills for it to be. The call of Jesus is to come down the mountain and into the lives of all who are lonely and oppressed. Our call is to follow. Our call is to pay attention. Our call is to listen. Our ministry is to come out of the sanctuary and into the lives of the lonely and the oppressed. God's chosen Son calls out to us to be his ministry, to be his voice in our world. By choosing Christ, we have become chosen, and we must listen to our call to be a voice in the world. In a moment of prayer, through the words of Scripture, in the midst of music and worship, God will reveal his mission for each of us. We must be alert and listen.

"Then from the cloud came a voice that said, 'This is my Son, my chosen; listen to him.'" —Lucy Pratt

ILLUSTRATION

WAKE UP.   Life is full of things that are designed to awaken us. (a) *There is sorrow.* Once Elgar said of a young singer who was technically perfect but quite without feeling and expression, "She will be great when something breaks her heart." Often sorrow can rudely awaken a man, but in that moment, through the tears, he will see the glory. (b) *There is love.* She looked at him. He looked at her as a lover can—"and suddenly life awoke." Real love is an awakening to horizons which we never dreamed were there. (c) *There is the sense of need.* For long enough a man may live the routine of life, half asleep; and then all of a sudden into life there comes some completely insoluble problem, some quite unanswerable question, some overmastering temptation, some summons to an effort he feels is beyond his strength. In that day there is nothing left for him to do but "cry, clinging to heaven by the hems." And that sense of need awakens him to God.

We would do well to pray, "Lord, keep me always awake to thee."—William Barclay[8]

SERMON SUGGESTIONS

Topic: Best of the Worst

TEXT: Gen. 45:3–11, 15

(1) What would you do with the worst possible situation in which you could imagine yourself? (2) Rather than complaining about the turn of uncontrollable events in our lives, we should attempt to find the positive elements. (3) This does not mean that we should like what has happened to us or that we should approve the ethics of contributors to our situation, but rather that we should affirm God's providence and his transcendent, creative power. (4) This attitude can give us hope in even the most unpromising situations. (5) Resolve to put yourself more into God's hands and live with victory.

Topic: Our Body in the Life to Come

TEXT: 1 Cor. 15:35–38

(1) *Situation:* We are confronted with the puzzle of the nature of our resurrection body. (2) *Complication:* Our present human body is adapted to the material, physical world and its requirements, and we find it difficult to imagine it beyond this life. (3) *Resolution:* God our Creator will give us a new body continuous with the old, suitable to our new place of existence.

WORSHIP AIDS

CALL TO WORSHIP.   "Then I heard all created things, in heaven, on Earth, under the Earth, and in the sea, crying: 'Praise and honor, glory and might, to him who sits on the throne and to the Lamb forever'" (Rev. 5:13 REB).

INVOCATION.   Holy God: you call us to worship, and by your Spirit prompt prayers and praise. . . . Fill us with such wonder that we may worship you, grateful for the mystery of your unfailing love for us, in Jesus Christ the Lord.—*The Worship Book*[9]

OFFERTORY SENTENCE.   "The land has produced its harvest; God, our God, has blessed us. God has blessed us; may all people everywhere honor him" (Ps. 67:6–7 TEV).

OFFERTORY PRAYER.   Gracious Lord, plenty and little are here, largesse and sacrifice are here, sudden gift and disciplined stewardship are here. Bless all that is in this offering and multiply it for your precious name's sake.—E. Lee Phillips

---

[8]*The Gospel of Luke* (Louisville, Ky.: Westminster John Know Press, 2001).
[9]Philadelphia: Westminster, 1970.

PRAYER.   Father, as we wait before you in this sacred place, we have come from many walks of life, bringing with us many needs and hopes and dreams. Meet us in power, we pray, as we expectantly wait in your presence for these brief moments.

Our needs are multitude and we cannot meet them all, so we turn to you asking that you be with us in our struggles, Father. We grow weary in the midst of the struggles and many times give up. Our faith is sorely tested and sometimes destroyed as we wage the battles of life against the many influences that converge upon us. We need your presence with us, that our resolve may not waver, that our courage may not fail, and that our hope may not be destroyed. Meet us in our struggles this morning and fortify us as we continue our journey across the days ahead.

Be with us in our successes, we pray. We know that success can be as dangerous to us as failure. Remind us that success can destroy the foundation of life if we do not maintain a balance in our priorities. Forgive us when we allow our achievements and successes to dominate life, separating us from higher callings and more noble service in your name. As only you can, when you are allowed to abide in us, keep us constant in life, no matter what we must manage—be it success or failure.

Be with us in the service and help us give to those about us. May we not become discouraged with others when they do not respond as we want them to. May we not expect others to immediately adopt our values and faith, but remember that we are seed planters. Therefore it is not our responsibility to make the seed sprout and grow, but simply to plant the seeds of faith and love and hope in the lives of those around us. Enable us also to see that help does not always mean service to the down and out of life, but that it needs to be given to people of all stations and situations where they are.

Now help us to worship you in spirit and in truth, that we may go from this gathering in this sanctuary renewed and inspired to be your disciples in the waiting world.—Henry Fields

SERMON
Topic: You Are What You Believe
TEXT: 1 Cor. 1:18–25

Donald Miller, the well-known minister and seminary president, tells about a woman who phoned him one Saturday night and asked, "Dr. Miller, what do I believe?"

"What do you mean?" asked Miller, not sure he had heard her correctly.

"I mean," she said, "what do I believe? You see, I've just come from a party where several people got into a discussion about their various beliefs. One woman was Jewish, and she told us what she believes as a Jew. Another was Roman Catholic, and she told us what Catholics believe. Somebody was a Christian Scientist, and he talked about what they believe. I was the only Protestant in the group, and frankly, I didn't know what to say. What do I believe?"

"That woman," said Miller, "must have come into the church on *confusion* of faith, not the confession of faith." World wars, several other major conflicts, and the great suffering that accompanied them have eroded many people's faith.

I. *The age of science and technology has made it increasingly hard to think in terms of religious causality.* Many people are inoculated with just enough understanding of the laws of physics to blind them to the great mysteries of the universe. They take a laboratory approach to life and, because they cannot quantify or qualify the role of the Creator, assume that the deity was only a "God of the gaps," imagined by primitive people to explain the natural phenomena for which they had no scientific explanations. Recent advances in medicine and communications, among others, have only further removed us from a sense of the presence of God. Wonder drugs and organ transplants have given many persons undue confidence in the power of physicians—a confidence that many physicians themselves will readily admit is probably misplaced. And the development of the media, especially TV and video, has provided humanity with such a vivid world of instantaneous diversion that many persons now go through life without confronting the void surrounding their consciousness.

"Who needs God, man?" asked one twisting, gyrating young man with an oversized cassette player on his shoulder and earplugs in his ears. "This is it!"

II. *The geometrical increase of knowledge in our time, with the relativism that invariably accompanies it, has also had a destructive influence on faith.* In a world filled with so much information, people don't know what to believe.

One religion teaches renunciation, another advocates embracing the world. What should a person believe? It is no wonder that professors of religion in colleges and universities are often respectful of all beliefs while having none of their own.

Confusion of faith, indeed! We admire the great modern heroes of the Christian way, such as Albert Schweitzer and Mother Teresa, but don't pretend to understand how they can be so single-minded. What happens when we no longer believe anything and can't act from a center of spiritual certainty, the way our forebears did? We lose our sense of direction. We are like globules of quicksilver racing this way and that, with nothing to steady or guide us.

If our society believes in God, we shall probably believe in God. If the society is not particularly interested in God, then we are not likely to be very committed to thoughts of a deity either,

Given a society like ours, then, which is admittedly only nominally religious and inclined more and more to secular, hedonistic inclinations, our programming for belief is at best rather indefinite and we are more likely to emulate such popular idols as Cher, Madonna, Michael Jackson, Sylvester Stallone, Lee Iacocca, and Donald Trump than St. Francis or Mother Teresa.

The ministers I meet feel increasingly helpless to try to turn people to God in such a world. Our efforts are so ineffectual, they say, in the face of widespread attitudes of selfishness and apathy, of the programming in the media and in the culture generally, which shapes beliefs not toward God but toward a cynical, self-serving lifestyle that is anything but spiritual and godly.

But fortunately, belief sometimes has a way of asserting itself against its programming. It did in the case of Saul of Tarsus, the highly trained Pharisee who claimed to have had a remarkable encounter with the Resurrected Christ on the road to Damascus and went on to become the hyperenergetic thirteenth apostle. It did in the case of Ignatius of Loyola, a soldier reared for battle and courtly love under the secretary of the Spanish treasury. Lying in bed with a wounded leg, he asked for a certain book to read. His attendants could not find it, so they brought him another book, *The Flower of the Saints.* When he had finished it, there was a visible change in his manner. Laying aside knighthood, he became an ardent follower of Christ. Eventually he founded the influential Society of Jesus.—John Killinger

SUNDAY, FEBRUARY 29, 2004

Lectionary Message

Topic: Walk the Walk, Talk the Talk

TEXT: Deut. 26:1–11

Other Readings: Ps. 91:1–2, 9–16; Rom. 10:8b–13; Luke 4:1–13

Our Old Testament lesson for today sounds tailor-made for Thanksgiving, or even better, for the church's fundraising campaign. Bring your money in a basket and lay it down at the minister's feet, and take an oath that you have really brought in 10 percent! Maybe it would work. Of course, there's the story in Acts of the husband and wife who lied about the percentage they gave and fell down dead.

But here we are, at the first Sunday of Lent, setting our minds on seven weeks of austerity and sacrifice, and here's this text that sounds more like Mardi Gras—"Rejoice in every good thing that the Lord thy God hath given unto thee." What does this text have to teach us about Lent?

I. *Lent, like first fruits, is part of community life.* To begin with, this passage, like the whole book of Deuteronomy, expects the worshiper to leave his or her home, schlep to Jerusalem, the place where God's name dwells, and worship at the Temple. While there, the worshiper will testify to how he or she has lived the rest of the year—"I haven't forgotten to give to the poor; I have given my contributions to the priest who lives in my town, I haven't gotten mixed up with the worship of the dead." This ceremony reminds us that our Lenten vows are not just private acts, but are part of our communal life, connected to how we worship together and to how we care for the needs of others. Lent isn't like a spiritual diet, where we make up for the excesses of the rest of the year. It is, or it should be, an outgrowth of our daily walk with God.

II. *Lent, like first fruits, is about trusting God with our best.* The worshiper brings the "first of all the fruit of the ground, which you harvest from the land that the Lord your God is giving you." It's a beautiful symbol. The farmer plants the crops and then harvests the first tender shoots that come up from the ground, giving them as an offering to God. The farmer doesn't know for sure that more will grow, but trusts God, believing that if God gave this much, God will provide more. Our vows should also be first fruits, offerings to God out of the bounty that we trust God will provide. If we make small promises—avoiding easy things, or doing without things that are bad for us anyway—what faith are we showing in God's ability to bless our lives?

III. *Lent, like first fruits, should reflect the way God has blessed us.* Maybe most important, the worshiper is instructed to recite the history of God's dealings with Israel, beginning with Abraham and running through the Exodus, and to testify that God has made good on the promises: "I profess this day unto the Lord thy God that I am come unto the country which the Lord swore unto our fathers to give us." In other words, don't bring the gift if you don't think God has fulfilled God's part of the deal. If you think you've been cheated—if you don't feel that God has richly blessed you—then keep your stuff at home.

What about you? God promised to be with you wherever you go. God promised to deliver you from whatever bound you, and to teach you how to live abundantly. Has God made good on that promise? And are your vows a testimony to God's blessings to you?

IV. *Lent, like first fruits, is a journey with an end.* The whole first-fruits ceremony begins when the farmer harvests the first shoots and sets them aside for the trip to Jerusalem. Then comes the journey itself—pilgrims coming to the "place where God's name dwells" from wherever they live. Then comes the offering and the testimony by the worshiper, and then finally, after bowing before God, the worshiper goes off to celebrate with the entire household. Lent is a journey, and it has an end at the Resurrection of Jesus, when the first fruits of our resurrection were raised and offered to God. Let today's text encourage us to make meaningful vows that connect with our whole life, vows that give God the best of our lives and that connect with how richly God has blessed us. And let us begin our walk today, knowing that it has an end in the renewal of our life.—Richard B. Vinson

ILLUSTRATIONS

TRIBULATION.   No one yet ever entered into the Kingdom of Heaven without tribulation; not perhaps the tribulation of fire and persecution, but the tribulation of a humble and contrite heart, of the flesh subjugated in the interest of the spirit, of a life poured forth like spilled wine in the service of others. If our religion is of such a pliable and elastic sort that it has cost us no pains to acquire, no self-denial to preserve, no effort to advance, no struggle to maintain, holy and undefiled—whatever else it is, it is not the religion of him who said, "Enter ye in at the strait gate. . . . Because strait is the gate, and narrow is the way, which leadeth unto life, and few there be that find it."—Robert J. McCracken

GOD'S LAW.   When God disciplines man through denial or sacrifice, even tragedy, it is not because God wants it that way but because men leave him no other avenue through which he can proceed. Man has real freedom relative to the will of God; he can block God partially, but never wholly. God cannot command and coerce the understanding and the love of man, but he can seek it and try to get men to give it in love and faith. He can seek it as a teacher seeks the confidence of a pupil or a father seeks the love and understanding of a son.

This much seems to be clear about the law of God. We cannot break it, but we can break ourselves upon it. We can disobey it, but we cannot escape it. It is the literal Hound of Heaven to one who seeks to escape it. But to one who accepts and obeys it with joy in his soul, it is indeed a strange delight. It means strength, peace, joy.—Harold A. Bosley

SERMON SUGGESTIONS

Topic: A Pilgrimage of Memory and Gratitude

TEXT: Deut. 26:1–11

(1) We should remember God's providence. (2) When the tokens of his grace are evident. (3) In the place of worship. (4) Because he has been with us in our defeats and victories. (5) Remembering with our gifts and our rejoicing.

Topic: Salvation Can Be Yours

TEXT: Rom. 18:8b–13

The ingredients of the experience: (1) the message proclaimed, (2) the truth believed, (3) the Lord Jesus confessed.

WORSHIP AIDS

CALL TO WORSHIP.   "He who dwells in the secret place of the Most High shall abide under the shadow of the Almighty. I will say of the Lord, 'He is my refuge and my fortress; my God, in him I will trust'" (Ps. 91:1–2 NKJV).

INVOCATION.   We acknowledge, O God, in ourselves the desire to seek our own way and to have our own will regardless of what it may cost us or other people. Open our eyes to these facts, unpleasant as they may be, and then interpret to us the teaching of thy Church, that we may be prepared to meet the crooked streak that runs through our world and finally be saved from it, through Jesus Christ our Lord.—Theodore Parker Ferris

OFFERTORY SENTENCE.   "But thanks be to God! He gives us the victory through our Lord Jesus Christ. Therefore, my dear brothers, stand firm. Let nothing move you. Always give yourselves fully to the work of the Lord, because you know that your labor in the Lord is not in vain" (1 Cor. 15:58 NIV).

OFFERTORY PRAYER.   Blessed beyond measure and imagining we come this morning to offer our thanks for the abundance that we enjoy even as we return our tithes and offerings to you for the continuing work of the Lord in the world. Grant us now the grace to give generously and honestly as we have been blessed, we pray.—Henry Fields

PRAYER.   O God, you have demonstrated your love for us and for all humankind by invading this planet in person. We praise you for your Spirit let loose in the world through Jesus of Nazareth.

Grant that the Spirit of his life lived on this common earth under these ordinary skies may be with us in all the tasks and possibilities of this season and all seasons.

Help us to show forth his eagerness, not to be ministered unto, but to minister; his sympathy with suffering of every kind; his courage in the face of his own suffering; his joy in doing your work even when it meant the discipline of a cross; his passion for truth and his compassion for others; his poise at all times, even when threatened by his enemies; his complete trust in you as God and Savior.

Grant us grace, grant us courage to follow him, even if far off.

O God, whoever else you are in the mystery and greatness of your coming, you are love— "love divine, all love's excelling." As we sense your love in Christ reaching out to us and to all persons, we would reach out to one another where there is any brokenness among us— in illness, in infirmity, in sorrow, in love, in disappointment, in failure. We pray the ministry of your word of grace that alone makes whole.

Called to the ministry of reconciliation, we pray not only for the overcoming of personal estrangements but also for the healing of the nations.

Grant us the love, faith, and hope to share the bread of life with which we have been so richly blessed. As the Church, may we be faithful to the world and the worldly mission to which Christ calls us, as he is among us as our living Word, teaching us to pray as family with all peoples.—John Thompson

SERMON
Topic: The Whole Course of God's Love
TEXT: John 3:16–17

I was once lost in Philadelphia. For some reason I can't quite comprehend, when lost I just continued to drive down one street after another. So on this particular occasion, I found my most horrid dream coming true. Streets narrowed and strange faces stared into my car—some with recognizable suspicion and others with obvious displeasure. There were homes without windows, children without shoes, and young men huddled around brown paper bags. An old lady, standing on her front stoop, made an obscene gesture and shouted something equally vile. Darkness was slowly settling over the city skyline.

Each corner turned took me only deeper into this incredible slum, teeming with burned-out buildings and broken-down lives. Then, as I turned one more corner, and as the street opened-up to a playground, I saw it.

Above my head, unceremoniously scribbled with a spray can, covering the broad side of a railroad overpass, were those words—words that I'd read and heard, perhaps hundreds of times; words with which I'm so familiar, seeing them there was like being greeted by the smiling face of a good friend. Even so, I read them as if for the first time: "For God so loved the world. . . ."

It's a phrase that need not be completed, because I knew where it was headed and what it would proclaim. And I was reminded: there, where I was lost in a world of strange, foul-smelling, disheartening, dilapidated living—there I was given this word about love. Not just any love, but God's love.

"Isn't it strange," I recall thinking. How strange that someone should scribble out those words above this world. A world that I imagined to be populated with poverty and polluted lives.

And yet, why not above this world in which we witness so much strife, struggle, bloodshed, and human bondage? Why should we assume for one minute that God's love has always been reserved for only the very best of creatures, as well as the most attractive aspects of creation? Wouldn't that drain the life blood from the very heart of this unprecedented word we've heard?

Our Christian faith would force us to think so. "In awful and surprising truth," writes C. S. Lewis, "we are the objects of God's love . . . not because we are lovable but because he is love; not because he needs to receive but because he delights to give"—which same truth is often hard to believe, isn't it?

Whenever I see love portrayed in much of contemporary culture, it seems so sweet and sentimental. Rarely, if ever, does such love allow for anything disfigured, unsightly, or unbecoming. Instead, love becomes a sanctuary, sheltering both the lover and the beloved from the harsh and hazardous side of life.

Now the culture no longer confesses that "God is love," but rather that "love is God." Which leads me to affirm what was said by another: "To say that love is God is romantic idealism. To say that God is love is either the last straw or the ultimate truth."

That's what I'm convinced our spray-can preacher knew when he scribbled out, "For God so loved the world . . ." And maybe whenever that mother who lost her child in a drive-by shooting looks at those words, maybe they don't wash away her pain, but maybe they still provide some soothing to her soul. And maybe whenever the homeless person pushes her shopping cart beneath that overpass, she reads those words as a promise she can't even put into words.

Perhaps in that place, where human hearts are burdened with discouragement and despair, maybe there this message is the only foothold for an endangered faith. Because for them, "to say that God is love is either the last straw or the ultimate truth."

Fortunately, for those who have faith in God's unrelenting love, it isn't really a question of either-or. The Christian faith affirms that both are held in tension. In so many circumstances, it's just because we're convinced that God's love is the ultimate truth that we can cling to that word as the "last straw," whenever push comes to shove.

It was and is in Christ that God loved and is loving this world into redemption and salvation—which means that God's love, in Christ, cannot be terminated; neither can it be worn down by this world's sickness-unto-death. God's love, unlike anything else we've ever known, is a power that continues to push both creature and creation toward future fulfillment.

I was once again reminded that this divine love—a force which, if in total control, would collapse all barriers and close all breaches—has not yet become the ruling force in this world. So those same words now took on another new meaning: they now pointed from the past, through the present, and to the future. They promised that this love, so patient, so passionate, and so very persistent, this love would one day win over this world.

And when it does, when that great day arrives, then there will be a harmony, a peace, and a communion such as the world has seldom seen. That love will then become our laughter. That love will then meet our deepest longings. That love will then mend our wounded hearts, healing those cracks caused by hatred and hard feelings. That love will then bring us home to brother and sister, home to unparalleled joy, home to a world washed clean of all corruption, calamity, and crying.

Our gut tells us that things aren't good at all, and they're steadily growing worse. All footholds seem to have fallen away. We're deeply troubled at the prospect of what tomorrow might bring. We're looking and longing for some sustaining word. Remember the spray-can preacher: "For God so loved the world . . ."

We have experienced, we will experience, much in this life. Some of those events will bring great joy, others will bring disabling sorrow. Some will taste of sweet success, while others will only offer the bitter tears of tragic conclusions. Some will cause us to question the love of God, while others will leave us speechless from the sheer magnitude of God's gracious provision.

That's why we would do well to remember what the reformer John Calvin once confessed. He said that "the true looking of faith is placing Christ before one's eyes and beholding in him the heart of God poured out in love."—Albert J. D. Walsh

SUNDAY, MARCH 7, 2004
Lectionary Message

Topic: Facing the Darkness
TEXT: Gen. 15:1–12, 17–18
Other Readings: Ps. 27; Phil. 3:17–4:1; Luke 13:31–35

Few things hurt worse than a failed dream. Maybe it's worse if part of the dream depends on someone else, someone you trust, living up to a promise. When he or she doesn't come through and your dream fails, you've lost not only part of your future, but part of your past and present as well, because of the collapse of your trust in your friend.

I. *Abram looks at the darkness and sees stars.* In this episode, Abram hasn't yet been named Abraham. Some years back, at age seventy-five, God promised Abram that he would have more descendants than he could count, and Abram believed God. When this story opens, he still has no heir, so when God next appears to him, Abram tells him straight up, "You have given me no child, so a slave born in my household will carry on my name. What will you give me? When will you make good on your promise?" And God takes Abram outside, out into the night, and asks him to count the stars: "That's how many descendants you will have, and they will be your own great-great-great-grandchildren." And Abram believes God. He looks into the darkness and sees the stars, and they give him enough light, enough hope, to go on.

Does he believe because he can't count the stars? No. He has been living in tents all his life, and he has looked up into the night sky since he was old enough to lift his head. Does he believe because of the extravagance of the promise? No. Earlier, God compared the number of his descendants to the grains of dust on the Earth, and Abram still has not one single child of his own. Again, nothing is different except that Abram and his wife Sarah are older. He has no more proof, no greater assurance, than when God first promised, and he has greater reasons to begin to doubt. So why does he believe?

II. *Abram looks at the darkness and sees only more darkness.* It gets worse, so I want to put off the answer to the question until we've seen the whole episode. When God first appeared to Abram, God told him to leave his ancestral home and walk until God showed him where to live. God had already promised him the whole land of Palestine—had told him to walk as far as he wanted in any direction and he'd still be on property that God was going to give to him. But so far Abram had been living on borrowed land, and in the chapter just before this one, his nephew Lot had been captured by the local warlords. So when God tells him, "I brought you here in order to give you this land," Abram again wants some kind of proof. "Can you give me a deed to the property? Can you assure me that I will have children and kin enough to work it and to protect it?" It isn't an unreasonable request. Abram has been promised a home and a family who can inherit it after him, and he wants to know how he can believe that God will pony up. Again, God takes Abram out into the night, but this time Abram doesn't see stars. Instead, he sees "a deep and terrifying darkness."

This time God gives Abram the bad news, straight up: "OK, you got me. I know I promised you a home, but I'm not going to give you this land, and it won't come into the possession of your descendants for a long time. In fact, first they will have to be slaves in a foreign land and be oppressed for four hundred years. But then they will come out and possess this land, from north to south, and they will live here in peace."

III. *Abram finds a way to believe.* We aren't told specifically how Abram reacted to this news. But the text says that the Lord and Abram made a covenant, so we must presume that he could look into the darkness and still find a reason to trust God, whose promises keep getting delayed and reconfigured. How does that work? How do you face the collapse of a dream and the foundation of trust on which it rested? How do you keep believing when you look out into the night and, instead of stars, see a "deep and terrifying darkness"?

Lent is a good time to think about this, because we know where it's leading: we are walking to Calvary. We are headed for Gethsemane, to hear Christ pray, "Isn't there any way this could turn out differently?" We are headed for Golgotha, to hear Christ cry out, "My God, my

God, why have you forsaken me?" And we each know something about the apparent collapse of dreams, the seeming failure of trust that Christ faced, only we know the end of his story but we don't know the end of our own. We don't know whether the Sunday after Friday will be Easter or just another dark and stormy night.

So how do we believe? I think the answer will be different for each of us. Some of us will hear a friend's voice as God's voice reassuring us with the same promises we've heard before—nothing new, nothing spectacular, but just what we need all the same. Some of us will find that prayer or the liturgy or some other moment in worship will be light enough to take us home. We will believe, in the end, the same way Abram did, by deciding that the God whose promises often seem elusive and slippery is still the God who is with us in the darkness, and that's enough.—Richard B. Vinson

ILLUSTRATIONS

SURPRISING DIMENSIONS.   The presence of the Kingdom in Jesus meant that the Kingdom of God was of a radically different order than people's expectations. Rather than representing the overthrow of the hated Roman Empire, it was present in weakness and suffering, where even the Son of Man had nowhere to lay his head (Luke 9:58), and where he came not to be served but to serve and to give his life as a ransom for the many (Mark 10:45). Thus the Kingdom was like a seed growing quietly (Mark 4:26–29), like a minuscule mustard seed, whose beginnings were so small and insignificant that nothing could be expected of it, but whose final end—inherent in the seed itself and therefore inevitable—would be an herb tree of such dimensions that birds could rest in its branches (Matt. 13:31–32).—Gordon D. Fee[1]

GOD'S TIMETABLE.   You can demand all the answers, neatly gift-wrapped. You can insist that God quickly resolve every trial and injustice in your life. You can hold out for the world, and your life within it, to become suddenly fair and rational, though they've never been so in the first place.

Or you can choose to lift up your eyes to the heavens, pour out your tears and grief and anger, and say in the very midst of them, "God, I have no clue what this turmoil is all about or where it is leading, but this is my resolution: I will put my trust in you, and I will praise you with all of my heart, unconditionally!"

The same God who has been there for you in the past is the God who is going to be there for you in the future. He will bring resolution in his own time, according to his own purposes. We become preoccupied with our circumstances; God is preoccupied with our character. He will allow the tough times for the higher good of our character until he is finished with the great work that is invisible to our earthly eyes.—David Jeremiah[2]

SERMON SUGGESTIONS

Topic: Faith as Righteousness
TEXT: Gen. 15:1–12, 17–18
(1) Faith is the basis of a right relationship with God. (2) Faith has to face the test of the yet

---

[1]*Listening to the Spirit in the Text* (Grand Rapids, Mich.: Eerdmans, 2000), pp. 170–171.
[2]*A Bend in the Road* (Nashville: Word, 2000), pp. 101–102.

unfulfilled promise: the unseen and the unrealized. (3) Faith leaves all to God, who will bring his promise to pass in the fullness of time.

Topic: Our True Homeland
TEXT: Phil 3:17–4:1
(1) *Problem:* If we center our life in this world, all will be for nothing in the end. (2) *Solution:* If we center our life in heaven, everything about us will be different and glorious—here and hereafter.

WORSHIP AIDS

CALL TO WORSHIP. "The Lord is my light and my salvation; whom shall I fear? The Lord is the strength of my life; of whom shall I be afraid?" (Ps. 27:1).

INVOCATION.   Lord God, deal with us in this our of worship as pleases you, that we may be so filled with the power of the Son of God that all else we do will reflect the God we serve.—E. Lee Phillips

OFFERTORY SENTENCE.   "Serve the Lord with gladness" (Ps. 100:2a).

OFFERTORY PRAYER.   Lord of life, though our gift today be great or small, bless our stewardship with maximum benefit as is your way and will.—E. Lee Phillips

PRAYER.   O merciful Father, who in compassion for thy sinful children didst send thy Son Jesus Christ to be the Savior of the world: grant us grace to feel and to lament our share in the evil that made it needful for him to suffer and to die for our salvation. Help us by self-denial, prayer, and meditation to prepare our hearts for deeper penitence and a better life. And give us a true longing to be free from sin, through the deliverance wrought by Jesus Christ our only Redeemer.—*The Book of Common Worship*[3]

SERMON
Topic: On the Way to Calvary—A Learner
TEXT: Luke 22:14–34

So much in life depends on what you do with your failures. Some people fail and stay stuck there—in the guilt and remorse of failure. That was Judas—he never got over it. Others fail and learn the valuable lessons that failure alone can teach—that was Simon Peter.

We read in the startling honesty of the Bible that while Jesus was on his trip to the cross, his chief lieutenant went AWOL . . . He copped out in the courtyard, around a fire, like a wimp.

And Jesus saw it coming, with Satan a part of the process.

Satan is one of the Bible's words for that other "mind," that other voice that rises in us to defeat us. And before you throw out Satan (literally, "adversary") as some prescientific,

---

[3]Presbyterian Church (U.S.A.), 1946.

prepsychological sort of understanding, I want to argue that Jesus has a point. There *is* something demonic about the way of the world: good intentions get lost, convictions get compromised, evil runs rampant.

For a disciple—such as Simon, or any of us—that failure and disappointment can be a *sifting*, a sorting out, a clarifying.

It's an interesting conversation here in Luke 22: "Simon, Simon, behold, Satan demanded to have you, that he might sift you like wheat" (v. 31).

You in verse 31 is plural—"Satan has desired to sift all of you like wheat." And they need it. The disciples have been with Jesus three years, and they're still into power struggles and jealousy. But in verse 32, *you* is singular: "But I have prayed for you that your faith may not fail; and when you have turned again, strengthen your brethren."

"I have prayed for you, Simon, to be an encourager to the others." Peter says, "I'm ready now!" And Jesus goes on to say, "Not quite, and you'll know that pretty clearly by tomorrow morning." (Three o'clock in the morning was what the Romans called the "cock's crow"— the third watch of the night.)

After that, Simon can be a wounded healer—that's what Jesus prays for. That's the best kind of healer—wounded, sifted, taught by experience. Some things you can learn only when the heat's turned up.

I. I think Simon might recall some things were he standing here this morning. He might say, *"Don't be too sure."*

Now, Simon has all the symptoms of overconfidence. Every time Jesus tries to warn him, he blusters and protests, "I'll never be culpable!" Hasn't Jesus himself nicknamed him "rock"? Is he not the acknowledged leader among the disciples? Still, he does what he said he'd never do.

We bemoan Simon's lack of courage, but what is courage? It is surely not the absence of threat or the denial of our fears. Usually it is shaking in our shoes, swallowing hard, and deciding to go ahead. Doing that is worth more than all the words and promises we spew out ahead of time.

Like courage, faith doesn't rest on absolute certainty either. I believe that when God feels most distant and our own awareness is most shaky, then it is that faith is closest to its most basic definition. That's when we trust God, believing that we are supported by his love, both in spite of unfavorable circumstance and in the absence of clear evidence.

I think that Simon would tell us, "Don't be too sure." Learn to live by a hard-swallowing courage. Leave words like *always* and *never* to God. Hold on to a faith that isn't so cocksure about all of the mystery of God, and about our relationship with God.

II. Then Simon might tell us, *"Don't lose touch."* I don't want to impose a twentieth-century understanding of human psychology on a prepsychological situation (we sometimes forget how recently in history the personality sciences bloomed), but my strong hunch is that Simon, like us, got victimized by more than fear or overconfidence. I believe he had some internal compulsions and insecurities that collaborated with the externals to help him stumble.

So when we fail Christ and our best Christian intentions, it could be because we've lost touch with those other voices inside us. We've failed to ask, "Where'd that feeling or attitude come from? What precipitated that action or reaction?"

For every one of us there are persons back there, experiences back there, that have grown up with us, that will compromise our conscious intentions. What are they? Where'd they come from? More important, have you owned them and given them over to Christ? Can you let them go?

III. The last thing Simon would say to us is, "Don't sell Jesus short." This may be the most important thing Simon learns. Jesus knows people. He knows Simon to be vulnerable, but not hopeless. He knows him to be sinful, but not worthless. He could see him becoming a cop-out, but not a throwaway. The great difference between Simon Peter and Judas Iscariot is at this point: Judas sells Jesus' renewing, forgiving love short; Simon does not. Judas fails and turns away; Simon fails and repents.

I love the cartoon that shows a fourth grader and his teacher in front of a blackboard full of unworked arithmetic problems. They are standing chin to chin and the fourth grader is saying, "I'm *not* an underachiever; *you're* an overexpecter!" Simon may have felt that about Jesus—we all do at times. But Simon learns something here that we must learn and relearn: there's something besides expectation with Jesus. There's also grace, and the grace is as real and as strong as the expectation.

Judas fails and walks away; Simon fails and comes back, so that when Easter morning dawns and he's told of Jesus' Resurrection, Simon is not alone. He is with a few other disciples—maybe sorting it out, licking his wounds, or getting the strength to start putting his life back together.

It's never too late—or too much—for Jesus and his people. Don't sell us short. Give Jesus a chance to turn you around and into the deepening believer he wants you to become. Don't be too sure, don't lose touch, and most of all, Simon says, don't sell Jesus short!—William L. Turner

SUNDAY, MARCH 14, 2004

Lectionary Message

Topic: Waiting for the Hammer to Fall

TEXT: Luke 13:1–9

Other Readings: Isa. 55:1–9; Ps. 63:1–8; 1 Cor. 10:1–13

September 11, 2001, we all stopped, shocked, grief stricken, mesmerized by the horror being shown over and over on the TV—the deaths of the people on the airplanes that crashed, of the people who jumped from the twin towers rather than perish in the flames, and then the awful knowledge of the death toll from the collapse of the two skyscrapers. When a well-known Christian leader opined that it happened because God was angry with the United States because of legalized abortions and greater tolerance of homosexuals, reaction against him was swift and probably much greater than he ever expected. We knew who had hijacked the planes, and we didn't think God had much to do with that.

I. *Was Pilate God's agent?* So can you imagine the reactions of those standing by Jesus that day as they broke the news to him about a group of pilgrims from Jesus' part of the country who had been killed by Pilate's soldiers as they worshiped at the Temple? We don't know for certain the details of this event, but an ancient historian tells how, during a festival, a group of pilgrims got a little rowdy and said some rude things to Pilate. He retaliated by putting plainclothes soldiers into the crowd and then giving the order to attack, with great loss of life among the worshipers. Jesus said, "Do you think they were killed because they were terrible sinners? No. I tell you, unless you repent, you will all perish in the same way."

In case they missed the point, Jesus followed up with a second example, this time using something that sounds more like an accident, when a tower fell on some bystanders. Were those killed more sinful than others living in Jerusalem? Nope, but unless you repent, you will all perish in the same way, said Jesus.

What do these two little stories mean? What Jesus denies seems clear enough: God wasn't using Pilate or a shaky wall to punish a particularly wicked group of Galileans or Jerusalemites. But the second part—does that mean that unless I change my ways, whoever I am, a similar fate awaits me? Must I go through my life waiting for the hammer to fall, waiting for the tower wall to collapse, waiting for the drunk driver to swerve in front of me, waiting for the cancer cell to eat me up? Does Jesus mean that we are all wicked, and that unless we get straight, God has a disaster with our name on it?

II. *Is the vineyard owner God?* The parable that follows seems at first to head in this direction—the unfruitful plant is given time to do better, but not an indefinite time. The gardener is successful in begging for an extra year to tend the plant and give it some attention, but he promises that if it doesn't produce, the owner can cut it down. Well, of course the owner can cut it down—it's his tree, and he's been waiting for fruit, and it hasn't given him anything. The owner can cut it down without waiting another year. But the gardener's comments—"Sir, let it alone for one more year, until I dig around it and put manure on it"—suggests that the owner may have been waiting but not doing much to encourage the fruitless tree.

If we assume that God is the vineyard owner, then God is the hammer, the profit-taking investor who is interested only in what produces. But the parable is ironic, surely; if the vineyard owner is meant to represent God, then who gives God permission to destroy what God created but on the condition that God wait a year? No, if God is in the parable, God is the gardener, or at least God is in the gardener's impulse toward patience. Wait—give it a chance, and give it better care, and then see what comes.

III. *Repentance is broader than we think.* Did God's voice instruct Pilate to kill the Galileans to restore his honor? Jesus says no. Did God push the wall over on the Jerusalemites? Again, Jesus said God didn't. But we do that sort of thing all the time. We injure each other by word and deed, we take our revenge for slights real and imagined, and we often feel completely righteous as we do it. We, the people of God, take out our frustrations on each other, and then we imagine that God, who is more powerful than we are, must do the same.

Luke uses *repent* more than any other New Testament writer, and in his Gospel it means to turn to God and accept God's good news of the Kingdom. Part of turning to God, according to Luke, is accepting Jesus' definition of God. God is the woman who kept sweeping the floor until she found the one lost coin. God is the father who welcomes home the wayward child and tries to woo in the unforgiving brother. God is the patient gardener asking for another year of tender care for the unproductive tree. You can cut it down, says the gardener; he doesn't say, "then I'll cut it down."

Let us repent, those of us who are in the Church, of our unforgiving and judgmental attitudes. Let us leave aside our wishes for God to destroy our enemies, and let us, like our Master, learn to leave them in the care of God.—Richard B. Vinson

ILLUSTRATIONS

LOVE THY ENEMY.   I think of a family in the Mount Vernon Place Methodist Church in Baltimore who had lost their only son during World War II. The day that war ended we had a service of solemn rejoicing in the church, and afterward, instead of joining the throngs on the street, I went to the home of this family and sat in the garden with them. We heard the noise of rejoicing swell up from the heart of the great city, and we too were glad the war was over. But in the quiet of the garden, our thoughts were on other things. Finally, as if speaking to herself, the mother said, "I don't hate anyone. I just can't bear to think of adding anything more to the grief of the world."

When I was in Japan visiting colleges and seminaries, I met a young man who had just returned from a student work camp in the Philippines. He told how he had been exposed for the first time to the murderous hatred of the Filipinos for the Japanese. When the airplane flying him from Japan landed in Manila, he was taken almost at once to the bronze statue of the beheaded woman that commemorated the savagery of the military rule of the Japanese army. He was stunned and wished he could go home. His hosts for the summer were a Filipino family who had lost two sons in the fighting. The Japanese student said, "These good Christian folk took me in as one of them. I found peace in their home."—Harold A. Bosley[4]

OUR CHURCH.   God has entrusted us with a treasure. God, however, is not to be held accountable for the way we have developed the institutional church nor the church as an occupational system. We have done that ourselves. It is our task, then, to change the mistakes we have made so that both clergy and laity can rejoice not only in the treasure but also in the institutional church and even in the church as an occupational system. At that point, both clergy and laity will find the goal we all long for, which is fulfillment in ministry.—Edward B. Bratcher[5]

SERMON SUGGESTIONS

Topic: When Love Prevails
TEXT: Luke 6:27–38
(1) The demands on us are difficult. (2) The example for us is inspiring. (3) The rewards to us are astonishing.

Topic: How to Succeed in Evangelism
TEXT: Luke 5:1–11
(1) In our own wisdom we fail. (2) By the Lord's wisdom we are challenged. (3) When we obey the Lord, we succeed.

WORSHIP AIDS

CALL TO WORSHIP.   "O God, you are my God; earnestly I seek you. My soul thirsts for you, my body longs for you, in a dry and weary land where there is no water. I have seen

---

[4]*He Spoke to Them in Parables* (New York: HarperCollins, 1963), p. 149.
[5]*The Walk-on-Water Syndrome* (Waco, Tex.: Word Books, 1984), p. 225.

you in the sanctuary and beheld your power and glory. Because your love is better than life, my lips will glorify you" (Ps. 63:1–3 NIV).

INVOCATION.   We thank you, O God, for giving us such revelation of yourself in your grace and providence that we can praise you, not only with our lips, but also with our lives and deeds. Give us today new experiences of your power and your glory, so that we can truly glorify you.

OFFERTORY SENTENCE.   "I am crucified with Christ: nevertheless I live; yet not I but Christ liveth in me: and the life which I now live in the flesh I live by the faith of the Son of God, who loved me and gave himself for me" (Gal. 2:20).

OFFERTORY PRAYER.   Loving Lord, who gave so much for us and to us, help us to see more clearly that your pattern of life is our model today. We pray that in that spirit we may bring to you our offerings, tokens of what we wish to do in everyday dedicated living.

PRAYER.   Walk with us, O God, in the plain paths where the day-by-day routine settles down to a test of private perseverance, unheralded by the accolades of praise or bright reward. If the heavenly vision grows dim and our hearts are weary in well doing, lay thy hand upon us and steady our steps that we may press onward, even in darkness, toward the light ahead. If we are alone and the task seems more than we can do, or if done, not at all welcomed by the world, reveal thy presence at our side that we may labor with thy help. Turn us from the dreams of far glory to work in the commonplace circumstances of this mortal world, and disclose to us the miracle of thy grace in unexpected places. Even so, may thy will be done on Earth as it is in heaven, through Jesus Christ our Lord.—Samuel H. Miller

SERMON
Topic: Dreaming Heavenly Dreams
TEXT: Gen. 28:10–22; Rom. 8:18–25

Have you ever had a life-changing dream or vision?

Some have.

In literature we could cite the dream of Dorothy of Kansas that carried her away to the Land of Oz and became a life-changing event for her. Throughout the course of her dream down the yellow brick road, Dorothy was a wanderer, a traveler, in search of herself and her way back home. Before her dream, all Dorothy could think of was running off to a faraway land. After her dream, Dorothy was changed, as she realized that there was no place like home.

Then there is Ebenezer Scrooge, whose experience of the three Christmas ghosts could be interpreted as a bad dream that resulted in his life being drastically changed as well. Before his Christmas dream, Scrooge was a stingy, miserly, hateful old man. After his dream, Scrooge was generous and happy to be alive.

And then there is Jacob—deceitful, conniving Jacob, who stole his brother Esau's birthright and blessing (that is, the place of prominence at the head of the family and the greatest share of the ancestral property). Jacob, who was forced to flee his home to escape his brother's anger, had a life-changing dream as well. But Jacob's dream was more than just fleeting thoughts that danced through his head as he lay there in the wilderness. No, Jacob's dream was much more than that.

This morning when I use the term *dream* I want to make it clear that I don't mean to limit dreams to those fantasies that float through our heads while we are sleeping. I would like for us to think of dreams in a broader sense. By dreams I mean God-inspired visions for the future, which might come to us while we are sleeping or just as easily in our waking hours. Martin Luther King Jr. had a dream, you will remember. It was a dream of a new day of justice, equity, and racial harmony. A dream is a vision, an ideal, a goal, a plan of action for the future. As we look at Jacob's dream, we see that his was this type of dream.

I. *It is interesting to note* when *life-changing, heavenly dreams come to us.* Jacob's dream occurred on the night he left home. He had become a wanderer, and a guilty, burdened wanderer at that. As I have already stated, he was fleeing from an angry brother, Esau, because he had stolen the birthright and family blessing in exchange for a bowl of stew.

Jacob was uncertain and afraid. He had set out on an uncharted future. He had not lived in such a way as to deserve a dream or vision from God, but he was at a time in his life when he desperately needed one. Strangely, Jacob's soul was such that God could speak to him at this point in his life.

Like Jacob, we often feel ourselves to be in spiritual exile. We sometimes feel like poor, lonely travelers upon the Earth. As with Jacob, when we are most vulnerable, when we feel that we are in spiritual exile, when we feel most alone in the world, God often comes to us.

II. *Just as interesting is* where *we may be when life-changing dreams come to us.* God has a reputation of imparting dreams and visions in some of the most unlikely places. Consider Moses out in the desert in front of a scrubby bush. There couldn't be a more desolate place than that, yet this is where God chose to call Moses to deliver his people from bondage in Egypt. It is interesting to note that Moses was also one who had been on the run. Having killed a man in Egypt, Moses had fled for his life to the desert, where he was tending his father-in-law's sheep. And that is where God spoke to Moses, giving him a vision and a dream.

Then there was the prophet Elijah. He was hiding in a cave, fearing for his life, when God spoke to him in the still, small voice and imparted a vision for the future.

And likewise here is Jacob, in the most unlikely place—on a bleak, desolate hilltop of barren rock out in the wilderness.

Often God speaks to us and imparts dreams and visions when we are in the most unlikely places in our lives. At such unexpected times and places, we, like Jacob, may be longing either consciously or unconsciously for a spiritual experience to show us that even in the most desolate place in our lives there can break through an experience that bridges the gap between heaven and Earth. We long for an experience like Jacob's that can impart guidance and hope.

III. *So, then,* how *to be recipients of God's life-changing dreams is of utmost importance.* Being vulnerable, Jacob was perhaps more open and receptive to a word from God at that particular time than at any other time in his life previously. The good news is that even a scoundrel like Jacob who is open and receptive can become a new person, can be changed by God. A dream or vision or word from God is what makes the difference.

The truth is, sometimes we need to step out of our own way so we can receive what God wants to impart to us. Sometimes we just need to relax in God's grace and let God speak to us and lead us where God wants us to go. For none of us is yet who God wants us to be; we are works in progress. And none of us is where God wants us to go; we are on a spiritual journey.

In the story of Jacob we see a picture of Jacob as he was and a picture of the Jacob he could become. We see a picture of Jacob with his broken past and a picture of Jacob with a promising future. Perhaps it would be so of us as well, if we could stand back and look at ourselves. We might see the person we have been and the person we can become.

In his dream, Jacob heard divine promises. Some of God's promises to Jacob included God's presence with him on his journey, God's safekeeping as he went, and God's blessing of others through Jacob's life and person.

Is it not possible that God wishes to speak to us, as he spoke to Jacob, to impart heavenly dreams and visions, to remind us of divine promises, and to show us a picture of the person we can be? And is it not possible that God wishes to speak to this church collectively this morning to impart a heavenly dream and vision of what this church can do and be in the future, to remind this church of God's faithfulness, and to assure this church of the divine presence in the journey?

The bottom-line good news in Jacob's story is that God's presence may indeed be identified in our spiritual journey. God is a promise keeper. God can be counted on to be faithful to us. And if we are open and receptive—especially in those most barren, desolate, and lonely periods of our lives—God may be ready to impart a word to us, to instill a vision, to inspire us with a heavenly dream.—Randy Hammer

SUNDAY, MARCH 21, 2004
Lectionary Message

Topic: Are We There Yet?
TEXT: Josh. 5:9–12
Other Readings: Ps. 32; 2 Cor. 5:16–21; Luke 15:1–3, 11b–32

Midway through Lent—time to look forward and back, like the cross-country runner who looks first at the heels of the runners in front of her, then back over her shoulder at the runners behind her and then thinks, "Can I hold steady for another few miles? Do I have enough saved up for a kick at the end?"

I. *They dedicated themselves to God voluntarily.* This chapter gives us three scenes that let us see both backward and forward in our Lenten journey. First comes the story of the mass circumcision. The narrator patiently reminds the reader that the generation that came out of Egypt with Moses got frightened at the border of the Promised Land and would not go in. So God marched them around in the wilderness until they died, and it was their children who gathered at Gilgal. This new generation needed to be circumcised, as a sign that they belonged to God and because it was required before they could eat the Passover meal.

The less said about the actual event the better, I think—all this talk of flint knives gives me the creeps—but we'll have to imagine it was a painful and humbling event for all these grown men who had been following Joshua all their lives. Not surprisingly, the Israelites had to stop traveling until the men were healed. But God found the silver lining: "Today I have rolled away from you the disgrace of Egypt." Circumcision is a humbling experience for an adult, but it was voluntary; now they showed that they were in control of themselves, that their bodies were their own, no longer slaves of the Egyptians but servants of God. In the same way, for us, our vows, our voluntary humbling, are ways for us to remind ourselves and to show the world that we belong to God and to no other. The prophets sometimes spoke of circumcision of the heart—a way to say that the real dedication to God happens when we put our wills under God's control.

II. *They celebrated their dedication to God.* The second episode is more pleasant to imagine—a Passover Seder. The people gathered in their camp and celebrated the meal that marked their deliverance from slavery. This Passover was even more special, notes the narrator, because they ate local food, unleavened bread made from grain taken from their new backyard. This Passover was a way of saying that while they were not quite home yet, they were on their way, and they could begin to enjoy some of the blessings of home.

The New Testament describes Jesus' followers as pilgrims, citizens of God's country, always on the move. Our Lenten journey captures that image perfectly, as we set aside aspects of this world to focus on our relationship with God. We eat the fruit of the land, as we must, to keep ourselves alive, but we belong to God.

III. *They found themselves on holy ground.* The final scene is my favorite. An unidentified warrior appears to Joshua, sword drawn, and Joshua asks the reasonable question, "Friend or foe?" "Neither," says the man, "I represent God." God is not Joshua's enemy, but neither is God Joshua's tame ally. God was in Egypt with Moses, leading the people out; God was with them through the wilderness, in pillars of fire and smoke; but often God shows up rather unexpectedly. Think about Abraham and Sarah's three visitors, coming to tell them they would indeed have a child. Think about Moses at the bush, discovering his heritage and his calling. Joshua didn't expect to find God at this time and in this place, but God was there with him then, and wherever you find God, that is holy ground.

So we look over our shoulders today and see behind us the sins we try to leave behind, and we wonder if we are making any progress. We look ahead and see we are not yet home. We can take vows, cutting off the sins "which so easily beset us"; and we can take communion, eating the bread and drinking the wine that reminds us of our true citizenship; and we can know, for a truth, that we are in midjourney, only halfway home. But that is no reason to despair. God is with us, wherever we find ourselves. We should fall to our faces, remove our shoes, humble ourselves, and rejoice to know that although we have not yet come to the end of our journey, every step of the journey is taken in the presence of God.—Richard B. Vinson

ILLUSTRATIONS

CHRIST MAKES OPTIMISTS.   The pessimist says of rain, it will make mud; the optimist says, it will lay the dust. The optimist says, I am better today; the pessimist says, I was worse yesterday. The optimist, when he sees a bee, says, there is a honey maker; the pessimist says, there goes the stinging bee. The optimist says, I am glad I am alive; the pessimist says, I am sorry that I must die. The optimist says, I am glad I am no worse; the pessimist says, I am sorry I am no better. The optimist discovers some good even in evil; the pessimist finds evil in good. Christ makes optimists of those to whom he gives the morning star; they see light in darkest gloom; they say the morning cometh, for morning is always coming somewhere.—W. E. Thorn[6]

---

[6]*A Bit of Honey*

THE ENLARGEMENT OF LIFE.   What was this guiding principle to be explored? Jesus Christ taught men to love others as God loves them, with the same redeeming passion which sees the dormant promise in the unworthy, the prophecy of something better in the unfit, and serves them in such a manner as will lift them to their higher capacity and fulfill their potential worth. This is the crusade to bring people to their best, what God intended them to be, and it changes a maladjusted society and begins a nobler civilization. It is a saving love bent on giving everyone a decent chance. The Christian attitude cannot keep out of politics, because it aims not only at economic reforms but also at higher standards of action and better laws. Its sense of social justice is prompted by concern for the soul of the community and the redemption of character in all classes. Here is the enlargement of life which Jesus Christ bestows, and it satisfies the urge to completeness, whereas a detached egotism comes to a dead end.—Arthur A. Cowan[7]

SERMON SUGGESTIONS

Topic: Putting God on the Spot

TEXT: Exod. 17:3–7

(1) Life inevitably brings us into unfavorable circumstances. (2) Our reaction may be bitter and complaining. (3) God often goes on blessing us despite our faithlessness and unworthiness.

Topic: When God Had Put Us Right

TEXT: Rom. 5:11

(1) We can expect to arrive at the destiny that God meant for us. (2) We can meet every trial bravely and joyfully as a stage on the way to that glorious destiny.

WORSHIP AIDS

CALL TO WORSHIP.   "Be glad in the Lord, and rejoice; . . . and shout for joy" (Ps. 32:11).

INVOCATION.   Lord, often our faith flags, and our desire to wait patiently is washed away in the impatience of constant demands. We often find it hard to still ourselves. Sweep over us now with the calm of your Spirit and fill us with the words of life that make the difference in all else we do. Through Christ, our Lord.—E. Lee Phillips

OFFERTORY SENTENCE.   "Greater love has no one than this, than to lay down one's life for his friends" (John 15:13 NKJV).

OFFERTORY PRAYER.   Lord, our God, let this offering be led by the Holy Spirit to save the lost, lift the discouraged, comfort the grieving, and encourage the saints in the building up of the body of Christ.—E. Lee Phillips

PRAYER.   Almighty God, Lord of the universe, God of our salvation, we praise you for your mighty power, your steadfast love, and your redemptive presence among us. We lift our voices to you in song; we lift our hands to you in prayer; we bring our gifts to you in offer-

---

[7]*Bright Is the Shaken Torch*

ing. We acknowledge that you are our creator, our redeemer, that you have brought us through many trials, and that you have given us good things of this world to enjoy. We belong to you. Yet we confess that we have often failed to hearken to your voice. Sometimes we have been preoccupied with business, conflicts in our home, or trouble with a neighbor or business associate. Some of us may even have let our hearts gradually harden against you through accumulations of bitterness and envy. Forgive us, put us on right paths again, and restore to us the joy of our salvation.

SERMON
Topic: Adultery—Forgivable but Not to Be Repeated
TEXT: John 8:1–11

The Gospel of John 8:1–11 tells of a woman caught committing adultery. According to the story, Jesus went to the Mount of Olives for the night, probably to spend long hours in prayer. Early the next morning he went to the Temple. There the people gathered around him, and he sat down and began to teach them. His teaching was disrupted by the teachers of the law and the Pharisees. They brought a woman who had been caught in the act of adultery. They made her stand before everyone and confronted Jesus with her sin. They pointed out that in their law, Moses commanded that such a woman was to be stoned to death. Our Lord must have known exactly what they meant for he was a student and teacher of his own rich religious heritage. Then they asked him for his teaching on the matter. It was a trap for Jesus, so they could accuse him. He could quickly be in trouble with the Roman or Jewish authorities. He seems to have ignored them for the moment by bending over and writing on the ground with his finger. They continued to pose questions, and then he straightened up. His answer still rings in the corridors of every real or imagined courthouse in the country dealing with such a matter. He said, "Whichever one of you has committed no sin may throw the first stone at her." Then he bent over again and began to write on the ground. When they witnessed our Lord's response, they left the area. Jesus was left with the woman still standing in his midst. Then he straightened up again and said to her, "Where are they? Is there no one left to condemn you?" She answered, "No one, sir." John closes the story by having Jesus say, "I do not condemn you either. Go, but do not sin again."

The problem is age-old.

For centuries the Jews had dealt with it in the Law of Moses. We commonly understand this Law to be found in the first five books of the Old Testament—Genesis, Exodus, Leviticus, Numbers, and Deuteronomy. In addition to the Ten Commandments, Leviticus chapter 20 and Deuteronomy chapter 22 specifically deal with adultery. For an ancient people, their thoughts are at a lofty level. They recognized the wrong involved, defined it, and prescribed punishment.

On other occasions Jesus speaks to the matter in ways that cut across the ideas of the ruling religious groups. The one that really must have blown their minds is found in Matthew 5:27–28. Jesus said, "You have heard that it was said, 'Do not commit adultery.' But now I tell you: anyone who looks at a woman and wants to possess her is guilty of committing adultery with her in his heart." Most men, I suspect, have difficulties with this one.

But let's not unduly digress from our initial story.

Notice in the narrative the attitude of Jesus the Christ compared to that of the teachers of the Law and the Pharisees.

A *trio of comparisons* is meant for our enrichment and enlightenment.

I. *They exposed her, but not Jesus, to public ridicule.* We see a group—really, a personification of self-righteousness—not only making charges but doing so in the most embarrassing way possible. There isn't much doubt about her guilt. The story does not argue for her innocence. We have the feeling that, if questioned, those pressing for prosecution could give all of the naughty details. They are a sophisticated lynching squad—ready, willing, and able to make her a spectacle for all to view. It has a kind of carnival air about it. If they had thought about it, tickets would probably have been sold to watch the event. No doubt there would have been many takers. Parts of the Old West must have taken their script from these men without knowing it.

While moral standards have to be upheld in order for civilization to exist, we have the uncomfortable feeling that these people were after more. The poor soul may have been guilty many times. We do not know. We know the group wanted to put Jesus on the spot. If they could just get him into serious trouble with the majority of the Jewish religious authorities, or better still, with the Roman rulers, their little staged event would be successful. In fact, the Romans did kill Jesus. Remember, he died by crucifixion and not by stoning. Perhaps of even greater significance was their own need to be above others. As upholders of the Law placed over and against her illicit amorous escapade, they looked quite good. A perceptive cartoonist could have a field day using such an idea. Of course, you and I would not want to carry that too far because we cannot actually know all the motives of such men at this point in time. At any rate, the worse she could be made to look, the better they looked. That sounds familiar, doesn't it?

Now, Jesus doesn't say to his brethren—and these men were in a sense his Jewish brothers—"You fellows are exactly right." He could very easily have given his approval to their actions and proceeded with the execution in an appropriate place. Maybe they were anxious to have his blessing and didn't know it. Often if a layperson can get the blessing of his or her pastor, that covers a multitude of sins. Of course, he can be given just the tip of the iceberg, which looks innocent, inviting, and worthy. I think it would have been so easy for Jesus to have told them how great, pure, and virtuous they were for having spotted her yielding to temptation and bringing her forth for judgment. This would have confirmed their understanding of the Mosaic Law, and left Jesus a comrade in arms. Of course, he doesn't do this. In fact, he does quite the opposite. From one standpoint, our Lord was an exceedingly poor politician. Surely he could have agreed with their actions and at some later time brought them around to his way of thinking. Not Jesus! He must do the work of the Father, and the Father was saying things they couldn't or wouldn't hear.

So much for the first third of the trio.

The second of the three comparisons merits our attention.

II. *They suggested she be stoned to death, but not Jesus.* While stoning may appear to you and me to be a terrible way to die, it had been common among the Jews for centuries. It was their form of capital punishment. Blasphemy, idolatry, and adultery were all punishable by stoning. Not everyone died that was singled out. For example, later in the eighth chapter of John, Jesus claims to have been part of the creation before Abraham. His opponents found this blasphemous, so they picked up stones to throw at him. He managed to slip away. In the fourteenth chapter of Acts, in Lystra crowds turned against Paul. They stoned him and dragged him out of town. They thought he was dead. However, some believers gathered around him and he got up.

The teachers of the law and the Pharisees were only doing what they felt was necessary. Sure, they were attempting to put Jesus on the spot, but their ancestors had been stoning people for centuries. They thought they were doing so for good reasons. The irritating problem was that Jesus was working beyond their understanding of consistency, legalism, and predictability. For their day and time they were models of religious thought and idealism. The flowering of their faith into Christianity was something most of them refused to accept. The faith of Abraham, Moses, David, and the prophets was aborted. They just didn't allow the essential, total fulfillment to come into their hearts and minds in the person of Jesus the Christ. The centuries since that time have been filled with sadness and desperation, because the Lord's people by and large have rejected him. Symbolically, their own adultery can be seen in the refusal to become a faithful part of the Church or of the bride married to her husband, the Christ. Paul tells us in Ephesians 5:23, "For a husband has authority over his wife just as Christ has authority over the Church, and Christ is himself the Savior of the Church, his body."

Jesus doesn't inflict the woman with a tirade on the awfulness of her sin, let alone stone her. He knows that she knows adultery is wrong. Sometimes you and I point a critical finger at people's lives, simply telling them what they already know about themselves. They need the Savior and not our low-grade lectures. Anyway, if we talk long enough and critically enough, we are probably saying more about ourselves than about them. Our Blessed Lord knows all of this infinitely more. Praise his name, he does not come at us with flaming nostrils and a wailing voice, reciting our sins, chapter and verse. Praise his name, he is not ready to shame us into submission by cataloging our infractions. Praise his name, any stones he may throw are those that have love in the center, with compassion and mercy for outer layers.

So much for the second third of the trio.

The final of three comparisons speaks to the meeting of a universal need.

III. *They left her alone, but not Jesus.* When it became obvious that Jesus would not be caught by their snare, they pulled out. Perhaps it was also due to their lack of genuine concern for the adulteress. Perhaps it was also a matter of lost prestige before the people. If you and I don't get our way, it's very easy to leave the situation or person. Our concern is often noticeably lacking for those caught in sin. If our judgment about a person or situation is questioned, we most likely feel the prestige factor slipping and we excuse ourselves. You and I might qualify as teachers of the Law and Pharisees.

To be left alone with Jesus must have been awesome and filled her with joy. We don't know if she shed tears. I think she did. We don't know if she audibly said, "I'm sorry. Forgive me." I think she did. I see her as a "fallen woman" in the presence of total purity, whose tears are trickling down both cheeks; . . . who prays for forgiveness and means it for the first time in her life; . . . who has brought to her mind those awful images of her betrayal of the marital vows; . . . who knows firsthand the meaning of liberation in the only sense in which it ultimately matters; . . . who forgives not only her accusers but her willing lover as well; . . . who leaves the presence of Jesus knowing that she is important in his sight; . . . who accepts herself as a child of God, guilty of the sordid and licentious to be sure, but at last washed in the blood of the lamb; . . . who can now be just as saintly as any woman who never broke her vows of marital faithfulness.

I wonder about you and me: Do we walk off and leave such persons to fend for themselves? Do we ignore them as just so much trash to be avoided? Maybe we like to be around them to hear their tales of exploitation, explicitness, and expletives. Indeed, what are our attitudes?

Maybe we feel good, even superior, knowing we have not physically been guilty of the act . . . until a voice whispers, "How many times have you wished for the right person, at the right time, and in the right place to make love?" Our Lord knew that her problem was not unique. He knew long before you and I that we seem to have a bad habit of condemning those whose sins do not tempt us very much. After all, it is so easy to say in our later years, "Isn't adultery a terrible thing!" It is so convenient, even smug, to say when we are happily married, "Good heavens, what a crime!" You and I do well to remember the words "except for the grace of God . . ."

Thus, we complete the trio of comparisons.

Adultery is not the unpardonable sin.

Having said that, however, let's keep a certain perspective. Nothing destroys a marriage quite so thoroughly as adultery. It is a sin that can be and often is forgiven, but it really isn't often forgotten. Satan will say, "Well, it happened once and it will happen again." If we do not begin the day with a forgiving attitude that places God's love first, the memory of the act will destroy the marriage through real or imagined infidelity.

Perhaps an even more wicked sin is the innocent spouse who "uses" the guilty one long after it has happened. I wonder how many men have towed the line under the threat of ruinous divorce settlements, becoming little more than four-year-old boys, living out their lives in quiet desperation? I wonder how many women have buried themselves in liquor, drugs, and other escape hatches because their husbands threatened to expose them to their children, relatives, and friends? There isn't a single drop of Christ's forgiving blood in such attitudes.

You and I are to be forgiving, but certainly not condoning.

Periodically, and at the time of temptation, it is well to repeat the question, "Wilt thou love, comfort, honor, and keep, in sickness and in health; and forsaking all others keep thee only unto your mate so long as ye both shall live?" and then answer, "I will" as many times as it takes to be confident that faithfulness is right.

Really, there is little that can be said about adultery that goes beyond our Lord's closing words to her. He says, "Go, but do not sin again." *Adultery is forgivable, but it is not to be repeated.*—Donald Charles Lacy[8]

SUNDAY, MARCH 28, 2004
Lectionary Message

Topic: Extravagant Love
TEXT: John 12:1–8
Other Readings: Isa. 43:16–21; Ps. 126; Phil. 3:4b–14

In John's Gospel, Jesus performs only seven miracles, and the last and most spectacular is raising Lazarus. Confronted by Martha and Mary, who blamed him for letting his friend die, Jesus calls Lazarus out of the tomb. Lazarus staggers out, still tied up in his burial bindings, and Jesus tells the bystanders to set him free. You'd think that everybody there would sign

---

[8]*Collected Works* (Franklin, Tenn.: Providence House, 2001), pp. 103–108.

up with Jesus on the spot, but in fact some witnesses go to the Temple leaders, and they decide to put both Jesus and Lazarus to death.

In the home of Mary, Martha, and Lazarus, however, it's time for a party in Jesus' honor. Jesus brought our brother back from death! What in the world can we do to say thank you? Let's cook, they think, and Martha puts on a feast and serves the guests. Apparently the disciples were there, too, and maybe some other family members. Jesus would have been seated at the main table, reclining on a couch or cushions, with Lazarus right beside him. Can you imagine the joy in that house?

Maybe that explains what happens next. Mary took the jar of burial perfume, the jar that their family would have used to anoint loved ones as they died, and poured the whole jar over Jesus' feet. Picture this now: a room full of men reclining in Roman style, propped up on their left elbows, eating with their right hands, taking their time with the meal, talking and enjoying themselves. Enter Mary, not with a bowl or rice or a jug of wine but with a small flask of perfume. She pours it all—John says a pound of it—on Jesus' feet, which were easy to reach because of the way he was stretched out. Jesus is at the center of the tables, so every eye is watching Mary as she does this. In fact, in a small room, the strong perfume must have been almost like tear gas—eyes are watering, and people are coughing and sneezing and trying to get some air as John remarks dryly, "The whole house was filled with the fragrance of the perfume." Then Mary lets down her hair—something respectable women never did in public—and began to wipe down Jesus' feet.

Now, in Luke's version, the woman who weeps over Jesus' feet and wipes them with her hair is a sinner, so her flamboyant, even suggestive actions fit with her reputation. But Mary, we presume, is a respectable woman—Why do something so personal to Jesus, something involving her own body? Mark's version has the woman anoint Jesus' head, symbolically marking him as God's chosen one, the Messiah. Why does John have her do this to Jesus' feet, especially since she wiped away the perfume after pouring it on?

The Gospel of John always has symbols on top of symbols. Jesus says that the anointing is right and that Mary had been saving the perfume for the day of his burial. When Jesus dies and is buried in Joseph of Arimathea's tomb, Joseph and Nicodemus bury him with about a hundred pounds of spices, a king's burial, but also a sign that they believe his death is final. Mary's act of preparing Jesus for burial, on the other hand, happens before he is dead. It is a sign that she—maybe alone among all those who have heard Jesus—believes that he is going to die, and she trusts that the man who raised her brother will himself be raised by God.

What Mary does also prepares for what Jesus himself does with the disciples when he washes their feet, wiping them with the towel tied around his waist. Jesus is going to lay his body down for the sake of his friends, and he tells them that what he has done for them they must do for one another. Mary is already doing this—washing Jesus' feet in the most extravagant and personal way she could, putting her whole self, body and possessions, at his disposal. Judas objects to the sacrifice—"Why wasn't it sold and the money given to the poor?"—knowing that he would use the money for himself. Mary is his polar opposite; she is completely transparent in her willingness to sacrifice herself and her money for Jesus.

In fact, her response is different from all other responses to Jesus' death. Judas betrays him, handing him over to those who want to kill him. Peter denies him, refusing to own up to their friendship in Jesus' most desperate hour. Nicodemus and Joseph, secret disciples, bury him with full honors, but out of fear they do not tell anyone they are doing this because they are devoted to Jesus. Even the disciple whom he loved stands at some distance, accepting the care of Jesus' mother, but doing nothing else to help Jesus through his execution. Mary's act is the only positive response, the only demonstration of faith in Jesus' words, the only act of sacrificial love for the one laying down his life for his friends.

What are our own responses like this Lenten season? Do our vows and our acts of devotion seem more like Mary's or more like what some of the others did? Let us resolve to love extravagantly, putting body, soul, and possessions at Jesus' disposal.—Richard B. Vinson

ILLUSTRATIONS

TRAVEL STAINS.   Friends, you and I all profess to be pilgrims on the road, and now we have arrived at another sacramental season. As we look back over the way we have traveled since our last one, and as we look at ourselves, must we not confess that much of the dust of the road has clung to us, yes, and even of the mire that those pilgrims find who wander off the road? Our lives have not had in them much to show whose we are and whom we serve. There has been too much vanity and worldliness and lovelessness and uncharitableness and evil temper. And the stains of these things are upon us, though we profess the name of Christ. But here is the Pilgrim's Hospice, where we can be cleansed from these travel stains, bathed in the mercy and love and grace of God.—D. M. Baillie[9]

RAINBOWS IN RAIN.   We were motoring in the Island of Maui, Hawaii, in a downpour of rain. Even the two-mile-high mountain Haleakala was obscured. Suddenly there was a break in the rain and a beautiful rainbow appeared, a graceful arc linking heaven and earth. Our hearts did leap up at this sudden vista of beauty in the storm, as we were reminded of the goodness and love and strength that make the character of God so wonderful. We were serving the Wananalua Church in Hana and had been given the book "Prayers from an Island" by Hawaiian pastor Richard Wong of Honolulu. Here is his lovely prayer about the rainbow:

> O God, Thou hast a merry way when Thou hangest rainbows in rain. So may we learn that life's secrets are hidden . . . joy embedded in pain . . . wisdom gleaming through suffering . . . strength growing through hardships . . . and fulfillments beckoning through problems. Teach us always to look through rain to find rainbows glistening. Amen.

God looks at the bow in the cloud, and remembers, and so may we!—Lowell M. Atkinson[10]

SERMON SUGGESTIONS

Topic: The Ways of the Tempter

Text: Matt. 4:1–11

(1) The tempter appeals to a bodily appetite; an obscure nervous feeling; ambition, which is wholly of the mind. (2) He proposes a useful miracle; a useless miracle; a gross sin. (3) He seeks to excite distrust of God; presumptuous reliance on God; worldly minded abandonment of God.—John A. Broadus

---

[9]*To Whom Shall We Go?*
[10]*Apples of Gold*

Topic: Modern Prodigals

TEXT: Luke 15:11–32

(1) Going away from God. (2) Suffering apart from God. (3) Rejoicing in return to God.

WORSHIP AIDS

CALL TO WORSHIP.   "The Lord hath done great things for us; whereof we are glad" (Ps. 126:3).

INVOCATION.   Today, O Lord, grant that we may become so aware of past providences that we shall have confidence and courage to face tomorrow and all the days and years and ages to come.

OFFERTORY SENTENCE.   "In the very truth I count all things but loss compared to the excellence of the knowledge of Christ Jesus my Lord. For his sake I have suffered the loss of all things, and esteem them but refuse that I may gain Christ and be found in him" (Phil. 3:8–9a, Montgomery).

OFFERTORY PRAYER.   Help us, O Lord, to distinguish between things of true and lasting value and things of empty and passing attraction, and set our hearts on all things worthy. Direct the use of these gifts, these tithes and offerings, that they may strengthen and support the works of faith, hope, and love, those enduring values that time and circumstances can neither steal nor erode.

PRAYER.   As the heavens declare the glory of God and the firmament shows his handiwork, so enter our lives that we may be channels through which expressions of your wonder and grace are made known to all people.

As we enter this new season of the year, we pause to thank you for the winter, that secret loom that weaves for us the tapestry of spring. We thank you for winter's nourishment of seed in hidden places of the Earth as rain and snow provide ingredients to bring the seed to life. We thank you for the treasures of darkness, the stars in their courses, shining in the night to guide travelers across the ages to their desired destinations. We thank you for the bright star shining in another winter night that brought wise men to a cradle and the Savior.

We thank you for springtime. We thank you for your faithfulness seen in the turn of the sun into its accustomed place. We thank you for full, running streams and the thrill of life in every root and branch—yea, every living thing. We thank you that springtime brings the resurrection of hope and joy, of beauty and goodness, and sets the hearts and souls of men and women to singing again. We thank you that the Lord's Resurrection came in springtime to release on the world bursting with newness the greatest and most sacred news of the ages— that in him we all have eternal springtime which abides in every changing season, even the darkest winters of the soul.

This morning as we worship, set our hearts to your music and let our lives be committed to your service. In this sacred hour, speak to every wandering life a word of direction, to every confused soul a word of enlightenment, and to every lost soul a word of salvation. Indeed, Father, may this be a day of transforming springtime in our lives and hearts as we wait in your presence, longing for your blessing and seeking your spirit through Jesus Christ our Lord.—Henry Fields

SERMON

Topic: On the Way to Calvary—A Failure

TEXT: John 12:1–11

The season of Lent (from the word for "springtime" and "lengthening of days") fits well the journey to the cross. The storytellers of Jesus' life cut to half speed or slow motion when they get to this part. John's Gospel gives nine chapters to the last five or six days, and the other Gospels give at least three chapters apiece.

So, as winter slows to make way for spring, we are urged by the biblical text itself to slow down, look inward, honestly confess, and open our lives more deeply to the purposes of God. That's what Jesus was doing on this journey—even down to the prayer in Gethsemane he was struggling with what it means for a person to say, "Not my will, but thine be done."

Now, there were others who struggled with that question, too—not as spectators to his journey, but as participants in it themselves. None is more mysterious or pathetic than Judas Iscariot. We met him last week in the home of Mary of Bethany. He looked at her impetuous and extravagant act of love and called it wasteful. Emotionally, he missed the point, so trapped was he in his own feelings.

Judas stands before us this morning a figure both despised and tragic. We value loyalty, so we loathe betrayal. Then why take time to remember a person we'd just as soon forget?

Because Lent is a season for remembering and examining and learning. Judas failed as a disciple, and we always learn more from failure than from success. Let's remember that Jesus failed, too—with Judas. Jesus failed—there's a shocking thought, isn't it? The divine Son of God struck out with Judas. The story of Jesus, like the rest of the Bible, is brutally honest. If the early church had wanted to cover up some things, you can be sure Judas would've been one of those things. Not his betrayal—a lot of people turned against Jesus that last week—but betrayal by one in Jesus' inner circle of twelve. The Scriptures are clear: he along with the other eleven was chosen by Jesus after a night of prayer. He along with the others was taught, then sent out to serve. He along with the others enjoyed some success in preaching, teaching, and healing.

Judas was, in every sense, a disciple. Mark's Gospel takes pains to tell us that. In this fourteenth chapter, where Judas does his worst, Mark describes him twice as "Judas, one of the twelve."

But in the end, Judas was Jesus' failure, because one thing is undoable, even for Jesus, and that's to change a heart and mind that are closed to him. Judas could live with Jesus for three years, but he would not yield to the possibility that Jesus was right and he was wrong— about how to be the Messiah, or about the nature of the Kingdom of God.

Jesus fails with any man or woman who closes mind and heart to him. I've known many of them, heard them say "not now" to the gospel for a lifetime. I've buried several of them. And I believe that God goes on loving them into eternity. How could he stop loving his own creation? But Jesus fails to change them and redeem them because they fail to allow it.

That's the failure of Judas. And there are two plain questions to be asked about him.

I. *How did it happen, this failure?* To be dogmatic in answering that question is to be dishonest. The actual evidence in the New Testament is very sparse. It's clear that the early church struggled with its own explanations about Judas.

Luke says that "Satan entered into him," but surely others were tempted, too. Jesus even addressed Simon Peter as Satan and a stumbling block on one occasion.

John's Gospel calls Judas a greedy person who at times hid his greed under a cloak of pious concern.

There *is* another clue. In both Gospels, the betrayal by Judas follows very closely the anointing of Jesus, by Mary of Bethany in John and by the unnamed woman in Mark.

Judas may have been a greedy man, but I think most of all he was a disappointed man. Jesus was not working out as he had hoped, did not fit his expectations. That may have justified his thievery in his own mind, since the cause of Jesus mattered less and less to him.

Now, his disillusionment was *not* instantaneous. In Luke's early list of the twelve, Judas is called the one "who became a traitor." Here in Mark 14, the story says *process*. In the first two verses of the chapter, the chief priests and scribes are looking for a way to arrest Jesus. In verses 10 and 11, Judas starts looking for a way to collaborate with them. Later on, Jesus, at the Passover table, says that the betrayer will be one of the twelve. Finally, in our text, Judas identifies Jesus with a kiss, and the deed is done.

Judas is the person who wouldn't let Jesus touch and reshape his understanding—and that will not only protect prejudice and ignorance, it will also shut down growth as a disciple.

Judas probably would end up where he started in his expectations. Discipleship for him became a fixed point instead of a journey of struggle and change.

Like Judas, we all bring baggage with us into discipleship. Some of it needs to be forgiven and discarded, some needs to be rechanneled, and some needs to be reshaped.

II. There's another question we must ask about Judas: *How do you deal with such a failure?* Judas didn't shrug it off. Matthew says he died a suicide. Acts says it was a fall. There is not necessarily a contradiction between the two. He *did* repent of his failure and betrayal, says Matthew, and he gave the thirty pieces of silver back. What he *didn't* do, apparently, was what he'd needed to do for years—open up his closed heart and mind to the grace of God.

Suppose he'd followed Jesus to the foot of the cross, there to ask for forgiveness and healing. "I have done an awful thing. I wish I'd never been born" (Jesus said he'd feel that way).

But Judas, as always, turned away from Jesus. That's not how to handle your failure as a disciple. Instead, come to Jesus, confess your failure and sin, and open your heart and mind to his healing and reshaping.

Failure is not the end of discipleship. It can be the beginning of it, as you bring your need for healing and forgiveness to Jesus. It can also, along the road, be the *expansion* of it. Judas missed that; but you and I don't have to.—William L. Turner

SUNDAY, APRIL 4, 2004
Lectionary Message

Topic: The Death of the Light
TEXT: Luke 23:44–55; or Luke 22:14–23:56
Other Readings: Isa. 50:4–9a; Ps. 31:9–16; Phil. 2:5–11

I. *They watched in darkness.* Darkness at noon is strange enough by itself, but when you are trying to watch a spectacle, it becomes especially noticeable. Darkness at noon might happen with an eclipse of the sun, but darkness extending from noon to 3:00 is unheard of. Then came the shout. Out of the darkness that familiar voice must have been startling—"Father, into your hands I commend my spirit." Then silence—darkness and silence. The crowd began to break up. People headed for home, mumbling, praying, wondering. One voice was finally heard. The Roman officer in charge of the Crucifixion spoke clearly, "Certainly this man was innocent." They had executed a righteous man. The other two were criminals, but this Jesus was innocent. The soldier would have trouble sleeping that night.

What about the followers of Jesus? They were standing at a safe distance, watching. Men and women who had been his friends, supporters, and students watched intently while he died in the strange darkness. They watched while a secret admirer came and removed the body from the cross. The women followed and watched while Joseph of Arimathea carefully laid the wrapped body in his own family tomb. They "saw the tomb and how his body was laid." There was a whole lot of standing around and watching going on. They were watching, but the darkness was inside them.

II. *What did they see?* What were they watching? Most of them had no idea yet just what they were seeing. Some that day were watching a man die who had posed a threat to their authority and influence over the people. Some that day were watching another criminal crucified for daring to question the authority of Rome over people's lives. Some that day were watching a dear and trusted friend die at the hands of sinners. Some that day were still wondering just who this man, Jesus of Nazareth, was. Whoever, or whatever, he was, he aroused the best and the worst in people. Wasn't it just a few days before that hundreds were acclaiming him the Lord's messenger as he rode that donkey into the city? Wasn't it he who had talked so much about light? And now it was so dark that they couldn't even see him die. They had no idea what they were watching.

What they seemed to be convinced of was that this was the end of something big. For some it was the end of worry that this man would start a revolution and get them all in trouble. For others it was the end of the best time of their lives—time spent with Jesus. His words had indicated that it was over. He had paraphrased a prayer that Jewish children were taught to say at bedtime: "Father, into your hands I commend my spirit." "Goodnight. Blow out the lamp. The day is over." It was the end.

They had no idea. It was truly the end of life as they knew it and the beginning of a brand new age. This was not just strange irony at work. This was God at work. In that enlightened age of Greek philosophy and Roman administration, nobody would have dreamed of God working this way. The death of an innocent man is a cruel twist of fate, but certainly no act of God. Darkness for three hours in the middle of the day is unusual, but scientists would be able to explain it—if not today, then certainly tomorrow. They had no idea.

III. *The light returns.* While people stumbled home wondering about it, praying about it; while his followers stood at a distance watching what they could, one man—one unlikely man—began to see some light. This Jesus was righteous. That was a start, a step in the right direction. Matthew 27:54 quotes the centurion: "Truly this man was God's Son!" For a Roman of that time, this might not have meant any more than that Jesus was a righteous man. Joseph of Arimathea at least gave the body a decent burial, but we don't know whether that was anything more than a way to protect the city from a transgression of the Sabbath laws. In other words, the scene Luke describes at the moment of the death of Jesus leaves us wondering if anybody in the world understood what was going on. Only God knew.

The meaning of the death of Jesus began to become clearer to a few people after his Resurrection. Those to whom he appeared began to see at least that God was involved in it somehow—that it wasn't just a tragic end of a hard life—but that somehow God was working toward a purpose in all this. Theologians have been trying to explain it all ever since, and nobody is able to get to the bottom of it. Theories of atonement focusing on blood, on sacrifice, on martyrdom, on substitution, on satisfaction—they go on and on and on. Maybe explanation and understanding do not describe the light that we are to seek.

The question for us is not, Do we understand the meaning of the Crucifixion of Jesus? The primary question is, Where do we stand in relation to that Crucifixion? Do we go home and shut ourselves off from the light of God? Do we get lost in the maze of philosophical and theological speculation about the Crucifixion? Do we throw ourselves into work and play so we haven't time to think about such things? Do we breathe a sigh of relief that we don't need to deal with this Jesus anymore? Or do we wait patiently for the light to break through?

It is no accident that the people to whom Jesus revealed himself after he was raised from the dead were the people who had waited patiently for the light of God to help them deal with the tragedy of the cross. It was to the women who went to the tomb as the light was dawning that Jesus showed himself. It was to the disciples meeting to pray and discuss the future that Jesus appeared. Apparently understanding is not nearly so important as positioning. If we keep ourselves turned in the direction of the light of God, we'll discover that we are also looking in the direction of the cross of Christ.—Bruce E. Shields

ILLUSTRATIONS

GRACE.   About six months before our new building was finished, I walked out on the roof and went up to the base of the forty-foot-high cross that sits atop our worship center. I love that cross because it is actually a part of the structure. The base of the cross descends thirty-two feet below the roof into the superstructure and acts like a keystone. It supports the twelve trusses that come to the center and symbolizes that the cross of Christ must be the cornerstone of our church. The cross is directly over the pulpit, symbolizing that we preach under the authority of the cross.

But as I stood at the base of that cross and looked out over the roof, I saw something that put goose bumps on my arms. Unknown to me, the company that had provided the insulation for the roof was the Grace Ice and Watershield Company. The insulation comes in six-foot sheets, and the word *GRACE* is printed in bold letters on every sheet. As I looked out from the cross, I saw the words *GRACE, GRACE, GRACE, GRACE, GRACE*—hundreds of times. I thought, *Maybe the Lord is trying to tell me something.* (Even I could catch the symbolism in that!) The church is to be covered with God's grace.

Jesus is described as being "full of grace and truth" (John 1:14). That's the kind of God we need to be portraying from our pulpits—a God of grace and truth.—Bob Russell[1]

SURPRISE AND ADVENTURE.   No one, before he becomes a Christian and enters the ranks of discipleship of Jesus, can even guess what miracles await him. The discipleship of

---

[1]*When God Builds a Church* (West Monroe, La.: Howard, 2000).

Jesus is something into which one must first jump to know what is involved. What is given to us by way of freedom, sovereignty, and whatever else may come to us (1 Kings 3:13; Matt. 6:33) will be clear to us not in calculable distance but only in actual discipleship itself. Who Christ really is and what we win with him is something we experience only when we dare to enter into a relationship with him. That is when the surprises begin. That is when the adventure begins.—Helmut Thielicke[2]

SERMON SUGGESTIONS

Topic: The Lord's Servant

TEXT: Isa. 50:4–9a

Like the Lord's Servant in Isaiah, Jesus Christ (1) spoke God's word, (2) was rejected by his contemporaries, and (3) trusted in God's vindication.

Topic: How to Put Your Rivals on a Pedestal

TEXT: Phil. 2:5–11

(1) Consider the example of Christ Jesus, who (2) did not snatch equality with God, though he was divine, but (3) renounced personal entitlements and (4) even died on the cross. (5) Therefore, God lifted him above all human attainments to universal acclaim for who is. (6) Thus we too can look to the interests of others, as well as to our own, knowing that God will do right by us.

WORSHIP AIDS

CALL TO WORSHIP.   "Listen! Shouts of triumph in the camp of the victors: 'With his right hand the Lord does mighty deeds'"(Ps. 118:15 REB).

INVOCATION.   O Lord, before whom all will one day bow, this day we bow before the Savior who comes riding on a lowly animal and proclaim him King of our hearts forever.—E. Lee Phillips

OFFERTORY SENTENCE.   "Serve one another in love. The entire law is summed up in a single command: 'Love your neighbor as yourself'" (Gal. 5:13b–14 NIV).

OFFERTORY PRAYER.   Lord, may our gifts this Palm Sunday be generous and grateful for the Savior who rides in our midst to sounds of acclamation. May we always proclaim Christ as Lord, and give accordingly.—E. Lee Phillips

PRAYER.   O God, whose creative power reaches back behind all beginnings and out beyond all endings, we marvel that you should come to us in our times—we who are creatures of time.

We wait before you, praying that our times be a time of the grace of our Lord Jesus Christ.

Open us to the insight to see that there is a sense in which the Church is here not because of us but in spite of us. There is a grace at work that is of your wisdom and power. There are times when we need to get out of the way, lest we get in the way of that new thing that you are doing in our day.

---

[2]*Faith—The Great Adventure* (Minneapolis, Minn.: Augsburg Fortress, 1985).

You have brought us from there to here and you will lead us from here to where you would have us be.—John Thompson

SERMON
Topic: Healing Broken Hearts
TEXT: Ps. 147:3

Heartbreak happens. It happens a lot, and it hurts—a lot. Maybe your first heartbreak happened when a pet died. But that wouldn't have been your last heartbreak—and probably not your worst.

For some children, severe heartbreak comes early, and it can change their entire lives. Most kids also run into some degree of heartbreak with friends while they're growing up.

There's deep heartbreak in parenting also. A mother and father may stand in a waiting room gasping "No, Doctor—not leukemia! Not our child! There must be some mistake. There must be something you can do!"

Heartbreak happens in many different ways. Your heart may break under blows being suffered right now, or it may break under the weight of the past, of memories from way back that you've never been able to deal with. Memories of being mistreated or molested by someone you trusted can leave you feeling rotten and unwilling to trust anyone. Memories of evil things that you yourself have done can crush you with guilt and regret.

Psalm 34:18 says, "The Lord is close to the brokenhearted and saves those who are crushed in spirit." You may have your doubts, but once you know what God is really like and you grasp the way he works, the healing can begin, and you'll find that the Lord is all you need.

Who is God? The Lord is a God of mind-boggling power, and at the same time he's a God of tender love and compassion. As Psalm 147 says, "He heals the brokenhearted and binds up their wounds. He determines the number of the stars and calls them each by name. Great is our Lord and mighty in power" (vv. 3–5). Maybe you've heard great statements from the Bible before, but they have left you unmoved. If so, you're not the only one to feel that way.

In Isaiah 49 God promises to rescue and restore his people. He starts off by saying, "In the time of my favor I will answer you, and in the day of salvation I will help you" (v. 8). But how do the people react? Do they shout for joy? Do they feel God's comfort and compassion? Far from it! They say, "The Lord has forsaken me, the Lord has forgotten me" (v. 14).

Why do we have such a hard time trusting that God will do what he says he'll do? We don't believe that God is greater than our circumstances.

But there's another reason we often have a hard time trusting God: we have a hard time trusting anybody. If you've been deeply hurt by people close to you, you've learned not to trust others or let them get too close. Being able to trust our parents is so important that when they fail it's hard to trust anybody, even God.

If you want to get beyond your hurts and your broken heart, then don't picture God merely in terms of the people you know. If you think God is somehow like the people who have abused and betrayed you, then of course you won't trust him. But the Lord says in the Bible, "I am God and not man—the Holy One among you" (Hos. 11:9). So don't get your picture of God from looking at the people around you.

There's only one person you can look at to get a perfectly clear picture of what God is like, and that person is Jesus. In Jesus God became a man. In Jesus we see just how far God will go to heal broken hearts. God keeps his promises, even if it costs him everything. Jesus, in fact, chose to die rather than abandon his people. This Lord comes to you now, with nail prints in his hands and Resurrection glory on his face, and he promises to bind up the brokenhearted.— David Feddes

SUNDAY, APRIL 11, 2004
Lectionary Message

Topic: Faith and Sight

TEXT: John 20:1–18

Other Readings: Isa. 65:17–25; Ps. 118:1–2, 14–24; Acts 10:34–43 or 1 Cor. 15:19–26

I. *Shock at the tomb.* Well, talk about a shock on top of a shock. Friday had been the worst day of her life. The one she thought had come to save the world—the one who had saved her—was executed by the authorities, and she couldn't do anything but stand by and watch him die. And now she had come to the tomb where they had laid his body; the tomb was standing wide open and no body was in sight. What a shock!

We have seen news clips of enough funeral processions in the Middle East to learn how emotional a time is the death of a friend or relative there. There is no quiet, stoic acceptance of death; there is, rather, loud and visible mourning at a time of grief. It is important, especially in those cultures, to pay one's respects to the dead. That's all Mary Magdalene had in mind that Sunday morning—doing her duty, paying her respects. I imagine she was thinking about what she would say to the guards or others who happened to be there when she arrived. She went early, perhaps so she wouldn't need to talk to many people. Then she arrived and found nobody, nothing. No guards, no mourners, no clergy, no sealed tomb, and no corpse. No corpse. First the cross, and now this: no corpse!

II. *Faith at the tomb.* So she ran to the disciples with the news that the corpse was nowhere to be found. They, of course, couldn't trust a hysterical female, so Peter and John ran to see for themselves. It's interesting how John records this for us in our text:

> The other disciple outran Peter and reached the tomb first. He bent down to look in and saw the linen wrappings lying there, but he did not go in. Then Simon Peter came, following him, and went into the tomb. He saw the linen wrappings lying there, and the cloth that had been on Jesus' head, not lying with the linen wrappings but rolled up in a place by itself. Then the other disciple, who reached the tomb first, also went in, and he saw and believed.

Notice how John got there first, leaned over, and peeked in, and then Peter caught up and walked right into the tomb. He then saw things in great detail: linen wrapping lying there and the head cloth neatly rolled up over here by itself. This was not evidence of grave robbers or secretive work. When John saw all this, he came to faith. At least he believed that Jesus was not taken away as a dead man, but rather had risen from the dead.

The men left the scene, and then Mary bent over and looked in and saw more than the men had seen; she saw two angels. Then she turned to face the garden, and saw a man she took for the gardener. It wasn't until she heard Jesus pronounce her name that she recognized him as the Risen Lord. So she went back to where the disciples were meeting and announced the good news, "I have seen the Lord."

III. *Faith at home.* It's hard for us to imagine how these words, "I have seen the Lord," would have been heard by these Jewish men. There are echoes in the words of their Scriptures. It was Job who, after hearing the theological reasoning of his friends and then hearing the thunder of God's own voice, said to the Lord, "I had heard of you by the hearing of the ear, but now my eye sees you" (Job 42:5). And it was the great prophet Isaiah, who declared, "In the year that King Uzziah died, I saw the Lord" (Isa. 6:1). Now here was this woman claiming that she had seen the Risen Lord Jesus. Would God give such a revelation to a woman first? That's almost as hard to believe as the Resurrection itself. But there it was. She was right about the open tomb—the empty tomb. Peter and John had seen that themselves. Now here she was telling them that she had seen the Lord and that he had given her a message for them.

What did she mean by "I have seen the Lord"? Was that wishful thinking? Was it hallucination? Had she had a vision of heaven? In what sense had she seen the Lord? John also believed after seeing just the empty tomb and the burial cloths. But what did he believe? We are not told that. We are told simply that he believed after having seen. Later Jesus would appear to ten of the disciples and they were forced to believe. Then, even later, Jesus would tell Thomas that people would be blessed who believe without seeing. Paul would write that faith comes from hearing (Rom. 10:17).

Christian faith, you see, is more than a decision that certain events have happened. Christian faith is entrusting ourselves to the living God, believing that God can overcome even death for us through our Lord Jesus Christ. It doesn't matter whether the evidence of God's power and love comes to us through the eyes or the ears; the important result is our trusting that the God who raised our Lord Jesus Christ from the grave will care for us for eternity.—Bruce E. Shields

ILLUSTRATIONS

MEANING.   This senseless death acquires a meaning only with the Resurrection of Jesus to new life with God, as known by faith. Only in the light of this new life from God does it become clear that the death was not in vain. That God, who seemed to have left him without support in the public gaze, did in fact sustain him through death. That God had not forsaken him who felt God's abandonment as no one had ever felt it before. That God, while publicly absent, maintained his hidden presence. This senseless human suffering and death thus acquire a meaning which man as he suffers and dies simply cannot produce himself, which can only be given to him by someone who is wholly other, by God himself.—Hans Küng[3]

CHANGE.   When we are no longer able to change a situation—just think of an incurable disease, say, an inoperable cancer—we are challenged to change ourselves.

This is brought home most beautifully by the words of Yehuda Bacon, an Israeli sculptor who was imprisoned in Auschwitz when he was a young boy and after the war wrote a paper from which I would like to quote a passage: "As a boy I thought: 'I will tell them what I saw,

---

[3]*On Being a Christian*

in the hope that people will change for the better.' But people didn't change and didn't even want to know. It was much later that I really understood *the meaning of suffering.* It can have a meaning if it changes oneself for the better." He finally recognized the meaning of his suffering: he changed himself.—Viktor Frankl[4]

SERMON SUGGESTIONS

Topic: God Has No Favorites

TEXT: Acts 10:34–43

(1) The grace of God is for people of every nation. (2) This good news came through Jesus Christ, the Lord of all. (3) Thus, everyone who trusts in Jesus Christ receives forgiveness of sins.

Topic: The Power of Christ's Resurrection

TEXT: 1 Cor. 15:19–26

(1) His Resurrection gives hope for the life to come, (2) promises that we shall be raised as he was raised, and (3) ensures that he will at last conquer all of God's enemies as well as our greatest enemy—death.

WORSHIP AIDS

CALL TO WORSHIP.   "The Lord is my refuge and defense, and he has become my deliverer" (Ps. 118:14 REB).

INVOCATION.   Lord of all, hear our worship of rejoicing and let our hearts be filled with gratitude for the gift of our salvation in Jesus Christ, whom sin could not conquer nor death hold.—E. Lee Phillips

OFFERTORY SENTENCE.   "So then, as often as we have the chance, we should do good to everyone, and especially to whose who belong to our family in the faith" (Gal. 6:10 TEV).

OFFERTORY PRAYER.   Holy God, let the Easter offering be reflective of the Resurrection of our souls from sin's hold to salvation's liberty through our blessed Redeemer.—E. Lee Phillips

PRAYER.   Almighty God, who hast brought again from the dead our Lord Jesus Christ and given him the name which is above every name, we rejoice this holy day with unutterable joy in thy great power and glory. By the might of thy Spirit, quicken us also, we beseech thee, that we may rise to newness of life and have a part in the working out of thy purpose of good for the world. Pardon and deliver us from all our sins. Bestow upon us thy healing and thy peace. And we beseech thee, grant us light upon our way and needed strength for our pilgrimage, until at length by thy great mercy we come to everlasting life.

We pray to thee for those dear to us who have gone before, whom we now name in our hearts before thee. Grant them thy peace, and in thy perfect wisdom and love, fulfill thy good purpose for them.

---

[4]*The Unheard Cry for Meaning*

We beseech thee for our brethren in all parts of the world, and most especially for those who are now in sorrow and affliction. O thou who art Father of mercies and God of all comfort, draw near to those in every place who cry for succor, that they may have hope both for this life and for the life to come.

Pour out thy Spirit upon thy Church, that it may do all which may serve and set forward thy blessed Kingdom. And we beseech thee, hasten the day when thy holy will shall be done on Earth as it is in heaven; through him who for our sake died and was raised, even Jesus Christ our Lord, to whom be glory for ever and ever.—Ernest Fremont Tittle[5]

SERMON
Topic: This Is My Message for You
Text: Matt. 28:1–10

"Do not be afraid," said the angel to the women at the tomb. "I know that you are looking for Jesus who was crucified. He is not here, for he has been raised, as he said. Come, see the place where he lay. Then go quickly and tell his disciples, 'He has been raised from the dead, and indeed he is going ahead of you to Galilee; there you will see him.' This is my message for you."

Death sometimes comes upon us with all the sudden, unanticipated fury of a summer storm. Yet frequently that's not the case. Instead, we witness death like the slow but irreversible setting of the sun. We see it in the developing sickness, the set of the jaw, the signs of flesh failing life. We hear it approaching in sighs and groans and labored breathing.

Long before that day when we are forced to say our final farewell; long before we look, through tortured eyes, at the last breath of life being drawn; long before that fateful day, we have already begun to grieve.

It begins deep in the darkest caverns of the heart and soul, hidden from the sight of human eyes. It begins in a daydream of despair, the lonely lilting of an inarticulate groan, a sigh too deep for words. Eventually we find that we are weeping—tears, tremors, troubled heart.

Death is not some abstract reality, some general principle at the closing point of life. Death is always and everywhere painfully particular. It is never simply that someone dies. It is always the case that my someone, or your someone, or their someone, dies!

I'm certain that's exactly what made the death of Jesus so very difficult for his disciples. Sure, to the average citizen, to the person who had merely a passing interest in this carpenter from Nazareth, to the visitor to Jerusalem, the death of Jesus made little or no difference.

But to his disciples? To his closest followers it was a calamity beyond description. Three years of songs and stories, of struggles and joys, of love and laughter, of dusty roads and memorable meals—and death had silenced their friend, and their faith.

Which is also what we know, isn't it? We know that death doesn't come merely to people in general, but to us and those we love in particular. Whenever we must, once more, stare into those cold, hard eyes of death, we find that our faith can fall silent, struck dumb in the presence of this powerful, this pain-inflicting foe.

---

[5]*A Book of Pastoral Prayers* (New York: Abingdon-Cokesbury, 1951).

And the memories that would console us will also become the source of our continuing sorrow, because what we miss most are those characteristics and qualities that are unique to the one for whom we grieve. We will never have them again—with anyone, for any reason. Only she could smile that way. Only he could say that right word at the right time. It's the particular that makes death painful.

Isn't the sharpest edge of our sorrow—that which cuts us to the quick—the singularity of our loss?

Long before death is done with us, we have been busy building relationships. Then, over time, we deepen in our devotion to and care for those we are learning to love. We can even find that we cherish the small and seemingly insignificant characteristics of the loved one's particular personality.

Well, I doubt very much that this would have been different with the disciples of Jesus. How could it have been? Like us, they had, over time, become personal friends with the one they had followed from village to village. Together they had crossed over some pretty rough terrain—physically as well as spiritually. They had roasted fish over an open fire, and they had broken bread while reclining at the same table. In short, the disciples had come to cherish this carpenter, with his calloused hands and compassionate heart.

Which is why his death cut so deep into their souls. Like us they had made an emotional investment in the life of Jesus—and even more.

Like us, when we deepen in love for another, they had invested in dreams and hopes and yearnings, all of which were suddenly cut short when that cross was raised on Calvary. Now death shrouded their longing and left them with a void at the very core of their characters. And haven't we too looked into that same void—as the chest stopped heaving, as the heart stopped beating, as the lid on the coffin was closed?

You realize, of course, that those same sorrowing disciples attended the tomb of Jesus expecting to discover the expected—that is to say, death. They came plodding along the pathway to his grave, to do what we do best when touched by death—they came to grieve. And we will surely miss the drama, the sheer force of this story, if we should think, even for one minute, that these mourners had the slightest notion that nothing would be as expected.

"Do not be afraid," said the angel to the women—which is, in and of itself, something of a wonder.

Fear is all we can know in the face of death, isn't it? We visit the grave, and what? We feel our own mortality nudge us from behind. Cemeteries are a grim reminder of the fact that one day our lives too will be measured out in a four-by-six-by-six plot of land. And tombstones are the signature of death, written in cold granite across the landscape of our lives.

But something fundamental has changed all of that—something of faith, something final, something with a future. "Do not be afraid," declares God's messenger to those early mourners.

Because for them, for us, for our world—by one act of grace beyond our wildest dreams—that tomb, on that first Lord's Day, was emptied of death and brimming with life. A messenger of God, standing within an empty tomb, announced for all the world that wondrous proclamation: In the crucified and Risen Christ, God had broken death's grip on creature and creation. A four-word declaration would from that day forward alter the entire course of human history: "He has been raised!"

Someone has rightly said that the Resurrection "comes from outside ourselves. It comes even from outside our knowing. It comes as the stunning surprise, the thing we could never imagine, illogical, implausible, the absurd solution—arising from no system we know or control. Its source must be God alone. Grace. It is a gift." Yet how can we lay claim to that gift—long before the grave becomes our bed?

That's the power of Christ's Resurrection! It claims us today. It means that death no longer has dominion over us. It means that we will never be alone in life, and never abandoned in death.

It means that God's mercy will sustain us in and through all sorrow, leading us ever forward to new life, beyond each and every loss. It means that Christ has surely blessed us and dressed us with an indestructible grace and a promise to prevail.

And when that becomes true in our lives, then perhaps we too will sing with the words of the psalmist (Ps. 30:11–12): "You have turned my mourning into dancing; you have taken off my sackcloth and clothed me with joy, so that my soul may praise you and not be silent. O Lord, my God, I will give thanks to you forever!"—Albert J. D. Walsh

SUNDAY, APRIL 18, 2004
Lectionary Message

Topic: Signs and Senses
TEXT: John 20:19–31
Other Readings: Acts 5:27–32; Ps. 118:14–29; Rev. 1:4–8

The Gospel of John comes to a neat ending with verses 30 and 31, although there is another chapter to come. We read here that "Jesus did many . . . signs in the presence of his disciples." We display signs so that human beings can access them with one or more of the five human senses: sight, hearing, smell, taste, and touch. This text deals with the human senses in some interesting ways, connecting them with faith in Christ.

I. *They experienced Jesus firsthand.* The original followers of Jesus experienced those signs first-hand. The following words open 1 John: "We declare to you what was from the beginning, what we have heard, what we have seen with our eyes, what we have looked at and touched with our hands, concerning the word of life." What those earliest followers of Jesus experienced with their human senses they declared to others so that they too could come to sense Jesus. That process has continued right down to the present, and here I am, declaring to you that you can know this Jesus.

John's Gospel says in verse 20:31, "These [signs] are written so that you may come to believe that Jesus is the Messiah, the Son of God, and that through believing you may have life in his name." In other words, the signs experienced in the sight of the disciples, which they have described vocally for the hearing of others, have now been written down so that the reader, using eyesight, and those who hear the text read, using the sense of hearing, may come to faith.

II. *We can experience Jesus, too.* So John's Gospel was written for us—for people who could not be present as the disciples were to experience the signs of Jesus' messiahship directly through our own senses. Therefore, we can apply our senses to the story narrated in the text.

Listen once again to the first few verses of our text, but listen this time for sensory words. See if you can sense what those disciples experienced.

When it was evening on that day, the first day of the week, and the doors of the house where the disciples had met were locked for fear of the Jews, Jesus came and stood among them and said, "Peace be with you." After he said this, he showed them his hands and his side. Then the disciples rejoiced when they saw the Lord. Jesus said to them again, "Peace be with you. As the Father has sent me, so I send you." When he had said this, he breathed on them and said to them, "Receive the Holy Spirit. If you forgive the sins of any, they are forgiven them; if you retain the sins of any, they are retained."

Locked doors, fear, Jesus appearing in spite of locks, Jesus speaking, showing them his wounded hands and side, the disciples feeling joy, then Jesus breathing on them—that was a multisensory experience. They saw him, heard him, felt his breath. No wonder they were happy, almost deliriously happy. But then there was Thomas.

Let's not be too hard on Thomas for wanting the same kind of sensory experience of the Risen Lord as the others had had. When he heard that they had seen Jesus, he said, "Unless I see the mark of the nails in his hands, and put my finger in the mark of the nails and my hand in his side, I will not believe." He only wanted to see and feel, just as they had.

And the next Sunday he got his chance, when Jesus came and graciously said, "Put your finger here and see my hands. Reach out your hand and put it in my side. Do not doubt, but believe." The senses are so much a part of this scene that the words get confused—"put your finger here and see . . ." Only blind people see with their fingers—or maybe not only blind people. The Creator has linked our senses in such a way that we can "feel" what we hear and see as well as what we touch. A well-written description will lead us to visualize the scene. A well-told story impels us to experience the event. We can sympathize or even empathize with people we have never met, if we read about them or hear about them.

That brings us to verse 29—a verse in which Jesus speaks about us. Here Jesus said to Thomas, "Have you believed because you have seen me? Blessed are those who have not seen and yet have come to believe." There are two primary dimensions of faith—past and present. When we hear the testimony of the original disciples of Jesus, we come to sense the actual historical reality of the divine person who walked this Earth in human form. We reach a hand over the centuries and see his hands, wounded for us. We see him healing and teaching. Our faith helps us to actualize the historical Jesus.

III. *We can touch eternity.* But our faith also helps us to know that Jesus is more than a martyr who lived in ancient times. We reach our hands into the dimension of eternity to actualize the Jesus who, as he promised, is with us always.

Right here, in the Church that the apostle Paul called the body of Christ, we can reach out and touch the Lord himself. Looking around us, we might wonder if that is all there is to this Jesus; but the experience of the first disciples was that there is always something more. Each time they thought they had Jesus figured out through their human senses, he pulled something else on them—and finally, he rose from the dead! That would blow it for me. We have not experienced the resurrection of somebody we watched die, and neither had they; but here he was, standing among them in spite of a stone tomb and locked doors. If God can arrange that, then God can take this unlikely looking group of human beings and make of us the body of Christ. The Risen Lord can live with his people, and we can reach out a finger and feel that he is here.

We can even pass a communion tray to the person next to us and say, "This is my body broken for you," and mean it. We can become the body of Christ, the Risen Lord. We can be sure that the Lord is in his congregation, and we can be just as sure that there is more to the Lord than we can see.—Bruce E. Shields

ILLUSTRATIONS

EXAMPLES OF FAITH.   Whether or not he intended to do so, the evangelist has given us . . . four slightly different examples of faith in the Risen Jesus. The Beloved Disciple comes to faith after having seen the burial wrappings but without having seen Jesus himself. Magdalene sees Jesus but does not recognize him until he calls her by name. The disciples see him and believe. Thomas also sees him and believes, but only after having been overinsistent on the marvelous aspect of the appearance. All four are examples of those who saw and believed; the evangelist will close the Gospel in 29b by turning his attention to those who have believed without seeing.—Raymond E. Brown[6]

THE BLESSING.   Yet it is true that the most blessed state is that of a faith which has no inhibitions to burst through. Just as it is best to believe that Christ is in the Father and the Father in him by a direct apprehension of the deity manifest in him, whereas to believe *for the works' sake* is a second best (xiv, 11), so it is most blessed to be able to believe in his deity and triumph over death by direct apprehension, because as we dwell with him we behold his glory: *blessed are they who saw not and have believed.*

St. Peter wrote to Christians who, like ourselves, had had no opportunity to see the Lord, and used the expression "Whom, not having seen, ye love; on whom, though now ye see him not, yet believing, ye rejoice greatly with joy unspeakable and full of glory" (1 Peter 1:8). We have not seen. Do we believe? Do we love? Can we claim the blessing—the "joy unspeakable and full of glory"?—William Temple[7]

SERMON SUGGESTIONS

Topic: Where Our Loyalty Lies

TEXT: Acts 5:27–32

(1) *Situation:* Life faces us with claims upon our loyalty. (2) *Complication:* We cannot serve two masters, and the master we choose may be the wrong one. (3) *Resolution:* The ultimately safe way is to obey God first and let that commitment determine all other loyalties.

Topic: Doxology

TEXT: Rev. 1:4–8

All praise to the living Christ, who (1) loves us, (2) freed us from our sins by his death on the cross, and (3) gave us royal status for priestly tasks.

WORSHIP AIDS

CALL TO WORSHIP.   "The stone the builders rejected has become the capstone; the Lord has done this, and it is marvelous in our eyes. This is the day the Lord has made; let us rejoice and be glad in it" (Ps. 118:22–24 NIV).

---

[6]*The Gospel According to John* (New York: Doubleday, 1970).
[7]*Readings in St. John's Gospel* (Harrisburg, Pa.: Morehouse, 1985).

INVOCATION.   O God, there is no end to your love toward us. In spite of our sins and failures, indeed because of these very things, you reach out to us through the cross of your Son, our Savior. We can praise you and thank you forever.

OFFERTORY SENTENCE.   This is the Christ we proclaim; we train everyone and teach everyone the full scope of this knowledge in order to set everyone before God mature in Christ; I labor for that end, striving for it with the divine energy which is a power within me" (Col. 1:28–29 Moffatt).

OFFERTORY PRAYER.   We are glad, O God, for this day and for this opportunity to extend our witness through the offerings we now bring. Bless those whose lives are touched with your grace and our faithful generosity.

PRAYER.   Almighty God, our Father, who has made this vast universe and can be named the owner of forever and the dispenser of eternal goodness, we come in all humility before you in this sacred hour. Though our steps have followed various paths to this hallowed place, yet in the stillness of our pulsating hearts we are one together. Our needs and concerns may vary in peripheral matters, but basically we share similar hopes and dreams, crises and fears. Here today we pray that you will silently and gently enter every trembling heart, that we might know the glad assurance of your peace and rest.

We gather here, Father, because we need to understand again your kind mercy and gentle forgiveness. We declare that you are light, but we constantly find ourselves walking in darkness. We call you peace, but we do violence to one another, to your creation, and even to ourselves. We call you joy, yet live our days in sadness and even bitterness. We call you hope, but spend much of life languishing in despair. We call you love, yet spend much of our energy despising and hating one another. We call you truth, but scatter the landscape of our lives with falsehoods and lies. We declare that you are faith, and crouch in fear even as we harbor distrust in our hearts. Lord Jesus, you have borne our pain and carried our sorrows away, and you have suffered and died for our sins, and this morning we come to ask you to forgive us again. Restore us to rightness and oneness with you, that we might be right with each other and the world and with ourselves.—Henry Fields

SERMON
Topic: Raised to Life with Christ
TEXT: Col. 3:1–4; Matt. 28:1–10

With some of the same power God used to bring Jesus from death back to life, God—in your personal commitment to and relationship with Jesus Christ—has raised you to life with Christ. Day-to-day living, then, is centered in that reality, and all that is superfluous and unnecessary about spirituality and discipleship is exposed as nonsense.

The life that God has given you through the Risen Lord, Jesus Christ, is the epitome of abundant life; you, as a child of God and a follower of Jesus Christ, are experiencing the best that life can be in this world. It is not to be cheapened by what is distracting, piddling, or unworthy of your time and attention. Just as surely as your life has been transformed, so also have your priorities and preoccupations been transformed.

So what is the bottom line of Christian faith? Because our religion is inseparably linked to Judaism, I'll point first to what I believe is the bottom line of faith in the Hebrew Bible, for that is foundational to Christianity, and then to the bottom line of faith in the New Testament.

In the Hebrew Bible, the bottom line of faith is, I think, expressed in the prophecy of Micah. In a dramatic scene, the prophet envisions God in dialogue with the people of God. The people, caught up in the ancient religious sacrificial system, ask, "What shall I bring when I come before the Lord, when I bow before God on high? Am I to come before him with whole offerings, with yearling calves? Will the Lord be pleased with thousands of rams or ten thousand rivers of oil? Shall I offer my eldest son for my wrongdoing, my child for the sin I committed?" (Mic. 6:6–7 REB). Then God answers—and interestingly, as if God is repeating something already spoken—"The Lord has told you mortals what is good and what the Lord requires of you: only to act justly, to love loyalty, and to walk humbly with your God" (Mic. 6:8 REB).

Here it is: the bottom line. There isn't a single thing suggested about doctrinal correctness. When we ask the Hebrew Bible what the bottom line of faith is, the answer we get is related to action: act justly, love loyalty in the sense of consistently expressing mercy or compassion to those in need, and walk humble with your God—that is, as one ever seeking to please and honor God through obedience. Incredible, isn't it?

Out of the whole massive and meticulous tradition of laws typically presented as absolutely required for all people, this prophet has God saying that most of the list isn't necessary or required. When you boil it all down, if you are a person of faith, you will act justly, you will love mercy, and you will walk humbly with God.

What does the New Testament add to this? Well, the New Testament says that such living is essential and that it grows out of a new motivation. The jailer asked Paul and Silas what he had to do to be saved. They answered, "Believe on the Lord Jesus and you will be saved, you and your household" (Acts 16:31 NRSV).

"Believe on the Lord Jesus and you will be saved." That is, trust the Risen Jesus Christ with your whole being; make him your Lord, which is to say, become his disciple; then you will be saved—delivered from the tyranny of sin's rule and given life abundant here and in the hereafter. You'll find yourself saved; you'll realize that you have been raised with Christ. Your life will have been transformed. You will have new goals, new impulses for service, new reverence and desire for the presence of God in your heart.

I want to tell you that the Resurrection of Jesus Christ from the dead is the great clarifier of faith essentials, and on this day we should not wonder, or have to wonder, about what we need to do in order to be a child of God or a community of faith. Doing what we need to do, I admit, is difficult, but seeing what needs to be done, what really has to be done, isn't difficult at all. God has given us the bottom line in a Risen Lord.

The enemies of Jesus were not the infidels. The enemies of Jesus were people of God who had gotten so caught up in the human-made details of faith, with their elaborately constructed extras, that the mere thought of faith in God as a simple, bottom-line kind of thing scared them and offended them. As with most people who get caught up in human-made religious rules, which from God's perspective clearly have nothing to do with real faith, they had come to trust their rules more than they trusted God. They were ritualistically perfect and they killed Jesus—not as angry murderers, but as pious and legalistically accomplished persons of faith.

Thorwald Lorenzen says we'll know we're walking the right paths when we are living as Jesus' disciples. The consequences of Jesus' Resurrection shape us into his faithful follow-ers. This discipleship, then, will lead us, formally and informally, in Christian communities, to the carrying out of Christ's mission of proclaiming God's love and living it out. Lorenzen says, "The church is only obedient to its Lord insofar as it understands itself as being sent to implement the concrete realization of that Lordship in the world."[8]

You have been raised. You have been saved. Salvation is liberation. You are free. Celebrate it! Rejoice! You can give your all living with and for God. You can use every bit of your energy pursuing a pure spirituality based in constant communion with God that will keep you focused only on what really matters. This focus will lead you to cry out against injustice and try to do something about it; will make you a person filled with mercy as was Jesus; and will keep you humbly and, no doubt, joyously walking with your God, the God who raised Jesus Christ, our Lord and Savior, from the dead.—David Albert Farmer

SUNDAY, APRIL 25, 2004
Lectionary Message

Topic: Do You See Him?

TEXT: John 21:1–14

Other Readings: Acts 9:1–6 (7–20); Ps. 30; Rev. 5:11–14

I. *Seeing the Lord is hard.* They had already seen Jesus twice since his Resurrection. You would think they would have recognized him the third time, even at a distance. But no—not until they began to haul in the fish did one of them figure it out.

"It's the Lord," he said. I wonder *how* he said it. Did he whisper it in Peter's ear? "Psst, Peter, it's the Lord!" Was his voice shaking with fear? "I-I-I-t's the Lord." Was he awe struck? "Whoa! It's the Lord!" Did he shout with excitement? "Hey, look! It's the Lord!" If you were playing that part in a drama, how would you intone those words? Maybe, "Well, duh—it's the Lord."

But before we go talking about how dense those disciples were, we should take a good look at ourselves. Jesus promised to be with his followers always, even to the end of the age. Do we really believe that? If we do, how often do we see him? How often do we recognize that he is at work in the world? Isn't it true that we most often conceive of Jesus as sitting on a majestic throne in the presence of God? That keeps him safely out of our way.

If you are like me, you probably don't stop even once a day and say, "It is the Lord!" Once a week, maybe—here in church at the Lord's table or during a hymn or sermon—we might become aware of the Lord's presence. Is that enough? He said "always," and we think "once a week."

Of course, seeing Jesus is different from seeing a family member or friend. Our eyes are accustomed to picking up the light that bounces off our fellow human beings. Our minds automatically interpret that light as another person. We even sense the presence of others by sound, smell, and touch. Our human senses are in play in all those circumstances of life that we call normal. That's just the trouble—we put a sense of the presence of Jesus in the cate-

---

[8]Thorwald Lorenzen, *Resurrection and Discipleship* (Maryknoll: Orbis, 1995), p. 310.

gory of abnormal or paranormal, and we wouldn't want to be known as abnormal. However, he gave us some hints as to how we can see him in a more normal way. We can train our brains to react to certain sights and sounds with "It's the Lord!"

II. *See him in those who help others.* What was Jesus doing when, according to our text, the disciple whom Jesus loved realized who Jesus was? He was cooking breakfast and giving these experienced fishermen advice on where to cast their nets. In other words, he was involved in simple service to people he loved. Don't we see Jesus when we notice somebody offering a cup of cold water in the name of a disciple? Don't we see Jesus when we see somebody reaching out to a person in need?

III. *See him in those who need our help.* Jesus also said once, "Inasmuch as you do it unto one of the least of these, you do it unto me." It is interesting that as he told the story of the last judgment, everybody asked him, "When did we see you?" He said, "When I was hungry . . . when I was sick . . . when I was in prison." The ones who didn't serve him said, "When did we see you hungry, sick, or in prison?" And the ones who did serve him asked the same question. But the point is not only that we see Jesus when we see somebody serving others; we also see Jesus in those others who need to be served.

Can we train ourselves and our children to begin to recognize Jesus in our communities? Can we begin to watch for the Lord at work with people who need him and who perhaps also need his Church? I challenge you—I challenge myself—this week, as we drive here and there, as we put in our work days, as we enjoy our homes, as we shop or learn in school, to watch for the Lord. Oh, he's here all right, and he's out there, too. Even if we go fishing, we might hear a voice say, "Hey there—it's the Lord!" Pay attention now, or you might just miss him.—Bruce E. Shields

ILLUSTRATIONS

SEEING THE LORD IN THOSE WHO SERVE.   There is a woman in the church where I am an elder who was attending services more or less regularly (but not every week). She was not involved with the church much more than that. She seemed shy and difficult even to engage in conversation. Then one day our benevolence committee recommended to the board and then to the congregation that we get involved in the Interfaith Hospitality Network. This is a group of congregations that offer their facilities for a week at a time to house and feed the homeless of the Johnson City area. This lady volunteered to help when the homeless came to stay at our church. Soon she was organizing our congregation's turns at keeping these people. She did it so well that the central organization offered her the job of helping to run the whole program. She has been doing that for over a year now—pouring her time, talent, and energy into helping those who are less fortunate than she is. All it took was for her to see a need that she could fill, and suddenly the rest of us were saying, "It's the Lord!"

SEEING THE LORD IN THOSE WHO NEED HELP.   There's an older couple who come by our church every once in a while. They usually show up at the end of a service and tell us about their need for help with the rent money. We keep nonperishable food in a pantry and we have a fund of money that we can use for such needs. We also direct people to other agencies where they can find help. All that is well and good but I wonder, do we see Jesus in them? I even visited the husband in the hospital once, but I can't claim to have been conscious of being in the presence of the Lord at the time. I hope the Lord will surprise me on that day and say "well done," even if I didn't know it was the Lord himself I was praying with.—Bruce E. Shields

SERMON SUGGESTIONS

Topic: The Transforming Power of the Gospel

TEXT: Acts 9:1–20

(1) *Then:* It changed Saul of Tarsus—"the chief of sinners." (2) *Always:* Through the centuries it has changed such people as Augustine, Francis of Assisi, Martin Luther, John Bunyan, and John Wesley. (3) *Now:* The gospel can change you, and through people like you God can change the world.

Topic: Worthy Is the Lamb!

TEXT: Rev. 5:11–14

Jesus Christ is worthy of the same kind of worship as the Creator: (1) because of who he is— God incarnate glorified; (2) because of what he did—he died, "the Lamb that was slain," for our salvation.

WORSHIP AIDS

CALL TO WORSHIP. "Sing praise to the Lord, you saints of his, and give thanks at the remembrance of his holy name. For his anger is but for a moment, but his favor is for life; weeping may endure for a night, but joy comes in the morning" (Ps. 30:4–5 NKJV).

INVOCATION. Gracious God, open our hearts to your reality, that we may see you in both your majesty and your love. As we contemplate your creation in its many aspects, grant that we may catch sight of you. Beyond the clouds of our doubts and fears, may we see the sunlight of your redeeming reality.

OFFERTORY SENTENCE. "Since you have accepted Christ Jesus as Lord, live in union with him. Keep your roots deep in him, build your lives on him, and become stronger in your faith, as you were taught. And be filled with thanksgiving" (Col. 2:6–7 TEV).

OFFERTORY PRAYER. Lord, as we travel the highways of life, give us a generous and sympathetic spirit for people in all kinds of circumstances. May we care enough for your Church and its ministers in the world that we will indeed bring the tithes into the storehouse, so that there will be plenty and to spare.—Henry Fields

PRAYER. Lead us, we pray, into the most holy of places this morning, Father. Let the consciousness of your presence fill our minds so that everything that is flippant and frivolous may be banished from our souls. Deliver us from carelessly approaching such holy times. Redeem us from our irreverent habits. Break up the bondage of any custom that has become our foe. May we never be imprisoned by the letter of the law, but rather be set free to be all possible in your name by the grace of Christ. Quicken our memories to recall the many times you have intervened with us and for us. Remind us of the boundless presence of your strength and comfort when we face the disasters of life. Let the warmth of divine solace scatter sorrow's shadow where shadows exist this morning. Let the glory of forgiveness be experienced as we lay our sinful burdens at the cross this sacred day. Encircle us with the wonder of real love that we may indeed learn to love as Christ loved.—Henry Fields

SERMON
Topic: God's Foolishness
Text: 1 Cor. 1:22–25

It seems to me that there are few things more presumptuous, or painful, than the pretense to strength and courage. I'm certain you know what I mean. Whenever life begins to wallop us about as though we were a Wiffle ball, most of us will claim to be made of firmer stuff. We wouldn't want people to see the cracks in our character.

The saints of society are those who can suck it in and stiff it out. They're the heroes of hard knocks. We admire their white-knuckled, bullheaded will to survive. Maybe we even consider such determined characters the last warriors fighting at the front lines of human weakness. Perhaps we do so because weakness frightens us.

We look to protect ourselves from pain, and all too often we send up a smoke screen, calling it strength. We attempt to masquerade our deepest insecurities behind a costume of courage, or a paper-thin shield of strength. Political prestige, material gain, personal power—in the end, they're all seen for what they truly are.

And we're aware that we make every effort to shield ourselves behind some pretty flimsy fortresses. So, what's the alternative? Are there any real options? Or are we stuck with the stiff upper lip?

I'm aware that the options I'm going to offer won't be all that appealing to those of you who think the only way to conquer fear is by a show of force. And I'm certain that for those who believe you should flex your muscle in the face of fear, what I'm about to suggest will seem somewhat spineless. But so be it!

I recently sat at the bedside of a woman who'd undergone extensive surgery for cancer. Oh, she had fears all right, and they fell from her eyes in small droplets of discouragement. They covered her skeletal face like the darkening clouds of a deepening disappointment. But it was in just that place of pain and puzzlement that her strength shined through. There, at the heart of her weakness, I witnessed something of a wonder.

Maybe my words won't say it as I saw it, but I'll try. I believe I saw Christ in the cracks of this woman's character. He seemed to reveal himself in the raw courage of this suffering saint who could do nothing, really, to change the course of her life. Here and there, through her feeble yet unwavering faith, I'm still convinced I witnessed the wonder of the Savior's strength in a shaken soul.

There was no pretense to power, no paper-thin shield of strength. She pounded her fists on the bed rail and demanded to know "Why?!"

She stammered out words that sounded more like a curse than a compliment. But then there was more.

There were moments when her eyes seemed to hold all the riches of heaven, times when her words were like oil poured on a festering wound. She would pray, and I swore I could feel the wind from angels' wings. There were times when Christ was so real in that room, I believed I heard him breathing. And in this woman's weakness, in her sickness, in her struggles, I beheld the Savior's strength in a shaken soul. The world will never understand such a wonderful reality.

But Christ makes possible a different kind of courage: a courage that doesn't conceal the wounds and weaknesses of human existence, a courage willing to take up the challenge of life's chaos and confusion.

I'm convinced that this kind of courage is contagious. Someone has said, "Keep your fears to yourself, but share your courage with others." That may be a bit of an overstatement. Yet I wouldn't be a bit surprised should the courage of Christ in one life beget a similar courage in another life.

Among the Japanese, the bamboo tree is a symbol of prosperity; the pine tree, a symbol of long life; and the plum tree, a symbol of courage. Now, the plum tree seems an unlikely candidate, don't you think? One would expect a much larger and sturdier tree to be the symbol of courage.

The explanation is that the plum tree blooms very early in the spring, when there's still snow on the ground. So you see, our courage is marked not simply by *what* we do, but by *where* and *when* we do it. The courage of Christ empowers us to stand firm—even in the face of our greatest failures and misfortunes.

When you're at your wits' end, when your back is against the wall, then the excuses you've fashioned for yourself begin to look pretty flimsy, don't they?

Even the pretense to power won't save us when death comes dancing at our door. Our moment of greatest weakness then becomes the time of Christ's greatest triumph, as he reaches out to redeem and restore us to life. So it would appear to be true: only the weak and wounded heart will surrender to the strength of the Savior.

The apostle Paul once wrote, "For religious folk demand miracles and nonreligious folk demand that things make sense, but we proclaim Christ crucified, a stumbling block to religious folk and foolishness to nonreligious folk, but to those who are called Christians? Christ, the power of God and the wisdom of God. For God's foolishness is wiser than human wisdom, and God's weakness is stronger than human strength."

I suppose Paul was referring to God's long love affair with humankind. At least it seems to me that this is God's "weakness." He loved us enough to walk smack dab into the heart of our hatred, our faithless ways, and our darkest fears. And he loved us enough to lay his life on the line for our salvation.

Is it any wonder then that "God's power is made perfect in weakness"? It was in the very weakness of human flesh that God chose to work out his wonder of redemption. When we are weak, then we're strong. But our strength and courage are merely the fruits of a faithful surrender to the Savior.

Well, then, I may not have the whole thing worked out; but this much I know: when that final hour comes and my feeble faith is being blown about like a feather, I won't be satisfied with tin-shield strength, or some stupid pretense to power. In that last desperate dance with death, I want only to know the comfort of a Christ-like courage—a power made perfect in weakness, a strength through surrender to a Savior who can truly save!—Albert J. D. Walsh

SUNDAY, MAY 2, 2004
Lectionary Message

Topic: Coming to Life

TEXT: Acts 9:36–43

Other Readings: Ps. 23; Rev. 7:9–17; John 10:22–30

All too often, many of us presume that this present existence is all there is. This is where we receive the glory, the praise, the accolades. This life as we know it becomes the embodiment for our very being; it defines who we are, what we do. It is this life that causes people to either remember us or forget us. In this present condition, where we operate out of the carnal and the natural, it seems the right thing to do. Yet this passage of Scripture shows us that life is more, so much more, than what we currently profess it to be. For each of us, life comes only when we are willing to die.

I. *To be alive in Christ and with Christ, we must die to self.* For any of us to receive our full measure and reach our full potential and purpose in relationship with God, we must first be willing to surrender to God all that we are, all that we presume to be, and all that others assume we are. We have to be willing to give up the things we feel are important, to let go of the things we hold near and dear. You see, as long as you or I hold on to thoughts, ideas, and actions that we believe are inherent to our significance in this life, we rob ourselves and deny ourselves the opportunity to bask in the wonder and awesomeness of God. For any of us, to be truly alive in Christ and with Christ is to let go of the natural in order to be filled with the Spirit.

The writer of this passage of Scripture speaks to the excellent virtues of the woman Dorcas. Her death brings about tears of sadness to the many who were affected by her life. Her passing causes others to reflect on the good works she had done on behalf of the Lord. Perhaps those who grieved questioned God's timing about this woman's death. Others may have been angry that the Lord would allow such a good person to die. Yet, for all of her goodness and godliness, Dorcas did die—it could not be avoided, especially if she truly desired to be alive in Christ and reign with him.

Each time we kill off the bitterness, the envy, the shame, the guilt, the anger, the loneliness, and so on that creep into our beings, we make room for the restoration of our joy, peace, contentment, hope, and love—all of which come from God and God alone.

II. *To be like Christ in this life is to be like Christ in his death.* If it is your desire to be like Christ in this present life—that is, to point others to God through your words and actions—then it is necessary for you to be like Christ in his death. To die like Christ is to allow yourself to be stripped of everything conceivable and imaginable so that God receives the glory and the praise. It is to understand that Christ descended from his throne in heaven to come dwell among regular folks like you and me. Christ's supremacy and his preeminence took a back seat to the desires of God. All that Christ was in heaven had no place on Earth. Christ died to self the moment he accepted his Father's assignment to go save the world. He became alive every time he responded or acted in ways that reflected his position with the Father.

Like Christ, when we accept the assignment to be all that God would have us be, we too must lay aside our issues, our idiosyncrasies, our very beings, so that we may do what God would have us do. It ceases to be about us and instead becomes all about God.

For you to be an heir to the Kingdom of God, you must imitate Jesus. This does not mean that you should act out of your own strength or will. Rather, it means that like Jesus you must humble yourself to the place where the Spirit of the Lord flows through you, so that as you think, act, and speak, you do so as a change agent for God—so that God becomes the central force by which you move and exist.

III. *Only by coming to God is there life.* It is only when you come to God, or allow God to meet you at your point of need, that you receive life. No matter what others may offer you, regardless of what others may say to you, it is only when the breath of God flows through your being and the word of God is spoken into your Spirit that you have true life. For all of Dorcas's success and achievements, only when Peter came and prayed for her as she lay on her death bed, and then called her name and gave her his hand, did Dorcas arise to live a new life.

Each time we seek out God for renewal and refreshment through praise, prayer, and worship, God calls our name and extends his hand to us, bidding us to come, to walk in the newness of life that he has for each of us.

The Lord wants us to have more than we presently have; he desires to give us an abundance and an inheritance that cannot be measured. By the same token, he desires that the praise and accolades given to us for our successes and achievements really go to him; after all, he is our Creator and Sustainer, the one who makes all things possible in us, with us, and through us—that is, of course, if we let him. And that's the key—our surrender, our death to the old nature, our death to our attitudes and behaviors that do not glorify or edify him. Truthfully, we should want to allow the Lord access to us, because in him, with him, and through him we gain so much. God is life, and because of this we have the opportunity day in and day out to come to him, so that we can come to life. Come just as you are; just come.—Cheryl L. Green

ILLUSTRATIONS

GOD'S WORK.   If I write a book on the spiritual meaning of medicine and one of my colleagues carries out some piece of experimental research in the laboratory, we are both equally in God's hand, both moved by the spirit of adventure he has put into our hearts, both instruments of his sovereign work. The work of all of us, whether it be scientific, technical, commercial, educational, artistic, industrial, agricultural, or manual, has its appointed place in the divine adventure of the world. We all play our part in the adventure. We all share in the divine joy of adventure, the joy of doing something useful, which has a meaning in the total purpose of the world—the joy of bringing forth fruit. That is the image that Jesus himself often used to express the meaning of human life (see John 15:5). Life is the current, the sap that flows into us day by day from God. Our work, all we do, feel, think, and believe—these are the fruits that it ripens in us.—Paul Tournier[1]

GOD'S SURPRISES.   Sometimes, when, after sin committed, I have looked for sore chastisement from the hand of God, the very next that I have had from Him hath been the discovery of His grace. Sometimes, when I have been comforted, I have called myself a fool for my so sinking under trouble. And then, again, when I have been cast down, I thought I was

---

[1]*The Adventure of Living* (New York: HarperCollins, 1979).

not wise to give such way to comfort. With such strength and weight have both these been upon me.—John Bunyan (1628–1688)[2]

SERMON SUGGESTIONS

Topic: But God Raised Him from the Dead

TEXT: Acts 13:15–16, 26–33

(1) God gave his best in sending Jesus Christ. (2) People did their worst in rejecting him. (3) Both God and the world gained a victory through what God made of it all.

Topic: What Heaven Will Be Like

TEXT: Rev. 7:9–17

(1) Celebration. (2) Worship. (3) Honor. (4) Service. (5) Fellowship with God and "the Lamb." (6) Life and happiness forever.

WORSHIP AIDS

CALL TO WORSHIP.   "Surely your goodness and love will be with me all my life. And I will live in the house of the Lord forever" (Ps. 23:6 NCV).

INVOCATION.   Help us, O Lord, to realize that our true home is in you and with you, wherever we are. With this assurance may we worship you and share our faith in song, in fellowship with other believers, and in openness to your Holy Word.

OFFERTORY SENTENCE.   "Set your affection on things above, not on things on the Earth" (Col. 3:2).

OFFERTORY PRAYER.   God of might and miracles, use what we bring to increase the message that Christ died for sinners and that all who will may come and find salvation and peace.—E. Lee Phillips

PRAYER.   You have called us to enter into your gates with thanksgiving and into your courts with praise, Father. How can we express the depth of our gratitude for the many blessings that have filled our lives? How can we utter praise that is worthy of your holiness? Our limitations keep us from fully speaking that which fills our souls. So we simply speak in broken words and sing the tunes uppermost in our minds as we pause in your presence today.

So come this morning singing the high notes of joy. Life has blessed them in special ways in recent days and from the pinnacle of their blessing they cannot but experience the wonder of great joy at their good fortune.

Some come chanting the soft cords of sorrow. Loss and pain, bad news and failure have visited houses once filled with laughter and hope, leaving behind broken hearts, empty places, and dashed dreams.

---

[2]*Grace Abounding to the Chief of Sinners*

Some come muttering the low notes of despair. Life has dealt them hard blows at every turn, causing years of frustration and depression that no bright promise seems able to chase away.

Some come gently singing hopeful tunes from the pit of their confusion. Life has for them been a constant leaving behind the familiar for the unknown, and all roots of life seem to have been severed, never to grow deep in the soil of security again.

Some come singing arias of hope and assurance. They have been through the darkness and they see ahead the light that has for so long eluded them. Now there is a new day dawning for them, and in the light of that day, hope springs eternal again.

Some come caroling the chords of thanksgiving. They have found the wonder of salvation, the key to fulfillment and the promise of life worth the name here and forever. No longer lost in the misty valleys of uncertainty, they now walk the sunlit hills of assurance, hearts filled with gratitude and lives given to service in Christ's name.

In so many ways we enter your gates this morning. Pray, Father, meet us as we come and do with us as you will. All we ask is that we have the assurance of your presence in all its power as we bow before you today in wonder, thanksgiving, and praise. Amen.—Henry Fields

SERMON
Topic: The Heart's True Home
TEXT: Jer. 29:1–7; 1 Pet. 1:17–23

The longing for home is a powerful force. A few months ago, business leaders from Louisville went to Atlanta to try to lure young adults who had grown up here and migrated to the big city to come home and build a career here. The struggle for homeland is at the heart of the conflict in the Middle East. The bloodshed in Israel won't stop until Palestinians and Israelis figure out how each side can call the same place home.

But you don't have to pick up and move away to know that longing for home. There's a sense deep in the heart of every human being that we're all on a journey, a continual quest to find the homeland, the place where we can rest and be at peace. We feel it acutely as teenagers when we feel like we're exiled in our own body and long to break free to find who we truly are. As we grow, we learn to be more at home in ourselves, some by coming to terms with who we are, some by losing ourselves in family or career, some by numbing that sense of being a wanderer by getting more and more things. But for all of us, that sense of being away from home and that longing to return is still there somewhere deep inside.

That's why a story like Homer's *Odyssey*, even though it's thousands of years old, strikes every generation as fresh and inspired.

Going home is one of the basic themes of human life. One of the things that makes the Bible so powerful is how it recognizes, names, and addresses our deepest longings. Listen to how the first letter of Peter addresses its readers in the opening verse: "Peter, an apostle of Jesus Christ, to the exiles of the Dispersion." And in the passage we read today, he says, "Live in reverent fear during the time of your exile."

He was writing to people who knew that no matter how comfortable and secure they were, there was some place else awaiting them, the true home that every heart desires.

Jesus has told us where that home is. In John's Gospel he says, "In my father's house are many dwelling places. I go to prepare a place for you, and when I go I come again to take you to myself." Jesus' life and work showed us what's in store for us at that home.

He showed us what we're made for, the place we long to reach at his side in the company of all the faithful. St. Augustine said it best over sixteen hundred years ago: "O Lord, our hearts are restless until they rest in thee."

And not only has Jesus shown us what we long for in our heart of hearts, but he has also freed us from the force that keeps us from getting there. We call that force *sin*. It holds us hostage and keeps us from entering the peace and joy and hope that Jesus has promised us.

But if we're hostage to a hostile force that keeps us from God, our ransom has been paid. 1 Peter 1:18 says, "You know that you were ransomed from the futile ways inherited from your ancestors, not with perishable things like silver or gold but with the precious blood of Christ, like that of a lamb without defect or blemish."

The idea that someone would lay down his life to free us from bondage isn't totally foreign to us. Jesus laid down his life for us to free us from a power far greater than that of any nation or human enemy. Peter compares what Jesus did for us on the cross to the Old Testament sacrifice of a lamb.

We no longer have to offer sacrifices because of our sins because Jesus did it for us, once and for all on the cross. He made the perfect sacrifice for us before God, and the love he showed was so perfect that it overcame the power of sin that keeps us from going home.

God gives us a part in the work God is doing along the way, the work God began at creation, the work of calling people home and setting them free. We're not freed to escape this world, where we journey on our way home. We're freed to make a difference in the world along the way.

That's what Jeremiah told the exiles in Babylon. In 587 B.C. King Nebuchadnezzar conquered Israel and carried the people to exile. You can imagine how they felt. Psalm 137 was written in exile. It speaks for all those who have been forced out of their homes. There are times when we resonate with those exiles. Life's sorrows make us feel as desperate as the Israelites in Babylon.

A remarkable thing happened while the Jews were away from home. It was in exile that the Jewish religion as we know it, as Jesus practiced it, began to take shape. In exile the people began to develop their identity as Jews, and they made a difference in Babylon. God used Daniel in exile to bear witness to the faithfulness of the Lord.

So Peter wrote to the Christians he addressed, "Live in reverent fear during the time of your exile."

We face the same challenges in our time of exile. We're expected to go along because that's the way things are done. Jesus shows us that something is wrong, that we are exiles, but even though we're at odds with the world around us, we care passionately about it.

Jesus was at odds with the world in which he lived. He knew how much more we should expect out of life. But he also saw something better. That's how he could eat with sinners and outcasts, people no one else with self-respect would associate with. He was secure enough in his identity and his purpose that he could engage with those who needed him most without becoming like them in their sin.

Jesus has our home prepared for us, and nothing that happens to us can take away that goal. Along the way he gives us the privilege of making a difference, of reminding the world that there's something better in store. Along the way we live as those who belong to a better place, a place where love is the standard, where compassion is the norm. That's not the way it is here, at least not all the time. But that's what Jesus has in store for us. We're not home yet, but we're on the way.—Stephens G. Lytch

SUNDAY, MAY 9, 2004
Lectionary Message
Topic: What's Heaven Like, and How Do I Get There?
TEXT: Rev. 21:1–6
Other Readings: Acts 11:1–18; Ps. 148; John 13:31–35

This is a Sunday in the church year when heaven is very much on some people's minds. It's true that we are in the Easter season, when we celebrate the Resurrection, and it's true that in a few weeks we will mark Ascension Day, when we commemorate the departure of our Savior into heaven until he comes again at the end of the age. But I think the real reason heaven comes to mind today is that it is Mother's Day, and many of us have mothers who are no longer living on this Earth. If you miss your mother and are confident that she enjoys fellowship with the living Redeemer in heaven at this moment, you may nevertheless wonder to yourself what heaven is *really* like. Playing harps for all eternity doesn't appeal to the majority of us, and sitting on clouds wearing white nightgowns may make for humorous cartoons, but it doesn't sound like something we'd look forward to—not forever and ever, anyway.

At the same time, the vague, sentimental, and often ludicrous images of heaven offered in contemporary culture don't satisfy, either. You know some of them: teddy bears and balloons left at the site of an accident where a child died, as though the child will use them beyond the grave; myths about an incredible number of black-eyed, white-skinned virgins awaiting men who are martyrs for Osama bin Laden's cause (one wonders what sort of heaven is promised to women within such a belief system, and whether they'd be interested); Walter Payton starring on some celestial football team. None of these images has anything to do with heaven as the Bible presents it. And if we believe in God's Word as the truth and are staking our eternal life on it, we should know what Scripture does and doesn't say about heaven and how we get there.

I. *There are no photographs in the Bible.* This seems obvious, doesn't it? Controversy about the Shroud of Turin aside, there were no cameras in the ancient world, nor attempts to substitute for high-resolution photos. The beautiful description of heaven found in Revelation is intended to be *evocative,* not a literal visual depiction. We quickly run into difficulties when we try to make it into something it is not. For example, I once read this passage with a friend during a devotional time when we were supposed to share a favorite text in the Bible. She took offense at the mention of "a bride adorned for her husband," because in her mind, that image reinforced patriarchal systems where women are valued only for their attractiveness to men. I asked her, "Do you remember your own wedding day—how you looked and how you felt?" Her expression softened as she looked into her past, and she smiled, "Oh, yes!" I said, "How you felt, and how you looked just now—that's what it's going to be like for all of us in the new heaven and new Earth, when we see Jesus face to face."

There are many things said about heaven in the New Testament. Some of these images overlap, and some are completely different from all the others. In Luke 16:23, the story of the rich man and Lazarus, heaven is being "in the bosom of Abraham; but in John 14:2, heaven is described (also in Jesus' words) as "many mansions." The martyr Stephen had a vision of heaven as he died, and he spoke of the Son of Man standing at the right hand of God (Acts 8:56). Paul says that we shall all be changed in an instant, in the twinkling of an eye, at the last trumpet, and we will be clothed with new, resurrection bodies (1 Cor. 15:52). One of the most reassuring passages about heaven is found in 1 John 3:2: "Beloved, we are God's children now; it does not yet appear what we shall be, but we know that when he appears we shall be like him, for we shall see him as he is."

Heaven is a state or condition as much as it is a place. Returning to the discussion about bridal imagery for a moment, my friend did not have a picture of love, but she did have evidence and expressions of love. Love is a quality of being, and so is heaven. Heaven is being with God (and 1 John 4:8 says that God *is* love) and with all who have died in Christ. The Bible offers evidence and expressions of heaven, the most important of which is the Risen Christ. Because he conquered death, today's reading from Revelation states confidently, "Death will be no more, neither shall there be mourning nor crying nor pain any more."

II. *You can't get there from here.* In the last few years, luxury cars have come equipped with a global positioning system, or GPS. As I understand it, once you program in where you want to go, the GPS will tell you where you are and how to get to your destination. It will not, however, drive the car; that's up to you. When it comes to heaven, both Christians and non-Christians sometimes act as though they have a GPS and will get to their destination through something they do: live a good life, follow the Four Spiritual Laws, attend church regularly, or whatever. But in this reading from Revelation we see that no one "gets to" heaven; rather, God's eternal Kingdom arrives without human volition. Heaven is a gracious gift, not a goal. In his farewell discourse Jesus said, "I go to prepare a place for you, and I will come again and take you to myself, that where I am, you may be also" (John 14:3). You see, heaven is a byproduct of our response to God's love. God takes the initiative in love and in promising us heaven. "We love him because he first loved us," reads 1 John 4:19; and nearly everyone knows John 3:16: "For God *so loved* the world that he gave his only begotten Son, that whosoever believes in him should not perish, but *have everlasting life.*"

What we have in the Bible is not a road map but an invitation to respond to that love, just as our mothers who died in the faith did. And friends, if you *do* respond by saying yes to the love of God manifested in Christ, you won't get heaven; heaven will get you.—Carol M. Norén

ILLUSTRATIONS

GOD WILL!   In one of her radio talks, Joni Eareckson Tada, a Christian who became a quadriplegic after a diving accident, spoke about this text from Revelation 21. She confessed that there were many times, particularly in the first few years after she was paralyzed, when she wept out of frustration for all she could no longer do for herself. She looked forward to heaven, where, in the new creation, she will be restored to wholeness. Joni found it ironic and humorous that although she will be able to wipe away her tears for herself—something she cannot do now—the Bible says God will wipe them away for us. What is more, there will be no more crying.—Carol M. Norén

A SPECIAL FUTURE.   John Greenleaf Whittier (1807–1892), the Quaker poet, seemed to have a special interest in heaven. One of his works, "The Eternal Goodness," has been set to music and is used as a hymn in many churches. Two particularly poignant stanzas are as follows:

> I know not what the future hath
> Of marvel or surprise,
> Assured alone that life or death
> His mercy underlies.
> I know not where His islands lift
> Their fronded palms in air
> I only know I cannot drift
> Beyond His love and care.[3]

SERMON SUGGESTIONS

Topic: God Can Be Counted On!
TEXT: Ps. 145:13b–21 NEB
(1) He keeps faith. (2) He imparts strength to the weak. (3) He provides daily bread. (4) He answers prayer. (5) He judges with care and justice.

Topic: When God Makes All Things New
TEXT: Rev. 21:1–6
Hostile forces will be gone—"no more sea." (1) God's presence will encompass and dwell among his people—"God himself will be with them." (2) The negative factors of human existence will be gone—"the former things are passed away." (3) A new order will prevail, in which we may drink freely and endlessly "from the water springs of life" (NEB).

WORSHIP AIDS

CALL TO WORSHIP.   "Let them all praise the name of the Lord! His name is greater than all others; his glory is above Earth and heaven" (Ps. 148:13 TEV).

INVOCATION.   Holy God, we pause to remember the truths of our faith and the mothers of our humanity, for often one is interwoven with the other, because we first knew to worship God when our mothers led us to the throne of grace. We recall and are grateful.—E. Lee Phillips

OFFERTORY SENTENCE.   "Let us run with endurance the race that is set before us, looking unto Jesus, the author and finisher of our faith" (Heb. 12:1b–2a NKJV).

---

[3]John Greenleaf Whittier, "The Eternal Goodness."

OFFERTORY PRAYER.   Lord, we bring all we own before you in stewardship; bless what is shared and all that remains, that God might be glorified.—E. Lee Phillips

PRAYER.   Wondrous Creator, you who have made us and not we ourselves, with gratitude we enter your presence with praise and thanksgiving. With adoration we voice your name as name above all names. Holy God, high and far beyond our earthly knowing, yet near and within, like the gentle beat of our heart, we are grateful that in your love and kindness you blew breath into our beings, and molded your holy image within us. Beyond our tears and our fears, we whisper our humble thanks.

Provider God, we pause this day to give thanks for our mothers and for all those women who have been mother and caregiver to us. Our hearts are flooded with wide emotions but we are, most of all, grateful for these who have birthed us to life, nurtured and sustained us, loved and sacrificed for us, and in their own way shown us your grace and face. As we come to your table this hour, we give thanks for all the tables of our lives, sacred places of nourishment and refreshment, community and home, grace and belonging.

Bless us all in your tender care, and fit us for heaven to live with you there, forever and ever, even in Christ.—William M. Johnson

SERMON
Topic: It's a Beautiful Life
TEXT: Matt. 5:1–6

If we were honest, we would admit a preference for the shortened or condensed versions of just about everything. "Give me the bottom line." "Just read me the headlines." That attitude can't help but spill over into our spiritual life. This year's emphasis on the Gospel of Matthew has convinced me that the Cliffs Notes version would not feed our souls. Even the form of this Gospel communicates.

This passage begins the first of five sections of the Gospel. It is very possible that this was a conscious effort to follow the pattern of Hebrew Scripture. The five books of the teachings of Moses were called the Pentateuch. Jesus, as if he were a new Moses, goes up on an elevated area symbolically called a mountain. Jesus, the teacher of an elevated way of living, has captured the imagination of countless generations.

One of the constant bromides that I heard when people discovered I was a pastor was built on this image of Jesus as the Great Teacher: "I don't need to go to church or believe any of the church's dogma to be a good Christian. All I have to do is live the Sermon on the Mount." Such statements are in part a legacy of an optimistic theology that developed in the nineteenth century and influenced the early twentieth. This theology is based on confidence in human progress. "Let's not talk about human sin or the reality of evil. No need to talk about the cross of Christ. Let's just isolate Jesus' best teaching and follow it."

As common as such statements were in past generations, you rarely hear them today. The reason for the change may surprise you. A George Barna poll indicated that 58 percent of all people don't know who is the author of the Sermon on the Mount. Of those who hazard any guess at all, Jesus is in the lead. But citing his most recent polls, Barna says that "Billy Graham" is gaining fast as the answer to that question If a majority of people read the sermon, they may be in for an even bigger surprise. One of novelist Rose McCauley's characters says,

"You can receive a sacrament and you can find salvation, but you can't live the Sermon on the Mount."

This frames the question, doesn't it? As we enter the twenty-first century, we have gone through scientific, sexual, and information revolutions. Is the Sermon on the Mount now impossible, outmoded, and simply irrelevant? Perhaps the irony is that here in Matthew 5, 6, and 7 is what every person and century aspires to—*the beautiful life.* The place to start is the portion of Jesus' teaching often called the Beatitudes. The very title suggests a vision of life that is beyond the Hobbesian view of life as "brutish, nasty, and short." Hobbes's description comes to mind as we here in this community are reeling from the news of multiple murders of the youngest and most vulnerable. Don't such obscenities wipe out the possibility of calling life beautiful?

If the predatory violence and systemic injustice of our world is to be transformed, we will need a vision from beyond our nightly news. I am reminded of a time when racial violence was being overcome by nonviolence. Those who risked their very lives for this cause often saw no sign of victory in that dark night. They encouraged one another with the words "Keep your eyes on the prize." They had a vision of a life that was better than what they were experiencing. We want such a vision, but we skip over the Beatitudes. In the church they are neglected and outside the church they are unknown. I grew up going to church. The eight Beatitudes were printed on big ol' thick pencils that were handed out in Sunday school class. By using your thumb and index finger and the index finger of your other hand, you could flick the person next to you in class with that Beatitude pencil. You could hit your target with the side that said, "Blessed are the meek." It seems to me that in the church we are always misusing the things closest at hand. What's really said in the Beatitudes could be a new vision for millions inside and outside the church. As the Barna poll suggests, we forget who preached the Sermon on the Mount. It was Jesus. As Matthew describes it here, it was preached primarily to the disciples, or learners. By the time these words were written down, the disciples were viewing this teaching from the other side of Mount Calvary. The teacher had been crucified and the impossible had happened. He had been raised from the dead. Living now in the power of the Resurrection, is it impossible to love your enemies or for the mourners to be comforted?

The Beatitudes have been called the Commandments of the New Testament. But perhaps as Hugh T. Kerr has suggested, they are not so much laws or commands as attitudes and invitations. The word *blessed* is used eight times. Read what follows any of the eight *blesseds* and it will blow you off your pew. Those who mourn, who have had everything of value snatched from their lives, will *not* be comforted by platitudes. They will be comforted only in time, by God—by seeing God in a new way, as the God who gave his only begotten Son, as the grieving God who becomes the comforting God. This word, *blessed,* can be translated "fortunate" or "happy." Those who mourn know better than that. God's comfort is not based on the surface happiness of always having the things or people we want in our lives. Being blessed is not a happiness based on what we have or who is in our lives.

Today I am convinced that the key to all the Beatitudes is found in verses 3 and 5. The Latin versions of the Bible, and some early manuscripts such as the Codex Bezae of Cambridge, put "blessed are the poor in spirit" and "blessed are the meek" together. I believe that, as in Hebrew poetry, it is the same thought repeated in similar phrases: "Blessed are the humble." "Blessed are the teachable."

The best translation for *poor in spirit* is "those who know their need for God." They are not so puffed with a hollow air of importance that they feel no need for the God who created all things. When my covenant group was meeting in Washington, D.C., I used one of the breaks to visit the Einstein Planetarium, and I felt in that darkened sphere the immensity of the cosmos, of creation. Then and there I remembered P. T. Forsyth's observation, "How vast a creation, but how vaster still a salvation." That the author of the cosmos is also the author of my redemption—what a humbling and energizing thought.

It is unfortunate that in our language, *meek* rhymes with *weak*. There's no cringing cowardice in *meek*. The book of James uses the word to mean "those not too proud to learn." We do not deny the gifts we have, but standing in the shadow of the cross, we admit how much we have to learn about offering those gifts and ourselves to God. It was Einstein who said, "Many a day I realize how much my own outer and inner life is built upon the labors of my fellow man, both living and dead, and how earnestly I must exert myself in order to give in return as much as I have received." The beautiful life is knowing that you have received all by grace and that the greatest blessing is to give in return. The blessing of being poor in spirit (or knowing one's need for God) and the blessing of being meek (or teachable) are one and the same Beatitude. The beginning and the ending of the beautiful life is humility.

We miss the power and beauty of humility because we misunderstand it. In Dante's *Purgatory* there are statues depicting humility to assist in "soul making." The first sculpture seems a strange example of humility. It is King David whirling and dancing before the Ark of the Covenant. In that moment, he was so caught up in the delight of the Lord, he forgot himself. Therefore he was most fully alive, beautiful.

Humility is not cringing and cowering before God, it is being secure in God's grace. It is not a false modesty that draws attention to itself like Dickens's character Uriah Heep. Theologian Amos Wilder, in studying the Beatitudes, is convinced that here is the ethics not so much of obedience, but of grace. They imply God as gracious giver, humankind as humble receiver. I can only say, "Amen."—Gary D. Stratman

SUNDAY, MAY 16, 2004
Lectionary Message
Topic: Return to Eden—A Story of "Now and Not Yet"
TEXT: Rev. 21:10, 22–22:5
Other Readings: Acts 16:9–15; Ps. 67; John 14:23–29

"May the Force be with you." How many people out there are Star Wars fans? As time goes on, the sci-fi action series seems to get more popular. Perhaps its popularity is connected to its theme: the age-old battle between good and evil. After much distress and hardship, good triumphs over the Dark Lord. The city responds in celebration. Finally the Dark Lord's reign has ended and a new season filled with peace, justice, and prosperity has come.

Is this not what our hearts yearn for? A time of justice. A time of peace. A time when there won't be so much pain in the world. A time when there won't be so much pain in our own lives. We want that time to come. We want to see *that* kingdom come.

I. The book of Revelation gives us hope that a time of jubilee and celebration is indeed coming. The author, John, is writing to Christians who are under siege. They are being persecuted by the Roman Empire. Torn between their culture and their faith, they struggle to remain loyal to Christ and avoid the temptation to yield to their persecutors. Amid this tension, John writes down his vivid prophecy. Unfortunately, we've lost touch with John's style of communicating. We no longer write in his style, speak his language, or use his imagery. Despite these obstacles, his message rings clear. A battle rages between God and Satan, and God is the ultimate victor. His Kingdom is transformed into a new heaven and a new Earth. Jerusalem is established anew.

II. This new Jerusalem that John describes in Revelation is a glorious place. It is a redeemed Garden of Eden. There, "death will be no more; mourning and crying and pain will be no more" (Rev. 21:4). There will be no more wars or famine. The nations will be healed. A river of living water will flow constantly from the Lord's throne. The trees that line its banks will bear fruit all year long. It is in this glorious new city, this new Garden of Eden, where God will be united anew with his people. There he will rule the new heaven and the new Earth, and there we will find God's glory shining. In this new Jerusalem, the Lord will be the light.

I long to see that sight: the glory of the Lord so concentrated and bright that the sun and moon are no longer needed to cast light onto our world. I long to be in the presence of the Lord Most High. I long to see the river of life and the ever-blooming trees. His return has been so long in coming. When Lord? When will you return to rule? When will you shine your light upon your people?

III. I want to take a moment here to talk more about the use of light in this section of text. The author makes a point to contrast light and darkness. The light is God, his glory and holiness. It fills the whole city. But more than that, it is symbolic of all that is good and righteous. The nations will walk by this light. The light will allow them to walk without physically stumbling, but it will also become a part of their lifestyle. They will no longer stumble spiritually. Nothing unclean, nothing unholy, nothing false will be allowed there. There will be no night. There will be no darkness. All of creation will be transformed. The physical darkness, along with the spiritual darkness, will be wiped away. In Acts 26:17–18, Jesus tells Paul, "I am sending you [to the Gentiles] to open their eyes so that they may turn from darkness to light and from the power of Satan to God, so that they may receive forgiveness of sins and a place among those who are sanctified by faith in me." Revelation 21:22 to 22:5 gives us a beautiful picture of what this will look like in the new Jerusalem. Those who are in the new city will be surrounded by God's light and God's power. There will be no darkness left. Satan will have been defeated. Light will reign. Glory, honor, holiness, righteousness, and love will abound.

This distinct contrast that the author makes between light and darkness made me think of this world we live in. Our world is not as black and white as the new world to come will be. There is much good here, but also so much darkness. Shadows cast dull silhouettes on the rays of light penetrating our lives. We hear so many stories of pain and hardship, stories about our Christian brothers and sisters across the oceans being persecuted, about the wars that divide nations and peoples, about the famines that claim the lives of thousands each year. We have our own stories of darkness, too. Perhaps we have been hurt by our loved ones, or have seen the pain of our friends and relatives as they have struggled to overcome a disease or illness. How long, O Lord, will we have to live in the midst of darkness? When will your new Jerusalem come?

IV. In seminary I had a professor who was very wise. In class he told us that the Kingdom of God is "now and not yet." "Now and not yet"—perhaps the new Jerusalem is here among us. Perhaps it is here, but only in part.

Jesus said, "I am the light of the world" (John 8:12). He shared that light with his disciples and asked them to let their lights shine before others so that they too could turn to God and give praise (Matt. 5:16). He called them to be lights to the nations, to spread the good news that Christ has risen. Jesus' call was not limited to his disciples two thousand years ago. His call is also for us today. It is for the now. We are God's light and God's glory here on Earth, now, as we wait eagerly for the "not yet." We can see the new Jerusalem only in part now. We can't possibly fathom how magnificent and holy it will be. As we wait, though, we get glimpses of its future glory. When we help someone in need, when we share what the Lord has done in our lives, when we sing a hymn of praise to our Creator, when we are broken and restored by God's grace, when we do what is right even when everyone else is doing wrong, when we forgive someone who does not deserve to be forgiven, when we live with a passion that conveys that we know the truth and that the truth has set us free—when we do all this, then we are lights. Then we get a glimpse of the coming glory of God that will fill new Jerusalem with light, liberty, and love.—Heather Proper

ILLUSTRATION

THY KINGDOM COME.   Man would like to break free from God, to make himself independent of God, to posit himself absolutely. In so doing, however, he overreaches himself. He cannot and will not succeed. Nor will the powers that he releases and that make themselves out to be lordless. "He who sits on the heavens laughs; the Lord has them in derision" (Ps. 2:1–4). He does that to us. He would not be God if the unrighteousness and disorder that man has brought on his individual and social existence, the lordship of the lordless powers, and the suffering that man causes himself and has to endure under this lordship, did not find a limit in him.

That they have this limit may be seen already in their own sphere in the simple fact that the Christian and the Christian community pray "thy kingdom come." The fact that along with everything else that happens it also happens that people can and will and, in all their weakness and confusion, do pray this proves the majesty and might of another kingdom, which as God's Kingdom is very different from the kingdom of disorder, the lordship of the lordless powers, to which the Christian and also the church are painfully enough exposed and even subject. Within the sphere of these powers, that other kingdom is obviously if inconceivably confessed and known. There is an open looking in its direction. A calling for it is heard, an invocation of God as its Lord and King. Among all other human acts, and in all humanity, the act of this invocation is to be noted too, and in it may be seen the limit which is set for the kingdom of human disorder—set by that other kingdom which in the form of the prayer for its coming is not only distant but also near and already present.—Karl Barth[4]

---

[4]*The Christian Life* (Grand Rapids, Mich.: Eerdmans, 1981), pp. 233–234.

SERMON SUGGESTIONS

Topic: A Pattern for Wise Decision Making

TEXT: Acts 15:1–2, 22–29

(1) Consider the opinions of those who have a real stake in the issues (v. 26). (2) Consider the will of the Holy Spirit (v. 8). (3) Consider the value of unanimity (vv. 25, 28).

Topic: The Church Triumphant

TEXT: Rev. 21:10, 22–27

(1) Filled with God's presence. (2) Illuminated by Jesus Christ, the redeeming Lamb of God. (3) Exemplary of the best in human government. (4) Universally accessible. (5) The home of those redeemed by the Lamb of God.

WORSHIP AIDS

CALL TO WORSHIP.   "May God be gracious to us and bless us, may he cause his face to shine on us, that his purpose may be known on Earth, his saving power among all nations" (Ps. 67:1–2 REB).

INVOCATION.   Holy God, in whose Son, our Savior, we find all our soul's need, bless our worship this day as we recall Jesus Christ, the only begotten of the Father, who in the fullness of time, having conquered sin and death, went away from us in a cloud, as one day he will return.—E. Lee Phillips

OFFERTORY SENTENCE.   "Let us be thankful, then, because we receive a Kingdom that cannot be shaken. Let us be grateful and worship God in a way that will please him, with reverence and fear" (Heb. 12:28 TEV).

OFFERTORY PRAYER.   O God, when we know that we are truly blessed, we cannot fail to bring our offerings to you, so that others may be blessed as the good news of Christ is proclaimed here and around the world. Thank you, God, for the privilege that is now ours.

PRAYER.   Let healing come to us today, Father, we pray. Hearts here are broken by life's adverse circumstances. Tears flow because of great loss in this world. Lives are misshapen by the disasters which rain down on us from so many quarters. May your healing and reclaiming presence encircle all sufferers with hope and wholeness. Remind us that we have one in Christ who has suffered in far greater measure than we shall ever experience and thereby makes us brave in all of life's circumstances. So we seek to meet you and be remade by you as we wait before you in Jesus' name.—Henry Fields

SERMON

Topic: Strange Providence[5]

TEXT: Gen. 50:20

The story of Joseph in Genesis 37–50 is the most beautiful biographical portrait in all of Scripture, outside the account of our Lord in the Gospels. This saga was so dramatic in plot, so

---

[5]The title and some of the themes of this sermon were suggested by a sermon preached in the Memorial Church at Harvard University by George A. Buttrick and published as "Strange Providence," *Survey*, Apr. 12, 1961, pp. 1–7.

emotional in tone, so insightful in purpose that Thomas Mann wrote a sequence of four novels based on this narrative without beginning to exhaust its significance.[6]

Today there is time to deal with only one of its many dimensions: the mysterious working of divine providence that lurks within its shadows. Here the truth is not couched in theory or abstract deductions, but it grows out of the development of the story itself. Three emphases in those passages focus on this theme (45:4–8a, 50:15–20b).

I. *The irrationality of evil.* Joseph is one of the most attractive characters in the Old Testament. His life offers a model that many might wish to follow. The virtues of wisdom, prudence, generosity, and forgiveness made him an ideal figure worthy of emulation. We would call him a "faired-haired boy," the kind of person "most likely to succeed."

These traits are seen especially in the way he impressed others. Though the eleventh of twelve sons, his father loved him more than his ten older brothers (37:3). Though later a slave, Joseph found favor with his master, Potiphar, who put him in charge of all his affairs (39:4). Even when he landed in jail on false charges, he so impressed the warden that he was put over all the other prisoners (39:21–22). Finally, when called before Pharaoh to interpret his strange dreams, he so dazzled the monarch with his insight that he was put over all the people (41:40).

Despite his incredible attractiveness, Joseph's life was a series of calamities from the time he was seventeen until he was thirty years old. First, he was thrown into a pit by his brothers, who almost killed him (37:18–20). From thence he was sold into slavery and taken down to Egypt (37:28). Then he was tricked and falsely accused by Potiphar's wife (39:7–20). Left to languish in prison, he seemed to be forgotten even by those whom he had helped in times past (40:23).

Why did a series of such unjust calamities befall one who was so attractive? Jealousy, greed, lust, revenge, and selfishness—the sources of evil lie close to the surface for all to see. How petty yet how cruel are its motivations. Joseph could not rebuff the dotings of an aged father, or change the fact that he had grown a handsome face, or disguise his brilliance in discerning the signs of the times. These were his gifts, a rich endowment to be sure. Yet he never asked for any of them, or spoke until requested, or tried to push himself on others. Is it a curse to be talented? Even if his abilities made him a bit proud or even conceited as some suppose,[7] does a touch of vanity merit the brutal treatment he received?

Any doctrine of providence begins with the fact of human perversity, for all of us are just cocky enough, or insecure enough, or prejudiced enough, to wreak havoc on our most attractive competitors, even when they have done little or nothing to deserve it. For some cruel reason, we want revenge for not being as bright or gifted as someone else may be. We are forever looking for scapegoats on whom to dump our failures. If we cannot win by fair means, then we will resort to foul means in a calculated effort to come out on top.

Mark it well: there is no justice in this life that ensures that what we get is what we deserve. As John F. Kennedy famously observed, life is not fair! For example, a promising

---

[6]The magisterial tetralogy, published in Germany from 1933 to 1944, was translated into English as Thomas Mann, *Joseph and His Brothers* (New York: Knopf, 1948) and has long been available in a one-volume edition.

[7]For an unflattering view of Joseph's character, see Maurice Samuel, "The Brilliant Failure," *Certain People of the Book* (New York: Knopf, 1955), pp. 299–350.

young leader in one of my churches chose to fail at everything in his marriage, and ministry, but then in frustration blamed it all on me! Abraham Lincoln was detested by those close to him who could only snipe at his greatness. Supremely, Christ caught hell on a cross just for doing good to others! We often suppose that virtue carries its own reward, but the blunt truth is that practicing virtue can stir the slumbering rattlesnakes of sin to strike with deadly force.

II. *The tenacity of faith.* How severely did sin's assaults tempt Joseph to indulge in bitterness, cynicism, defiance, and revenge? What we today sometimes call disillusionment or depression is often the result of unplanned, unprovoked, and undeserved misfortune. The loneliness of pit and prison is an incubator of such despair, especially when we can identify no sensible explanation for our plight. It is at least bearable to "get what is coming to us" as our just desserts, but when the blows of rejection are manifestly unfair, and especially when they come from our immediate family, the pain takes on a dimension of pathos.

Yet Joseph clung to the ancestral faith of his fathers, to his own covenant with God, and to its promises for the future. Note that he did this by inner resolve, without any outer bolstering. There is not a single theophany or miracle in the whole account! Unlike his father, Jacob, Joseph heard no heavenly voices; he could not return to some hallowed place such as Bethel for inspiration; he had to trust a God who was working unobtrusively behind the scenes. Never once does the story speak of direct divine intervention; instead, faint traces of a providential plan had to be inferred amid the ambiguity of life.

Moreover, Joseph was not swayed from his dependence on God either by failure or by success. As soon as he was exalted in Potiphar's house, he could have become cocky and succumbed to the insistent seductions of his master's wife. Or when he became Pharaoh's prime minister, he could have lorded it over the Egyptians who had once despised him. Or when his father Jacob died, he could have taken revenge on his brothers, who had thrown him into the pit and then sold him into slavery. But he allowed neither cynicism nor conceit to tarnish the purity of his faith.

Instead, he always sought the guidance of God. Potiphar promoted Joseph because "he saw that the Lord was with him" (39:3). Joseph resisted Potiphar's wife, not because he might get caught or because he might betray his master, but because it would be a "sin against God" (39:9). When he could have tried to impress Pharaoh by interpreting his dream, Joseph instead said, "God will give the answer" (41:16, 25). When he was in a position to condemn his brothers, he chose rather to reinterpret their treachery as a circumstance that God could use for his own purposes (45:5, 7).

For us, as for Joseph, faith in God's providential care always arises against the lashings of doubt. We have to stick by our convictions even when there is no apparent reason to do so. Miracles and special revelations are nice if they come, but their absence is no sign either that our faith is defective or that God has withdrawn his providence. For us and for Joseph, the contest is between one brave heart and the fickle finger of fate. So it was when Jesus stayed his course, even to a bloody cross, willing to play out the cruel hand that had been dealt him by entrusting the verdict to the vindication of God.

It is debatable whether failure or success is the greatest hindrance to faith in the providence of God. Only those who are not swayed either by defeat or by victory prove in the greatest test of life whether God is working out his gracious plan. If we make outward circumstance the determinative criterion, then we become overconfident in success and under-confident in failure. But if we make God's will the decisive criterion, then we view life not in terms of the way things are now, but in terms of the way they will finally end. Let us look now at what this invincible hope might involve.

III. *The vindication of God.* When our story reaches its climax, Joseph declares that there are two ways to view the very same thing: one, the way humans see it, and the other, the way God sees it. His brothers saw only that they had gotten rid of their brother by selling him into slavery, but God saw that he had sent Joseph on a saving mission to preserve life (45:5). Only one thing took place, the facts of which were not in dispute. But that act had two very different meanings, one born of envy and the other born of faith.

The reason there were two contradictory interpretations was that God was willing to use the evil intentions of Earth for his own divine purposes. Joseph was utterly realistic, both about human motivations and about their limitations. His brothers "meant evil" against him; but God "meant it for good" (50:20). His brothers and his God were both involved in the same event; both handled the same raw materials, but God had an overriding purpose that eventually prevailed over the purpose of the brothers. Joseph's brothers were free to sin, but God was free to direct the consequences of their sin into channels they never suspected and could not control.

What this means is that first appearances can be very deceiving. When Joseph landed in the bottom of a desert pit crawling with scorpions, neither he nor his brothers could see in this dastardly deed any hint of a grand plan "to preserve life" (45:5). So for us, God's will may be at work even in the darkest moments of life. His providence is no less real when it is hidden, mysterious, enigmatic, and radically secret. The tracks of God often seem ambiguous at best, which is why all of life is a call to faith validated by commitment rather than by circumstance.

Yet we are not dealing here with some fanciful theory or fond surmise. For we can see from the story how God used these very events to change the hearts of Joseph's wicked brothers. At one moment they wanted to kill Joseph because he was Jacob's favorite, but later the brother Judah was willing to sacrifice himself for the sake of the youngest son, Benjamin, when Joseph threatened to take the lad from his father (44:18–34).

The question posed for us by providence is, Will we give up on life when it unfairly lands us in a pit, or will we wait and hope and trust, not because of any supernatural sign from God, but because of our unshakable confidence in the goodness of God's character, coupled with the conviction that he will finally achieve his ends despite the freedom with which he has allowed us to sin? To be faithful is the option that each heart may choose regardless of circumstance. It is the committed heart that God can use to preserve and enhance life, even when others betray it in their efforts to achieve short-term solutions through destructive violence.

The question always comes: But what if Joseph had finally succeeded? What kind of providence would it have been if there were no great reversal at the end of the story? We already know the answer: "The Lord was with him" (39:3). That was the controlling inward condition of his life regardless of what outward circumstances might be. Jesus did not "win" his crown until after he endured his cross (Heb. 12:2), and we may not experience vindication when only thirty years of age as Joseph did. Like Joseph, our calling is not to succeed or to fail but to "preserve a remnant" (45:7), to ensure that there will be survivors who believe, which is why Joseph insisted that his bones be taken back to the Promised Land (50:25). He was glad to be exalted in Egypt, but he really lived for a future fulfillment that he didn't get to see within his lifetime.

Providence means that "God works in all things," even in the pits and in prisons, "for good" (Rom. 8:28), despite the fact that his gracious guiding is concealed in utter worldliness, in the darkness of human sin, in deepest tragedy. If God could use a cross to do us good, then he can use the worst thing that could ever happen to us for good. And to say that God can use even the basest intentions of evil to accomplish his purposes is to imply that, finally, he is willing to forgive evil because he can master it, change it, and use it for good ends. Joseph and Jesus found that to be true—what about you?—William E. Hull

SUNDAY, MAY 23, 2004
Lectionary Message
Topic: Two Prisons, Two Prayers, One Deliverer
TEXT: Acts 16:16–34
Other Readings: Ps. 97; Rev. 22:12–14, 16–17, 20–21; John 17:20–26

When I go to church on Sunday morning and listen to a preacher, one question that frequently comes to mind is, What is the preacher's relationship to the text? Over the years I have noticed that more often than not, male preachers speaking about a narrative passage tend to identify with the most powerful person in the story. Female preachers, on the other hand, often invite identification with the object rather than the subject of the action, or highlight an obscure character who might otherwise be overlooked. Then, of course, there are those preachers who place themselves a great distance from the text, admitting no intersection between it and their lives.

Why give attention to the perspective from which the preacher speaks? Because people in the pews often follow the preacher's lead in identifying with a Bible passage—and sometimes that identification can cause us to overlook other important aspects of the text. We can be so focused on some "facts" that we miss others.

In the account of Paul and Silas and the Philippian jailer, the most common perspectives seem to be (1) the wonderful faith of Paul and Silas, and (2) God's miraculous power to loosen their bonds, just as the angel unfettered Peter in the Acts 12 account of another deliverance from prison. These are the "facts," but focusing on other data yields an equally important lesson: this story describes two prisons, two prayers, and one deliverer.

I. *Two prisons.* The prison in which Paul and Silas were held was far more grim than any holding cell in the United States today. They were in stocks, a torture device that kept their legs apart at all times. They had already been beaten with rods, and their clothes and skin were torn. The stench of ordure, sweat, and blood added to their misery. They languished in total darkness; the jailer had to bring in lights to determine that no one had escaped during the earthquake.

The unnamed jailer was also a prisoner, though his bondage was not so obvious. He was a pawn of the Roman government, fearful lest he himself be executed because those entrusted to his charge had escaped. He was loathed and probably cursed at by those he kept in shackles. And without faith in Christ, he was Satan's hostage, bound by sin and death. For the first half of the narrative in Acts 16, he is fearful and despairing, clearly feeling trapped by his circumstances.

II. *Two prayers*. In these dreadful circumstances, Paul and Silas were praying and singing hymns. The Bible does not say they were lighthearted or oblivious to their situation. It is far more likely they were praying for strength and deliverance, just as we would in such conditions. Paul had witnessed God's miraculous power in the past. He himself had been healed of blindness after the Damascus Road encounter with Christ. He had been a channel for divine healing for a crippled man in Lystra, and he probably knew of Peter's deliverance from prison. Yet Paul also knew of Christians suffering or martyred for their faith: Stephen; James, the brother of John; and the disciples of Jesus he had persecuted before his conversion. Paul knew that faith was not an automatic "get out of jail free" card. Paul and Silas probably prayed and sang using the language of the psalms, which would have included praise, supplication, and lament.

The jailer's prayer was simple and just as sincere: "Men, what must I do to be saved?" The Bible says the jailer fell down before Paul and Silas, trembling—surely a posture of humility and reverence as well as fear. The jailer prayed for salvation. Even if he didn't know what salvation would entail, he recognized that it would come only through the God whom Paul and Silas served.

III. *One deliverer*. God's mercy was manifested in both prisons, though in different ways. What's more, we can say that God used the prisoners to answer the other prisoner's prayers, and vice versa. Paul and Silas were delivered from darkness, chains, hunger, and untreated wounds because the jailer ministered to their physical needs. The jailer was delivered from life without Christ and without salvation because Paul and Silas preached the gospel to him, and baptized him and his family.

I believe that by the power of the Holy Spirit each person can become a channel for God's deliverance and mercy today. It is wonderfully reassuring to know that whatever happens, God's will is ever directed toward his children's good. It is a great comfort to realize that the Lord hears our prayers, whether they are uttered in fine literary form such as the psalms, as spontaneous cries for help, or as "sighs too deep for words" (Rom. 8:26). And it is a privilege to participate in Christ's work of delivering people from whatever prisons hold them.—Carol Norén

ILLUSTRATION

EACH FROM HIS PRISON DELIVERED.   I was visiting a sociable old church member in the hospital. Clarence wanted a roommate he could talk to, someone who would relieve the tedium of being hospitalized. When I arrived, however, he complained bitterly that although the man in the next bed was about the same age as Clarence, and they came from the same town, the man was so standoffish he wouldn't even tell Clarence his name. He ignored everything Clarence said. Slightly embarrassed, I glanced over at the man to see if he'd overheard this criticism. The man smiled at me and said nothing. Then I noticed a sign over the bed, which said the man was a deaf mute. I turned to Clarence and explained that his roommate wasn't unfriendly but handicapped. Unappeased, Clarence retorted, "Well, he could have *told* me he was a deaf mute if he wasn't so unfriendly!" Clarence had one thing correct: the man hadn't spoken to him. But he missed an equally important fact: the man could not talk. We too miss important data in a pastoral situation—or in a text—when we become too focused on one perspective or another.

In *The Wasteland*, T. S. Eliot wrote:

> I have heard the key
> Turn in the door once and turn once only
> We think of the key, each in his prison
> Thinking of the key, each confirms a prison.[8]

In the Acts 16 narrative, Paul and Silas are delivered from prison, but the jailer is also delivered from a prison of sorts. The good news is that no matter what prison holds us, God has the power to deliver us.

SERMON SUGGESTIONS

Topic: Making the Most of a Bad Situation
TEXT: Acts 16:16–34
(1) Paul and Silas are thrown into prison. (2) Nevertheless, they pray and witness. (3) Consequently, God brings about a significant conversion.

Topic: When Jesus Christ Comes Back
TEXT: Rev. 22:12–14, 16–17, 20
(1) It *will be* a blessed occasion for those who are cleansed of their sins through the blood of the Lamb. (2) It *can be* a blessed occasion for those who will accept the water of life freely offered.

WORSHIP AIDS
CALL TO WORSHIP.   "The Lord reigns, let the Earth be glad; let the distant shores rejoice" (Ps. 97:1 NIV).

INVOCATION.   Gracious Lord, bring us out of the clouds with which our doubts have surrounded us, and lead us step by step into the sunshine of your love, that our joy may be full.

OFFERTORY SENTENCE.   "Keep your lives free from the love of money and be satisfied with what you have. For God has said, 'I will never leave you; I will never abandon you'" (Heb. 13:5 TEV).

OFFERTORY PRAYER.   Lord, allow our gifts to match our commitment, that with words of praise and gifts from the heart, the Lord Jesus might be glorified and the Kingdom of God enriched.

PRAYER.   O God, we thank thee for this universe, our great home; for its vastness and its riches, and for the manifoldness of the life that teems upon it and of which we are a part.

---

[8]T. S. Eliot, "The Waste Land, V: What the Thunder Said."

We praise thee for the arching sky and the blessed winds, for the driving clouds and the constellations on high. We praise thee for the salt sea and the running water, for the everlasting hills, for the trees, and for the grass under our feet. We thank thee for our senses, by which we can see the splendor of the morning and hear the jubilant songs of love and smell the breath of the springtime. Grant us, we pray thee, a heart wide open to all this joy and beauty, and save our souls from being so steeped in care or so darkened by passion that we pass by heedless and unseeing when even the thorn bush at the wayside is aflame with the glory of God.

Enlarge within us the sense of fellowship with all the living things, our little brothers, to whom thou hast given this Earth as their home in common with us. We remember with shame that in the past we have exercised the high dominion of man with ruthless cruelty, so that the voice of the Earth, which should have gone up to thee in song, has been a groan of travail. May we realize that they live not for us alone but for themselves and for thee, and that they love the sweetness of life even as we do and serve thee in their place better than we in ours.

When our use of this world is over and we make room for others, may we not leave anything ravished by our greed or spoiled by our ignorance, but may we hand on our common heritage fairer and sweeter through our use of it, undiminished in fertility and joy, so that our bodies may return in peace to the great mother who nourished them and that our spirits may round the circle of a perfect life in thee.—Walter Rauschenbusch

SERMON
Topic: Church Without Borders
TEXT: Eph. 2:12–22

How big is your church? Every pastor has to field the question, especially when meeting someone from his or her past or from his or her hometown. Bankers carry on conversations about the volume of controlled capital. Pastors count heads. The inquiry about church size is an invitation to brag, to declare the scope of success. Signs of achievement come in one-liners. "We broke an attendance record last month." "We had to bring in chairs on Sunday." "Our attendance on Easter Sunday was enormous." "We are the biggest church in three counties." "We grew by 20 percent last year."

Mass evangelism was reinvented by Billy Graham following World War II. A spiritual hunger following the war years sent people out in search of God. Graham's organization was bigger than the local church and suggested that God might be bigger than church competition and denominational loyalty. Seeing thousands of people gathered in sports stadiums and hundreds of people move toward the front during the invitation hymn "Just As I Am" was exhilarating. Yet Graham never started a church, and to this day he is not the pastor of any congregation.

I suspect that the mass appeal of Graham's crusades had something to do with the rise of the superchurch and the electronic church in the past three decades. A few years ago, an article in *Christian Century* featured one of these churches that had just moved to a new campus on the edge of a large city. The size of the church was defined by the number of bathrooms in the structure, with an appropriate distinction between the public facilities and the private, "executive" washrooms. An article in the *Wall Street Journal* noted that one superchurch sent parking lot attendants and greeters to Disney World for training. Because they are self-contained and independent, the superchurches are sometimes called "minidenominations."

The church growth movement may be misnamed. Rather than reaching the unchurched or growing the Kingdom of God, the trend toward the superchurch has been a shift in church population from smaller to larger congregations. The appeal of the big and the lure of success has put the small "family" church at a disadvantage. Some of the experts predicted a few years ago the complete disappearance of the small church in America. To survive in the next generation, a church must maintain a critical mass of three hundred or so members. *How big is your church?* may be a question about survival as well as about size or success.

I am not convinced that churches have outgrown the need for personal intimacy or that the appeal of family in church life is over. I suspect that God has a bigger measuring stick for churches than counting bathrooms, budgets, or heads. How big is your church? The witness of the New Testament challenges the standards of measure based on our business models of success.

I. *The Church is bigger than national or ethnic identity.* I recall a conversation with Ewell Smith, a deacon in my first pastorate. Ewell joined the Navy and saw more of the world than he ever thought existed. I recall one spring when we were gathering an offering for home missions, Ewell offered one of his observations on the state of the universe. He had noticed the vast number of churches in America compared to Japan and several of the Pacific islands he had visited. Ewell said he saw no point in taking money for missions at home with all of the churches around. He would put his missions dollars in the foreign fields where they could reach the unreached.

Like a lot of other observations, Ewell's made some sense, especially for the time; but the world situation is changing. *Home* and *foreign* are losing their distinctive meaning in this global era. We are learning to think of one world. People from every point on the compass are settling in our cities, and the Christian world mission is as valid in your neighborhood as it is in a Third World nation. The Iron Curtain of the old Soviet Union has disappeared and the Berlin Wall has been demolished. In this world without borders we are reminded that the Christ who has broken down the dividing wall between Jews and Gentiles is removing all of the other barriers. The old idea that salvation was limited to people of Hebrew descent ended with Christ.

The problem in the early Church was a simple division between Jew and Gentile. Although the Jews had lived under foreign domination for three centuries before Christ, they held to their hope that one day all of the nations would fall at their feet. Gentiles were forbidden to enter the inner courts of the Temple, and Gentile dominance was a direct affront to the Jewish belief in God's election of the Jews as God's own people. Paul was a Jew, well educated in Jewish theology and culture and convinced of the exclusive claims of his people on God. When Paul met Christ, he also confronted his cultural bigotry. We have a difficult time understanding the radical transformation of this man in giving up circumcision as the boundary of God's grace. When the walls came tumbling down in Paul's head, they began to fall in his world.

Ephesians uses popular hate language to describe the Gentiles as *atheists*, "strangers to the covenants of promise, having no hope and without God in the world." But Christ is our peace, breaking down walls, removing hostility, and reconciling both Jew and Gentile to God and to each other.

My home church grew to its maximum size during my early teens. Attendance edged over a thousand on Sunday mornings and became particularly high during a period of controversy and conflict. Over the years, the town changed, the congregation aged, and the culture shifted toward the Hispanic population moving into the aged housing. With attendance down to slightly over one hundred, the church has just called a Hispanic pastor. By the gospel measure, this church has never been bigger.

II. *The Church is bigger than the local congregation.* The Ephesian vision of the Church has global proportions. Unlike other letters attributed to Paul, this Epistle is not addressed to just one congregation. Here the Church is the body of the faithful, transcending time and place, culture and race, and united under the leadership of Christ, bonded into one body by the one Spirit. James R. Graves profoundly influenced Baptists in the South during the Civil War era. Graves believed that only the local congregation can be the Church. He pulled up the covers of exclusion over Baptist identity to reject all other denominations and all but Landmark Baptists from the community of salvation. His God was a local deity limited to the provincial world of his own definition.

Christ has broken down the walls of division between church signs and politics as well as between race and culture. The cartoon *Kudzu* by Marlette shows up in numerous national publications. The preacher Will B. Dunn is often pictured as the coach of a church league team, offering words of wisdom in the game of life. A recent cartoon shows the batter waiting for the other team to resume the game while Will says, "This happens every time we play the Baptists! They squabble amongst themselves, and somebody winds up going off and forming another team!"

We Baptists have a bad history of multiplying by division. There is a better way. Christ is our peace. The Spirit of God is the Spirit of unity. Shortly after I began my ministry in Louisville, the associate pastor and I were searching for a new name for our newsletter. Then I noticed a poster on his wall: "People are lonely because they build walls instead of bridges." We prayerfully named our newsletter *The Bridge.*—Larry Dipboye

SUNDAY, MAY 30, 2004
Lectionary Message

Topic: Special Delivery
TEXT: John 14:8–17 (25–27)
Other Readings: Acts 2:1–21 or Gen. 11:1–9; Ps. 104:24–34, 35b; Rom. 8:14–17

When the clerk at the post office asked me how I wanted to send my package, I told her, "Whatever way will get it there quickest." She gave me a form to fill out in triplicate. When I finished, she looked it over and asked, "Do you want us to require the addressee to sign for it, or can it just be left at that address?" I said the latter would do; frankly, it was more important that I be able to document that I had *sent* it as quickly as possible than that the person at the other end had *received* it personally the next day. Whenever he got it and whatever he did with it did not matter that much to me.

I. *We must sign for God's delivery.* On this Sunday of the church year, we remember and celebrate the giving or "delivery" of the Holy Spirit to the Church. We call the day *Pentecost*, which means "fiftieth day," because the original event occurred on the fiftieth day after

Passover. For the Jews, Pentecost was the festival that celebrated the giving of the Law. The Holy Spirit was not manifested for the *first* time on the Christian day of Pentecost, described in today's reading from Acts 2. As one of three persons of the Trinity, the Spirit was present from the beginning of the world; in fact, Genesis 1:2 says that the Spirit of God was moving over the face of the waters at creation. The Spirit inspired the writers of the Old Testament and filled the prophets so they could witness to God's Word to their generation. It was the Spirit who enlivened the "dry bones" seen by Ezekiel (Ezek. 37:1–14). In the New Testament, too, the Spirit is manifested at different times prior to Pentecost. For example, at the baptism of Jesus the Spirit descended like a dove. In his sermon at the synagogue in Nazareth, Jesus quoted Isaiah and declared, "the Spirit of the Lord is upon me" (Luke 4:18). What is promised in today's text from John 14, and fulfilled in Acts 2, is the delivery of the Holy Spirit as the *abiding* presence of Christ in the Church and in individual Christians.

It should be noted, though, that the Holy Spirit is not given to just anyone and everyone. Although the writer of Acts quotes the prophet Joel saying, "God declares, 'I will pour out my Spirit on all flesh'" (Joel 2:28), the Spirit filled the disciples of Jesus who were present, not the crowd. It is not uncommon these days to hear people say, "I'm not religious, but I'm very spiritual." We have to wonder just what spirit they're talking about, because the Holy Spirit is quite definitely religious! The Spirit is also more than the contemporary *Weltgeist* or the *esprit de corps* that binds a social or political group together. The Spirit delivered at Pentecost was given only to those who had "signed on" as followers of Jesus Christ.

II. *Obedience is the address for this special delivery.* We don't normally think about obedience in connection with Pentecost. Yet a careful reading of chapters 13 to 15 in John, and Acts 1 and 2, demonstrates that obedience is a major theme and is inextricably linked to receiving the Holy Spirit. In John 14 alone, Jesus says, "If you love me, keep my commandments" (14:15) immediately prior to promising the gift of the Spirit; "If anyone loves me, he or she will keep my commandments" (14:23); and "Do as the Father has commanded me, so that the world may know that I love the Father" (14:31). The disciples would not have been in the right place for the outpouring of the Spirit if they had not followed the ascending Lord's order not to depart from Jerusalem but to wait for the promise of the Father—which was the promise of the Holy Spirit (Acts 1:4). In his Pentecost sermon, Peter challenged the crowd, "Repent, and be baptized, every one of you, in the name of Jesus Christ, for the forgiveness of your sins; and you shall receive the gift of the Holy Ghost" (Acts 2:38). These chapters list the commandments Jesus wants his disciples to obey; the chief of these are loving God with all our heart and soul and mind, and loving our neighbors as ourselves. Repentance, believing and being baptized in the name of Jesus, waiting where God wants us to wait, living as God wants us to live, and loving God and neighbor—these are a long way from "being spiritual but not religious."

III. *What does God's "special delivery" bring?* By now you may be thinking that receiving the Holy Spirit is more trouble than it's worth, and that Christians don't have much to celebrate at Pentecost. But following God's commands simply puts us at the right address to sign for gifts we all desire—and they're free! The Holy Spirit conveys knowledge, truth, peace (John 14:17, 26–27). Other gifts of the Spirit may include the utterance of wisdom, faith, the power to heal and work miracles, to prophesy, to distinguish between spirits, to speak or interpret *glossolalia,* or the gift of tongues. "All these are inspired by one and the same Spirit, who apportions to each one individually as he wills" (1 Cor. 12:8–12). It is through the grace of the Holy Spirit that Christians enjoy love, joy, peace, patience, kindness, goodness, faithfulness, gentleness, and self-control (Gal. 5:23). Who wouldn't want all these gifts? Who wouldn't celebrate having them? And all of them are part of God's special delivery, sent at Pentecost but still available today. Are you where our Lord wants you, in order to receive the gift promised by Jesus Christ?—Carol M. Norén

ILLUSTRATIONS

YES OR NO.   Paul explains that the Holy Spirit was given to believers as a deposit or down payment on our future inheritance and as God's seal on believers, to show that they are his own people (Eph. 1:13–14). And Paul makes it very clear, if the Holy Spirit lives in you, you have life; if not, you do not belong to Christ (Rom. 8:9–11).[9]

A SIGN.   It is unfortunate that Christians in the United States and elsewhere seem to use the Holy Spirit as a *shibboleth* to separate themselves from other Christians rather than unite them in one Lord, one faith, and one baptism. I recall sitting next to a stranger one week who introduced himself as a representative of a particular "charismatic" group. As we listened to the prelude, he whispered to me, "So, do you think the Holy Spirit is here?"—the implication being that traditional organ music did not lend itself to the spontaneity he valued. I smiled at him and answered, "Of course the Spirit is here. Jesus says that wherever two or three are gathered in his name, he is in the midst of them." That man's critical attitude can also be found at the other end of the liturgical spectrum, in worshippers who shudder at any manifestation of strong emotion or experience during the service. It would be a wonderful sign of the Holy Spirit's presence if we could rejoice with one another at the richness and variety of ways Christ makes himself know as we worship him.

SERMON SUGGESTIONS

Topic: Babel Reversed

Text: Acts 2:1–21 (compare Gen. 11:1–9)

(1) The spirit of man—centrifugal: pride separates humankind. (2) The Spirit of God—centripetal: the work of God unites: "And it shall be that whoever calls on the name of the Lord will be saved."

Topic: If You Are God's Child

Text: Rom. 8:14–17

(1) You will follow the leading of God's Spirit. (2) You will recognize God as your Father and your belonging to him as a child, not as a slave. (3) You will inherit God's promises to Christ as did those who have suffered with him.

---

[9]Michael M. Jones, "God's Second Gift" in Michael Diduit, ed., *The Abingdon Preaching Annual: 1998* (Nashville: Abingdon Press, 1997), p. 204.

WORSHIP AIDS

CALL TO WORSHIP.   "I will sing to the Lord all my life; I will sing praise to my God as long as I live" (Ps. 104:33 NIV).

INVOCATION.   O Christ, who brought into our dull, drab lives so much brightness and so great a glory, raise us to higher levels, where we may in thy name and by thy power go out and turn the desert into a flowering place and make the lives of men and women leap for joy because of thee.—Theodore Parker Ferris

OFFERTORY SENTENCE.   "Even though the fig trees are all destroyed, and there is neither blossom left nor fruit, and though the olive crops all fail and the fields lie barren; even if the flocks die in the fields and the cattle barns are empty, yet I will rejoice in the Lord; I will be happy in the God of my salvation" (Heb. 3:17–18 Living Bible).

OFFERTORY PRAYER.   We have been assured, O God, that we belong to you, and we praise your name because you care for us. Even in the most difficult times we can count on you. Help us in all circumstances to be good stewards of your grace, knowing that there is always something to place on your altar, something that may in truth be more important than money.

PRAYER.   Almighty God, on this day you opened the way of eternal life to every race and nation by the promised gift of your Holy Spirit: shed abroad this gift throughout the world by the preaching of the gospel, that it may reach to the ends of the Earth; through Jesus Christ our Lord, who lives and reigns with you, in the unity of the Holy Spirit, one God, for ever and ever. Amen.—*Book of Common Prayer*

SERMON

Topic: To Walk in the Way of Love
TEXT: Eph. 4:31–5:2

It's a subject for which poets and preachers are never short on material, and about which they seemingly never grow tired of speaking. Perhaps that's because there's a richness, an intricate texture, a mystery, and a multifaceted dimension to the word and the world it creates. I'm referring, of course, to *love*.

Charlie Brown approaches Lucy and says, "Our Sunday school teacher tells us that we must love all of humanity." In the next frame Lucy says, "I've no problem with that! I'll gladly love humanity in general. It's the *particular people* I can't stand!"

We all, sooner or later, grow weary of hearing poets and preachers speak of love. The word simply begins to lose all meaning, while all around us and within us the love shared often smacks of pretense more than passion. I'd have to say that we find it difficult to love individuals in particular, because to do so requires great risk.

When you relate to people in particular, you risk being abused, mistreated, manhandled, and maybe even mauled! With genuine love you open yourself to every aspect of that persons' quirks and quarrelsome ways, and you also become vulnerable to a wide variety of potential victimizations. You discover a complicated world of delight and disappointment, of fulfillment and frustration, of harmony and heartache. We seldom make the effort to expend the energy to enhance and enlarge the limits of our love. Sadly, we become comfortable, if not complacent, with our confinement of love. The rewards may well be attractive, but the risks remain unappealing to most.

Genuine love gets out there along the front lines of life and deals directly with the difficulties, disappointments, and discouragements of relationships. Still, have you ever noticed how easily we can extinguish the flickering flame of love? Love anyone, anything, and your heart will be wrenched and knocked about, and possibly even broken. Of it's own accord, the human heart will almost always chose those pathways of love that promise maximal rewards and minimal risks. So, the enlargement of the human heart can be accomplished only by some larger love.

Well, the apostle Paul has already seen our situation: "Put away from you all bitterness and wrath and anger and wrangling and slander, together with all malice, and be kind to one another, tenderhearted, forgiving one another, as God in Christ has forgiven you."

Paul points to the real problem when he admonishes us to "forgive one another, as God in Christ has forgiven you!" For Paul, then, *forgiveness* is the very foundation and the foremost expression of Christlike love. Mere human love is temperamental, unpredictable, liable to change with any circumstance, subject to a vast array of insecurities, and all too often timid. However, "whichever way the wind blows, God is *still* love."

And whenever I read the Gospels, this is what I'm told. Our God's love made its most memorable mark on this world in the humility of a manger and in the scandal of a makeshift throne—in the shape of a cross! So, if we wish to see God's love, we need to look no further than this: to Jesus Christ.

Paul's words were those lyrics of a hymn that, I would imagine, the congregations of Ephesus sang for joy every Sunday: "Therefore be imitators of God, as beloved children, and live in love, as Christ loved us and gave himself up for us, a fragrant offering and sacrifice to God." An even more graphic—and I might add, accurate—translation of the same passage puts it this way: "Walk in the way of love!" Do you know what that means?

Renowned pastor Donald Grey Barnhouse once amply described such Christlike love as the key that will unlock the deepest dimensions of devotion, dedication, and discipline: "Joy is love singing. Peace is love resting. Long-suffering is love enduring. Kindness is love's touch. Goodness is love's character. Faithfulness is love's habit. Gentleness is love's self-forgetfulness. Self-control is love holding the reins!"

Such love is the only risk that bears the rewards of reconciliation and redemption, and such love is the province of our Savior, who alone can pour out and perfect its power in each and every Christian heart.—Albert J. D. Walsh

SUNDAY, JUNE 6, 2004
Lectionary Message

Topic: Fishing for Men
TEXT: Rom. 5:1–5
Other Readings: Prov. 8:1–4, 22–31; Ps. 8; John 16:12–15

Ours is a day of meeting the needs of persons dissatisfied with aspects of their lives. Indeed, much, if not most, of the marketing of goods and services involves creating dissatisfaction within consumers so they will want to buy the product or service being promoted. Not sexy enough? Buy this toothpaste to give you that irresistible smile. Too drab? Put yourself behind the wheel of this sleek auto and watch their heads turn.

Unfortunately, we fail to see that our real needs continue to go unmet regardless of the gains we make in this life. Fortunately, however, the Bible reveals our real needs and how they can be fulfilled. In the passage before us, we find that being declared righteous by God (that is, being justified) provides the fulfillment of three of our greatest needs.

I. *We have peace with God* (Rom. 5:1). Before we repented of our sins and believed on Christ, we were enemies of God. Does that sound too harsh? Consider what Paul wrote in verse 10 of the same chapter: "For if while we were enemies we were reconciled to God through the death of his Son, much more, having been reconciled, we shall be saved by his life" (NASB). Because God has declared believers righteous (justification), we are no longer his enemies; rather, we have peace with him. Notice, too, that this peace was procured not by anything we did. It was accomplished "through our Lord Jesus Christ."

To those who are sensitive about the gravity of their sin and the unapproachable holiness of God, Paul's words bring deep comfort. Jesus himself has satisfied the just demands of the Father. By faith in Jesus and in his atoning work, the believer no longer cowers from the wrath of an angry God. He is now instructed to "draw near with confidence to the throne of grace, so that we may receive mercy and find grace to help in time of need" (Heb. 4:16 NASB).

II. *We have hope in God* (Rom. 5:2, 5). When we think of hope, we usually think of something anticipated that may or may not occur. The child *hopes* she will receive the doll for Christmas, the woman *hopes* that the man she loves will ask her to marry him, the retiree *hopes* his pension is secure. When the Bible speaks of hope, though, the thing anticipated is as certain as if it had already been received (see, for instance, Acts 2:26–27; 2 Cor. 1:7; Col. 1:5, 27; Titus 1:2, 2:13; Heb. 6:19–20; 1 Pet. 1:3).

Because of the salvation that God has graciously granted, believers no longer have to face life with uncertainty or despair. They don't have to worry about what the future holds for them. They "exult in hope of the glory of God." Notice, though, that this "exultation in hope" is not man centered; rather, it is God centered. The rejoicing is "in hope of the glory of God." It is unto God's glory that persons are justified, and the Christian rejoices in that glory (see Eph. 2:4–8).

III. *We have security in God* (Rom. 5:3–4). Most of us love security. We want to know that the economy will be dependable, that our company will continue to prosper, that our spouses will always love us, and that our favorite sports team will usually win. What does God use to show us that we as believers are secure in him? Tribulation. Could anything be more strange? While we desire comfort, God reveals his love to us through tribulation. Paul can therefore exclaim that "we also exult in our tribulations." Did not Jesus say, "A disciple is not above his teacher, nor a slave above his master. It is enough for the disciple that he become like his teacher, and the slave like his master. If they have called the head of the house Beelzebul, how much more will they malign the members of his household!" (Matt. 10:24–25 NASB). Suffering for the sake of Christ identifies the believer with his Lord and is cause for rejoicing. The persecuted disciples were "rejoicing that they had been considered worthy to suffer shame for his name" (Acts 5:41b NASB).

Someone has well said, "God is more concerned with our character than with our comfort." Paul shows us that through tribulation we gain perseverance, through perseverance we gain tested character, and through tested character we gain hope. And this "hope does not disappoint," because God, though the Holy Spirit who dwells in us, reveals his love to us.—William G. Moore

ILLUSTRATION

To those living in a comfortable culture who find suffering for Christ as something to be avoided at all costs, this well-known episode from the annals of history provides a needed corrective. When Edward VI died in 1553, Nicholas Ridley supported the ill-fated attempt to elevate Lady Jane Grey to the throne. With the ascension of the Roman Catholic Mary to the throne, Ridley, along with other Reformers, was imprisoned. In 1554 he was taken with Thomas Cranmer and Hugh Latimer to Oxford, where attempts were made to get them to renounce their views of transubstantiation and papal authority. Ridley and Latimer were condemned to be burned at the stake in 1555. The following, a condensed excerpt from John Foxe's *Acts and Monuments* (1570), chronicles their execution:

> Dr. Ridley, entering the place [of execution] first, earnestly holding up both his hands, looked towards heaven; then shortly after, seeing Mr. Latimer, with a cheerful look, he ran to him and embraced him, saying, "Be of good heart, brother, for God will either assuage the fury of the flame, or else strengthen us to abide it."
>
> He then went to the stake and, kneeling down, prayed with great fervor, while Mr. Latimer followed, kneeled also, and prayed with like earnestness. After this, they arose and conversed together, and while thus employed, Dr. Smith began his sermon to them.
>
> Dr. Ridley, then, with Mr. Latimer, kneeled to Lord Williams, the vice chancellor of Oxford, and the other commissioners, who sat upon a form, and said, "I beseech you, my lord, even for Christ's sake, that I may speak two or three words."
>
> And whilst my lord bent his head to the mayor and vice-chancellor, to know whether he might have leave to speak, the bailiffs and Dr. Marshal, the vice-chancellor, ran hastily unto him and, with their hands stopping his mouth, said, "Mr. Ridley, if you will revoke your erroneous opinions, you shall not only have liberty so to do, but also your life."
>
> "Not otherwise?" said Dr. Ridley.
>
> "No," answered Dr. Marshal. "Therefore, if you will not do so, there is no remedy: you must suffer your desserts."
>
> "Well," said the martyr, "so long as the breath is in my body, I will never deny my Lord Christ and his known truth. God's will be done to me."
>
> They were then commanded to prepare immediately for the stake. Then the smith took a chain of iron and placed it about both their waists; and as he was knocking in the staple, Dr. Ridley took the chain in his hand and, looking aside to the smith, said, "Good fellow, knock it in hard, for the flesh will have its course."
>
> They then brought a lighted faggot and laid it at Dr. Ridley's feet, upon which Mr. Latimer said, "Be of good comfort, Mr. Ridley, and play the man! We shall this day light such a candle, by God's grace, in England, as I trust never shall be put out."[1]

---

[1]"A Tale of Two Martyrs," *Christian History*, 1995, *48*, 18.

SERMON SUGGESTIONS

Topic: God's Majesty Shared

TEXT: Ps. 8

(1) In the created order. (2) Especially in humankind, created in God's image.

Topic: When We Are at Peace with God

TEXT: Rom. 5:15

(1) We can enjoy the prospect of our glorious destiny with God. (2) We can regard even suffering in a different light, rejoicing in its positive benefits. (3) We can know the love of God as it floods our hearts through the Holy Spirit.

WORSHIP AIDS

CALL TO WORSHIP.   "O Lord our Lord, how excellent is thy name in all the Earth!" (Ps. 8:1a)

INVOCATION.   O God, the reach of your love and presence are without limit and worthy of all praise. Grant us now, just where we are, the grace to worship you acceptably, in spirit and in truth.

OFFERTORY SENTENCE.   "Set your mind on God's Kingdom and his justice before everything else, and all the rest will come to you as well" (Matt. 6:33 REB).

OFFERTORY PRAYER.   We trust you, our Father, to provide for our needs, and you have blessed us in so many ways beyond our expectations. Now grant that through our offerings we may extend the fruits of your grace for the blessing of others.

PRAYER.   Fill us, O Christ, with thy Spirit. Give us the power to do the things we want to do but are not able to do in our own strength. Take the raw material of our lives and refine it. Cool our tempers, soften our speech, enlarge our understanding, deepen our love. When the test comes, we will trust in thee and not in ourselves, knowing that by thy Spirit we will be able to do all things. Amen.—Theodore Barber Ferris

SERMON

Topic: Recovering a Lost Spiritual Life

TEXT: 2 Kings 6:1–7

A miracle may be regarded not as antinatural but rather as supernatural. That is, it does not negate natural law but brings into play higher laws that do not necessarily deny the natural laws but work within them.

No Christian should find it hard to accept the supernatural. The miraculous change in human nature brought by the indwelling of Christ and the work of the Holy Spirit has to be the supernatural work of God, for we all know the terrible tendency of human nature to drag us down. Yet the power of God can keep us up!

I believe that God also has supernatural power available to the backsliding Christian who has a sinking spiritual life. He is willing to use his almighty power to lift us up again if we are in a position of defeat. If we truly belong to Christ, we already share in the very nature of God (2 Pet. 1:4), and his indwelling Holy Spirit wants to fill and flood our souls with fresh power to rise again in spiritual life.

Second Kings 6:1–7 is a perfect Old Testament picture of the power of God available for the individual. Elisha and his theological students faced problems of restricted accommodation (vv. 1–2). They worked as a team to build a new place for their residence and study, with Elisha working with them (vv. 3–4). The thud of the ax and the crash of falling timber soon gave way to a wail of distress as one young theologian felt the handle in his hands grow suddenly light as the borrowed ax head slipped from its cleat and arced swiftly over his shoulder and into the Jordan River behind him (v. 5).

Now it was lost, seemingly forever. The young man stopped and asked Elisha for help. The two cooperated in the restoration of the ax as God's power caused it to float up to the river's surface (vv. 6–7).

Here is a story that records that something essential to the progress of the Kingdom of God had gone down and had to come up again. The whole story pictures for us the conditions for the effective restoration of a sinking spiritual life.

I. *God will restore your lost power to live for him when you admit what you have lost.* Here is a young man who lost something while doing the Lord's work. He was building a school to help train prophets of God. Can you imagine how his young, strong limbs would rejoice in their ability to serve God? He turned to his leader and friend, Elisha, and asked for God's help.

How many of us today have that much sense? It is so easy to lose your cutting edge in God's service, to have the spiritual life sink, and so easy just to keep on going through the motions.

II. *God will restore your lost power to live for him only when you acknowledge where you lost it.* Elisha's questions and the young man's answer were most specific. "And the man of God said, Where fell it? And he showed him the place" (2 Kings 6:6).

Where was it, exactly, that you lost touch with God's power? Confess exactly where you lost touch with God if you plan to renew that fellowship.

This man found what he had lost exactly where he had lost it. If you dropped your cutting edge because of sin, disobedience, or carelessness, you may need to retrace your steps to that point to find it again. Temper, anger, criticism, bitterness, jealousy, and any one of a hundred other spiritual failures may mark the spot for which you search. Seek the Spirit of God to find it and even a man of God to help you, as this young man did.

III. *God will restore your lost power to live for him when you do your part in its recovery.* Elisha told the man to take up the floating ax head, "and he put out his hand and took it" (v. 7).

God and man must work together at the recovery of a sinking spiritual life. He expects us to admit what we have lost, to acknowledge where we have lost it, and to act our part in its recovery. God does his supernatural work for us, but he will not do what we can do for ourselves. He can take your poor, feeble effort of will and magnify it by his power into a miracle of restoration and renewal.

The Lord waits to claim the freshly surrendered areas of your life and fill them with his power. He will blend his supernatural resources to your personal needs when you fulfill these conditions.

The oceans of God's pardoning grace can restore a lost spiritual life. The surging currents of his power await only the commitment of your will and the playing of your part in fastening the links of faith and action that will allow that supernatural power to flow. The iron will swim! And as it does you will exclaim as David did, "This is the Lord's doing; it is marvelous in our eyes" (Ps. 118:23).—Craig Skinner[2]

SUNDAY, JUNE 13, 2004
Lectionary Message

Topic: Total Provision
TEXT: Gal. 2:15–21
Other Readings: 1 Kings 21:1–10 (11–14), 15–21a; Ps. 5:1–8; Luke 7:37–8:3

How can I be right with God? How good do I have to be for God to accept me? Can I ever be good enough for God to accept me? Numberless persons have grappled with these and similar questions, and major religions and philosophies have attempted to answer them.

Those concerned about their place in eternity will often attempt to earn God's favor through a variety of ways. Many are convinced that a life of moral purity will win God's approval. Others follow regimens of asceticism, some rely on their giving to religious and other benevolent causes, and many bank on church attendance and keeping the rules and regulations of their particular sect. All such efforts amount to the same thing—attempting to satisfy God through living a life of good works.

Answering the substance of these questions drove Paul to write his Epistle to the Galatians. So certain was he of the right answer and so jealous was he over the eternal destiny of these believers that he pronounced a curse on anyone, human or angel, who provided a different answer (Gal. 1:8–9).

So how can we be right with God? Although every religious system devised by humans demands obedience to a set of laws or a code of ethics, each system falls short of what God demands. And what does God demand? Perfection (Matt. 5:48). And what mortal has satisfied this requirement? Paul answers elsewhere: "For all have sinned and fall short of the glory of God" (Rom. 3:23 NASB). Each of us is equal; none of us has satisfied God despite our best and most sincere efforts.

I. *Only by faith is a person justified—or declared righteous—by God* (Gal. 2:15–16). Paul knew all about trying to satisfy God's demands by attempting to keep the law. Living as a Pharisee and judging according to human standards, Paul had considered himself blameless concerning obedience to the law (Phil. 3:5–6). He came to understand, though, that his standard of blamelessness was woefully insufficient; only the righteousness of Christ would do. To those who would call upon believers to add law—obedience to faith in Christ, Paul could respond with "been there, done that."

Paul shows us that we do not earn righteousness; rather, we are *declared* righteous. Through faith in Jesus Christ, the believing person is justified by God. Such a declaration utterly removes

---

[2]*Back Where You Belong* (Nashville: Broadman Press, 1980), pp. 65–75.

works or merit from the salvation equation. The guilty sinner is graciously given what he or she could never earn (Eph. 2:8–9).

II. *Attempting to satisfy God's righteousness by adding works to faith is an act of sin* (Gal. 2:17–18). Men from Jerusalem professing to be Christians had claimed that Paul and other Jewish Christians were sinners because they were eating with Gentiles (see vv. 11–13). When Peter distanced himself from Paul and the Gentile believers, Paul confronted his hypocrisy (v. 14). Paul clearly shows that those who add law to faith are the real sinners (v. 18).

Christians are tempted to think that although they are saved unconditionally by God's grace, they still must *do something* to secure divine approval. Such efforts are futile because they are always, at best, imperfect. We need to heed James's warning: "For whoever keeps the whole law and yet stumbles on one point, he has become guilty of all" (James 2:10 NASB).

III. *For the Christian, obedience to God is the grateful response of having been declared righteous through faith in Christ; obedience is not an attempt to earn righteousness* (Gal. 2:19–21). Here we see the reason for Paul's indignation toward those who would attempt to add law-obedience to faith. While believers "are his workmanship, created in Christ Jesus for good works" (Eph. 2:10 NASB), obedience to God and the performance of good works are done out of gratefulness for the gift of salvation, not in order to gain divine approval. Attempting to secure God's favor through obedience is particularly egregious, because such efforts denigrate the graciousness of the gift of salvation provided through the atonement of Christ.

Paul recognizes a truth that puts to flight the notion that we by our own effort can live in a pleasing manner before God. Paul acknowledges that the old Paul, the one consumed with self-righteousness (Phil. 3:4–6), is no longer alive. The new life he now lives is "live[d] by faith in the Son of God, who loved me and gave himself up for me" (v. 20).—William G. Moore

ILLUSTRATION

GOD ALONE PROVIDES.   Imagine that you are invited to dine with the president of the United States but you have only rags to wear, clothing unfit to be worn in the presence of such a dignitary. Learning of your plight, the president purchases for you a set of clothes that you never could have afforded. Gladly you put them on, and then, inexplicably, don a weather-beaten, scruffy, holey old hat that no one would wear in public. You want to add something of your own to the gift graciously provided.

While this illustration pales in comparison, it points to the incongruity of attempting to add our futile efforts to the all-sufficient sacrifice of Christ. Well do we recall the words of Isaiah: "For all of us have become like one who is unclean, and all our righteous deeds are like a filthy garment" (Isa. 64:6 NASB). May those who have repented of their sins and believed upon Christ rejoice in the salvation that he alone so graciously has provided, recognizing that God alone provides what he requires.

SERMON SUGGESTIONS

Topic: Strength for the Journey

Text: 1 Kings 19–18

(1) Our life situation may lay murderous stress on us. (2) In our despair we may even wish to die. (3) Yet God makes unexpected resources available to enable us to carry on with courage.

Topic: How the Christian Life Works

TEXT: Gal. 2:15–21

(1) Not by obedience to even the finest rules and regulations—the Law. (2) Rather, by a faith in Christ that lets Christ live out his life in and through our human life.

WORSHIP AIDS

CALL TO WORSHIP.   "Give ear to my words, O Lord; consider my meditation. Hearken unto the voice of my cry, my King and my God: for unto thee will I pray. My voice shalt thou hear in the morning, O Lord; in the morning will I direct my prayer unto thee, and will look up" (Ps. 5:1–3).

INVOCATION.   Almighty God, who can do for us what you can do? Despite all our reverses and misfortunes, we still come to you in prayer, in worship, and in service, knowing that whether now or in eternity you will be glorified and we will be blessed.

OFFERTORY SENTENCE.   "May the Lord direct your hearts toward God's love and the steadfastness of Christ" (2 Thess. 3:5 REB).

OFFERTORY PRAYER.   Almighty God, our Creator, stir in these gifts to make of them tools to bring many to Christ, and us to a stewardship of priorities that puts God first.—E. Lee Phillips

PRAYER.   God of grace, we worship in your presence this morning. How often would we practice brutality and do damage beyond repair to one another if we were not aware of the wonder of God's grace alive in life and abroad in the world? How unforgiving we would be toward one another if we forgot the power of forgiveness embedded in your grace! How quickly the compassion needed among us would die and the unmerited love necessary to create social sensibleness would disappear. Grace has touched our hearts and remolded them in Godlike fashion. How could we but worship the God of grace and the God of glory?—Henry Fields

SERMON

Topic: The Christian's Cross

TEXT: Matt. 16:21–25

In the name of relevance, contemporary churches have talked much about "applied Christianity," about being the "scattered Church in the world," and about "the cross in the marketplace." Such talk is not only appropriate but also essential. The critical question, however, is this: Can we really carry the cross into the marketplace when we have so nearly lost it in the Church?

Prophets, who still enjoy less and less honor the closer they are to home, often charge Christian churches with forsaking the gospel and living off a civil religion that is a smooth blend of everything. How clearly do we distinguish between Christian and cultural values? Dietrich Bonhoeffer condemned the German churches in the 1930s "for avoiding a confrontation with the evils of Nazism by retreating into liturgism."

Perhaps the only thing that can save the world is also the only thing that can save the Church—the cross. If Christians are not only to redeem others but also to work out our own salvation, we must rediscover the cross.

Throughout his ministry Jesus seemed to have a growing awareness of the coming cross. When it came, it was not forced on him. Jesus could have refused it. How else do you explain the mighty inner struggle that began on the plains of the wilderness and lasted until the anxiety in dark Gethsemane? He is our Savior because he *chose* the cross, because he chose to make our cross his cross.

Now what of the other cross? What of the cross Jesus said you must bear if you are to follow him? Consider what the Christian's cross is not.

I. *The Christian's cross is not synonymous with poverty.* Jesus and his little band were not exactly affluent, it is true. Jesus had almost none of the earthly security we wear ourselves out to gain. We are still trying to find a "needle's eye" in Jesus' world big enough for a camel to get through, because we don't know what to make of our own wealth.

Jesus knew what wealth can do to a person. It can so weight him down that he can't even walk across the street to get to God. But Jesus didn't require a vow of poverty from all his followers. If we are to bear our crosses genuinely, it will be necessary for some of us to become poor. We'd better know that. But the Christian's cross is not synonymous with poverty.

II. *The Christian's cross is not synonymous with persecution.* One reason Jesus' cross was such a stumbling block to the Jews and such foolishness to the Greeks is that it was inconceivable to both that the Son of God would die like that.

You may have known people who so thrived on feeling persecuted that they destroyed their marriages and homes and personalities. The most extreme from of self-centeredness may be that which manifests itself in a martyr mentality. When Jesus said, "Blessed are they that mourn" (Matt. 5:4), he didn't mean we were to start looking for ways to suffer in order to be blessed.

If you really bear a cross, you can probably count on some kind or degree of persecution. But the Christian's cross is not synonymous with persecution.

III. *The Christian's cross is not synonymous with piety.* I will tell you quite candidly that you will probably not get any cross-bearing credit in heaven for attending church on Sunday and on Wednesday nights, no matter how painful it is. The Christian's cross is not synonymous with piety.

Our crosses must be *moral* for us in the same way Jesus' cross was *moral* for him if there is to be any continuity between his cross and ours. Many an individual's supposed cross-bearing has been a subtle indulgence in pride.

Christ's cross was moral in that (1) it was a choice (a decision made in freedom); (2) it was a choice made in fidelity to a relationship and a conviction—"Nevertheless, not my will but thine be done" (Luke 22:42); and (3) it was a choice to assume *someone else's burden.*

The cross was not Jesus' cross, it was our cross. He carried *our* cross! We have said it and sung it thousands of times; he took upon himself the sin of the world. He was under *our* load by his own choice, and I know of nothing more moral than that.

If there is, then, any continuity between Christ's cross and my cross, I must come to this: *my cross is someone else's burden.* If I am merely bearing my own burden, so what? Pagans and animals do that. What morality is there in carrying my own load? My burden is only a cross when some free, moral decision has put it there, and when it is something from the shoulder of another.

IV. Finally, consider this: maybe some burdens are not crosses at all but are infinitely heavier and ultimately more deadly than genuine crosses. In other words, maybe there *is* a mysterious joy that comes from cross-bearing that never comes from mere burden-bearing. After all, Jesus said when we take up our crosses and follow him we *find* our lives by *losing* them (Matt. 16:25).

Behold, the yoke *is* easy and the burden *is* light!—C. David Matthews[3]

SUNDAY, JUNE 20, 2004
Lectionary Message

Topic: The Almighty Savior
TEXT: Luke 8:26–39
Other Readings: 1 Kings 19:1–4 (5–7), 8–15a; Ps. 42; Gal. 3:23–29

How many times have you heard someone in complete despair cry out that they were beyond saving? For that to be true, God would have to surrender his claim to omnipotence, because a power superior to his would have been found.

In Luke 19:20 we hear Jesus declare that "the Son of Man has come to seek and to save that which was lost" (NASB). And yet, seeking and saving "that which was lost" would require that Jesus exercise authority over the Prince of Darkness, the devil himself, for it is Satan who has blinded the eyes of those who fail to believe the gospel (2 Cor. 4:3–4). In this passage we find Jesus making just such an exhibition. This one who came to save sinners reveals that no power is able to withstand his will to accomplish his plan.

I. *The demons submit to Jesus, but only involuntarily.* They are not blindsided by Jesus, shocked to find out who he is. They acknowledge that he is the "Son of the Most High God." They realize his superiority over them and beg him not to torment them. These demons demonstrate the warning that James gave to those who trust that their belief in God is sufficient for their salvation: "You believe that God is one; you do well. The demons also believe, and shudder" (NASB).

The fact that demons are more powerful than humans was not disputed by the biblical writers. The seven sons of Sceva's attempt to practice exorcism met with a regrettable result (Acts 19:13–16). The people witnessing Jesus' expulsion of demons were astonished at such power: "And amazement came upon them all, and they began talking with one another, saying, 'What is this message? For with authority and power he commands the unclean spirits and they come out'" (Luke 4:36 NASB). The demons realized that Jesus could send them wherever he pleased.

II. *The people of the region refuse to submit to Jesus.* Is it not incredible that such a display of purifying power, the cleansing of this demon-possessed man, would meet with a plea by the people that Jesus leave their region? Whether the people fear the power of Jesus or the further loss of income, they fail to recognize the depth and extent of their own need for healing. Notice that they neither ridiculed nor persecuted him. They simply did not want him interfering in their lives.

---

[3]In James C. Barry (ed.), *Award Winning Sermons.* Vol. 2. (Nashville, Tenn.: Broadman Press, 1978), pp. 47–53.

Many today react similarly to Jesus. They do not mind Jesus as long as he does not interfere with their lives. They simply want to be left alone. Of course, the refusal of people to submit to Christ is only temporary, as Paul reminds us: "At the name of Jesus every knee will bow, of those who are in heaven and on earth and under the earth, and every tongue will confess that Jesus Christ is Lord, to the glory of God the Father" (Phil. 2:10 NASB). As has often been stated, people will submit either voluntarily or involuntarily, but submit they will.

III. *The changed man submits to Christ.* Understandably, the redeemed man wants to follow physically this one who has effected such a great change in his life. Jesus, though, has a different desire: "Return to your house and describe what great things God has done for you" (v. 39a). And the man does exactly what the Lord commands.

So should we joyfully submit to the one who has changed our lives. Before salvation, we saw ourselves as great sinners when compared to the holiness of God (see 1 Tim. 1:15). Like this man, we too should gladly tell others what great things the Lord has done for us. Do we not want others to know this great Savior? In addition, we should recognize that any commandment we find in the Bible addressed to followers of God should be joyfully obeyed. The apostle Paul reminds us, "For you have been bought with a price: therefore glorify God in your body" (1 Cor. 6:20 NASB).—William G. Moore

ILLUSTRATIONS

HIS WILL ALONE.   Bernard of Clairvaux understood the totality of surrender to God: "We read in Scripture that God has made all things for himself. His creatures must aim, therefore, at conforming themselves perfectly to their Creator and living according to his will. So we must fix our love on him, bit by bit aligning our own will with his, who made all for himself, not wanting either ourselves or anything else to be or to have been, save as it pleases him, making his will alone, and not our pleasure, our object of desire."[4]

WATCH FOR SOULS.   The following words of Charles Haddon Spurgeon, pastor of London's Metropolitan Tabernacle in the latter nineteenth century, challenge our twenty-first-century complacency toward those who do not know the Lord:

Surely, brethren and sisters, if you love him [Christ] and wish to be like him, you cannot look on this congregation without pity. You cannot go out into the streets of London and stand in the high roads among the surging masses for half an hour without saying, "Whither away these souls? Which road are they traveling? Will they all meet in heaven?" What! You live in London, you move about in this great metropolis, and do you never have the heartache, never feel your soul ready to burst with pity? Then shame on you! Ask yourself whether you have the spirit of Christ at all. In this congregation, were we all moved with pity as we should be, I should not have to complain, as I sometimes must, that persons come in and out here in want of someone to speak with them, to condole, to console, or to commune with them in their loneliness, and they find no helper. Time was when such a thing never occurred; but in conversing with inquirers lately, I have met with several cases in which persons in a distressed state of mind have said they would have given anything for half an hour's conversation with any Christian to whom

---

[4]Bernard of Clairvaux [1090–1153], *On the Love of God,* chap. 10.

they might have opened their hearts. . . . You used to watch for souls, most of you. Very careful were you to speak to those whom you saw again and again. I do pray you mend that matter. If you have any bowels of mercy, you should be looking out for opportunities to do good. Oh! Never let a poor wounded soul faint for want of the balm. You know the balm. It has healed yourselves. Use it wherever the arrows of God have smitten a soul [with conviction].[5]

SERMON SUGGESTIONS

Topic: When the Lord Passes By

TEXT: 1 Kings 19:9–14

(1) He may call us to account. (2) He may put us through strange, even terrifying, experiences before he speaks definitively to us.

Topic: Now That Faith Has Come

TEXT: Gal. 3:23–29 NJB

(1) You are no longer motivated by rules and regulations. (2) You are God's free children through Christ Jesus. (3) You belong to an undivided body of believers. (4) You inherit the blessing of the faith-principle promised to Abraham's descendants.

WORSHIP AIDS

CALL TO WORSHIP.   "As the hart panteth after the water brooks, so panteth my soul after thee, O God. My soul thirsteth for God, for the living God: when shall I come and appear before God?" (Ps. 42:1–2).

INVOCATION.   Lord of life, we pause today to give thanks for fathers who open doors to the world and give us insights into human character and the world of work. Let us find ways through our fathers to know that God cares for us always.—E. Lee Phillips

OFFERTORY SENTENCE.   "May the God of hope fill you with all joy and peace as you trust in him, so that you may overflow with hope by the power of the Holy Spirit" (Rom. 15:13 NIV).

OFFERTORY PRAYER.   We have trusted in you, O God, and we have found joy. Sustain and increase our joy, we pray, as we participate in your work in the world, even as we bring our offerings.

PRAYER.   Quietly we come into your presence this morning, Father, just to abide with you for a while and to be strengthened for the living of these days. It is a special day we call "Father's Day," a time set aside to honor fatherhood. We need that, for ours is a time of confusion about roles and commitments and futures and values and responsibilities. Maybe what we really need are some strong guidelines to follow that have the strength and stability of eternity about them to pass on to fathers and fathers to be. Maybe what we need to do is look

---

[5]C. H. Spurgeon, *Collection of Sermons* (Simpsonville, S.C.: Christian Classics Foundation, 1997).

again at what we already have been given by you in the Bible and make it a part of our foundation as we interact with our families as fathers.

We do not really know exactly what we need to pray for in this area, but there are some things we desire for the fathers of the land. Inspire them to follow moral values that will be worth passing on to those whose lives are entrusted to them. Give them strong faith in you that will not falter in the face of temptation and ridicule. Give them compassion for others that will serve as a role model for young eyes to see. Give them a spirit of encouragement that will be contagious to children and will let them know that they can accomplish more than they sometimes believe possible. Give them a sense of right that cannot be compromised when evil winds blow strong, demanding that wrong be enthroned. Give them a sense of fairness that will win them honor in the decisions they must make. Give them the gift of honesty that solid trust can be built into family relationships. Give them a heart of courage to send signals of protection and hope to those in their care. Give them a determination to remain faithful to life's commitments even when momentarily it seems feasible to cancel them. Give them a spirit of love that will bring warmth to cold situations and stability in the face of hate. Grant them forgiveness for their sins so that they will be able to forgive the sins of the family. Stir them to Christlikeness so that the ones nearest and dearest to their hearts may always have before them an earthly likeness of him who is Lord of all life and Savior of every person and situation.

If such qualities are cultivated in our father's lives, then there will indeed be raised up a generation to change the world for Christ's sake and to hasten the day when the kingdoms of this world become the Kingdom of our Christ, where he shall reign forever and ever. Pray, begin in us the transformation needed to hasten that day.—Henry Fields

SERMON
Topic: The Father Formula
TEXT: Prov. 15:1–10; Luke 15:11–32

It is very difficult to be a father these days. I think it has been very difficult to be a father in any generation. And it is equally difficult to be a mother in any generation. We know that. We know the difficulty there is in parenting, in helping to create a good family atmosphere.

I heard a commentator the other day say that the average American father spends about thirteen minutes a week listening to his children, and the average American mother spends about thirty-two minutes a week listening to her children. Neither of these is enough. There are entirely too many pressures on parents and on children. The pressures on parents pull them away from their children. There are so many demands on children that they don't value time with their parents anymore. We must strike a balance in life, find a way to spend more time together so that as we live with one another we can help one another and grow with one another.

Those families that have good fathers are blessed. Persons who have good fathers need to give thanks to God and appreciation to their father for the blessing he is in life. For those people who do not have good fathers, the rest of us need to pray for them, and support them, and share with them our strength and encouragement.

I want us to think together briefly this morning about five elements in a father's formula.

I. *Fathers, grasp your significance and importance.* Every one of us is a child of God. Every single one of us is important. But fathers, you need to hear, you are important.

In the story that Jesus tells in the Gospel of Luke, when the young man who runs away from home comes to his senses, what does he do? He comes into his "right mind" it says in some versions of Scripture. He decides to go home. He decides to go back to his father. So significant is his father in his life that he must be reunited with him. Now the young man isn't a father yet, but he is well on the road to being good material for fatherhood if he stays in his right mind. Everyone is significant and important.

II. *Fathers, be present to your children.* A father's love is spelled T . . . I . . . M . . . E. As one who now has grown children, I can look back and see all the times I didn't know how to tell time. If you are a young father, don't make that same mistake. It is never too late. Today we can begin to change our way of marking time—not by what we are doing, not by who we are, not by responsibilities, but by relationship. We need to spend time with each other.

The writer of Proverbs shares these insights: "A soft answer turns wrath away, but a harsh word stirs up anger. A gentle tongue is the tree of life, and yet it is a fool who despises his or her parent's instruction." What does all this assume? It assumes a relationship. It assumes dialogue between parent and child. It assumes understanding of speaking and listening, and listening, and listening, and that all takes time.

III. *Help your children know your values and your skills by your actions.* We can teach our skills and our values by our words, but our children will learn so much more by our actions.

When our children were small we went to see their godparents on one occasion. We drove up in front of their house. David, the father, was out front in the process of mowing the yard. The yard was only half mowed. There was equipment lying around. We saw him and his son Sean over on the sidewalk, and they were kneeling down looking at something. So we went over. As we got to them they greeted us, and David said, "I was trying to get the yard mowed before you got here, but I knew you would understand why Sean and I needed to watch this ant cross the sidewalk."

Our children learn our values by our actions. Sean that day learned his value, because he could interrupt a job. He could delay preparation for company. He was that important. And he heard about his value as his father told us what had happened, and we heard it, too. Teach value and teach your skills by your actions.

IV. *See the good aspects of your children first.* Don't ignore their bad qualities, but see their good qualities first. It is what the father in Jesus' story does. His two sons are both questionable people—differently, but questionable, both of them. Yet he can see their good qualities.

There is a particular son we know who lives in another state. His parents live elsewhere. The son calls with some regularity, but he never seems to call at the right time. You know how that is? You are always doing something when the phone rings. One night the father heard the phone ring. The father was in the midst of a project. He thought to himself, "Oh I hope that's not my son. I don't have time to talk to him right now." Then the idea went through his mind, "But what if my son never called." He ran to the phone and answered it joyfully. It was his son.

V. *A good time to laugh is any time you can.* We need to share the joy of living with our children. We are burdened down with pressures, but there is joy in each of our lives and we need to share that with our children. We need to share the joy of our faith with our children. Don't let that faith be something that pulls you down. If you don't know the joy of the faith, then your number one priority is to discover it for yourself. But if you know joy in the faith, make sure your children know it as well. It is the greatest gift you can give, joy in the Christian faith.

So, the formula for being a father is: grasp your significance and importance, be present and spend time with your children, teach your values and your skills by your actions, see the good qualities in your children first, and a good time to laugh is any time you can.

The call to Christian discipleship today is, for those of us who can, to give thanks for our fathers; and for fathers, to listen to your children.—Jim Standiford

SUNDAY, JUNE 27, 2004
Lectionary Message

Topic: No Sentimental Journey

TEXT: Luke 9:51–62

Other Readings: 2 Kings 2:1–2, 6–14; Ps. 77:1–2, 11–20; Gal. 5:1, 13–25

The idea that there is a price to pay to follow Christ comes as a great surprise to many in the twenty-first century. Christ is so often presented as the ultimate solution to every problem that the emphasis is on convincing persons that following him is a good deal they need to buy into. The Bible, though, presents a different Christ than is popularly presented. When Paul writes, "Indeed, all who desire to live godly in Christ Jesus will be persecuted" (2 Tim. 3:12 NASB), we are brought face to face with the reality that following Christ is not without a personal price.

Our problem, of course, is that we view Christianity as a man-centered religion. The reason Christ came was to make life more pleasurable for us. Such thinking, though, betrays a sentimental view of Christianity and is naive and foreign to the Scriptures. In the passage before us, especially in verses 57 through 62, we find the Lord addressing three obstacles to true discipleship.

I. *The obstacle of personal comfort* (Luke 9:57–58). Notice that this person, identified as a scribe in Matthew 8:19, sounded a commitment of, ostensibly, supreme devotion: "I will follow you wherever you go." This person would be no nominal follower of Jesus; rather, he would leave all he had known to follow Jesus. This declaration, one would think, should have elicited high praise from Jesus' lips. Instead, the Lord replied starkly that discomfort was his companion; he did not even have someplace "to lay his head."

Our Lord has revealed that, contrary to much popular thought of our day, following him may very well bring about discomfort, not comfort. While in many Western countries Christians have not experienced the loss of personal security and possessions that many of our brothers and sisters in Africa and Asia have faced, those who sincerely follow Christ can expect to pay a price for their discipleship. The reality of the costs need to be set forth clearly. Some follow Christ too quickly, moved perhaps by an emotional decision to become a Christian. Richard Lenski observes that such a person "sees the soldiers on parade, the fine uniforms and the flittering arms, and is eager to join but forgets the exhausting marches, the bloody battles, the graves, perhaps unmarked."[6] What personal comforts are we willing to give up for Christ's sake?

---

[6]Richard C. Lenski, *The Interpretation of St. Luke's Gospel* (Minneapolis, Minn.: Augsburg Fortress, 1961), p. 559.

II. *The obstacle of financial security* (Luke 9:59–60). A second would-be follower makes what appears to be a legitimate request, "Lord, permit me first to go and bury my father." Jesus' reply seems almost heartless: "Allow the dead to bury their own dead; but as for you, go and proclaim everywhere the Kingdom of God." There is, of course, more here than meets the eye. To "bury one's father" was a figure of speech meaning to continue in business with one's father until the father's death, at which time the inheritance would be divided. Leaving before that time would mean forfeiture of part or all of the inheritance.

Are we willing to follow Christ if it means a change in our vocation? What if we are faced with an ethical decision at work because we are instructed to do what would violate biblical values? To follow what Christ teaches may mean the loss of our employment. Are we willing to overcome that obstacle?

III. *The obstacle of dual allegiance* (Luke 9:61–62). Once again, a would-be follower makes what appears to be a reasonable petition: "First permit me to say good-bye to those at home." What could possibly be wrong with that? One is about to leave, perhaps forever, and wants to bid farewell to one's relatives and friends. Jesus, though, sees through the not-so-innocent request. Following him means saying good-bye permanently to everyone and everything that draws the disciple's affections away from Christ.

Many would follow Christ but for fear of losing a boyfriend, a wife, a parent, or a cherished friend. Others fear the loss of their earthly hopes and aspirations. The question persists: Are we willing to forsake all for Christ? Morris well states, "Jesus points out that the Kingdom has no room for those who look back when they are called to go forward."[7]

Those who would truly follow Christ cannot be superficial followers. Our Lord applauds no half-hearted devotion but requires single-minded allegiance. The rolls of our churches already include too many nominal Christians. Let's not add to their number.—William G. Moore

ILLUSTRATION

HOW CAN I BLASPHEME MY KING?   Those who see Christ as their very life will, by his grace, find no obstacle to following him. On February 22, 156, Polycarp, the bishop of the church at Smyrna, was arrested at a country farm where he had taken refuge. For two hours he prayed aloud for individuals and the church throughout the world. At the arena, the proconsul attempted to get him to deny the Lord Jesus. Polycarp declared, "Eighty-six years I have served him and he has done me no wrong. How can I blaspheme my king?" He was burned alive before the arena spectators.[8]

SERMON SUGGESTIONS

Topic: Our Unknown Allies

Text: 1 Kings 19:15–21, esp. v. 18

(1) *Problem:* feelings of isolation and loneliness. (2) *Solution:* (a) the Lord's sometimes too secret disciples and their coming forward in times of crisis, (b) the cloud of unseen witnesses urging us on, and (c) the presence of the living God, who will never leave us nor forsake us.

---

[7]Leon Morris, *The Gospel According to Luke: An Introduction and Commentary* (Grand Rapids, Mich.: Eerdmans, 1974), p. 180.

[8]"Polycarp, Martyrdom of," *Zondervan Pictorial Encyclopedia of the Bible,* Vol. 4. p. 816.

Topic: A Paradox of Christian Experience
TEXT: Gal. 5:1, 13–25
(1) We are free from the rigors of the Law. (2) We are bound by the constraints of love.

WORSHIP AIDS

CALL TO WORSHIP.   "I will remember the works of the Lord: surely I will remember thy wonders of old. I will meditate also on all thy work, and talk of thy doings. Thy way, O God, is in the sanctuary: who is so great a God as our God?" (Ps. 77:11–13).

INVOCATION.   We confess, O God, that sometimes we are puzzled when heavy burdens are heaped upon us and costly challenges confront us. As we seek to worship you, strengthen our faith and focus our hearts to do your will.

OFFERTORY SENTENCE.   "Be patient therefore, brethren, unto the coming of the Lord. Behold, the husbandman waiteth for the precious fruit of the Earth, and hath long patience for it, until he receiveth the early and latter rain" (James 5:7).

OFFERTORY PRAYER.   Help us as individuals and as a congregation to be able to see and do that which is within our power to provide for the needs of ministry in the community and the church. Make us obedient stewards who are gracious and generous in giving to Kingdom causes, we pray in Jesus' name.—Henry Fields

PRAYER.   In this hurried world, Father, we forget to take time to reflect on truth and life and our reaction to both. Help us this morning to find truth and see life in such a way that we will leave this place redirected for the living of these days.

We have heard the invitation of Jesus saying, "Come unto me." It has echoed and re-echoed in our minds and souls. At times it has been like someone knocking at the inner doors of our soul. Sometimes it has been like a still small voice calling to us. At other times it has been the clear, unmistakable voice of the church bidding us "Come." We know that we should obey that call, yet we put if off. Be patient with us, Father, we pray. You know how we shut doors in our lives and close our listening to voices we do not want to hear at the moment. How do you stand the stubbornness of our self-determined wills? We want to take the talents you have given us, our lives, our wealth, and all the assets with which we have been endowed and spend them as we please. Indeed, we are prodigals in a far country.

This morning, help us to become as he was in the closing days of his wandering. Make us smart enough to realize that you are our Father and that without you we are truly bereft. Give us the courage to turn homeward, not for what we want to get from you, but simply because we have come to our senses and know that only in you is life, now and forever. Oh, Father! Here today may we experience your welcome, your forgiveness, and something of restoration, which only you can provide.

Let others be blessed today with your healing presence, we pray. Fill the hearts of the lonely, satisfy the hunger of the searching. Comfort the depths of the sorrowing. Grant peace to the disturbed peoples and nations of the world. Work in us to build a stronger, more noble place, where children's laughter will ring through the hills instead of the cries of fear, where health will be the order of the day and not devastating illness and disease, where life will be full and free and where poverty and untimely death will be no more.

Let this hour be yours, Father, and from it may we go in Christ's name.—Henry Fields

SERMON
Topic: Clothed with Christ
TEXT: Gal. 3:23–29

The Trinity Church Rectory, many of you may know, sides onto Newbury Street. So one of the extra benefits of being your rector is the privilege of watching shoppers from around the world walking up and down the street carrying bags with exotic Italian names printed on the out-side. It is quite a fashion boulevard, my street, with people making distinctive statements about who they are by the clothes they wear and the fashions they have embraced.

Of course, if I think the people on Newbury Street are exotic, they probably think I am, too. Before I came here this morning I put on a certain set of clothes, clothes that define who I am—black shirt, funny white collar. I wouldn't be the same person you see now if I came, say, in shorts and a T-shirt, or in my pajamas. No, my clothes help to define me; they tell me and they tell you something of who I am. You could even say they change the reality of who I am. Of course, you decided who you wanted to be this morning, too, and I can tell you wanted to be pretty impressive!

The usual way we talk about being a Christian is by saying that what really matters is what is going on inside you, in your soul; that externals aren't nearly as important as inter-nal things.

In our New Testament lesson this morning, St. Paul is talking to the Galatians about the change that happens when people are baptized. In Christ, he says, you have all been made God's children. But apparently they must not have felt that clearly, so he has to remind them by talking about clothes: "As many of you as were baptized into Christ have clothed your-selves with Christ." All the labels people put on each other, labels like Jew and Greek, male and female, don't mean much because they have now put on Christ. In fact, in Romans Paul says, "Put on the Lord Jesus Christ." It is as if we take on something external.

We live in a time obsessed with feelings—How do you feel about him or her, about this or that? Does this feel right to you? How does our worship make you feel? How does Ivory soap make you feel? Yet many of the most important things in life have to do not with feel-ings but with commitments we first make and then follow through on, regardless of how we feel. The feelings come later.

It happens that way in marriage, for example. One of the great problems that marriage is having, as are other committed relationships, is the widespread belief that commitment is based on feelings. If you feel in love, you get married, and you stay married as long as you feel that way. No surprise, then, when marriages don't do very well. Marriages aren't about feelings; they are about promises—promises to stay there, to work at loving a sometimes not very lov-able person. And it is out of the promises, out of the staying there, that the depth of feelings grows. We are not promising to feel in love every moment, we are not promising never to feel angry or hurt, or never to be drawn elsewhere. No, we are promising to be there "until we are parted by death."

It often happens that way at work, too. Most of us don't wake up in the morning and ask ourselves if we feel like going off to our desks or to see a client or to look after some kids. No, we get up and do what we've committed ourselves to doing.

And doesn't Sunday morning work a little like that, too? You don't always wake up feeling like a Christian, like coming to church here. Maybe you once knew why you were doing this, but at least on some days you're not sure. But look at you, you got up anyway, you came here, and you are going through the external motions—saying the prayers, singing the hymns—and at least often enough it all works on you, and by the end of the service you really do feel connected to God again.

There are some Christian traditions that require people to experience consciously the reality of their faith before they can be baptized. Other traditions, such as ours, emphasize that the external act of baptism will draw out our faith. That is why we baptize unknowing infants—not because we believe they have made some conscious decision about faith, but because we are helping them to put on Christ and to grow up in a community whose members are themselves learning what it means to live in Christ.

When we baptize a child, the priests make the sign of the cross on the forehead of each of these children and pronounces that they are Christ's own forever. Making this sign was apparently a practice the church borrowed from the Roman army. When a man became a Roman soldier, he was "branded," marked by the sign on the emperor's forehead to show that he now owed allegiance to the emperor. The sign of the cross on the forehead is an external sign of the one to whom we belong.

Putting on Christ is for all of us only the beginning. It is in the daily living that it yields its meaning.—Samuel T. Lloyd III[9]

SUNDAY, JULY 4, 2004
Lectionary Message

Topic: Ministry from the Margins
Text: 2 Kings 5:1–14
Other Readings: Gal. 6:(1–6) 7–16; Ps. 30; Luke 10:1–11, 16–20

Whenever God casts his big play, we expect him to cast big-name stars and to set the big scenes center stage. But God likes to cast unknowns and to put most of the action in the shadows and margins. The God of the patriarchs and prophets likes to work in unexpected people and places. He likes to do ministry from the margins and with people we might consider marginal for ministry. In the wonderful account of the healing of the leprous Syrian warrior, Naaman, we discover multiple evidences that God is at work in unexpected people and places:

1. *God was at work in a military victory of Israel's border enemy, Syria, through the leadership of its general, Naaman.* We do not expect God to be at work in the successes of our enemies, but he is.

---

[9]The author acknowledges William Willimon for contributions to this sermon.

2. *God was at work in the captivity of the Israeli border girl and her subsequent purchase into the home of Naaman.* We do not expect God to be at work in our experiences of reduced circumstance and status, but he is.
3. *God was at work in the unexpected petition of a neighboring king when the Syrian king asked the Israeli king for a favor.* We do not expect God to be at work in the neediness of our enemies, but he is.
4. *God was at work in the lack of hospitality that Elisha showed to Naaman.* We do not expect God to be at work in our experiences of unmet expectations, but he is.
5. *God was at work in the muddy waters of the Jordan River.* We do not expect God to be at work when the waters of obedience are muddy and humiliating, but he is.

As we really become committed to seeing and serving God in Christ, we will become better at cooperating with his ministry from the undersides of life. As we do ministry from the margins, God will give us wisdom and timing to answer four of life's tough questions. These questions are embedded in the Naaman story, where a little captured Israeli girl found God's answer to the first of these questions.

Tough question 1: *"Why tell your enemy where to find help when they need it?"* This nameless girl witnessed to her mistress the healing available for Naaman in Hebrew Samaria. Never underestimate the long-term effects of ministry to and with children. This girl loved her enemy, and God used her to move Palestine toward peace through the healing of Naaman. Be God's instrument by being compassionate to your enemies. Evangelism is one beggar telling another beggar where to find bread.

Naaman's lieutenants applied God's answer to the workaday world's toughest question.

Tough question 2: *"Why risk your boss's temper, and your career when an opportunity could be lost due to your boss's pride?"* Naaman was offended when the prophet Elisha refused to come out and personally and formally greet him. He was humiliated that he was being asked to "wash" in the muddy waters of the Jordan River when his homeland waters were renowned for their clarity. Yet these soldiers courageously risked reframing Naaman's perspective rather than see his quest for healing fail. Mentoring upward to those in authority over us is a divine ministry from the underside. Expect God to work through you when you try it. Be God's instrument by risking the right time and way to mentor your boss, teacher, or parents, so that they receive God's help when they need it most.

Elisha, court prophet in a second nation, showed his loyalty to God by answering everyman's question about self-preservation.

Tough question 3: *"Why get involved when it puts you and God on the spot to produce?"* Elisha exposed himself and his God to failure by speaking up for God in the court of public opinion and commerce. Be God's instrument by speaking up so that God's answers are considered in the court of public opinion and problem solving. Be God's instrument by seeing God's hand in unexpected events. Elisha saw God's hand in the Aramaic king's healing request.

Naaman himself answers the tough faith question:

Tough question 4: *"Why obey when the command doesn't make much sense?"* Isn't it remarkable that when Naaman was diseased he was prideful and expectant of the best treatment, but when he was healed he became humble and grateful for the least service? Be God's instrument by being obedient even when the way is muddy and unclear. Whenever we immerse ourselves in full obedience to the command of Christ, do we not experience a newness of life and attitude? As the chorus of the old hymn exhorts, "Trust and obey, for there is no other way to be happy in Jesus, but to trust and obey."—Rodrick K. Durst

ILLUSTRATIONS

GOD WITHOUT BORDERS.   Medecins sans Frontieres (MSF), better known in English as "Doctors Without Borders," was founded by a group of French doctors who claimed neutrality and impartiality in moving across borders to bring medical missions to people regardless of politics, religion, or race. MSF now has headquarters in more than twenty countries and medical missions in eighty countries. We need to believe in God without borders and to practice impartiality in taking Christian ministry across every frontier we face and fear.

INSTRUMENT OF THE LORD.   Simon Burch is a physically malformed, diminutive teenager in a movie that bears his name. In a tense scene in the study of his pastor, Simon expresses his faith and self-esteem by unexpectedly announcing, "I am an instrument of the Lord. I don't know when God will use me, but he will." What a shot of adrenaline our self-esteem experiences when we too see ourselves as God's instruments.

SERMON SUGGESTIONS

Topic: The Payoff
TEXT: 1 Kings 21:1-3, 17-21
Wrongdoing by leaders has dire consequences: (1) for the oppressed, (2) for the oppressors, (3) for the people in general.

Topic: Planting the Right Crop
TEXT: Gal. 6:7-18
(1) Avoiding self-indulgence—sowing to the flesh. (2) Living in glad obedience to God—sowing to the Spirit. (3) Waiting in patient faithfulness—persisting in doing good.

WORSHIP AIDS

CALL TO WORSHIP.   "Sing a song to the Lord, all you his loyal servants; give thanks to his holy name. In his anger is distress; in his favor there is life. Tears may linger at nightfall, but rejoicing comes in the morning (Ps. 30:4-5 REB).

INVOCATION.   Lord, in not every country is liberty available, in not every land may individuals worship as they please, in not every state is freedom of choice a possibility. We worship today as a grateful and much blessed people.—E. Lee Phillips

OFFERTORY SENTENCE.   "The Earth is the Lord's, and the fullness thereof; the world, and they that dwell therein" (Ps. 24:1).

OFFERTORY PRAYER.   All things belong to you, O God, and we all belong to you. Aware of what we are and whose we are and of the service we can render to your Kingdom, we bring to you a portion of what you have put into our hands and homes. Bless us with a deepening appreciation of our stewardship, through Jesus Christ our Lord, who gave his all for us.

PRAYER.   Lord of our land, beneath whose bending skies our people move and live, we thank thee for every sign of thy great purpose in forming this lovely world. Thou art the maker of all that is beautiful, noble, and right, and in some part of every living thing a benefit waits to be discovered and used for the community of people and nations everywhere. We thank thee especially for our homeland, for its forests, fields, and rivers, and for the genius of our people in making a nation with its widespread industry, culture, and learning under the aegis of thy name. We honor with gratitude and praise the founders of this country, the vision that urged them on, their wisdom in forming a government of and for the people, and their dream of the rule of justice and the freedom to exercise it. We bless thee as we receive daily the fruits of this rich heritage, for the strong zeal it gives us to live by, and for the impulse to build and expand for the sake of the common good.

To thee we commend now our country—those who govern and those who serve; be thou their refuge and trust until thy day will break and "Earth will be fair and all her people one." In the saving name of Jesus our Lord and Savior, we make our prayer.—Donald Macleod

SERMON
Topic: Show and Tell
TEXT: Mark 1:1–11, 14–15

Maybe it is because the circus is in town, or maybe it's because, as an adult, I have trouble focusing on one event at a time. Whatever the reason, the phrase "three ring circus" has been on my mind. We use the term loosely to refer to an area where a lot of activity is taking place. But it means more than that to me. You see, my earliest positive childhood memories revolve around the Shrine Circus and Fireworks Display.

What I remember most is standing on the wooden bleachers to be able to see poodles jumping on and off the backs of ponies moving briskly around in the circle. Nothing like that every happened in my neighborhood. It was the greatest! What I did not realize was that while I was transfixed, to my right the darkened center ring was the scene of quiet but intense preparation. When the moment was just right, the great center ring was bathed in light, and the death-defying drama going on there mesmerized my young eyes and dwarfed anything that went on before it.

That palpable memory comes back when I try to feel, as well as hear, the transition taking place in the story we have read this morning. Before this passage, we saw the people spellbound by the striking dress, diet, and prophetic preaching of John the Baptist—especially the preaching. For hundreds of years, the people of Israel had not heard the voice of a prophet. They could not take their eyes off of John even though that is just what John was trying to accomplish. He kept pointing to one who would come after him. He was not worthy to carry that one's shoes.

Now the imprisonment of John forces us to move our eyes from John to Jesus, from Nazareth to Capernaum. What had been developing in the darkness of relative obscurity now leapt into the light. Jesus' very movement into the region of Zebulun and Naphtali was seen by Matthew as a fulfillment of prophecy. This land, named for two of the tribes of Israel, had been in the shadowy depths of captivity by Assyria. Yet as Isaiah recorded, these tribes had been among the first to see the great light of deliverance. Isaiah's prophecy looked even further ahead to the coming of the Messiah. This area, which came to be known as Galilee of the Nations (or Gentiles), was among the first to encounter the one called the Light of the World. His message, "Repent, the Kingdom of Heaven has come near," both attracts and repels.

The image of light used here is most helpful in understanding the ministry of Jesus. We are drawn to great sources of light, such as the sun, but we know we can't look directly into the sun. The saving truth is that we come to know the light by what it lights up. In the completely yielding, obedient Jesus of Nazareth, God shines through a human being so that we may "behold his glory." In seeing the fully human Jesus, we are also able to look upon "very God of very God." All that it is possible to see of the fullness of God in a human body is seen in him.

Even more of this image of light is revealed as we witness Jesus calling his first four disciples. We know that objects penetrated by the light absorb some colors and reflect others. Something similar happens when we see and hear God in Christ. If we respond to his invitation to know him and follow him, the one true light is reflected in us through our distinct personalities. There are many hues and colors of disciples. God, who created the various human temperaments, redeems them all to be used in God's service. All we come to know of the four disciples called here reinforces that truth.

Simon Peter was the epitome of the no-nonsense all-action person. He did not want to see which way the wind was blowing. You don't have to guess what he really thought. He has been called bold and impetuous—two views of the same temperament. Dr. Kendle has rightly said that Peter reminds us of the world of the old spiritual: "Sometimes I'm up, sometimes I'm down, sometimes I'm almost on the ground." Indeed, Peter came up with the initial confession of Jesus as the Messiah. Not understanding the implications of his confession, he sought to hold Jesus back from his ascent to the cross. Peter was bold, impetuous, and called to show and tell the good news of God.

Andrew could not have been more unlike his more prominent brother. He did not charge ahead to speak the first word. He did not lead the advance troops. He was the support staff. He did not jump out front; he brought others. He brought Peter to Jesus. When thousands were hungry, he brought a small boy with a smaller lunch to Jesus' attention. Three out of the four disciples mentioned here were a part of the "inner circle," with Jesus at the raising of Jairus's daughter, at the transfiguration, and in the Garden of Gethsemane. Andrew was not recognized in this way. No matter—Andrew was supportive, inviting, and called to show and tell the good news of God.

James showed no diffidence in wanting, with his brother, John, to be in the front ranks when the reign of King Jesus began. When James asked for such a place, we notice, Jesus did not rebuke his ambition. Such ambition can be used by God. What Jesus did ask of James and John was, Can you undergo the baptism of suffering and death that I will undergo? Always confident, James's answer was a resounding testimony of being able. The elder of the two brothers, he hid not behind his mother or brother. He knew what and where he wanted to be. What he didn't know was what it would cost. James was ambitious, assertive, and called to show and tell the good news of God.

John should be the easiest to name; wasn't he the beloved disciple? Yet, when we read the descriptions across the Gospels, an even clearer picture develops. Along with his brother, John, he was passionate in wanting to call down fire from heaven onto the Samaritan village that would not receive them. He believed that such an affront, such an injustice to the Lord's disciples, should be punished. When John told Jesus that he and other disciples had forbidden a man to cast out demons in the name of Jesus, he displayed the same fiery sense of justice. Perhaps this disciple, who was loved, had yet to learn the power of loving even the outsider. Nonetheless, John was passionate, fiery, and called to show and tell the good news of God.

All of this diversity is good news for us. The one common denominator is the one in the center ring. The more that these and countless other men and women allowed the light of the world to be reflected through them, the more they found their true and unique identities as witnesses. They showed us the way of the witness by showing up. All four immediately left the security of their present lives. This speaks more to the world around us than any well-rehearsed "personal testimony." We proclaim who we are and whose we are by what we let go.

Each found a way to tell the good news of God in Christ through his own personality. The same can be said for Lydia and the women at the well, Mary and Martha. Each could speak a good word for Jesus Christ that was authentic to where they were at the time. Scholar Eugene Peterson is right: true witness is no "sea lion stuff." There is no need to embellish what we know of God, to puff it up in sea lion tones, to impress, move, and motivate. God asks only our honest report. God will do the rest.

Let us notice most of all that those called from their nets that day did not become instant disciples or instant witnesses. Our showing and telling the love of God begins immediately, but we are called to row in that witness all of our days. Matthew's Gospel shows the pattern of sending out the disciples in twos. The boldness of Peter must rub shoulders with the resourcefulness of Andrew. The true witness is not a lone ranger; we grow committed in prayer and ministry with one another.

From growing in the body of Christ come opportunities to let go of our nets of security and to show and tell of the one in whom we trust. The story has been told of the wounded soldier trapped in "no man's land." He felt completely cut off and abandoned. As he slipped in and out of consciousness, he realized that someone had crawled out to be next to him despite the fierce enemy fire. It was the chaplain. He had quietly begun to talk to him, giving him water and praying for him. After some time, the soldier spoke, "This Jesus you speak about, is he the one who brought you out here?" The response was, "Yes." So the soldier continued, "Then I do want to know more about him."

Sometimes the "showing" opens up the "telling." Amen.—Gary D. Stratman

SUNDAY, JULY 11, 2004
Lectionary Message

Topic: Building Inspection Failure

TEXT: Amos 7:7–17

Other Readings: Ps. 82; Col. 1:1–14; Luke 10:25–37

Amos was a Southern Palestinian syrup farmer and sheep rancher. In the midst of this dual career, his nation, Judah, fell under the domination of the expanding, prospering nation, Israel, just to the north. The classic dichotomy of the rich becoming richer and the poor paying for it, particularly the farming communities, fed Israel's economic boom. That these good times were a sign of divine favor was assumed. Thus the worship centers were full and hearers there feasted on the "health and wealth" preaching of the court priests, especially of high priest Amaziah from his cathedral pulpit in the ancient Hebrew religious center of Bethel.

While Amaziah's hearers had "padded pews in air-conditioned auditoriums," Amos stood in the dusty marketplaces of Bethel to launch his street ministry. His Spirit-honed preaching took only seven sermons to get Amos into trouble. Amaziah acted to have the royal court of King Jeroboam II revoke Amos's street preaching license and temporary visa. He contended that what Amos was preaching was traitorous and libelous to the administration of Jeroboam. "Amos is raising a conspiracy against you in the very heart of Israel. The land cannot bear all his words" (7:10 NIV). In its plan to protect the increasingly good life for the few, the political administration of Jeroboam and its religious affiliate, Amaziah, had developed a low tolerance for truth. They had forgotten three basic realities about truth in the public place.

I. *Truth is not libelous or traitorous.* Many expect government and religion to get along. Some expect government to get in line with their religion. Others expect religion to get in line with their government. Both views tend to spin the facts to support their position. Prophetic faith, however, operates in a "no spin zone," wherein the truth is spoken out of a love for all the people in the land. When such truths are spoken and welcomed, then the famous Amos "waters of justice" will begin to roll down and set right and refresh the entire community (5:24).

1. *The community that welcomes prophetic truth refuses to put truth up for sale.* When truth is not for sale, it is often unwelcome. Amaziah misread Amos. Amos wasn't seeking support as a professional seer. Amos was a God-called spokesperson sent to warn of an impending crash and crush ahead for Israel (7:14–15).
2. *The community that welcomes prophetic truth knows that preachers are not hirelings.* Pulpits are to be free of any constraint other than to present a spokesperson who can authentically say, "Now, then, hear the Word of the Lord" (7:16).
3. *The community that welcomes prophetic truth knows that denial or suppression of truth magnifies its consequences.* God refused to intervene against the consequences facing high priest Amaziah when he attempted to suppress the truth borne by God's messenger. "Your wife will become a prostitute, your sons and daughters will fall by the swords, your lands will be divided, and you will die in a pagan country" (7:17).

II. *Truth does hurt.* Whenever truth goes against civil religion, our temptation is to see prophetic truth as economic treason or as cultural cynicism. Christianity can drift into the service of the good life, for some. Righteousness may not benefit our retirement savings, but such righteousness pleases Holy God immensely. The labor pains of truthful confession and admission beget hope-filled living for all.

1. Hope-filled living requires humiliating honesty about our ethical condition.
2. Hope-filled living finds God's mercy upon repentance and restitution for our sins.
3. Hope-filled living practices restitution and restoration.

III. *Truths show us where we are not plumb.* Apparently, Amos had acquired a carpenter's plumb line. With this plumb line, he had taken to checking the public buildings of Bethel. He tagged as "condemned property" those structures that operated out of plumb with the truths of God's covenant. Amos acted as a God-appointed building inspector. God was revoking Jeroboam's contractor's license and God was revoking Israel's use permit for his promised land. You and I need to acquire some plumb lines capable of keeping our lives true to God and his Kingdom ways.

1. *Holy Scripture serves reliably as a plumb line for Christian living and loving.* Either the Bible will separate you from sin, or sin will separate you from the Bible.
2. *The Spirit of Christ serves as a plumb line to quicken our consciences as we daily surrender to his leadership and mission for our lives.* His Spirit brings Scripture to mind for correction, instruction, and training in plumb ways (2 Tim. 3:16).
3. *Communion with our local church serves as a powerful plumb line, as fellow members encourage and admonish one another to a life worthy of the high calling of Christ Jesus.* May our lives demonstrate the attractiveness of new construction as we build our lives with the Jewish Carpenter. Whatever is not plumb with him must go now!

—Rodrick K. Durst

ILLUSTRATIONS

TRUTH.   On November 5, 1733, John Peter Zenger began to publish the *New York Weekly Journal.* This journal made numerous scathing criticisms of the colonial government of William Cosby and resulted in the arrest of Zenger on November 17, 1734. After waiting ten months in jail, Zenger's case finally came to trial. In a landmark decision establishing the freedom of the press in America, the jury found Zenger innocent when it determined that his articles were based on fact. The jury determined that "the truth is not libelous."

SCRIPTURE CORRECTS.   Sixteenth-century radical Reformation leader Balthasar Hubmaier (1481–1528) declared, "I may err and make mistakes, but a heretic I can never be, for I can always be corrected by the Word of God."

SERMON SUGGESTION

Topic: The All-Time Favorite Text
TEXT: John 3:16 (NKJV)
Why do we love it? (1) It appeals to our instinct of self-preservation: we do not want our lives to come to nothing. (2) It appeals to our sense of need for cosmic support: only the love of God can satisfy our deepest hunger for security. (3) It appeals to our sense of what is right and fair: it is for everybody.

WORSHIP AIDS

CALL TO WORSHIP.   "Rise up, O God; judge the Earth, for all the nations are your inheritance" (Ps. 82:8 NIV).

INVOCATION.   O God, help us to see and understand where and what we are as individuals and as citizens of a nation, and in that experience to come to realize more and more that we belong to you. Make us increasingly the kind of learners who will glorify your name.

OFFERTORY SENTENCE.   "With all my heart I shall give thanks to the Lord. . . . He has won renown for his marvelous deeds; the Lord is gracious and compassionate" (Ps. 111:1, 4 REB).

OFFERTORY PRAYER.   We thank you now, O Lord, for all the blessings that we continue to receive, and we bring to you a portion of our material possessions, that your blessings may go forth in special ways for the advancement of your Kingdom.

PRAYER.   We have heard, Father, that no person can serve two masters: that we will either hate the one and love the other, or else we will hold to the one and despise the other. This morning we would discover anew the one Master of life, whom we can serve with love and honor and devotion. So often we forget whose we are. This morning remind us and call us to the Lord Christ with a freshness and enthusiasm that will empower us as we go about the living of these days.

How we thank you for the body of believers known as the Church. Help us together to discover more clearly what it means to be followers of Jesus. Enable us to realize that we are not all the same, that we do not all possess the same talents or occupy the same place in society or possess the same amount of this world's wealth. But let us never forget that your Spirit working in us enables us to do ministry through the gifts you have given to us in the place where you have set us. Remind us anew that we do not have to do what others are endowed to do, but rather that we may use our abilities to complement those about us as we share in the privilege of serving the Lord day by day.

So this morning we come to pray for each other. We ask that your healing, sustaining, redeeming love reach out through each of us to touch each member of our church family. May those who have been disturbed because life has become so difficult for them gain perspective and a vision of how to take the difficult situation and use it creatively for their good and your glory. May those who walk in loneliness day after day find not only eternal friendship in you, but also earthly friendship to scatter the loneliness in those of us who seek to care and love and minister in Jesus' name. May those walking through some dark valley have faith enough to say, "Even though I walk through the very valley of the shadow of death, I will fear no evil, for thou art with me." Free those who are ill from fear and anxiety, that they may be open to receiving the health of your healing grace.

Beyond our doors we pray for the agony, the brokenness, the brutality, and the suffering of the world. Show us how to implement better the truth of Jesus, so that the day will soon come when swords are beaten into plowshares and spears into pruning hooks, and people learn war no more. Lead us to peace and worthy service, Lord Jesus, we pray.—Henry Fields

SERMON
Topic: Does God Hear Us When We Pray?
TEXT: Rom. 8:26–27

Does God really hear us when we pray? The answer, let it be said at once, is yes, he does. "When I was in trouble, I called unto the Lord and he heard me." But it is not so simple as that, and it is not enough simply to say that and nothing more.

One of the reasons you wonder from time to time whether God hears you when you pray is that it is almost impossible for you to visualize it. Isn't that true? Nevertheless, you picture

God in human terms, as the great Cosmic Executive with the management of the universe in his hands. Then you go on to picture him getting calls from all over the inhabited world.

When you stop to think of the number of people and the vast variety of requests they make of the God of the universe, and of the calls that cancel out each other, the whole thing seems fantastic.

You may have a less personal picture of God. Your image of God, as you think of him either consciously or unconsciously, is the God of the sun and the planets, the great cosmic God who keeps the universe going; and if you have that sort of picture of God, you can hardly imagine him being interested in the likes of you and your rather unimportant needs and desires.

In this picture of God, it isn't that it is too much for God; it is beneath him. He is too great to bother with all these little concerns that rise up like mist from the surface of the Earth. You can worship him, but you can't expect him to single you out for special attention.

Whatever your picture of God may be, it becomes increasingly difficult for you to visualize the fact that God hears you individually, so you may come to the conclusion that he doesn't hear you at all, and if he doesn't hear you, there isn't much use in praying.

Just a couple of suggestions: First, because you are a human being you are bound to visualize; you will never get away from pictures entirely, and the deeper the thing is that you are thinking about, the more you will depend on pictures.

When you think of God, nine times out of ten you think of some picture of God, and my suggestion is that on the whole, the bigger picture of God you have the better it is. In other words, I think you are on safer ground with the picture of the big cosmic God than you are with the picture of the senior executive. Both pictures have drawbacks and dangers, but the larger picture is more likely to be the better one.

As you grow, your picture of God ought to grow, and as you increase in imagination, understanding, and depth of perception, you ought to reach out to greater depths of God's nature until God becomes vaster, more wonderful and majestic, than he was when you were a child. After all, it is so in the Bible. God appears in the opening chapters of Genesis in very human terms, as a God walking in the garden in the cool of the day, and in the last chapters of Revelation as the great cosmic energy of love who is making all things new. This growth in man's picture of God is right; it is natural.

This suggestion may help. Think of God not as someone at the other end of a long-distance telephone call, but as a living Spirit within you. In other words, try to think of your prayers not as long-distance calls by which you are trying to reach someone way out there, hundreds of miles away, but as intensely local calls by which you are communing with someone who is already with you. It isn't altogether impossible to believe that the life that took the trouble to become you is aware of your troubles and your needs.

St. Paul talked about the body being the temple of the Spirit of God. I've also come across a line in his Epistle to the Romans that was made clear to me for the first time when I read J. B. Phillips's translation of the Epistle: "We do not know how to pray worthily as sons of God, but his spirit within us is actually praying for us in those agonizing longings which never find words." In other words, St. Paul is saying that the longings you have in you, the reaching upward of desires that you may never know how to express, these longings are the Spirit of God in you praying for you. This may help you to overcome the feeling that God is far away.

And remember, finally, that there are things you cannot visualize and yet you know they are true. I cannot really visualize the love of parents for ten children, and I cannot really picture how it can be that when one of the children dies the parents suffer no less anguish because nine others survive. Yet I know this to be the mystery of love, and I believe this to be the mystery of God.

There is another, more practical reason you sometimes wonder whether God hears you, and this is that you don't get an answer. No answer, no one home.

But not *quite* so. The situations are not altogether comparable. In the first place, you don't expect a verbal answer to prayer as you expect it from a letter or a telephone call or a conversation. The answers to prayer come in the course of events, in the things that happen to you.

There is another possibility, of course, and that is that the answer is no, that God heard you but his answer is no, or not yet. Even though it is hard to take no for an answer from anybody, let alone from God, we know, and we know beyond the shadow of a doubt, if we have lived very long, that we are not always going to get everything we ask for in prayer. What about the words of Jesus when he said, "Whatever you pray about and ask for, believe that you have received it, and it will be yours"?

James and John asked him to give them places of priority, to let them sit on either side of him in his Kingdom. Do you remember what his answer was? "You don't know what you are asking. You may be able to drink of my cup and be baptized with the baptism with which I am baptized, but to give you places on either side of me, this is not for me to give; they will be given to those for whom they have been prepared." Jesus was saying point-blank that there were some things he couldn't give them no matter how often they asked for them or how much they wanted them. Nor could God. Jesus was saying in the first instance that when you pray, you pray with the simple trust and confidence of a child. He was saying in the second instance that you also pray with the humility of a child, knowing that not everything you want and ask for will your Father give you.

You know also that Jesus did not get everything he asked for. On the very last night of his life, Jesus asked to be spared from the agony of death.

When we ask for things in absolute confidence and trust, as he taught us to ask, we ask also with the same kind of humility, always adding to our prayer, "Nevertheless, not my will but thine be done."

And we shall always have before our eyes the vision of the cross on which he died, after he had asked to be spared. His prayer was not granted, and as he was dying upon that cross, he continued to pray for his enemies first, for the lost ones around about him in the same plight, for his friends, and finally for himself.—Theodore Parker Ferris

SUNDAY, JULY 18, 2004
Lectionary Message

Topic: The Fruit of Injustice
Text: Amos 8:1–12
Other Readings: Ps. 52; Col. 1:15–28; Luke 10:38–42

Amos was likely a visual learner. God taught and inspired the prophetic ministry of Amos by using visual object lessons. From a swarm of locusts, Amos learned the devastation of the judgments we fail to avoid. From a brush fire, Amos learned the power of divine wrath to consume whatever refused to dwell within the boundaries of the covenant. From a plumb line, Amos learned that whichever practices of God's people are not true to covenant righteousness are then subject to destruction. Now, in a fourth object lesson, Amos learns that Holy God does have the capacity and will to punish. For this object lesson, recorded in Amos 8, God showed Amos a basket of ripe fruit.

I. *Truth requires perception* (vv. 1–2). "What do you see, Amos?" What Amos perceived in the ripeness of the fruit was the ripeness of Israel for divine judgment. "The time is ripe for my people; I will spare them no longer" (8:3 NIV). Whenever a people acquires a taste for the sweet fruit of injustice, God will unleash a flood of consequences to spoil that fruit. The fruit of injustice spoils quickly.

II. *The sweet profitability of injustice is temporary, because the people least able to pay usually fund it.* Great prices and high profits for the *haves* are usually at the expense of the *have-nots*. Amos preached a God who couldn't get to sleep at night because he could not get the "trampling of the needy . . . and the cheating of the poor" out of his mind (8:4, 5). "I will never forget anything they have done" (8:7 NIV).

III. *God will not spare his children his rod.* God disciplines his children first, others after. He disciplines those whom he loves (Heb. 12:7). How could God's name have respect in a world where injustice was tolerated within God's covenant community? Because spiritual discipline is a sign of spiritual legitimacy, we must make sure that we have songs of suffering in our hymnbooks. Amos warned that orders of worship filled with songs of joy would need to be changed to worship filled with songs of mourning whenever God's children tolerated and profited from injustice in their community (8:3).

IV. *God will handle you in the same way you handle the humble* (8:4–7). Jesus declared, "Blessed are the merciful, for they shall receive mercy" (Matt. 5:7). Amos was embarrassingly specific about merchant strategies to cheat the poor through skimpy measurements, price gouging, and "dishonest scales." He warned of Yahweh's anger.

(a) If God's people will not voluntarily repent and restore the poor, then God will "make all of you wear sackcloth and shave your heads" (8:10 NIV). In the early Church, apostolicity was based on whether or not the gospel of Jesus Christ was preached and the poor were remembered (Gal. 2:10). To forget the poor is not merely to fail to remember them; it is to dismember them.

(b) If God's people plug their ears to God's call to repentance and fairness with the poor, then God will simply cease speaking to that people. "Men will stagger . . . searching for the Word of the Lord, but they will not find it" (8:12 NIV). God will not allow us to disconnect our relationship with him from our relationship to the people in humble circumstances around us.

(c) When God's people cannot hear God's words, they lose their identity. Without sufficient bread, humanity cannot live at all. But neither can humanity live by bread alone. Bread without the word of the Lord is anxiety. It is the bread of anxious toil.

V. *Conclusion.* If we want to be better hearers of God's voice, let us ask him to make us more sensitive to the poor and humble around us. If we want to experience new depths of God's mercy, then let us invent ways to share and balance profits with the poor. We may need to consider higher prices as the better deal, if it translates into living wages for the working poor at the other end. If we want to see more credibility and apostolic power in our witnessing to Jesus, let's parallel our witness with creative and empowering ministries with the poor.—Rodrick K. Durst

ILLUSTRATIONS

PROFITING FROM POVERTY.   In the 2002 American best-seller *Fast Food Nation,* Eric Schlosser documented the poverty experienced by most fast-food workers in the United States, especially if they are immigrant people. These people are often abused verbally and underestimated due to their limited English skills. Yet in order to keep prices low for customers and profits high for corporate shareholders, fast-food stores are intentionally designed to need little or no training of workers and to maintain low wages with no benefits by having a high turnover of employees. These fast-food workers are like the cheated poor of Amos's day, and we are the ones profiting from their impoverishment.

EMPOWERING THE POOR.   In *Leading the Church While Taking Care of Yourself,* Norman Shawchuck and Roger Heuser tell the story of WhaJa Hwang and her ministry to the poorest of the working poor in industrial areas of Korea. This Presbyterian laywoman worked with the poor and with manufacturers to create buying cooperatives. The products, such as laundry soap, most needed by the poor could be bought in price-reduced bulk amounts and distributed at discounted prices to poor individuals. As each cooperative matured, WhaJa Hwang repeatedly stepped aside and allowed the recipients of the cooperative to manage and grow that cooperative. Many of these people became open to the gospel of Jesus through this creative ministry of WhaJa Hwang.

SERMON SUGGESTION

Topic: Hospitality Rewarded
TEXT: 2 Kings 4:8–17; Heb. 13:2
(1) The story of the Shunammite woman. (2) The lesson: unexpected blessing may come to those who befriend and encourage God's servants.

Topic: Then, Now, and Hereafter
TEXT: Col. 1:21–29
(1) What we were (v. 21). (2) What we are (v. 22). (3) What we must do (v. 23). (4) What we can look forward to (vv. 24–27). (5) What helps us on the way (vv. 28–29).

WORSHIP AIDS

CALL TO WORSHIP.   "I will praise you forever for what you have done; in your name I will hope, for your name is good. I will praise you in the presence of your saints" (Ps. 52:9 NIV).

INVOCATION.   Gathered before you this morning, Father, we wait for the opportunity to encounter you in all the ways you come seeking souls. Each person brings separate circumstances to this hour for your consideration. All of us bring the need for divine intervention in our lives as we try to understand and manage the events surrounding us. Our wisdom is so meager. Our knowledge, even at its best, is so small. Our abilities to function in our own strength and foresight are far too insignificant. We know that without you we will fall and fail and flounder. So today, meet us in this sacred place, we pray, and lead us to do your will in all things, even as was done for those first followers whom Christ taught to pray [the Lord's Prayer].—Henry Fields

OFFERTORY SENTENCE.   "So now, since we have been made right in God's sight by faith in his promises, we can have real peace with him because of what Jesus Christ our Lord has done for us. For because of our faith, he has brought us into this place of highest privilege where we now stand, and we confidently and joyfully look forward to actually becoming all that God has had in mind for us to be" (Rom. 5:1–2 *Living Bible*).

OFFERTORY PRAYER.   Gracious Lord, we would yield ourselves to you to become good stewards of all that you have given to us, things both material and spiritual. As we give, bless us, we pray, and bless those whose lives are enriched by gifts greater than money.

PRAYER.   Eternal Father, because our Lord lives today, we live. But some of us have not felt the lifting power of that truth. We go about as those who know that our Lord was crucified, but hardly knowing that he was raised from the dead. We have been told that thou hast caused us to sit together in heavenly places with him, yet the sights and sounds and smells of Earth are still too much with us. May we hear in thy Word the trumpet blast of victory and rise with confidence, wide awake to what we are and what we should be doing. Help us to live on this Earth as those whose citizenship is in heaven but who are eager to bring the life of heaven to this Earth. Grant strength to those sorely tempted every day to live as if this world were all. Grant concern and tact to those who see others tempted and wish to help. And give us all knowledge of thy comradeship with us in our pilgrimage.

SERMON
Topic: A Child of God—Ishmael
TEXT: Gen. 16:1–10, 21:14–21

It was long ago and far away. The man would not come to church, especially not to worship. His wife was active in the congregation. He occasionally dropped by my office to talk. He was a public school teacher, very intelligent, a gentle soul with a deep sense of compassion and a special place in his heart for neglected children. On his first visit he apologized profusely for his absence from church and for taking my time. He did not presume to have any right to enter the building, much less to speak with the pastor. On the first visit, he told me he suffered from chronic depression and needed a minister with whom he could talk. He could not sit through a worship service without being overwhelmed by guilt. I secretly wondered what horrible deed this man had committed and kept waiting for a confession of some repugnant behavior, bracing against overreaction and shock. The horrible confession never came, and eventually I realized that this man could never hurt a flea. I kept trying to reassure him of God's forgiving grace. Intellectually he had no doubt that Jesus came to take away our sin, but emotionally and spiritually he never felt clean or worthy of God's love.

Reciting creeds and confessing sin were not the answer to this man's anxiety. The problem was not theological. He needed to talk and to be accepted by someone he identified with God's presence. He had been in therapy for years without any significant change. Medications relieved anxiety but did not alter his distorted sense of personal value.

I came to realize the legitimate priesthood in the work of ministry. I wished for the authority to send the man out to do some work of atonement and to pronounce absolution to set him free from his guilt, but nothing I said or did seemed to make any real difference. I learned of the man's death a few years ago and wished for him the peace he could never seem to find in life. Although my glimpse into his personal hell never seemed to help him, it was a gift to my understanding and compassion as a pastor. One day he told me about growing up on a farm with an abusive father. He was often beaten for some minor infraction of household rules. Children in his home were little more than farm animals. He was constantly beaten down and berated for being lazy or stupid. In his entire childhood he remembered only one word of affirmation from his father. He was ordered to dig a new latrine for the outhouse. His father growled a backhanded compliment that his work was better than usual.

Marian Wright-Edelman observed the cause for the defense of children in this world: this morning 100,000 children woke up homeless. In the time it took to pray the Lord's Prayer, an American baby was born into poverty. Before the end of a fourteen-minute sermon, a baby will die. Every minute, a baby is born to a teenage mother, and before we go to bed tonight a child will be murdered in our nation. Jesus seemed to be aware that the evil of this world can be prevented as well as forgiven.

I. *We are bending twigs.* I have a vivid memory of an oak tree in the yard beside a house on my walk to school as a child. Oak trees usually reach for the sky and provide shelter and shade for everything and everyone that has to cling to the ground. This tree was different. The trunk was parallel to the ground and the limbs were all on one side. More than once my friends and I stopped to climb the trunk and to mock the tree for its failure to stand upright. Recently, on a visit back home, I drove by to see if the tree was still there. It was gone, and I am left to wonder if it was real or imagined. That tree has stuck in my memory as an example of what happens to children when we bend them to the ground in their tender and innocent years.

The story of Ishmael is an offense to our spiritual sensitivity. We tend to write it off as a reflection of the ancient Near Eastern culture rather than an example of how we should treat our children. The patriarchal possession of concubines as well as the practice of polygamy are hard to reconcile with our current concept of Christian family and the critical importance of fidelity in marriage. The only good part of the story is the honesty. I never cease to be amazed at the biblical revelation of human warts even in spiritual heroes like Abraham. Furthermore, the tendency to attribute all human decisions and behaviors with the direct will and command of God raises serious questions about the moral authority of the God who commands holiness of life and love for one another.

The story appears to begin as a human solution to a divine problem. In the Covenant from God, Abraham and Sarah were promised a child—a double miracle. Not only were they far past the age of bringing children into the world, but Sarah had been stigmatized as sterile. In frustration, she invited Abraham to father a child by her slave girl Hagar. When Hagar conceived, Sarah reconsidered her generosity and demanded that Abraham send the unwanted woman and her unwanted child away. To Abraham's discredit, in spite of his expressed love for Ishmael, the patriarch of three of the world's religions sent the slave girl and her son into the desert alone, with nothing but a little bread and a skin of water.

More than one observer in this global climate of religious war has observed that this story identifies the point of departure for Judaism and Islam. The blessing (or curse) surrounded

Ishmael—"He shall be a wild ass of a man, with his hand against everyone, and he will live in hostility toward all his brothers" (Gen. 16:12)—and appears to have continued to bear fruit in all the generations to follow, including our own.

We have a heavy responsibility for the children of our world, and we reap what we sow in the lives of our children. We can never really measure the extent of harm that is done to the world in the abuse of children like Ishmael. Historians and psychologists have speculated about the beginnings of Adolf Hitler, Osama bin Laden, or Saddam Hussein. Even the Old Testament qualifies the maxim: "The fathers have eaten sour grapes, and the children's teeth are set on edge." Of course, all children are eventually responsible for their own decisions in life; but we cannot escape our community responsibility and the calling of the family of God to bend the twigs in the right direction.

II. *Suffer the child.* Behavioral psychologist B. F. Skinner thought he had the answer. He believed that all at-risk children should be put in group homes where the environment is carefully controlled. Jesus had a better response. He called his community of faith to welcome the children. I've always had a problem with the King James English in the story of Jesus with the children. Jesus commanded his disciples to let the children come to him, to "suffer the little children." I recall a few encounters with parents in which I was the "suffering" child. The archaic English may be more descriptive than originally intended. Jesus warned that it would be better to be cast into the sea tied to a millstone than to harm a child. If you welcome the child, you welcome Christ. Spiritually, he identified the Kingdom of God with the innocence and openness of children.

Marilyn was a young mother of five children in our church. She had a lovely voice for singing and was always in the middle of every church activity. One day she shared her story with the rest of us. As a child, her home was a tent on the edge of town. Her family was known as "poor white trash." She recalled thinking as a preschool child how she might end the misery of life by running in front of a car. Someone in that Alabama town invited her and her siblings to vacation Bible school and started her on a journey toward hope.

In spite of the rejection of Abraham and Sarah, God blessed Ishmael. To the credit of the Hebrew Scriptures, the promise given to Abraham and Isaac was also the blessing of God on Ishmael. In the eyes of God there are no illegitimate children—only children of God, adopted by divine grace.—Larry Dipboye

SUNDAY, JULY 25, 2004

Lectionary Message

Topic: The Three Little Sermons of Hosea

TEXT: Hos. 1:2–10

Other Readings: Ps. 85; Col. 2:6–15 (16–19); Luke 11:1–13

God is in the salvage business and business is good. The world is full of wrecked lives, families, communities, and nations. This Kingdom business has always been good, so God has always recruited and sent out first-rate coworkers. So desperate was the salvage work in eighth-century Palestine, that God sent out a famous crew we now call the Minor Prophets. Among these was a man named "salvation," or "Hosea" in Hebrew. Hosea began his salvage service in northern Palestine among the ten northern tribes in about 750 B.C. Hosea became identified with God's salvage mission to Palestine when God sent him some words to share.

I. *For effective mission, God requires willing men and women.* As prayer specialist E. M. Bounds once asserted, "Men are his method," and women are his way. God makes a new servant when he reveals himself verbally to faithful people. He drops his words onto these word-bearers and their task becomes to drop his words on others. Prophets and witnesses are heaven's mail carriers, and obedience at all levels, or any level, opens us to the fullness of servanthood.

Hosea became that servant and became a method God used to reach out to the northern Israelis. Redemption and restoration are at the core of the gospel mission. The people of northern Israel needed help to find their way back into covenant with God. Hosea was called to become their understandable messenger from heaven.

II. *Effective mission requires close identification with the receptors.* When theologians state that "God the Son, the Word of God, became incarnate," what they mean is that God took on skin to identify closely with us and to make his salvage plan effective. The sacrifices of identification usually feel like "downward mobility," just like God the Son was downwardly mobile in taking on "the form of a servant and was made into the likeness of humanity" (Phil. 2:7). Hosea identified with his people by taking a wife as they did. He married Gomer, "a woman of adultery." While biblical scholars are divided on the exact meaning of the text about Gomer's being a "woman of adultery," all agree that it means that just as God was in love with an unfaithful Israel and desperate to restore her, so Hosea married an unfaithful wife and was to love her into restoration. Hosea identified with her culture, but without compromising his message. He married Gomer with full Mosaic vows, instead of merely frequenting her services at the local Baal worship center and brothel.

III. *For mission to be effective, the message must be clear and uncompromising.* Hosea's gospel message conveyed the tension of judgment and hope. Our gospel message of the Savior must have this same authentic tension. Hosea's message communicated this tension in three sermons. He made these sermons personal and memorable by naming one of his children after each sermon. His children became his three "little sermons."

(a) Sermon 1. "A son!": *Acknowledge your Jezreels.* Hosea named his firstborn *Jezreel,* after the name of the location of the holy blood bath that Jehu had committed against the house of King Ahab. Jezreel stood for five Jehu-ordered operations resulting in at least several hundred killings (2 Kings 9–11). Those murders set Israel on a friendless path to shrinking land and increasing foreign debt payments. Jezreel was the terrible secret no one in Israel could talk about. But if sins are kept secret, those sins will make one's family sick, and God will make the secrets public. God called Hosea to speak the unspeakable so that sins could be acknowledged, restitutions made, and the community healed. All peoples have their My Lai Massacre, their Wounded Knee, their Auschwitz, or their "comfort women" episode. But these failures will never be atoned for until they are confessed. Jezreel means that God holds individuals and nations accountable—restitution must be made. There is more music to face after we sing "Just as I am." Forgiveness requires restitution as far as is possible and constructive.

(b) Sermon 2. "A daughter!": *Expect just desserts.* Hosea named his second child and sermon *Lo-Ruhamah,* which means "no affection." This middle child–daughter sermon means that real love requires discipline. Whoever Yahweh loves, Yahweh disciplines. Love without discipline is sentimentality at best and corruption at worst. Upon disciplining a beloved daughter, many a parent has heard the words, "I like Grandma better than you; she loves me all the time." Remember that God always preserves or reserves a remnant whenever he disciplines and judges. So look for hope in the midst of judgment.

(c) Sermon 3. "A second son!": *Practice reciprocity in all your relationships.* Hosea named his third child and sermon *Lo-Ammi,* which means "not my people." If we will not act as if we are God's people by how we live our lives, then God will not act in history as if we are his people. God owns us as we own him. "For he who honors me, I will honor" (1 Sam. 2:30). Remember, if we are fruitful in bearing or in receiving the bad news, then we will be given good news. God never judges without holding out hope. After all, God is in the salvage business. He loves welcome-home parties with overflowing cups and fatted-calf barbecues.

IV. *Conclusion.* For the Israel of Hosea's day, the calendar of accountability was counting down. Hosea prophesied during the first half of the eighth century before Christ. Within a decade or so of his death, death also came in his nation. In 721 A.D., the Assyrian army crushed Israel, dismantled it, and distributed its inhabitants as scrap throughout the Assyrian empire. In truth, some of us are living by that same calendar today. Either we are sliding down to destruction by increasingly sinful patterns, attitudes, and appetites, or destruction has already come and we sit now looking down at shattered careers, callings, marriages, and families. If the former experience is yours, Jesus is your Hosea. He can save and restore you, if you will fully acknowledge your need for him and his cross. If you will give yourself to him and learn of him, he will lead you in the restoring paths of righteousness.

If the latter experience of destruction is yours, Jesus is your Hosea, too. Give him the pieces of your life. God is in the salvage business. He is able to save. Look around you: any number of people in this church are demonstrations that what all the king's horses and all the king's men could not do, God in Jesus can. Not only did Jesus die to answer for your sin, but he also rose on the third day to give you newness of life, as the Pauline baptismal verse says. But Paul also informed us that Jesus will restore only those who fully surrender to him and his Hosea path of restoration. Will you make Jesus your Lord and Savior by walking in the Hosea path of restoration?

This salvage business of heaven is labor intensive and requires many workers to effect its harvest. The work can be heartbreaking when it fails, but it is heartmaking when it restores a lost man or woman to the covenant community. For those of us who have experienced and are experiencing his restoration, shall we not join Hosea's company and "be merciful to those who doubt; snatch others from the fire and save them; to others show mercy mixed with fear—hating even the clothing stained with corrupted flesh"? (Jude 22–23 NIV).—Rodrick K. Durst

ILLUSTRATIONS

ON ALERT.   All commercial pilots train to avoid a phenomenon called the "chain of errors." Whenever a U.S. jetliner goes down, the Federal Aviation Administration sends an investigation team. Inevitably the crash report shows that the cause for the crash was an unbroken chain of errors, and that if just one of those errors had been avoided, the chain would have been broken and the crash would have been avoided or the loss at least greatly lessened. The words God gave to Hosea and the words God gives to us are cockpit warning lights urging us to break our chain of errors and return to his flight pattern for our lives.

RESTORATION.   By age thirty-nine, Charles Colson was special counsel to the forty-fifth president of the United States. He relished his reputation as the toughest man on the White

House team. But then some of his operators were caught breaking into the Democratic Party's offices in the Watergate towers. Colson's president had to resign in disgrace from office, and Colson himself ended up pleading guilty to obstruction of justice. He was sentenced to Maxwell Federal Prison in Georgia in 1974. He found himself facing a shattered reputation and career. In the midst of his personal humiliation and public scorn, a friend shared of the newness of life that the friend had found in Christ. Later that night in his own car, Colson prayed to God, "Please take me. Take me just as I am." Colson's newfound peace stayed with him as he entered prison. There he prayed often with two redeemed drug dealers, a car thief, and a stock fraud criminal. Jesus restored Colson and gave him a mission. Today he leads the Prison Fellowship Ministry, which counsels in four hundred U.S. prisons, and he is one of the more respected voices in American evangelical circles. If Jesus is able to restore the Colsons of this world, what could he do with your life if only you would turn it over to him?

SERMON SUGGESTIONS

Topic: God's Providence at Work
TEXT: 2 Kings 5:1–5ab
(1) To guide the destiny of an alien nation (v. 1). (2) To overrule an illness to bring knowledge of God to Naaman (v. 2). (3) To use an ordinary servant girl to accomplish his purpose (vv. 3–5ab).

Topic: Christ Is Our All
TEXT: Col. 2:6–15
(1) In our living (vv. 6–7). (2) In our thinking (v. 8). (3) In our participation in the cosmos (vv. 9–10). (4) In our freedom from sin (vv. 11–15).

WORSHIP AIDS

CALL TO WORSHIP.   "I will listen to what God the Lord will say; he promises peace to his people, his saints—but let them not return to folly. Surely his salvation is near those who fear him, that his glory may dwell in our land" (Ps. 85:8–9 NIV).

INVOCATION.   Thou hast called us into thy presence, O God. Give us then light for our darkness and strength for every high purpose wherein we are weak; bringing us to do all that we do in quiet confidence, undisturbed, forever sure that thou wilt guide our steps and hold our feet from falling.—Paul Scherer

OFFERTORY SENTENCE.   "We are ruled by the love of Christ, now that we recognize that one man died for everyone, which means they all share in his death. He died for all, so that those who live should no longer live for themselves, but only for him who died and was raised to life for their sake" (2 Cor. 5:14–15 TEV).

OFFERTORY PRAYER.   You gave us the dearest and best you had to give, Father. We tend to bring to you the leftovers rather than the first fruits you should have. Lead us outside our smallness into your greatness, that we may give as you have given, we pray in Jesus' name.—Henry Fields

PRAYER.   Clear our vision this morning, Father, we pray. We are so blinded by what is visible around us that we fail to see the things of the Spirit that make the large difference in who we become, how we live, what we do, and where we eventuate as we travel this journey of life. As we experience the meaning of the sacrifice of the Lord this morning, we need to be able to see beyond the darkness of what is material into that which is luminously spiritual. All about us are barriers that prohibit our view of the wide vistas you desire us to see. Enable us this morning to get beyond those barriers, that we may envision what is real and eternal.

SERMON
Topic: The Divine Spark
TEXT: Acts 2:1–21

Several years ago, Nan Robertson wrote in the *New York Times* about a new "touch and see" nature trail at the National Arboretum. Her article focused on three teenagers who followed the trail and experienced it with a rare kind of sensitivity. They embraced the trunks of the trees to feel their mightiness and their great age. They gathered branches, snipped bunches of leaves, listened to the crackle of twigs under their feet and ran their fingers delicately over the bark of fallen logs. They perceived the density of the forest and the openness of the meadow beyond. Their senses filled them with awe and amazement.

These three young people—touching, feeling, sensing—found the experience "unbelievable" and were filled with wonder and appreciation. They were also blind.

Another blind person, Helen Keller, once said, "I believe that life is given to us so that we may grow in love. And I believe that God is in me, as the sun is in the color and fragrance of a flower—the light in my darkness, the voice in my silence."

Such people, whom we generally call "challenged," often develop sharper, keener, and deeper sensitivities than the rest of us. Because of a particular loss—sight, hearing, or whatever—they compensate by refining other senses to greater degrees. Helen Keller sensed, in an extraordinary way, the divine touch within her own life, believing deeply that God was within her. We come to this sanctuary week after week, hoping somehow to touch, to sense the Spirit of God, to get in touch with a word, an idea, or feeling that may bring inspiration or challenge or renewed commitment. I think that all of us, in some way, yearn for what we may call "the touch that gives life," or the "divine spark."

Many people look back on Michelangelo as the greatest artistic genius who ever lived. He left imperishable work in sculpture, painting, architecture, and poetry. In the "Creation of Adam" in his Sistine Chapel paintings, he has beautifully suggested the act of creation. And underlying the painting is the reverence and awe in which he held his subject. Adam lies elegant and athletically powerful, a heroic person in the "image of God," slowly stirring into life, arm reaching out toward his creator. God, borne by a group of angels and with the image of Eve tucked under his left arm, is all powerful. God's majestic body drifts easily within the dark swirl of his cloak, and he leans deliberately toward Adam's outstretched arm. Their fingers almost touch in what is one of the most evocative images of all time. The minute space between their fingers is suggestive of the first spark of life that jumps from one to the other. It is electric, powerful, dramatic. There is in that painting, powerfully portrayed for each beholder, the touch that gives life.

The spark that Adam is about to receive is the spark of spiritual awareness, of enormous vitality, of incredible potential, the image of God. And that divine spark is the potential within every child of God—from the infants we touch in baptism to the eldest among us.

What a precious gift—our humanity, our personhood, that indestructible spirit that, when tapped, affirmed, and developed, frees us from fear and timidity, to touch life again—to touch life at many points. The gift of the Holy Spirit is given. That's fantastic, exciting. But the possibilities of that gift are not forced upon us by a manipulating God. We are not coerced to develop and enhance our possibilities. This means that in order to *keep* in touch we have to *reach* out.

Adam is not simply lying inert and lifeless. His arm stretches toward the source of power. His fingers reach for the hand of his creator. That says to me that I need to be receptive, that I must open myself to the experiences that may touch my life with growth and that will fan into flame that divine spark. The initial spark is given—my life, my being, my individuality, my potential. Knowing that there is a welcoming, loving source of empowering energy—God the Creator and Sustainer—I can be encouraged to stretch out my own life, mind, heart, and soul to touch anew that powerful source. And I am able to discover the settings in which such inner resources can be brought to greater life.

Each of us can do that. We can all open ourselves to the experiences that renew the touch, the connection.

For many people there are great possibilities in worship—in the quietness and yearning of prayer, in the moments of communion, in the sudden flashes of new awareness and fresh ideas.

For others there are possibilities in the arts—in a new and deeper appreciation of a great cantata or symphony, in a fresh new look at a Michelangelo or Picasso, in a poetic verse that nurtures the moment by expressing the inexpressible, capturing your own feelings.

There are enormous possibilities in people, in moments that come to life, when a shared understanding flows between those who have really listened, not just with their ears but with all their senses—in a moment when the touch barrier is shattered and you reach out to embrace another; in a moment when you risk yourself in honest sharing and a new level of intimacy is experienced. I'm sure that each of you can make your own list of the settings in which you can get in touch.

For the church—the company of covenant people—there is a further dimension. As we experience the touch that gives life, we are commissioned to share that touch with others. I am reminded of a little parable that emphasizes this for us. The man who wrote the parable spoke of feeling like a frog. Have you ever felt like a frog? The frog feeling comes when you want to be bright but feel dull, when you want to share but are selfish, when you want to be thankful but feel resentful, when you want to be big but feel small, when you want to care but are indifferent. Then he used a familiar, airy tale about a frog who wasn't really a frog but was a prince who looked and felt like a frog because a wicked witch had cast a spell on him. Only the kiss of a beautiful maiden could save him, and that seemed unlikely. Where do you find gorgeous women who want to kiss frogs?

But miracles do happen. One day a beautiful maiden grabbed him up and gave him a big kiss, and then—zap—there he was, a handsome prince. And you know the rest—they lived happily ever after!

Now what is the observation for the church? To kiss frogs, of course. Much of the world around us appears froglike. The media are filled with the difficulties and brokenness that perplex our society, and people experience so many levels of hurt and pain. And a part of our touching, our mission as disciples of Jesus, our ministry as a covenant congregation, is to reach out, to touch, to "kiss frogs," bringing a message of hope and reconciliation and healing.

To do so, we need to make commitments to life's healing processes. Life takes on deeper meaning as we become makers of promises. For then we are in touch with convictions, with trusting relationships, with covenants that bring us together.

Commitment is a key word in our religious faith, for the faith itself urges us to a responsible commitment, which is to see in Christianity a way, a style of living that reflects the model we see in Jesus. Listen to these words: "In Christianity, stripped of its . . . additions, subtractions and divisions, Christianity as Jesus taught it, is the cure for all the social ills of humanity." Do you know who said that? It wasn't a Christian minister—an idealistic, dreaming "pulpiteer." It was Albert Einstein. "Christianity as Jesus taught it"—living by loving, by serving, by making your life count.

What is required of us is that we should seek to fulfill the condition of the Spirit's coming by doing our work as well as we can, hoping that the creative Spirit will take our best work and dwell in it and elevate it above anything we could accomplish. We cannot predict, or command, or contrive the Spirit's coming. If mysteriously and by its own good pleasure the Spirit comes to dwell in our house, it will give us what we could not have produced without it. Said Hemingway, "Most of the time I write as well as I can; occasionally I write better." There is a power that is not in us but that may come *through* us, and it is inexhaustible.

Perhaps, at least partially, that's what our hope and faith are about. As we face the distress among the nations, the signs of catastrophe, and our own confusions and fears about the future, "Let us be found going beyond ourselves"—living as men and women responsible in love for the continuing construction of the human community, using our imaginations to create avenues of service to others and to God, for our promises and commitments can only live in the inexhaustible spirit of God.—Robert Langwig

SUNDAY, AUGUST 1, 2004
Lectionary Message

Topic: Take Me Higher
TEXT: Col. 3:1–11 (12–17)
Other Readings: Hos. 11:1–11; Ps. 107:1–9, 43; Luke 12:13–21

The music is very different, but the dream is the same. Rock singer Scott Stapp of Creed thrills the audience of thousands when he sings:

> Can you take me higher?
> To the place where blind men see?
> Can you take me higher?
> To the place with golden streets?
> Let's make our escape.
> Come on, let's go there.
> Let's ask, can we stay?

Up high I feel like I'm alive for the very first time
Up high I'm strong enough to take
These dreams and make them mine.

The same sentiment comes from the old hymn as the congregation sings:

Lord, lift me up and let me stand,
By faith, on heaven's tableland,
A higher plane than I have found:
Lord plant my feet on higher ground.

We want to move to a higher level of living. How do we get there? These words from Colossians encourage us to "set [our] minds on things that are above." How does that really work?

I. *Put away.* If we are ever going to really soar in life, we must first put away those things that will hinder our flight. Paul lists two kinds of weights that will keep us from going higher.

(a) *Sins of the flesh.* These "earthly" sins are the kind in which people are used as objects to possess. Verse 5 contains the list: fornication, impurity, passion, evil desire, and greed (which is idolatry). The temptation is great to think that any one of the items on this list will take us higher. We are constantly bombarded with messages from our culture that teach us to live the "good life" with all the gusto we can. While there may be momentary pleasure in this list, eventually the thrill fades and we are left with an empty feeling. The world is full of stories of people who flew high as a kite only to come crashing down to the ground.

(b) *Sins of the Spirit.* Verse 8 contains a list of sins in which people are used as objects to destroy. These sins are attempts to rise high by keeping everyone else low. "Anger, wrath, malice, slander, and abusive language from your mouth" and lying are ways that we seek to bring someone else down so we can feel more important. You know how it works: when I do not get a promotion, I start to criticize the performance of the person who did. When I do not get a good grade on a test, I talk about how ugly the girl is who earned an A. Such "abusive language from your mouth" may make you feel good for a while, but you will never really get higher in life with that kind of attitude.

II. *Put on.* If we really want to go higher in life we need to do more than just put off the sins of the flesh and the spirit. Paul writes on to say that we "set our minds on things that are above" by putting on the character of Christ. "Clothe yourselves with compassion, kindness, humility, meekness, and patience. Bear with one another and, if anyone has a complaint against another, forgive each other; just as the Lord has forgiven you, so you also must forgive. Above all, clothe yourselves with love, which binds everything together in perfect harmony" (vv. 12–14). Each one of these words describes the character of Jesus. We put on Christ, and he takes us higher.

Perhaps the great hymn of Philippians 2:5–11 will help us understand. Paul encourages us to "let the same mind be in you that was in Christ Jesus." That is how we "set our minds on things that are above." We begin to take on the "mind of Christ." Through his own obedience, humility, and death on the cross he demonstrated every one of the qualities mentioned in Colossians 3:12–14. Then the climax of the Philippians passage tells us, "Therefore God also highly exalted him and gave him the name that is above every name." You can't get any higher than that!

Do you want to go higher in life? Whether the music of a rock group or an old hymn is the song of your heart, we all want to move to a higher level of living. When we "put on Christ" we rise high with him. We begin to live out the character of Christ. Life is lived on a higher plane. Have you discovered the difference?

Set your mind on Christ—and soar!—David W. Hull

ILLUSTRATIONS

SOARING.   In the year 1886 an eccentric inventor in Denver, Colorado, tried to fly. Known as the "Ornithopter Man," he used chicken feathers to make for himself a set of wings. His plan was to leap from the roof of his barn and fly. A large crowd gathered to watch as he failed to fly and instead fell into the hog pen and broke his leg. Interviewed by the press after his fall, he declared, "I made a big mistake. I should have gotten my feathers from eagles instead of chickens." If you really want to go higher in life, be careful what you use to get there.[1]

CRITICS.   A young musician's concert was poorly received by critics. The famous Finnish composer Jean Sibelius consoled the artist with a pat on the shoulder and the words, "Remember, Son, there is no city in the world where they have erected a statue to a critic."

SERMON SUGGESTIONS

Topic: When a Prophet Is More Than a Prophet
TEXT: 2 Kings 13:14–20a
The prophet, representing God, signifies forces more powerful than military might (v. 14b). Putting this truth under the Lordship of Christ, we know that (1) God may delay his action, but he will act at the proper time; (2) God may appear to be defeated, but he can win even by a cross; and (3) therefore, God can be utterly trusted, both in life and in death.

Topic: Living in a New and Different World
TEXT: Col. 3:1–11
(1) We seek a higher and better life. (2) We enjoy complete security in Christ. (3) We anticipate a glorious life with Christ hereafter (compare 1 John 3:2).

WORSHIP AIDS

CALL TO WORSHIP.   "So they cried to the Lord in their trouble, and he saved them from their distress; . . . Let them give thanks to the Lord for his love and for the marvelous things he has done for mankind" (Ps. 107:19, 21 REB).

INVOCATION.   Lord, cause us to withdraw from the world and draw nearer to the heart of God in our worship today. Turn us from all that would turn us from you, and feed us with the bread of life, through Christ our savior.—E. Lee Phillips

---

[1]Claude Broach, *Waiting for the Wind.*

OFFERTORY SENTENCE.   "Every good gift and every perfect gift is from above, and cometh down from the Father of lights, with whom is no variableness, neither shadow or turning" (James 1:17).

OFFERTORY PRAYER.   We acknowledge, O God, that every good thing that comes to us is ours through your providence. Grant us grace to let some of those good things that we enjoy be experienced by others as we are good stewards of your blessings.

PRAYER.   We thank thee, O God, for all the people in our lives through whom thy power and love and strength have come to us; open our eyes to the fact that when we need help there is always help available; take away our pride and our suspicions and our fears until we stand before thee in all our naked reality, waiting only upon thee, knowing that in some human shape our help will finally come to us, through Jesus Christ our Lord.—Theodore Parker Ferris

SERMON
Topic: Sword, Not Peach
TEXT: Matt. 10:34

Jesus seems to understand that his mission is something like the bow of a boat. As it pushes forward, it forces the water in front of it to one side or the other. Confronted with the question of Jesus and his Kingdom, we have to take sides, and with the stakes and issues involved, we end up in disagreement, controversy, and conflict. "I have come to bring not peace but a sword." The presence of light in the world disturbs those who like to live in the dark.

Maybe you understand why it happens. I just know that in my fraternity at Davidson almost forty years ago, there was a freshman who did not drink beer or other alcohol. As far as I know, I never heard him make a big deal about it. He never tried to make any of the parties alcohol free. He never made fun of the drunken escapades of the brothers. He was willing to be the designated driver for anyone who asked him. But there was just something about this sober, nondrinking presence in the midst of those alcohol flowing parties that just bothered the brothers something fierce. They bullied him and teased him, tormented him and tried to put alcohol in his drinks, and called him names. The presence of a sober person in the midst of their drinking caused hostility and conflict. Jesus says the Kingdom of God comes to bring the blessings of God, but it always comes first with division, conflict, and controversy.

"A student can never expect any better than the teacher gets. A servant will not be given better status than the master." These were Jesus' words to his disciples as he was talking to them about their mission into the world. They were to go into the world two by two to share the good news that God's love is for both the Gentiles and the Jews, that God's love is for those who need it rather than for those who earn it, that God's love is seen in the person of Jesus Christ, not in the keeping of some set of rules. They were to go and remember that they would not be any better received, any better treated, any better welcomed than Jesus was. Jesus came to bring light that disturbs the darkness. The darkness has flexed its muscle and abused the light. Those who are children of the light will get the same response.

The conflict and controversy come from all around. It will not be easy to know who the children of darkness are. The Rev. David Benke, president of the Lutheran Church Missouri

Synod, joined with religious leaders from around America at Yankee Stadium as part of a civic grieving over the loss of human life in the wake of September 11, 2001. He joined with Jewish, Sikh, Muslim, and Hindu religious leaders. Pastor Benke offered a petitionary prayer in the name of Jesus the Christ. Now Pastor Benke is being charged by other members of the Lutheran Church with participating in a worship service with infidels and pagans and he could be expelled from the Lutheran Church Missouri Synod for his sin.

Jesus knows that those who go forth in his name will meet the same kind of resistance, attacks, and opposition that he encountered. The students will not be treated better than the teacher. Those who go out in Christ's service simply go knowing that there will be flack.

There are three promises given by Jesus to his disciples in the words that follow, all of them given so that the disciples will not be afraid as they go forth. Three times Jesus says to his disciples, "So have no fear, do not be afraid, go forth in confidence. Do not be afraid."

Go forth in confidence. "Do not be afraid, because nothing is covered that will not be revealed. Nothing is hidden that will not be made known." What the disciples have learned from Jesus on the journey and as they have lived with him, what they have been told by Jesus, and what they go forth and preach may sound pretty strange and very controversial. It may sound like the prediction of the sinking of the Titanic before the ship was launched. What the disciples say about grace free from the Torah, what we say about the love of God for all people, what we offer as gift, others will say has always been purchased by works. But do not be afraid, for the Kingdom presses in against history and there will be a full and public revelation that will vindicate the good news. There will be the fall of kingdoms that put their trust in their own power; there will be revolutions so that those who have been rich will become poor; there will be Holocaust ovens, and AIDS, and Enrons; and every time people begin to believe that they are getting better and better in every way by their own efforts, there will be another "ethnic cleansing." Do not be afraid, but go forth and share the good news, because there will be a full and complete revelation that will clearly show, like God's voice in the whirlwind with Job, who has spoken for God aright.

Do not fear those who kill the body but cannot kill the soul. Go forth and share the light and the love of the new Kingdom, and do not fear those who physically attack and batter you. Do not fear, because God's eye is on you, the hairs on your head are counted. God is watching, and God, who has provided all that is needed for the sparrow, cares even more for his children and has provided for their eternal blessing. Do not be afraid for your reputation, because there will be a full disclosure that will show you to have been in God's service and those who opposed you to have worked against the Kingdom. Do not be afraid of those who can hurt your body or even take your life, because God loves you so much more than the sparrow and he has provided so much more for you in his Kingdom.

"Do not be afraid, for everyone who acknowledges me before men on Earth, I will acknowledge before my Father who is in heaven. But whoever denies me before others I also will deny before my Father who is in heaven." Jesus says, " I will know you if you admit to knowing me. I will call your name. I will give you identity. You will be one of mine and I will identify you."

Those who go out in joyful witness to the love of God that has blessed them from their birth will encounter conflict and opposition. It happened to Jesus, and the servant ought not expect to be treated better than the master. But Jesus gives us three promises:

1. Do not be afraid, because all the secret, dirty, selfish, exploitative deals will be exposed and the Kingdom will become visible and your work and witness will be seen in its rightful place. Your witness will be seen as faithfulness to the grace of God.
2. Do not be afraid, for the God who loves the sparrow and who has provided for that sparrow all that it needs for its full life loves you even more and has prepared for you the full joy of the Kingdom.
3. Do not be afraid, for as we go out and acknowledge Jesus in our witness before others, Jesus is helping us to discover our real names and he will call them out and acknowledge us by name and invite us into the glory of his Father.

—Rick Brand

SUNDAY, AUGUST 8, 2004
Lectionary Message

Topic: Find Us Faithful
TEXT: Heb. 11:1–3, 8–16
Other Readings: Isa. 1:1, 10–20; Ps. 50:1–8, 22–23; Luke 12:32–40

The ancient Greeks had a race that added a new challenge to the usual elements of speed and endurance. Each racer carried a lighted torch as he began the race. The runner's goal was not just to cross the finish line first; equally important was the task of keeping his light burning. If the torch went out, he was disqualified.

Faith invites us to run the same kind of race. Our goal is to keep the Light of Christ burning in our lives throughout the race. In the wonderful Hall of Fame of Faith described in Hebrews 11, Abraham and Sarah are examples of faith that keeps the light burning.

I. *Faith looks to the future.* Throughout this great chapter on faith, the emphasis is on the future. Faith looks to God's tomorrow. "Now faith is the assurance of things hoped for, the conviction of things not seen" (v. 1). Even when we do not know exactly what will come in the future, faith is always forward-looking. When Abraham set out on his journey of faith, he headed "to a land I [God] will show you" (Gen. 12:1). No land was in sight when he began the trip. He really did not know where he was going, but the act of faith led him and Sarah into the future. In eager anticipation of God's future, "he looked forward to the city that has foundations, whose architect and builder is God" (v. 10). In fact, most of these great heroes of faith mentioned in Hebrews 11 followed God out of obedience but did not always arrive at their destination (vv. 13–16). Faith is a pilgrimage that keeps moving forward.

Faith is an investment we make now for a return that will come later. This idea goes against our culture's emphasis on instant gratification. We want to live only in the now. "Forget yesterday, don't worry about tomorrow, just enjoy today." In our world of microwaves, e-mails, and cell phones, it is hard to wait for long, much less for tomorrow. Why should we even bother? Because that is what faith calls us to do! Faith is always looking to the future. Faith is always planting seeds that will grow into trees whose shade we will never sit under and enjoy.

II. *Faith remembers the past.* Hebrews 11 was written to help people remember the legacy that had been left from yesterday. Look at how many verses were given to a walk down the memory lane of faith. Stories were told to remind people of what God had done in the past. Memories of what God has already done help us to believe in what God is going to do. They also remind us that we are now enjoying the shade of trees that we did not plant. The faithfulness of earlier generations of our church has made a place for us to worship and fellowship. By remembering their faithfulness, we can be encouraged to be found faithful ourselves.

Faith always looks back to see what God has done in our lives. Sometimes we cannot know that in the present. The struggles of today are so great that we do not see clearly the work of God in our lives. We can only imagine it in the future. The possibilities for tomorrow are only hopes that have not yet matured into reality. Faith is built on sacred memory. Maybe that is why Abraham was able to "set out, not knowing where he was going." He and Sarah remembered what God had done for them in the past, and that allowed them to obey when the call came to move into an unknown future. They "considered him faithful who had promised" (v. 11). Why? Because their memory told them what God had already done in their lives. We remember the movement of God in the past, and that gives us strength for the present and hope for the future.

III. *Faith supports the present.* The word for *assurance* in the first verse is literally "things put under." In other words, it is a word for a foundation that supports a structure. Faith is not just looking to the future or remembering the past; it is also what supports us in the present. Because of what we believe God will do in the future (our "conviction of things not seen") and because of what we remember that God has done in the past, we support our lives on the reality of God who is with us in the present.

The foundation of God gives us power for living today. Can any story be more of an example than the account of Abraham and Sarah? "By faith he received the power of procreation, even though he was too old—and Sarah herself was barren" (v. 11). That same power of God is available to us for the challenges we face today. Are you building your life on that kind of foundation? It is the only way to run the race without your light going out!—David W. Hull

ILLUSTRATIONS

FAITH WORKS!   A man stopped to watch a Little League baseball game. He asked one of the youngsters what the score was. "We're losing 18 to 0," was the answer.

"Well," said the man. "I must say you don't look discouraged."

"Discouraged?" the boy said, puzzled. "Why should we be discouraged? We haven't come to bat yet." Faith looks to the future!—Stan Toler[2]

TIME OUT.   A young boy enjoyed building sand castles at the beach. A problem developed when every day older bullies came along and kicked down his creation. One day, on his way to the beach, the little boy had an idea. He passed by a construction site where he found a concrete block. Placing this block as the foundation, he built his castle once again and waited for the arrival of the bullies. They came, they kicked, and they never bothered him again!

---

[2]*God Has Never Failed Me, but He's Sure Scared Me to Death a Few Times* (Tulsa, Okla.: Honor Books, 1995).

SERMON SUGGESTIONS

Topic: Down at the Potter's House

TEXT: Jer. 18:1–11

(1) *Situation:* God's people are in his hands, to be shaped for a noble and beautiful purpose. (2) *Complication:* However, God's people thwart God's loving purpose by the stubbornness of their hearts. (3) *Resolution:* God's people may be reshaped and made useful by turning from their evil ways and amending their conduct.

Topic: Longing for a Better Country

TEXT: Heb. 11:1–3, 8–19 NEB

(1) By faith giving up familiar and limited horizons. (2) By faith embracing the unseen and unknown as if it were already present.

WORSHIP AIDS

CALL TO WORSHIP.   "The grace of our Lord was poured out on me [Paul] abundantly, along with the faith and love that are in Christ Jesus" (1 Tim. 1:14 NIV).

INVOCATION.   All of us, O Lord, have to confess our unworthiness of your grace, if we are honest. But we worship you with gratitude and new commitment as we experience your mercy that has made us your very own people. Therefore, let us sing with joy and pray with expectation, now and in the days ahead.

OFFERTORY SENTENCE.   "Offer unto God thanksgiving, and pay thy vows unto the most High, and call upon me in the day of trouble: I will deliver thee, and thou shalt glorify me" (Ps. 50:14–15).

OFFERTORY PRAYER.   God of grace, our faithfulness to you transforms every tragedy into triumph. Grant that our gifts shall now extend your mercies to others in their need and deepen our sense of participation in your mighty works in our needy world.

PRAYER.   To whatever thou has called us, O God, and at whatever cost, let it be. Only dost thou lead us, lest we stop anywhere when thou art saying "Come," and by the gift of thyself make us strong; through Jesus Christ, our Lord.—Paul Scherer

SERMON

Topic: The Blight of Backward-Looking

TEXT: Luke 9:62

I remember when I first learned to plow as a child while spending the summer on my grandparents' farm. The first impulse was to look *down:* to avoid rocks and roots, to check the depth of the blade, to watch the earth being broken. The second impulse was to look *back* over my shoulder: to see how far I had come and how well I had done. I quickly learned that the best way to look was straight *ahead* to the end of the row and to head directly for that goal without a glance in any other direction.

For centuries farmers have been seeking to plow a straight furrow. Plowed ground can be a work of art, but it requires total concentration and a sharp focus. Jesus applied this proverbial truth to the work of the Kingdom: you cannot plow a straight row for God if you are forever looking back over your shoulder (Luke 9:62).

I. *The backward look.* But why would some want to turn their head in the opposite direction when a possibility as wonderful as the Kingdom of God was set before them? Jesus answered by providing three examples of would-be disciples who were deflected from their goal by divided loyalty. All three diversions were related to family ties, one of the deepest pulls on the human heart.

The first volunteer mirrored easy optimism, the boundless enthusiasm of a gung-ho disciple (v. 57). But Jesus quickly shattered his brash impulsiveness with the reminder that he would have to forfeit the security of hearth and home in living life with Jesus as a vagabond, even a fugitive and refugee (v. 58). The man was sincere but shallow, his commitment true but thin. He had not counted the cost of a self-denying devotion. So he looked away, trading the Kingdom for a pillow on which to lay his head.

The second recruit heard Jesus' call but related it to conflicting duties at home (v. 59). When he asked for time to tarry until his father was in the grave, Jesus replied that there are always enough of the spiritually dead around with nothing better to do than to bury that which has died (v. 60). A soldier called to battle does not throw down his weapons and begin digging graves as soon as comrades begin dying all around him—and the Kingdom summons is just that urgent. Procrastination cannot be justified because events will not wait even for the Grim Reaper to do his work. The issue is one of defining life's highest priority. To be at one's post even when a father dies is to declare in unmistakable terms where life's deepest loyalties lie. Aging parents are not the only life-and-death issue we face.

The third volunteer (v. 61) wanted to do exactly what Elijah had allowed Elisha to do before leaving home to follow him (1 Kings 19:19–21). But Jesus had just refused in verses 54 to 55 to be a New Elijah (compare 2 Kings 1:10, 12) and now he refused to do it again. A divided mind was not adequate for the challenges that lay ahead. Courtesy had its place, but there was little time to observe social conventions when catastrophe was about to fall. The motto of Jesus as he set out to inaugurate a new age was "Now or never—now forever!"

Lurking in the backward look is always a hint of divided loyalty nicely captured in a story told by Bennett Cerf:

> In Java they tell of a young man who spied a beautiful maiden on the high road and followed her for a mile. Finally she wheeled and demanded, "Why do you dog my footsteps?" "Because," he declared fervently, "you are the loveliest thing I have ever seen, and I have fallen madly in love with you at sight. Be mine!" "But you have merely to look behind you," said the girl, "to see my young sister who is ten times more beautiful than I am." The gallant cavalier turned and saw as ugly a wench as ever drew breath in Java. "What mockery is this?" he demanded of the beautiful girl. "You lied to me!" "So did you," she replied. "If you were so madly in love with me, why did you turn around?"[3]

---

[3]*Pulpit Digest,* Nov.-Dec. 1978, p. 65.

II. *The hand on the plow.* All three sayings of Jesus in response to these would-be disciples are breathtaking in their radicality. They cut like a sword into the heart of the family. They seem to confirm the criticism of Nietzsche that Christianity is a religion for heroes and not ordinary people. But before dismissing these examples as hopelessly extreme, note that discipleship is defined as "following Jesus" (vv. 57, 59, 61) and that Jesus himself first did whatever he demanded of others.

It was Jesus who could not go home again (v. 58) even though his family had implored him to do so (Mark 3:31–35). He did not stay at home until his parents were dead and buried (v. 59), but assigned that responsibility to others (John 19:26). He did not go to Jerusalem with the best wishes of his family (v. 61), but entirely on his own initiative, without their support (John 7:3–9).

Jesus' attitude underlying this relationship to his family is best seen at the beginning of this passage: he "set his face" to go to Jerusalem (Luke 9:51). There was no way he could look back if his face was fixed like a flint (Isa. 50:7). Nothing could turn him back, whether it be the deadly hostility of his enemies or the fearful cowardice of his friends (Mark 10:32). He simply brushed aside every problem, such as the refusal of the Samaritans to provide overnight lodging (vv. 53–56). He was mastered by a magnificent obsession that refused compromise. His final journey to Jerusalem was a study in concentration, in unswerving resolution, in nonnegotiable determination. He had put his hand to the plow and nothing could loosen his grip.

For us, acceptance of Jesus means putting our hand to the plow. It begins with the radical reorientation of life around a future goal. It involves setting forth without delay for a distant horizon. It means living for God's tomorrow rather than for our yesterdays. Commitment alone is not enough, for one can be tenaciously committed to the promised future that is yet to be actualized. When we become Christian, our position may be little changed, but our direction is set facing tomorrow. With the gospel chorus we sing, "I have decided to follow Jesus; no turning back." We literally leave an old world behind, even if our immediate family does not understand, as we journey toward a new world with a new family of faith that shares our awesome dream (Mark 10:28–30).

The great British preacher W. L. Watkinson once took his grandson to the seaside, where they met an old minister very disgruntled with his many infirmities and, to make matters worse, suffering from a slight touch of sunstroke. When they left the grumbling old man, the grandchild turned to Watkinson and said, "Granddad, I hope *you* never suffer from a *sunset.*" That is the watchword of the Kingdom: forward to the sunrise, not backward to the sunset.[4]

III. *Fitness for Kingdom service.* The key demand of our text is not just to be saved but to be "fit," that is, able to function in useful fashion, "fitted to God's work." We are not called to *enjoy* the Kingdom but to *plow* it, to make something *grow.* The farming imagery suggests the familiar parables of sowing and reaping, of getting out a crop.

The negative possibility of being unfit implies a decisive act of judgment. We recall the story of Lot's wife (Gen. 19:15–17, 24–26) that Jesus mentioned with the admonition, "Remember Lot's wife" (Luke 17:28–33). (Albert Brewer shared with me the story of a Sunday school teacher who taught her children how Lot's wife turned into a pillar of salt. "That's nothing," replied a little boy, "my mother looked back while driving this week and turned into a telephone pole!) Jesus' warning does not require an outright rejection of the past. We

---

[4]William Barclay, *The Gospel of Luke*, Daily Study Bible, 2nd ed. (Philadelphia: Westminster Press, 1956), p. 134.

can learn from the past without living in the past. The past is full of familiarity, security, and nostalgia, but it is also full of failure, pride, and fear. Only the future offers a clean slate, the chance to build life afresh around the rule of God's Kingdom.

The harshness of Jesus stands like a hard rock across the path of discipleship. Does he expect too much of us? Does he judge us unfit if we cling to our families, if we cherish our own flesh and blood, if we love hearth and home more than a dangerous trip to Jerusalem? Jewish scholar Claude Montefiore once remarked that these un-Jewish sayings of Jesus produced un-Jewish results. A single-minded devotion to the Kingdom of God leads to spiritual breakthroughs, but a double-minded person receives nothing from the Lord (James 1:8) because of his or her divided loyalties.

Notice that fitness is based not on how talented we are or on how much work we do, but on our unswerving loyalty. The plowman who does not look back is giving the task his best, his all, and that is the only thing Jesus requires: to live for a dream, to press toward a goal, to claim a new future. It is not how far we have already come but where we are heading with all of our hearts that really counts.

Evangelist Sam Jones used to hold "quitting meetings" where people could resolve to quit drinking, quit cussing, quit fighting, or just quit sinning in general. One man caught up in the spirit of the occasion vowed, "I'm going to quit being a quitter!" That is the key to victorious discipleship: instead of forever trying to repair a broken past, resolve to leave it behind, walk away from it, and start claiming the promises of tomorrow rather than burying the mistakes of yesterday.—William E. Hull

SUNDAY, AUGUST 15, 2004
Lectionary Message

Topic: Running with Perseverance
TEXT: Heb. 11:29–12:2
Other Readings: Isa. 5:1–7; Ps. 80:1–2, 8–19; Luke 12:49–56

A scene near the beginning of the movie *Forrest Gump* set the stage for the rest of the story. As a young boy, Forrest had to wear leg braces to help straighten his back. Bullies would pick on him and his friend Jenny. One day Jenny called out, "Run, Forrest, run!" As he hobbled along in his braces trying to escape the bullies, all of a sudden a dramatic scene occurred. His leg braces began to pop off and he built up speed as Jenny shouted words of encouragement in the background. Forrest was off and running for the rest of his life. Maybe this picture from a movie classic will help us interpret these wonderful words from the Bible.

I. *The cheering crowd.* The first word of Hebrews 12 takes us back to the previous chapter. "Therefore" the writer begins. The previous chapter had highlighted the roll call of faith. Now that the history lesson has been given, the reminder comes that we are "surrounded by so great a cloud of witnesses." We have our cheering section of saints who have gone before us and prepared the way. They challenge us to be faithful as we run the race of faith. We are not alone as we seek to serve Christ.

Our cheering section may be the heroes of the Bible or the Christian church, or it may be made up of family, friends, and church members who helped to shape our faith. We can see their faces and hear their voices. They cheer for us and surround us. Is not the church to be a place where a "great cloud of witnesses" gathers to cheer and encourage one another in faith? Are you a part of a community that can encourage you in your spiritual formation? Are you one who is cheering for the faith development of someone else? We run best when someone is cheering for us.

II. *The extra baggage.* The only way to run the race with perseverance is to turn loose some of the extra baggage we carry in life. Notice that this extra baggage has two parts to it. We are to "lay aside every weight and the sin that clings so closely." Obviously sin that clings to us is like having our legs in shackles, which prevent us from running. Through repentance and confession we lay aside the grip of sin and we are set free to run.

We are also to set aside "every weight." This is mentioned separately from sin. This weight is some of the values and priorities we adopt that may not be sin but that keep us from being our very best. For example, in the area of stewardship, we may be hindered by debt from spending that is out of control. Our debt load keeps us from doing what we might want to do in our giving. There are even those times when good things weigh us down and keep us from running the race of faith. Work and family are values we all hold to be dear. However, if they control our lives at the expense of our relationship with Christ, they are braces hindering us from running the race of faith.

III. *The purpose.* Our purpose in the faith is to run for a long time. We are not to be flash-in-the-pan or shooting-star Christians. God wants us for the long haul. The race of faith is entered to be "run with perseverance." Many people get off to a dramatic beginning in their Christian experience. The important question is not how exciting was your beginning as a follower of Jesus, but how faithful is your journey through life?

A second element of our purpose is obedience. Not only are we to persevere as Christians, but we are also called to run "the race that is set before us." Our role is not to design the race-course or to determine its length. Instead, we are to follow the path marked out by our Lord. Imagine a runner who decided where he or she would run during the course of the race. That is grounds for immediate disqualification. Instead, we are to run the race we did not design.

IV. *The goal.* The only way to excel in this race of faith is to keep our eyes on the goal. In a race, the runner often fails by taking his or her eyes off of the finish line. So we fail when we do not fix our eyes on Christ, "looking to Jesus the pioneer and perfecter of our faith." That is really the key to running the long race of faith. We do not play our lives for the adoration of the crowd, but we live with the goal of following Jesus.

Jesus shows us the way in this long race of faith. He persevered and "endured the cross" because he knew of the "joy that was set before him." Rather than playing to the crowd who shamed him on the cross, our Lord was obedient as he followed the race that was set out for him. From his seat at the "right hand of the throne of God" he beckons us to follow and run the same race.—David W. Hull

ILLUSTRATIONS
THE REAL GOAL.   "A friend of mine described a colleague as great at running the 'ninety-five-yard dash.' That is a distinction I can do without. Lacking the last five yards makes the first ninety-five pointless."—Max DePree[5]

---

[5]*Leadership Is an Art* (New York: Dell, 1989).

TRIUMPH.   At the 1992 Olympics in Barcelona, Spain, the cheering section of the great cloud of witnesses made all the difference in finishing the race. As the gun sounded for the four-hundred-meter run, Great Britain's Derek Redmond had great hopes of winning the gold medal. But as he entered the backstretch, Redmond fell to the track due to a torn hamstring. By an act of sheer will, he struggled to his feet and began hopping toward the finish line.

Suddenly Derek's father jumped out of the stands and past a security guard. He threw his arms around his son. In a voice choked with emotion, he whispered, "Come on, Son, let's finish this together." The crowd cheered and wept as they watched the father half-carrying his wounded son down the stretch and across the finish line.

SERMON SUGGESTIONS

Topic: The Time Test for Prophets
TEXT: Jer. 28:1–9
(1) All of us are eager for good news in troubled times. (2) But "prophets" too eager to please may give false assurances and reckless advice. (3) Therefore, the wisest course is to keep an open mind, a steady heart, and a loyal spirit; and to wait for the outcome of events to prove the truthfulness of the prophet.

Topic: A Study in Contrasts
TEXT: Heb. 12:18–19
(1) We Christians have not come to Mount Sinai with its fearsome judgments. (2) Rather, we have come to Mount Zion, the heavenly Jerusalem, with its incredible grace. (3) Therefore, we respond with grateful obedience and genuine worship.

WORSHIP AIDS
CALL TO WORSHIP.   "Bring us back, Lord God Almighty. Show us your mercy, and we will be saved" (Ps. 80:19 TEV).

INVOCATION.   As we face our many problems and challenges day after day, continue, O God, to bring us back to yourself and your way, that we may enter into new depths of fellowship and joy in your service.

OFFERTORY SENTENCE.   "Bear ye one another's burdens, and so fulfill the law of Christ" (Gal. 6:2).

OFFERTORY PRAYER.   Gracious Lord, help us to understand and feel the reality of Christian love that makes our offering more than a mere ritual. Because of what we do now, may someone's burden be lighter and the work of your Kingdom more effective.

PRAYER.   Make us free, Lord; then shall we be free indeed! Teach us the deep meaning of freedom, that we may experience the wonders of its presence with us throughout the journey of life as we encounter varied situations, conditions, and interchanges along the way.

Lead us to freedom from selfishness, we pray. So much of the trouble we face comes from our individual and collective selfishness. Let a new day dawn in our hearts and lives so we turn our attention from our desires and demands and spend our efforts meeting the greater needs of the world and the closer needs of others, doing so after the fashion of Christ.

Lead us to freedom from prejudice. Remind us that prejudice goes far beyond racial attitudes that see one race and culture as superior to others simply because of the accident of birth. Help us to see that prejudice is a destructive attitude that, unless managed in Christlike fashion, will darken the skies of every relationship and event of which we are a part. Make us open to learning from one another rather than trying to force all others to conform to our taste and attitudes.

Lead us to freedom from possessiveness. Let us hear again the words of the psalmist who has called all your creation to the truth that "we are his people and the sheep of his pasture" and that "you own the cattle on a thousand hills and the wealth in every mine." Enable us to see and understand that what we call ours is simply a gift of trust given by a loving Father to be managed and used by us for his glory and our benefit while we travel through life. Set our eyes on the higher treasures worthy of good stewards of your creation—treasures that set us free to make this a better world for all those around us.

Lead us to freedom, to faith, we pray. Deliver us from being cloned into another's image of what they believe we should be as a special creation of yours. Rather, lead us to the truth that calls us to the highest and noblest characteristics possible for us as individuals who seek to follow Christ and do his will. May our practice of faith not be cramped by legalism, the egos of others, or imagined images we think we should emulate. Indeed, let us be true imitators of Christ as he lives and moves and works in us to bring us to the fullness and glory of true sons and daughters of God.

Lead us to freedom from our sins, O Lord, we pray. They burden us down, force us into pathways that are wrong, stifle our hopes and efforts, and destroy our very souls. This morning, touch each of us with the power of the cross and cleanse us by your Holy Spirit from all unrighteousness, that we may be set free to become all that you have ever intended us to be and desired that we should become. Save us from ourselves and make us completely yours, even now as we wait and worship before you in Jesus' name.—Henry Fields

SERMON
Topic: Courage You Can't Explain
TEXT: Ezek. 37:1–14; Rom. 8:6–11

If you've ever been to the valley of dry bones, you can appreciate Ezekiel's description. It's a low spot, a depression hemmed in on all sides. It's full of bones that once belonged to mothers and fathers and sons and daughters, individuals who laughed and hoped and loved. But now death has taken such a toll that every characteristic that distinguished one person from another has long disappeared. And in case there was any lingering hope that there might be a future for those who had been slain, Ezekiel was led all around them, and after his ghastly tour he assured, "they were very dry." End of story. Time to mourn their death and move on.

God showed Ezekiel that vision of a hopeless valley because God had sent Ezekiel to Israel to proclaim God's Word, and Israel's future looked as promising as the future of those bones. The nation had ceased to exist. It had been conquered by the Babylonian Empire and taken into exile. There was no hope for the Israelites. The glory of Kings David and Solomon was long gone. The people's fate, generation after generation, was to be refugees with no place to call their own, with their destiny in the hands of their captors. Their future was as bleak as that of those modern-day Palestinian suicide bombers who have so little to lose that they blow themselves up so they can become martyrs in their struggle to have a land of their own.

Many of us have visited that valley of dry bones, and you can understand those for whom that valley defines life. After all, it's where we all wind up eventually. We might find some fleeting pleasure on our way there, but the valley is our destination. Macbeth summed it up when he heard of the death of his wife: "Life's but a walking shadow . . . a tale told by an idiot, full of sound and fury signifying nothing." Why should we hope for more in the end? The psalmist even confirms it: "All flesh is grass. The grass withers, the flower fades."

There's logic in living our lives based on what we know about our flesh. It is frail and mortal and destined for the valley, so it makes sense to do everything we can to delay that end and to make sure that the road there is as painless as it can be. We see the way of the flesh in nature. I was sitting at my desk and a movement outside my window caught my attention. It was two bright red cardinals flitting from branch to branch in the tree not ten feet from the desk where I sat writing this sermon. They were fighting, establishing dominance. The stakes were huge: mating rights, territory, food, survival. They fluttered and pecked each other until one of them gave up and flew away. That's the way our flesh protects and provides for itself. Flesh threatens our flesh, so we fight back with the power of the flesh. And the valley grows fuller and fuller. The United States has one of the highest rates of capital punishment in the world. We employ the death penalty as our weapon of the flesh, countering murder with death, trying to assuage grief with more death. Flesh upon flesh upon flesh.

Paul sums it up in the eighth chapter of Romans: "To set the mind on flesh is death." Flesh knows only death as its goal. That doesn't mean that our bodies are bad. Elsewhere, the New Testament affirms that our bodies are temples of the Spirit. We should treat them with respect and honor. But to live by the flesh means that we assess the world according to that with which we're most intimately familiar, our flesh. And if we set our minds on the flesh, where can that lead us but to the valley of dry bones?

God offers us an alternative to the flesh, but we're reluctant to take it. You can understand why. We're afraid—afraid to let go of a mind-set, a way of living that the rest of the world, from those redbirds to our penal system, has relied on and taught us from birth. That's why fear is such a common reaction whenever God comes to a person and offers another way. When Jesus appeared to his disciples after he conquered the power of death on Easter, he had to tell them not to be afraid. We fear to give up those things that have served us for a lifetime. We're all too aware of what is out there. We're genetically programmed to fight our hardest to stay out of the valley as long as we can. To let go of what we know, what we're familiar with, what's tried and true, even if it's not ultimately effective, is terrifying. The risk is too great. So we cling to the flesh that promises us protection, the flesh that is headed for the valley just as surely as the flower fades.

But there is another way. It's not hidden or secret. Everyone has caught a glimpse of it. Everyone has experienced it, if even for a fleeting moment. Death and evil can't squelch it. How do you explain the determination of those firefighters to save lives when they started up the stairwells in the World Trade Center on September 11, knowing that loaded with sixty pounds of gear it would take a minute to climb a floor, and the fire was eighty stories up?

Who hasn't had those times when you were convinced that there's hope for the world in spite of everything? The way of flesh isn't the only way. There's something else going on. We've all seen it.

Ezekiel saw it in his vision. He spoke the Word of the Lord to the dry bones. He saw the power of that Word to join the bones together, to connect them with sinews, to cover them with flesh, to restore their skin. And then the Spirit came into the valley. It came from the four winds, from every corner of the sky, as mysteriously and as powerfully as it came into the clay God had fashioned into a human body on the sixth day of creation and gave life to Adam. And God told Ezekiel, "I will put my spirit within you, and you shall live, . . . then you shall know that I, the Lord, have spoken, and will act, says the Lord."

There's another way, the way of the Spirit, and that's how we know the Lord. Everyone has seen signs of hope and redemption. But some see hope and joy as exceptions to the hard and fast ways of the flesh. They see acts of love and grace and mercy and justice as oases along the way to the valley, resting spots to revive us for a while on our weary way. That's what we see when we see goodness through the eyes of the flesh. But for those who live in the Spirit, those signs show us another destination. They're not exceptions to the rule of the flesh, but alternatives to it. Yes, we acknowledge the flesh and its weakness, but we see that it's not the flesh that holds our destiny. It's the Spirit, which will one day transform the flesh, just as it transformed the flesh of Jesus on the day of his Resurrection.

On the cross he experienced death as complete and final as those bones in Ezekiel's valley. But that same Spirit that breathed life into Adam, that breathed over the valley of death—that same Spirit breathed life into the dead body of Jesus, who is our Risen Lord.

So to those who have committed their lives to Jesus, Romans 8:9 says, "But you are not in the flesh; you are in the Spirit, since the Spirit of God dwells in you. . . . If Christ is in you, though the body is dead because of sin, the Spirit is life because of righteousness." Christ changes the place for which we're destined. It's not the valley of dry bones; it's the mountain of the living Lord. We see that goodness and love and courage aren't exceptions to the rule of death, but evidence that the Spirit is at work overcoming death.

We see evidence of the power of the Spirit all around us. It takes courage to give our lives to it, to give up the convictions of the flesh with which we're so familiar. The power of the flesh, of hatred and violence and self-interest, is easy to see. But Christ gives us the power of the Spirit. We know where the real power is. Romans says, "If the Spirit of him who raised Jesus from the dead dwells in you, he who raised Christ from the dead will give life to your mortal bodies also through his Spirit that dwells in you." In Christ life wins. Always. Have courage.—Stephens G. Lytch

SUNDAY, AUGUST 22, 2004
Lectionary Message

Topic: Empowered
TEXT: Jer. 1:4–10

Norman Vincent Peale tells about walking by a tattoo parlor in Hong Kong one day. Many designs were displayed in the window, but one caught his eye: "Born to Lose." Curious about this simple design, Peale asked the shop owner if people really wanted these words imprinted on their bodies. The owner answered that his last customer had just had those very words placed on his chest. In amazement Peale asked, "Why? Why would anyone want to be branded with such a gloomy statement?" The old Chinese man shrugged his shoulders and said, "Before the tattoo is put on the chest, the tattoo is on the mind."

Is there good news that can help people change the tattoo that is on their mind? The story of Jeremiah is God's way to help us see a new picture of ourselves in our minds.

I. *The problem.* Many people do not believe in themselves. This inferiority complex comes from a lack of self-esteem. There is an "excuse me for living" cloud that hangs over the head of someone who moves through life with no self-confidence. When "born to lose" is implanted in the mind, it shapes the way we live.

Such an attitude can cripple us spiritually. We think so little of ourselves that we may not be open to what God wants for us. The call of Jeremiah gives us an example. In response to God's claim on his life, Jeremiah replied, "Ah, Lord God! Truly I do not know how to speak, for I am only a boy" (v. 6). That was his way of saying, "I don't believe I can do what you are asking of me." So what is your excuse? It may have nothing to do with age or the ability to speak, but chances are most of us have made our excuses at one time or another.

II. *The hope.* There is good news for those of us who may not fully believe in ourselves. God believes in us! That is our hope. In a progression of four statements, God teaches Jeremiah, and us, that he believes in us.

(a) *"I formed you."* We are a creation of the Master. Our value is determined not by ourselves but by the one who gave us life. Just as a painting is more valuable if it is painted by one of the master artists rather than by you or me, our lives have tremendous value because God made us.

(b) *"I knew you."* This can also be translated "I chose you." It is the next step to show how God believes in us. A potter may form a vessel but decide she does not like it and start all over. God not only formed you, he also chose you. In the very beginning, when all of creation was formed, God "saw that it was good" (Gen. 1:18). The same blessing came from God when you were formed.

(c) *"I consecrated you."* After choosing us, God sets us apart for something special. That is what it means to be consecrated. Jeremiah was set apart to be a prophet. That may not be your calling, but God has a plan for you and your life. This purpose for your life comes from God's belief in you.

(d) *"I appointed you."* After setting Jeremiah apart, God gave him a commission. This was a special assignment, or appointment. It showed God's trust in the man who thought he was too young for the task. We have a divine appointment and assignment waiting for us as well.

Through the progression of these four blessings from God, we hear loud and clear that God believed in Jeremiah. Can you also hear God believing in you?

III. *The power.* We are empowered to live out God's appointment when we believe in God. After Jeremiah protests and offers his excuses, God reminds him that the power for the journey does not come from within us. It comes from above us. Verses 7 to 10 encourage Jeremiah to remember God's presence with him and God's words in his mouth. Even in our weakness we grow strong because of God's strength in our lives. Many years later the apostle Paul understood this same truth when he wrote, "My grace is sufficient for you, for my power is made perfect in weakness" (2 Cor. 12:9).

The story of Jeremiah teaches us an important lesson. God believes in us even when we do not believe in ourselves. Nobody is born to lose. If we believe in the God who believes in us, we are empowered with the wonderful words, "Do not be afraid of them, for I am with you to deliver you, says the Lord" (v. 8). We are born not to lose, but to live the abundant life!—David W. Hull

ILLUSTRATIONS

TRUST.

> I cannot do without Thee
> I cannot stand alone;
> I have no strength or goodness
> Nor wisdom of my own.
> But thou, beloved Savior
> Art all in all to me
> And perfect strength in weakness
> Is theirs who lean on thee.[6]

TRANSFORMATION.   In the musical *The Man of La Mancha,* the grand idealist Don Quixote meets a harlot named Aldonza. He announces, "You will be my lady, and I give you a new name—Dulcinea." Throughout the play she laughs at him and scorns him. He continues to believe in her and the potential of her life, even when she does not believe in herself. At the end of the play Don Quixote is near death when a beautiful woman of grace and charm comes to visit him. He asks, "Who are you?" She stands so that he can see her fully. "Don't you remember? You called me your lady. You gave me a new name. My name is Dulcinea!"

SERMON SUGGESTIONS

Topic: On Being Unhappy with God

TEXT: Jer. 20:7–13

(1) The reaction to a sense of God's injustice. (2) The occasion of overwhelming compulsion to speak for God despite disappointment and frustration. (3) The prelude to a radiant conviction of God's final justice.

Topic: Our Spiritual Olympiad

TEXT: Heb. 12:1–2, 12–17

(1) A race threatened by sin. (2) A race with Jesus as the pacesetter. (3) A race with joy beyond the suffering. (4) A race with steadfastness as the requirement.

WORSHIP AIDS

CALL TO WORSHIP.   "In thee, O Lord, do I put my trust: let me never be put to confusion. Deliver me in thy righteousness, and cause me to escape: incline thine ear unto me, and save me. Be thou my strong habitation, whereunto I may continually resort: thou hast given commandment to save me; for thou art my rock and my fortress" (Ps. 71:1–3).

---

[6]Author unknown

INVOCATION.   Our Father, open our hearts to your love; open our minds to your truth; open our wills to your service. Grant us prevailing faith for every challenge, and opportunity to glorify you in our lives.

OFFERTORY SENTENCE.   "A generous man will himself be blessed, for he shares his food with the poor" (Prov. 22:9 NIV).

OFFERTORY PRAYER.   Lord, we, all of us, whether our money is little or much, are rich with what we can do for others. Your grace in Jesus Christ has given us an abundance to share. We pray that you will receive whatever we have to give and use it to supply the needs of others, wherever they are and whoever they may be. May this offering be used to supply what people need the most, whether it is the gospel message or a crust of bread.

PRAYER.   Thy kingdom come, O God, and when it comes let us not be blind or dumb or stubborn, too set in our own ways, to take it in. We have no choice. We can be taken in by it or washed away by it. Help us to see always those who are already in it, who shine like lights in our dark world. Gather us together and keep us close to each other, that we may give to those who are looking and longing for the life they want. Amen.—Theodore Parker Ferris

SERMON
Topic: If You Want to Walk on Water
TEXT: Ps. 40:1–5; Matt. 14:22–33

You have, no doubt, heard it said of someone that there are those who think he could walk on water. Or so and so thinks he himself could walk on water. We are all aware that no one we know can *really* walk on water. "Walking on water" is a figure of speech. In other words, the person is superhuman, beyond reproach, invincible, capable of extraordinary things.

I would like for us to look at that last definition—"capable of extraordinary things." We all also have known, or at least heard about, those who have proved themselves capable of extraordinary things, sometimes in spite of great obstacles or handicaps. They could almost walk on water. The saying comes, of course, from the story we have read about Jesus walking toward the disciples on the sea, and about Peter, who tried to walk with him.

This story was originally used in the early Church to bring comfort and strength to the early Christians suffering persecution and tribulation. The disciples in a storm-tossed boat is symbolic of the Church tossed by the storms of persecution and trouble. It could be symbolic of a church tossed about by turmoil or an uncertain future. From our perspective, the sea in the story represents anxieties and the unseen dark powers that might threaten us. As we think about walking on water, about attempting extraordinary things, or about setting out to achieve the seemingly impossible, there are some important principles to keep in mind.

I. *It goes without saying that if we want to walk on water, we must first get out of the boat.* You can't walk on water if you are not willing to get your feet wet. A problem with a lot of people is that they go through life without ever getting out of the boat, in a manner of speaking. They are content to rock along without ever taking any chances and experiencing anything different or new.

We all know that mediocre actions beget mediocre results. Those who never get out of the boat in life will always see life in the same way and will never get a glimpse of the vast possibilities that life has to offer.

II. *Just as true, if we want to walk on water, we must first overcome our fear.* When the disciples saw Jesus walking toward them on the water, "they cried out in fear." When Peter tried to walk toward Jesus, "he became frightened." Peter was both courageous and cowardly. First he had the courage to step out of the boat onto the water; then, when he thought about the tossing waves of the sea, he became afraid. Is it not so with us as well? Are we not this time courageous and bold and ready to take on the world, and then at another time timid and fearful and afraid to attempt anything?

As we face the challenging task, that extraordinary deed, all kinds of fears swirl around us, like the swirling waves of the sea. There is fear of the unknown. There is fear of failure. There is fear of ridicule. But we cannot let fear of the unknown paralyze us and keep us from action. And we cannot let fear of failure keep us from trying. And we cannot let fear of ridicule hold us back.

To give you an example, when I began my doctor of ministry degree, I was very anxious and intimidated at the thought of going to a school in Chicago where I knew there would be graduates from Harvard Divinity School. I entertained fears that I would not be accepted, that I would stick out like a sore thumb, that I would be ridiculed and shunned by the other class members. But thankfully I was able to overcome my fears and go to that first class anyway. And all my fears proved to be totally unfounded. For within a few minutes of the first class session I felt accepted and affirmed. And I soon learned that I had a contribution to make to the class and could converse with the best of them.

I could have let fear keep me from what proved to be a wonderful, growing experience. If we would walk on water, attempt extraordinary things, we must first overcome our fears. Most certainly, if we want to walk on water, we must step forth in faith. We cannot be half-believers. To *accomplish* extraordinary things we must in faith *attempt* extraordinary things.

The story before us emphasizes the need to keep our eyes of faith on Christ and not focus on the storms around us. As long as Peter kept his eyes of faith on Jesus he did well. But when he focused on the wind and waves, he began to sink. So it can be with us. As long as we keep our eyes of faith on God, we do well. But when we take our eyes of faith off of God and focus on the storms and problems around us, we may begin to sink.

A few months ago, a piece of siding came loose near the top of our chimney. The only way to get it repaired was to bring out my twenty-foot extension ladder and climb up there with a hammer and some nails and fix it. Some of you know I am not particularly fond of tall ladders. But the job had to be done and I was the only one to do it. Well, as long as I kept my gaze upward, toward the top of the chimney, I was OK. But if I took my eyes off the chimney and looked to the ground below, I was in danger of being paralyzed by fear.

So it is with our faith. If we keep our eyes of faith on God, we do well. But if we forget God, take our eyes of faith off God, and let ourselves become obsessed with the storms around us, we begin to sink.

Just months ago we were all anxiously watching and waiting as massive efforts were undertaken to free nine coal miners who were trapped underground in Pennsylvania. The experience of the nine miners huddled together in the dark was not unlike the experience of the disciples who were huddled together in their little storm-tossed boat in the dark of night.

We have heard it said that God was with those miners throughout their ordeal. This story of the coal miners and the story of the disciples say that no matter how dark the night or how bleak the circumstances, God is present. No matter how severe the tribulations or how strong the winds, God is present with us.

God comes in the time of crisis, when human resources have been exhausted, as Jesus came walking to the disciples in the storm-tossed boat. God comes in the darkest watch of the night, as Jesus came to the disciples in the darkest watch of the night. Faith may not enable us to actually walk on water, but it can enable us to believe, against all evidence, that God is with us in the midst of the storm. And faith can often help us do extraordinary things.

Now is the time for us to attempt extraordinary things, to meet the challenges head-on, to walk on water, if you will. We can do so only if we first get out of the boat, overcome our fears, and step out into the future on faith.—Randy Hammer

SUNDAY, AUGUST 29, 2004
Lectionary Message

Topic: The Labor of Love
TEXT: Heb. 13:1–8, 15–16
Other Readings: Jer. 2:4–13; Ps. 81:1, 10–16; Luke 14:1, 7–14

The simple strains of a campfire song may say it best: "And they'll know we are Christians by our love." Perhaps that is what the writer of Hebrews meant in this last chapter of the book. After recounting the roll call of faith in chapter 11 and encouraging Christian perseverance in chapter 12, a final, practical word about Christian living is offered. In specific ways we are challenged to live out our faith. The labor of love means:

I. *Community in the Church* (v. 1). "Let mutual love continue" (NKJV). Another translation says, "Keep on loving each other as brothers" (NIV). The word in Greek is *philadelphia*. The word for mutual love in Greek is *philos* and the word for brother is *adelphos*. Put those together and you have the concept of "brotherly love," "mutual love," or "community love."

Too many churches are torn apart by anger and hatred, division and strife. If we are ever going to communicate the message of God's love to the world, then the community in our church needs to reflect that kind of love for one another. Before we can ever love the world for Christ, we must demonstrate a mutual love within the church for one another. Let the world know that you are Christian by the way you love others within the church.

II. *Hospitality to strangers* (v. 2). "Do not neglect to show hospitality to strangers, for by doing that some have entertained angels without knowing it." Hospitality to strangers in the early Church was essential to the spread of the gospel. Without many hotels, Christians would take in other Christians as they came to town. This practice goes back to the days of Moses (see Lev. 19:34). The reference to entertaining angels was most likely rooted in the story in Genesis 18:1–21 in which Abraham and Sarah entertained three strangers who turned out to be messengers from God telling of the promised son.

Our social setting is different today than in the days when Hebrews was written. We have plenty of hotels and seldom provide lodging for Christians moving through our city. So how does the principle still apply to us? Just look around you this morning. Is there someone here who is a stranger to you? What have you done to share a word or a touch of hospitality with that person? We are encouraged to move to the next level in our labor of love. God wants us to do more than just love one another. We can let others know that we are Christian by the way we welcome strangers.

III. *Empathy for prisoners* (v. 3). "Remember those who are in prison, as though you were in prison with them; those who are being tortured, as though you yourselves were being tortured." Our ministry to others will be only as deep as our empathy for their needs. If we distance ourselves from them and simply do not care, we will be able to pass by without getting involved. That is why the writer says, "as though you were in prison with them."

Do you see the progression here in the levels of love? It is pretty easy to love those who are already in our community. It is more challenging to show hospitality to a stranger, but at least the stranger has come to us. Now God is calling us to move beyond our comfort zones to empathize with someone who is not near to us. The labor of love continues to move us out into God's world to expose others to the good news. Let the world know that you are a Christian by the empathy you show for those in all kinds of prisons.

IV. *Faithfulness in marriage* (v. 4). "Let marriage be held in honor by all, and let the marriage bed be kept undefiled; for God will judge fornicators and adulterers." The admonition to love moves to the intimacy of the marriage bed. Literally, this labor of love now hits close to home. To live out our Christianity means that we are to be faithful not only to Christ but also to our spouses if we are married. This was one way that the early Christians could show how they were different from a culture where promiscuity was prevalent. Does that sound familiar today? Let the world know that you are a Christian by living a life of sexual purity, if you are married or if you are not.

V. *Contentment with possessions* (v. 5). "Keep your lives free from the love of money, and be content with what you have; for he has said, 'I will never leave you or forsake you'" (v. 5). One final word about love has to do with the love of money. Remember, the problem is not money but the *love* of money. By knowing that Jesus will never "leave you or forsake you," we can learn the art of contentment with what we have (see also Phil. 4:11–13). Once again this is a way we can demonstrate the difference that our faith makes in our lives. In a society that is overcome with materialism, let the world know that you are a Christian by using things and loving people rather than loving things and using people.—David W. Hull

ILLUSTRATIONS

HOSPITALITY.   Singer John Charles Thomas, at age sixty-six, wrote to syndicated columnist Abigail Van Buren: "I am presently completing the second year of a three-year survey on hospitality or the lack of it in churches. To date, of the 195 churches I have visited, I was spoken to in only one by someone other than an official greeter, and that was to ask me to move my feet."[7]

THINGS.   George Lucas, *Star Wars* creator, describes how the young Anakin Skywalker became the evil Darth Vader in the movie *Attack of the Clones*. He turned into Darth Vader because he got attached to things. He couldn't let go of his mother, he couldn't let go of his girlfriend. He couldn't let go of things. It makes you greedy. And when you're greedy, you

---

[7]Quoted in "Eutyches and His Kin," *Christianity Today*, June 3, 1977.

are on the path to the dark side, because you fear you're going to lose things, that you're not going to have the power you need.[8]

SERMON SUGGESTIONS

Topic: Who's to Blame?
TEXT: Ezek. 18:1–9, 25–29
(1) We, not our parents or ancestors, are responsible for the consequences of our own wrong-doing. (2) Moreover, we cannot blame God: he does allow us to sin and suffer for it; however, he grants us the freedom to change our ways and truly live.

Topic: Tokens of Brotherly Love
TEXT: Heb. 13:1–8
(1) Practicing Christian hospitality. (2) Ministering to prisoners. (3) Avoiding greed. (4) Following true Christian leaders. (5) Trusting the ever-living Christ.

WORSHIP AIDS

CALL TO WORSHIP.   "Sing for joy to God our strength; shout aloud to the God of Jacob" (Ps. 81:1 NIV).

INVOCATION.   O God, let our worship and our relationship to others be like a song of joy that honors you and draws the people around us and the people we meet nearer to you.

OFFERTORY SENTENCE.   "Consider carefully what you hear," [said Jesus]. "With the measure you use, it will be measured to you—and even more" (Mark 4:24 NIV).

OFFERTORY PRAYER.   Give us, gracious Father, hearts with something of your generosity, so that our giving will be more free and uncalculated and a source of joy day by day.

PRAYER.   O God of mercy! Thou knowest the bitterness of poverty and the barrenness it spreads on life. Thou knowest how it darkens and tempts and embitters the soul, and divides man from his brother, and makes faith in thy goodness and care seem well nigh impossible. When poverty is a needed discipline, may thy children bear it with patience, and find in it liberty of soul and enrichment of the world within. But too often it is not of thy sending. Too often it comes from the selfishness and greed and wrongdoing of men. Be present with thy help and blessing in homes thus made sad. Forbid that within them the voice of unbelief, or envy, or rebellion should be heard; but may trust in thee, and gentle patience and prudent forethought, sustain the life of the soul against every threatening ill. Put into the hearts of all good men a love for the poor. Raise up to those who are in need wise friends and counselors, through whose ministry thou mayest provide a way of relief. And grant, O Lord, that justice and brotherly love may prevail. May we not only deliver the poor man from his distress, but may we also, in the strength of thy spirit, attack and overthrow every evil power that works

---

[8]*Time*, Apr. 29, 2002.

impoverishment and hardship to thy children. Hear our prayer and grant that those who are poor in this world's goods may be rich in heavenly treasure, honor, peace, and love, through Jesus Christ our Lord.—Samuel McComb

SERMON
Topic: Healing and Anger
Text: Mark 3:1–6

Perhaps you saw the security surveillance video of the woman attacking her four-year-old child in the parking lot of an Indiana shopping center broadcast on a Thursday. The video was broadcast nationally to help locate and arrest the woman and to allow police to check for injuries to the child. In addition to locating the child, the national broadcast seemed to have had a punitive objective. It was an exposé of parental misconduct and a warning that George Orwell's Big Brother is watching. The incident was appalling to see, and concern for the child certainly justified the public exposure. The repeated demonstration of an adult striking a small child around the head and face was sufficient to arouse my righteous indignation. What could a four-year-old child have done to provoke such behavior from any adult, much less from a parent? Anger with a clerk over a refused refund was reported as a possible cause, and we assume that the child just happened to get in the way. Anger has a way of getting passed around and creating more anger. Assuming that the store clerk was the catalyst, the mother's anger was passed on to the child, who is probably old enough to be angry in her own right at the injustice of her mother's behavior. After the video was broadcast, police reported more than a thousand calls from an outraged public. I wonder how many blows for justice were struck on Friday?

Walter Wink calls violence "the spirituality of the modern world." He says that violence has been accorded the status of a religion, demanding obedience to death. He calls it "the myth of redemptive violence." The entertainment industry has made a business of inciting public anger toward mythical characters representing darkness. Children are subjected repeatedly to cartoons, movies, and television dramas that arouse anger at the villains and allow vicarious revenge as the hero rises to the occasion and batters, shoots, stabs, blows up, humiliates, mutilates, and obliterates the devil enemy. By the age of eighteen, the average child has logged 36,000 hours of television, including 15,000 murders. The audience is more than casual observer. We and our children are drawn into the act and repeatedly pass through the cycle of fear, anger, and violent revenge in doing battle with evil. Wink observes the bland comparison of the children's sermon in worship with the sixteen acts of violence observed by our children every evening on TV. And we wonder why domestic violence appears to be rising.

We have learned to expect the cycle of threat, fear, anger, and violence to run in sequence in dealing with the evil of this world; and we find the tape running through its cycle in our emotional response to real life, just as it does when we are entertained in the comfort of our homes. In Mark, Jesus responded to his critics with anger, and it appears that the whole scene might have turned into a brawl, with Jesus the hero punching out the self-righteous Pharisees, sending them home with bloodied heads, torn tunics, and a resolve never again to mess with the Galilean. Read it again. The way Mark tells it, the story would never sell in prime time television: "He looked around at them with anger; he was grieved at their hardness of heart and said to the man, 'Stretch out your hand.' He stretched it out, and his hand was restored."

Injustice provokes anger. Anger is a normal human response to threat, and in the Gospel it is an appropriate response to perceived injustice that threatens the innocent and the weak. The issue of healing on the Sabbath was a persistent point of conflict between Jesus and the Pharisees. According to the Law, violation of the Sabbath was punishable by death (Exod. 31:15), but this response seems to have passed into antiquity by the time of Christ. Mark registers two statements of Jesus interpreting the Law before the incident in the synagogue. First, the Sabbath was made for the people, not the people for the Sabbath. Jesus recognized a human center in the purpose of the Law that seems to have escaped many of his peers. The second statement was an issue of authority: the Son of Man is Lord of the Sabbath, and the Law is subject to interpretation by the revelation of God in Christ.

Mark leaves the impression that Jesus was acting in defiance of the Pharisees against the Law in the healing of the man with a deformed hand on the Sabbath. Jesus could have avoided the confrontation by waiting one day. This evidently was not a life-or-death situation that required immediate action, but it appears to have been a contest of wills and a challenge to authority. The story is told by Matthew and Luke as well, but only Mark records that Jesus acted in anger, and this is the only place in the Gospels where Jesus expressed anger (*orge*). When the disciples blocked the children from coming to Jesus (10:14), he was "indignant" (another word for *anger*) toward his disciples. Again, the situation was a matter of injustice.

Dale Moody, one of my teachers, told of hearing a lecture in theology while on study leave at Oxford in England. One of the British students arrived late and whispered to his American friend, "Has he come to the wrath?" Moody observed a peculiar interest in the wrath of God at Oxford. He went on to note that divine wrath is a constant response in the Bible to the sin of the world. Jesus reveals the tough love of God in his cleansing of the Temple, in his pronouncement of woes on the Pharisees, in his chiding of the disciples on behalf of the children, and in his healing of the man with the deformed hand. Dahlberg write, "The compassion and mercy of Jesus find an element of their strength in his very capacity for anger (as much as for sorrow) whenever he finds the gracious will and purpose of God met with human hardness of heart."

In Christ, anger provokes healing. At the cross, Jesus had every right, by my standards, to resist arrest, to defy the angry crowd, to condemn the Roman soldiers, and to curse God and die. Yet he submitted to injustice in silence, as the lamb walks to the slaughter; he kept his focus on the grace of God even with Pilate; and as he died he forgave his executioners. Jesus revealed the wrath of God as anger on behalf of the weak and the oppressed—as anger that is an expression of healing grace. Strange that he was not angry in defense of himself.

The call in Romans to heap coals of fire on the head of the enemy is not an act of revenge, but a call to repentance. In Eastern culture a sign of repentance was to carry a basket of smoking embers on top of one's head. The teaching of Jesus is not that we are to knuckle under and yield to the power of evil in this world, but we are to bring the wicked to repentance. Wink tells a story from Angie O'Gorman about the need to take the teaching of Jesus seriously. She tells of being awakened in the middle of the night by a man kicking down her bedroom door and cursing as he approached her bed. She considered the options of screaming, resisting, or running, and decided that the only hope for either of them was to meet as two human beings. She asked what time it was, and he replied. She proceeded with small talk until the intruder's voice seemed calm, then she asked him to leave. He said he had no place to stay. She then offered him the sofa downstairs and sat up in bed for the rest of the night while he slept. In the morning they ate breakfast together and he left, never to be seen again.

Who among us is not sick with fear and anger at the attack of the terrorists on innocent victims in the World Trade Center, or sickened by the report of a ten-year-old Palestinian child shot for throwing stones at a tank? In our anger, can we follow Jesus into healing? Jesus looked with anger, he was grieved at human insensitivity, and he healed. Go and do likewise.—Larry Dipboye

SUNDAY, SEPTEMBER 5, 2004
Lectionary Message

Topic: Rights and Choices
TEXT: Jer. 18:1–11
Other Readings: Ps. 139:1–6, 13–18; Philem. 1–21; Luke 14:25–33

When I was a child growing up in the Methodist Church, one of the most moving but also intimidating services was the annual covenant service, usually held on or around New Year's Day. I was impressed by what seemed to me to be both dedication and utter recklessness in a section of one congregational prayer:

> I am no longer my own, but thine.
> Put me to what thou wilt, rank me with whom thou wilt.
> Put me to doing, put me to suffering.
> Let me be employed by thee or laid aside for thee,
> Exalted for thee or brought low by thee.
> Let me be full, let me be empty.
> Let me have all things, let me have nothing.
> I freely and heartily yield all things to thy pleasure and disposal.[1]

I would look around at my teenage friends and the older adults in the pews and wonder, "Do they know what they're saying? Do they really *mean* this?" The questions were not a commentary on the quality of discipleship in that congregation, but rather an attempt to come to grips with what it would mean to be completely yielded to God in all things.

The covenant service is not widely used in recent days, and I suspect that one reason is that our values are so at odds with the tenor of the covenant being renewed. We are ill at ease with turning our will over to another, even if that other is God. Our consumer-oriented culture believes fervently in an individual's right to choose, whether the matter under consideration is deciding between new cars or different lifestyles. Small wonder, then, that our contact with Jeremiah 18 is usually limited to infrequent singing of "Have Thine Own Way,

---

[1]"A Covenant Prayer in the Wesleyan Tradition," *United Methodist Hymnal* (Nashville, Tenn.: United Methodist, 1989), no. 607.

Lord" in mainline churches. The idea of being clay on a potter's wheel, subject to the pot-ter's choices, is as unwelcome to our ears as it was to Jeremiah's contemporaries. Jeremiah was God's mouthpiece to call the house of Israel to repent of the bad choices they had made. They chose to worship the queen of heaven (Jer. 8:16–18) and other idols, as well as to give lip service to Yahweh. They chose to remember the Davidic covenant but ignore the older covenant made with Moses. They chose to ignore God's laws. They chose to please them-selves, so being likened to clay and subject to the will of the potter was antithetical to their values. We are as stubborn and self-willed as they were, and like them we often insist on the right to make choices that are obviously damaging to ourselves and our future. Long-time church members want the music and worship style of their choosing. Motorcyclists insist that wearing a protective helmet should be a matter of individual choice. And of course the term pro-choice has come to mean the belief that a pregnant girl or woman should have the right to determine whether or not to kill her unborn child.

I. *God is "pro-choice," too*—but not in the sense we usually mean. God is pro-choice in that he created human beings with wills, the power to discern, and the ability to act on their choices. From the very beginning, in the Garden of Eden, the Almighty endowed humans with decision-making capacities. Adam was invited to name the birds of the air and the beasts of the field (Gen. 2:20). Adam and Eve were given their choice of the fruit of all but one of the trees in the garden, and although they were commanded not to eat of the tree in the middle of the garden, they had the freedom to choose obedience or disobedience. In the other Scrip-ture readings for today, we see choices being offered to people. In the Epistle, Paul presents Philemon with a choice: will he receive Onesimus back as a brother in Christ, or punish the runaway slave? Jesus' words in Luke's Gospel challenge listeners to decide whether they will renounce all or turn back from being his disciples. And despite the image of inanimate clay, even in Jeremiah 18 readers are offered a choice: "If the nation concerning which I have spo-ken turns from its evil, I will repent of the evil that I intended to do to it" (Jer. 18:10).

In every choice since the Fall, it should be noted, we are limited to two basic choices: *with* God or *against* God. And as author George MacDonald wrote, "All that is not God is death."[2] Why? Because God is the source of all life. If we turn away from life, what alternative is there but death?

II. *God has "rights," too.* The image of God as a potter appears elsewhere in the Bible. Isa-iah acknowledges the potter's sovereignty in this way: "Yet, O Lord, thou art our Father, we are the clay, and thou art our potter; we are all the work of thy hand" (Isa. 64:8). Paul put it more bluntly: "Has the potter no right over the clay, to make out of the same lump one ves-sel for beauty and another for menial use?" (Rom. 9:21). Paul, like Jeremiah, sees God's right to create, re-create, and destroy as cause for celebration rather than fear or rebellion, because the Lord's will is always directed toward our good. Our God does not wish "that any should perish, but that all should reach repentance" (2 Pet. 3:9).

A preteen was arguing with his mother about what he would wear on a visit to his grand-parents' house. He didn't like the clothes she had set out for him and brushed aside her rea-sons for wearing them: because your other clothes are dirty, because Grandma and Grandpa gave you that shirt and it would please them to see you wear it, and because clothes are a

---

[2]George MacDonald, quoted in Sheldon Vanauken, *A Severe Mercy* (New York: HarperCollins, 1977), p. 106.

way we show respect or disrespect for people. "I still don't see why I can't wear whatever I want!" he protested. "Because I said so, and I'm your mother," replied his mother, ending the discussion. God has the "right" to reshape us, to cut us down or build us up, to do whatever pleases him, simply because he is God. Our choice, says Jeremiah, is how we respond to the Divine Potter.—Carol M. Norén

ILLUSTRATION

HOOKED.   One of the characters in Susan Howatch's novel *Absolute Truths* is an artist who has been estranged from God and the church. In a mildly irreverent conversation with a bishop visiting her studio, Harriet reaches the insight that her work as a sculptor has much in common with God's creative and redemptive process. She says,

> Of course God couldn't forget [the world after the first creative blast]. No creator can forget! If the blast-off's successful you're hooked, and once you're hooked you're inside the work as well as outside it, it's part of you, you're welded to it, you're enslaved, and that's why it's such a bloody hell when things go adrift. But no matter how much the mess and distortion make you want to despair, you can't abandon the work because you're *chained* to the bloody thing, it's absolutely woven into your soul and you know you can never rest until you've brought truth out of all the distortion and beauty out of all the mess. . . . It involves an indestructible sort of fidelity, an insane sort of hope, an indescribable sort of . . . well, it's love, isn't it? There's no other word for it. You love the work and you suffer with it and always—*always*—you're slaving away against all the odds to make everything come right.[3]

SERMON SUGGESTIONS

Topic: When We Are in a Position to Help

TEXT: Ezek. 33:1–11

(1) We are responsible for doing something constructive. (2) This may mean the giving of timely warning to wrongdoers. (3) But the final responsibility belongs to the person warned.

Topic: On Sharing the Blessing

TEXT: Philem. 1–12

(1) The rewards of Christian faith. (2) The requirements of Christian faith.

WORSHIP AIDS

CALL TO WORSHIP.   "Examine me, O God, and know my mind; test me, and discover my thoughts. Find out if there is any evil in me and guide me in the everlasting way" (Ps. 139:23–24 TEV).

INVOCATION.   Lord, let this hour of worship reflect the clean hands and pure hearts we wish were ours and pray will be ours, and we look for ways to keep our hands and hearts clean and pure, the better to share with others the glory of our God.

---

[3]Susan Howatch, *Absolute Truths* (New York: Ballantine, 1994), p. 377.

OFFERTORY SENTENCE.   "When someone is given a great deal, a great deal will be demanded of that person; when someone is entrusted with a great deal, of that person even more will be expected" (Luke 12:48b NJB).

OFFERTORY PRAYER.   Father, we bring our offerings now to be joined with those of many others as we cooperate to accomplish some of your purpose in the world. May every tithe, every gift, and all offerings be magnified by power that they may ably serve your purposes in Christ, we pray.—Henry Fields

PRAYER.   O loving God, whose wisdom and power underlie the best of all the work we plan and do, you are for all time the master craftsman of the Earth and of the universe around us. We thank you that there is always some kind of work for us to do, and from you we receive direction for our use of heart and head and hands. We name with gratitude the world you have made, the vast numbers of laborers in industry, the administrators in commerce, and the knowledge among all of us that work is good and that at its best it reflects your will for our human nature and society. We rejoice over the leadership of the marketplace, the hands who turn the wheels of progress, and the minds and skills of those whose ability and genius have made our country the benefactor of lands and people who lack the privileges of ours. We thank you for that other dimension of labor where your Spirit reminds us that we are creatures with a calling, that we are heirs of your goodness every day, that the routine of work can include the joy of friend with friend, and that the pride and satisfaction of a job well done still inspire the workman's heart.

We bring before you now the skilled and unskilled workers of this nation, the men and women who toil for daily bread. You are the Lord of all life; bid that injustice, greed, and unfair dealings depart from the fabric and fiber of our economic systems and federations of labor. As we plan and build our cities, towns, and towers, may we not lose sight of our need to shape our life according to your pattern for a new Kingdom for all humanity. Help us to add to our every product that quality of life and service that gives to our society a good foundation and makes us all coworkers in a purpose whose ends are true and right. May all our workers be not only builders of things, but also shapers of a heritage that comes from honesty, duty, and prayer. Keep all of us faithful to your higher law so that our common life may be marked by boldness and conscience, steadfast purpose, and deeds and works as our best offering to our God. Give us to recognize the sacredness of both ordinary and professional labor, and in all the calendar of daily care may the vision of the larger good constrain and control our aims and obligations. Lord, keep us human, kindhearted, and well-meaning in every intention so that in our pursuit of various paths of service we shall follow our uncrowned king and find new life in him. Now, unto you, the King eternal, immortal, invisible, the only wise God, our Father, be all honor and glory, dominion and power, forever and ever.—Donald Macleod

SERMON
Topic: Looking Back
TEXT: Exod. 5:20–23, 14:10–12, 16:2–7, 17:2–3

Joseph Heller called it *Catch-22*. His novel about the insanity of war was set on an airbase in Europe during World War II. The novel is a cynical comedy about the antics of military personnel flying bombing raids over Europe. Yossarian is trying to grasp the logic of the military command. Orr wants out of the war. According to Heller, "Orr was crazy and could be grounded. All he had to do was ask; and as soon as he did, he would no longer be crazy and would have to fly more missions. Orr would be crazy to fly more missions and sane if he didn't, but if he was sane he had to fly them. If he flew them he was crazy and didn't have to; but if he didn't want to he was sane and had to." This is explained to Yossarian as the simple logic of a catch-22: *Sometimes insanity is normal.*

A similar logic operates in the Exodus. The Jews were slaves to the Egyptians. Life under the Pharaohs was unbearable. The people were cut off from the land of their ancestors and denied the freedom to worship their God. They had lost their identity and all hope for the future in the brickyards of Egypt. Anyone would have been crazy to choose slavery, to prefer Egypt to freedom; but the pain and cost of the Exodus was sometimes more demanding than slavery. In case you haven't noticed, Exodus contains a lot of whining. It may have been the original catch-22.

When Moses demanded release for his people, the Hebrew leaders complained. Moses had only made the situation worse. Then Moses took the complaint "upstairs." He did not want the job anyway, and God had done nothing to relieve the oppression. Ten plagues later, it would seem that everyone would have learned to respect the power of God. Pharaoh and the Egyptians had. But a funny thing happened on the way to the wilderness. The people looked back on an approaching army. They looked forward and saw nothing but water. They looked around and God was nowhere in sight. Then they cried out to the Lord but blamed Moses. "Let us alone and let us serve the Egyptians." They were ready to return to Egypt. "Better to serve the Egyptians than to die in the wilderness!"

After passing through the sea on dry land, one miracle later, the Jews arrived in the desert of Sinai fresh out of unleavened bread. They forgot the agony of bondage. Suddenly they could only remember eating bread in the brickyards, so of course they accused Moses, "You have brought us out into this wilderness to kill this whole assembly with hunger." Then Yahweh provided manna from heaven, with careful instructions on its meaning and use. Again the Jews began to have warm fuzzy feelings about the security of slavery. "Why did you bring us out of Egypt, to kill us and our children and livestock with thirst?"

The circular logic here would be laughable if it were not so familiar. The people wanted to be free, but they did not want to be responsible for their freedom. They wanted the blessings of Yahweh, but not the discomfort and insecurity of trusting God. They wanted a great leader, but they did not want to follow. They wanted the Land of Promise, but they did not want to make the journey. It seems that the God of miracles was not quite miraculous enough for them.

I. *To go, you have to leave.* We really should not be shocked or surprised at the persistent reluctance of the Jews to turn Egypt loose. Everybody wants to go to heaven, but no one wants to die to get there. The elder, retired pastor in my congregation was struggling with Parkinson's and quoted to me the words of the gospel song, "This world is not my home." Then he chuckled and added, "But I'm not homesick." The concluding scene of *Fiddler on the Roof* is a definition of the Jewish people. The inhabitants of a Russian Jewish village are being forced to pack up and leave. Tevye finds the identity of his people in the Exodus. He says that the Jews are always having to leave a place.

Exodus is about leaving Egypt to gain the Promised Land, leaving slavery to embrace freedom, giving up the security of a predictable life for the uncertainty of the life of faith, leaving the dominion of the gods to live in the power of Yahweh. It means turning loose the past, giving up who you were in order to become what you can be. Most of us have some trouble leaving Egypt. Periodically we stop and look back to some spot in our lives and fantasize about what might have been if this or that. The story is bad public relations for the Jews, but resistance to change is something that most of us recognize in ourselves.

The journey out of Egypt reminds me of family motor trips when our children were small. Typical wails would rise from the back seat, "Daddy, I'm hungry," or "I need to go to the bathroom," or "How much longer do we have to drive?" or "I'm car sick." Shortly after we moved here, our adult children joined us for a trip to Texas. About thirty minutes into the fifteen-hour drive, our twenty-four-year-old son whined from the back seat, "Are we there yet?" We remembered the good old days and shared some laughter of relief.

II. *To see, you have to look.* Gilbert Rendle in *Leading Change in the Congregation,* calls the spiritual journey of change "Welcome to the Wilderness." He wonders why the Jews needed forty years to accomplish a transition that could have been made in forty months or less. But the Exodus was more than a geographical journey from one place to another. It was a transformation of the people of God. Rendle observed that the people needed time in the wilderness to make the spiritual journey within the movement from place to place. Even the chaos and pain of the wilderness were necessary companions in the journey to promise.

Some of the most painful experiences in our lives are also the most revealing and the most transforming. Wilderness experiences can be eye-openers. Sometimes we have to break out of the ghetto of the way things are to see that our boundaries are prison bars and to understand that going back is not going to get us out. Walter Brueggemann said that it takes eyes to see the Exoduses happening all around us. He names the pain and delight of growing up, and the upheavals and changes that make persons free and that open up institutions. Then he proclaims, "The Holy One, within and without, has not stopped freeing people and calling them to rejoice."

With all of his personal hang-ups and leadership flaws, Moses had one quality that kept him going. He had the view from the top of the mountain. He was close to God, and in that nearness was a vision of the promise of God that lay ahead for the Jews. This is not the kind of vision that is often touted in the world of politics and corporations. It is not the ability to predict the future or a charismatic personality that makes people willing to follow you into hell. It is more than the power of positive thinking that sends us down the tracks saying, "I think I can."

First, the vision of Moses was insight into human nature. Only with an understanding of the people and a mirror to self can we find the power to forgive and to redirect our vision. Yes, they were stiff-necked, opinionated, and immature; and so was Moses. God was able to see something more in the people than they could see in themselves.

Second, the vision of Moses was confidence in the nature of God. Moses could not see the Promised Land any better than the smallest child in the wilderness, but he was learning to trust in the God who is always ahead of us, standing squarely in the middle of promise. Moses stood on the mountain looking ahead with God, and he led his people to follow the vision.—Larry Dipboye

SUNDAY, SEPTEMBER 12, 2004
Lectionary Message

Topic: Common Wisdom, or "Tax Collectors and Sinners, Oh My"

TEXT: Luke 15:1–10 NRSV

Other Readings: Jer. 4:11–12, 22–28; Ps. 14; 1 Tim. 1:12–17

Now all the tax collectors and sinners were coming near to listen to him, and the Pharisees and the scribes were grumbling and saying, "This fellow welcomes sinners and eats with them."

So he told them this parable: "Which one of you, having a hundred sheep and losing one of them, does not leave the ninety-nine in the wilderness and go after the one that is lost until he finds it? When he has found it, he lays it on his shoulders and rejoices. And when he comes home, he calls together his friends and neighbors, saying to them, 'Rejoice with me, for I have found my sheep that was lost.' Just so, I tell you, there will be more joy in heaven over one sinner who repents than over ninety-nine righteous persons who need no repentance.

"Or what woman having ten silver coins, if she loses one of them, does not light a lamp, sweep the house, and search carefully until she finds it? When she has found it, she calls together her friends and neighbors, saying, 'Rejoice with me, for I have found the coin that I had lost.' Just so, I tell you, there is joy in the presence of the angels of God over one sinner who repents."

I. *The common wisdom: separation.*

Hear for a moment some of the wisdom of the ages:

- "Associate yourself with men of good quality if you esteem your own reputation, for 'tis better to be alone than in bad company."—George Washington

- "Be very circumspect in the choice of thy company. In the society of thine equals thou shalt enjoy more pleasure; in the society of thy superiors thou shalt find more profit. To be the best in the company is the way to grow worse."—Francis Quarles (1592–1644)

- "Every man is like the company he is wont to keep."—Euripides (485–406 B.C.), "Phoenix"

- "Tell me what company you keep and I'll tell you what you are."—Miguel de Cervantes (1547–1616)

- "No company is preferable to bad, because we are more apt to catch the vices of others than their virtues, as disease is far more contagious than health."—C. C. Colton (1780–1832)[4]

- Do not enter the path of the wicked, and do not walk in the way of evildoers."
—Prov. 4:14 NRSV

---

[4]All preceding quotations taken from www.quotationspage.com.

- Whoever walks with the wise becomes wise, but the companion of fools suffers harm.—Prov. 13:20 NRSV

II. *The common response: criticism and self-righteousness.* There is lots of wisdom here, so the Pharisees and scribes—the wise, learned, and righteously religious of Jesus' day—would certainly have seen themselves in good company when they grumbled and said, "This fellow [Jesus] welcomes sinners and eats with them." Now that is an accusation worth listening to—why would anyone of good standing want to hang around with "tax collectors and sinners"? These people are the biblical version of our own smelly, drug- and alcohol-addicted street people, and our corporate thieves who fatten themselves while their employees lose all hope of retirement. Not exactly the best company to cultivate—and common wisdom strongly suggests that such company will either drag us down or lift us to greater morality and goodness. Jesus, of all people, should have known that he would be far better off shunning those unacceptable people and spending his time with those who clearly sought higher things.

In the passage before us, Luke 15:1–10, Jesus responds to those criticisms by telling three short stories. The third one is familiar to most people as "The Prodigal Son" or "The Parable of the Prodigal and His Brother." Today, we're going to look at the first two stories and see what we can learn about God's wisdom, which in this case seems to be far, far different from common wisdom.

III. *The common goal: repentance.* Both stories end essentially the same way: "Just so, I tell you, there will be more joy in heaven over one sinner who repents than over ninety-nine righteous persons who need no repentance" (v. 7), and "Just so, I tell you, there is joy in the presence of the angels of God over one sinner who repents" (v. 10).

The goal, then, seems to be repentance, the *metanoia,* the profound life change of mind and heart and soul that brings about reconciliation between God and God's created ones. Now, let's look closely at these stories and see how that repentance is described.

There are two main characters: first, a shepherd who has a hundred sheep; second, a woman who has ten silver coins. In each case, something is lost. The shepherd loses one of his sheep and the woman loses one of her coins. When they find what they have lost, they call their friends and neighbors together to rejoice. Easy enough so far—aren't we all pleased when we find something we've misplaced?

IV. *The uncommon wisdom: reconciliation.* A deeper look, however, makes this assessment a little more problematic. First, what do these stories have to do with keeping bad company? After all, they are spoken in response to the criticism of the religious elite of the society. Second, the lost ones, that is, the sheep and the coin, don't actually do anything. They don't go looking to be found, and more than likely they would not even be aware of their state of lostness. Instead, the protagonists, the active participants, go looking for the sheep and the coin. The shepherd not only goes looking, but does so at some risk of losing everything, for this shepherd leaves the rest of the sheep in the wilderness, vulnerable to all sort of negative possibilities. So, where's the repentance? Where's the seeking of forgiveness and the active movement and sorrow on the part of the one who is lost and separated from its rightful place?

It's not there. The action is all on the part of the people, the shepherd and the woman, who represent God in these stories. What we see is a fascinating piece of a picture of a being so passionately in love with these creatures that this being is willing to leave everything behind in the search to find that which is lost, even when the lost ones make no effort to raise their awareness of their lostness or to work to be found again.

Jesus lived out that lesson—he left behind respectability and uplifting company and the society of the educated and religiously competent. He went after the tax collector—that greedy person who would fatten his pockets at anybody's expense and suffered no pangs of conscience in the process. Jesus welcomed the sexually impure, the outcasts, the ones who just couldn't make it, who somehow missed the boat when it came to the ability to pull themselves up by their own bootstraps, who were trapped in a pattern of unrighteousness and degradation.

Truly there is something just a bit upside-down about this, both from the modern point of view and from the perspective of the religious listeners in the first century. Could it be that the economy in the heavenly places is upside-down? That it really will leave behind the productive, the good, the perfect, and the found and launch a major search, and a uneconomically sound one at that, for the lost, the imperfect, and the bad? Is that heavenly economy really willing to sacrifice everything for the sake of the one?

Yes, that is indeed what these stories tell us. The heavenly places are, in a word, righteous places where the marginalized are treated as those who are no longer marginalized. They are places where those who have are asked to leave it all behind and look for those who have not. It is a place of deep rejoicing, where those who have been lost and didn't even know they were lost or that someone was looking are found again. It is a place of uncommon wisdom.—Christy Thomas

ILLUSTRATIONS

JOY IN HEAVEN.   In the area in which I live, northwest Texas, extended lack of rainfall and excessive and debilitating heat are normal for the months of July, August, and September. Every once in a while, though, a thunderstorm will blow through, giving us a moment's relief. Most who live around here, many of whom are farmers and ranchers, carefully watch the weather reports, hoping against hope that one of those rare thunderstorms will blow through and water the fields and fill the stock ponds and replenish the rapidly shrinking lakes from which we get our water. On those infrequent days when it does happen, the phones begin to ring. "Is it raining over there? We've got a nice one here. Bet we got nearly an inch!" says the fortunate one. Because the storms tend to be spotty, others will answer, "Nope, nothing here yet, but I'm sure hoping it will make it this way. Surely do need it. Glad you were able to get some there." So we anxiously look, and excitedly rejoice when it comes. And in the aftermath of a truly good storm—we call them "gully-washers" here—we jubilantly note the rising water tables, the lowering water bills, and a blessed few minutes to be outside without melting from the heat. No need for umbrellas—it feels wonderful to get wet this way.

Perhaps the joy we get over a few minutes of long-awaited and eagerly anticipated rain here gives us a picture of the major joy in heaven when some other lost one is found again. Maybe the angels are getting wet, as are we, with one another's tears of joy at those moments.

LOST AND FOUND.   I lost one of my children once—most parents do manage at one time or another to misplace a child, especially as they get a bit older and start pushing for more independence. Anyway, on this particular day my youngest son had gone to a nearby mall with a friend for the afternoon and had neglected to let anyone know he was leaving or when he would be back. It led to a frantic search, phoning neighbors, friends, and finally the police. When he turned up on his own, he wondered at all the commotion, not realizing that he was the cause of it. He genuinely didn't know that he was lost and was bewildered at so much energy being expended to find him. Could it be that when we see Jesus face to face, we too are going to be astounded at the amount of energy that has gone into finding us and reconciling us to God—and will we also be shocked to discover just how lost we are?

SERMON SUGGESTIONS

Topic: When God Is Forgotten
TEXT: Hos. 4:1–3, 5:15–6:6
(1) Faithfulness, kindness, and knowledge of God are absent. (2) Distress may lead us to return to God for healing, which he promises to those who seek him.

Topic: Amazing Grace
TEXT: 1 Tim. 1:12–17
The grace of God toward us is truly amazing. (1) In its nature: it is God's favor toward the undeserving. (2) In its result: it makes useful to God the most unpromising sinner. (3) In its significance: it provides an example of what God can do for anyone.

WORSHIP AIDS
CALL TO WORSHIP.   "The Lord looks out from heaven on all the human race to see if any act wisely, if any seek God" (Ps. 14:2 REB).

INVOCATION.   You have not forgotten us, O God, when we have often gone away from you. Even now, you look beyond our motives to our need. Help us all to turn to you, so that the lost and the almost lost may be found and so that we all may know afresh the joy of belonging.

OFFERTORY SENTENCE.   "Everyone is to give what he has made up his mind to give; there is to be no grudging or compulsion about it, for God loves the giver who gives cheerfully" (2 Cor. 9:7 Moffatt).

OFFERTORY PRAYER.   Lord, here is our monetary offering. It is but seed to be planted in your service. May there be sufficient seed to bring forth a good harvest as it is broadcast in the fertile soil of your purpose, to germinate and blossom and produce fruit fit for your Kingdom. Amen.

PRAYER.   O God most holy, who art righteous altogether, who sees not as man sees but clearly and justly and compassionately, forgive us our religion when it makes us self-righteous, exclusive, bigoted, unforgiving. Forgive us for being the Pharisee who prays, "I thank God that I am not like other men are." It was Jesus' self-identification with every person in his or her need that loved that person into the fulfillment you had ordained for them. Grant us his love that calls out the best in the other—whoever the other may be—mate, daughter, son, neighbor, adversary.

Grant to us the truth—the courage—to give ourselves to the discipline of the love that discovers joy in bearing a cross. "Who for the joy that was set before him endured the cross, despising the shame." In your love marshaled at the cross to break down all barriers separating man from man, race from race, nation from nation, may we discover those resources to beat down the boundaries of our exclusiveness until our sense of estrangement from any person is completely lost in a sense of brotherhood or sisterhood.

O God, you so loved the world that you gave to the uttermost—your only Son. May we be instruments of this love. For a world broken by struggles for power, we pray for the experience of your love that reconciles; for persons made lonely by the death of a loved one or friend, we pray for the assurance of your presence; for those suffering sickness and infirmity, we pray for your strength and health; for those wrestling with difficult decisions, we pray for guidance—the light of your way.

For those who have responded this morning to the call sounded through this church to be your disciples in this time and place, we pray for the blessedness of the tie that binds our hearts in Christian love. With them may we be faithful to your Word in Christ to be the Church, the community of the Resurrection.

And now, O Lord, grant to each one such a commitment to ministry that his or her task may be not a burden but a delight. Through him, whom to know is perennial joy, even through crosses to bear; who teaches us to pray together [the Lord's Prayer].—John Thompson

SERMON
Topic: To Will and to Work
TEXT: Phil. 2:1–13; Matt. 21:23–32

A tiger attacked a little boy six years of age at a school assembly. It was part of a presentation by a company that goes around to schools. The tiger had been involved in this presentation. They were in the process of leading it out on a leash. As they made their way to the doorway, the tiger leaped over a row of chairs and attacked the little boy, grasping the child's head in its jaws. Luckily the principal was nearby and was able to wrestle the little boy out of the jaws of the tiger. A spokesperson for the company that owned the tiger said later, "It wasn't really an attack. It was just a case of a playful tiger." My guess is, if you would ask that little boy, he would say, "That's a wild animal!"

There are elements of wildness in all of our lives. Sometimes we bring that wildness to a situation, and other times the situation or other people bring it. You have had the experience of going to an occasion and thinking that everything was going to be calm and delightful, and then something erupts and disrupts the whole event. You have probably had the experience of going with fear and trembling to meet a certain person, because you knew they had a volatile personality, and they turned out to be so calm and mellow on that particular occasion. We just never know, but there are elements of wildness in all of life.

The mega-message or theme of Scripture, from Genesis to Revelation, is that God moves life from chaos to creation. Another way of saying it would be, from wildness to creativity. Or we might also say, from separation to salvation. Our salvation is a healthy relationship with God and with those around us. God's work as recorded in all of Scripture is a movement and an invitation for us to be a part of that movement, from chaos to creation, from wildness to creativity, from separation to salvation.

In the Gospel lesson, our passage comes after Jesus' entry into Jerusalem on Palm Sunday, and after his cleansing of the Temple by driving out the moneychangers. There are many who would describe that scene as being wild.

When Jesus was in the Temple driving out the moneychangers, the authorities thought he was wild, out of control. He had stepped over the line. So they asked him, "By what authority do you do these things?" Jesus did not answer their question, but rather asked a question of his own: "Was John's baptism a baptism from heaven or from humans?" Jesus was not playing games. If these authorities perceived John's ministry as being inspired, and were willing to say so, then they would be receptive to Jesus. In other words, Jesus was asking them about their will. He was asking then, "What are your conscious choices about John and me? How do you understand us? Are you in God's flow of moving from chaos to creation, from wildness to creativity, from separation to salvation?"

Jesus gave them a second chance. He told them a parable in the form of a question. A father had two sons. He asked those sons to go and do some activities for him. The first son said, "Of course father, I will do it," but did not follow through. The second son said, "No father, I won't," but later repented and did what his father asked. Jesus said, "Which one did his father's will?" The religious authorities said, "Obviously the one who did what his father asked."

What Jesus is doing is what God has asked him to do. The tax collectors and the prostitutes who have repented are doing what God has asked them to do. But these so-called religious authorities are saying they will do God's will, but they are refusing to do it. They are not doing what God has asked them to do. Jesus' authority is based in his humble obedience to what God has asked him to do. The authority of the converts is in their transformed lives of doing what God has asked them to do. The so-called authorities' lack of authority is in their refusal to do what God has asked them to do.

Who is wild in this passage? Is it really Jesus? I don't believe so. The wild ones are the religious authorities, because they are refusing to move with the movement of God. They are refusing to end chaos and be a part of creation, to leave their wildness and move to creativity, to leave separation and move toward salvation.

In the Philippian congregation there was a bit of wildness, too. Now I am not talking about somebody spiking the punch at the potluck. That is one form of wildness, but that is not what was going on here. This was much more serious. These people were putting up entrance requirements for the Church. There was one group in the Church that said first you have to become a Jew before you can become a Christian. You have to be circumcised before you are acceptable in the Christian faith. The other group said no, if you are a Gentile you can come straight into the Church. It was a big fight. My guess is that the word *wild* is tame for describing the fight.

Paul wrote to this congregation and called them to be of one mind, because they weren't. He called them to agree around the mind of Christ, which did not grasp equality with God but humbled himself and became obedient even to the point of death.

That's the great movement from chaos to creation, from wildness to creativity, from separation to salvation. That is what God is doing in our lives. Paul was calling the people to come together around that movement, to be a part of it. He said, God is at work in you. It is not something you do all on your own. You and I don't have the power to enter into this movement on our own, but with God's help we can. "God is at work within you to will and to work God's good pleasure." To make conscious choices, that's our will; to act, that's our work. God is at work in us to help us make the right decisions, and then act on those decisions, to be a part of God's activity in the world. This is not something we do alone. It is something with which we have great help.

When we perform the marriage ceremony, we don't ask, "*Do* you love this person?" but "*Will* you love this person, for better or worse, for richer or poorer, in sickness and in health?" *Will* you work on the relationship? God has put up with a lot of stuff, but God wills and works for our well-being. God has made conscious choices and worked through the eons for our well-being.

Let me end with an insight that comes from the Native American tradition. A Native American grandfather was talking to his grandson about his feelings. The grandfather said, "I feel like there are two wolves in my heart that are fighting. One is a ferocious, violent, angry wolf, and the other is a loving, compassionate wolf." The grandson said, "Grandfather, which wolf in your heart will win?" The grandfather answered, "The one I feed."

God is at work in our lives to will and to work God's good pleasure.

Thanks be to God. Amen.—Jim Standiford

SUNDAY, SEPTEMBER 19, 2004
Lectionary Message

Topic: Surprise Ending
TEXT: Luke 16:1–13
Other Readings: Jer. 8:18–9:1; Ps. 79:1–9; 1 Tim. 2:1–7

I was almost to the end of a mystery by one of my favorite authors. For several chapters the clues had been falling into place, and I looked forward to the denouement by the detective and his best friend, two of the recurring characters in the series. I was horrified, then, when at the penultimate page the detective was shot several times. What was worse, the final page was ambiguous enough that I couldn't be certain whether he lived or died. What was the author trying to communicate? What about the other characters in the story? What about the series? Was that it?!

I. *Jesus challenges our expectations.* The bewilderment and frustration I felt were, I suspect, similar to that felt by the people who listened to Jesus as he told the parable in today's Gospel reading. Here too was a story with an unanticipated ending that defied listeners' expectations. The Pharisees scoffed, according to the text. But the other listeners may have scratched their heads—because this story is confusing. We have as much difficulty sorting it out as did those who heard the Savior speaking the words. At the beginning of the passage, Luke indicates that Jesus was addressing the disciples, but at the end, a different group responds to his words. The parable itself seems to have multiple endings. First, the dishonest steward is commended by the master for his shrewdness. Then Jesus apparently advises his listeners to make friends for themselves by means of unrighteous mammon. The parable closes with the famous saying that no servant can serve two masters; one cannot serve God and mammon. The absence of a tidy wrap-up to the story is at odds with our culture's tendency to package stories and major news events into commodities for the mass market.

II. *Jesus challenges our values.* We can try to write it off as a sloppy editing job by the author of Luke, but perhaps we should instead examine the source of our own discomfort.

Many of us wish that Jesus had not spoken favorably of someone so patently dishonest as this steward was: someone who reminds us of corrupt politicians, or of self-serving executives who put stockholders in peril while lining their own pockets. But a closer look at verses 10 to 12 demonstrates that our Lord did not commend the steward's dishonesty; he drew attention to the man's determination and preparation for the future. This may make us more uncomfortable than dishonesty, given how people in the United States—including Christians—squander the world's resources and save little of their own income. We do not prepare much for the future, much less give our full attention to it. And Jesus' words that "you cannot serve God and mammon" are antithetical to the values of a consumer-oriented culture. Some groups that identify themselves as Christian have touted a "prosperity gospel," suggesting that a fat bank account is a sign that God looks with favor on us and our faith. For these and other reasons, the Master's words may offend as well as confuse us.

III. *Jesus challenges us to live another way.* So why did Jesus use a "bad" man as a good example? For all his dishonesty, the steward demonstrated three virtues for followers of Jesus to emulate.

(a) Like the steward, Christians should be *careful and shrewd.* God has entrusted resources to Christians as individuals and as communities. We are to be "wise as serpents and innocent as doves" (Matt. 10:16), keeping in mind God's priorities and purposes.

(b) Jesus also challenges his disciples to follow the steward's example of *connecting with people.* In verse 8, the Master notes that "the sons of this world are more shrewd in dealing with their own generation than the sons of light." Unlike the Pharisees and Sadducees, who enjoyed distinguishing themselves from those among whom they lived, the steward cultivated relationships with a particular purpose in mind. For the Christian, that purpose is to show forth Christ as Lord.

(c) Finally, Christ challenges us to have the same *sense of urgency* that motivated the steward. Like the character in Jesus' story, we too will have to give an accounting for ourselves. We are stewards of time, energy, money, and other finite resources in this life—all gifts from a gracious God. How shall we respond to such generosity? The response Jesus seeks, and that the Spirit enables, is the urgent and unflagging determination to proclaim the gospel faithfully through our words and lives. Then, for all our shortcomings, we will hear our Master's commendation, just as the steward did.—Carol M. Norén

ILLUSTRATIONS
See the first three illustrations in Section VII of this book, "A Little Treasury of Illustrations."

SERMON SUGGESTIONS
Topic: God's Love for Those Who Wander Away
Text: Hos. 11:1–11
(1) It begins at the beginning. (2) It persists through our rebellions. (3) It utilizes the consequences of disobedience. (4) It receives those who return with a broken and contrite spirit.

Topic: The Life, the Truth, and the Way
Text: 1 Tim. 2:1–7
(1) The life (v. 2b). (2) The truth (v. 3). (3) The way (vv. 5–6).

WORSHIP AIDS

CALL TO WORSHIP.   "Help us, O God of our salvation, for the glory of thy name: and deliver us, and purge away our sins, for thy name's sake" (Ps. 79:9).

INVOCATION.   We would glorify you, O God, by what we do in this service of worship, but especially in the everyday events of life. Help us to make wise choices day by day. And we pray that as we sing, meditate, and weigh our options, we will not fail to honor you.

OFFERTORY SENTENCE.   "If you would enjoy ample rations in my house, then pay all your tithes into the treasury, and see what I will do, says the Lord of hosts; see if I will not then open the very sluices of heaven to pour a blessing down for you, a harvest more than enough" (Mal. 3:10 Moffatt).

OFFERTORY PRAYER.   Take, now, what we bring to you, O God, and use it to bless all of us and all of those whose lives are touched by this witness of gratitude.

PRAYER.   Litany of confession:

> LEADER: O Jesus Christ, the Lord of all good life: enrich and purify our lives and deepen in us our discipleship. Make us humble, brave, and loving; make us ready for adventure. We do not ask thee to keep us safe, but to keep us loyal to thee, who for us faced death unafraid.
> PEOPLE: Amen.
> LEADER: From lack of reverence for truth and beauty, from prejudice and sentimentalism, from being contented with the mean and ugly—
> PEOPLE: O Christ, deliver us.
> LEADER: From the cowardice that dares not face new truth, the laziness contented with half-truth, and the arrogance that thinks it knows it all—
> PEOPLE: O Christ, deliver us.
> LEADER: From artificiality in life and worship, from all that is hollow, unreal, and insincere—
> PEOPLE: O Christ, deliver us.
> LEADER: From trivial ideals and cheap pleasures, from mistaking vulgarity for humor—
> PEOPLE: O Christ, deliver us.
> LEADER: From being dull and pompous, from being rude, offensive, and ill-mannered—
> PEOPLE: O Christ, deliver us.
> LEADER: From the blasphemy of cynicism about our brothers, from all false pride, intolerance, and contempt—
> PEOPLE: O Christ, deliver us.
> LEADER: From all uncleanness and unwholesomeness, from selfishness and self-indulgence—
> PEOPLE: O Christ, deliver us.
> LEADER: From the false piety that cannot laugh, from being self-centered in our

pity, from being narrowly ecclesiastical, and from loving systems more than we
love thee—

PEOPLE: O Christ, deliver us.

LEADER: From the disloyalty of being satisfied with things as they are, in the church and
in the world; and from failing to share thy indignation—

PEOPLE: O Christ, deliver us.

LEADER: From everything in our lives that may hide the true light of thee, who art the
light of the world—

PEOPLE: O Christ, deliver us.[5]

SERMON

Topic: Born of Promise—Isaac

TEXT: Gen. 17:15–22; Gal. 4:28–29

Maternal indignation is built into the structure of creation—an act of God, if you please. In
the story of Ishmael and Isaac, the whole question of favoritism and legitimacy is God's
doing. Abraham is ninety-nine years old. Sarah is ninety. Abraham fell on his face in reverence at the appearance of God. Later he fell on his face in laughter at the revelation that he
would father a child by old Sarah—already known to be barren. To Abraham's credit, the
patriarch pled with God for Ishmael's place in the family, and God blessed Ishmael.

So Sarah had a baby. I have seen a mother bird protecting her nest and a dog defending
her pups. The hostility of Sarah began as a reaction to the condescending attitude of Hagar;
but after the birth of Isaac and the family party celebrating his weaning, Sarah turned on
the teenage Ishmael. Sarah saw Ishmael "playing with her son, Isaac." The text implies that
Ishmael was either teasing or abusing Isaac. In addition to abuse, the whole issue of blessing and inheritance were at stake. Ishmael had to go. For Sarah it was probably about protecting her baby; but for the memory of Israel it was about the historical turn of events at
the bottom of God's promise. Centuries later the incident was still remembered as Paul in
Galatians described the two mothers as symbols of slavery and freedom: "Now you, my
friends, are children of the promise, like Isaac. But just as when the child who was born
according to the flesh persecuted the child who was born according to the Spirit, so it is now
also (4:28–29).

I. *God has a sense of humor.* The name *Isaac* means, "he laughs." With all of the laughter surrounding his birth, one gets the impression that Isaac may be a joke. Being politically
or socially correct in our context does not allow adults to laugh in ridicule of a child, but the
laughter of joy over the gift of a child is timeless, and the story about the conception and
birth of Isaac is humorous in any culture.

One of the funniest sermons I have ever heard was delivered by Bill Leonard, dean of
Wake Forest Divinity School. The message was on the humor surrounding the birth of Isaac.
Leonard observed, "Life, even spiritual life, is filled with irony and the unexpected, and some-
times all you can do is laugh." Sarah laughed at the revelation to Abraham that she was to

---

[5]*The Book of Common Worship* (Philadelphia: Westminster Press, 1966), pp. 101–102.

conceive and bear a child. Leonard wondered if Sarah laughed throughout the next nine months, about which hurt most, the rheumatism or the morning sickness. You can almost hear her cackle: "Sure, I'm going to have a baby! And Medicare will have to pay for it!"

Leonard, a church historian, went on to observe the humor in our Christian mission. He told of the nineteenth-century Presbyterian minister who approached a frontier woman with the question, "Are there any Presbyterians around here?" The woman replied that the woods were full of all kinds of varmints and that the preacher was welcome to check skins out back for any Presbyterian hides that her husband may have hung out to dry. Another nineteenth-century journal tells of an exchange between a stranger and the preacher in a frontier revival meeting. The preacher inquired, "Are you a Christian?" to which the stranger replied, "Sir, I am a theological professor." "My Lord," the preacher said, "I wouldn't let a little thing like that keep me from Christ!"

Biblical scholar Joel Kaminsky wrote about Isaac as a humorous figure in the Bible. He suggested that we have to let down our defense of the serious message in order to see the humor of the Old Testament. Much of the story of Isaac is a stand-up comedy act, and Kaminsky sees Isaac as a "schlemiel," the fall guy or bumbling fool in a slapstick story that sometimes reaches the level of the Three Stooges or the Marx Brothers. Kaminsky notes that Isaac seems always to be the passive pawn of the women in his life, including his mother Sarah and his wife Rebekah. As Abraham approaches the end of life, he sends out a servant to find a wife for Isaac. Isaac is not allowed to go to Mesopotamia or Egypt under any circumstances. Kaminsky wonders if Isaac could find his way back home and why he was not permitted to choose his own wife. On his first meeting with Rebekah, according to Kaminsky, Isaac's human dignity is compromised and, in shock, Rebekah falls off her camel. Even as an old man, Isaac is less than brilliant in Jacob's act to steal Esau's blessing. Ironically, the blessing that Ishmael could not take from Isaac was given by Isaac to the wrong son.

II. *The promise of God transcends the person.* Paul observed that the foolishness of God is wiser than human wisdom. He was addressing the foolishness of the cross, but the point extends to the acts of God through the ages. By human standards, Isaac should never have been born. L. Hicks observed that the picture of Isaac is weak both in character and in his portrayal in Genesis. Isaac is the conduit for the promise of God, but among the Patriarchs he seems to be inferior and somewhat out of place. Ishmael may well have been the wiser of the two sons, as well as the more physically robust; but never mind who is the greatest: the promise came from God. None of the characters in the story really stands out as the hero. Abraham is remembered for his faith, and Jacob for his shrewd dealings, but Isaac is just remembered. Oh yes, he was the father of Jacob and Esau. Furthermore, the entire family of God came to be identified with his son Jacob, or Israel.

We need to get over the idea that our children have to excel in everything they do. I recall when Whitney Cochran commented that successful parenting means your adult offspring are not in jail. His point was well taken. We need to encourage our children to strive for their highest level of performance in school and in life, and to accept them with love and pride in what they are able to accomplish. As I grow older, I have to apply this same grace to myself. Poor Isaac: he had to live in the shadow of a bigger-than-life father and a son who ran intellectual circles around him. Nevertheless, Isaac carried forward the covenant of God. Bless God, who saw in Isaac a channel of blessing to the whole world.—Larry Dipboye

SUNDAY, SEPTEMBER 26, 2004
Lectionary Message

Topic: God's Investment Strategy

TEXT: Jer. 32:1–3a, 6–15

Other Readings: Ps. 91:1–6, 14–16; 1 Tim. 6:6–19; Luke 16:19–31

Recently I had my first experience of being executor of someone's estate. Though it has been a lot of work (and isn't over yet), I have to admit I have learned a lot in the process. Discovering how my late friend had invested his assets, along with the difficulty of settling insurance benefits when the named beneficiaries had predeceased my friend, all made me want to become more savvy and intentional about stewardship of my own resources. So I was an "easy sell" when I saw a copy of *You're Fifty—Now What? Investing for the Second Half of Your Life.* The author, Charles R. Schwab, recommends keeping at least 50 percent of your portfolio in a diversified mix of stocks and stock mutual funds for as long as you live.[6] He notes that between 1802 and 2000, stocks out-performed all other assets.

Schwab's statistics may be correct, but we all know what has happened to the stock market *since* 2000. Although Schwab is CEO of one of the largest financial services firms in the United States, and although he speaks from experience, evidence and anxiety make me question his wisdom. I wonder whether he would say the same things in the current economic climate. Is it possible that our capitalist system and way of government is coming to an end? After all, other superpowers have fallen. Who is Schwab to care about me? What's in it for him, anyway?

These questions aren't so different from the ones King Zedekiah asked Jeremiah in today's reading from the Old Testament. There was no love lost between the two men. At God's command, Jeremiah had prophesied against Zedekiah's father, King Jehoiakim, for his greed, idolatry, and injustice, and his preaching likened Zedekiah to a basket of rotten figs, ripe for destruction. Zedekiah was a weak, puppet king placed on the throne by Nebuchadnezzar. He listened to false prophets and made bad decisions. Jeremiah warned that the nation would be destroyed and the people taken into exile by the king of Babylon. In short, Jeremiah was hardly the king's spin doctor or head of the local chamber of commerce.

I. *Zedekiah questioned Jeremiah's investment strategy.* We can therefore understand the incredulity that greeted Jeremiah's actions as recorded in chapter 32. The prophet had made a career of announcing that the end of life as they knew it was near. The land was in the hands of the Chaldean (Babylonian) army, and Judah was about to be swallowed up. In the face of this, Jeremiah went and bought a field at Anathoth from his cousin Hanamel, following the usual business procedures of the day, though he did seal the deed in an earthenware vessel so it would last a long time. Buying real estate in a land under siege seemed absurd. It appeared to be as crazy as putting your life savings in Enron stock. Common sense said there was no future in it.

II. *God directed Jeremiah's investment.* As Jeremiah testified (beginning in 32:6), he purchased the field because the word of the Lord came to him, telling him to do this. God had

---

[6]Charles R. Schwab, *You're Fifty—Now What? Investing Strategies for the Second Half of Life.* New York: Three Rivers Press, 2001, p. 16.

ordered him to take dramatic action before, such as wearing a yoke on his neck as a visual aid supporting the message that God would put Judah under the yoke of Nebuchadnezzar (Jer. 27:2, 6). In buying land in Anathoth, Jeremiah was not throwing good money after bad, but demonstrating his confidence in God's promise of restoration. Yes, Zedekiah would be the last king of Judah, and yes, Jerusalem would be burned and its people taken into captivity for seventy years. But eventually, Jeremiah prophesied, the people would return and the land would be cultivated again. God would cleanse his covenant people of their sin, and God alone would be worshiped in Jerusalem (Jer. 33:8, 9).

God would honor the everlasting covenant with his people, and the Lord's purpose would be fulfilled. People would turn away from their idolatry and once again glorify and serve the God of Abraham, Isaac, and Jacob. In other words, Jeremiah's investment proclaimed the Word of the Lord and served God's purposes. He was a confident steward of the divine promise, and he made it known to those around him.

III. *Where and how does God call us to invest?* There is not a direct correspondence between ancient Judah and twenty-first-century United States, nor between Nebuchadnezzar and Saddam Hussein. Our vocation is not identical to Jeremiah's. Nevertheless, I believe that God calls the Church and individuals to investment strategies that are as prophetic as Jeremiah's purchase of the field at Anathoth. We demonstrate conviction that "God has a future here" when our ministries and resources are directed to people and places that others would write off as a lost cause: prison chaplaincies, drug rehabilitation centers, outreach in places that have been abandoned by businesses and government services. We embody the prophet's courage when, empowered by the Holy Spirit, we speak unpalatable truths to corrupt leaders. We enjoy a share of Jeremiah's vision when we realize that the wisdom of the world is folly with God (1 Cor. 3:19), and when we embrace the ministry of Jesus, the one who came to call not the righteous but sinners to repentance (Luke 5:32).

I know of an old, mainline church that has ministered in its city for over a century. It has been home to an elementary school; offered hospitality to civic groups and Scouts; and baptized, married, and buried the poor in its neighborhood. A homeless shelter and a halfway house run by the denomination abut its building. The neighborhood has changed many times in a hundred years, and the congregation has dwindled in size. Unfortunately, the denomination seems to have decided that the church is no longer a "good investment," and it has withdrawn the supply of clergy. The surrounding area is starting to gentrify, and rumor is that the shelter and halfway house will be demolished, and luxury condominiums owned by the denomination will be erected in their place. This may be financially advantageous, but it is surely not God's investment strategy.

What should we be doing? Following in the footsteps of Jeremiah, John the Baptist, Jesus and the apostles, we should be fearless in warning people of divine judgment, but also faithful in proclaiming God's restoration. Investing in the wasteland of broken lives, we incarnate the transforming, redeeming grace of Jesus Christ for those exiled in sin. And why do we invest ourselves? Because God is faithful, and true security is to be found in his promises.— Carol M. Norén

ILLUSTRATION

THE HARVEST.   A farmer in Virginia's Shenandoah Valley is using agricultural methods that are the antithesis of most modern agribusinesses. For example, rather than feeding grain and processed food to cattle on feedlots, he houses them in an open-sided barn during the winter, where they consume hay and produce manure. Every few days the farmer adds a layer of wood chips or straw or leaves to the bedding, building a manure "cake" that's three-feet thick by winter's end. He lards each layer with a little corn. In March, when the cattle have gone out to pasture, he lets pigs loose in the area. They turn and aerate the compost in their search for the corn. The manure that stank a few months earlier is transformed into sweet-smelling compost, which can be spread to nourish the soil for the next growing season. To the casual observer, tossing good corn into cow dung is worse than a bad investment; it's stupid. But the farmer knows that in good time it will result in flavorful meat, richer soil, and happier animals. God sometimes calls Christians to invest ourselves—and perhaps even get dirty in the process—in ways that make no sense to the rest of the world. But we trust that in God's good time, the yield will be plentiful.[7]

SERMON SUGGESTIONS

Topic: The Outpouring of God's Spirit
TEXT: Joel 2:23–30, esp. 28–30
(1) God's best gift is the gift of his Spirit, with its inner enduring—"And it shall come to pass afterward," after all material favor. (2) God's best gift is for all humanity—young and old, men and women, rich and poor (see Acts 2:16–21).

Topic: What to Aim at as a Christian
TEXT: 1 Tim. 6:6–19
(1) A life of faith (vv. 12–13). (2) A life of unblemished character (v. 14). (3) A life of good deeds (v. 18). (4) A life of confidence about the future (v. 19).

WORSHIP AIDS

CALL TO WORSHIP.   "He that dwelleth in the secret place of the Most High shall abide under the shadow of the Almighty. I will say of the Lord, he is my refuge and my fortress, my God; in him will I trust" (Ps. 91:1–2).

INVOCATION.   Increase our faith and our courage, O Lord, to expect your providence to sustain us in challenging times. Help us to turn our hearts more and more toward you, our best refuge and our indestructible fortress.

OFFERTORY SENTENCE.   "Offer the right sacrifices to the Lord, and put your trust in him" (Ps. 4:5 TEV).

OFFERTORY PRAYER.   Here it is, Lord, our monetary offering for you this morning. Some bring a lot. Some can bring only a small amount. Others could do better if they would use wisely what you have provided. But these are our offerings today. They are yours now. We

---

[7]Adapted from Michael Pollan, "Sustaining Vision," *Gourmet*, Sept. 2002, pp. 80–81.

bless them to your care and use, as Christ's Kingdom cries out in need for what we give. Touch us with the wonder of generosity, even now, we pray in Christ's name.—Henry Fields

PRAYER.   Teach us, O God, how to be humble in praying, though we may not kneel; how to turn our sight to the inner world of life as we close our eyes; how to cease from restless labors while we fold our hands in peace. If, in prayer, thy mercy comes like healing on our unquiet hearts, teach us how to share it with one another. If life has left us shaken, be a rock for our questing feet, and if we have grown confused amid the storm of circumstance, be thou a mighty peace steadying our hands and hearts. Abide with us, we beseech thee, for Christ's sake.—Samuel H. Miller

SERMON
Topic: A Growing Faith
Text: 2 Pet. 3:18

Near the end of Jesus' earthly life, as he prepared the disciples for his departure from them in physical form, it became obvious that their faith still needed a lot of growing (John 14:1–11). In response, Jesus promised that his Holy Spirit would continue to guide them into truth, which they were not yet ready to grasp (John 16:12–15). This promise was abundantly fulfilled as the disciples, in less than one generation, moved beyond the most revered institutions of their ancestral faith, substituting baptism for circumcision as the rite of initiation into the people of God, substituting Sunday for Saturday as the day of worship, and substituting a host of local congregations scattered over the Greco-Roman world for the one Temple in Jerusalem as the unifying center of their faith. These incredible changes could never have taken place so quickly, or even taken place at all, had not the earliest followers of Jesus received from him both the mandate and the freedom to grow.

This transformation wrought by Jesus forever defined his faith as a religion of growth. The earliest Christians dared to assert that their Lord himself set the pattern by "increasing in wisdom and in stature and in favor with God and man" (Luke 2:52). What an amazing claim: even the divine Son of God needed to grow! As his many seed parables testify, Jesus saw the world as a place where God makes things grow (Mark 4:8, 28, 32). Paul recognized that, in the spiritual realm, we may plant and water but "God gives the increase" (1 Cor. 3:6–7). The church, like each of its members, "grows with a growth that is from God" (Col. 2:19). The goal of this growth is Christian adulthood, a maturity that Paul defined as "the measure of the stature of the fullness of Christ" (Eph. 4:13). The overriding imperative of Christian existence is "to grow up in every way . . . into Christ" (v. 15). It is no wonder that the last verse of what may be the latest writing of the New Testament calls on us to "grow in the grace and knowledge of our Lord and Savior Jesus Christ" (2 Pet. 3:18).

These urgings raise for us an important question: How may I have a growing faith? Here let me offer a half-dozen practical suggestions for your consideration.

I. *Realize that when you are "born again" (John 3:1–7) you are but a babe in Christ.* In Roman mythology, Minerva sprang fully grown from the brain of Jupiter, but we begin the Christian journey as spiritual infants. At first, "like newborn babes, we long for the pure spiritual milk, that by it we may grow up to salvation" (1 Pet. 2:2). But as we develop, we no longer depend on milk as do those "unskilled in the word of righteousness" because they are children. Rather, we need "solid food" that is for the mature "who have their faculties trained by practice to distinguish good from evil" (Heb. 5:13–14). Do not absolutize any stage of your faith, but believe that the best is yet to be. Make your own the confession of the apostle Paul, "Not that I . . . have already attained, but I press on" (Phil. 3:12).

II. *Adopt some spiritual giants as your heroes of faith.* These may come from Scripture, such as are recounted in Hebrews 11. Paul realized the importance of his neophyte converts serving an apprenticeship in the workshop of Christian living when he said to the confused Philippians (3:2, 18–19), "Join in imitating me, and mark those who so live as you have an example in us" (3:17). The story of the Church through the centuries is full of towering figures who, by their lives, show us the meaning of Christian maturity. But our selection of inspiring pacesetters is not limited to those "celebrity Christians" about whom we read because of their brilliant insight or heroic courage. You can find in this congregation a number of wise mentors who are much farther down the road to maturity than you have thus far traveled. Using a "buddy system" approach, ask one or more of them to share with you the secrets of their growth.

III. *Once you have tapped the wisdom of your spiritual elders, set your own specific goals for growth.* Inventory both your dreams and your discontents. What attitudes and actions do you want to discard as unworthy of your highest potential? What hungers of the spirit do you want to feed because they have been starved for nourishment? What aspirations will bring you the greatest sense of fulfillment if you are able to achieve them? Make some lists that you can look at and brood about in prayer. Seek to prioritize your purposes in a developmental sequence, and set yourself some deadlines for their accomplishment. Share these plans with your closest soul mates, asking them to help you be realistic in attempting the art of the possible. Most important, repudiate low expectations and let yourself be challenged by the promise of growth in God's tomorrow.

IV. *Translate your aspirations into action.* Commit yourself to a new pattern of conduct for each challenge you are seeking to meet. Stated simply, there is no couch potato growth! Merely sitting in church will not lead to spiritual growth any more than sitting in front of the television will lead to physical or mental growth. The key is to do something you have never done before so as to enlarge your fund of experience. If you want to "grow in grace" (2 Pet. 3:18) by becoming a more giving person, then decide to tithe. Should the change be too great to make in one leap, then resolve to increase your giving by 1 percent per year until you get to 10 percent. Or if you want to "grow in knowledge" (2 Pet. 3:18) of how to apply the Bible, agree to teach a Sunday school class. Should you have no background in this area, then start as a substitute or associate teacher, but do not stop until you reach your goal.

V. *Once you have begun to make real progress with the encouragement and reinforcement of your fellow Christians, then you are ready for the tougher challenge of taking on the enemies of our faith.* Some may want to practice by engaging in armchair combat with the likes of Karl Marx, Charles Darwin, Sigmund Freud, and Friedrich Nietzsche; but the real battle is joined not with these intellectual heavyweights but with the ordinary folk whom we see every day. There are more than a hundred million secularists or skeptics in America who, regardless of their spiritual heritage, are functionally irreligious. Can you counter their criticisms of the Christian Church? Or answer their questions about Christian doctrine? Here the point is not so much to defeat their position as it is to persuade them of your position. Can you commend your faith so winsomely that unbelievers will embrace it as their own? You will never know until you try, and you will grow only if you try!

VI. *Be patient in your efforts to grow, realizing that the achievement of maturity is the quest of a lifetime.* Expect progress to be slow and setbacks to be frequent. Think how often we go on a diet to lose weight, or embark on an exercise program to become physically fit, only to neglect these commitments once we tire of the disciplines they impose. Even in the spiritual realm we are easily distracted from our goals, frustrated by our failures, and wearied by our opponents, causing us to backslide and regress into patterns of immaturity, as did those addressed in the Epistle to the Hebrews (2:1, 3:12–13, 5:11–12). The only answer is to approach the Christian life with the relentless tenacity of an athlete determined to go the distance regardless of the effort required. Because our life here on Earth is but preparation for the life to come, we must constantly ask ourselves at every stage of the journey, Am I still "growing up in every way into Christ?" (Eph. 4:15).

If that description of the Christian life seems too daunting in its demands, remember that "God gives the growth" (1 Cor. 3:6–7), and Christ is his gift! To be sure, there is "a race set before us" that we must "run with perseverance" despite "every weight and sin which clings so closely." Yet we can run that race, not only "surrounded by so great a cloud of witnesses" to cheer us on, but also by "looking to Jesus," who pioneered the path we are called to follow (Heb. 12:1–2). Even though this involved enduring a cross of shame, he stayed the course until he perfected our faith and took his rightful place in heaven. We are not asked to do anything that Jesus has not first done for us. So let the heart kneel before him and whisper with the disciples of old, "Lord, increase our faith!" (Luke 17:5).—William E. Hull

SUNDAY, OCTOBER 3, 2004
Lectionary Message

Topic: Increase Your Faith
TEXT: Luke 17:5–10
Other Readings: Lam. 1:1–6; Ps. 137; 2 Tim. 1:1–14

I. *Difficult words.* Jesus said to his disciples, "If your brother sins, rebuke him, and if he repents, forgive him. If he sins against you seven times in a day and seven times comes back to you and says I repent, forgive him." To this the apostles replied, "Increase our faith!" Obviously Christ's followers felt incapable of measuring up to the standards he had set for them (see Luke 17:1–4). They wanted greater faith to lay hold of the power to live up to Jesus' standards, so they asked him to increase their faith. Jesus wanted his followers to see themselves as having a sense of duty. He therefore told them the story told in verses 6 to 10 of chapter 17. Verse 6 is figurative language that indicates that the power of faith is as unlimited as the power of God. As is always the case when Jesus' teaching is taken seriously, this is difficult stuff. Obedience in these matters is challenging, but it is obedience that enables us to be more like Jesus Christ himself. Jesus always stands against sin in perpetual rebuke and he delights in forgiving repentant sinners. His forgiveness is limitless, but how can ours be?

II. *Demanding responsibility.* Jesus called for demanding responsibility from his followers. It's interesting that the disciples did not ask for more love and tolerance in order to forgive. Nor did they ask for further understanding. Instead, they asked for their faith to increase so they could adequately rebuke and forgive others.

The connection between faith and forgiveness may at first blush not be an easy one. But the disciples had learned on other occasions when Jesus had said similar things to them. For example, in Mark 11:22–25, Jesus said, "Have faith in God. . . . I tell you the truth, if anyone says to this mountain, go, throw yourself into the sea, and does not doubt in his heart but believes that what he says will happen, it will be done for him. Therefore I tell you, whatever you ask in prayer, believe that you have received it, and it will be yours. And when you stand praying, if you hold anything against anyone, forgive him, so that your father in heaven may forgive you your sins." Here we see the connection between faith and forgiveness. Jesus explained the power that faith has to do wonders, concluding with the call to forgive. It was this understanding that informed the disciples' prayer in verse 5: "Increase our faith!" This prayer declared their faith. It is by faith that we even ask for faith.

III. *Delight in duty.* Faith, forgiveness, and service are closely connected in Jesus' teaching. In verses 7 to 10 we see a short parable about the life of a servant. The service of Jesus' servants is one of duty. Our attitude should be that we have done only what is required. Obedience is a matter not of honor but of duty. As Christ's followers we do not have the right to pick and choose what commands we will obey. Our tendency is to think we can earn our salvation or earn a relationship with God, but Jesus offered three rhetorical questions that can help us understand the key to relationship with him.

1. In verse 7 Jesus says, "Suppose one of you had a servant plowing or looking after the sheep. Would you say to the servant when he comes in from the field, 'Come along now and sit down to eat?'" The answer is no.
2. Then Jesus asks, "Would he rather not say, 'Prepare my supper; get yourself ready and wait on me while I eat and drink; after that, you may eat and drink'?" The answer this time is yes.
3. Finally Jesus asks, "Would he thank the servant because he did what he was told to do?" The answer is no. The only proper response, Jesus says, is, "We are unworthy servants; we have only done our duty" (v. 10).

Jesus drove home his point to his followers: forgiving, believing, and serving are all nothing extraordinary. They are what is expected of Christ's followers. This is the way believers are supposed to live. And when we live this way, we are at best "unworthy servants." Such a life of extraordinary duty is ordinary Christianity. The way to increase our faith is to be extraordinarily ordinary.

These demanding words warned Christ's followers against pride and presumption. The reason for these words is that everything is of grace. There is nothing in us on which we can stand. There is nothing we can claim, no ground for personal pride or personal accomplishment. We are indeed unworthy servants who have been graciously forgiven; thus we are to graciously forgive others. So we ask for faith so that God can do a work in our lives that will cause us to generously forgive others, and motivate us to faithful service until the day of Christ. Indeed, there is no ground for pride, only eternal praise.

The ultimate point of Jesus' story is that the nature of a master-servant relationship allows the master to make such demands on his servant. Because this is the case, how much more can God expect of his servants in his Kingdom. God's servants must recognize that whatever they do in God's service is still inadequate to deserve standing on their own. This demanding parable drives us to our knees and causes us to cry out with thanksgiving to God. Thanks be to God for his immeasurable grace.—David S. Dockery

ILLUSTRATIONS

KNOWLEDGE AND FAITH.   We don't know the millionth part of 1 percent about anything. We don't know what water is. We don't know what light is. We don't know what gravitation is. We don't know what enables us to keep on our feet when we stand up. We don't know what electricity is. We don't know what heat is. We don't know anything about magnetism. We have a lot of hypotheses about these things, but that is all. But we do not let our ignorance about all these things deprive us of their use.—Thomas Edison

INSTRUMENTAL FAITH.   The man who has faith speaks, and the power of God is demonstrated. This accords with the Synoptic emphasis on the power of Jesus' word and is further illustrated by statements made by Paul (Rom. 15:18–19; 1 Cor. 2:4, 4:20). This statement is not to be watered down by spiritualizing it. It simply means that the person who has the smallest possible amount of real faith becomes the instrument of God's unlimited power. On the other hand, we must recognize that faith is not a magic by which we control God. Nor is it synonymous with presumption. We cannot use it to back God into a corner and force him to produce a sensational show that will enable us to make the headlines.—Malcolm O. Tolbert

SERMON SUGGESTIONS

Topic: Why Seek the Lord?
TEXT: Amos 5:6–7, 10–15
(1) Injustice invites God's anger. (2) Injustice constructs its own punishment. (3) Injustice can be forgiven, justice achieved, and grace enjoyed.

Topic: How to Live in a Pagan World
TEXT: 2 Tim. 1:1–14
(1) With a sincere faith. (2) With a courageous testimony. (3) With a true message.

WORSHIP AIDS

CALL TO WORSHIP.   "How shall we sing the Lord's song in a strange land?" (Ps. 137:4).

INVOCATION.   Guide us, Lord, as we attend to our souls this day; deepen and broaden our understanding of the faith and of the Savior who loved us enough to die for us and waits in glory to receive us.—E. Lee Phillips

OFFERTORY SENTENCE.   "Offer the sacrifices of righteousness and put your trust in the Lord" (Ps. 4:5).

OFFERTORY PRAYER.   You have given your best for us, O Lord, and now we bring our offerings, such as they are, to you, and we pray that they may be used for your glory.

PRAYER.   Creator God, who indeed has made this day and all days, create in us, your children, a will and spirit to rejoice and be glad. In thanksgiving and praise, release our common sorrow and our personal sadness; may we remember and know anew that you are good. As we worship, may we too be led beside the still waters, may our souls be calmed, and may our inner self be refreshed and made whole. As we gather and worship around our Lord's table, O God, we are lovingly and redemptively reminded that you have spread the generous table before us. Cleanse us from all the unrighteousness of our ways as we prepare to meet you in the bread and cup. Wash our hands and our hearts. Erase the trash and debris from our walk and restore the joy in our journey with you.

Loving and accepting parent of us all, who wants to gather us under your wing as a hen gathers her chicks, we pray for our broken and dark world, ripped and torn by seething hate and ageless ill will, by blinding madness that bathes us in a constant flow of innocent blood. How long, O God, shall the helpless and innocent suffer so?

Merciful Redeemer, we pray for our country, often obsessed with the worst of ourselves, mindlessly enslaved to the absurd and grotesque. We are addicted to the folly and foibles of the rich and supposedly famous. O God, O God, deliver us from our foolish ways. Set upright our twisted and distorted view of reality. Tender presence, we pray for those suffering from the damage of disasters and for those who have lost loved ones in the line of duty.

God of the Church, the bride of Christ, we pray for ourselves as Church. As we gather each week for worship and work, may we seek your presence, wisdom, and direction. Bless and grace those who visit among us. Grant us wisdom and courage to be about the labors of the Kingdom. In worship and at the table, O God, come and redeem us, and make us your own, in Christ.–William M. Johnson

SERMON
Topic: Let Go of Ego
TEXT: Mark 1:14–15

I am unsettled by some current uses of the word *repent,* and the following is an effort to get at what Jesus meant in the Gospel for today.

I hear numerous preachers say, "Repent of your sins, and trust Jesus." Also, while driving down the Western Kentucky Parkway, I came upon a bit of fence-post preaching that said, "Repent of your sins and turn to God."

This sermon is a search for the meaning of *metanoia* as Jesus and John the Baptist used it, as a ground-clearing precondition for believing the gospel. *Metanoia* is a cognitive term meaning "to change one's mind." Jesus use doesn't seem to convey that moral cleansing is preparatory to salvation; rather, such cleansing happens only subsequently, as an ongoing project of the believer's life. Another word translated "repent" is *metamelomia,* which usually means "regret" or some other emotion of contrition. It troubles me that *metanoia* is being used less to mean a cognitive shift in meaning and more to mean a moral stance of "resolving to sin no more"—which, by the way, turns out to be a discouraging prospect (1 John 1:8)!

Contemporary usage seems to define *repent* as "turning from sins," which I believe was not the impediment that Jesus had in mind. The self-righteous ones to whom Jesus was speaking thought this was precisely what they had already done. The question arises, Can one forsake all sins in the instant it takes for one to be "born from above"? If *repent* is given the meaning "turning from sins," it seems to me that to forsake all at once every sin one has ever committed is impossible. And what about the sins the believer commits down the road after being saved (1 John 1:10)? As I read it, that is literally what the proposition to turn from sin is asking. When I hear or see "repent of your sins" interpreted as "turn from your sins," I assume that the whole catalogue is to be recalled, and each sin is to be recognized by name and confessed individually. If the penitent at that instant knows all the sins he or she has ever committed, and will ever commit, then the penitent either knows more than most or has forgotten too much. To sum up, there seems to be no scriptural ground for believing that "repenting of one's sins" can be done *carte blanche!*

The impossibility lies partially in the fact that some of my sins are buried in unmarked graves in my unconscious, and many of my sins were committed when I was ignorant of God's will and at the time knew no better. As my Christian experience becomes progressively enlightened, as my biblical knowledge increases, and as my fellowship with the Holy Spirit informs and energizes me, I am becoming aware of thoughts and deeds that were innocent at one time, according to what I understood, but are now wrong and should be indicted (Isa. 6:1–5). I could not have repented of all of these sins when as a fifteen-year-old I became a Christian. Yet the instant I put my trust in what Jesus did for my salvation, rather than in what I could do, I was saved (Eph. 2:8–10).

To be sure, forsaking our sins is important. When Paul says to put off the old person and put on the new (Eph. 4:22–24), the verb tense seems to indicate prolonged action. If correct, this putting off and putting on takes place continuously as we grow in grace as God's children. Never in a lifetime, though, will we exhume all those sins from the secret graveyards of our lives, or rouse them from the attics and closets and other hiding places. Then why bother if one is already God's child? The reason is simple: if the Holy Spirit makes one aware of a sin, past or present, that has not yet been owned and confessed before God, then the believer's fellowship with the Heavenly Father is impaired. If we assume that God knows all our sins and has forgiven them (which he did when we were saved), but then the Holy Spirit brings to light some prior sinful thought or deed that we ignore and leave to languish and fester, we will not be at peace.

When Jesus came into Galilee preaching his inaugural "repent and believe the gospel" (Mark 1:15), he used the word *metanoia* for "repent," which, as I have said, means "to change the mind." Forsaking one's sins is only indirectly what Jesus had in mind; the conviction and courage to forsake one's sins is only one of the fruits of the Christian life; it is not the whole tree!

Then what did Jesus mean by "repent"? What mind-set did his hearers need to change? The mind is that part of the human that thinks, feels, and wills, in contrast with the body. Therefore, Jesus was speaking to a cognitive condition resident at that time, most ostensibly in the Jews but also in all humans, and since. The Jews were confident that as descendents of Abraham and his seed (remember John the Baptist excoriating them in Matt. 3:7–10?) they were safely within the covenant that God made with Abraham. But they misunderstood the nature of the covenant. It required Abraham to abandon every security on which humans rely. Abraham's only security was the promise of God (Rom. 4:1–5). However, over the centuries this understanding was terribly deformed in the minds of the Jews.

As the Jews developed their beliefs on how to gain God's approval, their doctrines became self-centered, and in their self-absorption they closed themselves to the light of God's truth. In so doing, they gradually moved away from the original intention and challenge of the covenant. I once heard Rev. John Claypool say, "Only God is original; the rest of us just pass the biscuits!" Over the centuries, as they passed the biscuits, the Jews distorted God's intention by locating the problem outside themselves. It was God's attitude toward them that needed changing! This assumption drives the superficially pleasing but deceptive belief of salvation by works. In this assumption, the *evidence* is confused with the *cause*. The Jews banked on the idea that God could be appeased with ritual and sacrifice—by buying God off, as it were—and that a meticulous regimen of law-keeping would gain God's approval (Rom. 3:20; Titus 3:5–6).

In short, the sin that needed to undergo cognitive change was the sinful notion that one could save oneself. I hear Jesus saying that only when one is freed from this fatal conceit is one free to "believe the gospel." The gospel is that "God has come to Earth in the improbable figure of a small-town carpenter turned itinerant preacher, who was condemned as a common criminal, despised and abandoned, dead and buried—and then, in a moment that transformed the whole structure of reality, Jesus arose from the grave to become the greatest power in the universe, and the Lord of all human destiny."[1] As the apostle Paul put it, "For he hath made him to be sin for us who knew no sin, that we might be made the righteousness [all that God expects of us for salvation] of God in him" (2 Cor. 5:21).

It was this intractable, intransigent, and boastful conceit of the Jews (Rom. 10:3), and in all of us—a scornful indifference—that Jesus met head on with the call to "repent"! The notion that "the blood of bulls and of goats, and the ashes of a heifer" (Heb. 9:13), or whatever human device was thought to avail for salvation, had to go. The call was for the one thing that is most difficult for humans to do: let go of ego! Could this have been the "strait gate" and narrow way to which Jesus referred (Matt. 7:13–14)? Doubtless, it is not only improbable that without the brooding, convicting, and regenerating power of the Holy Spirit, a human being could do this, but the gift of the Holy Spirit even presupposes the impossibility (John 16:7–11).

What is the fruit of this "repentance"? What test was John the Baptist talking about when he instructed the Jews who came to him for baptism to "produce fruit in keeping with repentance" (Matt. 3:7–9)? The confirming evidence was to be "suitable or compatible," or kin to the repentance he was talking about. I believe that fruit to be a cognitive decision: "to as many as received him [not only by assent of the mind but by allegiance of the whole person] . . . even to them that believed [cognition] on his name" (John 1:12). John was calling for a change in perception to a complete abandonment of every other security and a dependence on Jesus Christ, who shed his blood for our sins (1 John 1:7). The penitent would no longer boast of vainglorious sacrifices or feel absolved because of conformity to the law (Rom. 8:3–5). As Jesus said to the crowd in John 6:28–29 when they asked, "What shall we do that we might work the works of God?" "This is the work of God, that you *believe* on him whom he has sent." Then, is the fruit to which John the Baptist referred—not deeds per se but *believing* in Jesus for salvation rather than in what one can do for oneself? This is the believer's *magnum opus!* Acknowledging and accepting Christ's finished work on the cross is the most worthy tribute we can bring to the feet of our Savior. The apostle Paul said in Romans 5:1–2 that we "access the grace of God by faith in Jesus Christ," and I say, glorying in this "access" is the greatest evidence the Christian can bear to convince another that a radical cognitive change has occurred by the grace of God.

Let John tell about the condemnation for which one should repent. "And this is the condemnation, that light is come into the world, and men love darkness rather than light,

---

[1] Peter Berger, *A Far Glory* (New York: Free Press, 1992) p. 6.

because their deeds [works to obtain salvation] are evil"—not consciously evil, but evil because in our self-absorption we are oblivious to the light of God's truth (John 3:19). The *light* is the loving self-disclosure that God has provided through the centuries—a way of salvation in Jesus Christ (John 8:12). If your sole trust is in Christ for salvation, you are "walking [living] in the light." If you mix works (Rom. 11:6) with grace, you are walking in the darkness, unheeding of God's revelation that Christ is the all-sufficient Savior.

Jesus came preaching the Kingdom of God, that God wants to reign from the inside (Jer. 31:33), and calling for renunciation of an imagined righteousness that is achieved by meritorious works (Rom. 10:3–4). "Give that up," he said, and with childlike faith accept the light that you are rejecting (John 1:5). This, then, is the righteousness that exceeds the righteousness of the scribes and Pharisees (Matt. 5:20). This commission the apostle received from the Lord himself: "To open their eyes, and to turn them from darkness to light, and from the power of Satan to God, that they may receive forgiveness of sins, and inheritance among them which are sanctified by faith that is in me" (Acts 26:18). And his commission to us?

Many years ago I heard the young Rev. Franklin Paschall preach the missionary sermon at the annual meeting of the district association, and he closed his compelling message with these lines that are to the purposes of this sermon:

Out of honor and into shame,
the Master willingly, gladly came.
And now since he must not suffer anew
As the Father sent him, so sendeth he you!

—John C. Huffman

SUNDAY, OCTOBER 10, 2004
Lectionary Message
Topic: Thanklessness and Thanksgiving
TEXT: Luke 17:11–19
Other Readings: Jer. 29:1, 4–7; Ps. 66:1–12; 2 Tim. 2:8–15

I. *Jesus heals ten lepers.* In this story we are introduced to what it means to live a life characterized by thanksgiving. Like many of the stories in Luke's Gospel, this one takes place in the midst of a journey. Jesus is now moving east to west along the boundary between Samaria and Galilee. His travels were hardly straight-line journeys, because they were filled with providential encounters with special people along the way. The encounter in this story takes place with the healing of ten lepers.

The miracle contained in this story has a double level of cultural tension because the main figure is both a leper and a Samaritan. Lepers were physically isolated and Samaritans were disliked for being racial half-breeds. The whole idea of a Samaritan leper receiving God's gracious healing was undoubtedly shocking to many who first heard this story, because they had written off people from both categories as being outside the boundaries of God's covenant people.

The story begins with Jesus entering the village and being approached by ten different lepers. The very fact that they came to him says volumes about Jesus. What they knew about Jesus told them that he was approachable. No doubt their hope for divine healing drove them to do the extraordinary. Still, they called to him from a distance, honoring the cultural understanding not to mix with other people. Leprosy was highly contagious and meant isolation until the condition cleared. In our text we see that the lepers cried out for mercy: "Have pity on us!" This is a cry for compassion, a request that Jesus no doubt heard frequently. Above all they wanted to be healed. Jesus' words in this context are startling. He told them, "Go show yourselves to the priest," for this is what the law commanded (see Lev. 13–14). A person would not or could not go to the priest until he or she had been healed. Thus everyone would understand that when Jesus said, "Go to the priest," full healing would indeed occur. When the lepers turned to do as Jesus had said, they were immediately healed. What an amazing picture of God's grace. The healings allowed these men to return to normal lives and to live no longer in isolation. Jesus' command to these lepers required faith on their part. How could ten people respond equally in faith? we might ask. Yet they were all cleansed. It was a mass healing. No doubt a wild celebration followed.

II. *Jesus hears from one leper.* There is one key point to this story that goes beyond the healing. It is the thankful heart of the Samaritan leper. The Samaritan leper was seized with an overwhelming sense of gratitude. Although the others were happy and thrilled, they did not return to Jesus to offer thanks. For the Samaritan, the ceremonial bill of clean health could wait. The work of grace that God was doing in his heart was more important to him than the ceremonial need. In verse 15 we hear this one say thanks to God in a loud voice. He had been loud in his pleading for healing, and now he was loud with his praise. It was as though he were crying out through a megaphone. "Mega-voiced" is the way the Greek text pictures his praise to God.

The Samaritan fell at Jesus' feet and thanked him. He recognized Jesus as God's agent of healing. He returned to Jesus with a heart giving glory to God and thanks to Jesus. He recognized God's power at work through Jesus Christ.

That the Samaritan returned to thank Jesus probably indicates that his heart had been changed as well as his body, that he had received salvation in addition to physical healing. Indeed, his faith had made him well. Jesus did not imply that salvation comes by having a disposition of gratitude, but he did say that where true saving faith exists, it will be accompanied by a profoundly thankful heart. The New Testament is clear that believing people have hearts that praise, glorify, and constantly thank God (see 1 Cor. 15:57; 2 Cor. 9:15; Col. 3:17; Heb. 13:15).

III. *What does Jesus hear from us?* The apostle Paul wrote in Romans 1 about people who were idolatrous. He said, "For although they knew God, they neither glorified him as God nor gave thanks to him" (Rom. 1:21). Grateful people are not only pleasing to God, they are also encouraging to those around them. They are lights in the darkness. Thankful people are different. We find ourselves in a thankless culture. May God give us thankful hearts that express thanksgiving to God and to his agents in our lives in this world.—David S. Dockery

ILLUSTRATIONS

ATTITUDE.   The heavenliest kind of Christian exhibits more bow than cloud, walking the world in a continual thanksgiving.—Christina Rosetti (1830–1894)

FITLY SPOKEN.   The Bible has wonderful examples of the power of speech and the blessedness of the "word fitly spoken" (Prov. 25:11). There was the incident of Naaman and Elisha. Naaman had come all the way from Syria to be cured of his leprosy, but when Elisha sent out his servant to meet Naaman and told him to go wash seven times in the Jordan, Naaman went into a rage and, turning his chariot about, started homeward. But one of his officers spoke the word in season and said to him, "My father, if the prophet had bid thee do some great thing, wouldest thou not have done it? How much rather, then, when he saith to thee, Wash, and be clean?" (2 Kings 5:13). Naaman saw the sense in this, put down his pride and anger, and went and washed in the Jordan, and his flesh became as the flesh of a little child.—Clarence Edward Macartney

SERMON SUGGESTIONS

Topic: Don't Preach at Us!
TEXT: Mic. 1:2, 2:1–10 TEV
Who are the people who do not want to be confronted with their wrongs? (1) Those who plan to take advantage of the helpless. (2) Those who are setting themselves up as examples of disaster. (3) Those who presume on the Lord's protection while they carry out their mischief.

Topic: The Unfettered Word
TEXT: 2 Tim. 2:8–15
(1) It is about the crucified and Risen Christ. (2) It is for the salvation and eternal glory of believers. (3) It deserves to be taught and proclaimed with scholarship and discipline.

WORSHIP AIDS

CALL TO WORSHIP.   "Shout with joy to God, all the earth! Sing to the glory of his name; offer him glory and praise! Say to God, 'How awesome are your deeds! So great is your power that your enemies cringe before you. All the earth bows down to you; they sing praise to you, they sing praise to your name'" (Ps. 66:1–4 NIV).

INVOCATION.   O God, let us be caught up in the joy and praise of your faithful people across the centuries. Grant that our songs may glorify you and that everything else we do in this service of worship may exalt your name.

OFFERTORY SENTENCE.   "Whatever you are doing, put your whole heart into it, as if you were doing it for the Lord and not for men, knowing that there is a master who will give you an inheritance as a reward for your service. Christ is the master you must serve" (Col. 3:23 REB).

OFFERTORY PRAYER.   Help us, O God, to be inspired as we give, by the one who gave all for us.

PRAYER.   Eternal God, whom the heaven of heavens cannot contain, yet who makest thine abode in humble and contrite hearts, here would we meet with thee, and feel for a moment in our souls the greatness of thy power. Here would we know the dignity of life and learn thy perfect law of liberty. Here would we rise to the height of thy upward calling, and deem ourselves thy sons and the heirs of immortality. We repent that we have despised our souls. When evil has made of us its prey, we have said, "These sins are not ours. They are a heritage of the past. Our fathers have sowed the wind; we reap the whirlwind." Thus have we sought to silence thy voice of rebuke. Reveal to us now the mystery of our greatness. Meet with each one of us alone. Fill each one of us with a sense of moral freedom, of personal worth, of our kinship with thee. May we, in the strength of thy visitation, rise up and shake off the bonds that bind us, and live henceforth as those whom thou hast made a little lower than the angels, and crowned with glory and honor.—Samuel McComb

SERMON
Topic: The Power of Jesus
Text: John 14:10

Reinhold Niebuhr has, I suppose, been one of the most severe critics of our civilization and culture, and yet when he was a younger man and still pastor of a church in Detroit, he wrote in his notebook something that we must not forget. Remembering who wrote it, its significance is greater than it otherwise would be. *"People must be charmed into righteousness."*

The one who has charmed more people into righteousness than any other is Jesus of Nazareth. The first thing people noticed about Jesus was his power. It was the first thing they talked about. He had power to heal the sick. The record puts it very simply: "Everyone with sick friends brought them to Jesus, and he cured them."

We must say that whatever power it takes to rearrange the various parts of a man's mind and body so he can function fully and freely, Jesus had it. He was not the only one who had it, mind you. People had had it before him, and people have had it since; but he had it to an intense and extraordinary degree, and used it in a unique way, for a unique purpose.

Also, allowing for the fact that his primary purpose in life was not to make people well but to make them good, nevertheless, the first experience that people had of Jesus' power was when he touched their broken bodies and their tortured minds.

He had power also over nature. There was a storm at sea that endangered his life and the lives of his friends; he stopped it. There was a hungry crowd that followed him out into the country to listen to his words; he fed them. He walked on the water; he changed water into wine; he raised the dead.

Again, allowing for exaggeration and extravagance, the inevitable enlargement of the original event, it is impossible to get away from the fact that in Jesus men saw someone in whom the higher order had power over the lower order. Just as a genius can take a violin made of wood and catgut and exert the higher order of his spirit over that lower order of material reality so that it sings with unbelievable beauty, so Jesus had this same sort of power over nature.

His words had power. When he spoke, people listened. They did not always understand and they did not always like what he said, but they listened.

The secret, I am sure, is to be found in the fact that when he spoke, he spoke not from a book but from his heart. He said harsh things—"Woe unto you, Scribes and Pharisees, hypocrites!" He said tender things, some of the most tender things, I reckon, that have ever been said—"Come unto me all ye that labor and are heavy laden, and I will give you rest." He made profound things plain; he put the truth in stories that people never forgot.

There was also power in his very presence. This is harder to describe. You have to feel it, you have to sense it as you read the Gospel narratives. He had the power to draw people to him. As they were drawn to him, they were often afraid of him, according to the stories; not always, I think, because they thought he would hurt them, but because they might hurt him and be unworthy of him.

I wish you could feel the power of his presence now. It is not something that anyone can tell you about; you have to feel it.

A person reading the Gospel for the first time would almost certainly get the impression that whoever Jesus was, and however accurate or inaccurate the stories about him might be, he was a man who had a strange and unprecedented power.

There are three or four things to be observed about the power of Jesus, and the first is that *the power did not come from Jesus himself.* "I can of mine own self do nothing," he said, according to St. John's Gospel. "The Father that dwelleth in me, he doeth the works." It is only when we are able to open our lives so that they can be channels for a power greater than ourselves that we are ever likely to be strong. "Of mine own self I can do nothing." Jesus said it. You may learn to say it. And he never used his power in his own behalf.

Another thing to observe about the power of Jesus is that *it was not the sort of power that enabled him to do anything he wanted to do.* He wanted, at least for a brief moment, at the end of his life, to avoid death himself, but he didn't; he couldn't. Why? Because his power was always under the control of his love. He loved people too much to force them into the Kingdom. He opened the doors, he showed them the way, but unless they were willing to respond to what he said and to what he showed them, they remained outside. He would not force them. He would not violate their integrity as persons. He loved God too much to usurp his sovereignty, and though he wanted to avoid death at his early age, when he saw clearly that it was the will of God that the cup would pass from him only if he drank it, he drained it to the dregs.

There are two kinds of power: one is the power that *drives,* the other is the power that *draws.* One is the power of a cannon, which drives its shot on its way to destruction; the other is the power of the sunrise, which draws men to itself. Jesus had both kinds of power. He used the first only occasionally, and with great restraint. He counted on the second, and by it has been drawing people to himself ever since.

In the long run, his real power was not in his success but in his suffering; not in his strength but in his weakness.

Paul speaks eloquently of the power of Jesus' Resurrection, and certainly no one would deny the reality of that power. But Jesus' real power over men is the power that comes from his cross, isn't it? The Resurrection is the seal of this power and the sign of its victory.

It is not the power of his healing, or of his own words, or of his mastery over nature, nor even of his presence. It is the power of his love revealed in his suffering—this is the real power of Jesus.

This is a new kind of power. It was new then and it is still new. This is the power of God. Any other kind of power corrupts. This power creates.—Theodore Parker Ferris

SUNDAY, OCTOBER 17, 2004
Lectionary Message

Topic: To Pray and Not Lose Heart

TEXT: Luke 18:1–8

Other Readings: Jer. 31:27–34; Ps. 119:47–104; 2 Tim. 3:14–4:5

I. *A call to persistent prayer.* Jesus told a parable to his followers, encouraging them always to pray and not to lose heart. The story Jesus told was indeed a fascinating one. It was told in the context of Jesus' encouraging his followers to live while hoping for the King's return. The promise of the inaugurated Kingdom will be consummated with judgment in the evidence of Jesus' total authority. It is in this context that Jesus exhorted his followers to faithful prayer. He told the story of the persistent widow and then concluded with this penetrating question: "Nevertheless, when the Son of man comes, will he really find faith on the Earth?" (v. 8).

II. *A model of persistent prayer.* Jesus drives his point home through the eyes of a widow who was particularly helpless and vulnerable because she had no family to uphold her cause. Only justice and her own persistence were in her favor. Constantly she came and asked the judge to intervene on her behalf. She did this so often that she began to wear out the judge. In his story, Jesus asks, "Will my God bring about justice?" It's an amazing comparison, for if an unworthy judge who feels no constraint of right or wrong is compelled by persistence to deal justly with the helpless individual, how much more will God answer prayer? God does not delay his support for his followers. He is hardly like the unjust judge who had to be badgered. The point of the story is not that God is like the judge who has to be harassed and worn down. He is quite the contrary. He is not like the unjust judge. Therefore, our prayer life should not fade. We should always pray and not give up.

III. *Challenges to persistent prayer.* But our prayer life begins to fade in a variety of life's situations. Prayer starts to fade when life is calm. When crisis comes we pray, and pray often. But when things settle down and God proves himself faithful one more time, the urgency dissipates and our motivation subsides. We tend to forget. God in Deuteronomy tells his people to remember him no less than twelve times. God says, when you got in trouble and prayed for intervention, when you needed protection and guidance, when you needed help, I was there. But when the storm passed, you remembered me no more. The point of this parable is to keep that from happening. God longs for consistency in the lives of his followers.

Our prayer life begins to fade when we seek other pursuits besides God. Almost all of our attempts to fill what Philosopher Blaise Pascal calls our God-shaped vacuum are really futile. Whether we are busy at work, whether we are continually absorbed in ourselves, whether we are running around outside the lines, whether life is off track because of greed or other sins, a gap in our relationship with God develops. During that time we need to tell God that he alone can fill the vacuum in our hearts and turn us back to him.

Sometimes our prayers fade because of disillusionment. We prayed and nothing happened. We thought of God's promises as magical, and yet there was no result. We need to recognize that most of God's promises are conditional and in some way are conditioned by our faithfulness.

Sometimes prayer fades because of discouragement. When we get to this place, we don't think God hears us or that he cares. We give up on prayer; we don't think it works. We begin to lose heart. It's at that time that the words of Jesus sink into our hearts afresh, telling us not to lose heart, to keep on praying. The Father does hear. He does care. He does have power. The Father may not answer every prayer, but for reasons we may not understand until we get to heaven, his ways are higher than our ways and his thoughts are higher than our thoughts. What God wants is for us to trust him. He calls today for us to refocus our prayer efforts in the midst of discouragement and disillusionment. We should always pray and not give up.—David S. Dockery

ILLUSTRATIONS

A REAL QUIET TIME.   I asked a couple who were living defeated lives if they kept the Quiet Time, and the naive reply came: "Yes, my husband and I sit and smoke in the quiet a half hour after breakfast." The modern equivalent of the Quiet Time! No wonder the husband had a nervous break. Those sincere but defeated souls found release and victory when they set up a real Quiet Time in which they took in the resources of the living God, instead of the pitiable substitute of nicotine. Breathing God deep into your inner recesses gives a lift with no subsequent let down.—E. Stanley Jones

PRACTICE FOR PRAYER.   It is by praying habitually that we learn best how to pray. The skill of the professional footballer seems to the unthinking onlooker to be natural and artless, but in fact it comes naturally only as a result of long and arduous practice. Ignacy Paderewski, the famous Polish pianist, once said, "If I stop practicing the piano for a day, I notice the difference; if I stop for three days, my friends notice the difference." In prayer, as in all cases of learning by doing, we shall make many mistakes, get fed up, and fail again and again. But these mistakes and failures, as in learning to ride a bicycle or to speak French, can be a valuable part of the process of learning. Resolve then to put into daily practice all that you know about prayer, and all that you read in this book which applies to your own life and situation. *Solvitur ambulando*—just as some of the problems of life are solved not by thinking them out but by living them out, so the art of prayer is learned, and its difficulties overcome, by praying.—Stephen F. Winward

SERMON SUGGESTIONS

Topic: Is God on Top of Things?
TEXT: Hab. 1:1–3, 2:1–4
(1) The prophet questions God's just governance. (2) God counsels patient waiting for God's good time. (3) Meanwhile, those who are truly righteous will find their answer in faithful living.

Topic: Duties of a Good Pastor
TEXT: 2. Tim. 3:14–4:5, esp. 4:5 NJB
(1) Keep steady all the time. (2) Put up with suffering. (3) Preach the gospel. (4) Fulfill the service asked of you.

SERMON
Topic: In the Power of the Spirit
TEXT: Acts 1:6–8

Our text indicates that Christ has given power to his Church to carry light into the darkened world. Let's look at that challenge.

I. *Christ indicated that the church had been given power to be God's instrument to carry salvation to the world.* We are to go into the dark corners wherever humanity is and tell them the good news of Christ. However, instead of being the transforming element within the world, the church often seems to be merely a reflection of the rest of society. Many people can see no distinction whatsoever between those within the Church and those outside of it. Some wonder what difference a church makes in many communities, except for the building itself.

It seems to me that in the New Testament the very purpose of the Church is to be the living, vital organism that extends God's redemption into the world. But the church cannot be God's instrument if we take the approach, "Let somebody else do it." If we are constantly trying to pass responsibility to someone else, and not assume any for ourselves, the work of the Church can never get done.

The Church can't be God's instrument in the world if it does not have the financial support of the people. We wonder sometimes why a church makes no impact. A church can't be God's instrument if it is only introspective, if it spends its time looking at its "churchliness." The Church has to go into the world as God's redemptive messenger.

II. *The Church seems to have had the most impact through the centuries when it has been a missionary church.* Throughout its history, the Church seems to have grown most when it has been concerned for others. Jesus told his disciples to go into the world. They began right in Jerusalem, then moved to Judea, to Samaria, and then to the outermost parts of the world. As they carried this message forward, the Church came into being, and others were attracted to it.

III. *The contemporary Church will have power when it has the proper motives for missions.*

(a) *Our first motive comes to us from the love of Christ.* We love because he first loved us. We are able to love other people when we have been properly loved. We are told that children who have never been loved by their parents can never really love somebody else. You and I should be able to be the extension of God's love into the community, because we have sensed God's love through Jesus Christ, through God's great sacrifices for us.

(b) *Our second motive is the commission we have from Christ.* The best translation of the Great Commission from Jesus is "as you are going, you will be teaching, you will be preaching, you will be baptizing." Jesus assumed that his disciples would be going. We have a commission from Christ to share the good news with other persons, no matter where we see them.

(c) *A third motive comes from our awareness of need.* Wherever we see men and women in need, that is where we want to share the good news of Jesus Christ.

(d) *A fourth motive is to be of service, as our Lord was.* Jesus said, "The greatest of all is the servant of all." We seek to serve wherever we are. This means that sometimes we have to get our hands dirty. The Christian faith is a crosslike way of living. The real Christian faith is concerned with getting our hands dirty as we reach down to where there is human need. We are called not merely to look, but to do and be.

We don't have to be professional holy persons to serve God. We can serve God through whatever vocation we have in life if we are willing to put God's Kingdom first.

The Church, indeed, exists by mission. Whenever we lose our sense of mission, we have lost our reason for being. We will be empowered by God to take the light into the dark world when we commit our lives more fully to doing what God would have us do in the world.— William Powell Tuck

SUNDAY, OCTOBER 24, 2004
Lectionary Message

Topic: Have Mercy on Me
TEXT: Luke 18:9–14
Other Readings: Joel 2:23–32; Ps. 65; 2 Tim. 4:6–8, 16–18

I. *Two approaches to God.* The problem with this parable is that we have heard it too often. We have heard the parable of the Pharisee and the tax collector so much that it has become to us like an old story that has lost its power. Yet this powerful story rightly understood strikes at the core of our own self-righteousness. It shows us what we think about ourselves and what we think about God. There are two prayers in this story—one by a Pharisee and one by a publican. One leads to relationship with God, the other leads to separation from God. We have heard the story so often and it seems so simple that we often miss the point.

II. *The approach of the Pharisee.* In verse 10 we see that two men went up to pray. There were periods for prayer, scheduled daily in connection with the morning and evening sacrifices at the Temple. People could go to the Temple for private prayer at any time, but the context is probably such that the two went together at one of the previously scheduled times of prayer.

The Pharisee boasted, "I fast twice a week," which refers to the special mark of holiness perceived in the life of the Pharisees. The parable can be rightly understood only when we see the expectations for the two characters in their original setting. Everyone would have assumed that the Pharisee was the good guy and the tax collector was the crook. Pharisees had a very positive image and tax collectors had a very negative image. The Pharisee's prayer began well enough: "God, I thank you that I am not like these others—the robbers, evildoers, adulterers—or even like this tax collector" (v. 11). He was appropriately grateful that God had kept him morally clean. He had stolen from no one, he had been faithful to his wife. It is appropriate to thank God that we have not fallen into serious sin. We ought to be thankful for God's protective and preventative grace. Yet there is something wrong.

III. *The approach of the publican.* The Pharisee's prayer was more focused on himself than on God. The sense of "I" was prominent. In contrast, the tax collector was humble and focused only on his own shortcomings. The Pharisee had moved to the front of the Temple court and prayed loud enough for all in the court to hear. His prayer was self-absorbed, a self-congratulatory monologue. How easy it is for us to fall into the same trap today, to think that we are good enough in our lifestyles to somehow make God happy, that personal achievement is connected with the grace of God. We become competent in our own righteousness and begin to look down on others. What a stark contrast to the genuine humility expressed by the tax collector.

The tax collector stood at a distance. He would not even look up, but quietly uttered these words, "God have mercy on me, a sinner" (v. 13). The contrast is powerful. It sings with intensity.

The publican had no desire to compare himself with anyone else, but only pleaded for God's mercy. He said, in effect, "I am everything people think of me and more. I will not try to justify myself in any way." Instead he fell on the mercy of God, pleading for forgiveness. What opposite attitudes were present that day in the Temple—one self-assured, one lowly; one seeking to exalt himself only to find himself humiliated, one who humbled himself only to find himself exalted.

The tax collector, who had sinned by taking advantage of other people, repented and left the Temple justified. The Pharisee, who entered the temple feeling great, left unaccepted under God's wrath and depending on his own merits. In reality he had nothing on which to stand.

IV. *The approach that pleases God.* The Kingdom of God is filled with surprising reversals. The spiritual posture in our hearts says much about God's genuine work of grace in our hearts. Any person, any prayer, any motivation that depends on ourselves is doomed for all eternity. Those who have been declared righteous understand that that righteousness is totally outside themselves. They have been declared righteous by God's marvelous grace and mercy. We come into God's presence with only one claim: we are not worthy; thus we cry out, "God, be merciful to me, a sinner." Our only hope is in Jesus Christ. This hope is built on nothing less than Jesus' blood and righteousness. Such an understanding affects not only our singing, but also our praying. Do we pray like the Pharisee or the tax gatherer? Do we exalt ourselves or do we humble ourselves, waiting on God to exalt us in the proper time? We have no good works to plead; thus we fall on our face in front of God, begging to be forgiven. Jesus Christ came into this world to save sinners like us. He has indeed made forgiveness possible. But he came not for the good people but for sinners. Those trusting in their own goodness will be in for a terrible surprise, but those who trust in Christ alone will spend all eternity with him, thanking him and praising him for his marvelous and majestic mercy to us in Christ.—David S. Dockery

ILLUSTRATIONS

MOTIVE IN PRAYER.   In Maxwell Anderson's play *Anne of the Thousand Days* there is this exchange between Henry the Eighth and Thomas Boleyn:

> HENRY THE EIGHTH: God answers prayer. That's known. Every morning I go on my knees and pray that what I do may be God's will. I pray him to direct me—that whatever thought comes to my mind, whatever motion floods in my heart, shall be God's will—and I only his instrument. . . . I find such peace in this that not one morning my whole life long shall I fail these devotions.
>
> THOMAS BOLEYN: This is a noble thought, of course, but your Majesty realizes that it might be used as an excuse for . . . doing as you please.

JESUS' VIEW OF GOD.   Whatever happens, or when, if you look up you'll find his face there, and in it will be nothing but tenderness and the sure knowledge of victory! Victory for men and women beaten against a wall, who can still leave their anxieties to him—all these things they never will understand, that harass their souls—certain that he's going to work them out in the end. We can't see how or why God deals with us as he does, any more than a spaniel in a living room can grasp the mysterious movements of his master's thought. His master has the facts and the spaniel hasn't, and when you don't have the facts, nothing makes sense! People can leave their lives to God and stake all there is on his handling of them! Job did that, when calamity came rushing in on him. It stripped him of everything that made the months and years tolerable, and through no fault of his own! But there beyond, it was God, and the far-off, desperate cry of Job's soul still lingers on the Earth: "Though he slay me, yet will I trust him!"—Paul Scherer

SERMON SUGGESTIONS

Topic: The Worst of Times and the Best of Times

TEXT: Zeph. 3:1–9

(1) The Lord denounces moral corruption in leaders in government and religion. (2) Notwithstanding, the Lord breaks through with forgiveness and with conversion of the nations.

Topic: A Portrait of a Faithful Servant of God

TEXT: 2 Tim. 4:6–8, 16–18

(1) He prepares to meet his Lord. (2) He takes confidence from his service. (3) He anticipates a reward. (4) As long as he lives, he goes on trusting God to deliver him and at last to save him.

WORSHIP AIDS

CALL TO WORSHIP.   "Happy are those whom you choose, whom you bring to live in your sanctuary. We shall be satisfied with the good things of your house, the blessings of your sacred Temple" (Ps. 65:4 TEV).

INVOCATION.   O Lord, by your providence we are now in this holy place. Grant that what we say and what we feel shall be acceptable to you, for you are our strength and our redeemer.

OFFERTORY SENTENCE.   "And whatsoever ye shall ask in my name, that will I do, that the Father may be glorified in the Son. If ye shall ask anything in my name, I will do it" (John 14:13–14).

OFFERTORY PRAYER.   We confess, O God, that we often are inclined to ask for things and happenings that are beyond your purpose, yet we come to you asking that you rule out what is not pleasing to you or what may be harmful to us. We believe that the spreading of the good news of Jesus Christ is in every age your will; therefore we pray that we may be more and more conditioned to that purpose and willing to support the work of your Kingdom through our stewardship.

PRAYER.   How can we ever say thank you for the privilege of being your children, Father? Pondering the wonder of such a position reminds us of how great and gracious you are and how small and grasping we are by comparison. This morning we come as people respectable in our communities, people who lead acceptable lives among our peers, but who too often do not recognize our dependence on your strength, power, and guidance as we manage each day of life. Forgive us, Father, when we ignore you and try to be gods unto ourselves. Fill us, engulf us, and sweep us away with the tides of the spirit, that we may live and move and have our being in your righteousness. Search us out with the hounds of heaven when we seek to hide from you in the enticing fields of self-importance and respectability. Send legions of good news bearers to chastise us and direct us when we take a stand against you in the arena of our doing good for others, our good works among people.

Forgive us when we are bullheaded and insist on doing in your name that which is not your work or way in your world.

Forgive us when we invoke your name to assert our personal vanity and prejudice. Forgive us for our impatience with your moving among the events of life and for too often trying to make you act on our schedules. Teach us to wait for your time and to move with the rhythm of your purpose.

Help us to stand rigid, inflexible against all evil, all cruelty, all hatred expressed in the name of justice. But remembering our sins we humbly ask to know the mystery of your mercy, that being recipients of your grace we may be merciful and kind in all our interchanges with those who frequent our days.—Henry Fields

SERMON
Topic: Holding Hands and Walking Together
TEXT: Eccl. 4:9–12; Eph. 4:1–6

Learning to hold hands is one of the greatest and most intimate joys of life. Many of you can remember, perhaps, the first time you nervously held hands with that first sweetheart. Joining hands with that special person was the greatest thing in the world.

And then there is that special time in the marriage ceremony when the bride and groom are asked to join right hands to symbolize their uniting and becoming one.

But the joy and importance of holding hands is not limited to romantic love. There is the joy of a parent and child holding hands while taking a walk together. And there is the priceless experience of holding the hand of a loved one in the hospital or nursing home. There is also the joy of holding the hand of a brother or sister in the faith at a religious gathering or prayer circle meeting where concern or unity of the faith is being expressed.

I. *Learning to hold hands and walk together is one of the most important lessons to be learned in life.* Robert Fulghum, in his best-seller, states, "Most of what I really need to know about how to live and what to do and how to be, I learned in kindergarten. . . . These are [some of] the things I learned: Share everything. Play fair. Don't hit people. . . . Don't take things that aren't yours. Say you're sorry when you hurt somebody. . . . When you go out into the world, it is better to hold hands and stick together."[2]

Such was the message of the preacher of Ecclesiastes centuries ago. "Two are better than one" he said. "For if they fall, one will lift up the other; but woe to one who is alone and falls and does not have another to help" (4:9, 10).

But you see, learning to hold hands and walk in unity is not always easy. It requires something from us, as the apostle points out in Ephesians. Taking someone's hand requires humility on our part. Can you remember how embarrassed you were the first time you tried to reach for a sweetheart's hand? Or when you wanted to take the hand of another to show acceptance or unity? You may have found it to be a humbling experience.

Learning to hold hands requires gentleness and love on our part. We don't reach for another's hand when we are angry or want to hurt them. We take another's hand out of gentleness and as an expression of our love.

We need to learn to hold hands as we walk the road of life together. For when we do this, we look out for one another, we help one another; we lift up one another when one of us trips and falls.

---

[2]Robert Fulghum, *All I Really Need to Know I Learned in Kindergarten* (New York: Villard Books, 1988).

II. *Learning to hold hands and walk together is a symbol of our Christian unity.* Make every "effort to maintain the unity of the Spirit in the bond of peace," the apostle encourages. For there is only "one body and one Spirit . . . one Lord, one faith, one baptism, one God and Father of all" (Eph. 4:3–5)

In August 1995, a faith seminar was held in Nashville, Tennessee. Representatives from the Christian, Jewish, and Muslim faiths were invited to participate in a dialogue and panel discussion. This seminar interested me because I am for anything that will strengthen unity among all those who call upon God in faith. Evidently it interested a lot of other people, too. Although a hundred persons were expected to attend the event, five hundred showed up.

As I interpreted it, the bottom line of the seminar was that what is important in religion is faith in God, seeking the truth, and good deeds that spring from a heart and life of faith and love. It is these principles that can bring together all people of God in unity.

A few years ago, I served as a delegate to the annual general assembly meeting of my denomination, which meets in Jackson, Tennessee. One evening, three minister friends of mine rode with me to the Casey Jones Country Store and Restaurant for our evening meal. While we were in the restaurant, a storm came up. By the time we got back to First Church, Jackson, where the meeting was being held, the dark clouds looked ominous. Jagged lightning in the distance was a warning that a severe storm was just minutes away.

When I pulled into the church parking lot, my three friends got out of the car. I remained behind a few seconds, taking some notes, getting my papers together, and stuff like that. When I finally opened my car door and stepped out, Sam, one of my minister friends, was standing there beside the car. "Sam," I said, somewhat humbled and embarrassed, "were you standing here waiting for me?"

"Well, yes I was," Sam replied. "I didn't want you to have to walk by yourself. In the world we often have to walk alone. In the Church we need to learn to walk together."

Nobody likes to feel alone; nobody likes to walk alone. Life can be so much sweeter when we take the hand of another—whether it belongs to a family member, a member of our own congregation, a member of another denomination, or a member of another race or nationality—and walk together in harmony and unity.

And it is important that all members of a congregation join hands together as they walk toward the same goal, share the same vision, and share equally in the work and financial obligations of the church and its ministry.

Yes, learning to hold hands and walk together is one of the greatest joys in life and one of the most important lessons we can ever learn. As Sam said, "We need to learn to walk together." For no one likes to walk alone.—Randy Hammer

SUNDAY, OCTOBER 31, 2004
Lectionary Message

Topic: The Zaccheus Principle
TEXT: Luke 19:1–10
Other Readings: Hab. 1:1–4, 2:1–4; Ps. 119:137–144; 2 Thess. 1:1–4, 11–12

I. *The resourcefulness of Zaccheus.* Zaccheus was a chief tax collector. He stood at the top of the collection pyramid. He was a very wealthy man, though his wealth was probably improperly gained. This background is important for understanding the crowd's reaction to Jesus' encounter with Zaccheus. As Jesus moved through Jericho, Zaccheus longed to see the now-famous teacher. The crowd prevented Zaccheus, who was short in stature, from seeing Jesus as he moved along. Zaccheus was never short on resourcefulness, however, so he ran ahead and climbed the sycamore tree. Jesus spotted him through the crowd. He stopped and said, Come down, because he wanted to stay at Zaccheus' house that day. He must do this, he said, because that was what his ministry was all about. The Son of Man had come to seek and save those who were lost. Zaccheus gladly welcomed Jesus into his home. He wanted to see the famous teacher, but now he was able to visit with him face to face. The religious leaders judged Jesus as a sinner for associating with the likes of Zaccheus. Indeed, Zaccheus was a sinner. But Jesus did not write off sinners; instead, he called them to himself. He reached out to them with the grace of God.

II. *The response of Zaccheus.* This powerful story pictures the initiative that Jesus takes with sinners. He reaches out to accept us where we are, inviting us to turn to God. Zaccheus demonstrated how one should properly respond to the gospel. He recognized his failures. He confessed his sins. He sought to make restitution for what he had done. Indeed, he evidenced a new life, a change of heart, and embarked on a new direction. The transformation of his heart toward God was evident for all to see.

Zaccheus's life was characterized by divine transformation. He declared, now I will give half of my possessions to the poor, and if I have cheated anybody out of anything, I will pay back four times that amount. Zaccheus's willingness to give 50 percent of everything he had went far beyond the requirement of a tithe. From what he had left over, he pledged to make restitution to those he had cheated. The Gospels tell us that it is easier for a camel to go through the eye of a needle than for a rich man to enter the Kingdom of God. The story of Zaccheus is a picture of his entrance through the eye of a needle and his living to tell about it. God accepted this greedy, dishonest tax collector. Jesus went into his house. When Jesus left, Zaccheus was a different person, all because of the divine encounter with Christ.

III. *Repentance and restitution.* Jesus said to Zaccheus, "Today salvation has come to this house, because this man too is a child of Abraham" (v. 9). Jesus said that Zaccheus was now a true Jew—not only of the lineage of Abraham, but also one who walked in Abraham's path of faith (see Rom. 4). Jesus no longer recognized the tax collector as someone excluded from the heart of Jewish society; instead, he declared him righteous in God's sight and a member of the family. Zaccheus was a new man. The giving away of his fortune was evidence for all to see.

A change like that which took place in Zaccheus was impossible except for the work of the Son of Man in his life. Salvation came to Zaccheus because Jesus sought him out. Yes, Zaccheus climbed the tree to see Jesus, but it was God who prompted and worked in his heart to cause the search. Indeed, God compels us to come to him. The story of Zaccheus is a picture of how God works in our lives to create a desire to seek Christ. In Zaccheus's seeking, he was sought. The Son of Man has indeed come to seek and to save those who are lost. He says to those in the sycamore trees of our contemporary society, Come down, I want to dine with you. He says, I will give you a new heart. I will give you a new life.

Verse 10 is not only a key verse in this story, but a key verse in Luke's Gospel. It is a summary of Jesus' purpose. Jesus became incarnate to bring salvation, to bring meaning and purpose and eternal life to sinners. He came to offer and embody the Kingdom of God. Indeed, in this story we find the picture of the mission of Jesus—the lost who can be sought and saved.—David S. Dockery

ILLUSTRATION

OUR TASK.   Zaccheus, the unlikely convert, was genuinely changed. Jesus saw that his experience ran deep. It was no passing fancy. It was no seed springing up quickly in shallow soil only to wither as quickly as it had appeared. New life had begun. Jesus responded by saying, "Today salvation has come to this house." What had happened to Zaccheus was what Paul described when he wrote, "If any man be in Christ, he is a new creature: old things are passed away; behold, all things are become new" (2 Cor. 5:17).

In this incident was Jesus' philosophy of evangelism. Here Jesus showed us by what *he* did what *we* ought to do. If we do not seek out the rejected, the morally homeless of this world, and if we do not see them as individual souls made for God, then we may discover that even in our "churchiness" we are working for ourselves, not for Jesus Christ, that custom and convention mean more to us than the Kingdom of God. Jesus declared, "The Son of man came to seek and to save the lost" (Luke 19:10 RSV). As those who represent him today, we have no greater task ourselves.—James W. Cox[3]

SERMON SUGGESTIONS

Topic: When God's Spirit Is Present

TEXT: Hag. 2:1–9

(1) It is a call to courage. (2) It is a reason for industry. (3) It is a source of confidence.

Topic: God Will Do What Is Right

TEXT: 2 Thess. 1:5–12 TEV

(1) In rewarding those who suffer for Christ. (2) In dealing with those who make them suffer.

WORSHIP AIDS

CALL TO WORSHIP.   "Though anguish and distress grip me, your commandments are my delight. Your instructions are upright forever; give me understanding and I shall live" (Ps. 119: 143–144 NJB).

INVOCATION.   As we bring many problems to our meeting together, O Lord, we come with the assurance that you are present with us in the Holy Spirit and in your relevant Word to deal with our every need. Speak to us now, we pray, in song and sermon and fellowship with those who worship with us.

OFFERTORY SENTENCE.   "I am not trying to make life easier for others by making life harder for you. But it is only fair for you to share with them when you have so much and they have so little. Later, when they have more than enough and you are in need, they can share with you" (2 Cor. 8:13–14a CEV).

OFFERTORY PRAYER.   Great and loving God, fill the needs of many souls through this offering, that it may go where it is most needed and speak strongly of God.—E. Lee Phillips

---

[3]*Surprised by God* (Nashville, Tenn: Broadman Press, 1979).

PRAYER.   God of faith and hope: We seek to be your people today. Keep us from being intimidated by either the past or the future.

When in retrospect we review the pilgrimages of our predecessors in the faith, we are tempted toward unreality. Recognizing their accomplishments and faithfulness, we forget or overlook their pains, failures, and setbacks. Seeing them as more than human, we decide we can never be like them or never labor as they labored. Keep us in touch with truth, God. Enable your work to be done by people just like us.

We can be faithful even though we have known fear.
We can achieve goals even though we have desired to give up.
We can do good even though we have done evil.
We can be instruments of your grace even if we see ourselves as unworthy.

Keep us from being intimidated by either our past or our future. When we assess all that needs to be done and the gifts required to do it, we are tempted to shrink back. We see all that is wrong in our lives as individuals and the weaknesses in our institutions. We feel more prone to despair than to hope. Redeem us by your truth.

Intentionally you have called us. We are your divine choices for carrying out the Church's mission in the present. Those whom you call you strengthen. Those whom you send out you accompany. We are not exceptions. Thus, allow our commitment to you to be encouraged by your confidence in us. Informed, not intimidated, by our past; challenged, not intimidated, by our future, in this present moment we offer ourselves to you in faith and in hope in the name of the one who unites the past and the future, Jesus Christ our Lord.—Welton Geddy[4]

SERMON
Topic: Trusting God's Providence—Moses
TEXT: Exod. 2:1–10

Every child of the Church remembers the story of baby Moses, a survivor of attempted genocide. Moses is the Egyptian name of a Hebrew child. As the story goes, a Pharaoh arose to rule Egypt who did not remember the obligation to Joseph and his family. This Pharaoh began to fear the growing Hebrew population. God's promise to Abraham was working. The first attack was on the spirit. Pharaoh enslaved and oppressed the people. Then, like his Nazi counterpart three thousand years later, he decided to manage the "Jewish problem" with executions. After a failed attempt to use Hebrew midwives to eliminate the male babies, Pharaoh ordered all Hebrew baby boys to be thrown into the Nile. Then Moses was born. After his mother hid the infant for three months, she lovingly placed the child in a waterproof basket in the reeds along the shore of the river and left his sister to guard the baby. Pharaoh's daughter discovered the child in the brush and immediately claimed him for her own. Then she unknowingly hired his own mother to nurture and nurse the baby.

By anyone's measure, Moses was a blessed child, a protected child, a child of divine providence. The story is intended to show God's special provision for this special child. We are supposed to look only at the positive in the story. God provided conditions, timing, and peo-

---

[4]*Prayers* (Valley Forge, Pa.: Judson Press, 1993), p. 36.

ple to protect one special Hebrew baby, but the question haunts us: What about the others? Do all children come under God's special love and care, or just the chosen few?

I. *You are God's providence.* In the Bible, providence is defined through another special child: Isaac. Abraham heard a voice calling for him to sacrifice his only child to prove his faithfulness to God. Kierkegaard called it the "horrible decree." This decree was self-inflicted genocide. But Abraham, thus Isaac, was given a reprieve. In the place of Isaac, Abraham sacrificed a ram caught in a thicket. He named the place, "The LORD will provide" (Gen. 22).

Providence comes from the word *to provide,* meaning to look ahead. Providence comes from a loving God—a God who looks ahead, who provides for the protection of the innocent and the helpless.

As I speak, children of our world are dying of war, hunger, disease, and neglect that could have been prevented by responsible adults. We have every reason to ask just how God's providence works. What about all of the Hebrew babies thrown into the Nile? For that matter, what about the Egyptian babies who died in the Passover? The baby Jesus survived Herod's insane attempt to purge Bethlehem of all rivals to his throne, but what about the wail of devastated mothers? "A voice was heard in Ramah, wailing and loud lamentation, Rachel weeping for her children; she refused to be consoled, because they are no more" (Matt. 2:18).

Page H. Kelley focused on two messages in the Exodus: First, *the mystery of divine election reminds us that God's grace is at work in our lives in ways that totally transcend our own efforts or abilities.* Kelley notes that the two midwives in the story of Moses are the only two people in Egypt who were said to have feared God. It appears that the Hebrews had forgotten God, but God had not forgotten the people. Second, *the message suggests a divine prejudice toward the weak, the downtrodden, and the oppressed.* The world runs on in freedom from divine control. Evil sometimes prevails, but God is revealed in defense of the little ones.

The lady was a loving mother and a devoted Christian, but her life was troubled. Her husband was irresponsible and negligent toward his family, she was periodically hospitalized for depression, and her daughter seemed bent on self-destruction. This dear lady had a naive faith. She told me on several occasions that God would rescue her daughter. To her, trusting God meant doing nothing. I never could convince her that God's providence included the gift of two parents to her daughter. They had a responsibility both to God and to the child. In an oppressive world, God gave Moses a wise and loving mother. We are God's providence.

II. *Your children are God's providence.* The story is brief but artistically written. The mother hid her child as long as possible. Then she lovingly made him an ark, something like Noah's. She did not toss the child into the current of the river, but carefully placed him where he could be safe until he was found. You can read between the lines that she already knew this to be the place where Pharaoh's daughter bathed. She did not abandon her child. She left a sister to watch over his safety. Finally, she managed to get herself hired as her baby's nursemaid. God's providence was at work through responsible people in Moses' life, including a mother who seemed to have the wisdom to turn loose her child at the right time and in the right place.

Releasing our children to allow them to grow up to become responsible adults in a dangerous world is probably harder than nurturing and protecting them, and I cannot declare to you that nothing bad ever happens to Christian families, to loving parents, and to promising children. From the day we moved to Louisville, the town was buzzing with talk of troubled waters ahead for our children. The courts were considering a busing integration plan to force racial integration on segregated neighborhoods. When the order came down, there were riots in the streets, rocks thrown at school buses, and angry people calling for boycotts of the schools. I wanted to hide my children in a closet to protect them from the world. Some parents did put their children in private schools to avoid the situation. When our turn came, our daughter had to leave for school at 6:15 A.M. to attend a high school in the inner city. I had a sense of what Moses' mother must have felt in leaving her child in a basket on the shore of the Nile. It is a dangerous world.

But God's providence is not only about the protection of Moses; it is also about the movement of God's people from bondage to freedom, from despair and oppression to promise. Of course infants need to be protected, but eventually our children need to be released to fulfill God's purpose in their lives, whatever the risk and whatever the cost.—Larry Dipboye

SUNDAY, NOVEMBER 7, 2004
Lectionary Message

Topic: Playing a Deadly Game
TEXT: Luke 20:27–38
Other Readings: Hag. 1:15b–2:9; Ps. 145:1–5, 17–21; 2 Thess. 2:1–5, 13–17

Games—we love to play games. As human beings we are fascinated by our games. Games are good—for they can and do provide physical exercise and mental stimulation, as well as develop our coping and management skills—not to mention providing a respite from the pressures of everyday life.

There are games we play that we should not. These are the games we use to avoid dealing with the harsh realities that life can bring us, or to get what we want in life. About thirty-seven years ago Eric Berne wrote *Games People Play*—an analysis of the ways people relate to each other and why. His basic thesis is that *"games are substitutes for the real living of real life."*[1] Often we play games because we do not want to get down to the real human business of honest-to-God interaction. We would rather live at a superficial level of societal games than talk about who we are and what we feel.

I. *We can play games instead of dealing with life, as did the Sadducees.* They had heard of this rabbi from Nazareth and they came to confront him. The Sadducees were an interesting religious sect. Their family heritage was the aristocracy, and they devoted themselves to the study of the Torah. They were liberal in their approach to politics—they had closely aligned themselves with the Romans so they might have some power over the governing of their land. They were conservative in that they rejected all religious authority save that of the first five books of the Hebrew Scriptures, the Pentateuch. Whereas the Pharisees considered oral tradition, interpretation, and the Prophets to be authoritative, the Sadducees did not. If a teaching was not in the Torah, the Sadducees wanted nothing to do with it.

II. *"In the resurrection, whose wife will the woman be?"* The Sadducees posed this conundrum. Jesus was gaining in popularity and the Pharisees had been unable to stump him. Now it was the lawyers' turn and they would not be denied.

---

[1]Eric Berne, M.D., *Games People Play* (New York: Ballentine, 1996), p. 18. Originally published 1964.

I can imagine Jesus looking at them with both amusement and dismay. He would have been amused because he knew the answer to their question. *They were starting from the wrong place and in so doing had predetermined their final destination.* They assumed that Moses was the end of God's revelation. They assumed that when the Pentateuch was finished God had said all that God would ever need to say. Further, they assumed that their interpretation of Moses was correct.

What did they understand? *The Sadducees believed that if there was another life it must mirror this one.* Further, because Moses did not said anything explicitly about a resurrection, then there must not be one. God was confined to the box of their making, the box of Moses' understanding—and they were not about to let God out of that box.

III. *Jesus' answer was incredibly simple, yet not simplistic.* The Sadducees were wrong about eternal existence: it is nothing like earthly existence. Their assumption about the possibility of eternal life was wrong. Further, their assumptions that this life is connected in type and quality to the next were wrong, dead wrong. To answer them, Jesus merely quoted Moses, who called God "the God of Abraham, Isaac, and Jacob." Jesus then stated that these men must be alive, for "God is not the God of the dead, but of the living."

How obvious this must have seemed to the Sadducees. Can we not see them slinking off to the hole in the ground from which they had come? "Teacher, you have spoken well" is what some of them said to Jesus.

IV. *The Sadducees were playing a game with Jesus, a deadly game.* It's the game of "gotcha,"[2] of "I'm smarter than are you and I'm going to prove it." There was just one problem—Jesus was not playing a game.

V. *The context is this—Jesus was in Jerusalem for the last time.* This was the final week of his earthly existence. Jesus knew what was coming—the signs were ominous and obvious. This question about eternal life was not a theoretical one to be bantered about in a game of theological gotcha. This question of eternal life was real for Jesus—this is where he was. Just as a person on death row or in the last stages of cancer does not deal in trivialities, so Jesus was not about to play games with the Sadducees. Death was on the horizon, the Pale Rider was approaching, and this was neither the time nor the place for gamesmanship.

Jesus' most severe criticism of the Pharisees and Sadducees comes in Matthew's Gospel immediately after the passage that is our text. Jesus raked them over the coals, not for their lack of knowledge but for their refusal to act on what they knew. They had the keys to the Kingdom—they knew what God wanted—but not only did they refuse to go in, they would not let anyone else go in either. Religion for them was just a theological game of biblical proof-texting—that is, seeing who can quote the most verses and prove their point best—not a matter of life and death.

VI. *Life was not meant to be a game, however.* As has been said, "Life is not a problem to be solved, but a mystery to be lived." Life requires openness, honesty, and the willingness to be engaged by others at the deepest level of one's soul. Theological tennis or congregational chit-chat will not suffice for real life.

A minister once attended a trial in his hometown where a lawyer friend was defending a man accused of first-degree murder. If convicted, this man stood to receive a sentence of

---

[2]Dean Lueking, "The Gotcha Game," *Christian Century,* Oct. 28, 1998.

death. The trial was difficult. The attorney argued, pleaded, and literally begged the jury to look at the evidence and not be swayed by emotion. Finally the verdict came back—"not guilty." The lawyer literally collapsed on the table as his emotions gave out. Later the minister and the lawyer were drinking coffee and the minister said, "You were incredibly passionate in this trial. I wish I could be that passionate in my sermons." The lawyer replied, "To you it is just a sermon and you give them every week. To me, it was a matter of life or death."

VII. *The Pharisees were playing a deadly game—and it cost them dearly.* What about us? What deadly games are we playing?

"Some die by shrapnel, some die by flame. Most die inch by inch playing silly, little games."[3]—Robert U. Ferguson Jr.

ILLUSTRATIONS
HABIT.   [Babbitt] stopped smoking at least once a month. He went through with it like the solid citizen he was: admitted the evils of tobacco, courageously made resolves, laid out plans to check the vice, tapered off his allowance of cigars, and expounded the pleasures of virtuousness to every one he met. He did everything, in fact, except stop smoking.—Sinclair Lewis[4]

ON OUR GROUNDS.   Jesus used arguments that the people he was arguing with could understand. He talked to people in their own language; he met them on their own grounds; and that is precisely why the common people heard him gladly. Sometimes, when one reads religious and theological books, one feels that all this may be true but it would be quite impossible to present it to the nontheologically minded man who, in the world and the Church, is in an overwhelming majority. Jesus used language and arguments that people could, and did, understand; he met people with their own vocabulary, on their own grounds, and with their own ideas. We will be far better teachers of Christianity, and far better witnesses for Christ, when we learn to do the same.—William Barclay[5]

WORSHIP AIDS
CALL TO WORSHIP.   "The Lord is gracious and merciful, slow to anger and abounding in steadfast love. The Lord is good to all, and his compassion is over all that he has made" (Ps. 145:8–9 NRSV).

INVOCATION.   O Lord, as we find comfort in your love and grace, grant that we find strength to refuse to presume upon your compassion by playing dangerous games with what is true and right. To that end, focus our hearts anew upon your purposes for our lives.

OFFERTORY SENTENCE.   "And my God will fully satisfy every need of yours according to his riches in glory in Christ Jesus" (Phil. 4:19 NRSV).

---

[3]Source unknown.
[4]*Babbitt*, chap. 4.
[5]*The Gospel of Luke*, Daily Study Bible Series (Louisville, Ky.: Westminster John Knox Press, 1975).

OFFERTORY PRAYER.   As we increasingly distinguish between our desires and our true needs, we believe that your riches in glory will truly satisfy the deepest yearning of our hearts. Make us, we pray, instruments of your loving purpose in our giving and receiving.

PRAYER.   O God, whose Spirit searcheth all things and whose love beareth all things, encourage us to draw near to thee in sincerity and in truth. Save us from a worship of the lips while our hearts are far away. Save us from the useless labor of attempting to conceal ourselves from thee who searchest the heart.

Enable us to lay aside all those cloaks and disguises we wear in the light of day and to bare ourselves, with all our weakness, disease, and sin, naked to thy sight.

Make us strong enough to bear the vision of the truth, and to have done with all falsehood, pretense, and hypocrisy, so that we may see things as they are, and fear no more.

Enable us to look upon the love that has borne with us and the heart that suffers for us. Help us to acknowledge our dependence on the purity that abides our uncleanness, the patience that forgives our faithlessness, the truth that forbears all our falsity and compromise. May we have the grace of gratitude, and the desire to dedicate ourselves to thee. Amen.—W. E. Orchard

SERMON
Topic: Judah and Tamar
TEXT: Gen. 38:1–30

Well, now you have heard the text they assigned to me: Genesis 38. You want it? I can make you a good deal. The story itself is bad enough, but its setting is even more unsettling. This account of Judah and Tamar interrupts one of the best-known stories of the Bible—the one where Judah and his brothers sell their young half-brother, Joseph, into slavery. In fact, it is Judah's idea to sell Joseph to the Midianites, to have some profit from the dirty deed. Now, somebody pointed out to me that this kept them from killing Joseph on the spot, which might put a more positive spin on it; but I think Judah was just greedy. Anyhow, chapter 37 ends with the Midianites selling Joseph to Potiphar, and chapter 39 picks up Joseph's story with Potiphar buying Joseph from the Ishmaelites. So chapter 38 could very easily be left out, and we could dismiss early and have a nice day. That would work for me. How about you?

Sigh—but I promised I would preach on this text, and my Old Testament preaching class has been bravely helping me to think it through, so I guess we had better work on it.

This account would make an interesting plot for about thirteen episodes of a TV sitcom, although perhaps not in prime time. It would be rated X in movie theaters. How in the world, then, do we treat it in a religious setting? Spilling semen, sex with the daughter-in-law, mistaken for a prostitute, twin babies by the father-in-law—that is not exactly what good, American Christians expect to hear in a family-values church on Sunday morning. But there it is, in the Bible; and try as we may, we can't get rid of it.

You know, come to think of it, Genesis is full of stories of dysfunctional families. Adam and Eve's boys—talk about sibling rivalry! And Judah's father, Jacob, wasn't exactly a paragon of virtue either. Jacob's grandpa, Abraham had several blotches on his record—even had a child by his wife's servant girl. Do we detect a pattern here? Maybe we could get more than thirteen episodes out of it. Sex and sibling rivalry—HBO didn't invent it and neither did John Steinbeck. These have been problems accompanying human sin since, as they say, time immemorial.

So maybe the important question here is not, Whose fault is it? or How did it get started? Or even, What can we do about it? Maybe the really important question is, What does God do about it?

Let's think about the result of Tamar's deception and Judah's response to it. The result dealt with explicitly in the Genesis text is shown by the use of the word translated "righteous" or "in the right" in verse 26. It is the only place in the Hebrew Bible where the word *tzedek* appears in the feminine form. Judah recognized that even in this situation, where nobody appeared to be acting in what we would recognize as a righteous way, Tamar, the Canaanite woman, of all people, was more righteous than he was—an Israelite patriarch.

The recognition and testimony of Judah appears to have changed him in an interesting way. The reader of Genesis soon finds Judah pledging himself as surety for his half-brother, Benjamin, to convince their father to let the youngest go with them to buy grain. (43:8–10). Then, from 44:14 on, Judah is reported as the leader of the family. It is now "Judah and his brothers" who come to Joseph; it is Judah who pleads with Joseph for Benjamin (44:18–34); and when they bring Jacob and their families to Egypt, Jacob appoints Judah to lead the way (46:28). This is no longer the Judah who leaves his father and brothers to make his fortune among the Canaanites (38:1). This is now the patriarch of the tribe whose name was to become the name of the whole people—Judah, Judea, Jew. God can change a deserter into a leader.

The story doesn't end there. The sons of Judah and Tamar are listed as Judah's descendants, and one of them, Perez, shows up on some interesting genealogy lists. The book of Ruth ends with these verses: "Now these are the descendants of Perez: Perez became the father of Hezron, Hezron of Ram, Ram of Amminadab, Amminadab of Nahshon, Nahshon of Salmon, Salmon of Boaz, Boaz of Obed, Obed of Jesse, and Jesse of David" (4:18–22). That's pretty high company for a baby born of what we would call the illegitimate union of a widow and her father-in-law. But that's not all.

Matthew begins his genealogy of Jesus with these names: "Abraham was the father of Isaac, and Isaac the father of Jacob, and Jacob the father of Judah and his brothers, and Judah the father of Perez and Zerah by Tamar, and Perez the father of Hezron" (Matt. 1:2–3). Also, Luke's genealogy, while moving in the opposite direction does not overlook Perez and his father, Judah, when it states that Jesus was a "Son of Amminadab, son of Admin, son of Arni, son of Hezron, son of Perez, son of Judah" (Luke 3:33).

One additional interesting note concerns Tamar. She was also involved in Matthew's genealogy. Have you ever looked closely at the women named in that list? Did you even know that women *were* named? There are five women in the list. The first is Tamar: "and Judah the father of Perez and Zerah by Tamar" (v. 3). The second is, of all people, Rahab, the prostitute who helped Joshua take Jericho and who is listed here as the mother of Boaz. The third is Ruth, that pushy female who (with the advice of her mother-in-law, Naomi) practically seduced Boaz into marrying her. The fourth is listed as "the wife of Uriah," whom we know as Bathsheba, the mother of Solomon. The list continues with the names of fathers until the very end, where we read, "Joseph, the husband of Mary, of whom Jesus was born, who is called the Messiah." Five women whose relationships with their mates were questionable at best are the only women listed in Matthew's genealogy of Jesus—and Mary is the only Jewish woman among them.

And all the people said, *So what?* I guess it's time to start preaching. This is a sermon about God. Remember? Our primary question of this text is, What does God do about it? We are so used to asking what *we* should do about things that we sometimes forget who is really in charge here. Are we serious when we talk about the reign of God or not? Do we mean anything by it when we address God as Lord? One more question: Do we actually expect God to do anything?

We have seen in our text and in its aftermath how God can use the least promising of situations and the least promising of people to accomplish the Divine will. I won't take a poll here today to see how many of us might have been prostitutes or how many had anything to do with prostitutes. I don't want to know. But I can tell you one experience I had in a class several years ago. It was my methods and models of biblical exegesis class and we were discussing what the reader brings to the interpretation situation. I asked the class members to reflect on the situation in their lives in which they first really heard God speak to them through the Scriptures. Several students mentioned rather mundane times in their lives. Then one said, "Six months in prison did it for me." Stunned silence followed as we all wondered what to say next. God brings some of his least-promising people to seminary and shocks all of us into realizing that it is God who does it and not us. By the way, this student of long ago continues in effective ministry to other unlikely saints.

The list of God's surprising saints isn't limited to the genealogy of Jesus. It also includes Simon Peter, Matthew, Mary Magdalene, Saul of Tarsus, Augustine, Erasmus, John Milton, John Newton, Raccoon John Smith, Dwight L. Moody, Billy Sunday—and the list goes on, into your life and mine.

You want the bottom line on this? Here it is:

God can use a fisherman with foot-in-mouth disease.
God can use a tax collector with questionable ethics.
God can use a prostitute so brazen that she would walk right into somebody else's house.
God can use a persecutor of believers who voted for Stephen's assassination.
God can use a profligate philosopher.
God can use a bastard son of a medieval bishop.
God can use a blind poet in prison.
God can use the captain of a slave-trading ship.
God can use a Kentucky boy from the back woods with little formal education.
God can use a shoe salesman from Chicago.
God can use a star baseball player.
God can use a smart-mouthed, jazz-obsessed trombone player.
God can use a—

Well, you get the picture. God can use even you, if you put yourself at God's disposal.—Bruce E. Shields

SUNDAY, NOVEMBER 14, 2004
Lectionary Message

Topic: Preparing for the Apocalypse

TEXT: Luke 21:5–19; Isa. 65:17–25

Other Readings: Isa. 12; 2 Thess. 3:6–13

Are you ready for the end of the world, for Armageddon? Evangelists the world over are tuning up for the millennium. Speculation that the terrorism and the Middle East crisis will bring about the end of the world as we know it, the Apocalypse, is running rampant in many circles.

Apocalypticism, the view that life is progressing toward a definite end, was a result of a definite worldview that arose in Israel. Rather than view life as cyclical, the Hebrews saw it as linear, as moving from one point to another. Earthly life had a definite beginning, that is, creation, and will have a definite ending, the consummation of the ages, also known as the Day of the Lord. History is not just an account of what transpires, but the battleground of a cosmic war between the forces of good and evil. There will be wars, rumors of war, violence, and oppression, but the faithful should not worry: God will win in the end.

Apocalyptic literature arose and flourished in popularity when persecution and oppression were the norm of the day for the Hebrews. They continued to believe that although they were suffering in the present, one glorious day God would come in the form of the Messiah, overthrow their persecutors, destroy all evil, and establish the Kingdom, with Israel, God's chosen people, at the head. Symbols were used to communicate truths that eluded human language, but the basic tenet held fast: God would vindicate the righteous. The time of peace and prosperity of which Isaiah spoke would indeed become a reality.

After the Resurrection and Ascension, the early church remembered that Jesus had spoken of his Second Coming. These first believers were Jews, so they naturally transferred their beliefs about the Day of the Lord to this promised event. The first coming of the Messiah had not produced what they believed would happen, that is, the Kingdom of God in its fullness; but the Second Coming would. The first-century Christians fervently believed that the Christ would come again in their lifetime.

A problem developed in the early Church: Jesus did not show up as anticipated. So, by the end of the first century, the Revelation (Apocalypse) of John was written for the purpose of encouraging and strengthening these believers in a time of persecution and turmoil. Christians were dying for their faith, and others were abandoning their professions in order to save their hides—or their necks, as the case may be.

How then should we live? How can we make any sense out of this chaos we call apocalypticism? What should be our approach to life and to the Apocalypse?

I. *We begin by recognizing that while all of life is lived under the Lordship of Jesus Christ, the Kingdom is not yet present.* We live in a tension between the now and the not yet, between this earthly existence and our heavenly home. We live in this tension lovingly, with grace and freedom, because as the children of God we know that life is moving toward an ultimate fulfillment. In Greek there are two words for "the future." One is *ta mellonta,* which denotes a future constructed out of the past and present. This future we can predict because we have a record on which we can base our predictions. The other word is *parousia,* which denotes the future as coming to us from beyond us. It is this word that the New Testament uses when it speaks of the Second Coming. These believers realized that Christ would be bringing to us a future that is beyond and above us, that we could never anticipate or plan. John strains at the limits of language in chapter 21 as he describes the beauty and glory of the New Jerusalem, the Kingdom of God. These are not literal descriptions but attempts to portray a wonder, a beauty, a holiness far beyond our ability to comprehend. We live now in anticipation of that Kingdom, as a sign to the world of the Lordship of Jesus Christ. Jesus will not only be Lord in heaven; he is also Lord here and now.

II. *We live as people of faith, believing that the purposes of God are being worked out even when we cannot fathom them.* History is linear, not circular, and as such is moving toward the goal, not just repeating itself in some unending, meaningless fashion. We are not just to sit around waiting for Jesus to come, but we are to be discovering where God is active and to get busy with God. A healthy eschatology, that is, a healthy sense of what God is doing in this world, has always been at the center of a healthy faith. If we have no sense of calling, no sense of God's presence in our lives, then we need to examine the nature of our faith and experience.

III. *We live as people who look forward to the resurrection and the Kingdom of God.* We do not need to freeze our corpses with liquid nitrogen in the hopes that one day science will be able to resurrect us on this Earth. We do not need to look to cloning of organs and so on to give us immortality. (Quite frankly, I would like a different body the next time around.) We need only to know that one day we will be resurrected for life on a new Earth that will be far greater than we can possibly fathom.

IV. *We are people who live by faith, not by fear.* Those who build bomb shelters, stockpile food, and wait for Armageddon may be sincere, but they are misguided. We must reject any and all theories that purport to know the time and date. Jesus said it was none of our business—and we should take it at that. We must also reject interpretations of apocalyptic literature that focus on literalism and in so doing seek to ferret out a corresponding event for every event portrayed. This literature is symbolic, not literal, and the revelation is limited by language. It is the difference between describing a maple tree in the fall when the leaves are yellow, and seeing a maple tree. It is the difference between describing the Rocky Mountains and seeing them rise up in all their majesty.

Scripture teaches us that Jesus is the Alpha and Omega, the beginning and the end. We are no more to fear the Apocalypse than we are to fear the Beginning. Persecution and oppression have been a part of every age, and will be until the end. The passage from Isaiah 65 speaks of an age of peace and reconciliation, an age of longevity and restoration. To a people in exile who had known nothing but war and oppression their entire lives, for whom hopelessness and fear ruled the day, this passage brought hope. In our world, lions and lambs do not lie down together; but in the Kingdom of God they do.—Robert U. Ferguson Jr.

ILLUSTRATION

BEING PREPARED.   A certain man moved into a cottage equipped with a stove and simple furnishings. As the sharp edge of winter cut across the landscape, the cottage grew cold, as did its occupant. He went out back and pulled a few boards off the house to kindle a fire. The fire was warm, but the house seemed as cold as before. More boards came off for a larger fire to warm the now even colder house, which in turn required an even larger fire, demanding more boards. In a few days the man cursed the weather, cursed the house, cursed the stove, and moved away.—Fred B. Craddock[6]

SERMON SUGGESTIONS

Topic: The Time Will Come

TEXT: Mal. 4:1–6

(1) When the wicked will be rendered powerless. (2) When the righteous will come into their own.

Topic: What to Do Until the Lord Returns

TEXT: 2 Thess. 3:6–13 NEB

(1) Work. (2) Do not give aid and comfort to the unnecessarily idle. (3) Do not tire of doing right.

WORSHIP AIDS

CALL TO WORSHIP.   "Behold, God is my salvation; I will trust and not be afraid; for the Lord God is my strength and song, and he has become my salvation" (Isa. 12:2 NASB).

INVOCATION.   Today, O God, grant that we may draw water from the springs of your salvation as we joyously worship you in song and thanksgiving. Let our celebration witness to those who know you already and to those who need to know you. May we all "hear the Word of the Lord."

OFFERTORY SENTENCE.   "But thanks be to God, who gives us the victory through our Lord Jesus Christ. Therefore, my beloved brethren, be steadfast, immovable, always abounding in the work of the Lord, knowing that your labor is not in vain in the Lord" (1 Cor. 15:57–58 NKJV).

OFFERTORY PRAYER.   O God, because of what Jesus our Lord has done for us and continues to do for us, we rejoice to be able to contribute to the extension of your work in the Church, in the community, and in the wide world. Now bless these offerings, we pray, as we are already blessed ourselves.

PRAYER.   O Lord, our God, we desire to feel thee near us in spirit and in body at this time. We know that in thee we live and move and have our being, but we are cast down and easily disquieted, and we wander in many a sad wilderness, where we lose the conscious experience of thy presence. Yet the deepest yearning of our hearts is unto thee. As the hart panteth after the waterbrooks, so pant our souls after thee, O God. Nothing less than thyself can still the hunger or quench the thirst with which thou has inspired in us. Power of our souls! Enter thou into them and fit them for thyself, making them pure with Christ's purity, loving and lovable with his love.

---

[6]*Craddock Stories* (St. Louis, Mo.: Chalice Press, 2001).

In the multitude of our own wants, we would not forget the want of others. Look upon those who especially need thy comfort. Be present in thy consoling pity with those who grieve because death has robbed them of loved ones, who weep for a sunshine that never returns. Let them realize that the realms of death and life alike are thine. Solace all who mourn with a grief that saps the mind and breaks the heart, and grant them to believe that though weeping may endure for a night, joy cometh in the morning. For those who are anxious and overstrained, laden with burdens that are not of thy sending, we beseech thy heavenly benediction. Give them freedom of heart, peace of conscience, the rest of lying still in thy hands, the joy of surrendering all their cares to thee, who carest for every creature thou has made. Whatever be the need or the desire, do thou supply it according to the riches of thy grace in glory by Christ Jesus. Amen.—Samuel McComb

SERMON
Topic: A Standard of Giving—A Stewardship Meditation
Text: Mal. 3:8–12; Luke 21:1–4

How much of my income should I give to God? What percentage of our family's take-home pay should we regularly contribute to the work of the church? Such are questions that every devoted, conscientious disciple of Christ must wrestle with. It is not possible to grow in one's spirituality and relationships with God without addressing the stewardship question, the question of how much of my income God would have me give to the work of his church. Herb Miller points out in his book *The Vital Congregation* that the Bible makes twenty-six direct references to the words *steward* and *stewardship*.[7] Jesus spoke about money and stewardship as much as or more than any other subject.

In considering how much to give to God:

I. *We cannot base our standard of giving on what someone else gives.* We cannot look at someone else who might throw a dollar or five dollars in the offering plate and say, "Well, I will give as much as that person gives." Jesus drew attention to the poor widow who threw two copper coins into the Temple treasury. He said she gave more than the rich folks who threw in large sums of money. The reason was that the poor widow threw in the last two copper coins she had. She gave everything. The rich people, on the other hand, threw in out of their abundance, what they had to spare, what they had left over after they spent, invested, and enjoyed the rest of their money.

We cannot base what we give to God—whether it be little, as in the case of the poor widow, or much, as in the case of someone like Bill Gates—on what someone else gives.

II. *We should not base our standard of giving on what the church needs.* This is often the method that is used in church stewardship campaigns. The total amount of the projected budget is divided by the number of members or families, and each one is expected to give that amount. But that is a poor theological method of Christian stewardship.

You see, such a standard of giving would vary from church to church. You might attend a small country church that needed only $20,000 a year to operate. But then you might move to a new, growing church that would need three or four times that much to operate and perform

---

[7]*The Vital Congregation* (Nashville, Tenn.: Abingdon Press, 1990).

ministry in the community. So if you were taught to give on the basis of what the church needs, your level of giving to God would change every time your family moved from one community to another.

Our relationship with God should not be that way. Our commitment to God and his work should be constant and should not be based on what the church we are attending needs to survive. If the church were to receive surplus funds, over and above what is needed just to survive, there are many excellent mission points to which that surplus could go. After all, it is God's money anyway.

Let me give you an example. In Texas there is a church that had the distinction down through the years of being the "oil well church." For you see, on the premises of that church there are several oil wells, even on the front lawn. This was a church that many pastors sought because it had the reputation of being a wealthy church.

Having the oil wells to support the church programs conditioned the members to give virtually nothing. After all, the church didn't need it. The whole question of what God would have me give—the oil wells notwithstanding—didn't matter much to the members of the oil well church. But then the oil bust came, when the price of Texas oil fell out the bottom. Can you guess what happened to the oil well church's budget, ministry, and programs? They fell out the bottom, too. For the people had been conditioned to give on the basis of what the church had needed in the past. When the church was broke and had no money, the people were not spiritually mature enough to give what they should have been giving all along—money that could have been going to increased outreach, missions, or social services.

God and Christian stewardship do not work that way. If this were the case, everybody would seek out the wealthy, well-endowed church, where not much would be required of them.

III. *The only acceptable standard of giving is what God would have me give.* It is not what someone else gives; it is not what the church needs; it is what God would have me give, based on what I earn.

After considering all I give to the government in taxes, after considering what our family spends on eating out or other forms of entertainment, after considering what we send to the bank so we can drive that car we want to drive, how much, what percentage of our income, would God have us give to the work of his church? You see, it boils down to a matter of priorities and how we choose to spend what we earn.

I think it is sad that we might consider sending 20 or 25 percent of our income to the IRS for taxes and social security and then be satisfied with giving only 1 or 2 percent of our income to God. Have you ever thought about that? What was it Jesus said in this regard? "Render unto Caesar the things that are Caesar's, and unto God the things that are God's" (Matt. 22:21).

The prophet Malachi put it bluntly when he asked, "Will anyone rob God?" The answer: If we give God what rightly belongs to him we will be blessed. It just might be that the more of our income we withhold from God, the more of a struggle we will have to make ends meet.

The opposite is also true. The prophet promised that when we give our full tithes and offerings to God, we will be blessed. What we have left after we give to God will go further. Unexpected benefits will come our way. The windows of heaven will open and pour down for us overflowing blessings.

What is the bottom line when it comes to our personal standard of giving? Not what my neighbor gives, not what we think the church needs, but what God would have each of us give, based on what we make and after we consider how much we spend on all the luxuries of life. We will not grow in our spirituality and relationship to God if we fail to address this issue. But there is the promise that we will be blessed abundantly when we, in gratitude for all God has given us, give as he would have us give.—Randy Hammer

SUNDAY, NOVEMBER 21, 2004
Lectionary Message

Topic: Was Jesus Really God?
TEXT: Col. 1:11–20
Other Readings: Jer. 23:1–6; Luke 1:68–79, 23:33–43

There is a commercial on television that breaks me up. A Chihuahua is trying to catch Godzilla. He has a box with a stick holding it open, a string is attached to the stick, and the end of the string is in his mouth. He is waiting for Godzilla to come so he can catch him in the box. As he calls "Here lizard, here lizard," he peeks around the corner, sees Godzilla knocking over buildings, and with a look of sheer terror on his face says, "I think I need a bigger box."

As finite human beings, we all fall prey to the temptation to place God in a box, in an airtight system that we can comprehend. If, however, we continue to grow in our faith, we discover a radical truth: God is always bigger than our boxes.

There is one fundamental belief that we nevertheless accept so easily, so gently, that it boggles my mind. It is the Godzilla of Christian belief—yet we act and speak as if it would fit into our little boxes. The central affirmation of Christianity is the Trinity, that God is one being who consists of three persons: God the Father, God the Son, and God the Holy Spirit—not three gods, but one God with three distinct, separate, yet interrelated persons.

The whole concept of the Trinity raises the question of whether Jesus was and is really God. This is a good—no, a great—question. Christianity rises or falls with this question. Why do we affirm a doctrine that is not even named in the Bible?

I believe in God as Trinity because this is how God has revealed God's self in Holy Scripture. As early as the narrative of the creation of mankind in Genesis 2, God says, "Let us make mankind in our image." Did we hear that? God is speaking but is using the plural pronoun, not the singular, in reference to God's self. What does it mean that Scripture uses plural pronouns to refer to God? Obviously there must be a multiperson dimension to God that is unlike what we experience on Earth.

How can this be? Any second grader knows that 1 plus 1 plus 1 equals 3, not 1. If, however, we go beyond the normal space-time dimensions with which we are familiar, this equation is entirely possible. Physicists and mathematicians are currently experimenting with what is known as string theory, which seeks to discover a set of laws that unify the observations of quantum physics. Briefly speaking—and understand that string theory is pure speculation at this point—string theory requires at least eleven dimensions of space and one of time in order to work. We are accustomed to only three dimensions of space—height, width, and depth—and one of time—forward. Mathematics can demonstrate four dimensions of space, but we have not been able to experience the fourth one. String theory works on twelve dimensions of space and time—something that boggles our minds.

If string theory is true, then God must be greater than his creation, so God must have more than twelve dimensions of space and time. It is at this point that mathematics could easily demonstrate how a being could be three and one at the same time. In fact, anything greater than two time dimensions would give the being a capacity for being eternal.[8] And we thought 1 plus 1 plus 1 equals 1 was difficult to comprehend! God and our universe are much more complex than we have ever dreamed.

When we come to the New Testament, we discover that there can be no doubt: Jesus is the Son of God, and God has revealed God's self as Trinity. Our Epistle text from Colossians affirms that "he is the image of the invisible God, the firstborn of all creation." Jesus is as close to God as this Earth will ever see until the end of the age. Jesus is God—not *a* son of God but *the* Son of God.

Throughout the New Testament we find the affirmation over and over again that Jesus is our Lord—a term that any self-respecting Jew would use only to refer to God. Paul, Jew of Jews, again and again asserts that Jesus is all God.

To affirm that Jesus is God is a tremendously huge leap for many of us if we approach theology from a completely rational perspective. Jews and Muslims alike often reject Christianity because of the Trinity and because of our belief in the divinity of Jesus. However, if we look at the experience and witness of the early Church and of Christians through the centuries, and at our own experience, we discover that we have a mountain of evidence that Jesus was and is God the Son.

- Would the disciples have laid down their lives for a good man?
- Would the early Church have found the power and perseverance to endure the persecution of the first and second centuries?
- Would the apostle Paul have left the secure confines of Judaism for the torture and pain of following Jesus the Christ?

To accept the Incarnation (that Jesus is God the Son) and the Trinity (that God reveals God's self as Father, Son, and Spirit, three in one) is to accept that God has and still does personally come to us. It is to accept that in Jesus we see God with a face on, that the Creator of this universe has indeed visited planet Earth in the form of the Son—and still does in the form of the Spirit.

What does it matter if we believe in the Trinity, or not? Belief in the Trinity can and should change how we live in at least three ways:

- To accept the Trinity is to acknowledge that God is beyond our human comprehension. We need bigger boxes—and that very admission brings about a humility that is a prerequisite for a relationship with God.
- To accept the Trinity is to acknowledge that the God of the universe is the God we meet in Jesus Christ, the God revealed in Holy Scripture.

---

[8]As related by Chris Longine on the Internet. A professor at Clemson University confirmed this, though he underscored the completely speculative nature of string theory at this stage.

- Why is this important? The major Christian sects and heresies of our day reject the Trinity. Most cults that have sprung up out of Christianity reject the Trinity. The New Age movement, which is syncretic eastern mysticism and not really anything new, does not affirm the Trinity. Believing in the Trinity distinguishes those who are Christian from those who are not.

- To accept the Trinity is to accept that relationship, community, and sharing—that is, love—are at the heart of the very existence of God.

- Colossians tells us that "through him God was pleased to reconcile to himself all things" and in so doing helps us to understand that self-giving is at the heart of who God is. Jesus is our way back to God.

Some years ago, at the Seattle Special Olympics, nine contestants were gathered at the starting line for the one-hundred-meter dash. The gun went off and they began to run—all but one boy, who stumbled, fell, rolled over on the asphalt, and began to cry. The other eight heard the boy, stopped, and returned to him. Every one of them. One girl with Down's syndrome bent down and kissed him and said, "This will make it better." Then all nine linked arms and walked to the finish line together. The stadium exploded with cheering for more than ten minutes.[9]

Here we have a portrait of God—Father, Son, and Spirit—walking arm in arm with us to the finish line—the Father who created us, the Son who redeemed us, and the Spirit who sustains us—all ensuring that we finish the race. Praise be to the Triune God. Amen.—Robert U. Ferguson Jr.

ILLUSTRATIONS

SELF-FORGETTING.   The main point in our religion is this: There is a deathless glory at play in the coming of Christ into our world, and into one life. It is not as one woman said of a sunset, "It's a wonderful sunset for such a little place." A wonderful sunset can happen anyplace. There is a deathless glory in any life that opens its doors to the coming of Christ. That is the breathtaking thing about our gospel, is it not? It catches the breath with wonder and hopefulness, with the idea that God himself has stepped into the need and poverty and anguish of a world that has in it evil and incurable disease and battlefields and scaffolds, and for each of us old age and dying powers. Unless in the Christian religion we find a lift into self-forgetting, outgoing emotion, we can miss its true power.—Halford Luccock

A PICTURE OF GOD.   If I were to paint a picture of God, I would so draw him that there would be nothing else in the depth of his divine nature than that fire and passion which is called love for people. Correspondingly, love is such a thing that it is neither human nor angelic, but rather divine, yes, even God itself.—Martin Luther (1483–1546)

---

[9]Author unknown. Printed as told by Bob French in *A Third Serving of Chicken Soup for the Soul*, edited by Jack Canfield and Mark Victor Hansen (Deerfield Beach, Fla: Health Communications, 1966), p. 70. The application of this to the Trinity was shared by Stephen Portner in a sermon published on the Internet, June 2, 1998.

SERMON SUGGESTIONS

Topic: Seasons of Joy and Gladness

TEXT: Zech. 7:1–10 RSV

(1) Self-serving religion (vv. 5–7). (2) God-serving religion (vv. 9–10; see also 8:18–19).

Topic: Keeping the Faith

TEXT: 2 Thess. 2:13–3:5

(1) In what you believe. (2) In how you live. (3) In the ways you worship (compare New Oxford Annotated Bible).

WORSHIP AIDS

CALL TO WORSHIP.   "How happy are the people who worship you with songs, who live in the light of your kindness! Because of you they rejoice all day long, and they praise you for your goodness" (Ps. 89:15–16 TEV).

INVOCATION.   O God, in Jesus Christ you are truly the one who has every right to rule our lives and who deserves our most joyous praise. Help us to open our hearts to your Word and your Spirit, that we may serve and worship you as those who are truly your own special people.

OFFERTORY SENTENCE.   "But thanks be to God, who gives us the victory through our Lord Jesus Christ. Therefore, my beloved, be steadfast, immovable, all excelling in the work of the Lord, because you know that in the Lord your labor is not in vain" (1 Cor. 15:57–58 NRSV).

OFFERTORY PRAYER.   Lord, bless this offering of appreciation during this season of bounty, that it may be used to multiply and bless the church of the Lord Jesus Christ.—E. Lee Phillips

PRAYER.   Christ, be with us as we try from day to day to work out the thorny questions and problems that perplex us, and as we try to use the talents and gifts that have been given to us so that other people may be helped and benefited by them, and we ourselves may enjoy them and delight in them. Help us to find in you the motivating spirit that will guide, direct, and keep in control all the rest of us so that we may move on in joy and gladness, in the freedom to live without fear. Amen.—Theodore Parker Ferris

SERMON

Topic: An Attitude of Gratitude

TEXT: 1 Cor. 1:4

Let me tell you about an interesting man. He was a Jew of great and profound learning. Tradition says he was below average in height and nearly bald. Many predicted that he would become the leader of his people against the hated Romans. Because he was a Roman citizen, this would have been a shrewd political stratagem. He could not believe in the significance of a certain religious sect. Therefore, outright persecution and persistent intolerance were the ways in which he related to it. His heart, mind, and soul worked with magnificent dedication for any cause he thought was right.

Many of his contemporaries visualized a special place in history for him—until it happened! He became sidetracked. Another Jew's spirit caught hold of him. Many said it was a shame he had to become part of a minority group that really stood no chance against either the Jewish religious elite or the Romans.

What amazed his former religious and political colleagues the most was that he now gave thanks all the time for the people and things about him. It seemed that a teasing phobia had seized him. Everything he wrote had to have an expression of gratitude in it. He was often in prison and his life was continually in danger. He never knew when his next breath would be the last one.

Someplace in every book of the New Testament written by St. Paul you will find expressions of gratitude. He was a man who literally lived in a thankful mood. His attitude of gratitude produced a certain very uplifting spiritual fragrance.

The fourth verse of the first chapter of First Corinthians begins, "Always, I thank my God." Many of us say: "When I get my way, I thank my God," or "When I have my ego inflated, I thank my God," or "When the company gives me a promotion, I thank my God." St. Paul says, "*Always* I thank my God."

Here is an attitude of gratitude that both opens the windows of heaven and promises the spiritually good life here and now. It ushers certain treasures into our lives.

I. *Respect for life and death.* When a baby is born, give thanks! Here, in miniature, is the image of God. He did not ask to come into the world. He did not select his parents. He had nothing to do with choosing the clothes he wears, the food he eats, or the place he lives. Yet in a few pounds is a human being with all sorts of potentialities.

Will he be president of the United States? Ask his mother. She knows perfectly well that the chance that he will attain this office is almost like putting him in a canoe and telling him to paddle across the Pacific Ocean. Yet don't you dare tell her that he can't make the grade. Her son is capable of anything.

Fathers, do you love that little slobbering and burping bundle of joy? He is putting a rather sizable dent in your pocketbook, isn't he? He cries as though he, not you, were the head of the house.

Is the child more than an additional member of the family? Is there genuine respect for the new life that may seem to be competitor? All babies—male or female, wanted or unwanted, big or little, wet or dry, normal or abnormal, fat or skinny, pretty or ugly—deserve to be treated with thankfulness.

When a human being draws his last breath, give thanks! A man's eyelids are pressed shut. This life is over.

A wife shrieks in horror: "He wasn't ready! Oh, he is lost forever!" How does she know he isn't ready? Justice is in the hands of God. Human souls can communicate; they cannot trade places with one another.

A lovely lady, active in the church and in other organizations, dies suddenly at the apparent peak of her productivity. A civic leader remarks, "What a shame to lose the efforts of such a woman. Her death is surely premature." How does he know her work isn't finished? The work of eternity goes on. There may be some indispensable people, but only for a moment.

"Always, I thank my God"; therefore, I have respect for every life and every death.

II. *Reverence for God as Creator.* God is the source of all that "was, is, and shall be."

When one approaches this truth in a receptive mood, it is stunning. We become so small and insignificant that we want to squirm, until we remember Jesus Christ. He entered history to become our Savior and Lord. This one great act takes the sting out of our helplessness and shows us we worship a God who refuses to forsake his children.

> If your God is a magnificent Heavenly Father who cares so much for you and me
>   that he sent his only begotten Son to die upon a cross and rise from a tomb,
>   give thanks!
> When you view the stars in the heavens, give thanks!
> When you see the sun shine, give thanks!
> When the rains come, give thanks!
> When the snow falls, give thanks!
> When there is a stale scrap of food on the table, give thanks!
> When you see great factories produce a bountiful supply of good, give thanks!

Christians are not called upon to worship God through nature or any other aspect of creation. Nevertheless, they are to hold him in reverence as Creator.

Always give thanks for the special place of human beings. It could be that there are superior beings on Planet X. Of what relevance is this to your understanding and worship of God, or to your duties to him, his Son, and his Son's Church? If those superior beings are out there, undoubtedly our discovery of them will affect us. However, you and I must live one day at a time. The Sermon on the Mount, which we have had for two thousand years, contains principles we have not yet practiced or even fully believed.

Thanksgiving must never be confined to the fourth Thursday of November. I can think of no more humanly devastating crime.

III. *Responsibility for coworkers in the community.* It is in the attitude "Always, I thank my God" that a final treasure comes into our midst: Give thanks that there are others to help your spiritual growth.

There are two extremes in the religious life that cause the Church to suffer. One says, "God and I can work out anything. I don't need anyone else." Jesus didn't even attempt this long, tortuous road. Perhaps God and you *can* solve your problems; but be careful: it isn't a simple case of you asking you and you telling you what you should do. Fellow Christians and non-Christians belong. Enjoy them!

The other extreme maintains, "I can't do anything alone. I need help from every dedicated Christian all the time to make it through the pearly gates." While this may sound like a very religious stance, it is frequently a mask for what has many names. It is best understood by the word *parasite*—that is, one who feeds off the labors or assets of another without giving anything in return. A human being does not grow spiritually by having others continually cater to his whims. Always thank God for those saints who will walk the second and third mile with you, but never expect a free ride. No sincere person devoted to Christ and his Church desires to be a religious freeloader.

St. Paul understood and practiced the art of positive thinking head and shoulders above any of our modern-day exponents. What is more positive in our total approach to life than to breathe the air of *"Always,* I thank my God"?

I sincerely commend to you this frame of mind and temperament of heart. It is a "spiritually complete" philosophy of life.—Donald Charles Lacy[10]

SUNDAY, NOVEMBER 28, 2004
Lectionary Message
Topic: Hope—Preparation for Christmas
Text: Isa. 2:1–5; Matt. 24:36–44
Other Readings: Ps. 122; Rom. 13:11–14

"Hope" is the thing with feathers—
That perches in the soul—
And sings the tune without the words—
And never stops—at all—

—Emily Dickinson

If there were such a thing as an endangered species list for virtues, hope would be on it. For too many, the bird of hope has ceased to sing its tune. How sad, especially as we begin the season of Advent and move into Christmas. Of all the seasons of the church year, this is one of anticipation, of excitement, of that I'm-so-excited-I-can-barely-stand-to-wait-until-Christmas feeling. Can we remember those years when as children and maybe even as teenagers the thought of Christmas caused our bodies literally to shake with excitement? What happened? Simply put, we grew older, we grew wiser, we lost our innocence, we learned that reality rarely equals the anticipation.

The process of tempering expectations with reality is what we call *maturity.* All of us must come to it; but in doing so, if we are not careful, we will lose our dreams and visions. Maturity should change our dreams and refocus our vision, not diminish them altogether. Unfortunately, life is hard and has the ability to wipe out our dreams altogether.

The Bible is a book of hope, a book filled with the persistent belief that despite the trauma and tragedy of life, God is still working. The message of the Bible is that no situation is without hope. The basis of hope is God's ability to transform any situation, no matter how hopeless, into one of hope.

It was this hope that sustained the Israelites through the destruction of the Northern Kingdom by Assyria and then through the total annihilation of Judah and the Babylonian exile. The vision of Isaiah 2:1–5 came in the middle of war. Through this vision God promised Israel that one day God's Temple would be exalted as the highest mountain on this Earth, that it would be a gathering place for all the nations, that all persons would come to learn of God and would live in God's ways, beating swords into plowshares and spears into pruning hooks. Our hope is not that this world is getting any better or any safer. Our hope is that Jesus Christ is Lord, and will rule as Lord for eternity.

---

[10]Adapted from *Collected Works* (Franklin, Tenn.: Providence House, 2001), pp. 146–149.

I. To begin with, *we must be prepared.* In the text from Matthew 24, Jesus warns us that we must be ready for the coming of the Son, for we will never know the hour or the day. We just never know when Christ will show up, for Christ does so at the oddest hours.

A conversation turns to serious matters—and Christ shows up.
An ordinary worship service led by ordinary people with ordinary gifts—and Christ shows up.
A time of prayer and meditation not unlike thousands of other times—and Christ shows up.
In the middle of mundane and tedious chores—Christ shows up.

How do we prepare ourselves so that we are ready when Christ shows up? We must learn to ask the right questions and to avoid giving shallow answers to them. What are some of the right questions we need to ask time and again?

Where is Christ in my life, in the events that are transpiring around me?
Where is Christ in the lives of my family and friends?
Is my life open to the presence of Christ or is it closed to the Spirit?
Would I recognize Christ in whatever form Christ chose to come?

II. *We focus on the Christ who is Christmas.* If we would focus on Christ, then we must ask the question that John's disciples asked of Jesus: "Are you the one who is to come or should we seek another?" Is Jesus the Christ? All of life hinges on that one question. If Jesus is the Christ, then nothing else on Earth is the same. For if Jesus be the Christ, then my priorities must change to reflect those of Christ. If Jesus be the Christ, then my entire life is to be lived in a radically different manner. If Jesus be the Christ, then church is not just a group of people but a community of hope whose commonality is Jesus. As Phillips Brooks wrote, "The hopes and fears of all the years are met in thee tonight."

Our slender sliver of hope is the way of Jesus Christ, but that way is not now nor has it ever been easy. As G. K. Chesterton put it, "Christianity has not been tried and found wanting; it has been found difficult and left untried." We have tried to domesticate Jesus, to tame Jesus, to change Jesus—and every time we do so we lose the essence of Jesus. Following Jesus can never be reduced to a formula or a simple phrase. Following Jesus requires obedience to a Lord whose ways are so different and whose path is so challenging that most people are unwilling to follow him.

When asked about the focus of her ministry, Mother Teresa said, "I preach the Jesus of the New Testament, not the Jesus of peoples' imaginations." The Jesus of the New Testament is quite different from the baby in the manger. In fact, this Jesus is quite disturbing in the obedience he demands and the places he shows up. But it is only this Jesus who brings the power to transform our meager manifestations of existence that we call life into genuine expressions of life worthy of the name. In that transformation we find the hope that makes life meaningful, for if the Spirit can transform our sinful lives into images of Christ, then just imagine what will take place in the fullness of the Kingdom of God!

Christ gives to us a new identity that precedes our birth and extends beyond our death—and in that identity is hope. As children of the Loving Father, we have the secure hope that whatever happens here, God will see us safely into the Kingdom. We have developed images of this hope that express our understanding of the transforming power of God in our lives and in our world. These images of hope nurture us through this roller coaster we call life. In a book of photographs titled *Images of Hope,* the authors chose such images as

- An open gate
- A tailor in a Rwandan refugee camp
- A homeless man reading a book amid garbage
- A fallen statue of Stalin

What are your images of hope? Mine would include the following:

- A sanctuary such as this—symbolizing communities of faith who gather week after week to study, pray, work, and worship together
- An offering plate—symbolizing the persons who give of their time and resources that we might touch others with the love and grace of God
- A hymn book—symbolizing the song that Christ puts in our hearts
- A Bible—symbolizing the Holy Scriptures, which have nurtured God's people for thousands of years
- A children's Christmas pageant, complete with bathrobes, aluminum foil stars, and a baby doll Jesus—for as long as we keep telling the story there is hope for this world
- A manger, a cross, and an empty tomb—in them lies the greatest hope we could ever have, that in Christ Jesus this world has been blessed by the presence of God

—Robert U. Ferguson Jr.

ILLUSTRATIONS

HOPE'S COMPANIONS.   Hope should not stand alone. When God encourages us to hope, he reminds us of the other relevant factors: the record of his past performance, the reliability of his promises, the power of his love, the certainty of a great future. There are three great realities that endure: faith, hope, and love. The three belong together, and the greatest is love (1 Cor. 13:13).—Donald T. Kauffman

TWO ORDERS.   The historical order is not separated from the eternal order. What is new in the prophets and in Christianity, beyond all paganism, old and new, is that the eternal order reveals itself in the historical order. The suffering servant of God and the enemies by whom he suffers, the man and the cross and those who fainted under the cross, and the exiled and persecuted in all periods of history have all transformed history. The strong in history fall; the strength of each of us is taken from us. But those who seem weak in history finally shape history, because they are bound to the eternal order. We are not a lost generation, because we are a suffering, destroyed generation. Each of us belongs to the eternal order, and the prophet speaks to all of us: Comfort ye, comfort ye, my people!—Paul Tillich[11]

---

[11]*The Shaking of the Foundations* (New York: Scribner's, 1948).

Sermon Suggestions

Topic: When God Has His Way
TEXT: Isa. 2:1–5
(1) The one true God will be recognized. (2) The teaching of God will be sought. (3) The judgment of God will bring peace.

Topic: Day Is Near
TEXT: Rom. 13:11–14
Therefore, it is urgent (1) to renounce the deeds of darkness, and (2) to armor ourselves with Christ Jesus—his truth, his love, his deeds.

Topic: King of Kings
TEXT: 2 Sam. 5:1–5; Col. 1:11–20
(1) The glory of an earthly king (2 Sam. 5:2b). (2) The glory of the heavenly king (Col. 1:18–20).

WORSHIP AIDS

CALL TO WORSHIP.   "I was glad when they said to me, 'Let us go to the house of the Lord!' . . . For the sake of my relatives and friends I will say, 'Peace be within you.' For the sake of the house of the Lord our God, I will seek your good" (Ps. 122:1, 8–9 NRSV).

INVOCATION.   Allow us, O Lord, to approach this advent season with an air of expectancy and a humbleness of spirit that longs, and looks, and openly awaits the inbreaking of deity into humanity, through Christ our Lord.—E. Lee Phillips

OFFERTORY SENTENCE.   "Therefore, my beloved, be steadfast, immovable, always excelling in the work of the Lord, because you know that in the Lord your labor is not in vain" (1 Cor. 15:58 NRSV).

OFFERTORY PRAYER.   You are preparing our hearts, holy God, as we approach again the celebration of the birth of the Son of God. Inform our giving with expectation, that others may hear and believe. In Christ's name.—E. Lee Phillips

PRAYER.   O God, whose throne is set eternal in the heavens: make ready for thy gracious rule the kingdoms of this world, and come with haste and save us, that violence and crying may be no more, and righteousness and peace may bless thy children; through Jesus Christ our Lord, who lives and reigns with thee and the Holy Spirit, ever one God.—*Book of Common Worship*

SERMON

Topic: The Form of the Christian Life
Text: Luke 16:19–31; Deut. 26:1–10a; 2 Cor. 4:8–11

Every life has a form—a pattern of thought and action. Many of us once lived in a world that had, at least on its surface, a common understanding of what is right and wrong. Today we are becoming increasingly aware of wide differences; some people can steal, kill, and destroy randomly, while others live peaceable, respectful lives.

What makes the difference? I suggest that the difference lies in what we permit to shape us. The form of our lives is determined by the influences we allow to have their impact on us—that is, the people, the things, the thoughts, and the aspirations that take up most of our time.

I. *Luke 16:19–31: Formed by the world.* Here is a picture—not a pretty picture, but a clear picture—of a person who has permitted his love of money to form his life. Verse 19 describes him in terms that leave no doubt that his money and what it could buy for him were the things highest on his scale of values.

His life was formed by the idea that other people could be bought and sold or commanded to do his bidding. As a result, even after he died he expected to be served. He apparently had never tried to relieve the suffering of Lazarus on Earth, but now he asked Abraham to send Lazarus to relieve his suffering in Hades. And when that did not work, he asked that Lazarus be sent to warn his rich brothers.

Those whose highest aspiration is amassing possessions or power forget the worth of persons as creations of God and treat one another as means to satisfy their own cravings. This leads to sexual immorality; to theft, both direct and sophisticated; and ultimately to murder.

I have the impression that none of you here today is interested in such a form of life. Yet we are all in danger of being shaped in that way by the world in which we live. It doesn't take deep analysis to see that there are people all around who want us to buy their products, to pay for their services, or to support their causes. We are surrounded by influences that try to shape our decisions into worldly life forms. There must be a better way to form a life.

II. *Deuteronomy 26:1–10a: Formed by memories.* Here is a picture of a life-forming influence that produces a much better outcome. This influence is memory. One Old Testament scholar has said, "Memory shapes identity."[12] God saw to it that his people, the Israelites, never forgot who they were and how they had become God's people. These instructions given to them for their offerings to God in the Promised Land show how memories of God's goodness shape people who appreciate what they have and give the Lord the credit.

Note how the pronouns in this recitation change: "My ancestor; he . . . us . . . we . . . I . . ." A person who identifies that closely with the history of the people who were specially blessed by God grows into a special shape.

Such a person would find it hard to misuse any produce of God's creation, and especially to take advantage of other people made in God's image.

We should certainly see to it that we and our children are in a position to be influenced by our memories of God's creation and of God's continued care for us, his children.

But the Christian has more than such general memories.

III. *2 Corinthians 4:7–11: Formed by the cross.* We remember Jesus. We go to Bible classes where we study the life of Jesus. We hear preachers remind us about the Crucifixion and Resurrection of Jesus. We remember with all our senses the death of Jesus each time we take Communion, each time we celebrate the Lord's supper. We remember Jesus.

---

[58][12]James A. Sanders, *God Has a Story, Too* (Philadelphia: Fortress Press, 1979), cited in Richard Lischer, ed., *Theories of Preaching* (Durham, N.C.: Labyrinth Press, 1987), p. 196.

And what a difference that makes! Paul describes in this paragraph from 2 Corinthians what it means to live the Christian life. Here is his description of the form of the Christian life: The Christian life is shaped by the central act, the climax of the life of Jesus himself. The Christian life is in the shape of a cross, "always carrying in the body the death of Jesus, so that the life of Jesus may also be made visible in our bodies."

The world might throw in our teeth the taunt, "I thought you Christians were supposed to live a triumphal life." And we can testify that a cruciform life, a life in the form of a cross, *is* triumphant, because it was through the cross that God accomplished our salvation and it was through the resurrection from the dead that God promised to all of us eternal life.

"Take up your cross daily and follow me" is the way Jesus put it to his disciples. Carrying a cross, or living a cross-formed life, is a struggle; but it is the struggle of Christ himself, and we have the assurance of his presence and power to help us with it.

IV. *Letting Christ's cross shape us.* Outside influences shape our lives. There is no escaping that. Our families shape us, our friends shape us, our organizations shape us, our schools shape us, our work shapes us, our recreation shapes us, our reading shapes us, our radio listening shapes us, our film and television viewing shapes us.

Everything that is put into our minds works to shape our lives. There is no escaping that, but there is a way to control it.

V. *Choosing to give God equal time.* We can choose to spend time with the Bible, so that God's input has a chance to counteract the input of the world.

We can choose to spend time in prayer, so that we can draw power from the Lord to make the right decisions.

We can choose to spend time with God's people, so that God's society can influence our development.

We can choose to meditate on the importance of the cross of Christ in our lives, so that our lives grow to look more and more like his—lives of loving, sacrificial service.

Let us commit ourselves to the God who created us and who wants to continue to shape us. Let us determine to put ourselves in the attitude and the opportunity to be formed into the likeness of Christ, our crucified and Resurrected Lord. Let's allow God to have his way with us.—Bruce E. Shields

SUNDAY, DECEMBER 5, 2004
Lectionary Message

Topic: The Authenticity of Our Hope

TEXT: Rom. 15:4–13 NIV (see also Isa. 11:1–10)

Other Readings: Ps. 72:1–7, 18–19; Matt. 3:1–12

The theme of hope is especially appropriate for this time in Earth's history, when so many people feel hope*less*. Since September 11, 2001, our whole world seems to have a lot more fear and hopelessness than in recent memory. A new reality seems to have hit home; there is a new awareness of the uncertainty, danger, and evil that lurks all around us. Many people aren't sure if life really does have purpose and meaning, or if there really is a bright future ahead for them.

So, to those in this era who so desperately need hope, our text speaks with great relevance, because it opens in Romans 15:4 with the theme of hope, and closes with it in verse 13. How fitting for the Advent season. According to Paul, this hope is authentic because it is based on undeniable *truths:*

I. *The Scriptures were written to teach us how to endure hardship and to create courage.* Paul explained, "For everything that was written in the past was written to teach us, so that through endurance and the encouragement of the Scriptures we might have hope" (v. 4). Paul made it clear that in the midst of those difficult times in ancient, pagan Rome, believers could look to God for success and happiness. He reminded them that all of Scripture was written to help them endure ("have perseverance," NASB) as they faced hardships, doubts, and worldly temptations. He specifically said that the Scriptures provide "encouragement" to look at things from God's perspective rather than from the standpoint of the "insults" of their enemies and "the failings" of the weak among them (vv. 1–3).

II. *Christ has accepted us, forgiven us, and made us part of a unified, worldwide family.* Paul said, "Accept one another, then, *just as Christ accepted you*" (v. 7; emphasis mine). He made it plain to the Romans that Jesus had first accepted them, despite their flaws and shortcomings. He had made both Jews and Gentiles part of his family.

Armed with this knowledge, we today can in turn accept and embrace others who love the Lord, even if they are different and imperfect. We can become "servants" to others just as Jesus became a servant to Jews and Gentiles alike (v. 8; Phil. 2:6–8). Paul pleaded, "May the God who gives you endurance and encouragement give you a spirit of unity among yourselves as you follow Christ Jesus, so that with one heart and mouth you may glorify the God and Father of our Lord Jesus Christ" (vv. 5–6).

By becoming a unified, loving community that reflects the love of Christ, we give the world a precious "Christmas gift."

III. *Jesus has either already fulfilled or is in the process of fulfilling the promises and prophecies given to the patriarchs of old.* According to Paul, the great messianic promises and prophecies going back to the time of Adam, Abraham, Moses, Daniel, and John have been, and continue to be, fulfilled in Jesus Christ (Gen. 3:15; Isa. 53:2–7; Dan. 2:44–45; Luke 24:25–27). Notice how he puts it: "For I tell you that Christ has become a servant of the Jews on behalf of God's truth, *to confirm the promises made to the Patriarchs,* so that the Gentiles may glorify God for his mercy" (vv. 8–9; emphasis mine).

In other words, the Romans—and we today—can have hope and assurance because Jesus is the fulfillment of those powerful, gospel-based promises. The promises made to Abraham, Isaac, and Jacob have been kept in Christ.

IV. *The hope that Paul speaks about is also based on the truth of Christ's future rule over all the nations of the world.* Paul cites Isaiah 11:10–12 when he says, "The Root of Jesse will spring up, one who will arise to rule over the nations; the Gentiles will hope in him" (Rom. 15:12). Jesse was the father of David, and the Messiah was to be the "Son of David" (Matt. 21:4–10). This is clearly a messianic reference to Christ and to events following his Second Coming, when he will reign over all the nations of the Earth (Dan. 2:44–45; Matt. 24:30; Luke 21:27–30; Rev. 22:1–5; Matt. 25:31–34). Jesus will overthrow all corrupt human governments and rule with righteousness and true justice—and make all things new and perfect. His people (Jews and Gentiles) will live in peace and joy forever and ever.

No longer will we have to worry about corporate greed, political corruption, and crushing oppression. Our hope is valid, because it is based on the certainty and authority of the eternal Kingdom of Christ, which will fill the whole Earth.

V. *Each of us has been promised the power of the Holy Spirit.* Paul concluded this pericope with these words: "May the God of hope fill you with all joy and peace as you trust in him, *so that you may overflow with* hope *by the power of the Holy Spirit*" (v. 13; emphasis mine). Hope was assured to the Roman Christians through the promised indwelling of the Holy Spirit in their lives. As we surrender to God today, we too can be certain that God will freely give us of his Spirit, and the power that comes with that Spirit.

We don't need to be afraid of anything with the Holy Spirit in control of our lives. Joy and peace are ours, not only at Christmas, when we sing "Joy to the world" or recite the words of the angels at Bethlehem ("Glory to God in the highest, and on Earth peace to men on whom his favor rests," Luke 2:14), but every day! No wonder Paul said, "'Rejoice, O Gentiles, with his people. . . . Sing praises to him all you peoples.' . . . Overflow with hope" (vv. 10–11, 13).

So let us all glorify God in word and deed; let us sing hymns of rejoicing and praise to his name, for the great hope that we have. For our hope is absolutely authentic, and founded on undeniable truths.—Kenneth B. Stout

ILLUSTRATIONS

HOPE TO THE RESCUE!   To the man who drove his car through a guardrail on a dangerous curve and off a cliff into the tops of some rugged trees, hope was the difference between life and death. He dangled upside down by his seatbelt for days with serious injuries, no food or water, and no one aware of his plight. He said the only hope he had was that someone would spot the damaged railing and discover him, or that the weak battery in his cell phone was sending out a strong enough signal to help rescuers locate him. He hung onto this slim thread of hope until, amazingly, he was rescued. Ultimately, the cell phone was the key. Today our only hope is in God, but we don't have to worry about the batteries of divine power going dead. Hope in God continually recharges our prayer signal to heaven—and we will always be rescued from wherever sin takes us and be given eternal life.—Kenneth B. Stout

THE POWER OF HOPE.   The life of actor Christopher Reeve, known especially for his movie role as Superman, is a living metaphor for the word *hope*. Several years ago he was thrown from a horse while attempting a jump in a cross-country equestrian competition. He suffered a severe spinal injury and near-complete paralysis, and almost died. To this day he is in a wheelchair and unable to perform many normal tasks. But he, with the help of his devoted wife, has been a fighter and a person of great hope. I recently saw an interview with him on CNN's Larry King talk show. Reeve spoke inspiringly of how hope has kept him going under the most daunting of circumstances. He has exercised an extraordinary hope in spinal cord research, in new and old physical therapy techniques, and in God. He has said for years that he believes he will one day walk again. Most doctors held out little or no hope of him recovering any significant movement below his neck, but recently, after years of seeing little change, he has been able to do some things that have shocked the medical world and forced doctors reevaluate the benefits of certain therapies. Reeve's hope and his hard work have begun to pay off. He is able to breathe for up to an hour or so without a respirator. For the first time he has feeling over his whole body. He can move his fingers. He can move every joint in his body and push off with his legs from the side of a swimming pool—with assistance. Of course, he's worked very, very hard and fought through terrible pain. But the hope that he can recover further—even walk—drives him forward, and no one knows what he will be able to accomplish before he is done. Hope is powerful for anyone, but for the Christian, hope is even more of a force because it is placed in a loving, all-powerful God who is a sure thing!—Kenneth B. Stout

SERMON SUGGESTIONS

Topic: The Ideal Ruler
TEXT: Isa. 11:1–10
(1) His spirit (vv. 2–5). (2) The conditions of his reign (vv. 6–9). (3) His ultimate success (v. 10).

Topic: God's Truthfulness
TEXT: Rom. 15:4–13
(1) Foreshadowed in the Scriptures of the Old Testament (v. 4). (2) Confirmed in Jesus Christ (vv. 8–12). (3) Made the basis of hope for the future and of the joy and peace that spring from this hope (v. 13).

WORSHIP AIDS

CALL TO WORSHIP.   "Praise the Lord, the God of Israel! He alone does these wonderful things. Praise his glorious name forever! May his glory fill the whole world" (Ps. 72:18–19 TEV).

INVOCATION.   Our gracious Lord, there is no end to occasions for praising you. As we pray for the glory that is yours to be experienced in every part of our world, grant that we may experience a portion of that glory as we worship you today in this place.

OFFERTORY SENTENCE.   "Love never gives up; and its faith, hope, and patience never fail" (1 Cor. 13:7 TEV).

OFFERTORY PRAYER.   O God, we bring these offerings to you in the confidence that they, in your providence, will be used to deepen experience of your grace, whether here in this congregation or in distant places where the good news is lived and proclaimed. May we never give up our efforts, in spite of frequent difficulties, knowing that because of love, our faith and hope and patience will never fail.

PRAYER.   Hungry, we wait before you, Father. Oh, we do not always identify what we are struggling with as hunger, but basically that is what it is. Some of us struggle with problems that to us seem to have no easy solution. While we would not say so, we are hungry for a God-given solution to the besetting struggle with which we daily deal.

Some of us are hungry for a remedy for ruptured relationships. We fume and fuss and blame and work out human solutions. But what we need to see is the divine solution that truly makes all relationships come out right, as you want right done among your children. What we need is the courage to do the right we already know, as well as what you reveal to us in the struggle of getting along with one another.

Some of us are hungry for understanding by others. Efforts made to communicate seem to be met with closed minds and preconceived attitudes. The barriers seem to rise higher when we try to break them down, and life becomes frustrating and painful.

Some of us are hungry for expressions of human love. The knowledge that we are loved by you hasn't registered, because it has not been genuinely demonstrated by some human being who reaches out to love us in spite of all our evident unloveliness and need.

Some of us are hungry for companionship. The lonely road has been walked for a great distance, and companionship would make the journey more pleasant and less frightening.

Some of us are hungry for salvation. Long have we struggled with overpowering temptations and with the sins that yielding brings. We have tried to resist and change, but the grip of the temptations and the sins is overpowering. There is a hunger to be freed from such a grip, that life may be whole and clean and promising again. We cannot in our own strength escape the maze in which we find ourselves. We look for some star of deliverance, and long for its coming to guide us. Bread of life, child of Bethlehem, Son of God, come today, we pray, to satisfy our hungers, set us free, and make us whole, we pray.—Henry Fields

SERMON
Topic: Working at Peace
Text: Mark 1:1–3

Matthew, Mark, Luke, and John begin the story of Jesus differently. Matthew describes Jesus' family tree, Luke describes his birth, and John describes his cosmic stature, but Mark begins with an affirmation: "The beginning of the good news of Jesus Christ, the Son of God." From this affirmation, he moves directly to the word of the prophet Isaiah, who spoke of an age of justice, a time when the Messiah would come and make the crooked ways straight. The messenger that God would send first would be "one crying out in the wilderness," which does not denote someone "out in right field," as we might assume. Matthew's Jewish audience would have known that a messenger from the wilderness would likely bring a message of salvation, a message from God, for the wilderness had long been the home of true prophets. Thus Mark quickly set the stakes high. Something tremendous was about to happen—a new Exodus, a new Kingdom, a new Prince, who elsewhere is called the "Prince of Peace."

This is the Sunday in Advent when we traditionally focus on peace. For Mark's listeners, peace was not just a Christmas sentiment. If you traveled deep into the heart, soul, and mind of an ancient Hebrew, you would find a word, and that word would be *peace,* or more properly, *shalom.* In part, *shalom* meant what we popularly take to be peace: serenity, tranquility. But it also meant many other things: safety, blessings, prosperity, and the presence of justice.

The word was (and still is) often used as a greeting or a farewell. As a word of welcome, it expresses God's presence in a moment. As a goodbye, it commends someone to God's care. Language often recognizes a risk in parting, so we say "good-bye"—a shortened version of "God bless ye"—or "Adieu" (French) or "Adios" (Spanish), both of which mean "to God" and imply that we entrust the other person to God as we part. Shalom is a more explicit statement of faith and request for God's blessing than these other words. It wishes for someone not just the absence of what is wrong and unjust, but also a prayerful hope for what is good and just.

We, however, have emptied *peace* of much of its power, have boiled it down to an absence of war, have made it something we wish for. This idle wishing for peace has become so commonplace that we chuckle at the beauty pageant contestant wishing for "world peace." Yet peace is something we cannot simply wish for; we must always work for it. Few things worth having come without effort. Lost weight, increased bank accounts, and good grades all require work. An apt analogy for working at peace is working at marriage. We don't work at falling in love, but we would be wise to work at staying in love. A friend who was counseling a couple about to be married noted the apparent differences between them: she was a churchgoer, he was an avowed atheist; she was a preppy dresser, he was a devotee of torn blue jeans and tattoos; she was a business major, he was a philosophy major. When asked how they planned to negotiate their differences, they asked in amazement, "What differences?" If wishing to be in love did the trick, then taking out the trash, skipping the meeting to make time for our spouse, having the courage to admit when we are wrong, and practicing patience would be unnecessary. But just wishing for it won't get it done.

One form that the peace we work for can take is the presence of justice in our world. It has been said before but bears repeating: peace is not simply the absence of conflict, but rather the presence of justice. For example, was there peace in the American colonies the day before Lexington and Concord? No. There was not yet armed conflict, but there was no peace in the rich biblical sense. The only question to be answered was whether the absence of peace would lead to war or not.

If peace is the presence of justice, then peacemaking becomes more than the diplomatic resolution of potential armed conflict. Peacemaking involves bringing the love of Christ to bear on the roots of conflict. Rodney King, the man who found himself in the public spotlight during the Los Angeles riots that followed his beating by police, said something that caught the nation's attention: "Can't we just all get along?" This is a fair question, a good question, but ultimately an insufficient question where biblical peace is concerned. The proper question for a peace rooted in justice is, *What actions must we undertake to establish a mutual respect and even a love for one another?* Why does a healthy family avoid destructive conflict? Because they have all made a commitment to get along? No, the key to peace in any family is mutual love and respect.

Peace, however, is not simply something we want to come to our world and our societies. We also long for peace in our own lives. What does it mean to work for personal peace? John the Baptist gave us a clue. Mark 1:4 contains the epitome of John's message: repent and forgive; move away from doing it the wrong way and move toward the right way, with the confidence that we are forgiven and loved by God.

But repentance is not a one-time event. We don't so much *do* repentance as *practice* repentance, and this does not mean *practice* simply in the religious sense. Practicing repentance is not altogether different from practicing basketball. How do you get good at shooting a basketball? Shoot it at the basket. If it goes in, keep doing it that way over and over. If it doesn't go in, don't do it that way again, and try it a different way. In short, work at it.

Working at peace in our lives is more of a trial-and-error process than we sometimes realize. Peace can be revealed to us, or granted to us, but sometimes we just keep groping in its direction, trying to gain on it as we go. Do you want the peace of Christ this Christmas? Simply wishing for it won't make it so. But be of good cheer and take heart this Advent season, for we have indeed received "the beginning of the good news of Jesus Christ, the Son of God." A voice cries out in the wilderness, and it tells us to keep trying, keep searching for peace, knowing that we are both wholly inadequate and wholly forgiven.—Chris Caldwell

SUNDAY, DECEMBER 12, 2004

Lectionary Message

Topic: A Survival Guide for the Oppressed

TEXT: James 5:7–10 NIV

Other Readings: Isa. 35:1–10; Luke 1:47–55; Matt. 11:2–11

A popular tool in today's society is the "survival guide." There are survival guides for nearly every situation: for new teachers, for those facing divorce, for those hiking in the wilderness, for domestic violence, and yes, even for candle making.

In the first six verses of chapter 5, James gave a strong reprimand to the wealthy for their oppression of the poor; but in verses 7 through 10, he turned to advise and encourage the poor, who were the target of injustice and persecution. Essentially, James offered a brief survival guide for those facing oppression while waiting for the Lord's return. He wants the oppressed to know God's will for them as they agonized and suffered under the boot of the worldly wealthy. So he counseled them to do four things.

I. *Wait patiently for the Lord's coming as a farmer waits for his crops to ripen.* "Be patient, then, brothers, until the Lord's coming. See how the farmer waits for the land to yield its valuable crop, and how patient he is for the autumn and spring rains" (James 5:7). Notice that he was clearly talking to poor believers who were being mistreated by the rich. He advised them to wait patiently. This is the theme of the whole pericope: waiting patiently, or *makrothym,* which means long-suffering, loving, expectant waiting on the Lord.

This needed to be said because these abused people would have been severely tempted to strike out at the overlords who were directly responsible for their misery. But James called for cooler heads to prevail, and he pointed to an analogy that the poor could relate to: they were to wait like a farmer waits for the rains that will ripen his crops. They could understand this because many of them were the planters and harvesters working the fields of the rich (see v. 4) who depended on the early and later rains of October and November and April and May. When they buried the seeds at planting time, they knew there was nothing they could do to speed up the crops' maturation. But they also knew that eventually the rains would come— and with them, the harvest.

We live in an instant-gratification world that demands satisfaction and results now. We want next-day mail and instant credit approval. But we too must wait.

II. *Stand firm in the conviction that the Lord's coming is a certainty.* "You too, be patient and stand firm, because the Lord's coming is near" (James 5:8). Once again, James called for patient waiting, but here he added the idea of "standing firm" (*sterizo,* or "strengthen your hearts," NASB). This command seems to suggest that they should do more than passively wait; instead, they were to put forth intensive, decisive effort to fortify themselves with courage to stand against sin and difficult circumstances with even greater determination.

Today we too need to stand firm. Like soldiers on the front lines of battle, we must stand firm and not give ground to evil forces or doubt. We too need to rise above present trials and hardships, with hearts strengthened by our walk and talk with Jesus in our devotional life.

But how can we today be patient and stand firm when James says that "the Lord's coming is near"? Here we are, almost two thousand years since James's day, and the Lord Jesus has not yet returned. All of the apostles anticipated the soon return of Jesus. They knew that no one knew the precise "day or hour" (Mark 13:32). What they meant by "near" or "imminent" is that it could happen in a short period or at any time. This means that we must always be ready, while at the same time being patient.

III. *Wait without grumbling and complaining against one another, believing that God is judging not only your oppressors but also yourselves, according to how you treat one another.* "Don't grumble against one another, brothers, or you will be judged. The judge is standing at the door" (James 5:9). James made it clear that they were responsible not to grumble (*stenazo,* that is, "complain," NASB) about either other believers or unbelievers. James saw grumbling as a clear and present threat to patient waiting and healthy spirituality. He stressed that God will judge us on this issue and that this judgment will be as real and near as the coming of the Lord.

The fact is that grumbling and complaining threatened to destroy both the peace and the patience of James's readers. When people experience difficulty, they begin blaming and attacking those who are closest and dearest to them, as well as those who may actually be responsible. But this normal response misses the wonderful opportunity we have to make the point that a calm, patient trust in God can see us through anything.

IV. *Wait patiently in the face of suffering as did the true prophets of the past.* James concluded, "Brothers, as an example of patience in the face of suffering, take the prophets who spoke in the name of the Lord" (Rom. 5:10). Here James hit the issue of suffering head-on. But instead of simply lecturing them to endure trials and suffering, he tried to inspire them by asking them to reflect on the example of the true prophets of God who had suffered in the past.

James presumed that his listeners understand Jewish history. Many of God's faithful prophets had been ridiculed and put to death for speaking out for God and for living countercultural lives. They were often politically incorrect, and paid dearly for their godly, correct faith and patience. He knew that the minds of his readers would quickly trip back over the road of history and remember prophets like Daniel, Zechariah, Jeremiah, and Job and all that they had been through. James's readers would also have remembered that for each of these prophets, the suffering was well worth it in the end.

In conclusion, then, we see that James indeed gave his readers an authentic survival guide to help them face and endure oppression. As we read his words afresh today, we too can find help to wait patiently and survive these present, trying days of Earth's history.—Kenneth B. Stout

ILLUSTRATIONS

THIS TOO SHALL PASS AWAY.   In her book *Light from Many Lamps,* Lillian Eichler Watson writes about the legend of an Eastern monarch who sought a phrase or motto from his wise men that would enable him to meet any crisis or hardship throughout his life. The wise men supposedly came up with the simple phrase, "This too shall pass away." According to the story, this phrase was engraved on his ring, and it helped him through many a trial. The legend and the phrase caught on and were passed on through the centuries until, more than a hundred years ago, an American editor, Paul Hamilton Hayne, came across it. He was so impressed with it that he wrote a brief story about it and eventually a poem. His simple lines were embraced by the public, and many demanded a copy, which they carried around with them in their purses and wallets. It is fitting to read it as we prayerfully consider the words of James 5:7–10:

Art thou in misery, brother? Then I pray
Be comforted. Thy grief shall pass away.
Art thou elated? Ah, be not too gay;
Temper thy joy: this too, shall pass away.
Art thou in danger? Still let reason sway,
And cling to hope: this, too, shall pass away.
Tempted art thou? In all thine anguish lay
One truth to heart: this, too, shall pass away.
Do rays of loftier glory round thee play?
Kinglike art thou? This, too, shall pass away!
What'er thou art, where'er thy footsteps stray,
Heed these wise words: This, too, shall pass away.[1]

THE DANGER OF COMPLAINING.   Paul warns about complaining like some of the Jews did against Moses during their wilderness wandering (1 Cor. 10:10). Their constant complaining and grumbling grew into rebellion against both God and Moses, and they finally had to be destroyed. Their constant grumbling kept may of the Israelites from waiting patiently and from being able to enter the Promised Land. Paul concluded, "These things happened to them as examples and were written down as *warnings for us,* on whom the fulfillment of the ages has come" (1 Cor. 10:11; emphasis mine). We who live in this end-time period will do well to take Paul's counsel to heart and stop complaining and start praising God for his goodness.—Kenneth B. Stout

SERMON SUGGESTIONS

Topic: A Word for the Discouraged
TEXT: Isa. 35:1–10
(1) God will reveal himself gloriously in his creation (vv. 1–2). (2) Because of who God is, the downhearted can have new strength and confidence (vv. 3–6a). (3) The way will be clear and inviting for the service and worship of God (vv. 6b–10).

Topic: Patience—Until the Coming of the Lord
TEXT: James 5:7–10
(1) What is patience (vv. 7–8)? (2) Why is patience a problem (v. 9)? (3) Who exemplifies patience (v. 10)?

WORSHIP AIDS

CALL TO WORSHIP.   "His mercy extends to those who fear him, from generation to generation. He has performed mighty deeds with his arms; he has scattered those who are proud in their inmost thoughts" (Luke 1:50–51 NIV).

INVOCATION.   Let your mighty work be done in us, O God, as we worship you and as we open our lives to your guidance and your love for all humankind.

---

[1]Lillian Eichler Watson, *Light from Many Lamps* (New York: Simon & Schuster, 1988). Originally published 1951.

OFFERTORY SENTENCE.   "Do not neglect to do good and to share what you have, for such sacrifices are pleasing to God" (Heb. 13:16 NRSV).

OFFERTORY PRAYER.   Here are our gifts of gratitude, Father, expressed in this coinage of the land. May these gifts represent not our stinginess and littleness, but our generosity and love.—Henry Fields

PRAYER.   Lord, make us instruments of your peace. Where there is hatred, let us sow love; where there is injury, pardon; where there is discord, union; where there is doubt, faith; where there is despair, hope; where there is darkness, light; where there is sadness, joy. Grant that we may not so much seek to be consoled as to console, to be understood as to understand, to be loved as to love. For it is in giving that we receive, in pardoning that we are pardoned, and in dying that we are born to eternal life.—Attributed to St. Francis of Assisi[2]

SERMON
Topic: The Gift of Joy
TEXT: Phil. 4:4–9; Zeph. 3:14–20

For many of us, joy is, at best, ephemeral and, at worst, always beyond our reach. At times we almost grab it; maybe we actually catch it for an instant, but just as quickly it is gone. We spend our lives in a state of frustration, or maybe in a state of depression, because the sense of joy or the level of joy that we want and that we think *could* be ours if we just got the formula correct escapes us.

Don't measure the joy level in your life against purely external indicators of what you take to be joy in someone else. Who told us that the way to understand and evaluate ourselves is through comparing ourselves to others? That is one of the most distorting perceptions of reality that we can take on, but somehow, from adolescence on, we place ourselves in a kind of competition with others around us.

Joy does not, will not, come from anything exterior. Unless or until we make room for joy deep down inside, it will forever elude us.

Don't assume that joy is generic, that those objects or circumstances that give someone else joy will necessarily give you joy. We are all very different from one another. What brings her joy, even if you had it in duplicate, wouldn't necessarily bring you joy at all. So you get exactly the same black velvet dress and you wear it to an important function—not one at which she will be in attendance, of course—and everyone comments on how lovely you are in the dress; you agree, but you don't feel a bit different inside.

Your path to joy is your own. It will not be identical, in any sense, to anyone else's. We cripple ourselves trying to walk toward joy the way we believe someone else is doing it. We must have the courage to walk our own path, and not all sections of that path will be clearly marked. The path to joy will require us, at times, to launch out in new, untried directions made known to us only by the quiet leading of God's Spirit.

Don't take joy to be an emotion or a state that should be constant. The individual who is emotionally healthy experiences the whole range of human emotions: happiness *and* sadness,

---

[2]*Book of Common Prayer*

exhilaration *and* depression, self-confidence *and* self-doubt, spiritual satisfaction *and* spiritual restlessness, joy *and* sorrow. We are not one-dimensional; that is not how God created us, and if we try to function in that way, we become *dys*functional.

This is a very important matter. There are those of us who somehow come to believe that once we become Christians, we aren't supposed to have concerns or problems or any days without joy. I can't figure out where in the world we get that idea. Certainly not from the Bible, and not from the life of Jesus.

We people of God are not promised insulation from any problem or tragedy common to the rest of humanity. What we Christians are promised is that whatever curve life throws us or whatever evil we bring upon ourselves, it is not the last word.

We heard the subject of joy addressed in both our Scripture lessons, from the prophet Zephaniah and from the apostle Paul. Both men were calling their readers to rejoice, to have joy, based on confidence in God and on God's involvement with humanity.

In Zephaniah's case, he urged his people to rejoice based on the confidence that they would not always live in submission to foreign powers; and what was more, the foreign powers— Assyria, Babylon, and Egypt—could not squeeze the life out of God's people. There would come a great day of judgment, the Day of the Lord, at which time the enemies of God and of God's people would be defeated, and the true people of God—though only a remnant of them might survive the fallout of evil's demise—would then live on (Zeph. 3:11–12).

Are you hearing all of this? In the midst of an ungodly age and with only the "poor and lowly" surviving, there will be joy. Do you see any external reason here to have joy? None at all. Nevertheless, the word from God is, "Zion, cry out for joy; raise the shout of triumph, Israel; be glad, rejoice with all your heart, daughter of Jerusalem." God is in control regardless of all appearances to the contrary.

The word from Paul is similar. He and his readers anticipated the immanent reappearance of the Christ in this world of woe, and with it, the ending of the age, but regardless of the timing of that event, Paul said, "The Lord is near; do not be anxious, but in everything make your requests known to God in prayer and petition with thanksgiving. Then the peace of God, which is beyond all understanding, will guard your hearts and your thoughts in Christ Jesus" (Phil. 4:5b–7 REB). If we can, with God's help, we prayerfully rid ourselves of debilitating anxiety and replace it with *God's* peace.

The enemies of our inner peace, who steal our joy, will not go away and stay away, but occasionally, in spite of them, joy can break through and fill us with light enough to press on.—David Albert Farmer

SUNDAY, DECEMBER 19, 2004
Lectionary Message
Topic: Joseph—The Forgotten Father in the Christmas Story
Text: Matt. 1:18–25 NIV
Other Readings: Isa. 7:10–16; Ps. 80:1–7, 17–19; Rom. 1:1–7

When we look at the birth of Jesus, Mary, his mother, deservedly gets most of the attention, aside from the child himself. But what about the man in the story? What about Mary's hus-

band, Joseph? Could the birth of Christ have occurred as God intended without his participation and faith as well as Mary's? Unfortunately, Joseph gets little attention, little honor, little recognition as a player in the original Christmas story. I think we have missed the blessing
of this man's inspiring role in the birth account as the earthly father of Jesus. Like Mary,
Joseph also demonstrated great courage, sacrifice, and faith in the incarnation of our Lord.
Let's look at the *facts.*

I. *Joseph was a righteous man who knew how to temper justice with mercy and how to act
with grace in a time of shame and humiliation.* The passage opens with this simple account:
"This is how the birth of Jesus Christ came about: His mother Mary was pledged to be married to Joseph, but before they came together, she was found to be with child through the
Holy Spirit" (Matt. 1:18). Now think about this from Joseph's perspective. He was engaged
to this sweet young woman, perhaps as young as twelve or fourteen years old, and he discovered, to his shock and dismay, that she was pregnant. Now this was a serious problem
for both of them, because being engaged in those days was binding and equivalent to being
legally married today.

Here's where we first notice something very special about this man. While he had every
right to be angry with and to condemn Mary, he instead displayed a rare and marvelous
grace. Instead of trying to protect and preserve his *own* reputation by publicly repudiating
her, he moved quickly to protect and preserve *her* reputation. He decided to quietly arrange
for the signing of the necessary legal documents to divorce Mary, which required at least
two witnesses.

Technically, Joseph had the right to profit from the divorce by impounding Mary's dowry
and perhaps even recouping the "bride price" that he had paid for her. But Joseph, the man
of grace, took no such action.

II. *Joseph was a man who, when commanded by God, acted in complete and immediate
obedience.* Now, of course, as the story continues, God sent his angel to correct Joseph's mis-
understanding and to instruct him about how he should act toward Mary: "Do not be afraid
to take Mary home as your wife, because what is conceived in her is from the Holy Spirit"
(vv. 20–21). Mary was not an adulteress after all. In fact, she was the one young bride in all
of human history who had been given the high privilege of being impregnated by the Holy
Spirit. She alone had been given the honor of becoming the mother of the Messiah. Mothers
from Eve to Sarah, from Rachel to Ruth, and on down the stream of time had hoped and
prayed to be the *one* who would be mother to this special boy—the Savior of the world.

And how fortunate that made Joseph! No, he would not be a man of shame, misfortune,
and disgrace. He would be the man the angel called him: "Joseph, son of David," caretaker
and earthly father of the ultimate Son of David—the Messiah himself. How could it be?

According to the text, Joseph acted quickly and without hesitation on what the angel had
commanded: "He did what the angel of the Lord had commanded him *and took Mary home
as his wife*" (v. 24; emphasis mine). I like what one commentator has said about Joseph's
quick obedience: "The role of Joseph was humble yet indispensable, and his prompt com-
pliance with the angel's instructions made a great deal of difference, both to Mary and to
public opinion." Oh that there were more Josephs today who were as quick to obey God
when duty is made clear.

III. *Joseph was a man of self-discipline and commitment to God's plan.* Now, think about
what the text says next about Joseph: "He took Mary home as his wife, but he had no union

with her until she gave birth to a son, and he gave him the name Jesus" (v. 25). He had no sexual relations with her. Now that's saying something for a vigorous new husband. To give up his right as a husband to sleep with his attractive, young wife in order to help fulfill God's prophetic plan was no small thing. His self-denial made a huge statement to the world about the authenticity of the Virgin Birth. What if he hadn't controlled his passions?

According to the age-old word from the Lord, the virgin would *conceive* as a virgin and *give birth* as a virgin. Jesus was not born of a human father, as some have tried to say—*no way!* That fact was driven home by Joseph's decision to act in self-sacrifice and faith, by the Spirit's power, in forgoing sexual pleasure with his wife, Mary. How long did he restrain himself? The Bible doesn't say, but it is obvious that it was a substantial period of time until the birth, certainly several months.

IV. *Joseph was a man who protected, provided for, and helped shape the life of Christ!* The story doesn't end there, even though the text does, for Scripture makes it plain that Joseph went on to help protect the baby Jesus' life time and again (Matt. 2:14–23), to train him, and to provide for his basic earthly needs until Jesus moved from childhood to adolescence to manhood (Luke 2:51). Joseph taught Jesus to be a fine, careful carpenter, like himself, and surely many, many other lessons, as a loving father would.

To my knowledge, not one bad word is spoken of Joseph. Jesus became known as "the carpenter's son." Let us never forget that that carpenter was *Joseph,* and that Joseph was a righteous man, a man of grace and mercy, a man of quick obedience, a man of self-discipline, and a man who nurtured Jesus through life as a loving father.

Let us imitate his admirable life of faith and service to his son—*God's* son—Jesus, the Christ!—Kenneth B. Stout

ILLUSTRATIONS

FAITH IN THE FACE OF THE UNKNOWN.   The fact that Joseph was able to manifest such strong faith and courage in this most unique and difficult situation, when his new wife was about to give birth to the Messiah, is impressive. What doubts and questions must have arisen in his heart about how he was going to explain all of this, and about what it would be like to be the earthly father to this special child. I am reminded of the words of James Allen: "Where faith is there is courage, there is fortitude, there is steadfastness and strength. . . . Faith bestows that sublime courage that rises superior to the troubles and disappointments of life, that acknowledges no defeat except as a step to victory; that is strong to endure, patient to wait. . . . Light up, then, the lamp of faith in your heart. . . . It will lead you safely through doubt . . . and over the treacherous places of uncertainty."[3]

THE MAN BEHIND THE TIGER.   Tiger Woods is known as the greatest golfer of our day. Most people agree that he is going at such a torrid pace that he will likely break most of golf's prestigious records and even surpass the great Jack Nicklaus. His name and fame make him perhaps the most recognized and admired sports figure in the world today. But he is respected for more than his golf achievements. He is also admired for his maturity beyond his years, his grace under pressure, his determination, and his great work ethic. He is a man of princi-

---

[3]Source unknown.

ple and integrity. He is confident yet humble. Woods attributes much of his development as a golfer and a man to the strong influence of his father, Earl Woods. The senior Woods trained Tiger in Tiger's childhood days and later exposed him to some of the finest golf instructors in the world. He made many sacrifices to pay for Tiger's lessons and to attend his matches. He spent much time talking to his son about discipline, practice habits, integrity, and how to maintain a well-rounded, balanced life.

Oh that more fathers would be such powerful shaping, caring forces in the lives of their sons and daughters today.—Kenneth B. Stout

SERMON SUGGESTIONS

Topic: A Great Light
TEXT: Isa. 9:2–7
(1) Messiah's deeds (vv. 2–5). (2) Messiah's character (v. 6). (3) Messiah's program.

Topic: The Incomparable Grace of God
TEXT: Titus 2:11–14
It is incomparable (1) in its outreach (v. 11), (2) in its demand (v. 12), (3) in its promise (v. 13), and (4) in its source (v. 14).

WORSHIP AIDS

CALL TO WORSHIP.   "Let your hand rest on the man at your right hand, the Son of Man you have raised up for yourself. Then we will not turn away from you; revive us, and we will call on your name. Restore us, O Lord God Almighty; make your face shine upon us, that we may be saved" (Ps. 80:17–19 NIV).

INVOCATION.   Lead us, O God, through the deep waters of our days to a new understanding and appreciation of the new life that came into the world in Christ Jesus; and so stir our hearts and minds that we will see in him something new to live by and live for, so that our lives will have new meaning and joy. Amen.—Theodore Parker Ferris

OFFERTORY SENTENCE.   "Like good stewards of the manifold grace of God, serve one another with whatever gift each of you has received" (1 Pet. 4:10 NRSV).

OFFERTORY PRAYER.   Lord, let our Christmas offering this day be tinged with the light of that first Christmas and suffused with the glow from the stable where God kept his promise.—E. Lee Phillips

PRAYER.   It is Christmas everywhere, Father. For weeks we have heard the songs and carols of the season, sung the hymns, and listened to the anthems extolling the birth of the Lord. Over and over we have been reminded of the swift passage of time as we approach that day of days celebrating the occasion of Christ's birth. In the midst of such prolonged emphasis, we often grow weary of the music, jaded with the preparations, and tired of the season before it is completed. Yet, when we pause and meditate on the meaning of the coming of the Lord and try to understand something of your purpose for Christmas, we are filled again with amazement and wonder. During these remaining days of concentrated celebration, when so many are frayed and weary, bring us again to the remembrance of your gift to us and its meaning for all humankind. Restore unto us the joy of thy salvation and renew a right spirit within us. Remembering again the deep meaning for the season, we will declare your ways to transgressors, and sinners will be converted unto you.

Many among us cannot celebrate joyfully, Father. Life has dealt them severe blows and their faith has been shaken. Some have become so ill that Christmas celebration is more of a burden than a blessing. Others, walking in loneliness, feel like strangers standing outside the party looking in. Some even wonder if there will ever be a joyous Christmas for them again. Let the bright star of Bethlehem shine in their skies, we pray. Through the darkness of their night let the angelic news be sung. Over the pathways leading to Christ's presence may they journey and for themselves see this thing that has come to pass, which the Lord has made known unto us. And may those of us more able to celebrate his coming seek out the ones needful of his presence and power and bring them to his consolation.

Now we commit the hour into your hands. Overrule our agenda if necessary and have your way with us as we wait and worship before you, we pray in the name and power of Christ. Amen.—Henry Fields

SERMON
Topic: From Here to Eternity
Text: Heb. 1:1–12

I remember conversations about some of the more reputable examinations that students had to endure in my seminary days. I had one teacher who preferred to give simple true-false exams that were graded in class, thus eliminating the necessity of a graduate assistant or grader. He was also known to allow a class vote on disputed questions. Too bad if you were right and in the minority when the vote was taken.

At the other extreme was the mythical teacher who asked the mythical question, "Discuss the universe and give three examples." The exam question was supposed to be a joke, but in recent years several books have emerged that seem to take the question seriously. One is physicist Stephen W. Hawking's 1988 book *A Brief History of Time: From the Big Bang to Black Holes.* This book is actually comprehensible and somewhat entertaining. His chapter "Black Holes Ain't So Black" makes you wonder if Hawking is from East Tennessee instead of England. The scope of the title is slightly broader than one person should be allowed in one lifetime, much less than one book should be allowed. But Hawking dares to raise ultimate questions: Was there a beginning of time? Will there be an end? Is the universe infinite? Or does it have boundaries? By anyone's measure, this is a pretty big assignment for a two-hundred-page book, and Hawking, by his own admission, is anything but a prophet.

Then there is Karen Armstrong's 1993 best-selling book, *A History of God.* At the outset, the book appears to be a fraud. It does not pretend to tell the whole story of God. Armstrong, a former Catholic nun, deliberately overstates her subject. Who knows? Maybe the pretentious title was concocted by the publisher in order to attract readers. To the author's credit, the subtitle injects a note of honesty, limiting her study to a "4,000-Year Quest for Judaism, Christianity, and Islam"—hardly the whole history of God.

Christmas seems to be the gospel in miniature—a little baby born in the little city of Bethlehem in the little Roman province of Israel. People who visit the Holy Land are shocked at its size. Biblical places that seem bigger than life in our minds are in a postage-stamp-size world. The mystery of Advent is the macroscopic message located in a microscopic piece of the world. The big story does not fit as well in the Christmas narratives as it does in the Advent reflections in other places in the Bible. The prologues to John and to Hebrews sound pretentious. They reach out to the bounds of the universe, and in a few strokes of the pen they presume to encompass both Hawking's and Armstrong's subjects, the history of time and the history of God.

Barclay called the first line of Hebrews "the most sonorous piece of Greek in the whole New Testament . . . a passage that any classical Greek orator would have been proud to write." The eternal God, who has been speaking through the prophets throughout the ages of human history, has in the last days spoken the final Word in a Son.

I. *God speaks.* The first message of our Bible begins at the beginning of time, with first things—the first light, the first day, the first night, the first life, and finally the first human-, ity. The poetry of creation in Genesis is about the God who speaks. It appears to us that language is a distinctly human creation. We set ourselves apart from the rest of the animal world with sounds of complex communication and libraries stuffed full of books. According to Genesis, the word begins with God, and perhaps the word more than anything else in all creation distinguishes the human being as having been made in the image of God. The creation mythology of the Assyrian neighbors describes a world made from a war between the gods. Almost as if in response to Hawking's question, the Jews declared the universe to be a creation, an orderly work of art made with purpose and set in motion with meaning. The finite world is the gift of the infinite Creator. The Spirit brooding over the waters of chaos began to bring order and meaning to the formless void, and the writer of Genesis finally located the creative power of God in the word spoken, "Let there be . . ."

Since the beginning, God has not ceased speaking. The Word of God has persistently crossed the chasm that divides God and creation. God has spoken in the committed words of covenant, uttering promises containing both curse and blessing. God has laid down the Law. From Mount Sinai, words emerged with Moses that were held sacred as the very message sent from God for the health and happiness of God's people. The Torah was the foundation for life in Israel because God had spoken in human terms. Finally, the Word of God emerged on the street corners of Jewish civilization in messages delivered by the prophets. Their sermons contained the classical imprimatur, "Thus says the Lord." They came on the horizon of history, speaking the very Word of God; and as in the creation, the Word of God was effective. God's Word is never spoken loosely or without action. God's Word does not come back empty. The event in history known as the exile was not a historical accident. It was the judgment of God on the sin of the people delivered first in the words of warning from Jeremiah, but the word finally exploded in human history in war, defeat, and ultimately exile.

In the Jewish mind, no one could get any closer to God than in the words of covenant, the words of the law, and the words of the prophets that have been passed down through the centuries:

Word of God, across the ages,
Comes the message to our life;
Sources of hope forever present
in our toil and fears and strife.

The Holy Scriptures contain the very Word of God to humanity. They were carefully gathered and have been preserved and transmitted from one generation to the next. No miracle in the Bible is more wonderful than the miracle of the Bible itself. This collection of words forms the foundation of understanding God's will and way in the world, and it seems to say to all people of all time, "the Word stops here!"

II. *The Word in Christ is final.* We need to be careful in our declarations about lasting things. Charles Barton has recently written an article for *Senior Living* on buying a used car at age ninety. He thought his '93 Ford Victoria was going to be his final set of wheels, but 96,000 miles later he found a continuing need for dependable transportation.

Every generation has had a tendency to think of their questions as the ultimate concerns, their problems as the worst in history, and their solutions to be eternal. Every generation in time has been surprised that God has the last word. That is essentially what Hebrews says about the Son. "In these last days" is an ultimate statement that belongs with final matters. The Word spoken through the Son will be extended but never replaced. In an age when angel fantasies are more popular than the gospel, we need to hear the message that the Son is greater than anybody's angels. Angels are messengers essential to the communication of the Word of God through the ages, but prophets and angels are timely. The Word of God in Christ is timeless.

In a Christmas meditation, Roger Douglas tells the story of a four-year-old child named Suki. After her baby brother was born, she pleaded with her parents to leave her alone with her brother. The parents were somewhat apprehensive. They had read about how children are sometimes jealous of newborns. They feared for the infant's safety and for Suki's well-being if injury should occur to the baby. Finally, they agreed to let Suki have a few minutes alone with her brother, but in the interest of safety they kept the door from closing completely and they watched over their two precious children. To the parents' amazement, Suki leaned over into her brother's crib and asked the ultimate question: "Baby, what does God look like? I am beginning to forget." A child's fable? Perhaps. But the Word of God is that the Son is the image, literally "the character," of God. God is like Christ, the one we proclaim.—Larry Dipboye

SUNDAY, DECEMBER 26, 2004
Lectionary Message

Topic: Jesus—Our Brother by Choice

TEXT: Heb. 2:10–18 NIV

Other Readings: Isa. 63:7–9; Ps. 148; Matt. 2:13–23

In society today, brotherhood is highly thought of, even when the term is not used in the context of blood relationship. People talk about being so bonded to someone that he is "like a brother." Or they express closeness by saying, "He's the brother I never had." A recent, acclaimed TV mini-series was called *Band of Brothers*. It tells of a company of soldiers that fought courageously in some of the most difficult battles of World War II. Through common suffering, they formed a comradery that could best be described as a brotherhood.

In our text for today we find that the Creator himself has become our very real "brother," by assuming human flesh and suffering with us. We read in Hebrews 2, "So Jesus is not ashamed to call them [that is, us] *brothers*" (v. 11b; emphasis mine). And later the same chapter says of Jesus, "For . . . he had to be made like his *brothers* in every way" (v. 17; emphasis mine). But *why?* According to Hebrews 2:10–18, he did it to accomplish at least three vital goals that were necessary for our salvation.

I. *Jesus became our brother to destroy the Devil and the power he holds on death.* The writer of Hebrews states this first goal plainly: "Because the children [that is, human beings] have flesh and blood, he too [that is, Jesus] shared in their humanity so that by his death he might destroy him who holds the power of death—that is, the devil" (v. 14). The explanation is clear, though the process itself is an unfathomable mystery that cannot be explained by science or human logic. It is one of the great mysteries of God that the Son of God, Jesus, needed to become the Son of Man—that is, human—to save humanity from the devil and death.

No other religion presents its god as taking on humanity and fully experiencing human existence—even death. But that's exactly what Christ did in the Christmas story. He became one of us. He became a true brother by becoming human. He came to eat, sleep, thirst, get tired, and feel pain—just like we do—yet "without sin" (4:15).

The devil claimed that it was impossible to obey and serve God as God demanded, and that it was impossible not to sin. But Jesus' perfect human life was a judgment on the Devil and proved that his claims against God were wrong, because Jesus' perfect life and death—and subsequent Resurrection—paid the wages of sin for us. The Devil will be destroyed and stripped of his "power of death" (Heb. 2:14; Rev. 20:10, 14).

II. *Jesus became our brother to free us from the fear of death.* Not only did Jesus come to destroy the Devil and the Devil's power of death, he came to "free those who all their lives were held in slavery by their *fear* of death" (v. 15; emphasis mine). Is there any greater fear than the fear of death? The most difficult thing that most of us face in life is that we will die. One commentator states, "Fear is an inhibiting and enslaving thing; and when people are gripped by the ultimate fear—the fear of death—they are in cruel bondage." We all grow old, get sick, and die—or something else happens to us that cuts our life short. First-century philosophers tried to teach people to be calm in the face of death, but usually without success. Many tombs were etched with inscriptions of hopelessness (4:16).

Today people are afraid of dying from AIDS or cancer, or from terrorist attacks, whether by bomb, hijacked airplane, anthrax, small pox, or sniper bullet. A contemporary country spiritual is titled "Everybody Wants to Go to Heaven, but Nobody Wants to Die." Most of us fear death—even professing Christians. Our text tells us that Jesus came as our brother, to destroy not only the Devil and the power of death, but the "fear of death" as well (v. 15).

III. *Jesus also became our brother in order to be an authentic high priest who could rightfully atone for our sins.* Notice what Hebrews 2:17 says: "For this reason, he [Jesus] had to be made like his brothers in every way, in order that he might become a merciful and faithful high priest in service to God, and that he might make atonement for the sins of the people" (NIV). To "make atonement" for the sins of the people—literally, "to propitiate" for our sins (NASB; *hilaskesthai* in Greek)—means that Jesus had to "put away divine wrath" (or "show mercy").

In the plan to save humankind, two requirements had to be met.

(a) Jesus had to "be made like his brothers in every way . . . that he might become . . . a *merciful* . . . high priest" (v. 17; emphasis mine). Only as a human being, who comprehended and had fully experienced the raging force of the temptations of a human body, could Jesus acceptably serve as our merciful advocate.

(b) Jesus had to be a "*faithful* high priest in service to God" (v. 17). In other words, he had to live a life of faithful obedience, even in the face of the most severe temptation. Jesus had to be one who was "tempted in every way, just as we are—yet was without sin," according to Heb. 4:15. If Jesus had simply been human and merciful like us, it would have been insufficient. God the Father could not have accepted it. Jesus had to be both merciful, by understanding our weakness and the power of temptation, and faithful, by obeying God and his laws—even unto death.

Jesus became our brother and attained the three goals he had set out to achieve for our salvation: (1) to destroy the Devil and rip out of his hands the power to hold death over us, (2) to free us from the fear of death, and (3) to become an authentic high priest who can atone for all of ours sins—and make us strong to resist sin today.—Kenneth B. Stout

ILLUSTRATIONS

BECOME A BROTHER, SAVE A BROTHER!   I recently heard the story of a humble priest and his parishioners who lived in a Texas border town. Across the border, in Mexico, was a neighboring town full of poverty and despair. This town had a huge dump occupied by about 350 to 400 "dump people." They literally lived in the dump. They survived by digging through the garbage and eating the remnants of rotting food and drink, and by selling the plastic bottles, aluminum cans, and other junk they found. It was difficult, smelly, disgusting work. The priest and his congregation felt the need to minister to these people, so they prepared enough simple meals to feed about 125 people. They took the food to the dump people and found that God literally performed a miracle by stretching the small lunches to feed every one of the 350 to 400 people. They even had food left over, which they took to area shelters. It was a modern-day miracle. They decided to continue helping these people by bringing them food and clothes, and even by organizing them into a kind of "dump market." But to make a real difference, they knew they would have to do more than just give aid. So they began to work side-by-side with the dump people, digging through the trash on appointed days. They become brothers and sisters to them. At the risk of getting tuberculosis and other diseases and having to endure the terrible stench and indignity of such work, they became part of the dump "family." As they did, they found that the people responded to their grace and friendship, and in the end many of the dump people began to accept Jesus as one who cared for them. In turn, the church members found that their own lives were changed by what they saw God doing in the lives of these poor people. The ministry—and the sense of brotherhood—continues to grow to this day.—Kenneth B. Stout

LIVING ABOVE THE FEAR OF DEATH.   This is such a personal issue for my wife and me. In 1999 we lost our precious and only daughter in a tragic bus accident. She was just twenty-one years old, serving as a student missionary in Taiwan, with her life in front of her. How our hearts still ache because of her death. We miss her so very, very much. We also have a dear son, so our daughter has a brother. How wonderful to know that Jody loved Jesus and therefore has a second brother in him. And this Jesus, who has conquered death and the reason to fear it, will restore her to everlasting life at his Second Coming—along with all the righteous dead (1 Thess. 4:16–18; 1 Cor. 15:20–23, 51–55). Today we can live without the fear of death, knowing that it is temporary and that Jesus has become "the resurrection and the life" (Heb. 2:15; John 11:25).—Kenneth B. Stout

SERMON SUGGESTIONS

Topic: The Lord's Unfailing Love
Text: Isa. 63:7–9 NEB
(1) Despite our unworthiness. (2) In all our troubles. (3) By coming to us in person.

Topic: Our Highest Priest
Text: Heb. 2:10–18
(1) Identified with us in his enfleshment. (2) Suffered for us to make expiation for our sins. (3) Helps us when we are tempted.

WORSHIP AIDS

CALL TO WORSHIP.   "Let kings and all commoners, princes and rulers over the whole Earth, youths and girls, old and young together, let them praise the name of the Lord, for his name is high above all others, and his majesty is above Earth and heaven" (Ps.148:11–13 REB).

INVOCATION.   God of incarnation, fill our worship with the sense of awe and wonder so that we may find the profound in the simple and the mighty in the humble, as did the shepherds long ago who worshiped the Son of God lying in a manger, and this world has not been the same since.—E. Lee Phillips

OFFERTORY SENTENCE.   "For God loved the world so much that he gave his only Son. God gave his Son so that whoever believes in him may not be lost but have eternal life" (John 3:16 NCV).

OFFERTORY PRAYER.   We know, O God, that nothing we offer can compare with the gift of your Son for our salvation in this world and in the world to come. But with gratitude beyond description we come to you with our meager gifts, with the prayer that they may be multiplied by your grace to bless untold numbers who need you.

PRAYER.   Love incarnate, you came to Bethlehem, to plain shepherds and to angels ill-fitting the scheme of things, to wise men the powerful ignore, and to Mary, a pregnant teenage girl. You come still in the wonder of new birth, in quiet kindness, in anonymous goodness, to bring a new order of salvation, heaven permeable to your messengers, earth abode of angels, to tabernacle among us, full of grace and truth.

At this hallowed hour we pray for all sorts and conditions of men, but especially for the poor, the bereaved, and the alone; the wronged, the dumped, and the uninvited; those in prison and those who are appointed to die, and all who have not faith. That such souls would find effectual grace, your saving difference made flesh, turn hearts again to your Word and to its living center, our Lord, and let the beauty of this hour nurture discipleship, the settled will for plain duty done far from the approving crowd.

We pray for peace in our time and for the things that make for peace, in others and in ourselves, the indwelling life of your Son in crowning lowliness.—Peter Fribley

SERMON
Topic: The Beginning and the End
TEXT: Matt. 2:13–23

"Do not be afraid. I bring you good news of great joy that will be for all people. Today in the City of David a Savior has been born to you. He is Christ the Lord. This will be a sign to you: you will find a baby wrapped in swaddling cloth and lying in a manger." And the shepherds went and saw the child and went home glorifying God for all the things they had been told and had seen.

If we just stopped there it would be a great fairy tale. They all lived happily ever after. The Wise Men, being warned in a dream, went home by another way. And they all lived happily ever after. Perhaps that is the way we come out of Christmas. We have a beautiful Christmas and then we slip into New Year's celebration and move into the New Year on a pretty positive and upbeat note.

But like a thorn on a beautiful rose, there is this story of the slaughter of the innocents, this harsh political reality that those who are on top do not tolerate even the smallest possibility of opposition. Herod met with the Wise Men who had come to worship the one whose birth had caused the heavens to have a new star. What kind of being must be born to be signaled by a new star in the heavens? You and I have been offered the chance to name a star and have it recorded in some book someplace, but none of us thinks that our being born is so significant that the heaven's will mark it by the creation of a new star.

The Wise Men told Herod that they had seen a new star and they knew it signaled the birth of a great new king, and Herod did not take such news lightly. He dealt with the threat by killing all the three-year-old and younger male babies—killed them all to get rid of the one. We do something like that in chemotherapy—kill all the blood cells in hope of killing all the cancer ones and then hope you will grow new healthy ones. We have engaged in a war with a whole government in the effort to get one man. So Herod ordered the death of all the male children.

The angel of the Lord came to Joseph to tell him to take the child and Mary and flee to Egypt to hide until the threat was over. Run to Egypt for protection. Bob Dylan has an old standard now called "Shelter from the Storm." "Come, she said. I'll give you shelter from the storm." Egypt was the shelter from the storm for Joseph, Mary, and Jesus.

Joseph, Mary, and Jesus needed someplace to run, someplace to hide. So even those who had found favor with God and God's gift of love in human flesh needed to find some place to wait out the storm? We might have thought that those who had found favor with God would not encounter storms. We would like to hope that if you are in God's good graces you will not see danger and attacks. We are forever expecting that if we are blessed by God we will not see adversity. But the angel told them to flee, run away, take Mary and the baby and go hide in Egypt. There are times when even the Son of God simply had to take shelter from the storm.

We do not need to fight every battle. We do not need to be invincible all the time. We do not need to show how powerful and mighty we are in every crisis. Even God in human flesh needed simply to go somewhere out of danger for a while. If the angel told Joseph and Mary to take the child and flee to Egypt, the same angel bears the same message for us as we enter into the New Year. You and I do not need to stay and fight every storm that comes. There is no disgrace in taking refuge from a struggle. There is no need for us to pretend that we can handle every adversity that comes. We do not have to try to win every battle at all times. It may be best for us simply to find shelter and wait out the storm.

Or if you want to think in terms of the bigger story of the Scriptures, the flight into Egypt is simply the recognition that there is great wisdom in waiting to fight the battles at the right time. Jesus told his mother at the Wedding of Cana that his time had not yet come; it was not the right time. Throughout his ministry Jesus was constantly telling his disciples not to tell the crowd whom they believed him to be because the time was not right. Jesus had to grow in stature and in favor with God and man before he was ready for the struggle with Herod—his Kingdom versus the kingdom of this world. Egypt was a strategic withdrawal in order to await a more appropriate time. Even the Devil in the wilderness temptations withdrew from Jesus until a more appropriate time. There are some struggles, some adversities, some storms in life that will have to be faced, but the angel of God's love advises us to find some shelter from the storm and to face the battle at a better time.

Even that advice is not always welcomed by the world around us. We seem so eager and anxious to pick a fight. Just let the school administration say you cannot wear rings in your nose and immediately there will be a host of lawsuits. You and I know the kind of outrage that comes when somebody is told they are not old enough for something. But Jesus, Joseph, and Mary went into Egypt and ducked this fight, found shelter from this storm, and waited for a more appropriate time for Jesus to be about his Father's business.

One of the lessons a community organizer in Texas constantly used to give to the leaders of the group was that we did not need to fight every fight when it was presented. We could collect the fights and remember the issues, and then when we were ready and prepared, when we had the advantage, we could return to these issues and fight the fights. We had a tendency to try to deal with issues the way people at the state fair deal with that game about hitting the squirrels when they appear. Every time an issue would come up we thought we had to hit it. Jesus could not deal with the evil and death brought about by Herod now, as a baby. He fled and found shelter and waited until he was prepared.

There are times for all of us when we need to take shelter from a storm. If even the Son of God needed to find shelter from the slaughter of innocents, then there is no shame in our acknowledging that we need a shelter from our storm. If even Jesus did not fight every battle and had to wait in secret to confront his struggle, there is no disgrace for us to avoid our battles until we are better prepared.

As we come to the end of one year and stand at the beginning of a new year, we look around at one another and give thanks to one another for the protection, shelter, and comfort we have found in one another's company. We have come into this place each week seeking a little time to lick our wounds, a little time to rest, a little time for encouragement, a little time to put our monetary concerns into the great perspective of God's eternity. And we no longer feel like we have to solve all of our problems immediately. We no longer think we are by ourselves. We are reminded that God's purposes, God's will, and God's intentions are at work in the world, and we can rest and let God work his will while we take a breather.

We have come in here seeking a place of comfort and consolation from the attacks of time, decay, and illness, the onslaught of old age. We are given the shelter that God knows we are human. He knows we are made of dust, and God has promised that what he has made in love he will keep with him in eternity, so our time-bound pains are, as St. Paul claims, mere transitory nuisances.

The Church is to be, we are to be, the place that gives shelter, comfort, hope, and protection to those who are under attack and suffering the storms of life. The storm and assaults are going to come. As we look into this New Year, we, the people of God, need to prepare ourselves to provide the consolation, the comfort, and the hope to those who will be experiencing the destruction caused by the great economic factors at work in the world. The competition of the free enterprise system is what we are suppose to be so proud of, but there are going to be a number of people in our community who will be battered and beaten by those forces. Tobacco and textiles, tech stocks and drug makers—it may be the battle of the fittest, but we are called to be a shelter for those who are slaughtered in the process.

We as the Church are supposed to be the refuge for those who are victims and abused by the powers and forces of strength and might. We are a place of comfort, refuge, and hope for those working poor and poorly educated who are under attack from predatory loans, cheap imitations, drugs, and greed.

We as the body of Christ are to seek to be a place of safety, of comfort, of courage for all of us who are under constant attack from the fear of death, from the fear that our existence is an accident and our being here doesn't make a bit of difference, either to the world in which we live or to our own lives; and from the assault of regret, of failure, of guilt that we have not even been able to do the good and the beautiful we had hoped and tried to do.

The angel told Joseph to take Mary and the baby into Egypt and wait until Herod was dead. We do not have to fight every evil or every battle. We can wait, we can pick and choose some of the struggles we will endure. A place of hiding, a shelter, a refuge from the slaughter is a necessary thing, and that shelter is to be found now in the fellowship of faith. It is the calling of the Church to be a place of refuge, a house of prayer for all those who stand in need of prayer—a shelter from the storm.—Rick Brand

SECTION III

RESOURCES FOR CONGREGATIONAL MUSIC

BY PAUL A. RICHARDSON

The hymns listed here have been chosen for their relation to the Scripture readings for each week. Most are not merely compatible with the theme of the pericope; they also reflect the particular language, imagery, or content of the passage. The following letters preceding the titles of the hymns indicate the reading to which each hymn relates:

O = Old Testament
P = Psalm
E = Epistle
G = Gospel

Often several choices are provided, though some passages have no readily accessible companion in the hymnic literature. Sometimes the scriptural link, though evident, is not that of traditional usage (for example, "Joy to the World," typically sung at Christmas, is a paraphrase of Psalm 98). The use of a familiar text in a different context can prompt new awareness of both Scripture and hymn.

Because hymn texts have often been altered, even in their first lines, authors' surnames are provided as an aid to location. No judgments are made as to authenticity of attributions, nor are preferences expressed for particular translations. The texts are listed in alphabetical order within each grouping.

Seven hymns are identified in connection with three or more distinct passages. Learning and repeating these in their multiple relationships offers a way to expand a congregation's enduring repertory for worship. These are as follows:

"Christ, from Whom All Blessings Flow" (Wesley)
"Christ Is Risen, Christ Is Living" (Martínez)
"Christ, You Are the Fullness" (Polman)
"Come Down, O Love Divine" (Bianco of Siena)
"O Day of Peace That Dimly Shines" (Daw)
"Of the Father's Love Begotten" (Prudentius)
"Sing Praise to God Who Reigns Above" (Schütz)

If a hymn is widely published, no source is cited. For those found in only one of the following hymnals, the book is indicated after the title of the hymn using the following abbreviations:

BH = *The Baptist Hymnal*[1]
CH = *Chalice Hymnal*[2]
HWB = *Hymnal: A Worship Book*[3]
NCH = *The New Century Hymnal*[4]
PH = *The Presbyterian Hymnal*[5]
RS = *RitualSong*[6]
UMH = *The United Methodist Hymnal*[7]
WC = *The Worshiping Church*[8]

Particular mention must be made of *Hymns for the Gospels,*[9] an anthology of texts chosen specifically for use with the Gospel readings for most Sundays in the three-year lectionary. The abbreviation HG follows the title of each relevant hymn, even if that hymn also appears in one or more of the other hymnals.

Hymns identified with the psalm readings are closely related to the corresponding text, in keeping with the design of the Revised Common Lectionary, which intends that the psalm itself be a response to the first lesson. Because numerous recently published resources, including many hymnals, provide brief responses intended for responsorial or antiphonal use with the reading or chanting of the psalms, none of these is cited here. Rather, all hymns listed in connection with the psalms are metrical versions; that is, they are in traditional multi-stanza hymn form. Many of these come from *The Presbyterian Hymnal.* A more extensive collection of metrical psalm settings is the Christian Reformed Church's *Psalter Hymnal,*[10] which contains metrical versions of all 150 psalms.

Those who would use hymns not found in their own congregational hymnal are reminded of the obligation, both legal and ethical, to observe the copyright law. Each of the collections cited provides clear information about copyright owners and agents. Participation in Church Copyright Licensing International (CCLI)[11] or LicenSing[12] can make available a wide range of material without great cost or complex paperwork.

January 4
Jer. 31:7–14; Ps. 147:12–20; Eph. 1:3–14; John 1:(1–9) 10–18

O: See the references under December 12 for Isaiah 35, which has a similar theme.
P: "Now Praise the Lord, All Living Saints" (Anderson) PH

---

[1]*The Baptist Hymnal* (Nashville: Convention Press, 1991).
[2]*Chalice Hymnal* (St. Louis: Chalice Press, 1995).
[3]*Hymnal: A Worship Book* (Elgin, Ill.: Brethren Press, 1992).
[4]*The New Century Hymnal* (Cleveland, Ohio: Pilgrim Press, 1995).
[5]*The Presbyterian Hymnal* (Louisville, Ky.: Westminster/John Knox Press, 1990).
[6]*RitualSong: A Hymnal and Service Book for Roman Catholics* (Chicago: GIA Publications, 1996).
[7]*The United Methodist Hymnal: Book of United Methodist Worship* (Nashville: United Methodist, 1989).
[8]*The Worshiping Church* (Carol Stream, Ill.: Hope, 1990).
[9]*Hymns for the Gospels* (Chicago: GIA Publications, 2001).
[10]*Psalter Hymnal* (Grand Rapids, Mich.: CRC Publications, 1987).
[11]Church Copyright License, 17201 NE Sacramento Street, Portland, OR 97230 [www.ccli.com].
[12]LicenSing: Copyright-Cleared Music for Churches, Logos Productions, 6160 Carmen Avenue East, Inver Grove Heights, MN 55076–4422 [http://www.joinhands.com/hallway.taf?site_uid1 = 4039&hallway_uid1 = 4039&_UserReference = 53122101FFA911593B3CFBE8].

E: "Here, O Lord, Your Servants Gather" (Yamaguchi); "To God Be the Glory, Great Things He Hath Done" (Crosby)

G: "Christ Is the World's Light" (Green); "Christ Is the World's True Light" (Briggs); "God Has Spoken by His Prophets" (Briggs); "Hark, the Herald Angels Sing" (Wesley); "O Come, All Ye Faithful" (Wade; using the stanza, "God of God, Light of Light"); "O Splendor of God's Glory Bright" (Ambrose); "Of the Father's Love Begotten" (Prudentius); "Savior of the Nations, Come" (Ambrose); "Word of God, When All Was Silent" (Stuempfle) HG

EPIPHANY

January 11 (Baptism of the Lord)
Isa. 43:1-7; Ps. 29; Acts 8:14-17; Luke 3:15-17, 21-22

O: "How Firm a Foundation" ("K")

P: "The God of Heaven Thunders" (Perry), PH; "Worship the Lord in the Beauty of Holiness" (Monsell)

E: Though no hymns treat this specific passage, many relate to the coming of the Holy Spirit. See the listings for May 30 (Pentecost) and the weeks following.

G: "Christ, Your Footprints Through the Desert" (Stuempfle), HG; "Mark How the Lamb of God's Self-Offering" (Daw), NCH; "Songs of Thankfulness and Praise" (Wordsworth); "What Ruler Wades Through Murky Streams" (Troeger), NCH; "When Jesus Came to Jordan" (Green), HG

January 18
Isa. 62:1-5; Ps. 36:5-10; 1 Cor. 12:1-11; John 2:1-11

P: "Come, Thou Fount of Every Blessing" (Robinson); "Thy Mercy and Thy Truth, O Lord" (*The Psalter*, 1912), PH

E: "Christ, from Whom All Blessings Flow" (Wesley); "Come, Holy Ghost, Our Souls Inspire" (Maurus); "Come to Us, Creative Spirit" (Mowbray), WC; "Forward Through the Ages" (Hosmer); "Many Are the Lightbeams from the One Light" (Cyprian of Carthage); "Spirit, Working in Creation" (Richards), WC

G: "As Man and Woman We Were Made" (Wren), UMH; "Come, Join in Cana's Feast" (Stuempfle), HG; "God, in the Planning and Purpose of Life" (Bell and Maule), RS; Jesus, Come, for We Invite You" (Idle), WC; "Songs of Thankfulness and Praise" (Wordsworth)

January 25
Neh. 8:1-3, 5-6, 8-10; Ps. 19; 1 Cor. 12:12-31a; Luke 4:14-21

O: "Stand up and Bless the Lord" (Montgomery)

P: "God's Law Is Perfect and Gives Life" (Webber), PH, vv. 7-14; "Nature with Open Volume Stands" (Watts); O Let's Sing unto the Lord" (Rosas); "The Heavens Above Declare God's Praise" (Webber), PH, vv. 1-6

E: "Christ, from Whom All Blessings Flow" (Wesley); "God of Change and Glory" (Carmines), NCH; "In Christ There Is No East or West" (Oxenham)

G: "Arise, Your Light Is Come" (Duck; based on Isaiah 60 and 61); "Live into Hope of Captives Freed" (Huber), PH; "O for a Thousand Tongues to Sing" (Wesley; see UMH for relevant stanza); "The Kingdom of God Is Justice and Joy" (Rees), WC; "A Year of God's Favor" (Dufner), HG

February 1

Jer. 1:4–10; Ps. 71:1–6; 1 Cor. 13:1–13; Luke 4:21–30

E: "Gracious Spirit, Holy Ghost" (Wordsworth), PH; "Not for Tongues of Heaven's Angels" (Dudley-Smith); "Though I May Speak with Bravest Fire" (Hopson); "Where Charity and Love Prevail" (anonymous Latin)

G: "God Has Spoken by His Prophets (Briggs), HG

February 8

Isa. 6:1–8 (9–13); Ps. 138; 1 Cor. 15:1–11; Luke 5:1–11

O: "God Himself Is with Us" (Tersteegen); "Holy God, We Praise Your Name" (Franz); "Holy, Holy, Holy, Lord God Almighty" (Heber); "I, the Lord of Sea and Sky" (Schutte); "My God, How Wonderful Thou Art" (Faber); "Thuma Mina [Send Me], Lord" (South African), v. 8

P: "I Will Give Thanks with My Whole Heart" (Webber), PH

E: "Christ Is Risen, Christ Is Living" (Martínez); "This Is the Threefold Truth" (Green)

G: "Lord, You Have Come to the Lakeshore" (Gabaraín); "When Jesus Walked Beside the Shore" (Stuempfle), HG

February 15

Jer. 17:5–10; Ps. 1; 1 Cor. 15:12–20; Luke 6:17–26

O and P: The Man Is Blest Who, Fearing God" (Gower); "Like a Tree Beside the Waters" (Martin), NCH

E: "Christ Is Risen, Christ Is Living" (Martínez); "Christ the Lord Is Risen Today" (Wesley); "Sing with All the Saints in Glory" (Irons), UMH

G: "Blessed Are the Poor in Spirit" (Edwards), NCH; "Your Ways Are Not Our Own" (Bayler), HG

February 22

Gen. 45:3–11, 15; Ps. 37:1–11, 39–40; 1 Cor. 15:35–38, 42–50; Luke 6:27–38

P: Be Still, My Soul" (Schlegel), v. 7; "Fret Not for Those Who Do Wrong Things" (Webber), PH; "Give to the Winds Your Fears" (Gerhardt); "If Thou but Suffer God to Guide Thee" (Neumark; many variants)

G: "Forgive Our Sins as We Forgive" (Herklots); "Help Us Forgive, Forgiving Lord" (Stuempfle); HG

Transfiguration Sunday

Exod. 34:29–35; Ps. 99; 2 Cor. 3:12–4:2; Luke 9:28–36 (37–43a)

E: "O Come and Dwell in Me" (Wesley), UMH; "There's a Spirit in the Air" (Wren)

G: "Christ upon the Mountain Peak" (Wren); "Jesus, Take Us to the Mountain" (Vajda), HG; "O Wondrous Sight, O Vision Fair" (anonymous Latin); "Swiftly Pass the Clouds of Glory" (Troeger); " 'Tis Good, Lord, to Be Here" (Robinson), RS; "Transform Us as You, Transfigured" (Dunstan), HG; "We Have Come at Christ's Own Bidding" (Daw), NCH

LENT
February 29
Deut. 26:1–11; Ps. 91:1–2, 9–16; Rom. 10:8b–13; Luke 4:1–13

O: "As Saints of Old Their First Fruits Brought" (Christierson); "For the Fruit of All Creation" (Green); "God, Whose Farm Is All Creation" (Arlott), HWB; "Great God, We Sing That Mighty Hand" (Doddridge); "We Give Thee but Thine Own" (How)

P: "Be Not Dismayed, Whate'er Betide" (Martin); "Safe in the Shadow of the Lord" (Dudley-Smith), WC; "Sing Praise to God, Who Reigns Above" (Schütz); "Within Your Shelter, Loving God" (Dunn), PH

E: "Here, O Lord, Your Servants Gather" (Yamaguchi); "Immortal Love, For Ever Full (Whittier)

G: "Forty Days and Forty Nights" (Smyttan); "From the River to the Desert" (Dunstan), HG; "Jesus, Tempted in the Desert" (Stuempfle), RS; "Lord, Who Throughout These Forty Days" (Hernaman); "O Love, How Deep, How Broad, How High" (anonymous Latin)

March 7
Gen. 15:1–2, 17–18; Ps. 27; Phil. 3:17–4:1; Luke 13:31–35

O: "The God of Abraham Praise" (Dayyan)

P: "God Is My Strong Salvation" (Montgomery)

G: "O Jesus Christ, May Grateful Hymns Be Rising" (Webster); "Welcome, All You Noble Saints" (Stamps), HG

March 14
Isa. 55:1–9; Ps. 63:1–8; 1 Cor. 10:1–13; Luke 13:1–9

O: "All You Who Are Thirsty" (Connolly), RS; "Come, All of You" (anonymous Laotian); "Seek the Lord Who Now Is Present" (Green)

P: "God Is My Great Desire" (Dudley-Smith), WC; "O God, You Are My God" (Webber), PH; "O Lord, You Are My God" (Dunn), PH

G: "Come to Tend God's Garden" (Dalles), NCH; "Sovereign Maker of All Things" (Daw), HG

March 21
Josh. 5:9–12; Ps. 32; 2 Cor. 5:16–21; Luke 15:1–3, 11b–32

P: "How Blest Are the People Possessing True Peace" (Wollett), WC; "How Blest Are Those Whose Great Sin" (Anderson), PH

E: "God, You Spin the Whirling Planets" (Huber); "Love Divine, All Loves Excelling" (Wesley); "My Song Is Love Unknown" (Crossman); "O Come and Dwell in Me" (Wesley), UMH; "The First Day of Creation" (Troeger), CH; "This Is a Day of New Beginnings" (Wren); "Walk on, O People of God" (Gabaraín); "We Know That Christ Is Raised and Dies No More" (Geyer)

G: "A Woman and a Coin" (Vajda), CH; "Far, Far Away from My Loving Father" (anonymous), HWB; "Far from Home We Run Rebellious" (Stuempfle), HG, vv. 11b–32; "Our Father, We Have Wandered" (Nichols), RS; "Shepherd, Do You Tramp the Hills" (Stuempfle), HG, vv. 1–3

March 28

Isa. 43:16–21; Ps. 126; Phil. 3:4b–14; John 12:1–8

O: "This Is a Day of New Beginnings" (Wren)
P: "Let Us Hope When Hope Seems Hopeless" (Beebe), NCH; "When God Delivered Israel" (Saward), PH
E: "All That I Counted as Gain" (Joncas), RS; "Ask Ye What Great Thing I Know" (Schwedler); "Be Thou My Vision" (anonymous Irish); "Before the Cross of Jesus" (Blanchard); "When I Survey the Wondrous Cross" (Watts)
G: "Said Judas to Mary, 'Now What Will You Do'" (Carter), HG

April 4

Palm Sunday

Luke 19:28–40; Ps. 118:1–2, 19–29

P: "Open Now Thy Gates of Beauty" (Schmolck); "This Is the Day the Lord Hath Made" (Watts)
G: "All Glory, Laud, and Honor" (Theodulph of Orleans); "Filled with Excitement, All the Happy Throng" (Ruíz); "Hosanna, Loud Hosanna" (Threlfall); "Rejoice, O Zion's Daughter" (Stuempfle), HG; "Ride on, Ride on in Majesty" (Milman)

Passion Sunday

Isa. 50:4–9a; Ps. 31:9–16; Phil. 2:5–11; Luke 22:14–23:56

P: "God of Our Life, Through All the Circling Years" (Kerr); "God of the Ages" (Clarkson), WC; In You, Lord, Have I Put My Trust" (Reissner), PH
E: "A Hymn of Glory Let Us Sing" (Bede); "All Hail the Power of Jesus' Name" (Perronet and Rippon); "All Praise to Thee, for Thou, O King Divine" (Tucker); "At the Name of Jesus" (Noel); "Creator of the Stars of Night" (anonymous Latin); "Lord of All Nations, Grant Me Grace" (Spannaus), RS
G: "A Purple Robe, a Crown of Thorn" (Dudley-Smith); "Bread of the World, in Mercy Broken" (Heber); "For the Bread Which You Have Broken" (Benson); "Great God, Your Love Has Called Us Here" (Wren); "Jesus, Remember Me" (Taizé); "Jesus Took the Bread, Daily Gift of God" (Duck), NCH; "Kneeling in the Garden Grass" (Troeger), RS; "Lone He Prays Within the Garden" (Stuempfle), HG; "Now to Your

Table Spread" (Murray); "There Is a Fountain Filled with Blood" (Cowper); " 'Tis Midnight, and on Olive's Brow" (Tappan)

EASTER
April 11
Isa. 65:17–25; Ps. 118:1–2, 14–24; Acts 10:34–43 or 1 Cor. 15:19–26; John 20:1–18

O: "O Day of Peace That Dimly Shines" (Daw)

P and G: "Come, Let Us with Our Lord Arise" (Wesley), WC; "Open Now Thy Gates of Beauty" (Schmolck); "This Is the Day the Lord Hath Made" (Watts)

1 Cor.: "Christ Jesus Lay in Death's Strong Bands" (Luther); "Christ the Lord Is Risen Today" (Wesley); "Come, Ye Faithful, Raise the Strain" (John of Damascus); "Jesus Christ Is Risen Today" (anonymous); "Sing with All the Saints in Glory" (Irons)

G: "I Come to the Garden Alone" (Miles); "O Mary, Don't You Weep" (African American spiritual), UMH; "The Sun Was Bright That Easter Dawn" (Stuempfle), HG; "Woman, Weeping in the Garden" (Damon), CH

April 18
Acts 5:27–32; Ps. 118:14–29; Rev. 1:4–8; John 20:19–31

P: "Open Now Thy Gates of Beauty" (Schmolck); "This Is the Day the Lord Hath Made" (Watts)

E: "Christ the Lord Is Risen Today" (Wesley); "Jesus Christ Is Risen Today" (anonymous); "Jesus Shall Reign Where'er the Sun" (Watts; based on Ps. 72); "Lo, He Comes with Clouds Descending" (Wesley)

G: "Breathe on Me, Breath of God" (Hatch); "Chosen and Sent by the Father" (Clarkson), HG; "O Breath of Life, Come Sweeping Through Us" (Head); "O Sons and Daughters, Let Us Sing" (Tisserand); "Show Me Your Hands, Your Feet, Your Side" (Dunstan), HG; "These Things Did Thomas Count as Real" (Troeger); "Thine Is the Glory, Risen Conquering Son" (Budry); "We Walk by Faith and Not by Sight" (Alford)

April 25
Acts 9:1–6 (7–20); Ps. 30; Rev. 5:11–14; John 21:1–19

P: "Come Sing to God, O Living Saints" (Anderson), PH

E: "All Hail the Power of Jesus' Name" (Perronet and Rippon); "Blessing and Honor and Glory and Power" (Bonar); "Fairest Lord Jesus" (anonymous German); "See the Morning Sun Ascending" (Parkin), UMH; "Ten Thousand Times Ten Thousand" (Alford); "This Is the Feast of Victory for Our God" (Arthur); "What Wondrous Love Is This, O My Soul" (anonymous); "Ye Servants of God, Your Master Proclaim" (Wesley); "Ye Watchers and Ye Holy Ones" (Riley)

G: "More Love to Thee, O Christ" (Prentiss); "O Risen Christ, You Search Our Hearts" (Stuempfle), HG, vv. 1–19; "The Empty-Handed Fishermen" (Leach), HG, vv. 1–14

May 2

Acts 9:36–43; Ps. 23; Rev. 7:9–17; John 10:22–30

P: "My Shepherd Will Supply My Need" (Watts); "The King of Love My Shepherd Is" (Baker); "The Lord's My Shepherd, All My Need" (Webber); "The Lord's My Shepherd, I'll Not Want" (Huber); "The Lord's My Shepherd, I'll Not Want" (Scottish Psalter)

E: "Behold a Host, All Robed in Light" (Brorson), NCH; "Christ the Lord Is Risen Again" (Weisse); "Crown Him with Many Crowns" (Bridges and Thring); "For All the Saints Who from Their Labors Rest" (How); "Here from All Nations, All Tongues, and All Peoples" (Idle), WC; "John Saw the Number" [*Alabaré*] (anonymous Latin American), CH; "Lift High the Cross" (Kitchin and Newbolt); "O What Their Joy and Their Glory Must Be" (Abelard); "Ye Servants of God, Your Master Proclaim" (Wesley); "Ye Watchers and Ye Holy Ones" (Riley)

G: "Savior, Like a Shepherd, Lead Us" (Thrupp); "You, Lord, Are Both Lamb and Shepherd" (Dunstan), HG

May 9

Acts 11:1–18; Ps. 148; Rev. 21:1–6; John 13:31–35

Acts: "Spirit of the Living God, Fall Fresh on Me" (Iverson); see also other hymns on the Holy Spirit listed for May 30 (Pentecost) and the weeks following.

P: "All Creatures of Our God and King" (Francis of Assisi); "Creating God, Your Fingers Trace" (Rowthorn); "God Created Heaven and Earth" (anonymous Taiwanese); "Let the Whole Creation Cry" (Brooks); "Praise the Lord! Ye Heavens Adore Him" (anonymous English); "Stars and Planets Flung in Orbit" (Stuempfle), NCH

E: "Be Still, My Soul" (Schlegel); "Come, We That Love the Lord" (Watts); "For the Healing of the Nations" (Kaan); "Here, O My Lord, I See Thee Face to Face" (Bonar); "I Want to Be Ready" (African American spiritual); "In Heaven Above" (Laurinus); "Jerusalem, My Happy Home" (anonymous English); "O Holy City, Seen of John" (Bowie); "O Lord, You Gave Your Servant John" (Patterson); "O What Their Joy and Their Glory Must Be" (Abelard)

G: "Lord, Help Us Walk Your Servant Way" (Stuempfle), HG; "Love Is His Word" (Connaughton), RS; "We Are One in the Spirit" (Scholtes); "Where Charity and Love Prevail" (anonymous Latin)

May 16

Acts 16:9–15; Ps. 67; Rev. 21:10, 22–22:5; John 14:23–29

P: "God of Mercy, God of Grace" (Lyte), PH; "Let All the World in Every Corner Sing" (Herbert)

E: "I Want to Walk as a Child of the Light" (Thomerson); "O Holy City, Seen of John" (Bowie); "O Lord, You Gave Your Servant John" (Patterson)

G: "Come Down, O Love Divine" (Bianco of Siena); "May God's Love Be Fixed Above You" (Dalles), HG

May 23

Acts 16:16–34; Ps. 97; Rev. 22:12–14, 16–17, 20–21; John 17:20–26

Acts: "And Could It Be That I Should Gain" (Wesley)

P: "Earth's Scattered Isles and Contoured Hills" (Rowthorn), PH; "Sing Praise to God Who Reigns Above" (Schütz)

E: "Come, Ye Thankful People, Come" (Alford); "O Morning Star, How Fair and Bright" (Nicolai); "Of the Father's Love Begotten" (Prudentius); "The King Shall Come When Morning Dawns" (Brownlie); "Welcome, All You Noble Saints of Old" (Stamps), RS

G: "At That First Eucharist Before You Died" (Turton), RS; "Eternal Christ, Who, Kneeling" (Reid), HG

PENTECOST

May 30

Acts 2:1–21 or Gen. 11:1–9; Ps. 104:24–34, 35b; Rom. 8:14–17; John 14:8–17 (25–27)

Acts: "Filled with the Spirit's Power" (Peacey); "Like the Murmur of the Dove's Song" (Daw); "O Breath of Life, Come Sweeping Through Us" (Head); "O Church of God, United" (Morley), UMH; "O Holy Dove of God Descending" (Leech); "O Spirit of the Living God" (Tweedy); "On Pentecost They Gathered" (Huber); "When God the Spirit Came" (Dudley-Smith), RS; "Wind Who Makes All Winds That Blow" (Troeger)

P: "Bless the Lord, My Soul and Being" (Anderson), PH; "Many and Great, O God, Are Thy Ways" (Renville); "O Worship the King, All Glorious Above" (Grant)

E: "For Your Gift of God the Spirit" (Clarkson); "Praise the God Who Changes Places" (Wren), RS

G, first part: "God Is Unique and One" (Kaan), HG; "Holy Spirit, Truth Divine" (Longfellow); "Love Divine, All Loves Excelling" (Wesley)

G, second part: "Blessed Jesus, at Your Word" (Clausnitzer); "Come Down, O Love Divine" (Bianco of Siena); "May God's Love Be Fixed Above You" (Dalles), HG

June 6

Trinity

Prov. 8:1–4, 22–31; Ps. 8; Rom. 5:1–5; John 16:12–15

O: "Source and Sovereign, Rock and Cloud" (Troeger); "Who Comes from God as Word and Breath" (Michaels), CH

P: "How Great Our God's Majestic Name" (Dudley-Smith), BH; "Lord, Our Lord, Thy Glorious Name" (*The Psalter*, 1912); "O How Glorious, Full of Wonder" (Beach), NCH; "O Lord, Our God, How Excellent" (Anderson), PH

E: "Come Down, O Love Divine" (Bianco of Siena); "Come, Holy Ghost, Our Souls Inspire" (Maurus); "Come, Holy Spirit, Heavenly Dove" (Watts); "Creator God, Creating Still" (Huber)

G: "Holy Spirit, Truth Divine" (Longfellow); "Let Your Spirit Teach Me, Lord" (Clarkson), HG

June 13

1 Kings 21:1–10 (11–14), 15–21a; Ps. 5:1–8; Gal. 2:15–21; Luke 7:36–8:3

P: "As Morning Dawns, Lord Hear Our Cry" (Anderson), PH

E: "Alas, and Did My Savior Bleed" (Watts); "Alleluia, Alleluia, Give Thanks to the Risen Lord" (Fishel)

G: "Said Judas to Mary, 'Now What Will You Do'" (Carter), HG; "Two Fishermen, Who Lived Along the Sea of Galilee" (Toolan), WC; "When Jesus Came Preaching the Kingdom of God" (Green), RS

June 20

1 Kings 19:1–4 (5–7), 8–15a; Ps. 42; Gal. 3:23–29; Luke 8:26–39

O: "As Water to the Thirsty" (Dudley-Smith), WC; "Dear Lord and Father of Mankind" (Whittier; many variants; also relates to the Gospel); "Though Falsely Some Revile or Hate Me" (East Asia), NCH

P: "As Deer Long for the Streams" (Webber), PH, vv. 1–7; "As Pants the Hart for Cooling Streams" (New Version)

E: "Baptized in Water" (Saward); "Blest Be the Tie That Binds" (Fawcett); "Christ, from Whom All Blessings Flow" (Wesley); "In Christ There Is No East or West" (Oxenham); "One Bread, One Body" (Foley), UMH; "Pan de Vida" [Bread of Life] (Hurd and Moriarty), RS; "When Minds and Bodies Meet as One" (Wren), NCH

G: "Silence, Frenzied, Unclean Spirit" (Troeger; though based on Mark 1:23–27 and parallels, there are connections to this passage), HG

June 27

2 Kings 2:1–2, 6–14; Ps. 77:1–2, 11–20; Gal. 5:7, 13–25; Luke 9:51–62

O: "Swing Low, Sweet Chariot" (African American spiritual)

P: "How Long, O Lord, Will You Forget" (Woollett; based on Psalm 13), WC

E: "As Sons of the Day and Daughters of Light" (Idle), WC; "Lord of All Hopefulness" (Struther); "Of All the Spirit's Gifts to Me" (Green); "Spirit of God, Descend upon My Heart" (Croly)

G: "O Christ, Who Called the Twelve" (Stuempfle), HG; "O Jesus, I Have Promised" (Bode)

July 4

2 Kings 5:1–14; Ps. 30; Gal. 6:(1–6) 7–16; Luke 10:1–11, 16–20

O: "God of the Prophets, Bless the Prophets' Sons" (Wortman)

P: "Come Sing to God, O Living Saints" (Anderson), PH; "Wake, My Soul, with All Things Living" (Canitz), NCH

E: "Ask Ye What Great Thing I Know" (Schwedler); "Called as Partners in Christ's Service" (Huber), vv. 1–6; "In the Cross of Christ I Glory" (Bowring); "Lord, Make Us Servants of Your Peace" (Quinn); "Lord, Whose Love in Humble Service" (Bayly); "When I Survey the Wondrous Cross" (Watts)

G: "Let Us Talents and Tongues Employ" (Kaan); "Lord, You Give the Great Commission" (Rowthorn); "Not Alone, but Two by Two" (Daw), HG

July 11
Amos 7:7–17; Ps. 82; Col. 1:1–14; Luke 10:25–37

O: "Let Justice Flow Like Streams" (Huber), NCH
G: "Jesu, Jesu, Fill Us with Your Love" (Colvin); "They Asked, 'Who's My Neighbor?'" (Wesson); "We Praise You with Our Minds, O Lord" (McElrath); "We Sing Your Praise, O Christ" (Stuempfle), HG

July 18
Amos 8:1–12; Ps. 52; Col. 1:15–28; Luke 10:38–42

O: "Make a Gift of Your Holy Word" (Imakoma), NCH
E: "Christ Beside Me, Christ Before Me" (Quinn), WC; "Christ Is Risen, Christ Is Living" (Martínez); "Christ, You Are the Fullness" (Polman); "God of Creation, All-Powerful, All-Wise" (Clarkson), WC; "O Christ, the Great Foundation" (Lew), NCH; "Of the Father's Love Begotten" (Prudentius); "We Are Pilgrims on a Journey (Gillard; many variants); "When Peace, Like a River, Attendeth My Soul" (Spafford)
G: "Lord, Grant Us Grace to Know the Time" (Stuempfle), HG; "When Jesus Came Preaching the Kingdom of God" (Green), RS

July 25
Hos. 1:2–10; Ps. 85; Col. 2:6–15 (16–19); Luke 11:1–13

E: "Baptized in Water" (Saward); "Great Work Has God Begun in You" (Birkland), NCH
G: "Forgive Our Sins, as We Forgive" (Herklots); "Let All Who Pray the Prayer Christ Taught" (Troeger), PH; "Lord, Teach Us How to Pray" (Stuempfle), HG; "Lord, Teach Us How to Pray Aright" (Montgomery); "Renew Your Church, Her Ministries Restore" (Cober)

August 1
Hos. 11:1–11; Ps. 107:1–9, 43; Col. 3:1–11 (12–17); Luke 12:13–21

O: "Like a Mother Who Has Borne Us" (Bechtel), NCH
P: "Jesus, Thou Joy of Loving Hearts" (Bernard of Clairvaux); "Now Thank We All Our God" (Rinkart)
E: "Christ, You Are the Fullness" (Polman)
G: "Lord, Whose Then Shall They Be" (Stuempfle), HG

August 8
Isa. 1:1, 10–20; Ps. 50:1–8, 22–23; Heb. 11:1–3, 8–16; Luke 12:32–40

O: "Come, Let Us Reason Together" (Medema)
P: "Golden Breaks the Dawn" (Chao)
E: "Faith, While Trees Are Still in Blossom" (Frostenson); "For the Faithful Who Have

Answered" (Dunstan), NCH; "Forward Through the Ages" (Hosmer); "How Clear Is Our Vocation, Lord" (Green); "Rejoice in God's Saints" (Green)

G: "God Whose Giving Knows No Ending" (Edwards), HG

August 15
Isa. 5:1–7; Ps. 80:1–2, 8–19; Heb. 11:29–12:2; Luke 12:49–56

P: "O Hear Our Cry, O Lord" (Anderson), PH

E: "For All the Saints Who from Their Labors Rest" (How); "Guide My Feet" (African American spiritual); "I Sing a Song of the Saints of God" (Scott); "I Want to Walk as a Child of the Light" (Thomerson); "The Head That Once Was Crowned with Thorns" (Kelly); "They Did Not Build in Vain" (Luff), NCH

G: "Thou, Whose Purpose Is to Kindle" (Trueblood), HG

August 22
Jer. 1:4–10; Ps. 71:1–6; Heb. 12:18–29; Luke 13:10–17

E: "Come, We That Love the Lord" (Watts)

G: "By Peter's House in Village Fair" (Albright). HWB; "O Christ, the Healer, We Have Come" (Green), HG; "This Is the Day When Light Was First Created" (Kaan), RS

August 29
Jer. 2:4–13; Ps. 81:1, 10–16; Heb. 13:1–8, 15–16; Luke 14:1, 7–14

E: "For the Beauty of the Earth" (Pierpoint; the connection is made by using the original refrain: "Christ, our God, to thee we raise / this our sacrifice of praise"); "Jesus, Savior, Lord, Lo, to Thee I Fly" [Saranam] (anonymous Pakastani); "Jesus, Thou Joy of Loving Hearts" (Bernard of Clairvaux); "O Jesus, I Have Promised" (Bode); "Your Love, O God, Has Called Us Here" (Schulz-Widmar)

G: "Christ, the One Who Tells the Tale" (Leach), HG; "God of the Ages" (Clarkson), WC

September 5
Jer. 18:1–11; Ps. 139:1–6, 13–18; Philem. 1–21; Luke 14:25–33

O: "Have Thine Own Way, Lord" (Pollard)

P: "Search Me, O God" (Orr); "You Are Before Me, Lord" (Pitt-Watson), PH

G: "For God Risk Everything" (Troeger), HG; "Take up Thy Cross and Follow Me" (McKinney); "Take up Thy Cross, the Savior Said" (Everest)

September 12
Jer. 4:11–12, 22–28; Ps. 14; 1 Tim. 1:12–17; Luke 15:1–10

E: "Immortal, Invisible, God Only Wise" (Smith)

G: "I Will Sing the Wondrous Story" (Rowley); "Our Father, We Have Wandered" (Nichols), RS; "Savior, Like a Shepherd Lead Us" (Thrupp); "Shepherd, Do You Tramp the Hills" (Stuempfle), HG

September 19

Jer. 8:18–9:1; Ps. 79:1–9; 1 Tim. 2:1–7; Luke 16:1–13

O: "There Is a Balm in Gilead" (African American spiritual)

E: "God of Our Fathers, Whose Almighty Hand" (Roberts); "Lift Every Voice and Sing" (Johnson); "O Beautiful, for Spacious Skies" (Bates); "O God of Every Nation" (Reid)

G: "Lord of All Good, We Bring Our Gifts to You" (Bayly), WC

September 26

Jer. 32:1–3a, 6–15; Ps. 91:1–6, 14–16; 1 Tim. 6:6–19; Luke 16:19–31

P: "Be Not Dismayed, Whate'er Betide" (Martin); "Safe in the Shadow of the Lord" (Dudley-Smith), WC; "Sing Praise to God, Who Reigns Above" (Schütz); "Within Your Shelter, Loving God" (Dunn), PH

E: "All My Hope on God Is Founded" (Neander); "Fight the Good Fight with All Thy Might" (Monsell); "He Is King of Kings" (African American spiritual)

G: "Through All the World, a Hungry Christ" (Murray), NCH; "Thou, Whose Purpose Is to Kindle" (Trueblood), HG

October 3

Lam. 1:1–6; Ps. 137; 2 Tim. 1:1–14; Luke 17:5–10

P: "By the Babylonian Rivers" (Bash), PH; "I Love Thy Kingdom, Lord" (Dwight)

E: "I Know Not Why God's Wondrous Grace to Me He Hath Made Known" (Whittle); "Like a Mother Who Has Borne Us" (Bechtel), NCH

G: "Faith, While Trees Are Still in Blossom" (Frostenson); "Let Us Plead for Faith Alone" (Wesley), UMH; "When Our Confidence Is Shaken" (Green), HG

October 10

Jer. 29:1, 4–7; Ps. 66:1–12; 2 Tim. 2:8–15; Luke 17:11–19

O: "All Who Love and Serve Your City" (Routley); "O Jesus Christ, May Grateful Hymns Be Rising" (Webster)

P: "Let All the World in Every Corner Sing" (Herbert)

E: "Come to Me, All You Weary" (Young), RS; "How Clear Is Our Vocation, Lord" (Green); "Keep in Mind That Jesus Christ Has Died for Us" (Deiss), RS; "O God, Our Faithful God" (Heerman); "We Hold the Death of the Lord Deep in Our Hearts" (Haas), RS

G: "An Outcast Among Outcasts" (Leach), NCH; "Banned and Banished by Their Neighbors" (Stuempfle), HG

October 17

Jer. 31:27–34; Ps. 119:97–104; 2 Tim. 3:14–4:5; Luke 18:1–8

O: "Deep Within I Will Plant My Law" (Haas), RS; "O God, Who Gives Us Life and Breath" (Daw), HWB

E: "Powerful in Making Us Wise to Salvation" (Idle), WC
G: "Eternal Spirit of the Living Christ" (Christierson), HG

October 24

Joel 2:23–32; Ps. 65; 2 Tim. 4:6–8, 16–18; Luke 18:9–14

O: "Fear Not, Rejoice and Be Glad" (Wright), WC; "Return, My People, Israel" (Martin), NCH
P: "Mountains Are All Aglow" (Lim), UMH; "Praise Is Your Right, O God, in Zion" (Wiersma), PH; "Sing to the Lord of Harvest" (Monsell); "To Bless the Earth God Sends Us" (*The Psalter*, 1912)
E: "Awake, My Soul, Stretch Every Nerve" (Doddridge); "Fight the Good Fight with All Thy Might" (Monsell)
G: "O Savior in This Quiet Place" (Green); "In a Lowly Manger Born" (Yuki), HG

October 31

Hab. 1:1–4, 2:1–4; Ps. 119:137–144; 2 Thess. 1:1–4, 11–12; Luke 19:1–10

G: "When Jesus Passed Through Jericho" (Stuempfle), HG

November 7

Hag. 1:15b–2:9; Ps. 145:1–5, 17–21; 2 Thess. 2:1–5, 13–17; Luke 20:27–38

P: "O Lord, You Are My God and King" (*The Psalter*, 1912), PH, vv. 1–13; "Your Faithfulness, O Lord, Is Sure" (Patterson), PH, vv. 13–23
G: "In the Bulb There Is a Flower" (Sleeth), HG

November 14

Isa. 65:17–25; Isa. 12; 2 Thess. 3:6–13; Luke 21:5–19

Isa. 65: "O Day of Peace That Dimly Shines" (Daw)
Isa. 12: "Surely It Is God Who Saves Me" (Daw); "With Joy Draw Water" (McKinstry), NCH
G: "Here from All Nations" (Idle), HG

November 21
Christ the King

Jer. 23:1–6; Luke 1:68–79; Col. 1:11–20; Luke 23:33–43

Luke 1:68–79: "Blessed Be the God of Israel" (Quinn), BH; "Blessed Be the God of Israel" (Perry); "Now Bless the God of Israel" (Duck), NCH
E: "Christ Is Risen, Christ Is Living" (Martínez); "Christ, You Art the Fullness" (Polman); "O Christ, the Great Foundation" (Lew), NCH; "Of the Father's Love Begotten" (Prudentius); "We Are Pilgrims on a Journey" (Gillard; many variants); "When Peace, Like a River, Attendeth My Soul" (Spafford)
Luke 23:33–43: "A Purple Robe, a Crown of Thorn" (Dudley-Smith); "Jesus, Remember Me" (Taizé); "Lord, You Give the Great Commission" (Rowthorn); "Son of God, by God Forsaken" (Stuempfle), HG

ADVENT
November 28
Isa. 2:1–5; Ps. 122; Rom. 13:11–14; Matt. 24:36–44

O: "Behold a Broken World, We Pray" (Dudley-Smith), UMH; "Christ Is the World's True Light" (Briggs); "God Is Working His Purpose Out" (Ainger; also relates to the Epistle); "O Day of Peace That Dimly Shines" (Daw); "O God of Every Nation" (Reid); "Wake, Awake, for Night Is Flying" (Nicolai; also relates to the Epistle and the Gospel)

P: "With Joy I Heard My Friends Exclaim" (*The Psalter*, 1912)

E: "Awake, O Sleeper, Rise from Death" (Tucker)

G: "Waken, O Sleeper" (Forster), HG

December 5
Isa. 11:1–10; Ps. 72:1–7, 18–19; Rom. 15:4–13; Matt. 3:1–12

O: "Let Our Gladness Have No End" (anonymous German), HWB; "Lo, How a Rose E'er Blooming" (anonymous German); "Lord, Today We Have Seen Your Glory" (Balhoff), RS; "To a Virgin, Meek and Mild" (Boe and Overby); "O Come, O Come, Emmanuel" (anonymous Latin); "O Day of Peace That Dimly Shines" (Daw); "O Morning Star, How Fair and Bright" (Nicolai; also relates to the Epistle); "Who Would Think That What Was Needed" (Bell and Maule), NCH

P: "Hail to the Lord's Anointed" (Montgomery); "Jesus Shall Reign Where'er the Sun" (Watts)

E: "Help Us Accept Each Other" (Kaan); "Hope of the World, Thou Christ of Great Compassion" (Harkness)

G: "Comfort, Comfort Ye My People" (Olearius); "On Jordan's Bank the Baptist's Cry" (Coffin); "When John Baptized by Jordan's River" (Dudley-Smith), RS; "Wild and Lone the Prophet's Voice" (Daw), HG

December 12
Isa. 35:1–10; Luke 1:47–55; James 5:7–10; Matt. 11:2–11

O: "Awake! Awake, and Greet the New Morn" (Haugen; also relates to the reading from Matthew); "Strengthen All the Weary Hands" (McMane), NCH; "The Desert Shall Rejoice" (Grindal), PH; "When the King Shall Come Again" (Idle), WC

Luke: "For Ages Women Hoped and Prayed" (Huber); "My Soul Gives Glory to My God" (Winter); "Tell Out, My Soul, the Greatness of the Lord" (Dudley-Smith)

Matt.: "Are You the Coming One" (Stuempfle), HG

December 19
Isa. 7:10–16; Ps. 80:1–7, 17–19; Rom. 1:1–7; Matt. 1:18–25

O: "O Come, O Come Emmanuel" (anonymous Latin); "To a Virgin Meek and Mild" (Boe and Overby)

P: "O Hear Our Cry, O Lord" (Anderson), PH

E: "God of the Prophets, Bless the Prophets' Sons" (Wortman)

G: "Hark, the Herald Angels Sing" (Wesley); "Joseph Dearest, Joseph Mine" (anonymous German); "Of the Father's Love Begotten" (Prudentius); "The First Noel the Angel Did Say" (anonymous English); "The Hands That First Held Mary's Child" (Troeger), HG

CHRISTMAS
December 26
Isa. 63:7–9; Ps. 148; Heb. 2:10–18; Matt. 2:13–23

P: "All Creatures of Our God and King" (Francis of Assisi); "Creating God, Your Fingers Trace" (Rowthorn); "God Created Heaven and Earth" (anonymous Taiwanese); "Let the Whole Creation Cry" (Brooks); "Praise the Lord! Ye Heavens Adore Him" (anonymous English); "Stars and Planets Flung in Orbit" (Stuempfle), NCH

E: "My Faith Looks up to Thee" (Palmer); "O God, We Bear the Imprint of Your Face" (Murray)

G: "In Bethlehem a Newborn Boy" (Herklots); "O Sleep, Dear Holy Baby" (anonymous Spanish); "Our Savior's Infant Cries Were Heard" (Troeger), HG

MESSAGES FOR COMMUNION SERVICES

SERMON SUGGESTIONS

Topic: The Communion Cup

TEXT: 1 Cor 11:23–26

The Gospels tell us that at the Last Supper Jesus took a cup and blessed it. This cup was a part of Jesus' last supper as he celebrated the Passover with his disciples. Some early Christians claimed to have possessed the cup that Jesus used at the Last Supper. They called it the Holy Grail. Stories and miracles were centered around this particular cup for many years. A contemporary writer, Thomas B. Costain, wrote a novel I read as a teenager titled *The Silver Chalice*.[1] This novel was built around the cup of Jesus, how it made its way to Antioch, and the lives it touched.

In the Bible, the cup is a reference to the common drinking utensil that often played an uncommon role in peoples' lives. For example, there is a cup in the dream of Pharaoh's butler. Joseph interpreted this dream for the butler. Joseph had a cup hidden in the grain sack of his brother Benjamin as Benjamin and Joseph's family left to go back home. Through this entrapment, Joseph later revealed to his brothers who he really was. At the Last Supper, Jesus took a cup and blessed it as a part of the Passover feast. That cup has continued to be a part of the tradition of the Lord's Supper to this day.

The cup in the Bible is also symbolic in many ways. In some places the Bible refers to "the cup of bitterness," "the cup of agony," and "the cup that overflows," which the writer of the Twenty-Third Psalm noted. Think with me about some of these symbolic cups to which the Scriptures refer.

I. *The cup of salvation.* The psalmist wrote about the cup of salvation in Psalm 116. The psalmist said, "I will lift up a cup of salvation and call on the name of the Lord." Through the death of Jesus Christ, this cup is offered to all persons. It overflows with the bounty of God's love, grace, and abundance. The salvation from this cup has overflowed and run down through the centuries to where you and I can drink of that cup today.

Like a person standing with a cup under a waterfall, there is no way that our cup can contain all of the wonder that comes from God's love. God's salvation is beyond our understanding. It is abundant and free.

II. *The cup of the new covenant.* As we come to the communion table, let us also be reminded of the cup of the new covenant. Jesus shared the Passover meal with his disciples and then lifted his cup to proclaim the beginning of a new era. The cup of blessing was traditionally the last thing at this sacred meal. With his cup raised high, Jesus declared that this

---

[1] Garden City, N.Y.: Doubleday, 1952.

"cup was a sign of the new covenant." He had established a new relationship with his disciples. The old Sinai covenant, which was built on sacrifice of animals, was over.

The covenant was one of the great Old Testament images. It appears 286 times from Genesis 17 to Revelation 21. A covenant was made with Abraham, and with Moses at Mount Sinai. The covenant that God made with Israel was often broken by the Israelites and reaffirmed by God. Jeremiah promised that a new covenant would come, and this covenant would be a law written within their hearts.

Jesus declared that he had established a new covenant by his blood. The disciples, who were Jewish, would not literally want to drink blood. Jesus was saying that his death was a sign, a symbol of the outpouring of life and the creation of a new relationship with God.

Today, we can relate to God differently, because Jesus Christ has made this way to God possible for us. His new covenant was the one that Jeremiah said would be written on our hearts. The cup is a sign of the new covenant, a new relationship with God, brought about by Jesus Christ.

III. *The cup of suffering.* As Jesus bowed in agony in the Garden of Gethsemane, he prayed, "Oh Father, if it is possible, let this cup pass from me." What cup? The cup of suffering, the cup of agony, and the cup of death. The mother of two of Jesus' disciples said to him, "Lord, let my sons have the chief seats in your Kingdom." Jesus asked them, "Are you able to drink of the cup that I must drink?" They said, "Yes, Lord," but they really did not know what it was. "Are you able to drink the cup of suffering and agony that I must bear?" Jesus asks us. It is easy to say yes when we really do not know if we can.

The Lord's Supper was instituted within a context of suffering. Jesus knew that he was soon to be betrayed and that he faced the agony of the cross. Are we able to share in the suffering, to be his instruments to reach out in love to others and touch them? We are challenged by Paul to be ministers of reconciliation, to share the suffering of Christ. Are we able to do that?

IV. *The cup of service.* Do you remember that Jesus told his disciples, "As often as you give a cup of cold water in my name, you minister to me"? All the other cups—the cup of salvation, the cup of suffering, and the cup of the new covenant—lead us to the awareness that, having received such great love, we are now challenged to manifest compassion, mercy, and love through our lives. Our Lord reached out to the needy and hurting, and he has commissioned us to share the cup of compassion with them. We who have been reconciled by God reach out to bring reconciliation to others through God's love and grace.

We are now offered Jesus' cup. As we drink of that cup, our challenge is to go into the world and to share the love of God with others, so they too might drink from his cup. His cup is one of service, of self-giving love. To drink of Jesus' cup challenges us to be a part of the redemptive force in the world. We share Christ's cup only as we are his instruments in ministry in the world. Whenever we give a "cup of cold water" to someone in need, we serve our Lord.

As you eat the bread, reflect on the fact that Christ is the bread of life. As you drink the cup, remember that Jesus Christ is the one in whom you have life. As you drink, remember the cup of salvation. Remember the Christ who has suffered, died, and given us salvation. Reflect on the cup of suffering. Remember that you are united to Christ through the cup of the new covenant. When you have finished eating his bread and sharing in his cup, remember that you now go to bear the cup of service, in his name, into the world.—William Powell Tuck

Topic: Supper of Commitment
TEXT: Mark 14:12–25

One of the fascinating things to me about the Lord's Supper is its many facets. A meal, instituted by Christ and given to his Church to be enjoyed repeatedly, has become the vehicle for almost limitless meaning to those who participate in reverence, faith, and honest petition. Meditation on the meaning of the Lord's Supper brings fresh insight concerning its strong implications to the servant Church of a servant Lord.

> Christ's meal is a *supper of sharing,* displaying in one united act the solidarity of
>   Christ's people.
> It is a meal that *activates memory* and causes us to review Christ's redemptive acts on
>   our behalf.
> The supper is a means of *celebrating deliverance*—personal deliverance from wrong and
>   self-centeredness.
> It is an act that *renews our covenant* relationship with our Lord.
> The meal is a corporate *giving of thanks* for full life.
> In its use of simple, common elements, the supper removes our distinction between *the
>   common and the sacred.*
> Out of our participation as a body comes *strength for the continuing struggle* to be
>   Christ's people in a society that needs him and what he continues to do and say.

I have been amazed at the variety of lessons and the depth of meaning to be found in the vivid scene and the creative words of the Lord's Supper.

The thought has occurred to me that among the many significant meanings to be gleaned from our participation in this meal is the truth that we share a supper of commitment. Because we are mortal, we have to review our commitments periodically to keep fresh our awareness of that to which we have pledged ourselves. This is true in various areas of our living: marriage and family, friendships, vocations, community activities, and educational pursuits. If we are not careful and attentive, we forget or neglect to fulfill an original commitment.

One vital service that the Lord's Supper does for us is to keep before us the pledge we made in a moment of sincere response to the living Christ, and it allows us to renew that pledge. The supper is for those who are determined followers of Christ, and it does not allow us to forget the demands involved in such following.

If we participate in the Lord's Supper with understanding, we become aware that *we are renewing our commitment to Christ.* Commitment involves our total lives, our dedication of what we are and have, without reservation. In the case of the Christian, this commitment is to the person of Christ. I have been impressed with what people can accomplish when they are committed to a cause. I have seen serious, enthusiastic people undertake projects that I honestly thought were beyond their reach. Yet through their dedication translated into determined work, they reached their goal.

And the thought has impressed itself on me: Christianity is not a cause or merely a movement; it is a way of life in relationship to the Person of Jesus Christ. How much deeper and stronger should our commitment be to this person who gives full life than to anyone or anything else? Often I have wondered what would happen in churches, families, and neighborhoods if commitment to Christ came before every other commitment. What if our pledge to him were honored first? My mind cannot grasp the creative change that would result or the quality of life that would be produced.

If we don't have the rich, full, personal relationships we want, the depth of spirit in our churches that often is so conspicuous by its absence, or the healthy atmosphere of community that helps to nurture life, the primary reason lies in our shallow or nonexistent commitment to Christ. The Lord's Supper is a vehicle for the reverent, serious renewal of the pledge of our lives to Christ.

The meal we share is also a means of *recommitting ourselves to one another.* One puzzling observation I have made is that so few of us seem to understand that when we commit our lives to Christ, *we also commit ourselves to the members of his company.* We present a strange picture to those around us, I am sure, when we pledge ourselves to Christ and keep one another at arm's length or farther.

Christ made clear to his disciples that the person who is open to him must also be open to the other members of God's family. One of the most definite proofs of our being Christ's followers is our active care for one another. In John 13:35, Jesus said, "By this shall all men know that ye are my disciples, if ye have love one to another." And to love in the sense that Christ meant without committing ourselves to one another's highest good is impossible.

One early writer, recording information about the earliest Christians, wrote that what impressed those who viewed the Christians in action was their care for one another. The early Christians loved one another sincerely, and they showed it. The supper should cause us to review our commitments to one another in a love that runs the risk of being rejected, a determined goodwill that is not easily discouraged.

Finally, this shared meal reminds us that our commitment to Christ and to the members of his company is a *commitment to serve.* We stay ready to function in whatever capacity our abilities allow for the advancement of Christ's work. We do this in the knowledge that Jesus adopted the servant role and he called his followers servants. In his servant role, he was Master and Lord to those who made him so. If Jesus served people, how much more should his followers do so? For the servant is not better than his Master. We accept the benefits that Christ provides. Therefore we should seek to share these benefits with others.—Eli Landrum Jr.[2]

Topic: The Lord's Presence—In Our Fellowship
TEXT: 1 Cor. 10:16

"The cup of blessing which we bless, is it not a participation in the blood of Christ? The bread which we break, is it not a participation in the body of Christ?"

We might come to church, see the table set for observance of the Lord's Supper, and think or say, "There will be no preaching today!" Don't you believe it. The observance of the ordinance can be one of the most powerful forms of preaching. Indeed, it can be preaching at its best, involving the congregation and using the spoken Word, music, and vivid elements to proclaim eternal truth. Note 1 Corinthians 11:26: "For as often as you eat this bread and drink the cup, you proclaim [show forth, declare] the Lord's death until he comes." Thus, the ordi-

---

[2]*More Than Symbol* (Nashville: Broadman Press, 1983), pp. 96–98.

nance is a powerful means of Christian proclamation. I have a friend who led his son to faith in Christ by discussing the meaning of the Lord's Supper.

In addition to being a form of preaching, the Supper is also a symbol of fellowship. Our text reminds us that the cup is the communion of the blood of Christ and the bread is the communion of the body of Christ. We Baptists tend to shy away from the word *communion,* but the apostle Paul didn't. It is a powerful word. The Greek for *communion* is that familiar word *koinonia,* which means "fellowship with," "participation in," or "sharing." Here it means sharing in the effect of his broken body and shed blood that resulted in our salvation.

Jesus gave his blood, his life, for our redemption, that we might be heirs to and enjoy eternal life. "The blood of Jesus Christ his Son cleanseth us from all sin" (1 John 1:7b KJV). Jesus' body was sacrificed once for all on the cross, that death might be forever defeated. In Christ we are members of his body. Indeed, the Church is identified as the body of Christ. In that body there is oneness and unity: "Because there is one bread, we who are many are one body, for we all partake of the one bread" (1 Cor. 10:17). We who are many are one in Christ. In Ephesians 4:4–6, Paul underlined our oneness in fellowship when he wrote, "There is one body and one Spirit—just as you were called to the one hope that belongs to your call—one Lord, one faith, one baptism; one God and Father of us all, who is above all and through all and in all."

There is something special about eating together. Table fellowship creates close and meaningful relationships. An Englishman will invite friends to "come for tea." A man of the world will invite another to "have a drink." Business and professional men get together for lunch with clients and with one another in luncheon clubs. Courting couples go out to dinner together. We entertain friends in our homes at dinner parties. Our closest times together as a family are often those around the table. At our home we've found this to be a splendid time for sharing family concerns. Yes, there is something special about eating together, something highly symbolic. We need to remember that Christ is Lord of the dinner table as well as Lord of the communion table.

Notice the prominent place that eating and table fellowship occupies in the Gospel accounts. Some of Jesus' most memorable teaching was done around a table or at a meal. Recall his feeding of the multitudes, his attending banquets, and his appearing to the two at Emmaus. Indeed, the Risen Christ said by way of invitation, "Behold, I stand at the door and knock; if anyone hears my voice and opens the door, I will come in to him and eat with him, and he with me" (Rev. 3:20). When we eat together, we share at a deep level. This is equally true of our fellowship with the Lord. Actually, heaven contains a banquet hall where we'll eat together in the presence of God. Imagine! Sitting at a table, eating with God! Surely, the Lord's Supper offers us a glimpse of what it will be like to sit at the Lamb's table in glory.

The Lord's Supper is such an opportunity for table fellowship, sharing and communion. John wrote, "Truly our fellowship is with the father, and with his Son Jesus Christ" (1 John 1:3b KJV). Christ is the head of the family, and we are family members. He is host at the Lord's table, and we are his guests, sharing in fellowship with him.

More than this vertical fellowship in the presence of Christ and the Father, there is also a horizontal fellowship at the Lord's table. We eat together with other believers. They are our brothers and sisters in Christ. Here is the truest fraternity—around the table of our Lord. By our baptism we were united with the body of Christ. By periodically sharing at the Lord's table, we renew our companionship and strengthen our union and oneness with him and with one another. This is the observance, the symbol, that unites the Church. Just as we were united with the Church in our baptism, so our relationship is cemented and renewed at the Lord's table.

As we come to the table together, let us hear the reading of our (First Baptist Church, Greensboro, North Carolina) church covenant and be reminded of our common bonds:

As we trust we have been brought by divine grace to embrace the Lord Jesus Christ, and by the influence of his spirit to give up ourselves wholly to him, so we do now solemnly covenant with one another that, God helping us, we will walk together in him in brotherly love.

That, as members of one another for the glory of Christ in the salvation of men, we will exercise a Christian care and watchfulness over one another, and as occasion may require, faithfully warn, rebuke, and admonish one another in the spirit of meekness, considering ourselves lest we also be tempted.

That we will willingly submit to, and conscientiously enforce, all wholesome discipline of the church.

That we will uphold the worship of God and the ordinances of his house by regular attendance thereon, search diligently the Scriptures, observe closet or family worship, and seek to train up those under our care to the glory of God in the salvation of their souls.

That, as we have been planted together in the likeness of his death by baptism, and raised from an emblematic grace in newness of life, especially will we seek divine aid to enable us to walk circumspectly and watchfully in the world, denying all ungodliness and every worldly lust.

That we will remember the poor and contribute cheerfully of our means for their relief, and for the maintenance of a faithful gospel ministry among us, and for the spread of the same to the ends of the Earth.

That we will endeavor, by example and effort, to win souls to Christ, and through life, amid evil report and good report, seek to live to the praise of him who hath called us out of darkness into his marvelous light, to whom be glory and honor and power for ever and ever. Amen.

Let us approach the table for this observance. It is a symbol of our fellowship, with the Risen Christ and with one another. Let us break bread together. We will drink the cup together. We will find Christ present and real to us in this Supper, and we will find one another precious. May this kind of *koinonia* meal bind us to Christ and to one another, as we both remember and proclaim his death.—Alton H. McEachern[3]

Topic: The Bread and the Body
TEXT: Luke 22:14–23

In a letter written about 55 A.D. the apostle Paul reminded the little group of Christians in the Greek city of Corinth what had happened on the night before Jesus died. He told them that Jesus had had supper with his friends, that it had been a simple meal of bread and wine.

---

[3]*The Lord's Presence* (Nashville: Broadman Press, 1986), pp. 76–79.

Jesus had broken the bread, given it to them and told them to eat it, and said that it was his body, broken for them. And when he'd poured the wine out and given it to them he'd said, "Drink it, this is my blood; it is shed for you."

Christians have been doing that, in one way or another, ever since—for roughly two thousand years—and we are about to do it now, once again. The setting has changed, the language has changed, the world has changed, but the words are the same. The question is, What do we mean when we say that a small piece of bread is the body of Jesus Christ, and that the wine is his blood? And when we do it, when we eat and drink it, are we doing what we seem to be doing? Are we reverting to cannibalism? Are we withdrawing into some mystical act that has no relevance at all to a world that is filled with turmoil and confusion, torn apart with suffering and bloodshed?

"Take, eat, this is my body, which is given for you." It is time we stopped once again and thought about these words and what they mean to us here and now.

The first thing to do is to go back to the event itself: the Last Supper in the Upper Room, the meal Jesus planned and shared with the twelve men who were closest to him. One thing is as clear as day: as Jesus sat at the table with those twelve chosen friends of his—chosen to be his apprentices, his students—as he broke the bread and said as he gave it to them, "Take, eat, this is my body," and when the disciples ate it, it is as clear as day that they were not eating the body of Jesus, for the body of Jesus was sitting right there at the table in their midst. Why, then, did he say it?

First, because he was a Jew, and Jews by nature do not theorize, they dramatize. When the prophet Jeremiah was aware of the fact that the Kingdom of Judah was about to be swallowed up and completely conquered and forced into exile by Babylon, he talked about it to a certain extent, but he did something much more dramatic than that. He had a huge yoke made, and whenever he went through the streets of Jerusalem he wore it! No one could miss what he meant; he was dramatic, he acted out what he thought and believed. He knew that actions speak louder than words.

Jesus did the same thing, not only at the end of his life, but all through his ministry. One time people went to him and asked what he thought about paying taxes to Rome. Instead of giving a learned disclosure on the principle of taxation, he said, "Show me a coin." They gave him a coin and he said, "Whose face is that?" They said, "Caesar's." He said, "All right, if it belongs to Caesar, give it back to Caesar, and give to God what belongs to him."

Another time a man went to him and said, "Who is my neighbor?" and instead of giving a discourse in which he tried to define exactly who was and who was not a neighbor, Jesus drew a picture. A certain Samaritan came by and helped a man who had been stripped and robbed. He was the "neighbor," the Good Samaritan, who lives to this day. This dramatization was one of his natural ways of teaching, of communicating the truth to the learned as well as to the simple.

At this particular point he wanted to say something about his death. He knew that it was coming and that it was coming soon. He hadn't sought it; he was not at all like the fine Japanese novelist who deliberately committed suicide a few weeks ago to prove and commend his commitment to the old order of things. He wasn't like that. He tried to avoid death, as a matter of fact, up to the very end. When he saw that it could not be avoided without compromising the things he believed to be essential, he accepted it. And he was convinced, in ways that we may not and perhaps cannot understand, that his death would give other people life. But it has happened before on an infinitely smaller scale; the things that people have given, the self-sacrifices they have made, have been the bread of life to other people.

Jesus told them what he felt and believed, not by talking to them but by doing something. He took the loaf of bread, and when he broke it he said, "My body, broken for you: eat it, feed upon it; it will give you life." The implication is that he expected them to share not only in his life but also in his death. In other words, he expected them to share not only in his healing and preaching ministry, in all that he did and said to make life richer and fuller for people, but he also expected them to share in his suffering, and to join him as one of the burden-bearers of the race.

That is one thing that is clear. There is another thing that is equally clear when you look at the event. After Jesus died, a small group of his followers continued this simple meal. In other words, the event survived, and for a good and understandable reason. His followers believed, and there is no question about this, that his spirit was alive and that his spirit was everywhere. But they felt his lively presence particularly when they shared in this meal. That is when they felt it most vividly, and I think you can see why. For one thing, it was so like him. It was simple, so bare, so stripped of all the nonessentials of life that make up such a large part of the lives of other people. It was a continual reminder of the way he pared life down to its bare essentials. It was so like him to give and not to count the cost, not to hold back.

And it was so natural for them to feel something by doing something, not just thinking or talking about it. Sometimes you can do that; sometimes you can feel the presence of another person who is either absent or departed by talking about him. I can do that, but there are other times when I can feel it more vividly by doing something, by feeling the things that were associated with him. I have a small, private communion set that was given to Mr. Brooks in 1860 by one of his classmates after they graduated from the Virginia Seminary. I don't take it out very often, but when I do, to show it to people, somehow just the touch of it makes me feel his presence in a way that I don't when I simply talk and talk and talk about him.

Two things, then, are clear when we look at the event, the Last Supper. First, when Jesus said, "This is my body, take it and eat it," he was not referring to his own body of flesh and blood. When he first said those words, the bread and the body were not identical. Second, when his followers continued the meal after his death, they believed that the spirit of Jesus was alive and present everywhere, but they felt it more especially in that meal, and that the bread and the presence went together hand in hand.

As time went on and Christianity broke loose from its Jewish moorings, it became more and more intellectual. This almost always happens in the normal development of any event. When you fall in love, for instance, you don't at the very beginning stop and try to explain it or analyze it. You just do it. You enjoy it. You don't have time to think much about it, to analyze it. As time goes on, perhaps, you reflect on it, and if you are wise, you try to see what it means in the larger context of life. If you ever write your memoirs you may try to put it, years later, in its proper frame of reference—either as a passing romance or as the pole star of your life. But at the time, no. You are busy doing it, enjoying it, living it out.

This certainly happened to the first followers of Jesus. I think it is fair to say, in the colloquial language of our time, that there were people who "fell" for him. They were convinced that he was alive even though some of them had seen him die on the cross. They were absolutely convinced that he was the image of his Father, and they were sure that he was with them in this meal of bread and wine. They didn't try to explain it. As time went on they began to think about it, especially about the bread and the wine, and about the relationship between the bread and wine and the body and blood of Christ. If he said that the bread was his body and the wine his blood, they thought it must be so. But how could it be? How could those simple, material things be identical with the living, vibrant instrument that once spoke, walked, wept, and prayed? They must be changed. How?

Through the ninth, tenth, eleventh, and twelfth centuries they gradually worked out an explanation. They said that the bread and the wine are not changed in appearance; they look exactly the same as they did in the beginning. They have all the "accidents" of bread and wine—they taste the same, they look the same—but they are changed in "substance," in their essence, the way you might say a dollar bill is changed—it is still paper, it looks like paper, tears like paper, but you don't tear it because it isn't paper, it's money. The nature of it is different; it has been changed. The bread and wine have been changed from food and drink into the presence of a living body.

When does this change happen? At that time they said it happened when the right words of institution were said by the right man, the man ordained and commissioned with the power to say them. Those words are the same words that originally came from St. Paul: "On the night on which he was betrayed, he took bread: and when he had given thanks he broke it and gave it to his disciples, saying, 'Take, eat, this is my body, which is given for you.'"

Since the Council of Trent in 1545 this has been the explanation of the Roman Catholic Church, and it is called the Doctrine of Transubstantiation. It is easy for the plain man to take it to mean that the bread itself becomes the body of Jesus. The English Church never accepted this explanation, nor did it ever attempt another one. So, in this church we have no official explanation of what actually happens. I for one am thankful that we don't. The mystery remains, and one can still appreciate it without trying to explain it. The more you explain it, the more commonplace it becomes, and as so often happens, what begins as a mystery deteriorates into a miracle.

This means that we are left with the action only. We continue the meal, we say the words, we repeat the action, we share in the food, and we feel the presence. Some feel it more than others.

Some of you may say, I'm one of those who don't feel the presence—not intensely at least, if at all. I think about Christ and I care a great deal about the Church; the church means everything to me, and I couldn't live without it. But I sometimes feel the presence of Christ more when I am alone in the church and nothing is being said or done, or when I'm listening to music, or even listening to a sermon, or even when I'm out on the street or at home at my dining room table with the rest of the family. What about me?

I say to you (to the others perhaps I don't need to say anything), don't be ashamed of being the person you are, and don't ever try to be someone else; you can never do it. No two people are exactly alike. Never forget those two great Christians (those of you who are my age are old enough to remember them both, even if you never saw them): Rufus Jones, the Friend, the Quaker, who never went to any sacrament in his life; and Baron von Hugel, the faithful Roman Catholic who went to Mass every day of his life. When those two met they were absolutely in unison, grounded in their faith in God made man in Christ.

Also, remember that it is easy, and often very tempting, to draw back from suffering; the thought of blood may turn you away. You cannot get away from it. Life is full of suffering and stained with blood wherever you look, and there is nothing you can do to change that.

On Friday in the *New York Times* I read a review by Clive Barnes of a revival of Samuel Beckett's *Waiting for Godot*. There was one line that I noted. Clive Barnes wrote this in trying to interpret Beckett's extreme rejection of everything that means much to many of the rest of us: "Life is not the Charge of the Light Brigade; it is a succession of little deaths." I say the same, and I add to that: Life is not the Charge of the Light Brigade; it is a succession of little deaths, often followed by little risings, and it's the risings that make the deaths not only bearable but often beautiful.

Jesus knew that. He went through many a "little death" before he shed his blood, and he has helped others go through those "little deaths"—not actual deaths, but the giving up of this, the losing of that, the disappointment here, and the curtain that falls at the end of a chapter, the sting of grief, the darkness of despair. We have all gone through those little deaths over and over again, and he has enabled some of us to go through those little deaths in such a way as to make them little victories. Little deaths transfigured into little risings—that is what we see wherever and whenever the Spirit of Christ dwells in a man. What else is worth seeing?

Finally, be sure you take into account the drama and poetry in the biblical tradition of the Christian faith, for they play an enormous part in it, and until you understand them you will be misled at every turn, and miss half of the meaning and most of the glory.

When and if you come to the communion table, beware of the literal fallacy. It is a trap that has tripped up thousands of well-meaning Christians. They are like the conductor who sees the notes but has not yet learned to see beneath them. Be open to the greater truth, the presence, suggested by, communicated by, but never completely contained in the material things like bread and wine. In them the presence is felt and perceived in a unique way by those who are open to it. It is expressed, don't forget, only when you go out of this place to do likewise, in remembrance of him.—Theodore Parker Ferris

SECTION V

MESSAGES FOR FUNERALS AND BEREAVEMENT

SERMON SUGGESTIONS

Topic: Hope's Persistence

TEXT: Heb. 10:35–39

Gerry's life was not an easy one, for her and often not for those around her. She suffered from a debilitating mental illness that took a bright, energetic, beautiful, and sweet person and turned her into someone who was a puzzle to herself and to those closest to her. Not that she ever lost the core of who she was, but the illness affected her outlook on life and her ability to relate to people. When it was at its worst, she would lash out in anger at her friends, her church, and her husband. We all knew that at those times it was not Gerry speaking but the illness.

To honor her life, it is important that we be honest about her struggle and how it affected her life. Yet despite the limitations of her illness, Gerry never lost her love for the Lord nor her desire to share his love with others. In fact, her struggles, her love, and compassion for others may have deepened. It certainly strengthened her relationship with God.

Preparing for this service, her husband handed me several prayers Gerry had written. The intimacy with God they reflect and the longing for God's presence they express put them on par with some of the best writings on spirituality I have read. I was impressed with her deep love for God, her honesty about her limitations, and her strong desire that others come to know the love of God that sustained her. Lesser people would have given up. I could not help but wonder if under similar circumstances I would be so strong.

As I thought of her life and witness, Hebrews 10:35–39 kept coming to the fore. Gerry was a woman of hope. She knew that her only hope for making it through the day was Jesus. She knew that her only hope for eternal life was Jesus. She knew that the only hope for any of us is Jesus. The persistence of her hope gave her courage.

She knew what it was to endure suffering, and through that suffering to do the will of God. Gerry refused to let her suffering and her limits put an end to her life of witnessing. She did not shrink back, but pressed on in faith.

Listen to the closing words of one of her prayers: "In our most difficult times, he surrounds us with his angels, which means a lot to us. Our Lord remains with us forever. Keep tuned in with him, and he will keep you on the right path. Love God with all your heart."

I believe that Gerry has received "what was promised." I believe she received it even before her death. Her life is a plea to us: "Hope in God and find his promise."—Jim Holladay

Topic: Like Children Needing to Be Blessed

TEXT: Prov. 22:1; Mark 10:13–16

Matthew Robert Stockman. Matt and Jane, you named him even before he was born. No doubt great care went into choosing the words that would carry his identity through life. The writer of Proverbs says, "A good name is to be chosen rather than great riches." Though he did not choose it for himself, Matthew Robert's name would have given him something to live up to—the life and witness of both his grandfathers.

Matt, you and Jane are products of your fathers' faithfulness to the Lord, to their families, and to the church. No doubt you wanted to honor them by naming your first child after them. But more than that, I believe that with those names comes a hope—a hope that Matthew Robert would have grown into the values, character, and influence reflected by the men for whom he was named.

Naming our children is an expression of hope. Carl Sandburg once wrote, "A child is God's affirmation that the world should go on." We invest so much hope in the birth of our children. From the day we hear the words, "You're pregnant," we begin to dream and plan for that child's future. Having that hope dashed in the way you have creates a grief that many of us cannot imagine. Matthew Robert lived long enough for you to see his face and his smile, and to hear him cry. Then, almost as quickly as he had been born, he died. Matt and Jane, we cannot begin to know the depth of your grief. Words are so feeble. Know that we are here for you and will do whatever we can to bear you up in your grief.

And yet, we gather in the hope and knowledge that there exists one who does know your grief and whose words can speak to your sorrow. In an oft-quoted passage from Mark's Gospel, Jesus is confronted by some folks, most of whom were his own disciples, who believed that children did not matter. Mark says that Jesus "became angry." You see, in the Kingdom of God, children do matter. In fact, Jesus warned his disciples that if they were not willing to become children, they would not see God's Kingdom. Pretty strong words.

Mark ends this piece of narrative with these words, "And he took them up in his arms, laid his hands on them, and blessed them."

Matt, Jane, grandparents, aunts, uncles, friends—at this point this may be all we need to say, because it may be all that we can hear: "Jesus Christ has taken Matthew Robert Stockman up in his arms. All the hopes and dreams you had for him have become a part of Jesus' blessing."

As little children in need of God's blessing today, may we be willing to fall into the arms of Jesus so he can bless us, too.—Jim Holladay

AN ODYSSEY OF CONSOLATIONS
By James W. Cox

These messages were presented at various times during the editor's ministry as pastor.

Mrs. Ann Mary Wright

This afternoon we honor one who has brought joy and blessing to so many of us. I first met Mrs. Ann Mary Wright as I was finishing my first year in seminary. She and Mr. Wright had had a major role in the founding of the Memorial Baptist Church, and I had been called to be the first pastor of the new church. The Wrights did not join the new church for several years, but they helped sustain its growth in many ways, one of which was to provide room and board for the pastor as part of his compensation.

As the years went by, the Wrights became more deeply involved and active in all phases of the work of this church. Your air-conditioned comfort here on this hot afternoon is due to a generous gift of Mrs. Wright.

Yesterday, as I was thinking of Mrs. Wright and her many contributions to church and community, I thought of something I heard several years ago. Kenneth Scott LaTourette was a historian and professor at Yale University. He wrote the monumental *History of the Expansion of Christianity,* as well as other important works. He was talking once to a small group of us in Louisville. He said that the real history of the church does not have so much to do with popes, bishops, and preachers as it has to do with the deacon who comes early to the little country church on a wintry Sunday morning to build the fires so that the worshipers can be comfortable, or with the woman who uses her God-given voice to sing at funerals and bring comfort to the mourners. Dr. LaTourette said that these latter persons are the real makers of church history—not the popes, bishops, and preachers—but their names are not recorded for posterity, for we do not know who they are.

Today we do know who one of those persons is—and God knows, as he knows all such servants of his. So we honor Mrs. Ann Mary Wright today and thank God for her life and for the many things she has done, known and unknown, that have brought blessings to so many. Someone who ought to know said to me last night, "No woman in Frankfort has touched more lives than Mrs. Wright." I owe to her a personal debt of gratitude that I cannot begin to express. To my wife and her parents she has been as close as members of their own family.

The suddenness of Mrs. Wright's passing has stunned us, but we do not grieve as those who have no hope, nor as those who mourn the passing of one who has been cut down before life has hardly begun. We grieve for ourselves, not for her. Her life was full of years, full of friends, full of service to God and others. What more could one expect of life, or give to it?

Mark Twain once cynically said that life ought to begin at eighty, gradually go back toward childhood, and end with infancy, instead of the way it is, with three score years and ten or perhaps four score years. But the wisdom of God has decided otherwise, no matter how baffling the mystery of suffering and the infirmities of age may be.

The apostle Paul said, "No wonder we do not lose heart: though our outward humanity is in decay, yet day by day we are inwardly renewed. Our troubles are slight and short-lived, and their outcome an eternal glory that outweighs them far. Meanwhile, our eyes are fixed, not on the things that are seen but on the things that are unseen."

As I think of the life of Ann Mary Wright, three affirmations come through.

(1) *Our profession of faith is only a beginning.* It would be easy to believe otherwise. Many seem to think that the first expression of faith in Christ is all there is to being a Christian. That first profession is important, of course, just as the beginning of anything is important to all that follows. But Christians are challenged in the Scriptures to "grow in the grace and knowledge of our Lord and Savior Jesus Christ." Mrs. Wright's growing faith was shown in her singing, in her Sunday school teaching, in her mission activities, in her community service. As she gave of herself she grew in that grace and knowledge of her Lord.

(2) *True fulfillment in life is in giving more than receiving.* Of course it is good to be able to receive graciously, for when we learn how to receive, we learn how to give. We love God because he first loved us, and we love other people because of how God loves us, undeserving as we are. The person is to be pitied who lives only to get; such a person only half lives.

(3) *There is always something that one can do for others.* No life has to be useless. I have said many times, there is always one thing a person can do when age and infirmity have closed every other door: one can always pray for other people. As the poet Tennyson put it, "More things are wrought by prayer than this world dreams of." Fortunately, Mrs. Wright was able

to do more than just pray, important as that is and always will be. She was a gracious hostess and shared the hospitality of her home with so many people, even when, as very recently, she had to sit in a wheelchair to do some of her work. Like my own mother, Mrs. Wright never thought of retiring; there was always something worthwhile to do. Many times my mother reminded us that at her funeral she wanted Rudyard Kipling's "L'Envoi" to be read. It expressed her wish always to be busy with something worthwhile, and I believe it also captures the spirit of Ann Mary Wright:

> When Earth's last picture is painted
> and the tubes are twisted and dried,
> When the oldest colours have faded,
> and the youngest critic has died,
> We shall rest and, faith, we shall need it—
> lie down for an aeon or two,
> Till the Master of All Good Workmen
> shall put us to work anew.
> And those that were good shall be happy;
> they shall sit in a golden chair;
> They shall splash at a ten-league canvas
> with brushes of comet's hair;
> They shall find real saints to draw from—
> Magdalene, Peter, and Paul;
> They shall work for an age at a sitting
> and never be tired at all!
> And only the Master shall praise us,
> and only the Master shall blame;
> And no one shall work for money,
> and no one shall work for fame,
> But each for the joy of working,
> and each, in his separate star,
> Shall draw the Thing as he sees It
> for the God of Things as They are!

Sam Ridgway

It isn't given to us to be the final judges of any person, yet God has given us eyes to see and minds to weigh the words and acts of other people. When I think of Sam Ridgway I am reminded of a man in one of Jesus' parables: the man who was given five talents by his master and who doubled those resources by loyal service. The master said, "Well done, my good and trusty servant! You have proved trustworthy in a small way; I will now put you in charge of something big. Come and share in your master's delight."

A writer of one of the noncanonical books of the Old Testament said, "Let us now sing the praises of famous men, the heroes of our nation's history." Sam Ridgway would no doubt recoil at being called a hero, yet it is illustrious people like him who in great ways and small have pointed the way to a better life for all of us and who have a special place in the history of our local communities and even of our nation.

Sam Ridgway received remarkable gifts from many sources and used his endowments faithfully and gladly. A person looking for a model for useful and meaningful living can find it in his example in many ways.

He had faith in God and acknowledged it modestly, humbly, and honestly. I will long treasure the time of prayer we had together with Lucille last week. He knew that his time here was short, but he faced the future unafraid.

He loved his family and his extended family. He honored his father and mother by his life and accomplishments and by founding the Ridgway Memorial Library in their memory. And he wanted it known that his nephew had a significant role in establishing this memorial. He spoke with tender affection of Lucille and of her caring and her genuine Christian character.

He gave time and energy to many community enterprises and touched the lives of countless thousands.

He was a true patriot. He expressed it very simply and clearly to me in these words: "I love my country."

The same writer who said, "Let us now sing the praises of famous men" also said of the Lord God, "Where can we find the skill to sing his praises? . . . Honor the Lord to the best of your ability, And he will still be high above all praise. Summon all your strength to declare his greatness, and be untiring, for the most you can do will fall short" (Eccl. 43:28, 30).

This is a time when, having praised an outstanding man, we find in every human value and accomplishment the work of God. In a real sense, if we are anything, we are what we are by the grace and providence of God. Often God is at work in our lives when we are not at all aware of it; but his plan for us unfolds—and for those with faith and hope and love, God's will gets done.

It would be wonderful, wouldn't it, for each of us to be able at the end of our days to say with the apostle Paul, "As for me, already my life is being poured out on the altar, and the hour for my departure is upon me. I have run the great race, I have finished the course, I have kept the faith."

This is also a time to rest in the Lord. The psalmist said, "Rest in the Lord, and wait patiently for him." The challenge to fight the good fight of faith is important, but the command to wait patiently for God to work even apart from our strenuous human efforts is important, too. When we are too stunned and grief-stricken to do anything but simply trust God and give him room and time to work things out, it is enough. It may be quite a while between the planting and the harvest. Yet harvest time comes. "But the harvest of the Spirit," says the apostle, "is love, joy, peace, patience, kindness, goodness, fidelity, gentleness, and self-control."

So today we can be inspired and made thankful by a life well-lived.

> Lives of great men all remind us
> We can make our lives sublime,
> And departing, leave behind us
> Footprints on the sands of time.[1]

---

[1]Henry Wadsworth Longfellow, "A Psalm of Life."

We can be challenged to a renewed faith in God's plan for our own life, and we can be comforted by God's call to put our trust in him to bring all things that concern us to a perfect fulfillment at last.

First Lieutenant Billy Joe Beasley

When I first heard the news about our friend Billy Joe Beasley, it was hard to believe. But as many thoughts raced through my mind, three facts stood out: (1) his occupation was a hazardous one, he knew it, and he was willing to take the calculated risk; (2) he was doing something he enjoyed and that he did enthusiastically; and (3) his life was a vital part of the vast contribution that many heroic men and women are making to safeguard our freedom—that from the human and humanitarian side.

Then I thought of his religious faith and devotion, his clean living and noble example, his radiant enthusiasm and deep affections. We have been reminded again and again of his winsome personality and unspotted reputation. If anybody ever lived abundantly, he did—at home and abroad. His commanding officer wrote, "Bill was a good pilot. His approach to flying was enthusiastic and he worked hard at perfecting his skill. His cheerful temperament and kindly concern for people endeared him to all the members of the squadron. The men for whom and with whom he worked considered him an outstanding officer. He posed a determination to excel in everything he did."

We can say all of these things, yet many anxious questions remain unanswered in our saddened hearts. Perhaps if we could be raised high enough in our thoughts, we could gain a better perspective for all our problems. A relative of Billy's, in a consoling letter, wrote of his experiences in flying: "I feel that to look at the Southern Cross in a deep blue Pacific sky, the North Star, the Big Dipper, all the planets, to look down on all that expanse of ocean, the fields of grain, rivers, lakes, snow-covered peaks, green meadows, and to witness the handiwork of the Lord is reward enough for any man. . . . So many, many times I have seen the most beautiful sunsets, sunrises, rainbows, shooting stars, and other things of beauty, and my only wish was to be able to share them with Mother and Dad."

Now Billy Joe Beasley's life is being lived in a new dimension and he is exploring a world of beauty and reality that we have yet to see. If we let our faith put us in touch with that world of glory, our hearts find great consolations and inspirations.

A prophet in the Old Testament, whose visions, insights, and stalwart preaching are found in the book of Isaiah, can take us to dizzying heights of spiritual outlook that will remove the shadows of despair from our souls and clothe us in garments of heavenly glory.

I. *The prophet sees man in his weakness and frailty, and in the same moment sees God in his strength and glory.*

The voice of him that crieth in the wilderness, Prepare ye the way of the Lord, make straight in the desert a highway for our God. Every valley shall be exalted, and every mountain and hill shall be made low: and the crooked shall be made straight, and the rough places plain: and the glory of the Lord shall be revealed, and all flesh shall see it together: for the mouth of the Lord hath spoken it. The voice said, Cry. And he said, What shall I cry? All flesh is grass, and all the goodliness thereof is as the flower of the field: the grass withereth, the flower fadeth, because the spirit of the Lord bloweth upon it: surely the people is grass. The grass withereth, the flower fadeth: but the word of our God shall stand for ever [Isa. 40:1–8 KJV].

Man is so frail that we wonder, first of all, how he is born. Then it is amazing that he survives the hazards of infancy and childhood. If he reaches ripe old age, it is a miracle indeed! But through all the crises and changes are the fortunes; whether the outcome is life or death, this remains constant: God's glory is unsullied; his word remains fixed in heaven and his eternal purpose moves on to its final fulfillment.

It is therefore possible to read these comforting words:

Hast thou not known? hast thou not heard, that the everlasting God, the Lord, the Creator of the ends of the earth, fainteth not, neither is weary? There is no searching of his understanding. He giveth power to the faint; and to them that have no might he increaseth strength. Even the youths shall faint and be weary, and the young men shall utterly fall: but they that wait upon the Lord shall renew their strength; they shall mount up with wings as eagles; they shall run and not be weary; they shall walk and not faint [Isa. 40:28–31 KJV].

II. *Moreover, the prophet sees God in the majesty of his thoughts and ways:*

For my thoughts are not your thoughts, neither are your ways my ways, saith the Lord. For as the heavens are higher than the earth, so are my ways higher than your ways, and my thoughts than your thoughts. For as the rain cometh down, and the snow from heaven, and returneth not thither, but watereth the earth, and maketh it bring forth and bud, that it may give seed to the sower, and bread to the eater: so shall my word be that goeth forth out of my mouth: it shall not return unto me void, but it shall accomplish that which I please, and it shall prosper in the thing whereto I sent it. For ye shall go out with joy, and be led forth with peace: the mountains and the hills shall break forth before you into singing, and all the trees of the field shall clap their hands. Instead of the thorn shall come up the fir tree, and instead of the brier shall come up the myrtle tree: and it shall be to the Lord for a name, for an everlasting sign that shall not be cut off [Isa. 55:8–13].

Often we wonder why the young must die and why the good must suffer. It is an age-old mystery. Suffice it to say, at this point, that the God of love revealed in the face of Jesus Christ will do what is right and what is ultimately for the best. We cannot trace the end from the beginning, but God can. We do not know what one day will bring forth, but God does. We do not know where or how our life may gain its highest usefulness and significance, but God does.

The apostle Paul said, "We know that all things work together for good to them that love God, to them who are called according to his purpose. . . . For I am persuaded that neither death, nor life, nor angels, nor principalities, nor powers, nor things present, nor things to come, nor height, nor depth, nor any other creature shall be able to separate us from the love of God, which is in Christ Jesus our Lord" (Rom. 8:28, 38–39).

III. *Finally, the prophet sees the nobility of vicarious living—life that is lived for others, life that is lived out of concern for the groups to which one belongs, life that is prepared to be sacrificed for the good of all.* "Surely he hath borne our griefs and carried our sorrows: yet we did esteem him stricken, smitten of God, and afflicted. But he was wounded for our transgressions, he was bruised for our iniquities: the chastisement of our peace was upon him; and with his stripes we are healed" (Isa. 53:4–5).

The occupation that claimed the enthusiasm, the skill, the daring, and yes, the mortal life of our friend demands a willingness to live and die for others. But the sacrifices are not without rewards. The book of the Wisdom of Solomon (3:1–5) in the Apocrypha beautifully expresses it:

> But the souls of the righteous are in the hand of God, And no torment shall touch them. In the eyes of the foolish they seemed to have died; and their departure was accounted to be their hurt, And their journeying away from us to be their ruin: but they are in peace. For even if in the sight of men they be punished, their hope is full of immortality; and having borne a little chastening, they shall receive great good; because God made trial of them, and found them worthy of himself.

SPECIAL RESOURCES FOR LENT AND EASTER

SERMON SUGGESTIONS

Topic: C. S. Lewis: Hearing God in a Higher Key

TEXT: Isa. 55:6–9; Col. 1:16–20 NRSV

One definition of Lent I read is that it is "a time, in joy and sorrow, that the church proclaims, remembers, and responds to the atoning death of Jesus." Lent is also, as we all know, a time when we remember and get ready for Easter. This is a season when we Christians want to show the world we *really* believe that Jesus did not suffer and die on a cross for nothing, and we also *really* believe in the wonderful fact of his Resurrection.

But a big problem is that many people during a time like this, including many professing Christians and church members, never really change their routines at all; they continue to do the ordinary things. They get up, eat, drive their cars, read their newspapers, work, make phone calls, check their e-mails, tend to their children, go to the mall, watch TV, and then go to bed, without giving a single thought to God or Jesus or Lent, or to getting ready for Easter. To many folks, Lent is just another ordinary time.

I read about a man who was having trouble finding God. He had gone to church his whole life but had never (as he said) had an authentic experience of God. He said that his problem with special church times like this was that they all seemed so ordinary. Church had become ordinary: same order of worship, with some exceptions; same preacher with the same suit or robe on; same choir members; same people who sit in the same pews and say (more or less) the same things every Sunday; same special celebrations every year; same music; same Scripture texts and Bible stories; same church decorations; same way of celebrating Lent and Easter. He said, "I've been in church for a long time, and I've seen and heard it all!" Then he added, "Where are God and Jesus during Lent and Easter? I never sense or experience them. To me these are just special days and times I'm used to, and what I'm *really* getting ready for is eating hot cross buns and finding the best way to hide the Easter eggs for my grandkids."

This man is not alone. For many people, God and church and special days have become ordinary. There's no life-changing experience, no touch of holiness, no revelation, no inspiration, no spiritual happening. It's happened to me, too. Sometimes my mind wanders at church, even during Lent and Easter services. Occasionally I find myself thinking about everything but what I should not be thinking about, and even when I try to be good. sometimes nothing happens. Sometimes, special church seasons and celebrations like Lent become ordinary, even when I know for sure they are not.

I write and teach full-time about C. S. Lewis and J.R.R. Tolkien, and I have received great help with this problem of the ordinary from Lewis's writings, and from one in particular. On Sunday morning, May 28, 1944, Lewis preached a sermon at Mansfield College chapel in Oxford called "Transposition." It was reported that he was so overcome by emotion that he stopped in the middle of his sermon, said "I'm sorry," and left the pulpit. After receiving help, and after a hymn was sung, he returned and finished the sermon. It was obvious to everyone that he had some very personal feelings about his subject.

Someone has suggested that "Transposition" represents some of Lewis's very best theological thinking. It was really a sermon about God and about holiness. It was also a sermon that Lewis wanted to use to combat "the mind of his day"—today we would call this postmodern, anti-God thinking. Many of the "religious pessimists" in Lewis's England were saying and writing and complaining that the spiritual life of the Christian was a psychological projection (after Freud), or just an ordinary philosophy, as many say today about Christian spirituality. A Christian couldn't experience God, they said. Why go to church? God isn't there. Why bother with all the hymns and services and prayers and celebrations and rites and rituals? Besides that, aren't all churches about the same anyway?

One person has written that in preaching "Transposition," C. S. Lewis was really saying two things: (1) that there really is holiness in the ordinariness of life, and (2) that we can "hear God in a higher key" if we learn how he works in us and in this world. Lewis suggested to his audience that day that the Christian *should* look at so-called spiritual times (like Lent and Easter) "from above"—that is, with a godly and heavenly viewpoint. He also said that nonbelievers see these events and times without God in mind. For Lewis, a Christian's search for and devotion to God (which he called "joy") was not a psychological projection, not wishful thinking, not just another philosophy. Longing for God and devotion to him has been placed in us by God, and it is up to us to recognize and celebrate that.

Paraphrasing Lewis, a good working definition of *transposition* is "the power of the higher to come down and be incarnate in the lower." In plainer English, this means that God can, and does, change and use "low" or ordinary things and events, turning them into "high," rich, and meaningful things and events. Some examples of this are the miracles of Jesus, in which he often used ordinary things such as bread and wine to show God's power and who he was; or when great writers (such as Lewis) put "higher" thoughts into a "lower" form, like paper; or when great artists such as Beethoven, Mozart, and Michelangelo put the higher (their inspiration) into notes on a score or paint on a wall.

Now what does this mean for us? What makes the difference? How can one person feel the great exhilaration and joy of remembering and celebrating Lent and Easter, while another person sitting down the pew is thinking about how ordinary it all is and when are the services and special days at the church finally going to end?

Lewis would say that some folks have forgotten or have never been taught that God can change what we call ordinary into what he calls holy. The ordinary act or event is made holy when we offer it as service to God and in his name. Lewis would also say that instead of sitting at a Lenten service and waiting for "an experience" (or waiting for it to end), the Christian should remember that special times like this become *really special* if we offer ourselves to them rather than wait for them to "give us something."

Lewis always believed that he was to look and try to find God in everything, even things he was "used to." He also knew that most people would never have dreamed of looking for the Savior of the world in an ordinary cattle trough, or riding on an ordinary donkey, or hanging on an ordinary Roman obscenity called a cross, or standing beside an ordinary grave plot. Who would have expected, Lewis would say, that the Son of the Creator of this and all other worlds would spend his days with the down-and-outs of society and the physically and financially challenged, and allow ordinary Jewish kids to sit on his knee? Who would have known that Jesus would hold up as religiously important an ordinary loaf of bread, an ordinary towel, and an ordinary cup of cold water?

C. S. Lewis knew that God uses things and events we would never choose to show himself to people. He also knew (and wrote about it a lot) that God uses low, ordinary, sinful human beings (like those in church) to do his work. When this happens, lots of things and happenings and experiences become holy and "transposed." He once wrote that our real goal as Christians is that we should try to become "little Christs." When that happens, the ordinary really does start to become holy.

So how do we become "transposed"? How do we start to hear God in a higher key? I know a couple of things Lewis might say. He might quote from the old theologian Kierkegaard and remind us that when we come for worship at a special time like Lent, or any other celebration of the church, we should remember that God is watching us, and that God is the audience, not the other way around. We are the actors in the great play of life and God is our loving critic. How would he judge our performance of worship at a Lenten service, this year or any other? Lewis might also say (and this is straight out of the New Testament) that when folks like us are gathered together in God's name, God is right here with us, whether we can "experience" him or not. How do we remember and celebrate Lent and Easter with that in mind?

Most people are ready for a good time and an experience of some kind on a day like Easter, but the bad news is that unfortunately some of us never seem to understand the real meaning of Lent. The whole thrust of the biblical message, however, and the whole point behind Lewis's great sermon is that there is as much holiness in the ordinary as there is in the spectacular. We can hear God in a higher key, and that key is found in his love for us and in how we respond in faithfulness and commitment to that love.

So how would C. S. Lewis, who almost always tried to look at the world with God's eyes, advise us on how to approach this (always) special Lenten season? I don't know for sure, but one thing he might tell us is to use our imaginations and put ourselves right down there with the carpenter's son, right next to that ordinary donkey. Then Lewis might ask us how on earth would we feel if we knew in advance that all the celebration of that day was going to be cut dreadfully short later by a cross. Maybe then, as we sit in church, we could remember all that Jesus did for us and what he had to go through to help and save us.

Lewis might also possibly suggest to us that our friends and even the people we don't know in our church and in our community are God's special creations, that no one is ordinary in God's sight, and that we are to treat everyone we meet, and live next to, and sit next to, and work with, as if we really believed that. Finally, Lewis might remind us that everything we do at our church (or at any other), on this or any other day, is not ordinary if we do it first with God, not ourselves, in mind. That means any worship, any church celebration, any giving, any fellowship, any prayer, any forgiveness, any teaching, any visiting, any working—anything.

Do you remember the movie *Chariots of Fire*? When his sister asked him why he had to run in the Olympics instead of going back to the China mission field, Eric Liddell said to her, "When I run I can feel God's pleasure." That's the great news, because when we take the ordinary and offer it to God, we can feel and know his pleasure, and nothing ought to make us feel better than to know we are doing something that Almighty God himself enjoys and takes pleasure in.

We all know that in the end God looks on the attitude of our hearts. When Lewis was a youngster, he suffered many traumatic experiences at his early schools. At one of them, the headmaster beat the boys and traumatized them psychologically. For many years, even after he became a Christian, Lewis felt anger and resentment toward this man. Just before his death, Lewis wrote to a friend in America and told her, "Do you know, only a few weeks ago I realized suddenly that I had at last forgiven the cruel schoolmaster who so darkened my childhood. I'd been trying to do it for years. One is safe as long as one keeps on trying." Lewis kept on trying for nearly fifty years, and maybe that is another whole point. It is our attitude and our effort that really counts with God, especially during a special season like Lent.

I mentioned at the beginning that fellow who couldn't find God at church and couldn't experience Jesus and God during special church times like Lent and Easter. I hope that some-day he will read something Lewis wrote in his great classic *Mere Christianity;* these are some of the most famous and compelling words any Christian ever wrote, and they are the bene-diction to this sermon: "Give up yourself and you will find your real self. Lose your life and you will find it. Submit with every fibre of your being, and you will find eternal life. Keep back nothing. Nothing you have not given away will ever be really yours. But look for Christ and you will find him, and with him everything else thrown in." Amen.—Perry C. Bramlett

Topic: Sorting the Treasures
TEXT: Matt. 13:31–33, 44–52

One of the things that made Jesus such an effective teacher was his ability to show us ulti-mate truth in a very down-to-earth way. Take, for instance, the kingdom of heaven. How do you describe that? It seems so lofty, so distant from the mundane things that occupy us day in and day out. So Jesus used a myriad of pictures to describe it: It's like a mustard seed. It's like yeast. It's like a treasure buried in a field. It's like a pearl. It's like a fishing net. It's not any of those things, but it's like them all. Jesus' parables appeal to our common sense. They make what seems incomprehensible so compelling that it demands our very lives.

Take the parable of the treasure hidden in the field. Jesus told about a day laborer who was hired to plow a field. One day he was plodding along behind the oxen, turning over the fur-rows, with the sweat dripping off the tip of his nose in the hot afternoon sun. As he was plow-ing under the poplar tree, he rammed against something hard buried in the ground. "Probably just a root," he thought to himself, but he was curious enough to get down on his hands and knees and dig away the dirt. He uncovered a large box. Over the years the roots of the tree had pushed it toward the surface, and erosion had washed away the topsoil. He lifted the box out of the ground, opened it, and gasped when he discovered that it was filled with gold and silver and jewels. He looked furtively around him to make sure no one had seen him, then quickly put it back in the ground, covered it up, and finished plowing the field.

That scenario isn't as strange as it might seem. Two thousand years ago a person's wealth wasn't as secure as it is today. There was no Federal Reserve System to insure your bank deposit. In ancient Palestine you never knew when the next invading army of Seleucids or Herodians was going to come sweeping through the countryside and rob and pillage your vil-lage. In those uncertain times, the safest thing to do with your wealth was to bury it where no marauding soldier could find it. Sometimes a rich person would bury a treasure and never get around to digging it up. He might meet a sudden death before he ever had a chance to tell his children that their inheritance was buried out under the poplar tree in the north forty. Or he might die without any heirs, and his creditors would lay claim to the field, not having any idea of the value of their new property. Any number of things could happen that might make it possible for a treasure buried in a field to be left unclaimed.

Well, the laborer, after covering up his discovery, finished his work and nonchalantly collected his day's wages from the owner of the field, trying to look as if nothing out of the ordinary had happened. He headed off toward the village, but once he was out of the sight of his employer, he broke into a sprint. He barely made enough to live on, but being a man of common sense, he knew that any sacrifice he made to get a hold of that treasure would pay off thousands of times over. He gathered what possessions he had. He took a few jars of food off the shelf, packed up his extra clothes, folded up his bed, and immediately went to find a buyer for them. He didn't get nearly enough to buy the field, so he found someone to buy his one-room house. His neighbors thought he was crazy. He didn't even own a plow. What was he going to do with the field once he got it? But the next day he went to the owner of the field and told him he'd decided it was time to take the plunge and become a landowner. The owner of the field was puzzled, but if he could turn a profit by selling to this crazy peasant, it was no concern of his what happened to the sucker who bought it. So he sold the field, and in an instant the day laborer who had nothing became a millionaire. That, said Jesus, is what the kingdom of heaven is like.

Jesus told another story, of a merchant who traveled all over the world in search of fine pearls. The merchant's trained eye knew quality when he saw it, and he spent his life sailing to India and Greece and far-off islands in search of exquisite jewels for his well-to-do clientele. On one trip, in some remote corner of the Earth, far from home, he came across the most beautiful pearl he had ever seen. To buy it, he would have to sell his entire business, his home, everything he owned. But he was enough of an expert to know that here was the investment opportunity of a lifetime, and he would be a fool to pass it up. Back home the pearl would bring such a profit that he could retire and live in luxury for the rest of his life. So he made arrangements to sell everything he owned and went back and bought the pearl. That, said Jesus, is what the kingdom of heaven is like.

Sometimes we stumble on the riches of the kingdom of heaven in the course of our day-to-day life and it takes us completely by surprise, like coming across a treasure in a field. Sometimes we devote our whole lives to finding it, a spiritual quest that leads us to eastern religions, New Age, and self-help before we finally find what we truly desire in Christ. For some it is an experience of intense joy that makes us want to shout at the top of our lungs. For others it is that quieter sense of satisfaction that comes with completing a long journey.

Regardless of how we come across it, the kingdom of heaven that Jesus proclaims confronts us with our priorities. It forces us to sort out what's most important to us from all those things that don't matter very much.

After my brother and I left home, my parents were transferred to another city and moved into a smaller house. Every time I went to visit them in their new home, my mother asked me to sort through the drawers of my old desk and dresser. She asked me to take what I wanted to keep and throw out the rest. I didn't take her seriously. "How could my dear mother want to part with all those things that remind her of her darling son?" I thought to myself. There were some of my favorite toys from childhood, stacks of papers from kindergarten and elementary school, some poems I wrote for English class in junior high school, term papers from high school, my old yearbooks. I never was able to find the time to sort through them when I was visiting, but I was sure that one day Mom would enjoy reliving precious memories and marveling at how her boy had grown. This went on for about three years. She didn't nag me about it, but once a year when I went home, she reminded me that they really did need some space and she would appreciate it if I would sort through my things. She assured me that anything she wanted she had already saved. Finally, one day a month or so after I'd visited them, the UPS man delivered two boxes to my door from Tampa, Florida. They contained the so-called treasures from my parents' house. Before I realized what I was saying, I exclaimed, "Where am I supposed to put all this junk?" All of a sudden, these items had taken on a different value. A thousand miles away they were treasures, but finding a place for them in my house was a different story. I held on to a few yearbooks and a picture or two. But most of the stuff found its way into the trash.

All the time we're being forced to choose what's really important to us. Do we invest our lives in things of lasting value or in things that don't mean very much?

Several years ago, Tom Gillespie, the president of Princeton Seminary, told me about a trip that he and Mrs. Gillespie took to eastern Germany shortly after the reunification of Germany. They had escorted Mrs. Gillespie's mother back to the village she had left in the 1930s to come to America. She hadn't been back since. When they got to the village, Mrs. Gillespie's mother took them to the church where she had been baptized as an infant. The pastor's wife graciously showed them around and told them what it had been like for her and her husband to serve that church for the past twenty years. Their salary had been almost poverty level. Each Sunday there were only twenty to thirty people in worship. They had two sons who were bright and aspired to go to the university to study to be doctors or lawyers. Because she and her husband were Christians in a country that was officially atheist, her sons were denied admission to the gymnasium, or high school. After the Communist government fell, the townspeople were allowed for the first time to climb the hill that overlooked the center of the village. On top of the hill, looking down on the front door of the church, they discovered a spy nest. In it were cameras with powerful telephoto lenses, a video camera, and a notebook containing the names of members of the parish. Agents of the notorious Stasi, the secret police, had kept a lookout there. All the villagers who went through the door of the church had their pictures taken and their names recorded. That information was used when they looked for a job or their children applied for an education. Would anyone ever notice that you are a Christian? The East German government certainly noticed. And it cost something. The Christians in that East German village had sorted through what was important to them.

Jesus presents us with the opportunity to sort out what is important to us. He invites us to join him in the kingdom of heaven. Sometimes it looks insignificant compared to all those things that keep us busy and worried. But that kingdom can be in the smallest things—a visit to a nursing home, a Bible story read to a child, a ride to English lessons for a refugee family, a hymn on a Sunday morning. But like the mustard seed that grows into the largest of bushes, those small seeds of the kingdom are part of God's cosmic reclamation of the human race. Sometimes it looks as if what we're asked to choose will never come. God's kingdom seems to move so slowly. The good still die young, dictators still oppress, and more people died in the twentieth century's wars than died in all wars before 1900. But like yeast that permeates a loaf, God's Kingdom gradually, imperceptibly works its way through this world and changes it.

The cross that Jesus invites us to carry doesn't look very appealing when we compare it to the comfort and ease of a self-centered life. But we take it up because we know that once we've sorted out what's important to us and what is not, we will discover that the cross of

Christ is what gives us life. That's what lasts. We can never find what is most important to us until we lose ourselves in Christ. Why would you want to give your life to anything less? He is our priceless treasure.—Stephens G. Lytch

Meditations
By James W. Cox

The following meditations may suggest ideas for sermons during Lent and on the Sundays of the Easter Season. They may also be printed in church bulletins on any or all of those Sundays, with proper acknowledgments.

Topic: How People Find God
TEXT: Job 11:7–9; Jer. 29:11–13; Matt. 7:7; John 14:8–10

Finding God is difficult because we look for him so anxiously. If we trusted as we should, we would know God. Every experience of life would confirm his reality.

But for many of us, the simple faith, that awed innocence of childhood, is not possible. Early training has exaggerated the importance of the question mark. We take beliefs apart like clocks to see what makes them go. But like clumsy, inept children, we do not find it easy to put them back together.

We need God—how desperately we need him! We have scrutinized and dissected so many experiences of life that the romance and glow are gone. Pleasure has ceased to please. Money can no longer buy happiness. Youth marches toward decrepitude. No warm love of the Earth is beyond the chill of grief.

Thus our skepticism at last brings us back to God. At first our skepticism seems to devour God, but it actually succeeds in destroying our idols and sets us before God for life or death. We capitulate before our heavenly Father, find life's ultimate meaning in him, and start from there to put the wheels of life in place again.

It is Jesus Christ—the Way, the Truth, and the Life—who gives the clues, the directions, and the evidence we need.

O God, I need you; my heart yearns for you. Grant me faith to receive the little light possible for me today, and patience to wait and work for the brighter light tomorrow. Amen.

Topic: For Those Who Doubt
TEXT: Mark 9:24; John 20:24–31

Don't let your doubts upset you. Wisdom, however, will dictate a refusal to flaunt your doubts, a reluctance to become a storm-center of lifted eyebrows, flushed faces, and angry, unsympathetic voices.

Honesty before God is a great virtue, but a cocky display of our spiritual immaturity before our friends and the world is another matter.

The way to faith is a dangerous way. So is every road that leads anywhere. Perils lie hidden. Enemies lurk. Darkness looms. But a destination lies ahead that makes it worth every sacrifice and every courageous resolve.

One danger is that of mistaking an absence of buoyant emotion for a lack of faith. Our feelings are a poor weather vane for our spiritual progress. Some plants grow better when there is not much sunlight. Some souls do, too. Most of us would prefer to travel by day, but it is possible, sometimes necessary, to go by night.

Another danger, closely related to the first, is that of insisting on some comforting sign before we are willing to trust. Often the only sign given is a sign pointing to the wilderness. That sign may be a dissatisfaction with self, a discontent with mummified traditions or the urgency of appealing need. Whatever the occasion of our spiritual pilgrimage may be, the important fact is that it is the work of God. Even the wilderness is friendly if God is there. Mark records that when our Lord was tempted in the wilderness, he "was with the wild beasts; and the angels ministered unto him" (1:13). Jesus' greatest service came after the wilderness experience. The road to the Promised Land of the Israelites went by way of the wilderness.

God uses time and patience—ours and his—to bless these experiences for our spiritual growth. In many cases, we eventually see that some of our doubts were about matters of marginal importance; these doubts are then dissolved in larger concerns and certainties. In other cases, we come to realize that our doubts were basically self-doubt, peculiarities of temperament, or sheer prejudice. There may be still other reasons, but God always brings matters to a successful conclusion for one who is willing to be taught and led.

O God of truth, lead me to a better understanding of myself and of those things that should engage my faith and loyalty. O Lord, I believe; help my unbelief. Amen.

Topic: The Faith That Moves Mountains
TEXT: Matt. 14:31, 17:14–20; Mark 4:40; Luke 24:25

Did you ever envy the faith of another? It isn't hard to do. When you see a person radiant with optimism and confident that God will bring forth unfailing blessings, you can wistfully imagine what a difference such a faith would make in your own life.

Jesus, however, spent most of his time with the weak in faith. He was compelled to say to his disciples, in exasperation, "O ye of little faith!" They had seen his miracles. They had heard his teachings. They had lived in his presence. Yet they were men of little faith.

It seems that Jesus' disciples were well assured of God's power and of their Lord's ability to do signs and wonders. But they could hardly believe that they could have anything to do with it. It was this awkward faith with which Jesus had to work.

Nevertheless, Jesus bore with them: with Simon Peter and his unpredictable impulsiveness; with Thomas and his genial skepticism; with James and John and their immaturity and selfishness. Jesus believed, "If ye have faith as a grain of mustard seed, ye shall say unto this mountain, Remove hence to yonder place; and it shall remove; and nothing shall be impossible unto you."

The faith of the disciples was lamentably small, but given time and exercise, it removed the mountains of exclusiveness that shut off the soul of Israel from the rest of the world and it caused the followers of Jesus to be called, "These that have turned the world upside down." One day they ran like scared rabbits when trouble struck, but later they walked triumphantly into prison and up to crosses. It was the undaunted faith of Jesus that made the little faith of his disciples so mighty.

Is your faith small? That does not matter. The Lord's faith in you is great. You too can make the mountains disappear!

Strong Son of God, help me to value the modest faith you have given to me. Grant that I may not despise the day of small things but may stir up the gift of God within me. Amen.

Topic: The Effect of Wrong Living on Faith
TEXT: Ps. 139; Heb. 3:13

If I wished to practice my sins in peace, the first thing I would do would be to try to get rid of God. I would make quite a fuss over things in my religion that I could not understand. I would refuse to accept anything I could not understand. I would eliminate one item after another from my faith until at last I came to God himself, and by that time getting rid of God would not be so impossible a task. With God out of the picture, why should I feel guilty if I fail to live up to the moral code associated with this God?

This is not a far-fetched supposition. Of course an individual would not arrive at unbelief so obviously. The unbelief that grows out of moral problems transpires slowly and subtly. It may require the disobedience of years to bring its result. But it takes place in essentially the manner I have stated.

It is ironic, however, that the God thus eliminated is not the true and living God at all. The true God cannot be banished as if he were a mere figment of the imagination. His truth comes back to haunt our minds, his love to haunt our hearts.

The Laws of God are written into the very structure of the universe, and their presence is inescapable. With the psalmist we must say, "Whither shall I go from they presence?" We can banish an idol, but not the Lord God.

The God whom people try to eradicate is a God they fear will make them unhappy. Seeking happiness, these people imagine that they can find it in their own way. They get rid of God (so they believe); they enthrone their selfishness, lust, and passion; then they proceed to make a mess of life.

Our only hope for true and lasting happiness is in God. He has what we want but sometimes try to find apart from him.

The wise thing to do is to face our sins, admit them, and try to find a better solution than one we invent. If you are unsure of God, you need not worry, provided you are sincere enough to be willing to do what is right, regardless of what that is. Jesus was willing to submit his person and teaching to examination and experiment: "If any man's will is to do his will, he shall know whether the teaching is from God or whether I am speaking on my own authority" (John 7:17 RSV).

The reason that some people find it hard to believe in God is that they find it hard to forsake their sins.

"Search me, O God, and know my heart; try me and know my thoughts; and see if there be any wicked way in me, and lead me in the way everlasting."

Topic: The Things That Strengthen Faith
TEXT: Eph. 6:17; Rom. 15:4; Matt. 7:7, 18:20; Heb. 10:25; Matt. 7:21; John 7:17.

Because faith is the key to spiritual life and growth, the degree of our achievement and progress will be determined by the strength of our faith. The amount of faith, however, is not so important as the quality of faith. If the faith is real it can become strong.

A devout and intelligent study of the Bible will strengthen faith. The Bible is the inspired record of God's dealings with his people. In it we learn that God deals with his people not capriciously but righteously and lovingly. In it we discover the principles underlying his moral commands. In it is a message that is vindicated by personal experience. A careless, impatient, superficial reading of the Scriptures may result in a weakening of faith; but a serious, deliberate, profound study of the Bible will make one stronger in faith the further one goes.

A devout and intelligent use of prayer will strengthen faith. Prayer is the activity in which one begins to translate into experience what one has assumed to be true. Prayer breathes spiritual life into the dry bones of memorized Scriptures and perfunctory service. Prayer teaches the depth of the wisdom of the love of God through the discipline of unanswered prayer, as well as through the triumph of answered prayer.

A constant and discerning experience of Christian fellowship will strengthen faith. One believer is only half a believer. It takes the shared faith of others to round out our own faith. How divinely wise was our Lord when he sent out the disciples two by two. How humanly practical were the early Christians when they stayed close together in companionship, in study, in worship, and in work. The chill of loneliness does not strengthen faith; the supporting and nurturing warmth of Christian fellowship is absolutely necessary.

Obedience to the Christian mandate of clean living will strengthen faith. There will then be no need to distort the truth to rationalize our shabby character, no need to discard our faith to make room for things that do not belong in the Christian life. Our faith, thus free of the barnacles of selfishness, lust, envy, and hate, can then sail the high seas of courage and adventure.

Christian service will strengthen faith. Some of us are pale, stumbling, gasping believers whose amens and hallelujahs are too weak to intimidate the devil's housecat, precisely because we have grown our faith as sheltered spectators rather than as active participants in the onward march of the Kingdom of God. Give your faith, and it shall be given to you—good measure, pressed down, shaken together, and running over shall your heavenly Father give to you.

Heavenly Father, help me to grow in the grace and knowledge of my Lord and Savior Jesus Christ, through the strengthening of my faith. Grant me the courage, the will, and the persistence to do those things that cause faith to grow. Amen.

Topic: Is the Christian Faith Unique?
TEXT: Gal. 4:4; Rom. 12:8–10; 1 Cor. 15:1–4; Jude 3

We cannot subscribe to the ill-informed theory that one religion is just as good as another. There are religions that teach people to kill their enemies, that make human sacrifice a part of their devotion, that include sexual immoralities in their worship. Is the Christian faith no better than these? Of course it is! Every intelligent person would concede that. There are many religions that would not condone these atrocities. Even so, the Christian faith is to be distinguished from all religions.

The Christian faith differs from the many religions of the world in this important way: the Christian faith is grounded in facts, in history. What we believe about God comes from what he has revealed himself to be in certain decisive acts in human history. When the Bible speaks of "the mighty acts of God," it speaks of the means by which God made himself known to people.

The deliverance of the Israelites from slavery in Egypt was a mighty act of God in which Israel became conscious of the Lord's peculiar love and of his choice of them to carry out his purposes on Earth. As a result, Israel entered into a covenant that pledged the nation to obey the Lord God.

The incarnation of Jesus Christ was a mighty act of God in which sin and death were met in mortal combat, in which God gave Jesus Christ the victory, and in which those who trust in him become "more than conquerors."

Our faith is not based, therefore, on fine-spun theories or even on the most excellent ethical principles. It is founded on what God himself has revealed and proved to be true. When one takes hold of Jesus Christ, the secret is disclosed: "In him we have redemption through his blood, the forgiveness of our trespasses, according to the riches of his grace which he lavished upon us. For he has made known to us in all wisdom and insight the mystery of his will" (Eph. 1:7–9).

Heavenly Father, give me, I pray, the faith and willingness to trust your love proffered in your mighty acts. Anchor my soul to the truth in Jesus Christ. Amen.

Topic: The Foundations of Christian Assurance
TEXT: Ps. 37; Rom. 8:24; Heb. 6:19

Religious believers at times marvel at the seeming courage of some unbelievers.

Destitute of ultimate hope, the unbeliever grimly plods on. He has reduced life to an irreducible minimum and has accepted that as his own ultimate reality; he can never be disappointed, for he expects nothing. Bertrand Russell, writing from this point of view, once said, "Only on the firm foundation of unyielding despair can the soul's habitation, henceforth, be safely built."

But what kind of life is that? It is a life without tears, but also a life without real love. It is a life of detachment from suffering and pain, but also a life devoid of true sympathy. The cold grandeur of it does not commend itself to the heart in which the love of God is poured out through the Holy Spirit. The Christian life burns with aspiration and is redolent with hope. It is affirmation, not negation. It suffers, but it is glorified.

The Christian hope is built upon the love of God. Assurance comes from the conviction that the purpose of God toward us is a purpose of love and that whatever he does or will do is good.

The history of the Lord's dealings with his people discloses a purpose of love. Through slavery and deliverance, exaltation and chastisement, God's concern and care have been manifest.

When, in the fullness of time, God sent Jesus Christ, his unique Son, the world was confronted with the love of God in all of its vast dimensions. If God the Father is like God the Son, then he can be forever completely trusted. Thus we can anticipate the ultimate fulfillment of our highest aspirations and a reward for what we have presented to God upon this Earth's wide altar.

O God of grace, I trust my all to your love, assured that those who hope in you will not be put to shame. Through Jesus Christ my Lord. Amen.

Topic: The Things That Test Our Assurance
TEXT: Matt. 4:1–12

It is hard to believe that the heroic servants of Jesus Christ had no discouraging moments. I believe that they gained their triumphant hope by knowing and overcoming disappointment and despair.

Once we get the certainty of hope, we discover that it is buffeted from many sides. Rains descend. The flood rises menacingly. The wind blows without rest or mercy. Then we sigh prayerfully, "O Thou who changest not, abide with me."

If we know what to expect, perhaps we shall not be so easily upset when upsetting things happen.

Here, as in other connections, the opinions of other people have powerful influence. Some people are very much like the chameleon that changes color to suit its surroundings. We know people who find it easy to believe when others believe, too. But they are troubled by doubt and fear when others waver. In the interest of our steadfastness, however, we have to learn that a majority vote in the court of human opinion does not alter truth. Jesus did not ignore the burning aspirations of his contemporaries, but if he had tried to build his faith on their conflicting ideas, the world could never have looked to him as the Savior.

Again, delay in the fulfillment of their schedule causes some people to fear that the things they have confidently expected will never come to pass. "Hope deferred maketh the heart sick." More than that, hope deferred can all but destroy an ill-informed or impatient type of hope. The first Christians had to face the problem of the delayed return of the Lord. They went about with great courage in the midst of persecution, saying triumphantly and joyfully, one to another, "Maranatha—the Lord is coming!" But though the Lord delayed his coming and though the disciples surely felt keen disappointment, they were doggedly loyal, and hope did not die in their hearts. They knew that whether they slept or were alive at his coming, they belonged to him and they would be with him forever.

In the last place, a change of feeling makes some of us jittery about the future. Our emotions have more to do with the chemical states of our bodies than many realize. Most of us, however, know how our moods are affected by hunger and fatigue. It is to be expected, then, that even our spiritual outlook can be sorely tested by feelings that have absolutely nothing to do with the certainty of what we have believed. A clinical report on John Bunyan, author of *The Pilgrim's Progress,* would show him to have been a highly neurotic person. He was assailed by doubts and fears all his life, but he refused to be overcome by them and rightly attributed them to Satan. He persisted in believing in the love of God and held tenaciously to God's promises, regardless of black, noisome moods. He was stubborn enough, thank God, to believe that nothing, not even his feelings, could separate him from the love of God in Christ.

When I am tempted, O Lord, to resign myself to what I can see and feel, help me to place my baffled faith again in those things that are unseen and eternal. Amen.

Topic: The Blessed Hope
TEXT: Acts 1:9–11; Heb. 9:28; Matt. 24:36; Phil. 3:20–21; 1 Pet. 5:4; 1 John 3:2

Many wild ideas and predictions about our Lord's coming again have been advanced. So much so that earnest believers, in their bewilderment, put the thought out of their minds and try not to think about it. But the promises of Christ and the undaunted expectations of the first Christians keep bobbing up and compelling us to tackle the problem of the meaning of the Day of the Lord.

To leave our Lord's coming again out of our faith is to make all life a tragedy, all hope a farce, and all love an illusion. For his return signifies the ultimate fruition of all that is good, and the final defeat of all that is evil.

When Christ returns, it will not be a different Christ that we meet. It will be the same Christ. At his first coming, his righteous love meant salvation for some and judgment for others. All depended on the attitude of the person confronted. So it will be when he comes again. We shall have to do with the same God of grace. Therefore, it becomes possible to "love his appearing."

That great day will signal the final defeat of evil. All creation shares in our fallen condition. Therefore the evil in our hearts has its counterpart in the reckless elements. Paul saw that God had subjected the whole creation in hope. The divine purpose will be realized when evil's long day has come to an end. "For he must reign till he hath put all enemies under his feet" (1 Cor. 15:25). All that is contrary to his purpose will be either redeemed or destroyed.

Therefore the Lord's return will mean the triumph of God and his righteousness, and at the same time the triumph of those who have trusted in him. The Day of the Lord is a day of light, not darkness, for those who love him. It is a new beginning, not the end of anything good. "And he who sat upon the throne said, 'Behold, I make all things new'" (Rev. 21:5 RSV).

Believing these things, one's life on Earth in the here and now is changed. One can never be the same after perceiving the glorious destiny to be shared with Jesus Christ. "Journeys end in lovers meeting." "And every man that hath this hope in him purifieth himself, even as he is pure" (1 John 3:3).

The sum of it all is this: believing steadfastly in our Lord's coming again adds a new dimension to life. Some people look at life horizontally and are terribly frightened. Many dreadful things could happen and, no doubt, will happen. But when life is regarded vertically—that is, with God taken into account—the worst that people or Satan can do will not overthrow the ultimate purpose of God. This indicates that life has meaning beyond all human measurements. "We, according to his promise, look for new heavens and a new Earth, wherein dwelleth righteousness" (2 Peter 3:13).

But a word of warning should be added. Many people have been denied the comfort and inspiration of the Lord's return because of repulsive fanaticisms and wrong interpretations by sincere but misguided Christians. It behooves us, therefore, to seek to understand the deeper meaning of this doctrine so that its strength and purpose may give us the solid basis for a fresh and undaunted hope and may induce others also to "love his appearing."

O my Savior, grant that my life may know the vigor of confidence in thy return, and that no sin of mine may keep me from saying, Even so, come, Lord Jesus.

Topic: Heaven
Text: John 14:1–4; Phil. 1:20–26; 1 Cor. 15; Rev. 21

On a questionnaire about worries, one member of a civic club indicated that his chief worry was whether he would go to heaven. There would be a better world and happier people if this became a more widespread concern, if this concern was implemented by study, and if study resulted in assurance. "For every man that hath this hope in him purifieth himself even as he is pure" (1 John 3:3).

When we go to the Bible we find in different places various emphases with regard to the future life of the redeemed. At one time we read of the immediate bliss of those who are absent from the body and present with the Lord. At another time we read of the ultimate glory that comes through the resurrection of the body. There should be no confusion, however, with different phases and stages of the same general experience.

The Bible does not speak of a natural immortality. Immortality belongs naturally to God and he gives it to those who are in Christ Jesus. "This mortal must put on immortality" (1 Cor. 15:13).

The faith of the Bible is resurrection faith, not the pagan Greek idea of a natural immortality. Both the Old and the New Testaments affirm that there shall be resurrection; that is, the redeemed will be resurrected personalities in glorified bodies, more than disembodied spirits floating aimlessly in space or seeking another incarnation on Earth. Paul wrote, "But our commonwealth is in heaven, and from it we await a Savior, the Lord Jesus Christ, who will change our lowly body to be like his glorious body, by the power that enables him even to subject all things to himself" (Phil. 3:21–22 RSV).

We must remember, however, the words of our Lord to the penitent on the cross: "Today thou shalt be with me in paradise." There is no long wait before one enters into a state that is "far better" (Phil. 1:23).

A great deal of mystery surrounds the future life, for we are yet little more than unborn babes living in the womb of time. Human experience and biblical revelation, however, tell us all we need to know at present about the life to come.

(a) *Heaven is the fulfillment of the Lord's purpose for humankind.* The designs of God, so beautiful and meaningful in their beginning and in their development, will not end in ashes and dust. We are more than an ephemeral plaything of the deity.

(b) *Heaven is a corollary of the Christian faith.* Until Jesus, even the Jewish ideas of immortality were nebulous and unsatisfying. But Jesus assured us, "Because I live, ye shall live also" (John 14:19). Immortality is life by the power and in the personal love of God.

(c) *Heaven is respite from the fragmentary and imperfect, from the painful and disillusioning.* It is strength and freedom for new and eternally interesting tasks.

(d) *Heaven is reunion.* The Savior who redeemed us and others who have poured meaning and value into our lives by their sacrifices, their love, and their companionship will be there to make heaven complete. We shall see our Redeemer as he is, and we shall know one another with complete understanding, appreciation, and love, even as God thus knows us (compare 1 John 3:2; 1 Cor. 13:12).

O God of love and salvation, give us ever fresh glimpses of your eternal purpose, that we may be assured that the living of the Christian life is worth every sacrifice. For Jesus' sake, amen.

SECTION VII

A LITTLE TREASURY
OF ILLUSTRATIONS

ANGER.   Anger, in the prayerful hands of the people of God, can rise to be the channel of concern, commitment, and love that it deserves in the Church. And by the grace of God, with patience and Christian sensitivity, anger can become primarily a constructive force for the expression of ethical concern, personal commitment, and corporate action. After all, has not history shown us that some of the most important steps in the lives of nations and people have occurred only when they have become angry enough at some wrong that they have determined to invest themselves in its redeeming counterpart.—Daniel G. Bagby[1]

TODAY'S OPPORTUNITY.   Each one of us has certain opportunities in life that must be viewed in the light of the fact that time waits for no one. But praise be to God! We have today! How many "todays" we shall have, we cannot say. But we have today. Therefore, if the termination of any part of life, or of all life here, is to be a time of rejoicing in what has been accomplished, rather than a time of regret, then we must live today in the proper way before it is too late. How well the psalmist has expressed it: "So teach us to count our days that we might gain a wise heart" (Psalm 90:12). This, then, is my prayer: "God, give us a wise heart from the awareness of how rapidly time passes."—Kenneth A. Mortonson[2]

LIVING WITH DANGER.   The lesson found in any object will depend on the context in which we consider its meaning. For David, the arrow was a symbol of friendship. At another time, assuming that David wrote Psalm 91, the arrow appeared as an instrument of destruction (compare Ps. 91:5). Paul also used the symbol of the arrow as a sign of pending danger. He advised the Ephesians to ". . . take up the shield of faith, with which you can extinguish all the flaming arrows of the evil one" (Eph. 6:16).

The arrow is an excellent symbol of imminent danger. In silence, it can approach from any direction. When it hits our unprotected skin, it can do great damage. The same can be said of the thrust of evil and our unprotected soul. The impulse to do what is evil can come from anywhere. When it enters our life, it can create burning desires and turbulence in the heart and mind. If it is not removed, it will fester and infect the whole being.—Kenneth A. Mortonson[3]

LANGUAGE IN ACTION.   A plumber we know used his backhoe to look for a broken sewer line under a neighbor's lawn and was successful in his search. When asked by the lady

---

[1]*Understanding Anger in the Church* (Nashville: Broadman Press, 1979), pp. 149–150.
[2]*What? A Biblical and Personal Study of Life After Death* (Lima, Ohio: Fairway Press, 2002), p. 11.
[3]*What Do You See?* (Lima, Ohio: Fairway Press, 1999), p. 27.

of the house, "How can you stand that stifling smell?" his reply was, "Smells like bacon and eggs to a plumber, ma'am." The plumber's frame of the situation, focusing on his economic gain, probably helps him to tolerate a smell that most of us find repugnant.

As this example demonstrates, it is easy to create alternative views of the world with a mere turn of a phrase. Highlight the negatives, and a problem looks overwhelming. Accentuate the positives, and a solution seems just around the corner. Choose an image ("stifling smell"), and you have highlighted one aspect of your subject; choose another ("bacon and eggs"), and a new aspect emerges.—Gail T. Fairhurst and Robert A. Sarr[4]

ESTRANGEMENT.   We have all been quick to condemn the elder son, and rightly so, but there is something of his spirit in us all. Like him we have spoiled the atmosphere and disturbed the harmony of our Father's "house." We have polluted the world of nature. We have upset its delicate balance through our greed and through our indifference to the rights of others. We have ruined our lakes and rivers by making them the repositories of our waste materials and we have scarred our hills and mountains with our surface mining and our lack of reforestation. As a result our world is no longer a "Garden of Eden." It reflects and mirrors our estrangement both from God and from one another.—Samuel Robert Weaver[5]

FACING DEATH AND LIFE.   One of the main tasks of effective psychotherapy is to help people gain enough faith in the process of living so that they are willing to face death and dissolution, trusting in resurrection. A great deal of neurosis and psychosis arises from the resolute desires of individuals to avoid the unpleasantness of death and the effort of preparing for rebirth. Nothing binds one more firmly to emotional illness and immaturity than this childish requirement that life be pleasant at all times. Dying and rising are part of the eternal process. If we insist on wasting our lives hoping in vain for some other way out, we never get down to the real business of seeking and finding life and light and the kingdom of love. I often wish reality were different, but this seems to be what life is like.—Morton T. Kelsey[6]

GOD'S MERCY.   God has mercy on us. He says "yes" to us, he wills to be on our side, to be our God against all odds. Indeed against all odds, because we do not deserve this mercy, because, as we rightly suppose, he should say no to us all. But he does not say no he says yes. He is not against us; he is for us. This is God's mercy.—Karl Barth[7]

DEFEATING FEAR.   I know a fellow who has a fear of crowds. When encircled by large groups, his breath grows short, panic surfaces, and he begins to sweat like a sumo wrestler in a sauna. He received some help, curiously, from a golfing buddy.

The two were at a movie theatre, waiting their turn to enter, when fear struck again. The crowd closed in like a forest. He wanted out and fast. His buddy told him to take a few deep breaths. Then he helped manage the crisis by reminding him of the golf course.

---

[4]*The Art of Framing* (San Francisco: Jossey-Bass, 1996), p. 7.
[5]*The Gospel in the Gospel* (Charleston, W.V.: Mountain State Press, 1997), pp. 121–122.
[6]*Afterlife* (New York: Paulist Press, 1979), p. 250.
[7]*Deliverance to the Captives* (New York: HarperCollins, 1961), p. 87.

"When you are hitting your ball out of the rough, and you are surrounded by trees, what do you do?"

"I look for an opening."

"You don't stare at the trees?"

"Of course not. I find an opening and focus on hitting the ball through it."

"Do the same in the crowd. When you feel the panic, don't focus on the people; focus on the opening."

Good counsel in golf. Good counsel in life. Rather than focus on the fear, focus on the solution.

That's what Jesus did.

That's what David did.

And that's what the writer of Hebrews urges us to do. "Let us run with endurance the race that is set before us, looking unto Jesus, the author and finisher of our faith" (Heb. 12:1–2 NKJV).—Max Lucado[8]

MIXED MESSAGES.   Kids are receiving mixed messages when it comes to morals and values. Let's take sexuality, for example. From home they hear, "Don't do *it*" but not much more about the subject. From church (although it is hopefully changing for the better) they often hear either silence or, "Don't do *it* because *it's* dirty, rotten, and ugly." From the secular media they often hear, "Do *it*." The secular media is thrilled to sing, write, and make movies about sexual promiscuity. Kids today are much more influenced when it comes to issues like drugs, sex, and rock-'n'-roll from the secular media than from their mom and dad. It's time to bring it back home when it comes to teaching our children about morals and values. Morals and values education belongs first and foremost in the home.—Jim Burns[9]

TIME FOR THE CHILDREN.   I disagree with the parenting specialists who say that if you can't give your kids a quantity of time, then give them quality time. I think your kids deserve both. I find that my finest discussions with my own children come during the quantity times, not the so-called quality times. I'll be driving one of the kids someplace and—bingo!—the conversation goes to a very important topic. I just slow the car down and get in as much time as possible.—Jim Burns[10]

GOD'S RECTIFYING WORK.   I have to realize that what will finally be retained by God is not necessarily what I have done with the greatest piety, morality, faith, or searching out the will of God. . . .

All the acts which I have done expressly to serve thee, and also all the acts which I believe to be neutral and purely human, and also all the acts which I know to be disobedience and sin, I put in thy hands, O God, my Lord and Savior; take them now that they are finished; prove them thyself to see which enter into thy work and which deserve only judgment and death; use, cut, trim, reset, readjust, now that it is longer I who can decide or know, now

---

[8]*Traveling Light* (Nashville, Tenn.: W Publishing Group, 2001), pp. 99–100.

[9]*How to Be a Happy, Healthy Family* (Nashville, Tenn.: Word, 2001), p. 37.

[10]*How to Be a Happy, Healthy Family* (Nashville, Tenn.: Word, 2001), p. 107.

that what is done is done, what I have written I have written. It is thou that canst make a line true by taking it up into thy truth. It is thou that canst make an action right by using it to accomplish thy design, which is mysterious as I write now but bright in the eternity which thou hast revealed to me in thy Son. Amen.—Jacques Ellul[11]

TESTIMONY.   A little boy told his mother that he believed in Christ and wanted to be baptized. Since he was quite young, she was concerned. She wanted him to understand the significance of his decision. She explained that baptism brought some big responsibilities, like witnessing to his friends about his decision. "That won't work, Mom," he replied. "By the time I get to school I'll be dried off and they won't be able to tell." When members of a congregation are connected with Christ, people in the community can see it—even if they are dried off from baptism. It shows up in their serving.—Herb Miller[12]

INSPIRATION OF BIBLE.   It is to the God who is active in history, redeeming it and infusing it with meaning, that the Scriptures ultimately point. The inspired authors and editors of the Bible perceived giving an account of Israel's past as telling "his story." They saw God's hand at work in the calling forth of a consecrated people in patriarchal times, in the deliverance of Hebrew slaves from Egyptian captivity, and in the rise of a mighty Israelite nation in a land God provided. They heard God's voice in the ancient precepts from Sinai, in the lilting songs of David, in the sage wisdom of the prophets and apostles, and in the profound aphorisms of the Sermon on the Mount. They perceived God's faithfulness in the resilience and restoration of an often wayward people through times of oppression and exile. And they sensed God's love in the utter selflessness of a carpenter from Nazareth who "while we still were sinners . . . died for us" (Rom. 5:8).

It is as a witness to that sacred history, to the mighty acts of Israel's God in the affairs of nations and in the lives of people of faith, that the Bible most resoundingly sets itself apart from the other ancient texts. More than the precision of its historiography, it is the power of its inspired testimony and the resonance of its timeless message that has earned the Bible the fidelity and trust of countless millions through the centuries who, having read and believed, have encountered in their own experience the self-revealing God of the universe.—Jeffrey L. Sheler[13]

IN LOVE WITH LIFE.   *For your love to last forever, you must be in love with life.* Think in terms of the oxygen-mask instructions given by airline flight attendants. They say that passengers flying with children or others who need assistance should fasten their own masks first before trying to help someone else. If you don't make the choice to reach for oxygen for yourself, there's no point in your trying to help anyone else. You won't have the strength or ability to do it. That's how it is with love: Learn to love your own life first, and then you have the resources to give and receive love.—Gary Smalley[14]

---

[11]*The Politics of God and the Politics of Man* (Grand Rapids, Mich.: Eerdmans, 1972), pp. 71–72.
[12]*The Vital Congregation* (Nashville, Tenn.: Abingdon Press, 1990), p. 132,
[13]*Is the Bible True?* (San Francisco: HarperSanFrancisco/Zondervan, 1999), p. 256.
[14]*Making Love Last Forever* (Nashville, Tenn.: W Publishing Group, 1996), p. 7.

MONEY.   People can waste their money and their lives by directing all their wealth into temporal, earthly investments. History records in the words of famous wealthy people that there is no joy in such a life. John D. Rockefeller lamented, "I have made many millions, but they have brought me no happiness." Cornelius Vanderbilt commented, "The care of millions is too great a load. . . . There is no pleasure in it." John Jacob Astor once called himself "the most miserable man on earth." And Henry Ford looked back to a more carefree time when he "was happier doing mechanic's work."—John MacArthur[15]

GOD'S ACTION IN US.   God's love is God's ultimate action and it is given human form in Jesus Christ, and if God can invest himself and his love in the unlikely form of man born of a woman, who suffered as we suffer and died as we shall die, dare we invest less in humanity than God? Dare we invest less in ourselves and in our world than in God? Ought we not to take the sign of God's love for us in Christ as a sign that we are lovable and the world is worth loving? If that is so, can there be any possible limit to what we can attempt as God's representatives in the world? . . .

We become, then, you and I, not simply the objects of a benevolent, a wrathful, or an indifferent God, pieces of furniture to be arranged at will; rather, we are licensed, as it were, by the Incarnation to be the action, the activity of God in the world, for it is through us, our patience, that God will be known and served; indeed, the acts of God become the actions of the men and women who know and love him, and who seek to serve him.—Peter J. Gomes[16]

DECISIONS.   To make our decisions in faith is to make them in view of the fact that no single man or group or historical time is the Church, but that there is a Church of faith in which we do our partial, relative work and on which we count. It is to make them in view of the fact that Christ is risen from the dead, and is not only the head of the Church but the redeemer of the world. It is to make them in view of the fact that the world of culture—man's achievement—exists within the world of grace—God's Kingdom.—H. Richard Niebuhr[17]

BELIEF.   Belief is . . . not what some would have us believe. It is not a well-fluffed nest, or a well-defended castle on a high hill. It is more like a rope bridge over a scenic gorge, sturdy but swinging back and forth, with plenty of light and plenty of air but precious little to hang on to except the stories you have heard: that it is the best and only way across, that it is possible, that it will bear your weight.

All you have to do is believe in the bridge more than you believe in the gorge, but fortunately you do not have to believe in it all by yourself. There are others to believe it with you, and even some to believe it for you when your own beliefs wear thin. They have crossed the bridge ahead of you and are waiting on the other side. You can talk to them if you like, as you step into the air, putting one foot ahead of the other, just that: just one step at a time.—Barbara Brown Taylor[18]

---

[15]*Whose Money Is It, Anyway: A Biblical Guide to Using God's Wealth* (Nashville, Tenn.: Word, 2000), pp. 21–22.
[16]*Sermons* (New York: Morrow, 1998), p. 179.
[17]*Christ and Culture* (New York: HarperCollins, 1951), p. 256.
[18]*The Preaching Life* (Boston: Cowley, 1993), pp. 93–94.

THE DOXOLOGY.   "For thine is the kingdom, and the power, and the glory, for ever. Amen" (Matt. 6:13b).

The conclusion of this divine prayer, commonly called the doxology, is a solemn thanksgiving, a compendious acknowledgement of the attributes and works of God. "For thine is the kingdom"—the sovereign right of all things that are or ever were created; yea, thy kingdom is an everlasting kingdom, and thy dominion endureth throughout all ages. "The power"—the executive power whereby you govern all things in your everlasting kingdom, whereby you do whatsoever pleases you, in all places of your dominion. "And the glory"—the praise due from every creature, for your power, and the mightiness of your kingdom, and for all your wondrous works which you work from everlasting, and shall do, world without end, "forever and ever! Amen!" So be it!—John Wesley[19]

WITNESS OF A LIFE.   Queen Esther modeled seven secrets for having an Esther Effect.

Secret #1: Self-Confidence. Esther had confidence in her ability to fulfill the plan that God had for her. . . .

Secret #2: Self-Control. Esther had a passion about her purpose, yet she exercised great self-control. She took the time to plan how to best achieve her purpose, then she waited patiently on God's perfect timing. . . .

Secret #3: Courage. Esther calculated the risk of her actions and acted courageously. Courage means acting decisively, even in the face of risk, in whatever ways God directs you. . . .

Secret #4: Communication. Esther knew the art of listening as well as speaking clearly and courteously. . . .

Secret #5: Character. Esther had a strong character, and character dictates our attitudes and actions under pressure. . . .

Secret #6: Connection. Esther remained emotionally connected with those who could give her support through her difficult time. . . .

Secret #7: Calm Assurance. Esther was patient and had faith in God's control of situations and events. . . .—Dianna Booher[20]

FAITH THAT DARES.   Abraham, our father in faith, is not the only one for whom God did staggering things. He is also an invitation to believe and trust and risk and relinquish. He is the one who was fully convinced that God was able to do what God had promised (Rom. 4:21). Abraham was, in an awesome moment of faith, prepared to receive God's newness that was against all probability, but that set his life utterly new. Abraham might have said "Yes, but." He might have, if he were embarrassed and sophisticated. Such faith, however, is not enacted by those who are embarrassed. It is modeled by the daring who sing songs, who receive gifts, who make journeys, who confess more than they understand and who claim more than they explain. Faith is enacted by those who trust God, who imagines well beyond our resistant suppositions. Such imagination requires a dying and yields utterly new life.—Walter Brueggemann[21]

---

[19]*The John Wesley Reader,* compiled by Al Bryant (Waco, Tex.: Word Books, 1983), p. 78.
[20]*The Esther Effect* (Nashville: W Publishing Group, n.d.), pp. 20–22.
[21]*The Threat of Life* (Minneapolis, Minn.: Augsburg Fortress, 1996), p. 8.

HIS CALLING WILL BE BIGGER THAN YOU ARE.   The kind of assignments God gives in the Bible are always God-sized. They are always beyond what people can do because He wants to demonstrate His nature, His strength, His provision, and His kindness to His people and to a watching world. That is the only way the world will come to know Him. *Then the Jews were amazed and said, "How does He know the Scriptures, since He hasn't been trained?" Jesus answered them, "My teaching isn't Mine, but is from the One who sent me"* (John 7:15–16).—Henry Blackaby[22]

OUR PAINFUL YESTERDAYS.   Recently we said farewell to Charles Schultz, creator of the comic strip *Peanuts*. Some of you may recall one *Peanuts* strip where Linus, feeling anxious, says, "I guess it's wrong, always to be worrying about tomorrow. Maybe we should think only about today." Charlie Brown replies, "No, that's giving up. I'm still hoping that yesterday will get better." I need this channel marker called "Priorities! Put God first!" because only God can forgive and only forgiveness can make yesterday better!—William G. Enright[23]

TENSIONS.   We live with tensions illustrated by a caustic repartee between George Bernard Shaw and Winston Churchill. Shaw sent Churchill two tickets for the opening night of one of his plays, with a note: "Come and bring a friend—if you have one." Churchill wrote back a regret for opening night, but promised to come the second night, "If there is one."—James W. Crawford[24]

THE CROSS AND GLORY.   On the cross we see the depths which Jesus plumbed in his complete identification with the human situation. *"My God, my God,"* he said, *"why hast thou forsaken me?"* (Matt. 27:46; Mark 15:34). Many of Jesus' sayings are uninventable, but this one is supremely such.

Jesus was beginning to quote Psalm 22, so this saying of Jesus is not so much, as it were, a personal saying, but rather the beginning of the psalm, which Jesus was quoting to himself to remind himself of the servant of God in the ancient times who had begun in shame and humiliation and who had ended in confidence and glory.—William Barclay[25]

NEED FOR FATHER.   Basically, everyone needs a father. The father has a vital role. The mother represents nature, but the father introduces the son and the daughter to social relationships.

From your mother you get your body.

From your father you get your role in the social world.

The son has to play a role like that of his father, so the father is a model, either a positive or a negative one. You may be disgusted with the kind of life your father lives, but you have that model, and responding negatively to it will be your life. If he's not there, it's almost impossible to relate effectively from where you are in your family to the outside world.

---

[22]*Experiencing the Word Through the Gospels* (Nashville, Tenn.: Holman Bible, 1999), p. 230.
[23]*Channel Markers* (Louisville: Geneva Press, 2001), p. 9.
[24]*Worthy to Praise Jesus* (Cleveland: Pilgrim Press, 1991), p. 49.
[25]*Jesus and the Cross* (Louisville, Ky.: Westminster/John Knox Press, 2001), p. 31.

For the girl, the father is the first intimate relationship to the male principle in some way or other. With the father gone, the mother must play both roles, and I think the child, down deep, blames the mother for there being no father there. It's a sense of "you have deprived me of the person who would have been absolutely my guide and my messenger."—Diane K. Osbon[26]

WITHOUT A DOUBT.   Faith is a spiritual muscle that needs to be exercised in order to prevent atrophy, which makes our entire spiritual body weak. Faith is first a decision, then an exercise in obedience, then a gift from God as it multiplied. Our first step of faith is taken when we decide we will receive Jesus. After that, every time we decide to trust the Lord for anything, we build that faith. And whenever we decide *not* to trust him, we tear it down. Faith is our daily decision to trust God.—Stormie Omartian[27]

HUMAN GRANDEUR AND MISERY.   A rabbi observed that a person should carry in a pocket two stones, one inscribed with "For my sake the world was created," and the other with "I am but dust and ashes." And each stone should be pulled out, as the occasion requires, to remind us of who we are in God's creation.—Bernhard W. Anderson[28]

HEALING POWER OF PRAYER.   That prayer is psychologically therapeutic for the supplicant, benefiting him independently of any benefit that may come to those for whom his supplications are asked, has been long widely recognized. Dr. Alexis Carrel, a highly original though much criticized thinker who won the Nobel Prize for his work on suturing blood vessels and further recognition for his work on cancer research, was quite definite in his medical opinion of the efficacy of prayer. He called it "the most powerful form of energy that one can generate," and he claimed that "its influence on the human mind and body is as demonstrable as that of secreting glands."—Geddes MacGregor[29]

FAITH'S PARADOX.   The Cross of Christ became for all time the supreme symbol of faith's paradox. The Crucifixion was the worst and saddest thing that ever happened through the wickedness of man, yet also the best and most glorious thing that ever happened through the wisdom and power and love of God.—D. M. Baillie[30]

FEAR OF REPENTANCE.   One Christian leader, asked why he never mentioned repentance, smiled and replied, "Get 'em first, let them see what Christianity is, and then they'll see their need to repent." Tragically, this attitude pervades the church not only because we're afraid the truth will scare newcomers, but because it might also drive a number of the nodding regulars right out of their comfortable pews.

Repentance can be a threatening message—and rightly so. The Gospel must be the bad news of the conviction of sin before it can be the good news of redemption. Because that message is unpalatable for many middle-class congregations preoccupied with protecting their

---

[26]*Reflections on the Art of Living: A Joseph Campbell Companion* (New York: HarperCollins, 1991), pp. 56–57.

[27]*Praying God's Will for Your Life* (Nashville, Tenn.: Thomas Nelson, 2001), p. 169.

[28]*Out of the Depths,* 3rd ed. (Louisville: Westminster/John Knox Press, 2000), p. 198.

[29]*He Who Lets Us Be* (New York: Seabury Press, 1975), p. 158.

[30]*Faith in God* (Edinburgh: T. & T. Clark, 1927), p. 303.

affluent lifestyles, many pastors endowed with a normal sense of self-preservation tiptoe war-ily around the subject. And the phenomenal growth of the electronic church has only aggra-vated this trend, for while the Sunday morning pew-dweller is trapped, unable to escape gracefully when a tough subject like repentance comes up, the TV viewer has only to flip a switch or go out to the refrigerator.—Charles Colson[31]

HOPE.   Do we need hope? Yes. May Christians hope? Yes. Are we ever beyond hope? No. Is the greatness of our hope an index of the graciousness of God? Yes. Does our hope of salva-tion bring joy, energy, faithfulness, and a desire to be one of God? Yes, yes, yes, yes. May we hope that God will use us each day to his glory, even though we are not as yet perfectly sanc-tified? Yes. Is this glorious good news? Yes.

Good hoping to you!—or as some say, here's hoping!—as a way of life, as a source of strength, and as a fountain of joy in the heart from which praise and prayer will flow out con-tinually.—J. I. Packer and Carolyn Nystrom[32]

THE HARDER PATH.   If I had been at Gethsemane, I would have slept with the others. (Actually, my wife says my snoring might have kept the others awake, so my secret hope is that God can use me even sleeping.)

You see, there is a big difference between salvation on the one hand—which God brings to us with grace abundant and to me in the firm confidence of my heart—and holiness on the other hand, which is our task to work out with God's grace. I am saved in the glory of God, but very much in need of holiness. I praise God, but cry to Jesus to be waked up more often, for longer periods of time. Jesus hears my selfish cries, Jesus listens to my materialistic ambi-tions, Jesus yawns through my superficial blather, and says, Wake up! I need to change my ways to keep awake. I need to be less selfish every day, one day at a time. I need to put mate-rial things in their proper places, not right in front of me where I like to keep them; and this is a daily struggle. I need to choose the harder path, not the easier, to accept the things I can-not fix or understand, and to engage those things with faith. I am very bad at these steps in holiness and I doze off all the time. I need help and encouragement, and mostly perseverance. I ought not sleep while the Lord prays in agony.—Robert Cummings Neville[33]

GROWING IN FAITH.   Someone asked a church deacon if he were a Christian. He replied, "In spots." All of us must make the same confession. God has graciously come to us in Jesus Christ, called us, given us faith and means of grace—yet our Christian faith and Christian life is often "spotty." We have days of faithfulness and days of failure. We begin in faith, gain nour-ishment for our faith—yet do not feel that we grow in faith. On a larger scale, our Christian lives are lived in the context of the Christian church. The church itself is faithful and unfaith-ful. It gives us birth, nourishes us, and then lets us down when it too will not grow in accord with God's Spirit or is downright "un-Christian" in some of its attitudes and practices. The Christian life is a "mixed bag," a path of "zig-zag" through the pressures and temptations of

---

[31]*Loving God* (Grand Rapids, Mich.: Zondervan, 1983), p. 95.
[32]*Never Beyond Hope* (Downers Grove, Ill.: Inter-Varsity Press, 2000), p. 20.
[33]*The God Who Beckons* (Nashville, Tenn.: Abington Press, 1999), pp. 26–27.

life. We know that if we are ever to finish our course and ultimately live in God's reign, it will be solely by God's loving and forgiving grace alone. We want to grow in our faith, but our frailties and sins are often stumbling blocks along the way.—Donald K. McKim[34]

A PHYSICIAN/PSYCHIATRIST'S NEED.   When my sister died, a pastor friend came to see us. He said to us, in praise of her faith: "She was a real pillar of the Church." Ah! If he had known what a fragile, unquiet, tormented, anguished soul she had! I am perhaps a little more solid than she was, at least at certain moments, when I am carried away by a strong conviction. But to others, I am very like her. Thirty years ago a friend came up to me in the street and greeted me, looking me in the eye: "Good morning, Paul, how are you?" It may seem astonishing that I remember such an ordinary question so clearly. But the tone in which it was spoken was not ordinary. I felt that it meant, "You too have your difficulties and problems. Do you need any help?" I was so moved that I was afraid I was going to cry.—Paul Tournier[35]

WHAT ONLY GOD CAN DO.   A few years ago, Carl F. H. Henry and I were driving around Buckingham Palace on our way to Westminster Chapel, and I said quite casually and spontaneously, "Carl, do you have any regrets about life? What would you do if you could relive your life?"

He paused and then he said, "I would remember that only God can turn water into wine."

So often we all try to make things happen, and consequently we lose joy from seeing what God alone would actually do.—R. T. Kendall[36]

A SAINT'S REPENTANCE.   Augustine repented the sins of his ministry, all the rancorous dividedness, all the failed efforts at love and peace, that afflicted one unable to retire into some ivory tower. We know he blamed himself for some of this—in 423, when he was turning seventy, he had offered to retire from office when a bishop he consecrated turned out to be a destructive rogue. He wrote publicly to the pope:

> I have inflicted a tragedy in my hastiness and lack of due precaution. . . . As for me, Your Beatitude, I am debating whether to resign the exercise of my bishop's office and devote myself to merited penance, tortured as I am by fear and anguish over two possible outcomes—either that I shall have to see a church of God losing its members because of a man I imprudently made a bishop, or that (may God prevent this) a whole church may be lost, along with the man himself.

Those are the kinds of sins he went into solitude to atone for at this last opportunity.—Garry Wills[37]

REAL JOY.   I recall some years ago in a church I was visiting on a Sunday afternoon, a van pulled up in the church parking lot, and a bunch of young people got out. They looked

---

[34]*Introducing the Reformed Faith* (Louisville, Ky.: Westminster/John Knox Press, 2001), p. 153.
[35]*A Place for You* (London: SCM Press, 1968), p. 171.
[36]*All's Well That End's Well* (Cumbria, U.K.: Paternoster Press, 1998), p. 282.
[37]*Saint Augustine* (New York: Viking Press, 1999), p. 144.

like thirteen, fourteen, fifteen, maybe up to eighteen years old. I think there were ten or twelve young people who belonged to that church. They got out with bedrolls. It was the awfullest-looking bunch of kids you've ever seen, something like the cats would drag in. They were really in bad shape. I said, "What is this?" They had just returned from a work mission. They named the place where they went. In one week, those young people, along with other young people, had built a little church for a community. They were beat. Aw, they looked terrible.

They were sitting on their bags out there waiting for their parents to come. I said to one of the boys, I said, "You tired?" And he said, "Whew—am I tired!" Then he said, "This is the best tired I've ever felt."

Now that's what joy is. Do you feel that? "This is the best tired I've ever felt." I hope some day young people in this church get that tired. I hope we all get that tired. The best tired there is, is called in your Bible, joy.—Fred B. Craddock[38]

RESPONSE TO CRISIS.   This response to crisis—with strangers or friends or family—is part of our nature. Every day, every week, every year since time began, whatever the size or nature of the crisis, this has been true of the human community—a fact that must be laid alongside all we know of the horror of man's inhumanity to man. Few of us do not have a story to tell—of what we gave or what was given to us in response to "Help me, help me." We are capable of being agents of one another's revival. None of us can go all the way alone.

Even in the midst of the unbearable agonies of prisons and concentration camps, there are those who choose to help—to give to others: bread, shoes, comfort, whatever. These acts of compassion are the shining, diamond-tough confirmations of human dignity. This is keeping our affairs in order at the highest level. This is communion in its highest form—the ritual of the keeping of the living flame, held daily in the unfinished cathedral of the human spirit.—Robert Fulghum[39]

CONVICTIONS.   A conviction is not anything one must hasten to publish to the world: abundant confusion and grievous injury has, alas, been wrought, because one who was immature has published his immature conviction. Nay, let but the conviction grow in silence, let it but grow along with the courage gained with God, and then shalt thou, in whatsoever danger may assail thee, be certainly assured what courage can do. A spark in wood-shavings is extinguished with a glass of water, but when it has had time bit by bit to take hold of all the house, and at length utters a deep groan (what happens in our illustration happens actually in the spirit's experience which it illustrates), and it bursts out in flame—then say the firemen: Here there is nothing to be done, the fire has conquered here! Grievous is it indeed when the firemen say: Here there is nothing to be done; but joyous is it when the fire that has conquered is the fire of conviction, and they that are hostile say: Here there is nothing to be done! For the fire of conviction has had time bit by bit to take hold of a man, until, when the moment has come, with a deep groan it releases the blast of courage into the flames: then in suffering courage is capable—and this too can be called a thrilling sight, when

---

[38]*Craddock Stories* (St. Louis, Mo.: Chalice Press, 2001), p. 94.
[39]*From Beginning to End: The Rituals of Our Lives* (New York: Villard Books, 1995), p. 240.

burning zeal for a conviction consumes a man like fire!—is capable of wresting power from the world, and is able to transform shame into honour, ruin into victory.—Søren Kierkegaard[40]

CREATIVITY.   The ordinary person is immersed in a life that asks him to be creative in his own way, to leave his mark not on a statue or a poem but on those he loves or teaches or just stands by in hard times. Creativity for most of us is not taking a ceramics class in evening school as much as it is facing into every day with a vision of its promises and a willingness to die to something of ourselves in order to redeem these. The psychological reality of the process is lighted up by, but not radically different from, the struggle of the writer or the sculptor. What is striking, or course, is how these dynamics parallel the life theme of all of Jesus' teaching. We are given life not to hoard it nor to protect it but to invest it through committing ourselves, at the risk of suffering, to re-creating the face of the earth. The work of the Spirit is surely that of the faith we profess: to take on our flesh, that is, our own identity, and to suffer the deaths that are the necessary condition for our resurrecting ourselves and others with new life. We keep faith by responding with our total selves to this most fundamental of all religious experiences, the daily round of living and loving that defines life for most of us.—Eugene C. Kennedy[41]

A SPECIAL GIFT OF CHRIST.   He is the giver of the *new birth.* By the divine rebirth he gives men power to become the son's of God. When the Christian candidate emerged from baptism, he was clothed in new white robes to symbolize the fact that he had entered on a new life. The very word *candidatus* means *one who is clothed in white.* The difference which Jesus Christ makes to a man is so complete and so radical that nothing less is adequate to describe it than to call it a new birth. In him the coward becomes the hero, the sinner becomes the saint, and the man of the world becomes the man of God.—William Barclay[42]

STUBBORNNESS.   Pascal says that men never sin so cheerfully as when they do it with a good conscience; and often enough religious polemic is conducted by those whose conscience *is* good—that is why they can, if not cheerfully then certainly zealously, speak and act as they do. A friend once said that there are people who do not engage in thought but simply in the "rearrangement of their prejudices." They adopt an unyielding attitude because they simply will not listen to criticism nor open their minds to truth which they have not themselves arrived at.—Norman Pittinger[43]

CONKING OUT.   It was forty years ago I had a 1956 automobile. I will not name the brand because it might in some way be a problem for the automobile company. But my car was a lovely car, beautiful on the outside. Oh, I see the powder blue color of it now. But it was not hale and hearty for the cold of the northern climate. And I would get up early in the morning, and I'd have to start it before I was going on a journey, let it run a while. That car would

---

[40]*The Gospel of Our Sufferings* (Grand Rapids, Mich.: Eerdmans, 1964), p. 150.
[41]*Believing* (Garden City, N.Y.: Doubleday, 1974), p. 200.
[42]*Great Themes of the New Testament* (Louisville, Ky.: Westminster/John Knox Press, 2001).
[43]*Life in Christ* (Grand Rapids, Mich.: Eerdmans, 1972), p. 84.

run so beautifully, purr like a kitten. And as soon as I shifted into gear, it would conk out. Now, there are Christians like that, who have everything you would expect, look beautiful, sound good, but when it's time to shift into gear, they conk out.—James Forbes[44]

THE HOLY SPIRIT.   The church age has often been called the age of the Holy Spirit. The New Testament has far more explicit references to the person and ministry of the Holy Spirit than does the Old Testament. Over 250 New Testament passages include a clear reference to the Holy Spirit. These passages demonstrate that the Holy Spirit plays a vital part in the life of the true church, the spiritual body, of which Jesus Christ is the living Head. These passages reveal that Christ works in the life of each believer through the enabling of the Holy Spirit. The Holy Spirit is thus indispensable to the mission of the true church and to the purpose of each Christian. . . . If we are not rightly related to the Holy Spirit, then we are not experiencing the abundant life Jesus promised (John 10:10).—Robert Gromacki[45]

ACCOMMODATION WITHOUT COMPROMISE.   Luke presented the Areopagus speech as the model of Paul's preaching to the *pagan world*. It is Luke's summary, based on the actual preaching of Paul. It shows how Paul sought to build bridges as he reached out to the philosophers of Athens. His sermon drew largely from the Old Testament but presented ideas compatible with the thought of the philosophers, especially the Stoics. Recognizing this, it has sometimes been argued that Paul's efforts before the Areopagus were a failure, a "disastrous blunder," as one interpreter put it. Paul is said to have abandoned forever his attempt to reach the intellectuals and to have resolved to preach only the crucified Christ (1 Cor. 2:2). But Paul preached the dead and risen Christ in his Areopagus address (v. 31). It was at this point that he lost many of his audience. Paul knew there was no compromising on this central message of the gospel.

On the other hand, he did not fail to make all points of contact with his hearers that he legitimately could without compromising the gospel. His sermon is a model of missionary accommodation. His sermon was also no failure. He won one of the thirty members of the venerable court, not an insignificant percentage. And Paul never abandoned his desire to probe the depths of the gospel, to seek a full understanding of his faith in Christ. His letters have challenged the best of minds in every generation of Christians and will continue to do so. There may be anti-intellectual Christians; Paul was not one of them.—John B. Polhill[46]

HUMAN POTENTIAL.   A human being is not one thing among others; *things* determine each other, but *man* is ultimately self-determining. What he becomes—within the limits of endowment and environment—he has made out of himself. In the concentration camps, for example, in this living laboratory and on this testing ground we watched and witnessed some of our comrades behave like swine while others behaved like saints. Man has both potentialities within himself; which one is actualized depends on decisions but not on conditions. Our generation is realistic, for we have come to know man as he really is. After all, man is

---

[44]*Ten Great Preachers* (Grand Rapids, Mich.: Baker Books, 2000), p. 64.
[45]*The Holy Spirit* (Nashville: Word, 1999), p. xv.
[46]*Paul and His Letters* (Nashville, Tenn.: Broadman & Holman, 1999), pp. 212–213.

that being who has invented the gas chambers of Auschwitz; however, he is also that being who has entered those gas chambers upright, with the Lord's Prayer or the *Shema Yisrael* on his lips.—Viktor E. Frankl[47]

THE CHURCH.   We ought to be able to see in the Church a true spirituality, that process of breaking open and bringing forth the new qualities of a truly spiritual humanity. The Church, as community of the Spirit, should be the environment for the developing of full personhood. However imperfectly, the Church should be already exhibiting the eschatological kingdom of God, that final community of the Spirit toward which not only the Church but all creation is headed.—John Macquarrie[48]

THE PUREST FAITH.   The purest acts of faith always feel like risks. Instead of leading to absolute quietude and serenity, true spiritual growth is characterized by increasingly deep risk taking. Growth in faith means willingness to trust God more and more, not only in those areas of our lives where we are most successful, but also, and most significantly, at those levels where we are most vulnerable, wounded, and weak. It is where our personal power seems most defeated that we are given the most profound opportunities to act in true faith. The purest faith is enacted when all we can choose is to relax our hands or clench them, to turn wordlessly toward or away from God. This tiny option, the faith Jesus measured as the size of a mustard seed, is where grace and the human spirit embrace in absolute perfection and explode in world-changing power.—Gerald G. May, M.D.[49]

LUCK.   An old Chinese folktale tells of a farmer who owned only one horse. He depended on the horse to pull the plow and to draw the wagon. One day a bee stung the horse, and in fright it ran away into the mountains. His neighbors said, "We are really sorry about your bad luck in losing your horse." But the old farmer shrugged and said, "Bad luck, good luck—who is to say?" A week later his horse came back, accompanied by twelve wild horses, and the farmer was able to corral all the fine animals. News spread, and his neighbors returned and said, "Congratulations on this fine bonanza," to which the old man said, "Good luck, bad luck—who can tell?" The farmer's only son decided to make the most of what looked like good fortune and started to break the wild horses so they could be sold. But he got thrown from one of them and broke his leg. At the news of this accident, his neighbors came again, saying, "We are so sorry about the bad luck of your son's fall." And of course, the old man said, "Bad luck, good luck—who can say?" Several weeks later, war broke out among the provinces of China. The army came through the village and conscripted all the young men, but because the old man's son was so badly injured, he did not have to go.—Michael L. Lindvall[50]

FROM PRAISE TO SERVICE.   I was nurtured in an Associate Reformed Presbyterian congregation in which the Sunday service began by the people standing and singing a metrical

---

[47]*Man's Search for Meaning* (Boston: Beacon Press, 1959), pp. 136–137.
[48]*Paths in Spirituality* (New York: HarperCollins, 1972).
[49]*Addiction & Grace* (San Francisco: HarperSanFrancisco, 1988), p. 128.
[50]*The Christian Life* (Louisville, Ky.: Geneva Press, 2001), p. 73.

version of the One Hundredth Psalm. The practice had a basis in the psalm itself. Psalm 100 is an entrance song, composed for a processional into the place of the presence. It was liturgically appropriate, but I have come in retrospect to think there was more to it than mere liturgical correctness. Somewhere in the history of this practice—which, I was told, came over from Scotland with the Seceders—it had been discerned that Psalm 100 introduced the congregation to the praise of the Lord. It led the people through words that, had they ears to hear what they were saying, constituted them as what they should be and led to their doing what they should do.

Most of us in the congregation of my childhood knew the metrical psalm, versified by William Kethe, by heart:

> All people that on earth do dwell
> Sing to the Lord with cheerful voice;
> Him serve with mirth, His praise forth tell,
> Come ye before Him and rejoice.

—James L. Mays[51]

THE TRUE CHRIST.   Why not? I believe that the Christmas event, for all our magnificent Christmas windows and beautiful cards, provokes a crisis of recognition. I believe that what most of us hope for in a Savior is not what we get. I believe that what we look for, what we expect, what we want in a Christ blinds us frequently to the Christ who really comes. And I am persuaded that those of us in the Christian ministry are among the most sadly deceived. *"The Word came to the Word's own home, but those to whom the Word came did not receive the Word. The Word was in the world, . . . yet the world did not know the Word."* The Word, even Jesus Christ, comes to us as a stranger, as outsider—as one with no place to lay his head. He seeks a home among us, but cannot find one.—James W. Crawford[52]

BURNOUT.   Burnout is a surrender, Dr. Martin Luther King Jr. once said at a conference in 1964. A lot of us were sitting at a table talking about the subject because we had witnessed it in others and ourselves. He explained his somewhat startling choice of words this way: "We have just so much strength in us. If we give and give and give, we have less and less and less—and after a while, at a certain point, we're so weak and worn, we hoist up the flag of surrender. We surrender to the worst side of ourselves, and then we display that to others. We surrender to self-pity and to spite and to morose self-preoccupation. If you want to call it depression or burnout, well, all right. If you want to call it the triumph of sin—when our goodness has been knocked out from under us, well, all right. Whatever we say or think, this is arduous duty, doing this kind of work; to live out one's idealism brings with it hazards."—Robert Coles[53]

---

[51]*The Lord Reigns* (Louisville, Ky.: Westminster/John Knox Press, 1994), p. 61.
[52]*Worthy to Raise Issues* (Cleveland, Ohio: Pilgrim Press, 1991), pp. 62–63.
[53]*The Call of Service* (Boston: Houghton Mifflin, 1993), p. 141.

DELIGHTFUL DESTINY.   Christian hope suggests that man is destined for a City. It is not just any city, however. If we take the Gospel images as well as the symbols of the book of Revelation into consideration, it is not only a City where injustice is abolished and there is no more crying. It is a city in which a delightful wedding feast is in progress, where the laughter rings out, the dance has just begun, and the best wine is still to be served.—Harvey Cox[54]

CARING.   Many years ago, when I was serving as a student pastor in the Buckhead community in Atlanta during World War II, my wife and I were called in the middle of the night to the home of an elderly member of our little church who was dying. It was at the height of winter and a fierce blizzard was in progress, so the drive in our ramshackle old car took more than an hour and a half. When at last I stood in the door of my friend's room, he looked up at me and said in feeble tones, "You cared enough to come!" Is it theologically too elementary to say that one of the deep messages of the cross is that God cared enough for the likes of you and me *to come—and to die*? I can never forget what that remarkable British essayist Gilbert Keith Chesterton, overcome one day by a new consciousness of Calvary, cried out, "It was God himself upon the cross!"

I cannot understand it fully, but I know that when I look in its direction what happened on the cross brings me my salvation. And I know also that there have been millions of others like myself who have never comprehended its theology completely but who have been saved by it!—Earl G. Hunt Jr.[55]

TRANSFIGURATION OF TRAGEDY.   The cross and the resurrection of Jesus Christ become for Christians the focus of the divine activity. They assure him of God's providence, and they evoke his trust and hope. On the cross they see the compassion of the divine love, God's participation in the tragedy which marks and mars creation. But with the eyes of faith they apprehend through this passivity an activity which is transfiguring the total situation. Evil itself is being compelled to serve a deeper good. Divine and human are becoming at one.—Peter Baelz[56]

---

[54]*The Feast of Fools* (Cambridge, Mass.: Harvard University Press, 1969), p. 162.
[55]*I Have Believed* (Nashville, Tenn.: Upper Room, 1980), p. 75.
[56]*Prayer and Providence* (New York: Seabury Press, 1968), pp. 131–132.

EVANGELISM AND MISSIONS

SERMON SUGGESTIONS

Topic: Tearing the Roof Off for God

TEXT: Isa. 43:18–25; Mark 2:1–12

How disappointing! To have made plans. To have had a dream. To have gotten all excited about putting those plans into action and seeing that dream come true. To have made the emotional and physical effort to make that dream reality, only to be faced with the distinct possibility that it was all for naught.

Perhaps you have been there at some point in your own life and can identify with the four men who brought their friend to Jesus on a stretcher. When they made their way to the house where Jesus was teaching, a wave of disappointment must have flooded over them when they saw that there was no way to get in the door because of the crowd.

Yet in this delightful passage we see problem solving at its best. You and I can learn a lesson or two from the friends in the story.

I. *The first thing we see in this story is a problem.* A man was paralyzed. Whether he was paralyzed from birth or left paralyzed by some illness or accident, we do not know. But we do know that he was bedfast and helpless, having to rely on the sympathy of others for the basic functions of life.

But this man was also blessed in that he had some good friends who were willing to carry him to see Jesus. Whether the man himself had heard about Jesus and his power to heal, or whether one of his friends had heard of Jesus and suggested they take him is not known. But it doesn't really matter, because the main point is that they were willing to put forth the effort to go.

Now, you know how it is when we are getting ready for church—sometimes we are running a little late. So it was with the men in the story. They arrived at the house where Jesus was teaching and found that they couldn't even get near the door because the crowd was so great (a problem few churches have, I'm sorry to say).

"Oh, man, just look at that crowd!" we can just hear one of the friends say. "Man, how will we ever get in to see Jesus?"

They had a real problem. Their friend was paralyzed. They had expended all this time and effort to bring him to the Master, and they could not get anywhere near him.

II. *But these men also knew how to approach their problem.* They did so with faith, zeal, and persistence. They had faith in the power of Jesus to make a positive difference in their friend's life. They had faith that God wanted good, and not ill, for their friend. They had faith that they could overcome any obstacles that got in their way.

One of the many joys while our children were young was taking them to see the Ringling Brothers & Barnum and Bailey Circus, the so-called Greatest Show on Earth. It is quite an experience. One of the most breathtaking acts is the trapeze artist who climbs to the top of the tent, swings high into the air, lets go of the rope, and turns two or three summersaults in mid-air before catching the hands of her friend swinging from the other side of the tent. What leads one to attempt such a dangerous, seemingly impossible feat? It is faith—faith that her partner will be there at just the right split second to catch her.

So it is with faith in God—it is confidence that God is there for us, willing our good, even in spite of obstacles and the seemingly impossible situation.

Accompanying the men's faith was a burning zeal. They were zealous to get their friend to Jesus, and that is what they set out to do.

But the attribute that really proved their devotion was their persistence. When the way before them was blocked, they were persistent in finding a way to get their friend to the Master. Realizing that it was not possible to go through the door because of the crowd, they did not give up and say, "Well, we tried. Sorry, old chap; tough luck." No, instead they climbed up steps on the side of the house and tore a hole in the roof. (Palestinian roofs at that time were made of sapling poles laid flat across the walls of the house, with branches and twigs spread over the poles and clay patted down over the branches that was dried in the sun.)

Once they tore a hole in the roof big enough to pass their friend through, they lowered him down to where Jesus was sitting. If they could not get their friend to Jesus *through* the crowd, then they would get him to Jesus *over* the crowd. These friends were unique and a bit unconventional, to say the least. But they did not give up. They got the job done.

III. *Because of the men's approach to their problem, which included their faith, zeal, and persistence, the result was a positive outcome.* When Jesus saw what had taken place, and saw evidence of their faith and persistence, he said to the paralytic, "Son, your sins are forgiven you." Now, that strikes us as a strange thing for Jesus to have said, doesn't it? It helps to understand that in Jesus' day it was commonly believed that illness or physical problems such as paralysis were punishment *for* or a consequence *of* sin. It may be that the paralytic himself believed that his paralysis was because of unforgiven sin. We have no proof that Jesus believed that way, and I don't believe he did. And we certainly don't believe that way today.

Nonetheless, psychology and psychoanalysis have taught us that feeling forgiven is central to healing. It has been proven that deep-seated guilt and self-loathing can result in physical illness that imprisons both body and soul.

Perhaps Jesus was wise enough to know that the paralyzed man and those around him *believed* that his paralysis was because of sin, so he said, "Son, your sins are forgiven."

When questioned about his power to forgive sins, Jesus said to the paralytic, "Stand up, take your mat, and go to your home."

The application of this story to our personal lives and to the work of our church is at least twofold:

(a) *The story has something to teach each of us about the way we face problems in our lives.* Problems call for faith that God wants what is best for us, and faith that God wills for us to overcome problems that beset us.

Problems call for zeal and determination that lead us to be a bit unconventional sometimes, if necessary.

And they call for persistence that will not let us give up but lead us to approach our problem from many different angles so as to find a solution. What the men's ingenious persistence says to us is, when the way is blocked, try another way. When one attempt fails, make another attempt. As the old saying goes, "Where there is a will, there is a way."

(b) *The story also has something to say to us about evangelism in the church.* How good if we had the zeal of those friends to bring others into contact with the healing touch of Christ, believing that he can make a positive difference in their lives. How good if we should let nothing stand in our way of sharing the good news. How good if we had the zeal and determination to invite our friends, family, neighbors, and coworkers to worship and other church activities, in spite of any embarrassment we think it might cause us. How good if we were determined to overcome any obstacles that are standing the way of our outreach and church growth. What a difference it could make in the life of our congregation.

May God grant us zeal enough to tear the roof off for God (I am speaking figuratively, now, you understand), that is, to do whatever is necessary to enable others to be brought to the healing touch of Christ.—Randy Hammer

Topic: The Form of the Christian Life
TEXT: Luke 16:19–31; Deut. 26:1–10a; 2 Cor. 4:8–11

Every life has a form—a pattern of thought and action.

Many of us once lived in a world that had, at least on its surface, a common understanding of what is right and wrong. Today we are becoming increasingly aware of wide differences; some people can steal, kill, and destroy randomly, while others live peaceable, respectful lives.

What makes the difference? I suggest that the difference lies in what we permit to shape us. The form of a life is determined by the influences we allow to have their impact on us, that is, the people, the things, the thoughts, and the aspirations that take up most of our time.

I. *Luke 16:19–31: Formed by the world.* Here is a picture—not a pretty picture, but a clear picture—of a person who has permitted his love of money to form his life. Verse 19 describes him in terms that leave no doubt that his money and what it could buy for him were the things highest on his scale of values.

His life was formed by the idea that other people could be bought and sold or commanded to do his bidding. As a result, even after he died he expected to be served. He had apparently never tried to relieve the suffering of Lazarus on Earth, but he now asked Abraham to send Lazarus to relieve his suffering in Hades. And when that did not work, he asked Lazarus to be sent to warn his rich brothers.

Those whose highest aspiration is amassing possessions or power forget the worth of persons as creations of God and treat one another as means to satisfy their own cravings. This leads to sexual immorality, theft (both direct and sophisticated), and ultimately murder.

I have the impression that none of you here today is interested in such a form of life. Yet we are all in danger of being shaped in that way by the world in which we live. It doesn't take deep analysis to see that there are people all around who want us to buy their products, pay for their services, or support their causes. We are surrounded by influences that try to shape our decisions into worldly life forms. There must be a better way to form a life.

II. *Deuteronomy 26:1–10a: Formed by memories.* Here is a picture of a life-forming influence that produces a much better outcome. This influence is memory. One Old Testament scholar has said, "Memory shapes identity."[1] God saw to it that his people, the Israelites, never forgot who they were and how they had become God's people. These instructions given to them for their offerings to God in the Promised Land show how memories of God's goodness shape people who appreciate what they have and give the Lord the credit.

Note how the pronouns in this recitation change. "My ancestor; he . . . us . . . we . . . I . . ." A person who identifies that closely with the history of the people who were specially blessed by God grows into a special shape.

Such a person would find it hard to misuse any produce of God's creation and especially to take advantage of other people made in God's image.

We should certainly see to it that we and our children are in a position to be influenced by our memories of God's creation and of God's continued care for us, his children.

But the Christian has more than such general memories.

III. *2 Corinthians 4:7–11: Formed by the cross.* We remember Jesus. We go to Bible classes where we study the life of Jesus. We hear preachers remind us about the Crucifixion and Resurrection of Jesus. We remember with all our senses the death of Jesus each time we take Communion, each time we celebrate the Lord's Supper. We remember Jesus.

And what a difference that makes! Paul describes in this paragraph from 2 Corinthians what it means to live the Christian life. Here is his description of the form of the Christian life: the Christian life is shaped by the central act, the climax of the life of Jesus himself. The Christian life is in the shape of a cross, "always carrying in the body the death of Jesus so that the life of Jesus may also be made visible in our bodies."

The world might throw in our teeth the taunt, "I thought you Christians were supposed to live a triumphal life." And we can testify that a cruciform life, a life in the form of a cross, *is* triumphant, because it was through the cross that God accomplished our salvation and it was through the resurrection from the dead that God promised to all of us eternal life.

"Take up your cross daily and follow me" is the way Jesus put it to his disciples. Carrying a cross, or living a cross-formed life, is a struggle; but it is the struggle of Christ himself, and we have the assurance of his presence and power to help us with it.

IV. *Letting Christ's cross shape us.* Outside influences shape our lives. There is no escaping that. Our families shape us, our friends shape us, our organizations shape us, our schools shape us, our work shapes us, our recreation shapes us, our reading shapes us, our radio listening shapes us, our film and television viewing shape us.

Everything that has input into our minds works to shape our lives. There is no escaping that, but there is a way to control it.

We can choose to give God equal time.
We can choose to spend time with the Bible so that God's input has a chance to counteract the input of the world.
We can choose to spend time in prayer so that we can draw power from the Lord to make the right decisions.

---

[1]James A. Sanders, *God Has a Story, Too* (Minneapolis, Minn.: Augsburg Fortress, 1979), cited in Richard Lischer (ed.), *Theories of Preaching* (Durham, N.C.: Labyrinth Press, 1987), p. 196.

We can choose to spend time with God's people so that God's society can influence our development.

We can choose to meditate on the importance of the cross of Christ in our lives so that our lives grow to look more and more like his—lives of loving, sacrificial service.

Let us commit ourselves to the God who created us and who wants to continue to shape us. Let us determine to put ourselves in the attitude and the opportunity to be formed into the likeness of Christ, our crucified and Resurrected Lord. Let's allow God to have his way with us.—Bruce E. Shields

Topic: God's Water Blessing
Text: Gen. 1:1–5; Acts 19:1–7; Mark 1:4–11

As a child I was terrified of water. The first time our family went to the ocean I was four years old. My mom and dad took me by the hand and tried to lead me out a little way into the surf, but I was so terrified of the waves coming in that I screamed bloody murder. "What are you trying to do, drown me?" I yelled at my parents through hysterical sobbing.

In later years I would learn to love the ocean and would go there time and again. Some of our fondest memories of times spent with our own children were made at different seashores around the country.

The fact that water is such a vital part of our existence causes me to be almost embarrassed even to mention it. At the same time, how can we avoid thinking about it?

Life begins in water and from day one is sustained by water. Many scientists believe that life on Earth began in the sea. Perhaps that is why in many of us there is a longing to go to the sea.

The first verses of the Bible recount that "in the beginning when God created the heavens and the earth, the earth was a formless void and darkness covered the face of the deep, while a wind from God [or the Spirit of God, RSV] swept over the face of the waters." Before there was life as we know it, there was water—abundant, potential-filled, life-giving water.

After human conception occurs, the unborn infant is sustained and nurtured by the water of the mother's womb. As soon as the newborn baby makes it appearance from the womb in childbirth it is cleansed in the waters that come from the Earth. Soon the newborn child is nourished by the water found in its mother's milk. As long as we live, we will need pure drinking water to survive, and often in life we will suffer great thirst for it. A great percentage of the human body, we are told, is—you guessed it—water.

Long ago water became a primary archetype or universal symbol that has shown up in the literature of many cultures, so rich is its power to speak to the human condition. For instance, in that great American novel *The Adventures of Huckleberry Finn,* the Mississippi River is a primary literary symbol that speaks of the human journey into self-discovery and maturity.

It goes without saying that water is one of life's greatest blessings. We might even refer to it as "God's water blessing."

It should be no surprise that water found its way into the sacred rites of most of the world's great religious traditions. Water has significance in Judaism, Christianity, and Islam, as well as in religions of the east.

It is not insignificant that Jesus began his public ministry, according to Mark, by being baptized with water by John the Baptist. Mark begins his story about Jesus not with the birth narratives, as Matthew and Luke do, but with Jesus' baptism in the Jordan River. The book of Mark ends with Jesus giving instructions to his disciples to go into all the world proclaiming the good news and baptizing those who believe.

John's baptismal rite as recorded by Mark was tied to the confession and ceremonial cleansing of sin. As the repentant psalmist long ago said while confessing his sin against God, "Wash me thoroughly from my iniquity, and cleanse me from my sin. . . . Wash me, and I shall be whiter than snow" (Ps. 51:2, 7).

So John the Baptizer came calling the people to avail themselves of the waters of the Jordan in tangible expression of their desire to be cleansed from sin.

But why, we ask, did Jesus need to be baptized? Was he not sinless, the Son of God? Yet the truth of the matter is, Jesus insisted on it. He walked down to the Jordan River, where John was administering his "baptism of repentance for the forgiveness of sin," and prevailed upon John to do it. John, Matthew tells us, tried to prevent Jesus from being baptized. "I ought to be baptized by you," John said, "and yet you have come to me!" (Matt. 3:14 GNB).

Jesus didn't need to be baptized—or did he? Maybe he *did* need to be baptized—but not for himself. Maybe he needed to be baptized for us, as an example to all who would follow him. "It is proper for us," Matthew records Jesus saying, (Matt. 3:15 NRSV) to do this, "For in this way we shall do all that God requires" (GNB). Yes, I believe Jesus did it for us—to set an example for us, to teach us something, to show us the importance of it all.

Jesus saw baptism as important because it is a sign of doing what God requires. Baptism is a sign of righteousness, or a right standing with God. Baptism says that we have turned from being enslaved to a life of sin and have turned to a life of service for God. As a result of our repentance and baptism, our sins are washed away, as it were, with water serving as the holy symbol thereof.

Whenever we see someone walking down the street carrying clothes on a hanger covered with a plastic bag and bearing a laundry ticket, we know that person has just had his clothes cleaned. Likewise, when one comes forward to receive or to affirm her baptism, it is a sign to the world that God has cleansed her from all sin.

Jesus also saw baptism as being important because it is a sign of the spirit's presence in our lives. As Jesus was coming up out of the water from his baptism, "he saw the heavens torn apart and the Spirit descending like a dove on him" (Mark 1:10). Long before Jesus, the dove was a symbol of God's Spirit, and it has been so even more since the baptism of Jesus. John had said, "I have baptized you with water; but he [Jesus] will baptize you with the Holy Spirit" (Mark 1:8). If baptism says anything to us, it says that the Spirit is alive and working in our hearts and lives.

Baptism for Jesus was a sign of our adoption as God's children. Mark the Gospel writer seems to have believed that the affirmation of Jesus as God's Son did not occur until his baptism, when "a voice came from heaven: 'You are my Son, the beloved; with you I am well pleased'" (Mark 1:11). Through our baptism, God declares that we too are beloved children of God.

And baptism was important for Jesus because he saw it as setting one apart for Christian service. Jesus did not begin his earthly ministry without first receiving the sacrament of baptism. Martin Luther, the great reformer, viewed baptism as every believer's ordination to service in the world. Luther advised in his larger catechism that one should consider and recall one's baptism often. "A truly Christian life," Luther said, "is nothing else than a daily baptism, once begun and ever to be continued."

I have read that "a part of the act of baptism in the Church of India is for the candidate to place his own hand on his head and say, quoting the apostle Paul, 'Woe is me if I preach not the gospel.' This is part of the baptismal service of new members, not the ordination of ministers."[2] Christian baptism is the ceremony that sets us apart as witnesses, as servants for God in the world.

Most of you here have been baptized, either as infants or adults. What does that baptism mean to you? Did your baptism, if you received it as an adult, make any difference in your life? Have you ever thought of your baptism as being a commission from God—a setting apart—to go forth into the world and do good?

Well, we began by talking about how precious water is to life as we know it—"God's water blessing" we have called it. Within the context of the Church, this precious substance we call water—H_2O—becomes a real blessing in the lives of the faithful because it reminds us of our right standing with God, of the Spirit's presence in our lives, that we are beloved children of God, no less, and that we are set apart to do God's work in our world.—Randy Hammer

Topic: Recipe for Revival
TEXT: 2 Chron. 7:12–16

Those of us who try to look at current events through the eyes of faith, who try to get a biblical perspective on things, are starting to wonder. If the shock of events like this does not provoke lasting spiritual renewal, what will it take? What more could we want than to be shaken out of our lethargy and suddenly confronted with the prospect of death ourselves?

You know there is something wrong with the church when attendance is one-half the membership; when the rate of divorce among supposedly born-again folks is virtually indistinguishable from the rate among pagans; when the notes in a study Bible have more authority than the text itself; when in our worship we spend more time lauding ourselves for our love for God than confessing our sin; when the ripened harvest cries for reapers but we concentrate on filling our churches with spectators. These are the characteristics of many of the churches across this land. This is the picture of American evangelism as a whole, which by and large has been squeezed into the mold of the world and stands in desperate need of revival.

But what is revival? What kind of circumstances do we need to create to generate revival? Using a familiar text as a basis, this morning I would like for us to consider the Lord's prescription for revival. Turn to 2 Chronicles 7:11–16.

I. *Who needs revival?* This text identifies those for whom the Lord is concerned with two expressions: they are the Lord's people, and they are those "who are called by my name." The first expression is a simple statement of ownership: whereas the Moabites were known as "the people of Chemosh" (Num. 21:29) and the Ammonites as "the people of Milkom" (1 Kings 11:5, 23; Jer. 49:1, 3), the Israelites were "Yahweh's people." This truth is reiterated

---

[2]E. Paul Hovey, *The Encyclopedia of Religious Quotations.*

by the second expression, "they are called by the name of Yahweh." This too is a statement of ownership. Like a jar stamped with the seal of its owner, so Israel bears the imprint, the signature, of Yahweh. From this preliminary observation we conclude that when we speak of revival we speak of something happening to the people of God. The world does not need revival. America does not need revival. This nation has never been the people of God in the sense that Israel was. Being dead in their trespasses and sins, the people of America need rebirth. It is the Church, those who claim to be the people of the Lord, that needs revival.

But why should the Lord's people need revival? Some who claim the name do not. They are on fire, they bear the name of the Lord with joy, and they represent his will. But verse 13 envisions a people of God who stand under his judgment.

These judgments are sent by God upon his people to bring them to their senses—in the words of Amos, to cause them "to seek the Lord and live" (4:6–13).

Like the nation of Israel throughout most of her history, in many places today the Church seems to languish under the curse. Disaster follows disaster as leadership fails, churches fight and divide, God's people are discouraged, and people starve of famine for the Word of God. Meanwhile, our health-and-wealth gospel has duped us into thinking that believing in the Lord Jesus Christ is the answer to all of life's problems, and that it holds out to all takers automatic and unconditional title to all of heaven's best. But God is under no obligation to bless a wayward people. Those who claim the privilege of being his people but reject the call to holiness, those who are impressed with their own love for God but bear no fruit of his love for them, are the ones who need revival.

II. *Under what circumstances might revival occur?* How can spiritual renewal become a living reality? Our text offers us the recipe for revival in four short prescriptions.

(a) *Revival will occur only when the Lord's people are broken.* Verse 14 speaks of "humbling oneself." This (kana' niphal) is not the usual word for "to be humble," but it is a favorite of the author of Chronicles. For a positive example of what this means we may turn to Josiah, the boy king. You remember the story: While his people are renovating the Temple, they discover the Torah scroll. When they show it to Huldah the prophetess, she immediately receives a word from the Lord announcing that if the nation would not turn from its evil, the Lord would visit them with all the curses in the book. But the text tells us that Josiah's heart was tender; he humbled himself, tore his clothes, and wept before the Lord (2 Chron. 34:27).

My friends, revival begins with brokenness. Revival does not come to the proud, to the self-sufficient, to those who advertise their love for God with empty words. Sadly, in many quarters the Evangelical Church in America has adopted an arrogant and abrasive style that has little connection with our confession that we are only sinners saved by grace.

(b) *Revival will occur only when the Lord's people begin to pray.* The kind of prayer this text is talking about is anything but "a friendly conversation," "a chat with the Lord about myself," or "dialoguing with God." The weight of this Word is illustrated in Daniel 9:3. In the aftermath of the destruction of Jerusalem, and presumably counting on the promises offered by the Lord in this Word to Solomon, Daniel "prays, he pleads for grace, he fasts, he puts on sack cloth in mourning, and he sits in the ash heap." Daniel recognizes that he and his people do not deserve a hearing with God; all he can plead for is mercy.

It is not accidental that Augustus Toplady's classic hymn "Rock of Ages Cleft for Me" is rarely sung these days, and when we do sing it, we leave out the third verse (see the 1991 edition of *The Baptist Hymnal,* p. 342). We don't even understand what he was talking about when he wrote,

> Nothing in my hand I bring,
> Simply to Thy cross I cling;
> Naked, come to Thee for dress,
> Helpless, Look to Thee for grace;
> Foul, I to the fountain fly,
> Wash me Savior or I die!

Naked, helpless, and foul: this is our condition. This is what we must confess before revival will happen.

(c) *Revival will come only when the Lord's people seek his face.* But, you ask, why should one need to seek the face of the Lord? Has it been lost? If you asked some of the psalmists, they would say yes; to them it had become an enigma. Why has God hidden his face? But as Samuel Balentine[3] has observed, outside the psalms, God hides his face always as the result of sin (see, for example, Deut. 31:16–22; Mic. 34:1–4).

In short, when God hides his face, his people must examine their hearts for the cause. It always lies in human sin. When those who have experienced God's marvelous grace do not express their gratitude with wholehearted obedience, they ought not be surprised if their prayers go unanswered and God seems to have withdrawn. This contrasts with the contemporary casual, if not in-your-face, approach, "Here I am Lord, aren't you lucky?"

(d) *Revival will come only when the Lord's people abandon their sinful ways.* To understand this last expression, we may need to reeducate one another on what sin is. Now that we are enlightened, tolerant, nonjudgmental, and open to alternative lifestyles, we have dispensed with words like *sin, evil,* and *wickedness,* because they imply some kind of normative ethic. But revival will not come as long as we refuse to deal with sin for what it is. To the ancient Israelites, the sins included idolatry, trust in foreign powers, and exploitation of the weak. We may need to repent of our insensitivity to our spouses, our inhospitality to our neighbors, our hardness toward a needy student or neighbor, our dishonesty, bitterness, and pride. None of us is immune to any of these problems.

This, then, is the recipe for revival: humbling ourselves before God, earnestly pleading his grace, seeking his face, and abandoning our sinful ways. Sadly, we want revival without pain, renewal without remorse, and rejuvenation without repentance. But it will not happen without brokenness and earnestly imploring God's mercy.

But when that happens, and I pray that it will all over this land, what will be the result?

III. *What are the effects of revival?* Our text answers this question, too. In fact, in classic homiletic style, verse 14 closes with three glorious promises.

(a) *When the Lord's people pray with humble and penitent hearts, the Lord will hear them.* He will respond. He will not remain aloof, hidden forever. He will turn his face toward the supplicant.

---

[3]*The Hidden God: The Hiding of the Face of God in the Old Testament* (New York: Oxford University Press, 1983).

(b) *When the Lord's people pray with humble and penitent hearts, the Lord will carry off their sin.* This strikes at the heart of the human predicament. Sin needs to be admitted. Ironically, that is the only way it can be removed.

(c) *When the Lord's people pray with humble and penitent hearts, he will remove the effects of sin.* Here this is described in terms of healing the land, that is, to restore a state of shalom between his people and their physical environment.

Did you notice what is missing in these promises? God does not promise to make Israel number 1 in the world, the way she had been in the days of Solomon. Also, what may be especially significant for us, not a word is said about miraculous signs and wonders sweeping the land as evidence of revival. The effects are really quite unspectacular, but they strike at the root of human need. People who humble themselves before God receive assurance of forgiveness. What more could a wretched sinner want?

Could it be that our longing for revival is actually off base? Could it be that we are looking for a quick fix, a short cut that may in fact arise from a carnal desire to experience what others have experienced, without going through the pain of brokenness, penitence, and confession? Could it be that we are seeking revival rather than God?

Ladies and gentlemen, my brothers and sister, it is never too late to humble ourselves, to plead for forgiveness, to seek the Lord's face, and to turn from our wicked ways. May the Lord break our proud hearts and give us the humble spirit we need to acknowledge our wretchedness before him. May he be gracious and hear our confessions of our sin, and forgive us for our evil ways.

May the Lord, the great King of Heaven and Earth, be merciful to us. May he forgive our sins this day. May he bring healing in our hearts, in our homes, in our schools, and in our churches. For his is the kingdom, and the power, and the glory, forever. Amen.—Daniel I. Block

SECTION IX

RESOURCES FOR PREACHING ON PRAYER

BY W. MATT TOMLIN

Topic: Prayer Can Change Your Life
Text: Luke 18:9–14, esp. vv. 13–14

On one occasion, a fellow in the community was having a hard time; everything was going wrong, it seemed, in his life. So he said to one of the businessmen in town, "I'm really having a lot of trouble. I don't know what to do." The businessman replied, "Why don't you try praying—I've had pretty good luck with prayer lately!"

There are some strange ideas about prayer in the minds of many. Some think it is a lucky charm we use to get what we want. Some believe that it really doesn't make a lot of difference when we pray because this is a world of law and order and we are not going to get God to change the orderly process of the world to meet our needs.

But Jesus talked a lot about prayer. In our passage of Scripture he tells about two men who went into the Temple to pray. When the incident was over, one of them was the same as when he entered, but the other one was changed because of the prayer he prayed. The first man was of high moral character. He did everything he was supposed to do in the practice of his religion. The second man, a publican, was a charlatan. His life was full of dishonesties and he was hesitant even to come into the Temple to pray. The first man prayed a prayer that was proud and hollow. His prayer changed nothing about him. But the second man prayed with passion and humility, admitting his sins and asking forgiveness from God. His prayer changed him, and thereby changed his relationships with others. The message is clear: prayer can change your life.

I. *Why do we pray?* We are prayer and worship animals. Prayer is the one great imperative in our lives. We are the only creatures of God who have within us the capacity to recognize and respond to our maker in thanksgiving and prayer.

Prayer is an instinct within us; it is as natural for us to pray as it is for us to eat or drink to satisfy our physical needs. Prayer comes inevitably to all of us at some time or another. We pray when the great issues of life come to us, and we pray because the Bible tells us to pray.

II. *Then how shall we pray?* The Bible tells us to come directly to God—come right to him, openly and directly. We can come to him as a child comes to its father. We do not need someone to intercede for us. We have direct access to God.

And then we are to pray according to God's will. This is the kind of praying that Jesus did in the Garden of Gethsemane. We are to ask that God's will be done in our lives.

A little girl prayed, "O, God, please make Memphis the capital of Tennessee!" Her mother, overhearing, asked why she had prayed for that. She replied, "Because that's what I put on the test at school today!" We pray just as selfishly. We plead with God to give us what we want, not what it is his will for us to have. But Jesus always prayed that God's will would be done. We are to pray that God's will be done in our lives.

III. *What difference can prayer make?* If we pray will it change things? Let's divide prayer into two areas.

(a) *We pray to change circumstances,* and most of the time God's answer is not to change the circumstances. God sometimes denies our request in love, just like a father does with his children. God answers our prayers, but sometimes he says, "I will not or cannot change the circumstances." Yet sometimes he does change the circumstances to fit into his will. Paul prayed three times for God to remove his thorn in the flesh, but the answer was *no*.

(b) *Prayer will change you.* There are three ways that prayer changes us. First, prayer brings us closer to the person of God. We get to know him better. The more we pray the closer we get to God. Second, prayer brings us closer to God's will for our lives. Third, prayer brings us closer to the work of God. The more we pray, the more likely it is that we will do the work of God.

These are the ways prayer changes us. It brings us closer to the person of God, closer to the will of God, and closer to the work of God. Do you want your life to change? Then spend more time in prayer. God will reward you for it.

Topic: The Christian's Prayer Life
TEXT: Matt. 6:5–7; James 4:2–3

Power is what one is. Power is what one says. Power is what one does. But the greatest power is the power of prayer. Prayer is so powerful that kingdoms have been won, souls have been saved, churches have been built, lives have been changed, and people have been blessed. All of this has happened because of the power of prayer. People who live lackadaisical lives, weakened by the humdrum daily existence into which no excitement comes, can add a powerful dimension to their lives by increasing their prayer life. The reason that so many people live powerless lives is that they do not pray. Oh, they ask the blessing at meals and pray for God to bless them, but they have not learned the secret of *"praying without ceasing"* (1 Thess. 5:17 KJV).

When people have truly learned to pray in that great communion with God, homes have been changed, prodigals have been brought home, and miracles have been wrought. Is this kind of power reserved for a few special people who are the supersaints? Not at all. Every Christian can have this added dimension of power in his or her life if he or she is willing to pay the price of great praying. What are some of the questions that need to be answered about prayer?

I. *What does the Bible promise concerning prayer?* Certainly it is elemental to our faith that we are promised forgiveness for our sins if we ask for it in prayer. Over and over again the Bible promises us that if we seek God in prayer and ask for forgiveness, he will forgive. We are even told, "As far as the East is from the West, so far hath he removed our transgressions from us" (Ps. 103:12 KJV).

We are also promised in the Bible that through prayer we can gain a supply of wisdom. Paul wrote to the Colossian Christians, "For this cause we also, since the day we heard it, do not cease to pray for you, and to desire that ye might be filled with the knowledge of his will in all wisdom and spiritual understanding" (Col. 1:9 KJV).

The Bible also promises that prayer will bring provision for our needs. God will provide for us. He may not give us what we ask for, but he will give us what we need. Some of the most powerful praying is done when we covenant with someone else to pray specifically for something or someone.

II. *Why do we pray?* We pray because there is that need deep within for contact with and communication with God. We are praying beings. We cannot help but pray. We pray out of a deep sense of need for something that is greater and higher than ourselves. So we pray for strength from God, because we recognize our own inherent weakness. We pray to prevent worry. When we are convinced that God is near and that God is in control, worry is lessened and often eliminated. When we have been alone with God in prayer, we know that worry is fruitless and we turn it over to God. But most of all we pray to stay in close touch with God. God is our Father and we are his children. Children should stay in close touch with their father. It is when we are in close touch with God that life takes on meaning and we can become what we ought to be.

But what about those times when it seems that our prayers are unanswered?

III. *Why are our prayers not answered?* Sometimes when we think our prayers have not been answered, the answer is no, or not now, or later. But there are times when there is no answer to our prayers.

(a) *Prayers that are not offered cannot be answered.* We wonder why we do not often receive the blessings of God although we have never asked God for them. If we do not offer up our prayers, then God will not answer them.

(b) W*e pray with the wrong motives.* Why are we praying that prayer? Is it for our own selfish desires, or is it for God's will to be done in our lives and in the world? For prayer to be answered we must pray with the right motive. We often pray with the wrong spirit in our hearts. Is there sin in our hearts that we have never taken up to God for forgiveness? Have we understood that God will forgive our sins as we forgive others? Are we harboring some hatred toward someone else? Is there someone we need to forgive so we can utter our prayers with the right spirit in our hearts? We have to take care of these things that are hindrances to prayer before we can expect God to answer our prayers.

(c) *We do not abide in Christ and keep his commandments;* we are not earnest. I believe that many times we pray for God to do something in our midst but don't believe it is possible for him to do it. We have to pray believing in God's ability, promise, and desire to answer our prayers. We must be submissive to God's will. Remember that Jesus in the Garden of Gethsemane prayed, *"nevertheless not as I will, but as thou wilt"* (Matt. 26:39b KJV).

Topic: Powerful Praying
TEXT: John 14:1–14, esp. v. 14

Harry Emerson Fosdick told about a college roommate of his who had every resource a student could ask for. His room was equipped with adjustable furniture, special lights, a miniature library, stores of paper, pencils, pens, and unusual desk equipment of every sort, and he also had a device that held a book at the prescribed distance that could even turn the pages by an automatic method. This fellow would come into his room each night after dinner, put on his pajamas, adjust the lights, fix his book on the reading rack, sit down in his custom-made chair, and then go immediately to sleep. He had every resource available but he flunked out after one semester.

There are many people like that. They have all the resources of their faith at hand, but they have gone to sleep. Jesus says in John 14:14, "If you ask anything in my name, I will do it" (KJV). What a tremendous statement this is. Resources untold are at our fingertips if only we will reach out and take them. The disciples of Jesus knew what a staggering truth this is. One day they came to him and asked him not to teach them to fish, still storms, heal the sick, or even walk on water. They wanted to know how to pray. They knew that prayer was the key to the treasure house of God.

How do we go about putting this tremendous force to work in our lives? That is the question, and there are several things we need to recognize about prayer.

I. *Prayer is a way of life.* Prayer is not simply an emergency device. If we are instant in prayer, every little circumstance awakens the disposition to pray, and desires and words are always ready. But if we neglect prayer, it is difficult for us to pray. Paul advised his congregation to "pray without ceasing" (1 Thess. 5:17 KJV).

Prayer is at its highest and noblest when its purpose is not to get something but to get close to someone—the eternal Lord. To come into God's presence and wait before him, wanting nothing more than to be close to him, should be our attitude about prayer.

Prayer is not always asking, it is a way of life, a daily walk in communion with Christ.

II. *Prayer is a dialogue.* Here is where many of us slip up in our prayer life. In our relationship with God we tend to do all the talking. There ought to be a time of listening. Of course God does not always say what we want to hear. One of my favorite stories is about the agnostic who fell off a cliff but managed to latch on to a bush sticking out of the cliff. He was too far from the ground to let go. He cried out, "Is there anyone up there?" A voice answered, "Yes, this is the Lord." The man yelled, "Help me!" There was a moment of silence, then the Lord answered: "Let go of the bush and I will save you." There was another silence as the man looked down at the ground far below. Finally he yelled, "Is there anyone else up there?"

There are times when we want to ask, "Is there anyone up there?" when it seems our prayers have gone unheard. You see, listening to God involves a constant evaluation of our desires and motivations. We often pray to get what we want, but seldom do we pray for God to remake us into what we ought to be. Prayer at its best will draw us toward the spirit of Jesus.

There are three levels of prayer: (a) the childish level, where we simply say, "Give me"; (2) the adolescent stage, when we recognize the foolishness of childish prayers and give them up; and (3) the adult stage, when we begin praying for peace of mind, and when we start praying for others—for God to heal and restore the hurting and the wounded.

III. *Prayer is a new determination.* We do not really pray until we are willing to work. We have to be willing to put feet to our prayers. Prayer must issue in a new determination to do what must be done. It is being willing to allow God to use us to be the answer to our prayers. Our prayers are most effective when we keep working. Powerful praying is a daily walk, a dialogue with God, and a new determination. Keep praying until that kind of praying is your kind of praying.

Topic: Practice What You Pray
TEXT: Matt. 6:5–13, esp. v. 6

We are always admonished to practice what we preach. But what about practicing what we pray? Our prayers are as multitudinous as the stars in the sky and the sands of the seas. We ask God for everything. When the disciples wanted to know how to pray and what to ask for, Jesus gave them what we have come to call the Lord's Prayer, but in reality it is the disciples' prayer. So what does it mean to practice what we pray? How do you practice, "Thy kingdom come?"

God has the power to bring in his Kingdom, but when we do our part and the Church is built, it will be built with bricks and mortar, with sweat and labor and sacrifice, as people give of themselves and their resources. Kingdom citizens will bring in the Kingdom by the price they pay and the service they render.

Jesus said that he would leave a continuing witness in the world, and that witness is the Church. It is charged with the bringing in of the Kingdom in the world. It is the vehicle, the living, continuing expression of the body of Christ in the world. Believers, born-again Kingdom citizens, must by their energies, their sacrifice, and their work bring in the Kingdom. To pray "Thy kingdom come" means something; you have to practice what you pray.

I. *To practice what you pray when you pray "Thy kingdom come" means that you are a part of the Church.* You cannot separate the Kingdom of God from the Church. To pray "Thy kingdom come" means that you are part of the body of Christ in the world, and that you are going to be a part of his continuing Church. You cannot substitute the affairs of community for loyalty to and participation in the Church. There are many good causes in the world to participate in, but we should never substitute them for participation in the Church of the Lord Jesus Christ.

II. *When you practice what you pray, you are not only a churchman but a working churchman.* Bringing in the Kingdom and practicing what you pray goes beyond just being on the church roll, beyond being just one who comes to be married and buried at the church. A working churchman works to bring in the Kingdom. One gives time and energy through the church. Life makes many demands, but you have a prior commitment to the Lord Jesus Christ, in your life and in his church. It is the church that represents Christ in your community. It is the church that needs your labor and energies. You have a commitment to work in the church.

III. *When you practice what you pray you are a giving churchman.* There are a lot of folks who don't like to hear about money from the pulpit. But you cannot separate the Kingdom, being a part of the church, working in the church, and giving of your financial means. When we talk about working in the Kingdom and working in the church, it involves not only our sacrifice and energies; it also involves our support of the church with our financial resources, working through the church for the Kingdom of God.

Practice what you pray—not only "Thy kingdom come" but also, "Thy will be done on earth as it is in heaven." If we are going to send missionaries, we must give of our financial resources. If the church is to be a shining light, directing men and women to Christ, we must give our money. If the church is to "train up our children in the way they should go," we must give our money. If the gospel is to be preached and taught, we must give our money. If God's will is to be done in the areas of our stewardship, we must give our money.

You can't pray for God's will to be done in the lives of others if you are not willing for it to be done in your own life. If you pray for God's will to be done in the mission field, or during the church worship service, or in a revival, then you must first be willing for the will of God to be done in your own life. That's practicing what you pray.

You must bring your own life into conformity to the will of God before you can pray that the will of God be done on Earth among men, or that others be saved or brought into the church or do the work of God. You have to practice what you pray.

Practice what you pray. Help bring in the Kingdom. Be a part of the church. Be a working part of the church. Be a giving part of the church. Be willing for God's will to be done in your own life, and practice what you pray for.

SECTION X

CHRISTMAS AND ADVENT

SERMON SUGGESTIONS

Topic: Joy Running Over
TEXT: Isa. 61:10

One day when men and women lived in caves, some creative soul began beating two sticks together, and as she did, she began to develop a pattern, a beat, a rhythm. Then, sitting nearby, first one person and then another began tapping their toes, smiling, and feeling something good inside. So music was born, at the moment that someone hitched together human sounds and the human heart. If it happened on a Monday, then I suspect that by Wednesday of the same week, someone made the connection between God and this new thing called music.

As long as there has been worship, two things have been present: words and music. Why? Because our relationship with God has always been something of the mind and of the heart. Words, I hope you will allow, add something to worship. Wordsmiths like myself stand up and do the best we can to say who God is and what that means for us. Words can teach us about God and convey the passion of faith.

But—and this is no great surprise, yet it is nevertheless a great frustration for those of us who traffic regularly in words—there are limits to how well we can communicate, especially when it comes to conveying the emotion and passion of faith. Why does the poet say, "How do I love thee? Let me count the ways"? Because no sentence alone begins to get the idea across, and the best the poet can do is offer a list of loving images. Why is love like a "red, red rose"? Because the image comes closer to the idea than any dictionary definition. Words are simply limited.

So there comes a time when retired English majors like myself have to cede the stage to the musicians. Why? Because music has power that words alone do not have. Although many of us have teared up upon hearing a familiar line of poetry or verse of Scripture, it is the music that gets us consistently. Go to a nursing home and watch the expressions on the faces of the residents when the old hymns are played, then compare them to the expressions on their faces during the weekly devotional. Or consider the cumulative effect that all my preaching will ever have, then compare it to the power in the last fifteen minutes of Beethoven's Ninth Symphony. Which will say more about the majesty of God? Lest our musicians get too full of themselves, however, remember Oscar Wilde's quip as he endured a tedious concert. When told that the quartet had been playing together for five years, he responded, "Surely we have been here longer than that!"

As a specific example, consider the following contest in expressing joy. Listen as I bring all the passion and emotion I can to saying the word *joy:* "JOY!" Now listen as the choir takes a stab at it. [*At this point the choir sings the word* joy *fortissimo.*] No contest, right? My point?

Joy has roots so deep within us that words alone cannot express it. So Scripture says, "I will greatly rejoice in the Lord; my whole being shall exult in my God." When you peel it all away and get to the core, there you discover joy.

The choir won our little contest because they employed music and I did not. But there is a second reason: they were expressing joy together, as a group. Joy is best when shared. Although joy can be expressed when singing in solitude, it is best expressed by singing with others. Consider the joy of proclaiming Christ's birth. In Luke 2:10, one angel conveys the information: "I am bringing you good news." But the text says that as soon as this angel mentioned joy, "suddenly there was with the angel a multitude of the heavenly host, praising God and saying, 'Glory to God in the highest heaven, and on earth peace among those whom he favors!'" One angel was enough to announce the news, but it took a heavenly chorus to celebrate it. In one of the most joyful pieces of music there is, Beethoven's Ninth Symphony, we see the phenomenon. The choral part of the third movement, based on a poem by Schiller, "Ode to Joy," begins with a solo voice, but as soon as the word *fruede* ("joy") is sung, the chorus thunders in. One voice just won't do.

Joy has real meaning only when it is shared by others, and this is true not only where music is concerned. Why come to church? I would say, if for no other reason, because you can't really experience joy in its fullest sense by yourself or by watching a worship service on TV. Joy calls us to be with others; it calls us beyond ourselves, pointing us in the direction of God. C. S. Lewis, in *Surprised by Joy,* says that joy is not primarily about happiness or pleasure; rather, its supreme function is to be a signpost pointing beyond itself to God. Lewis is right. At the deepest part of who we are, joy is that thing deeper, more wonderful, and more powerful. It can come to us in times of happiness, but also in moments of sadness, such as when Isaiah (61:10) said to a defeated Israel,

> I will greatly rejoice in the Lord,
> my whole being shall exult in my God;
> for he has clothed me with the garments of salvation,
> he has covered me with the robe of righteousness,
> as a bridegroom decks himself with a garland,
> and as a bride adorns herself with her jewels.

Even though he lacked happiness, the author of these words still had joy, because he had a relationship with God.

As we continue in Advent, we would do well to ask ourselves, more thoughtfully than normal, What do we want for Christmas? Our wants tend to be surface things; therefore, in the words of Wordsworth, "getting and spending, we lay waste our powers."[1] My prayer is that this year we'll seek what we need for Christmas instead of merely what we want. This Advent season, may we be granted the gift brought by Christ, the gift offered by God, the gift so bountiful that a legion of angel voices was required to celebrate the gift we all truly need: joy!—Chris Caldwell

---

[1]William Wordsworth, "The World Is Too Much with Us," 1806.

Topic: The Time Is Fulfilled
TEXT: Mark 1:1–15

Christian psychologist Wayne Oates liked to talk about the "teachable moments" and "rites of passage" in the developmental process of growing up. Oates identified the critical stages when we are ready to learn, attempt new tasks, and accept new responsibilities in our lives as teachable moments. For example, when is a child ready to walk? The teachable moment occurs when several factors come together. It involves the physical development of legs strong enough to support the body's weight, and the coordination of mind and body for deliberate movement of muscles and limbs. It involves mental readiness—the ability to observe and to comprehend the mobility of others, the desire for freedom and for access to all of the things in range of observation, and the courage to launch into new experiences. It also connects with the expectations of family. We encourage and teach our infants to stand and walk, we help them to exercise their limbs, and we celebrate their first steps on a level that rivals Neil Armstrong's first step on the moon. We rush to find the camera, we call everyone in the house and even the neighborhood to gather and observe, and we register the event in history with announcements to extended family and friends.

When the second and third child comes along, parents are often surprised at individual differences. Not only do our children demonstrate unique abilities and limits in learning to walk, but they may never have the same facility with language or the same aptitude for math or music as their siblings, and they may vary significantly in the age of awakening to faith. Parents need patience to wait for the right moment. We can teach and encourage, but we cannot force our children to develop any sooner than they are ready. Just because a child is healthy and strong at twelve months does not mean they have the mental readiness to walk, and just because a child is small at eight months does not mean that walking is premature. We are never ready for some experiences. Just because the parents like music does not mean that the kid is ever going to be gifted or learn to play the piano. The same could be said of science, medicine, engineering, and theology. Perhaps the most important quality we can develop as parents, teachers, and pastors is discernment of the teachable moment—when the time is right to take the next step in life. Being five does not make a child ready for kindergarten, and turning twelve does not make the child ready for baptism, any more than arriving at twenty makes us ready for marriage. Wisdom in life calls us to pay attention not only to the passing of time but also to the moment of opportunity.

According to the Gospels, the world was like a child struggling to stand up and to take a baby step forward when Jesus came preaching, "The time is fulfilled, and the Kingdom of God has come near; repent and believe in the good news."

I. *The need is great.* A new poll conducted by the Pew Research Center was released last week: "What the World Thinks in 2002: How Global Publics View Their Lives, Their Countries, the World, America." It was based on 38,000 interviews conducted in forty-four countries. The poll reported a significant loss of public respect for the United States around the world since September 11, 2001. The director of the study, Andrew Kohut, observed that in spite of the global outpouring of sympathy for the victims and their families, there was a significant drop in support for America, especially among Islamic nations, but also among traditional allies in Europe. He went on to insert a "however." After some exploration of possible causes for America's decline in public relations around the world, the attitude toward the

United States is consistent with the global gloom about the international situation that came to light in the poll. The people who expressed disrespect for America seemed to have even less respect and hope for their own governments.

We live in a time of fear and despair. Wherever you go these days, people are in need of a lift, of a word of encouragement about the future, of good news to ballast the evil and depression of our age. I suspect that this is the reason for the popularity of flight into fantasy. The entertainment industry understands the situation. In times of anxiety, people are more interested in escape from reality than in facing fear, more concerned with security than with adventure. My parents were married in 1930. Because of the Great Depression, the entire world was struggling with unbelievable poverty and fear during the first years of their marriage, but I recall hearing Dad say that they always seemed to find money to go to the movies. Perhaps it was necessity that led to the rise of the movie industry during a time when people needed to escape from the world. There has to be some irony in the flight from a dark world of fear into a dark world of fantasy.

II. *The time is right.* John sounded the alarm and called his people to repent. If you envision Elmer Gantry exploiting naive, trusting people, you have not seen John. He came out of the wilderness exhibiting something of the radical change in life that he preached. The sin of the world was abiding in the sins of the people. Blame Rome if you will, but his message was not about the darkness of the world. It addressed the darkness inside of us. That is usually the case. We look at the context and plead helplessness. We are just victims of circumstances caught in the sweep of a world going to hell in a handbasket. John's sermon addressed the person. It was a call to reverse the direction of life. Baptism was his rite of passage for those who committed to change, and personal practice and behavior were the evidence. The time was right for John, and the time was right for Jesus.

Wayne Oates found a significant connection between the teachable moment and the understanding of time in the New Testament. In addition to the Bible's chronology, the measurement of history in terms of age and longevity, the gospel also speaks of the time of fulfillment. The Greek word *kairos* addresses the circumstances of a moment in time. *Kairos* is the time of opportunity, the time of fulfillment. It is the word Mark uses for the preaching of Jesus: "The time is fulfilled."

The time was ripe for John's alarm. The Kingdom of God was emerging in history. The time was right for the gospel, the good news of God's salvation. This was the teachable moment to hear of God's gift of *shalom,* peace on Earth toward people of goodwill. The word *euangellion* ("gospel") was already in use. The *euangellion* was the official, public announcement of an event of profound national importance. It often addressed the birth of an emperor, his arrival at the age of responsibility, or his accession to the throne. The good tidings of our gospel are about more than the birth of a child. They are about the presence of Emmanuel, God with us, and the authority of God over all creation. The time is now. The time is right.

Theologian John Killinger recalls the Simon and Garfunkel recording of "Silent Night" during the Vietnam War. The soft Christmas melody was punctuated with the sounds of gunfire and bombs with news reports of body counts and devastation. Killinger speculates that the first Christmas was like that. Behind the songs of angels and the wonder of shepherds was the rise of taxes, corruption in Herod's house, poverty in Jerusalem, and cruelty by Roman soldiers. Yet the time was right. God was Christ, reconciling this world to God's self. Today is the day of salvation. Hear the Word of the Lord.—Larry Dipboye

Topic: Coming to Conflict
TEXT: Matt. 10:34–42

On December 10, 1964, Dr. Martin Luther King Jr. received the Nobel Peace Prize in Oslo, Norway. Some folks strongly believed that he was more troublemaker than peacemaker. In his acceptance speech, King recited the current news on the conflict in Alabama and the murders in Mississippi and said, "I must ask why this prize is awarded to a movement which is beleaguered and committed to unrelenting struggle." He then stated his own conclusion "that nonviolence is the answer to the crucial political and moral question of our time—the need for man to overcome oppression and violence without resorting to violence and oppression."

Martin Luther King Jr. may have been a man of peace and nonviolence, but his life was centered in conflict and he died by assassination. He was accused of being a troublemaker and was often asked why he could not leave things as they were. For King and thousands like him, peace had to be associated with justice. From a Birmingham jail he wrote to Christian clergy who challenged his methods: "We know through painful experience that freedom is never voluntarily given by the oppressor; it must be demanded by the oppressed."

Another character in the catalogue of American rogues and radicals, Saul Alinsky, was active in his hometown of Chicago, but his genius in working for social justice spread across the nation. He was Jewish, but he worked with the Catholic Church in the development of parish political organization, and he rubbed elbows with numerous protestant ministers in confronting issues of racial justice. In 1972, a group of students from Tulane was planning a protest to disrupt the speech of a prominent politician defending the Vietnam War. Alinsky offered an alternative approach: dress up like the Ku Klux Klan and cheer every time the war is mentioned.

Alinsky was a rascal. He believed in justice, but he also believed in the power of conflict. He usually employed self-interest to accomplish worthy ends and often found himself at odds with clergy and idealists. His biographer wrote that Alinsky believed in the trinity of conflict, organization, and power. He was a social reformer, not a theologian.

Even as we celebrate the peace of Advent, we are reminded that Jesus was a troublemaker. He came to fulfill the teachings of the law and the prophets, to call us to a higher righteousness than that of scribes and Pharisees. He came for sinners. He offended the self-righteous of his time by keeping company with all of the wrong people. In light of the controversy surrounding his ministry, we should not be so shocked at his declaration: "I have come to bring not peace but a sword."

I. *The peace of God is rooted in justice.* When Ahab confronted Elijah, the king asked, "Is it you, you troubler of Israel?" The prophet retorted that it was Ahab who had troubled Israel by idolatry and corruption. Elijah set the stage for prophetic ministry. The primary tools of the prophet are challenge and conflict rather than compromise and conciliation. Ahab called it right.

During Advent, we read the vision of Isaiah about the one who shall be named "Wonderful Counselor, Mighty God, Everlasting Father, Prince of Peace"; but Jesus challenged the notion that he had come to bring peace to the Earth. Like Elijah before him, Jesus came to disturb the peace, not only of Israel but of the whole world. This is a text that most preachers prefer to avoid and most commentaries are hard-pressed to explain. Critics usually affirm the authenticity of texts such as this. Disciples would never put such words in the mouth of the Messiah. Jesus certainly did not raise an army or practice violence, but he did trouble authorities. He was neither a terrorist nor a politician, but he did demand mercy and justice, and he proclaimed a Kingdom that transcends all authorities of this world. The gospel of grace was not easy. With the gospel came both conflict within persons and a crisis of relationship among people.

Jesus sent out the Twelve with wise counsel about the mission of the Kingdom. He empowered them to heal and authorized them to preach. He warned of threats and resistance. The passage is usually explained as *eschatology*, the message of the ultimate end, but it is more than that. It is almost as if Jesus were answering a specific inquiry, like the complaints leveled at King and Alinsky by their friends. Jesus admitted to the truth in complaint. He uttered one of those shocking statements occasionally found in the Gospels that sets us back on our heels: "I have come to bring not peace but a sword." If that were not enough, he went on to say that he had come to create conflict in families—sons and daughters against parents. How can I preach this alongside the gospel of peace?

II. *In the real world, peace passes through the crisis of conflict.* Baptist minister Carlyle Marney challenged all of our set notions about the meaning of biblical peace. He noted that in the Bible peace is not some kind of divine United Nations. The *shalom* of God was never close to the *pax Romana,* the political calm that surrounded the political world into which Jesus was born. Carlyle Marney speculated, "If Christ had not been absolutely compelled by his obsession with the spiritual rule of Yahweh, he could, with the slightest bit of political ambition, have been the head of a vast new political region and a religion." Marney counts thirty-one forms of the word *peace* in the Bible, and 393 verses where the word is central. The birth of Jesus was announced by an angelic choir singing the *Gloria.* The promise of God was "peace on Earth among people of goodwill." But it was not the kind of easy peace we think of and ask for. Fred Craddock noted that the peace that Jesus opposed was status quo. Real peace is won on the battlefield of moral turmoil. It is peace that comes through a cross, that puts the cross right in the middle of all of our values.

Jesus was a radical. He loved God more than anything in the world, and he demanded that kind of radical love from his disciples. We attended a conference on the family a few years ago. It was filled with all kinds of great stuff about family values, healthy parenting, and spiritual growth. Then we came to the closing sermon. I could not believe my ears. The pastor stood in front of this community of peace and called for war on the family. Oh, he acknowledged the threats to family values that occupied our agenda. He affirmed our desire to build "Christian homes," as well as our vision of harmony and love around the home communion table. The he dropped the bomb. He challenged the idolatry of family. He challenged the family-first values of our pulpits and classrooms and declared war on our vision of perfection that ignores singles, the aged, and the divorced. He complained about people hiding behind the family to avoid the nominating committee calling for service in the church. Certainly our lives are consumed by too much to do these days, but is the church the sacrificial lamb for our altar of busyness? The preacher had the audacity to quote Jesus: "Whoever loves father or mother more than me is not worthy of me."

Jesus modeled what he preached. Early in his ministry he was called home by his mother and siblings, and he identified his family with those who do the will of the Father. He had no sympathy for the man who wanted to bury his father before following Jesus, and I doubt that he would sympathize with many of us in our begging to be excused from Christian service.

Anyone who has responded to the call of God knows that Jesus spoke the truth. If God comes first, you will be called to choice in your home. A healthy Christian family is centered not in itself but in the rule of God. Children do not need to be protected from the demands of the gospel. If the Church is a Kingdom value, then we cannot hide from service and stewardship behind family. When God comes first, the family grows in faith and love.—Larry Dipboye

Topic: A Christmas Reflection on Christmas Eve

A few years ago my husband and I had the opportunity to make a pilgrimage, joining thousands of others doing the same. We participated in the annual ritual for New Englanders and world travelers alike, driving north from Boston to take in the spectacle of the changing leaves. Appreciating the brilliant hues of red and orange and yellow, we marveled with all the other "leaf peepers" at the natural beauty of the region.

As many of us know, making such a pilgrimage also involves some other quaint New England traditions. Before we knew it, Matthew and I found ourselves participating in one of them as we combed through a large antique store filled with consignments of every kind. Surrounded by other wandering weekenders we searched for priceless treasures, hoping for the find of a lifetime that would have us featured on some antiques program like the *Road Show*.

Browsing carefully, it was about fifteen minutes into our hunt that I spotted a treasure. There, above an array of blue glass dishes and old pewter bowls, was a nativity scene made of figures about two and three feet high. I couldn't quite reach them to feel their weight, but the colors were deep and a few scratches only added to their charm. The chip on Mary's nose was clearly patchable with a little modeling clay. Even better, the price was right. The vendor's tag read simply, "Church Nativity Set: $45."

I quickly found Matthew in a nearby stall of old comic books and pulled him over, saying, "You've got to come check this out. I've found something that would be great for my office." He knows, you see, that in a minister's life there's no end to the use of good Christian kitsch, so he came over to take a look. "It's nice," he said. "It looks a lot like the one we used to have in the church where I grew up." Then he added, turning to look at me strangely, "But where is Jesus?"

Where is Jesus? What was he talking about?

I looked at that pastoral scene and then at Matthew and back again, and sure enough, baby Jesus was missing. Joseph stood over an empty trough and Mary gazed reverently at only painted straw. There was no Christ child lying in the manger—and I hadn't even noticed.

Tonight we gather to make sure that Jesus is not missing from our Christmas celebrations. Making our pilgrimage to this house of faith, we step away from all our other holiday traditions and from the frenetic pace of this season's festivities to put at the center of this sacred day the Christ child, God incarnate. Gathering to hear stories of faith and to sing songs of yearning, we pause to remember that even in our darkest hours God is present, reaching out with patient and enduring love. "Do not be afraid," we hear the angels say to Mary and then to the shepherds. "For we bring you good news of great joy for all people: to you is born this day a Savior, who is the Messiah, the Lord."

Certainly this is what we need to hear tonight. Like our ancestors of ancient times, as well as those of more recent generations, we come seeking peace in a time of war, hope for places of devastation, love where hatred gives life only to fear, terror, and greed. Disillusioned by the ruthlessness of human nature, we come looking for one who can lead us to be reconciled to God and to one another, asking ourselves this night: Can we, on this Christmas pilgrimage, find Jesus? Dare we admit that our Savior has gone missing from our lives?

Oh, baby Jesus, helpless child wrapped in bands of cloth, where are you? How have we misplaced your Spirit of mercy and love?

Looking for the Christ child this Christmas Eve, we find ourselves beckoned to Easter, called to travel not to Bethlehem first but rather to Calvary, where God's redemptive presence is most fully revealed. There, at the cross, we see a birth like no other, as the death of Jesus leads ultimately to the Resurrection of Christ. It is a scene filled with radical contradictions, where brutality is met by forgiveness, ridicule quelled with compassion, death defied by triumphant and eternal new life. Searching for hope on the Friday we dare to call "good," we find the worst of our human capacities transformed by God. "Do not be afraid," the angel said to the women at the empty tomb, and to us. "I know you are looking for Jesus who was crucified. He is not here; for he has been raised."

Yes, traveling to Calvary we find Christ in magnificent form, and we realize that Christmas is a time to receive God's gift of salvation, because that priceless Easter treasure is what lies in the manger. Gathering beneath the cross, we remember that in celebrating this birth we rejoice in the Resurrection, and are then eager to offer God our worship and praise. As inconceivable as it may seem, this is how God's revelation unfolds. Christmas, like Easter, turns the world upside-down. Christmas, like Easter, invites us all to be part of the story.

"Here am I, the servant of the Lord," Mary said upon hearing the miraculous news that Gabriel brought to her. She said yes to God's gift of grace, offering her very self as a vessel for the life of Christ. Then Joseph said yes, followed by the shepherds and the Wise Men. Over and over, people respond positively to God's offer of transforming grace, putting their trust in God's power, staking their lives on God's plan. The stories go on through the Gospels as one by one by one people arrive—lepers and prostitutes, tax collectors and Samaritans— all with the hope of finding a Savior. They look for God's mercy and acceptance, God's healing and redemption, and they find it in Jesus.

Now it is our turn. Moving through the centuries, the Christian story carries on, offering you and me the chance to participate in God's radical plan. For as we move from Calvary to Bethlehem tonight we see the transcendent Christ as an innocent child and realize that we are invited to embrace him, to hold his truth, to adore his presence. Helpless, that precious infant invites caring. Humble, he welcomes acceptance. Homeless, he seeks shelter and love. Born of a woman, our God leads us to be instruments of salvation, joining us together as one human family in which mercy is offered without pretense or prejudice, without privilege or pride. Christ comes to this Earth in humble and human form, welcoming each of us to participate in the miraculous unfolding of God's loving and just realm.

Another nativity set comes to my mind tonight, an image from my childhood. Every year we'd set out the family crèche on a table in the living room, with each figure put carefully in what we considered its most proper place. There were pebbles to scatter and a large, mountainlike piece of wood to set behind the stable. The crèche—perhaps like one you grew up with—was part of the many special traditions of our Christmastide.

That is, until one year when the scene was altered. Unlike that set I saw in Southern Maine, from which Jesus was missing, our cast of characters began to grow. First it was a little purple anteater, just the size of the sheep. Then Wylie Coyote arrived, perched on the rooftop, his arms outstretched with glee. For several weeks various plastic figures appeared, little green soldiers and cartoon characters standing alongside the shepherds and wise men as my little brother, Will, added his influence to that holy scene. Only four years old, he didn't realize that our nativity set was already complete. To him these toys were welcomed and each one of them belonged.

Of course, God's vision is always unfolding. The scene at the manger is never complete; even tonight our gathering testifies to the miraculous way the Christian story carries on. Through the child in the manger we're drawn together this night in unity and love—*despite* our differences and diversity and *because* of our differences and diversity—and we recognize together our common bond and deepest human needs. We are in the Church, in all its glory, in all its failings—realizing, as in the words of the great theologian Dietrich Bonhoeffer, that "the Church is nothing but a section of humanity in which Christ has really taken form. The Church is the man [or woman] in Christ, incarnate, sentenced and awakened to new life."

Yes, we gather here tonight as a testament to the living faith we receive in Jesus Christ, the humble child, the radiant Savior, celebrating the one who comes to bring justice and peace to this broken world. We come, one by one by one, to receive God's light and to lift that light up to the world.

Thanks be to God!

Amen.—Lael P. Murphy

Topic: Around the Stable with the People

All around the sanctuary, in the windows we have the traditional nativity scenes. These have been made by our Sunday school department, in the way the nativity scene has been shaped, crafted, refined, edited, and represented by Christians in the West for more than two thousand years. We are still startled when we see the expressions of the nativity scene from other cultures. It is surprising to see Mary in a Japanese dress or a black baby in the feeding manager. So, we have been revisiting the whole scene during the last few weeks. We have asked about the inn and where the animals were usually sheltered. We have examined the place and discovered that it was ordinary and average—a hotel with a barn for caring for the animals. The baby would have been put in one of the feeding cribs of these animals.

We have looked at the animals that would normally have been part of the traveling public—the camels, the donkeys, the oxen, a few goats—and at whatever animals the innkeeper might have had for his own use. It is important to keep the animals in our nativity scene, for they are part of God's good creation and they share in the promise of God's renewed and redeemed creation. When God brings in his promised future, the animals will be included.

So we have looked around the inn. We have noticed all of the animals, the feeding cribs, the water, and the saddles. It was a crowded place. That is the one thing that is missing in the traditional nativity scenes—the hustle and bustle, the crowd, and the noise of the people. There are lots of people in this story. After all, this was an inn, a crowded inn. This was the little hotel on a Saturday night, with the sign on the door, "No vacancy."

People and animals were packed into this place. We have eliminated a lot of people from this story as unnecessary. That happens so often in life. People get lumped together and thrown out of the picture because they are deemed unnecessary. There was the innkeeper and his family, and possibly some other relatives or servants—stable boys, cooks, waiters and waitresses. The innkeeper was the small business owner in the middle of the story. He was certainly very busy, exhausted, and overextended by the demands placed on his business. The people had been coming and going all day. They wanted this or that, they asked questions, they wanted service. Who made reservations in the first century? They just kept showing up and wanting a room.

We are not told much about the innkeeper. Each year, different pageants put a different spin on the attitude of the innkeeper. Did he tell Joseph in a mean and exhausted voice that there was no room? "I'm busy. I ain't got any more rooms." Was his offer of the manger an act of compassion or greed? Do you think the innkeeper charged Joseph for the space on the floor? Do you see the innkeeper looking at Mary, who was in labor, and out of compassion offering them the little space? Did the innkeeper's wife and children help Mary and Joseph to clean out a small corner?

The inn was full. That has to mean that there were people all over the place. Just imagine walking into a hotel lobby in Greensboro during the ACC [Atlantic Coast Conference] tournament—packed with people, all of them there for the same purpose. All of the travelers were at the inn because the Roman government had told them to come there to be counted. Having listened to all of the noise and complaints about the U.S. Census of 2000, you can imagine what kind of unhappy people were walking around the lobby. These people, like Mary and Joseph, had come seventy to a hundred miles to Bethlehem to be counted by the Roman government. We hate to drive to the post office to mail our income taxes. So you can imagine how resentful all these travelers were about being there. This was not a happy place.

All were there for the same purpose—to be counted—so the crowd was full of old and young. The rich and the poor were united under the law to come and be counted. There were people just arriving and those who had already reported and were checking out. Masters and slaves, Pharisees, Sadducees, Levites, Publicans—they were all there. Crippled and blind, the Roman government said, we need to know how many of you are in this province. They did not make exceptions. The crowd at the inn would have been made up of people of every status, rank, and wealth. Like the Christmas parade down Garnet, the crowd, the mob scene, at the inn would have had all kinds in it.

It would not be too much of a stretch to imagine that there were some Roman officials in the crowd. This was a Roman census and it seems likely that some Roman bureaucrats would have been sent to oversee the counting. They would have taken rooms in the inn and stayed there until the counting was done. Somebody had to be there to make sure the matter was conducted according to the letter and intent of the law. Who knows—perhaps the assignment of Roman Legions would have depended on the count, and if the count had been low, Palestine might not have gotten its fair share of the legions. Maybe that thirteenth legion would not have been given to Egypt but to Palestine if the census had not been done as it should have been. These functionaries of the state set up shop, took over the public building, pulled out their stylus and papyrus, and began making notes. Maybe the counting was being conducted in the courtyard of the inn. How many National Guard armories did they have in Bethlehem to hold such a counting?

It is into this chaos and confusion that Mary and Joseph came. They were most likely tired and hungry, bedraggled and exhausted from their trip. They had made a sixty- to seventy-mile trip. Whether in one day or two days, it is still a very long trip at about three to four miles per hour by foot. They needed a place to rest. There was no room available in this packed and noisy place, but the innkeeper said, if you can find room where the animals are you can rest there.

There were so many people—the innkeeper, his family, his staff, the crowd of people filling up all of the rooms the innkeeper had, the others who had come to be counted, those who had come to do the counting—and here came Mary and Joseph. Who in the world would ever have stopped to notice them?

Mary, a nice Jewish girl, devout and obedient, was probably a teenage mother. A nice Jewish boy named Joseph had been picked out for her by her family. She had been betrothed to Joseph but not yet ready to finalize the marriage; Joseph's parents thought they had made a perfect match for their son, but they were not yet ready for grandchildren. Then Mary turned up pregnant, and we all know the kind of rumors that get passed around about unmarried teenage girls. However, both Mary and Joseph were told by angels that this was different, and they both trusted the dream. Now they were married and had to go to Bethlehem because they were of the lineage of David. When the angel had come to talk to Mary about her calling, the angel had suggested that Mary was from the line of David. We know Joseph was. It may also be that Mary was descended from the priestly family of Levi if she was kin to Elizabeth by blood and not just by marriage. It is possible that she had family ties to both the priestly family of Levi and to Davidic ancestors. That would certainly have made her a good Jewish girl. This was a mighty young couple to whom God has entrusted such a precious cargo.

Mary delivered her child in the middle of the crowd of people and activities, and the coming of the child did not in any way lessen the crowd that was there. The screams and activities of childbirth in the middle of a crowded inn surely got lots of people involved: heat some water, get some rags. Take that kid Joseph out for some fresh air; he's looking a little pale. When the child had been delivered and they had gotten it cleaned and wrapped up, they put him in a manger so that Mary and the baby could get some rest. But the crowd only got bigger as the workers from the country come walking in, claiming that angels had told them to leave their sheep and come and see the miraculous act of God. The country people came and joined the small town crowd to look at this act of grace.

At some point the mob of people at the inn was also joined by those who had come from the East following a star. The Wise Men come with their gifts. Did these Wise Men get there on the night the child was born, or did they come on January 6th, or was it perhaps even three years later that they came and paid tribute? Why would Pilate kill all the male children three and under if the Wise Men had come at the time of Jesus' birth? In any case, we put them in the story.

It is important to remember that all of these people were present at the coming of God's grace. When God came to dwell with his creation, all kinds of people of all different ages, economic means, businesses, classes, and powers were present at Jesus' birth.

Shortly after the bombing of September 11, somebody sent me a moving and powerful e-mail. It was a series of magnificent photographs of mountains, lakes, beaches, sunsets, flowers, valleys, snow, and rivers. They were incredibly beautiful pictures, and written on each picture was some touching affirmation about the goodness of life and the value of people and the quality of relationships, and about how fragile and powerful human life is. Yet not one human face was shown. In this whole pictorial and verbal affirmation about the goodness of human life, about the power of love, and about the wonder of being human, not one single human face was present. It is possible to love humanity and not love people.

When God became human and dwelt among us, he came to a place that was packed with human faces. Maybe tradition has attempted to eliminate all the extra people as unnecessary so that we will not miss seeing who we have come to worship. Perhaps we have reduced the number so we can see the child more clearly, the way George W. Bush invited the children at his signing of the aid bill for Afghan children to step out of the way of the TV cameras so he could be seen more clearly as he signed the bill. But the story of the birth, as it is told, suggests that there would have been a wild mob where the child was born, and they would have heard his parents say, We will call his name Immanuel, which means "God with us"— God coming to reconcile all creation to his love. "All creation" means farmers and city folks, rich and poor, old and young, sick and well, black and white—all of them there, all of them present, all of them included as the ones to whom Jesus had come. Thanks be to God who has come to be with us, a crowd.—Rick Brand

CHILDREN'S SERMONS

January 4: Only God Knows What Time It Is
TEXT: Matt. 24:36
Object: A wall clock

Clocks, like this wall clock, tell time. The alarms on clocks loudly tell us when it is time to get up. We use clocks to inform us when to catch the school bus, when to eat lunch, and when to go to bed. The last one is not one of our favorites, is it?

Some of you have already learned to tell time. We tell time by learning to read the positions of the big and little hands on the face of the clock. The big hand marks the minutes, the little hand marks the hours. If there are digital clocks in your home, all that is needed to tell time is the ability to read the brightly displayed numbers.

There is another clock that is marking time. It is God's clock. God's clock began at the time of creation and has been running ever since. God's clock doesn't require batteries or have to be wound. It is ticking down to the time of Jesus' return to Earth.

No one knows what time it is on God's clock. That is, no one knows when Jesus is going to return to Earth. Jesus admitted that even he didn't know what time the clock said. Jesus also said that the angels don't know how much time is left. Only God the Father knows the time. Listen to this verse.

God asks us to be ready for Jesus' return at any moment. Some would like to know the time of Jesus' return so they can get ready at the last moment. These folks would prefer to live for themselves until the last minute, and *then* prepare for Jesus' return. When we feel that way we are not being faithful to the gifts and abilities that God has given to us, so Jesus' return will be like a thief in the night. We will be caught by surprise. When we live each day for Jesus by praying, sharing, and witnessing, we are doing the very things necessary to be ready for Jesus' return. If we live faithfully, we will be ready when Jesus returns.

When we ask, "What time is it?" we are asking what our clocks say according to human time. We also need to be aware of God's clock and live in faithful obedience. Let's be ready for Jesus to come back, whether he comes this afternoon or next year.—Kenneth Cox

January 11: The Password
TEXT: Ps. 100
Preparation: In addition to the morning Scripture reading, bring with you a copy of *The Message.*[1]

---

[1]Eugene H. Peterson, *The Message: The Bible in Contemporary Language* (Colorado Springs, Colo.: NavPress, 2002).

Psalm 100 has been an important part of the worship of God for a long, long, long time. At the time of ancient Israel, it was sung by those going to the Temple to praise God. The Pilgrims used a version of Psalm 100 that rhymed. It was like the hymn we sang this morning.

Now, I have a book called *The Message,* which gives us another version of this old psalm. Listen to this opening line: "Enter with the password: 'Thank you.'" What is a password? Yes, that's right; it is a word that allows something to be opened. What are you thinking of when you say that? You're not sure. Where might you use a password? Yes, on a computer. The password opens the door into your e-mail or the Internet. *Thank you* is one of the first things we say when we worship God. It opens us to all that God has done, is doing, and will do for us. It's not just for Thanksgiving Day. Remember, each day can begin with the password "Thank you." God never gets tired of hearing those words.—Gary D. Stratman

January 18: God Is Good

TEXT: 1 Chron. 16:34
Objects: Positive (+) and negative (–) signs written on a sheet of paper
Song: "God Is So Good"

Good morning, boys and girls. I'm glad you came to church today. Raise your hand if you're glad to be in church? [*Hold up the positive (+) sign.*] Is this the right sign? [*Wait for response.*] We may see this sign in many places. Perhaps we see it when working math problems. We may see a positive sign showing that something is right or safe. A negative sign may indicate something that is harmful or wrong.

Do you think God has signs he holds up when we are good or bad? [*Wait for response.*] No, he doesn't hold up signs. But when we listen, he speaks to our heart. This helps us decide what is right and wrong. When we live our lives close to God, we can hear him when he speaks. So the next time you see a + or – sign, remember to listen to that small voice that is God speaking to you. Will you do that? Then you will make the best choice.

First Chronicles 16:34 says, "Give thanks to the Lord, for he is good; his love endures forever." [*Say the first line of each stanza of "God Is So Good."*] "God is so good, he cares for me, I love him so, and I praise his name." [*Lead the children to sing each stanza. Ask the boys and girls to recall this song throughout the week. Pray that each child will realize the goodness of God's grace. Ask the pianist to continue playing as the children return to their seats.*]—Carolyn Tomlin[2]

January 25: Accept God's Simple Ways

TEXT: 2 Kings 5:13–14
Object: K.I.S.S. poster

This poster is a reminder to keep life simple. The letters KISS stand for "Keep It Simple Somehow." This is a useful reminder when life gets complex and hectic.

---

[2]Carolyn Ross Tomlin contributes to numerous Christian publications and leads conferences for women. Her husband is Matt Tomlin, pastor of Ward's Grove Baptist Church, Jackson, Tennessee.

God asks us to accept the simple way he works in our lives. After we accept the simple things, God reveals greater things to us. It is like a baby taking the first step in learning to walk.

A man named Naaman had to accept God's simple things. Many years before Jesus was born, Naaman was a famous, powerful military leader. He was friends with the King and rode the finest horses and wore fancy clothes. He had servants to bring him water when he was thirsty and food when he was hungry. Even though he was famous, Naaman caught leprosy. Back then there was no cure for this highly contagious disease. Sadly, Naaman faced losing his fame and fortune, and then he would die.

One of Naaman's servants was a little girl from Israel. When she heard that Naaman was sick, she told Naaman's wife that if he went to Israel and saw a prophet name Elisha he would be healed of his leprosy. So Naaman took his servants, horses, camels, and all sorts of gifts to Elisha's house. When Naaman arrived, Elisha didn't go out to see him. He sent a servant instead, to tell Naaman to go wash himself in the Jordan River seven times to get well. That's all Elisha said to do.

Naaman got mad because he expected Elisha to make a big deal of healing him. Naaman was a famous person and expected to be treated like a star. Also, where Naaman lived the rivers were nicer than the Jordan River. Naaman angrily turned to go home, still deathly sick. Along the way, one of Naaman's servants begged him to do the very simple thing that Elisha had instructed. Naaman put aside his pride and listened. Then he dipped himself into the Jordan River seven times. When he did this, he was completely healed. Listen to these verses.

Like Naaman, we may want God to work in our lives in the ways we have determined. God often asks us to do something very simple instead. If we will do the simple things, God will involve us in even greater things, but we must do the simple things first.—Kenneth Cox

February 1: Thanksgiving

TEXT: Phil. 4:4–7
Objects: Salt and pepper shakers, jars of peanut butter and jelly

Sometimes I bring objects out of the Time for Children bag and ask you to tell me what the objects are. Today we are going to play another game. When I bring something out of the bag, you tell me what goes with it. [*Hold up a saltshaker.*] That's right, it is salt and pepper that goes with it. You must have all known that, because there were so many hands lifted in the air. [*Hold up a jar of peanut butter.*] Knife is a good answer, but that's not what I have with me this morning. Yes, that's right. I have a jar of jelly. It really goes with peanut butter.

In our Bible reading this morning we are encouraged to pray about everything. We can talk to the Lord about big things and little things. We can pray at the beginning of the day and before we fall asleep at night. We can pray for our families and for our church. You know what goes with all of our prayers? Paul says we are to pray *with thanksgiving*. That means that whatever you tell God or ask of God, there is always room for thanking God. Thank God for the strength to play and to help others. Thank God for sending his Son, Jesus. See [*put your two hands together as in prayer*], thanksgiving goes with every prayer.—Gary D. Stratman

February 8: Jesus Loves You

TEXT: Matt. 19:14
Object: Mirror
Song: "Jesus Loves the Little Children"

Hello, boys and girls. I'm holding something that you might use every day. We call this object a *mirror.* Can you tell me how you use a mirror? [*Wait for response.*] Yes, you look into a mirror when you comb your hair. If you shop for new clothes you may look into a tall mirror to see how the clothes fit. Your mother or older sister may carry a small mirror in her purse for putting on makeup. A car has a rearview mirror and side mirrors to help you drive. So you see, mirrors are important in our lives.

But today I want you to look into this mirror I'm holding and tell me what you see. [*Pass around the mirror to all the children and allow them time to speak.*] You may see red, brown, blond, or black hair. You may see brown, black, blue, or green eyes. Your hair may be straight or curly. You may have freckles, wear glasses, or have braces on your teeth. When God looks at us, he does not see the things we see. He looks inside, at our hearts. He looks and sees how we love him and other people.

Did you know that Jesus loves children? He wants you to be part of a family that comes to church and obeys his laws. Matthew 19:14 says, "Jesus said, 'Let the little children come to me, and do not hinder them, for the kingdom of heaven belongs to such as these.'" [*Lead the children in singing "Jesus Love the Little Children." Lead them in prayer, asking God to bless all the children represented here today.*]—Carolyn Tomlin

February 15: Lift Your Voice and Sing

TEXT: Ps. 95:1–2; Eph. 5:19
Object: Hymnal
Song: "My Singing Is a Prayer"

Good morning, boys and girls. Isn't it wonderful to be in the house of the Lord today? Being in church always makes me happy. Church is a place to worship God. Let us name some ways we worship him. [*Wait for response.*] You hear Bible stories, bring an offering, pray, and sing.

Now, today let's talk about the importance of singing. When we come to church we should participate in as many activities as possible. You boys and girls may not know all the words to the songs, but you can still make a joyful noise unto the Lord. Singing comes from the heart; it's an activity that makes you happy. I don't believe that a person can be truly happy if he does not have a song in his heart. Do you? [*Wait for response.*]

When a song number is announced, you can turn to that page in the hymnal and follow along. Of course, you may already know many songs we sing regularly. If someone seated near you doesn't have a hymnal, offer him or her one.

When David was a shepherd boy, he wrote and sang songs while taking care of the sheep. Many of those songs are recorded in the psalms. For example, Psalm 95:1–2 says, "Come, let us sing for joy to the Lord; Let us shout aloud to the Rock of our salvation. Let us come before him with thanksgiving and extol him with music and song." In Ephesians 5:19, we read, "Speak to one another with psalms, hymns, and spiritual songs. Sing and make music in your heart to the Lord."

[*Pray and thank God for the ability to worship him in song. Ask the pianist to play "My Singing Is a Prayer" as the children return to their seats.*]—Carolyn Tomlin

February 22: God's Protective Wings

TEXT: Ps. 91:4
Object: Bird Pictures

These pictures of birds show the usefulness of their wings. Wings are used for flight. This stork is flying. Birds also use their wings to protect their young. In this picture the mother duck is shielding three young ducklings.

The mother uses her wings to protect her chicks in various ways. By holding a chick or duckling close in cold weather, she helps the baby bird to stay warm and not be harmed by the cold. After hatching, the chick is covered in soft, fluffy feathers called down, which is like hair. Later their feathers develop and can keep them warm. The mother's wings also protect the chick from other birds that might attack them, and the mother uses her wings to keep the chick from wandering off. Her wings nudge the chick back onto the right path.

The Bible compares the protection we receive from God to the wings of a bird. Listen to this verse.

God's wings are called a refuge, or place of safety. When a tornado warning is heard, we hurry to a place of safety or refuge, such as a storm shelter or a strongly built closet or hallway. When we feel in danger in the world, we hurry to the refuge of God by asking for his help through prayer. God's Word protects us like wings by showing us how to live.

These ducklings would be helpless without the protection and guidance of their mother's wings. We can feel safe in God's protection as we find refuge under his wings. God is faithful in caring for us; that means he will always be there to take care of us. When we feel safe we are free to enjoy life and become what God wants us to be.—Kenneth Cox

February 29: Rough Sandpaper

TEXT: Rom. 12:16b–21, esp. v. 21
Object: A piece of wood that is easily scarred, such as pine, and some sandpaper

Good morning, boys and girls. Today we are going to have an experiment to show you how a piece of wood can be like a person. I just love a smooth piece of wood that has been freshly cut. It smells good and it feels good. A piece of wood like this is just like a baby. When it is this fresh it is without any scars on the outside, but as it gets older and is used more and more, you begin to see marks here and there. [*Make some lines on the board with a pencil.*] A board gets more than marks; sometimes it also gets bumped and scratched and dented. [*Bump the board against another board, scratch it with a nail.*] Now the real problems are starting to show up, and if something isn't done pretty soon, the board will be replaced by another board and thrown away.

There is something that can be done for the board that will bring it back, fresh again, so that it looks like new. Does anyone have any ideas about how we can fix the board? [*Let them answer.*]

We could paint it, but another method that is used—and this should be done even before we paint it—is to sand it with sandpaper. Look what happens to the marks and the scratches when we sand it. Do you see them disappearing? We are making good out of something that looked bad.

People can do the same thing with their lives as we did with the board. A lot of people have things happen to them that we call sins. This kind of reminds us of bumps, dents, scratches, and marks. At first these things don't seem too bad, but as time goes along we find that the sins are really making us look awful. We find that just saying we are sorry or that we made a mistake is not enough. The Bible teaches us that we need to be forgiven for our sins by God and that we need to do something that will prevent us from doing bad things. It is when we start doing good things for people that we are like sandpaper. We can't do two things at once. When we are doing good, we cannot do bad. We need to overcome our sins by doing good for others. Sandpaper overcomes marks and scratches and love overcomes sin. So the next time you want to do something, make sure it is something good for someone else, and while you are doing it you will know that you are not only making someone happy, but you are also keeping yourself from doing something wrong. Overcome evil with good.—Wesley T. Runk[3]

March 7: Scribes Preserve God's Word
TEXT: Jer. 36:32
Object: A scroll or a picture of a scribe

This is a picture of a scribe. A scribe writes down the Word of God. A scribe named in the book of Jeremiah is Baruch. Listen to this verse.

The scribe had a very important job. In the day of Baruch there were no word-processing computers, typewriters, or printing presses. The scribe carefully copied all the words of God by hand onto a scroll. The scribe's tools were a sharpened reed or feather for a pen, and a container of ink. Being a scribe was a profession, like being a doctor or lawyer today. The scribe would commit his whole life to learning to copy correctly and write neatly. The scrolls that were made of God's Word were not owned by just anyone. At the synagogue the scrolls were kept in a special container and taken out and read on the Sabbath day.

The words of the Bible have been carefully preserved and transmitted to us over hundreds of years by scribes. If the scribes were like Baruch, who served Jeremiah, the original messages were written down exactly as the prophet dictated them. After years had passed, other scribes were careful to copy the original words for the next generation. We can be sure that the words of God have been passed down to us accurately because of the scribes.

We are very fortunate to have many individual copies of the Bible, but we should not take this privilege for granted. Our Bibles should be read each day and carefully studied throughout our entire life. Like the scribes, we pass along the Bible and what it means

---

[3]*Pass It On* (Lima, Ohio: C.S.S. Publishing, 1977), pp. 9–10.

to the next generation, and we can pass along only what we have carefully learned.—
Kenneth Cox

March 14: Jesus Is Our Best Friend

TEXT: John 15:13
Object: Picture of Jesus
Song: "What a Friend We Have in Jesus"

Greetings, boys and girls. I see that some of you brought friends to church today. We all need
friends. The right kind of friends are faithful. We can count on them in good times and bad.
Let me tell you about someone who can be your best friend. Listen and I will give you clues.

> He was born in Bethlehem in a manger.
> His mother was named Mary and his earthly father was Joseph, a carpenter from
>   Nazareth.
> He went with his family to the Temple in Jerusalem for the Feast of the Passover when
>   he was twelve years old.
> His knowledge of the Scriptures amazed all who heard him.
> When he was about thirty years old, he started preaching and healing.
> He made the blind to see, the lame to walk, and the deaf to hear.
> He was crucified on a cross for our sins.
> He rose again on the third day.
> He has gone to prepare a place for those who accept him and become Christians.
> He hears us when we pray and helps us make the right decisions.

Look at this picture [*hold up picture of Jesus*]. Who is this person? How many guessed the
clues as I read them. [*Wait for response.*] Remember, Jesus is the best friend boys and girls
can have. He will never leave or forsake you.

Listen as I read this verse from John 15:13: "Greater love has no man than this, that he
lay down his life for his friends." [*Lead the children in singing "What a Friend We Have in
Jesus." Pray that the children will realize that Jesus is a friend for life.*]

March 21: To Find God, Really Knock!

TEXT: Jer. 29:13
Object: A small board

Before doorbells were invented there was only one way to let somebody know you wanted to
come into their house: by knocking. This is what knocking on a door sounds like [*demonstrate*].

There is an unhappy story of a boy selling candy for a second grade class project. He went
from door to door without selling any candy. No one would come to the door. He was shy,
and this is how he would knock. [*Knock lightly on the board.*] In fact, the boy didn't want to
sell any candy, and he would sneak away from the door, relieved that no one had answered.
If no one came to the door, he wouldn't have to talk to the resident and try to sell the candy.
He thought that after he had been up and down his street without success, he could get his
mom or grandparents to buy all of his candy.

That's no way to sell candy, is it? To sell candy, the door must be approached confidently, and if there is no doorbell, the knocking should be loud enough to be heard inside, like this [*demonstrate*]. To knock too loudly is rude. When the door is answered, the seller should say, "Would you like to buy some candy? It is inexpensive and absolutely delicious!"

The Bible contains some verses about knocking. Jesus promised that if his followers would ask, seek, and knock, the way to truth and abundant life would open unto them (Matt. 7:7). Jesus also said that he knocks on the door of our lives wishing to come in (Rev. 3:20). The prophet Jeremiah spoke about how to seek God. Listen to this verse.

Sometimes when we ask for God's direction, we are like the little boy selling candy for his second grade class. We may pray once or twice and give up easily if we are not immediately answered. To discover answers to our questions about life, we are to seek diligently for God's direction. We are to pray, and to ask for help from others, such as our pastor or Sunday school teachers. Our parents can help us understand God's truth, or we can read the Bible to learn the answer. Seeking God is like knocking on a door. We must not be rude, but we must be confident in our attempts.

If you have a question or need guidance, call boldly upon the Lord and expect an answer. That is how God expects us to seek his help.—Kenneth Cox

March 28: Hands Help Others
TEXT: Matt. 8:3
Object: Picture of a hand, or a hand cutout; easel or standing chart
Song: "Jesus' Hands Were Kind Hands"

Good morning, boys and girls. I'm holding a picture of a hand. Look at your own hands. What do you see? [*Wait for response.*] Do you see five fingers on each hand? Hands are such an important part of our bodies. God gave us hands to help us with so many tasks. Let's make a list of ways we use our hands. I'll write as you tell me how you use your hands.

Buttoning clothes and getting dressed
Holding a spoon or fork while eating
Eating some foods with your hands
Rubbing or petting your dog or cat
Combing your hair
Holding a pencil
Turning pages in a book
Cutting with scissors
Helping your parents with chores

We could fill up this chart with "how we use our hands" and we would not be finished. Our hands tell others about our life. People who use their hands in their work may have rough, calloused hands. My father's were like that because he was a painter. A farmer's hands may appear rugged from the weather and from the soil in which he works.

Let's think about the hands of Jesus. How do you think they looked? [*Wait for response.*] You remember that Jesus probably worked in the carpenter shop of his earthly father, Joseph? A carpenter's hands would be rough and rugged. But I believe Jesus had kind hands also. He went about healing people and caring for the sick. He blessed little children with his hands. He washed the tired feet of his disciples. We could say that Jesus went about doing good things with his hands. Are your hands helping people?

Listen as I read from Matthew 8, verse 3: "Jesus reached out his hand and touched the man. . . ." [*Lead the children in singing "Jesus' Hands Were Kind Hands." Close in prayer, asking God to guide the hands of these children as they work and play.*]—Carolyn Tomlin

April 4: Jesus on the Cross
TEXT: Luke 23:34
Object: A picture of a crucifix

The cross above the baptistery is an "empty" cross. A figure of Jesus is not hanging on the cross. Statuary and pictures that depict Jesus on the cross are called crucifixes. I have a picture of a crucifix here for you to look at. You may see crucifixes on other churches or in hospitals and gift shops.

Crucifixes emphasize the death of Jesus for our sins. This is a sad picture, but one we must see in order to grasp the seriousness of sin. When Jesus died on the cross, he paid the penalty for our sins. Sins are the wrong things we all have done against one another and against God. We cannot pay the penalty for our sins because we are sinners. God has provided a way of forgiveness through Jesus' death. Everyone who believes in Jesus as Savior can pray for forgiveness and God will forgive them.

Empty crosses emphasize that Jesus did not remain on the cross but was resurrected from the dead. An empty cross helps us to remember the love of Jesus and that he is alive and reigning in heaven. Both crucifixes and empty crosses are important to portray the love and power of God for each one of us.

When Jesus was on the cross, he uttered seven important statements. One of the things Jesus said was a prayer asking God to forgive all those who were involved in his Crucifixion. Listen to the verse that contains that prayer.

When we look at a crucifix, it is comforting to think that Jesus prayed for our forgiveness there. He prayed for us because he loves us. Instead of being angry and full of revenge, Jesus was filled with love and mercy. Jesus wants us to become his disciples and receive the gift of eternal life. As you consider the love of Jesus on the cross, give your heart to him and commit your life to serving him.—Kenneth Cox

April 11: You Have Potential!
TEXT: Mark 12:30
Object: Package of seeds
Song: "More About Jesus"

Boys and girls, I'm holding something in my hand that has great potential. Inside this little package is something that can grow and become much larger. [*Hold up the package of seeds.*] Yes, this is a package of seeds. Let me ask you this: If these seeds stay in this package, away from the sun, soil, and water that God provides, will they grow and produce what they were intended? [*Wait for response.*] What would happen? [*Wait for response.*] That's right: nothing. They would just stay as they are. Soon they would loose their power to grow roots, leaves, and fruit.

How can we relate this lesson of the seeds to how Jesus wants boys and girls to grow in the Kingdom? [*Wait for response.*] Let's suppose you never make the decision to give your life to Christ. Of course, you may grow tall. You may accomplish much in life. But something just won't be quite right. You won't reach your full potential.

Or perhaps you are a young Christian. You are regular in church attendance, you obey your parents, and you pray and read your Bible. Can you think of other ways we can be better Christians? [*Wait for response.*] Yes, we should tithe our money.

Now, let me ask you: Which illustration shows a person reaching his or her full potential and growing more like Christ? The child who never accepted Christ? Or the one who lives for Christ each day? Which do you want to be like?

[*Read Mark 12:30: "Love the Lord your God with all your heart and with all your soul and with all your mind and with all your strength." Close with a prayer, asking the children to put God first in their lives. Ask the pianist to play a stanza of "More About Jesus" as the children return to their seats.*]

April 18: How God's Word Becomes *Real*
TEXT: Ps. 119:11
Object: A chisel, a hammer, and a rubber stamp

To write words on wood, a chisel like this is used. The chisel is placed over the wood and struck with a hammer. The chiseler must be very skillful.

Most writing that we do today is printed on paper using word processors on computers. In the past, however, words were printed on paper by setting type on a printing press. Each letter had to be set by hand, inked, and then pressed against the paper. A printing press is like this stamp. See, the letters are molded into this rubber and placed on an inkpad. After being pressed onto an empty page, the words are clear and readable. [*Demonstrate.*]

Words can also be engraved in stone. On buildings, inscriptions are made on cornerstones and over doorways. Words can be etched onto jewelry, too. One of the most interesting places to have words written is on our hearts. Listen to this verse. The word *hide* means to put God's truth in a safe place, like concealing a special treasure that we don't want to lose.

When we have memorized a Bible verse, what do we say? We say, "I know it by heart." That is, I can repeat it. I have a verse memorized. Listen as I say it. [*Demonstrate.*] Hiding God's word also means that we have learned its truth. We can learn the truth of a verse by being obedient to its commands. We can memorize the verse that tells us it is better to give than to receive, but that truth will be meaningless until we put it to work. If we share food with those who are hungry, we always feel good inside after we have done it—even better than when we get a present. Thus, hiding God's word means knowing not only the words, but also their truth through experience.

Do you have any Bible verses hidden in your heart? Let's memorize God's Word and then put it to work. As we do, we will learn about God and love him.—Kenneth Cox

April 25: The Teachings of Jesus
TEXT: Matt. 13:3–9
Object: Bible
Song: "Tell Me the Stories of Jesus"

Hello, boys and girls. I'm glad you chose to come to the House of the Lord today. I'm holding the greatest book ever written. [*Open the Bible.*] Do you know that the Bible is on the best-seller list every year? That's amazing when you consider all the books published annually. The New Testament is filled with stories that tell about the work of Jesus. Jesus used parables, or stories, related to life in Bible times when he taught the people.

You may ask, do the stories told long ago relate to today's problems? The answer is a definite yes. Families, churches, and boys and girls face the same difficulties as the people who lived in the time of Jesus faced.

One of my favorites stories is the parable of the Sower. Listen as I read from Matthew 13:3–9.

A farmer went out to sow his seed. As he was scattering the seed, some fell along the path, and the birds ate it up. Some fell on rocky places, where it did not have much soil. It sprang up quickly, because the soil was shallow. But when the sun came up, the plants were scorched, and they withered because they had no roots. Other seed fell among thorns, which grew up and choked the plants. Still other seed fell on good soil, where it produced a crop—a hundred, sixty, or thirty times what was sown. He who has ears, let him hear.

What did Jesus want the people to hear? [*Wait for response.*] Yes, the lesson was that our lives influence people if we choose to walk with Christ. Think about the parable of the sower throughout the week.

[*Pray, asking God to be with each child and his or her family this week. Ask the pianist to play "Tell Me the Stories of Jesus" as the children return to their seats.*]

May 2: Don't Forget Your Gift
TEXT: Deut. 16:16
Object: An empty gift bag

This is a gift bag. Gift bags are a great invention because the present is put into the bag with some tissue paper and no wrapping paper or ribbons are necessary. There is also no need for Scotch tape and gift-wrapping skill. After a gift has been received in one of these, the bag can be saved and recycled. We have a shelf in a closet filled with gift bags, and I help the environment by reusing them.

What would you think if one of your friends brought an empty bag to your birthday party? A pretty bag containing only tissue paper would make you wonder how that friend felt about you. A birthday present expresses friendship and admiration. With all presents, it is not the gift or the expense that is important; it is the thoughtfulness in choosing the present.

When we come to church we come to worship God. We are not coming to be with our friends, though our friends are here; we are coming to worship God, to sing praises to him and to listen to his voice. When we come we are to bring our offerings, too.

In the Old Testament there were three religious events that God required all of the Israelites to attend. The special times were called the Passover, the Feast of Weeks, and the Feast of Tabernacles. When God's people attended these celebrations they were instructed to bring a gift to God. They were not to come empty-handed. Listen to this verse.

Our gifts and offerings are important to God. Our donations to God show what we think of him when we come to worship. When we give it is not the amount that is important, it is the thought in our hearts. We should give freely and out of a sense of gratitude.

I know you wouldn't give an empty gift bag to a friend for his or her birthday. When we come to church we shouldn't come empty-handed. When your parents give you some money to place in the offering plate or turn in at Sunday school, you are completing a very important part of worshiping God. It pleases the Lord when we joyfully give to him.—Kenneth Cox

May 9: Making Your Home Happy
TEXT: Prov. 22:7
Object: Picture of a house
Song: "Happy the Home When God Is There"

Good morning, boys and girls. It's good to see you in church. Today we are talking about ways to make our home a happy place. Look at this picture I'm holding. By looking at the outside of this house, you can't tell much about the people who live there. You might say that the yard is neat, and the outside of the house is well cared for, but you know nothing about the people—whether they are a happy family or not.

Having a home that is a happy place is important to God. God planned for families, and he wants children to have loving parents. Did you know that if you grow up in a happy family, you are more likely to have that same type of home when you marry and have children of your own? What we learn, we want to continue.

Let's talk about how boys and girls can make a difference in their homes. Can you share some ideas that work for your family? [*Wait for response.*] You are saying that everyone needs responsibility in a home, which means that children should share in the workload and have chores. Then families should spend time talking. Turn off the television and enjoy conversation, games, and sports. Take time to laugh and be happy. Stay on a budget and refrain from asking for things you want but don't need. Plan meals so that everyone eats at the same time. Enjoy pleasant conversation during mealtime. Of course, there are many other things we could add.

Proverbs 22:6 says, "Train a child in the way he should go, and when he is old he will not turn away from it." [*Pray that each child will have a Christian home where parents seek God as their guide. Ask the pianist to play "Happy the Home When God Is There" as the children return to their seats.*]—Carolyn Tomlin

May 16: God Is Our Creator
TEXT: Eccles. 3:11
Object: A single flower
Song: "All Things Bright and Beautiful"

Good morning, boys and girls. Isn't this a beautiful morning? I brought this small flower to show you just one thing God created. This flower grew from a tiny seed. The seed sprouted, produced roots in the soil, sent up a stem, grew leaves, and finally produced this flower.

That's amazing, isn't it? I've seen flowers and plants growing out of rocks—where almost nothing grows. When we think about creation, God certainly had a plan.

In the song "All Things Bright and Beautiful" the writer speaks about the great and small things God created. Can you help me name some things that are great? Let's see, there are elephants, camels, giraffes, hippopotamus, eagles, and other large birds and animals. Next, let's name some small creatures: a mouse is small. What about an ant? Then there are kittens, puppies, gold fish, and others.

Then God provided cold wind in the winter and warm summer sun. He made the fruit to ripen for us to enjoy. He gave us a marvelous body, with lips to taste the food. Because he wanted us to see this beautiful world, he gave us eyes to take in every thing he made. What a plan! What a Creator!

Ecclesiastes 3:11 speaks of God's creations: "He has made everything beautiful in its time." Listen as I read the chorus and the first stanza of "All Things Bright and Beautiful," written by Cecil Alexander, who lived from 1818 to 1895.

> All things bright and beautiful,
> All creatures great and small,
> All things wise and wonderful;
> The Lord God made them all.
> Each little flower that opens,
> Each little bird that sings,
> He made their glowing colors;
> He made their tiny wings.

[*Lead the children in singing this selection. Lead them in prayer, thanking God for the beautiful world he created for us to enjoy. Ask the pianist to continue to play as the children return to their seats.*]

May 23: The Devil Is Like a Lion
TEXT: 1 Pet. 5:8
Object: Picture of a lion

This is a picture of a lion. Lions are frightening. I prefer seeing lions at a zoo locked up in a cage. I would be uncomfortable if I were close to a lion, because they are predators. Predators are animals that live by killing other animals. In Africa, lions hunt antelope, an animal that looks like a deer. The Bible compares the devil to a lion. Listen to this verse.

A lion hunts its victim in two ways. First, it looks for an antelope that has wandered from the herd. Off by itself an antelope is easy to attack. Second, if there is not a solitary antelope, the lion seeks to identify the weakest animal in the herd. When the lion runs after and scatters the herd, the weakest antelope will be the slowest and the easiest to catch.

The devil operates in the same way. First, the devil tries to tempt and destroy one of God's children who is not active in a congregation of believers. When a Christian is not active in the fellowship of other believers, he becomes isolated and weak. He is like a burning stick pulled out of the fireplace. Alone the stick quickly loses its flame. Second, the devil tempts our weaknesses. If we don't pray and read our Bibles, we grow weak spiritually and can be mislead into sin.

We shouldn't let this truth about the devil frighten us. God has warned us so we will be safe. First, God will take care of us when we are at church and gain strength from our teachers and Christian friends. Worshiping together also unites and builds us up. When we are close to God and his people, we become strong in the Lord. Second, we must remain alert spiritually. When we study our Sunday school lessons, and read our Bibles each day and pray, we are not likely to fall into the devil's trap for weaklings.

It is best to see lions when they are locked in a cage in the zoo. The Lord has provided a way for us to live safely as the devil prowls around seeking to harm us. When we are close to God and his people and on guard spiritually, we can be safe from the devil, as from a lion behind bars in the zoo.—Kenneth Cox

May 30: Giraffes Are Great
TEXT: Acts 1:8
Object: A giraffe

This is a giraffe, the world's tallest mammal. Giraffes may stand more than eighteen feet tall, and their necks account for nearly half their height. The giraffe has two to four small, skin-covered, hornlike structures on its head, and a long, tufted tail. Giraffes are able to use their extremely long tongues for cleaning their eyes and ears. They are speedy runners. They are found only in Africa, south of the Sahara desert.

If giraffes had feelings as humans do, they might feel very odd or different. In fact, they might even question why God put them on Earth. They are here to fill a special place in nature, and they are also beautiful to look at. Giraffes cause us to marvel at God's creation.

We might feel like a giraffe. We may not be like other people, though we want to look like them and have similar abilities and possessions. We may wonder about our purpose in life.

One purpose for which God has made us is to witness. Listen to this verse. If every believer in Jesus would witness to their faith, the gospel would spread over the world in a matter of months, and millions of people would be saved.

God has placed us in our families to be witnesses. Because of your unique ability to make certain friends and because of your family ties, you are specially equipped to tell others about Jesus. Some of your friends would not listen to me talk about Jesus because I am a stranger to them. Your aunt or uncle might not want me to present the gospel, because they don't trust me. However, your friends and family members will listen to you because they know, love, and trust you.

Giraffes have a special place in the Kingdom of God. We have a special place, too, because of our unique circle of family and friends. God's purpose is for us to use our connections to share his love and grace.—Kenneth Cox

June 6: Jesus, the Light of the World
TEXT: 2 Cor. 4:6
Object: Drawing of the sun on paper
Song: "Sunshine in My Soul"

Hello, boys and girls. Did you notice that we are having a beautiful day today? Isn't God good to us! Look at this picture of the sun I'm holding. The sun is really amazing, and just think: God put it into our universe. Let's talk about what the sun provides. [*Wait for response.*] Let's see, you say the sun provides warmth, the sun melts the snow, the sun makes plants grow, the sun heats our homes, and the sun warms the Earth. We could make a long list of how the sun benefits the Earth.

Have you ever thought about what our life would be like without the sun? For example, plants would not grow, you wouldn't have daylight hours to play outdoors, and you couldn't see the beauty of God's Earth if everything was dark all the time.

The next time you are outside and feel the warmth of the sun, thank God for making it part of our world. Just as the sun is the light of the world, Jesus is the light of our lives. He puts the sunshine and happiness in each boy and girl.

Le me read a verse from 2 Corinthians 4:6: "For God, who said, 'Let light shine out of darkness, made his light shine in our hearts.'" [*The children will enjoy singing a verse of "Sunshine in My Soul." This familiar song praises God for the glorious and bright feeling that comes when Jesus is the sunshine of our lives. Pray that each child will accept Christ as Savior.*]— Carolyn Tomlin

June 13: Labels
TEXT: Jer. 22:3
Object: Various containers with descriptive labels

There are laws in our country that apply to product labels. Breakfast cereal boxes must state the amount of calories and vitamins in their products. Grape drinks are required to disclose what percentage of the liquid in the can or bottle is actually grape juice. These laws protect purchasers from being mislead, and they convey that what is advertised on the outside is really on the inside.

God has some labeling concerns, too. When we call ourselves Christians, we are saying we belong to God. We should not just say we are disciples of Jesus; we must also be authentic in our words, thoughts, and actions. God said through the prophet Jeremiah that his people were to do some real things. Listen to this verse.

Jeremiah proclaimed that God's people were to rescue those who had been robbed. God didn't want his children to ignore victims of crime. Believers were to protect people who had recently moved from a foreign country. These aliens couldn't speak the language and weren't used to local customs, so the dishonest could take advantage of them. Widows and orphans were to be respected and kept from harm, too. The Lord said that if believers carried the label of being his people, they should protect those who couldn't protect themselves.

In some television shows, detectives search for the villain who is guilty of a crime. When that evil person is brought to justice, we say, "All right!" When we protect the innocent and do acts of justice, God says the same thing in heaven. We may be tempted to think that someone else will right the wrongs in our world, but actually we must become that someone or no one will complete the good deed.

It is so easy to be a Christian in name only. We may protect the label of "Christian" by coming to Sunday school and telling people which church we belong to. To the Lord the most important thing is "being." We must be genuine in our commitment to Jesus Christ.

It's nice to know that a label accurately describes what is in the box. God wants us to be the same way. He wants our words, thoughts, and actions to be like the label we hold out to the world, to show that we are truly God's people.—Kenneth Cox

June 20: A Great Big Bunch of Love

TEXT: 2 Cor. 4:13–18

Object: An invisible armful of love

Good morning, boys and girls. How are you on this special day? [*Let them respond.*] Do you know what day this is? [*Let them tell you.*] Right. This is Father's Day. Today we are especially nice to our fathers because today we want to thank them for all of the wonderful things they do. I have a great gift with me today, boys and girls, which you could give to your dads. Would you like to see it? [*Let them respond.*] Well, here it is. How do you like it? [*Hold out your arms as if holding a huge package. Let the children respond.*] Can't you see this gift? [*Let them respond.*] Why, this is the best gift of all. Let me tell you about it, then maybe you will be able to see what it is.

This gift could make all of the troubles in the world go away! Wouldn't that be wonderful, boys and girls? You see, this gift is sort of catching. You know how you can catch a cold or the measles from someone else? Well, when you give this gift away, it spreads, and other people catch it, too. Can you guess how big this gift is? [*Let them guess.*] Well, this gift can be as big as you want it to be. It will be at least as big as your heart.

Another wonderful thing about this gift is that it will last forever if you want it to. How long do your toys usually last after Christmas Day? [*Let them respond.*] Sometimes your Christmas presents don't even make it to the next Christmas. Some of them get broken or lost. Some of them get too small for you. Gifts don't last a very long time, do they boys and girls? Well, this gift—if you treat it right—will last forever! You will never outgrow it.

Another strange thing about this gift is that even though you give it away, you still have it! Did you ever give someone a present that you really wanted yourself? [*Let them answer.*] It is really hard to give away something that you love very much. Well, with this gift, even though you give it away, you still have it! Can anyone see what this gift is? [*Let them guess.*] This wonderful gift is *love.* Even though you can't touch it or weigh it or put it in a box, it is very real, isn't it, boys and girls? [*Let them respond.*] Your parents give you lots of love each day. Because love is catching, you have lots of it now that you can give to other people. Who are some of the people who would like a little bit of your love? [*Let them answer.*] Those are good people to share your love with, boys and girls. Most of all, on this Father's Day, let's all give a great big bunch of love to our dads, so they will know how much we care about them. Will you do that, boys and girls? Good. So will I. God bless you. Amen.—Wesley T. Runk[4]

June 27: We Are to Fish for the Lost

TEXT: Luke 5:10b–11

Object: A fishing pole

This is a fishing pole. I'm going to cast it over there. Let's see if we can catch something. I don't seem to be getting any bites. Let's be quiet and see if a fish will get on the line.

---

[4]*On the Move with Jesus* (Lima, Ohio: C.S.S. Publishing, 1984), pp. 49–50.

This is silly, isn't it? There's no water here, only carpeting. This is a church and no fish are hiding under the pews. To catch fish we must go to the lake or ocean. We'd also have to put a hook on the line and use some bait.

Jesus specially selected twelve men to be his apostles. These apostles were with Jesus most of the time for the three years of his ministry. The first apostles that Jesus selected were fishermen. Jesus told them from that day forward that they were to "fish" for men. Listen to these verses. These men understood that their special calling would be to seek out the lost as they used to locate fish.

Jesus' command to us is the same. We are to be fishers of men and women, boys and girls. We "fish" by telling folks about Jesus and what he has done for us. Some think we are doing all we need to do in God's Kingdom by coming to church. Attending church is important. We learn the truth about God through our Bible study classes. We pray and sing praises to God during worship and gain strength from one another. But if that is all we have done, we haven't done the most important task. Jesus still wants us to go to people who are not Christians and teach them about him. We can't catch any fish in this sanctuary. Folks won't come to know Jesus as Savior if we wait for them to find us and come to church. The majority of lost people will not come to church. We must go where they are.

Jesus called seeking the lost "fishing." We can fish for souls by asking our friends to come to Sunday school with us. Also, we are fishers of men when we pray for those around the world who have never heard the name of Jesus. Let's be sure to tell others about Jesus and become fishers of men.—Kenneth Cox

July 4: God Bless America
TEXT: Ps. 33:12
Object: American flag and a Bible
Song: "America the Beautiful"

Good morning, boys and girls. [*Hold up the flag and Bible.*] How do a flag and a Bible go together? I was thinking about how very grateful I am to live in a country that is free. We have a great nation. We can come to church and worship God as we please. In some countries, that is not possible. You and your family would be persecuted and punished. I think we often take our freedoms for granted.

Let us talk about some freedoms we have in America. Can you name some? [*Wait for response.*] Our country provides public schools for all boys and girls. In some countries only the wealthy attend school. In some, only the boys are allowed to go. Most of us live in homes where parents love us and care for us. Our neighborhoods are safe and you can play outdoors. In some countries, war has been going on for years. Playing outside the home is very dangerous.

We also live in a beautiful country. The land forms vary from coastline to mountains to deserts to plains and flat country. Fertile land produces food for our citizens. Towering mountains frame the valleys. Rivers provide fish and water transportation. Yes, America is a great and beautiful country. But for America to stay great, we must never forget to thank God for our freedoms. So the next time you see a flag, think of the Bible, too.

Psalm 33:12 says, "Blessed is the nation whose God is the Lord." [*Ask an adult to read the stanzas of "America the Beautiful." Close by thanking God for blessing our nation and ask him to help us to always choose to obey his will.*]—Carolyn Tomlin

July 11: God Sends the Rain

TEXT: Job 5:10

Object: Glass of water

Song: "For the Beauty of the Earth"

Boys and girls, I am so happy to see you today. You are as welcome as a rain after a dry spell. How many of you have heard that saying? [*Wait for response.*] It means that when the Earth is dry and the crops are wilting and drying up, farmers need rain.

Now, this glass of water I'm holding represents rain that God sends down onto the Earth. Rain is something that people cannot make. We have to wait for conditions to be right and for God to bless us with this precious resource that we call rain.

Let's talk about the ways our Earth uses rain. What comes to mind? [*Wait for response.*] Let's see, animals must have water to drink, fish must have water to swim in and to live, and plants must have water in order to grow strong roots, stems, leaves, and fruit. How is water necessary for families? Yes, we use water for cooking our meals, for washing our clothes, and for bathing. Then we enjoy recreational activities in which water is required, such as swimming, boating, and water skiing.

I've made it a practice that when the first drops of rain fall, I rush outside and enjoy the unique smell. Why don't you try that next time, too? And don't forget to thank God for sending water to nurture the Earth.

The Bible mentions rain many times. In Job 5:10 we read, "He bestows rain on the Earth; he sends water upon the countryside." [*Say a prayer thanking God for the Earth he created. Ask the pianist to play a stanza of "For the Beauty of the Earth" as the children return to their seats.*]—Carolyn Tomlin

July 18: How to Be Cleansed from Sin

TEXT: Isa. 1:18

Object: A bar of soap

This is a bar of soap just out of its wrapper. It smells pure and clean. It's fun to be at the lake or beach all day swimming and building castles in the sand. However, at the end of the day it is good to clean up. In the bath, we use soap to remove all the sticky sun block lotion and gritty sand. Afterward, when we put on clean pajamas, there is a special sensation of being clean.

It's good to be clean spiritually. We become dirty spiritually when we sin. We all sin because we are all imperfect. When we have done something wrong, like broken a friend's toy and not told him about it, we feel bad inside. Our conscience hurts us and a frown may darken our otherwise happy face. That frown is deeper than our skin; it goes into our inner being. When we are unclean we can come to God for forgiveness. Listen to this verse.

There are two ways for us to become clean spiritually. First, we have to be truthful with those around us. If we have broken the toy of a friend, we must tell that person about the accident. If it was our fault, we must offer one of our own toys in exchange. When we replace what they lost, we are making restitution. The second way to become clean is by asking God's forgiveness. When we wrong someone on Earth, we also sin against God in heaven. All sin hurts God. By offering us forgiveness, God has provided a way for us to cleanse ourselves from our wrong actions. All we have to do is bow our heads and ask for forgiveness from God. God always forgives us because he is faithful. After we have taken these two steps for forgiveness, God wants us to smile again and accept the spiritual cleansing he has given.

God has provided this powerful way of forgiveness through Jesus' death on the cross. Jesus paid the penalty for all of our wrongs because we were unable to provide a way of forgiveness on our own.

It's a good sensation to be clean physically. It's even better to feel right with others and be forgiven by God. Then we are clean spiritually.—Kenneth Cox

July 25: Jesus Values Pennies
TEXT: Mark 12:42–43
Object: Two pennies

Pennies aren't worth much. I remember that when I was in junior high school I watched a boy throw pennies across the street into a field. He said he didn't like pennies because they crowded his pockets. Some folks won't bend over and pick up a penny if they see one lying on the street. They don't believe the little copper coin is worth the trouble.

One day Jesus told his followers how much he valued two very small coins. A poor woman came to the Temple and donated two coins of small value, like pennies. Jesus noticed the offering and said she had given more than the rest because she had given all she had to live on. The coins revealed the commitment in the woman's heart. Listen to these verses.

Out attitude about money and possessions will determine much about our future. If we are willing to give generously to the church and to others in need, we will be blessed. When we give it is not the amount but the attitude that is important. It is possible to be proud and to think that we have earned all the money we have. That feeling makes us more likely to keep our money. But if we believe that God has provided our jobs and health, we will be generous. Our giving will flow from grateful hearts. It is easy to be cold and to begrudge giving and sharing. However, if we open our hearts, we can give and then manage what remains to meet all of our needs. Remember, Jesus knew the heart of the poor woman who gave two small copper coins. He also knows our hearts.

Let's give our hearts to Jesus in everything. Let's serve faithfully, seek the lost diligently, and give generously.—Kenneth Cox

August 1: Walking Like Jesus
TEXT: Luke 5:11
Object: Cutout of a footprint
Song: "Footsteps of Jesus"

Hello, boys and girls. I'm glad to see you today. Every one of you left something behind you when you came to church this morning. Do you know what it was? [*Wait for response.*] Here's another clue: look behind you now. Perhaps you see them, perhaps you don't. The answer to this riddle is *footprints.* [*Hold up the cutout of a footprint.*] Your footprints follow you everywhere you go. Whether your footprints are visible or not depends on the surface— such as grass, sand, concrete, or carpet.

The disciples left their work and followed Jesus. Those who made their living as fishermen left their nets and followed him. Our missionaries who serve in foreign countries must leave behind extended family members, their jobs, and their homes and go to a new location when they are appointed. You boys and girls do not know what Jesus has planned for your life. You must be ready to obey his call and follow him wherever he leads. However, you can walk like Jesus even when you are young. Keep your eyes on what is right, pray that God will guide you, and listen to his voice. Following Jesus is the only way to real happiness. You too can follow in the footprints of Jesus.

Listen as I read from Luke 5:11: "So they pulled their boats up on shore, left everything and followed him." [*Close in prayer, asking God to guide the footprints of these children as they go through life. Ask the pianist to play "Footprints of Jesus" as the children return to their seats.*]—Carolyn Tomlin

August 8: Jesus Taught His Disciples
TEXT: John 8:2
Object: A globe

In just a few days school will begin. It is time to get your school supplies together and be ready for a new year of teachers and classes. By learning at school we are fighting the enemy of ignorance. Ignorance means to not know something. If we say we are ignorant about repairing cars, we are not saying we are dumb; we are admitting that we don't know how to fix cars.

Ignorance works against us. Ignorance is like trying to walk on a broken leg. Walking on a broken leg is painful and causes further damage to the leg.

Some examples of human ignorance are amusing. Christopher Columbus is credited with sailing from Spain and discovering America in 1492. In those days, some people thought the world was flat, not round like this globe. In their ignorance they feared that Columbus, along with his ships and men, would sail off the edge of the world and die. Long ago doctors believed that bleeding someone would cure their illnesses. The physicians would cut their patients and let their "bad blood" flow out to bring healing. Since those days we have learned that the Earth is round and that bleeding causes harm to patients. We have removed these harmful results of ignorance through our growing knowledge.

Jesus taught. Listen to this verse. As a great teacher, Jesus taught his disciples how to pray, that it is more blessed to give than to receive, and to love their enemies. In every lesson Jesus aimed to reduce harmful ignorance about God. As Jesus' followers learned to pray, they discovered the miraculous power of God. As Jesus taught about giving, selfish men and women learned how good it felt to share their possessions with those in need. Also, as the disciples accepted the need to love their enemies, they got rid of bitterness and anger. Jesus' followers learned and were helped in this life and in eternity.

Remember, there is nothing wrong with being ignorant. When we say we don't know, we are also saying that we are willing to learn and remove harmful ignorance. It is good to remove ignorance about the world, about medical care, and about God. We especially need to teach those who have never heard about Jesus. In the world there are millions of people who are ignorant about how much Jesus loves them. Jesus commanded his followers to go into all the world and teach. When the lost learn about Jesus they come out of the darkness of ignorance and into the light of knowing God.—Kenneth Cox

August 15: Disciples

TEXT: John 8:31–36

Object: Any snapshot of a person or persons. It would fit well to have a picture of the children. Also have a picture of Jesus.

What do I have in front of me? That is correct; it is a picture. Now I am going to lift it up and ask you to describe it to me. That was fast; yes, it's a picture of children from vacation Bible school! OK, OK. I am getting that many of you are in this picture.

Now, before I showed you this photograph, where was it kept? You all saw it. It was in my Bible. That reminds me of this morning's Bible story. In it Jesus says, "If you abide [stay] in my word, you are my disciple." A disciple is a learner. If we keep studying God's Word and learn more about who Jesus was and what he did for us, we will become his disciples.

We speak of the twelve disciples, but there are many more than that. Watch as I put the picture back in the Bible. It is a reminder that when we stay in God's Word through family devotions, Sunday school, vacation Bible school, and worship, we become more and more free to follow Jesus wherever he leads. Even more than that [*take out from the Bible the picture of Jesus*], we will be more like Jesus. That doesn't mean we will look like him physically. But we will love people even when they don't act so lovely toward us. We will pray and trust God. This will happen because we have learned to stay in God's Word. Thanks for being here.—Gary D. Stratman

August 22: Getting It Together

TEXT: Eph. 2:13–22

Object: Two pieces of rope

Good morning, boys and girls. How many of you would like to be a Boy Scout or a Girl Scout? Boy Scouts and Girl Scouts learn many things and have lots of exciting adventures. But one of the things they learn that I like best is how to tie knots. How many of you know how to tie a knot? [*Let them answer.*] There are special knots for sailors and mountain climbers, and then there are just regular knots for people like you and me. Tell me one kind of knot that you can tie. How many of you know how to tie your shoes? That takes a special kind of knot.

Knots are really fun, but they also tell us a very special story about the way God helps people like you and me. I brought with me today two pieces of rope. When you see what happens with these pieces of rope, you will understand something new about Jesus. This piece of rope, the big piece, is God, and this piece of rope, the little piece, is you or me. The two pieces of rope can be as far apart or as close together as you want them to be. God and people are like that also. You can be as close to God as you want to be or you can live like you've never heard of God. But no matter how far from or close to God you are, you are not together. You are still two pieces of rope. God had a plan, a very special plan, and he called that plan Jesus. God, the big piece of rope, took a hold of a little piece of rope and made a knot with the little piece of rope. The knot is called Jesus. Jesus brings together God and people like you and me. The Bible has a special word for this knot: *reconciling.* It means bringing two persons or things together. God brought you and me together with him in the knot called Jesus. That's a pretty wonderful plan and it makes a lot of sense. It is something that none of us can do ourselves; only God can do it.

The next time you tie a knot or see someone else tie a knot, I hope it reminds you of this story and how Jesus is the knot that brings God and us together. In Jesus' name, amen.— Wesley T. Runk[5]

August 29: Clean Inside and Outside

TEXT: Matt. 23:25
Object: A bowl smeared with mud on the inside

Would you be willing to eat ice cream from this bowl? Well, I guess not; it is filthy on the inside. Even though the outside of the bowl is sparkling clean, there is mud on the inside. If we ate ice cream from this dish, the mud would get all over the ice cream. Not only would the mud spoil the taste of the ice cream, but the grit would get in our teeth. Eating mud is not healthy either, so we would not want to eat ice cream from this dish. We enjoy having ice cream, but we would insist on a clean dish.

Jesus encountered some people who were like this bowl. On the outside they wore beautiful flowing robes and smiled. They had titles that brought them respect. There were others like them who had formed a type of club. They never called attention to the wrongs that were done by the others. In the minds and hearts of these leaders were selfishness, greed, and unkindness. Jesus therefore said that they were like bowls clean on the outside but dirty on the inside. Listen to this verse.

We are sometimes like this dish. We clean the outside of our lives and not the inside. We are unclean inside when we have anger, hatred, and bitterness in our thoughts. We may try to disguise them on the outside with a smile, but we still know about them. God does, too. Jesus instructs us to be honest, loving, and kind in our hearts and minds. We may think it is impossible because so many in the world have unclean thoughts and actions. God promises that he will help us to be clean on the inside. He offers forgiveness and the power of the Holy Spirit to guide our thoughts and minds.

Eating ice cream from a dish that is dirty on the inside is not very appetizing. It is not desirable to live in a world that is filled with people who are smiling on the outside but frowning on the inside. With God's help we can be clean inside and out and make a better world.— Kenneth Cox

September 5: Learning from the Teacher

TEXT: Matt. 5:1–2
Object: A Bible
Song: "Jesus Was a Loving Teacher"

Hello, boys and girls. Today we're talking about how we learn. Sometimes our parents read us a story that gives an example of how we should live. Perhaps our Sunday school teachers tell us Bible stories. [*Hold up the Bible.*] The Bible has been handed down for many generations as a book of God's Word. This book tells us that Jesus was a loving teacher who taught people to love and pray. He was patient with all people, even when they did not understand. Do

---

[5]*On the Move with Jesus* (Lima, Ohio: C.S.S. Publishing, 1984), pp. 61–62.

you know what the word *patient* means? [*Wait for response.*] It means to take plenty of time, not to rush.

One way we learn is by seeing and using our eyes. Another is by hearing and using our ears. Then we learn by touching and using our fingers. Aren't you glad that God gave you such a wonderful body to help you learn?

One of the ways that Jesus taught was to tell stories called parables. When Jesus taught in parables and related these to the people's lives, they understood what he was teaching. Because many people wanted to hear him teach, he often took a small boat out on the water. The people gathered on the shore and listened to his words. He taught in another location in Matthew 5:12: "Now when he saw the crowds, he went up on a mountainside and sat down. His disciples came to him, and he began to teach them."

[*Lead the children in singing "Jesus Was a Loving Teacher." Close in prayer, asking God to watch over each child during the week. Ask the pianist to continue playing as the children return to their seats.*]—Carolyn Tomlin

September 12: Friends
TEXT: Phil. 4:2, 3
Object: A pair of gloves

How many of you know what I am holding in my hands? That's right, a pair of gloves. Why do we call them a pair of gloves? Yes, you need two gloves because you have two hands. So you always need two gloves at all times. Well, OK, except when you are playing golf. Now, back to the pair of gloves. These two have so much in common; look how they fit together when I fold my hands. You wouldn't want to separate one from the other or lose one of them.

In the Bible we read of the apostle Paul's friends, Euodia and Syntyche. Those names may sound strange to us, but they were Christians and leaders in the Church. Paul says that their names were in the book of life. They were not strangers to God. Paul called them fellow workers who shared his hardships as missionaries of the good news of Jesus Christ. But now they were separated due to some argument; they didn't seem to be able to work together for God. As one glove can be separated from the other, so we can be separated from one another by not forgiving one another (for instance, if we have an argument on the playground, or if jealousy gets in the way when a friend gets a prize that we didn't). I hope you will always move toward forgiving your friends. When something separates you, God can make you, one again. [*Put on the gloves and fold your hands.*] Amen.—Gary D. Stratman

September 19: Don't Be Deceived by the Liar
TEXT: 2 Cor. 11:14
Object: Posters of the names of Satan

The Bible calls Satan by several names. These are some of the descriptions used for the evil one: the devil, our adversary, Beelzebub, and the prince of this world. Jesus called him the father of lies. Jesus said that Satan's native tongue was the language of lies (John 8:44). The Scripture also says that Satan disguises himself as an angel of light. He does this to make his lies more believable. Listen to this verse.

One disguise that Satan wears to make his lies more attractive is the costume of a friend. The evil one wants to mislead by making us think he wants to help us. He may speak to us through another human being and persuade us to shoplift some candy because it will be a thrill. He may tempt us to copy answers off someone else's paper during a math test because he wants us to get the best possible grade without doing our homework. The devil may entice us to take a bike that doesn't belong to us because we will have fun. All the time he has on the mask of a friend when he is actually our enemy.

If we believe the devil's lies we must pay the price. Instead of having a thrill, we get caught shoplifting and lose the respect of our parents. Instead of making better grades by cheating, our paper is taken up by our teacher and we get a zero. And the bike that looked like so much fun is impossible to hide, and we are too embarrassed to return it to its owner.

It is scary to think that the devil wants to trick us and ruin our lives. Satan can tempt and mislead any unsuspecting human being.

How can we protect ourselves? By loving the truth. Jesus is called the way, the truth, and the life. We love and learn the truth by reading the Bible, by listening in Sunday school, and by coming to church. The more we love the truth, the safer our lives will become. Then, when we hear a lie, we will notice the falsehood because it won't sound like the truth. When we know the truth, a lie, no matter how friendly, will make us suspicious. When we know the truth, we become safe in the loving arms of Jesus. Furthermore, the truth will set us free (John 8:32).—Kenneth Cox

September 26: Gifts

TEXT: Luke 1:67–79

Object: Wish-list (all paper products stores sell decorated to-do lists or reminder pads on magnets for the refrigerator, or you can make your own marked "List for Santa")

This is the time of year when something like this is very popular. It's a long paper with lines on it. What could you write on those lines? Yes, things to pick up at the store. Maybe a list of special events during the holidays. But at Christmastime, what list comes to mind? That's right: a list of presents or what you would like to have.

Sometimes our praying to God is just like a wish list. We pray asking for good health, for a family member who lives far away to be back here for Christmas. These are all good things, and Jesus does tell us that we should *"ask, seek* and *knock."* These words remind us that God is the giver of every good and perfect gift. But isn't there more to prayer than asking? Look at the Bible story this morning. Notice what Zechariah calls God in his prayer—"the Most High." In his prayer he recognizes God's tender mercies and loving-kindness.

God used Zechariah to tell the world that Jesus has come as our Savior. Zechariah also reminds us that our daily prayers are more than a wish list. We can thank and praise God for being God and for giving every good gift. Amen.—Gary D. Stratman

October 3: Changing in the Spirit

TEXT: 2 Cor. 3:12–4:2

Object: A heating pad

Good morning, boys and girls. How many of you have a heating pad? [*Let them answer.*] Aren't they great? I think that a heating pad when you are sick is one of the best things I know. As a matter of fact, it seems to make you feel better than all of the medicine. Do you remember the last time you had a cold and felt just terrible? You were shivering one minute and so very hot the next that you knew something had to be wrong. After your mother gave you medicine, she might have asked you if you would like the heating pad. The best part of the heating pad is the little switch that comes with it. Sometimes you put the pad on your cold feet and sometimes you like to lay it under you; but you always hold on to the switch. Do you remember what the switch looks like? [*Let them answer.*] That's right, it usually has colors on it, and one of them is hotter than the rest. You can have it on warm, pretty warm, or hot. You can change it by degrees. Most people start out with hot and then change it to pretty warm and then back to nice, plain warm. You keep changing the heat by degrees with the little switch. How many of you remember that switch? [*Let them answer.*]

Do you know that Jesus is changing you by degrees just like you change the heating pad by degrees? Did you know that his Spirit is changing you every day so that you will be a little more like him all of the time? That's right. God is working on you through the Spirit to change you little bit by little bit, so you are becoming more like him every day. Isn't that great? We are changing by degrees. Do you remember the heating pad and how you would push the switch and how you would never know when it got a little cooler or a little hotter? All of a sudden is just was not as hot or as cold as it was before you moved the switch. That is the way the Spirit of God is working inside of you. Every day that you learn and practice the things Jesus teaches you, you find that you are becoming more like Jesus. I think that is wonderful and I am sure that you think so, too.

The next time you take a look at your heating pad, look at the switch and see what I mean. Turn it on to warm first, then move it up to hot. You will not know when it got hot, but pretty soon you will feel the difference. You will have changed the heat by degrees. The Spirit of God is changing you and making you more like the Lord Jesus every day. That is one of the ways God works, and I think it is one of the best. Amen.—Wesley T. Runk[6]

October 10: Storing up Treasure
TEXT: Luke 12:34
Object: Pecan or other nut
Song: "Great Is Thy Faithfulness" (2nd stanza)

Boys and girls, I'm glad you chose to come to church today. Let me share with you something I saw this morning before I came to Sunday school. I looked outside and there were two squirrels gathering pecans. Did you know that squirrels like pecans, jut like we do? As I watched, I realized that the squirrels were not eating the pecans at that time. They were holding them in their mouths—that's how squirrels gather food—and carrying them one by one back to a nest high in a tree. As soon as they deposited a nut, they returned for another. This activity continued as long as I watched. Now, let me ask you this question. Why were they carrying the nuts back to the tree? [*Wait for response.*]

Yes, they were gathering or storing food for the winter. In the fall, these are their treasures. Later in the winter, the ground may be frozen or covered with snow, and the squirrels will

---

[6]*On the Move With Jesus* (Lima Ohio: C.S.S. Publishing, 1984), pp. 15–16.

not be able to find food at that time. So, before cold weather comes, they prepare for the future. That's smart, wouldn't you say? One day they will wake up in their nest and see the snow. All they will have to do is pull a pecan out of their nest and eat breakfast. Then they will snuggle down and go back to sleep.

During the fall, let us be reminded as we watch God's creatures provide for the future that we should do likewise. Christians, who love God, store up treasures in heaven when we obey him and help others.

Listen as I read from Luke 12:34: "For where your treasure is, there your heart will be also." [*Lead the children in singing the second stanza of "Great Is Thy Faithfulness." The words of this stanza speak of summer, winter, springtime, and harvest and the order of the universe God created. Close in prayer, asking the children to remember always the greatness of God.*]— Carolyn Tomlin

October 17: A Treasure Hunt
TEXT: Mark 1:29–39, esp. v. 37
Object: Hide a jewel box somewhere in the chancel

Good morning, boys and girls. Today I need your help to find something that seems to be missing and is really a great treasure. I know that you will be a great help to me because it is somewhere in the front of the church. It isn't lost, but it is hidden, and I can tell you that it is very valuable. How many of you like to look for things that are hidden? [*Let them answer.*] Good. Now let me tell you what it looks like. [*Describe your jewel box and make it sound as valuable as you possibly can.*] Remember, we are looking not only for the box but for the most gorgeous jewels that you can imagine. Take good care and hunt quietly until you have found it. [*When someone has found the box, have him bring it back, then look through the box to make sure nothing is missing.*] That was good work and you did it so quickly. I am proud of you for both finding the box and making all of the people who use it happy again.

Finding that jewel box reminds me of the time when Jesus needed some rest after a very hard day of teaching people and healing them of their many diseases. Jesus was exhausted and needed to be by himself for a little while, so he got up very early one morning and went out to a very lonely place where he could pray. But while he was gone, the people came to where he was staying. They brought other people who were sick and crippled and asked for Jesus. The disciples, who were also tired and still asleep, thought that Jesus was close by but they could not find him. Peter, John, James, and all the others looked here and looked there, but they could not find Jesus anywhere. The people were going crazy because they wanted to see Jesus very much and no one seemed to know where he was. Finally, the disciples started a search like you did this morning. They hunted everywhere until they found him. Jesus was more valuable to the people than a jewel box. He was as important to them as life. They wanted Jesus and they were willing to hunt for him for as long as it took to find him. They searched and searched until they saw Jesus in his lonely spot praying. Quickly they ran up to him and told him how hard the people were looking for him and how glad they were to discover him when they thought he was lost. Jesus was glad to see his disciples, but he told them he had to move on to other places where there were other people who needed him as much as the people did in this village.

The next time you see a jewel box or something very valuable, I hope you will remember the day you searched for one in the front of the church and how you found it. Then you will also remember the day the disciples searched for Jesus and found him praying to his heavenly Father. How many of you will remember? That's wonderful. Amen.—Wesley T. Runk[7]

October 24: Standing Room Only

Text: Mark 2:1–12, esp. v. 2
Object: Some signs (Standing Room Only, Full, Sold Out)

Good morning, boys and girls. How many of you have ever gone to a really good movie and could not get in because all of the seats were taken? [*Let them answer.*] Maybe you went to a game or tried to get into a parking lot and there were so many cars that they could not take one more in the lot. If you did any of these things, then you will have seen the kind of signs that I brought with me this morning. Look at these signs because I am going to tell you a story that you will always remember about Jesus. [*Hold up the signs and let them read them very slowly.*] These are the kinds of signs you see when you have gotten to the place you wanted to go and there was no room for you to get in.

A long time ago Jesus was having a wonderful time traveling through small villages and the countryside. Wherever he went he healed the sick people and preached about God and his wonderful world. The people came from everywhere. As soon as they heard that Jesus was coming, they would begin looking for him and making plans for how to get the sick people in their family to Jesus so he could heal them. Men would run ahead for miles to announce to their friends that Jesus was coming. One day on such a trip the people hurried up and put away their work, cleaned up their houses, and looked for ways to carry their friends who were sick to a place where they could meet Jesus. You must remember that they didn't have cars, busses, or trains. They had to carry people on stretchers or put them in carts.

Jesus came to town and went to the biggest house he could find and began to teach. Pretty soon the crowds were so great that there was no room in the house. It was full and sold out, and there was no standing room. All of the space was gone. Most of the people stood outside and hoped they would get to see Jesus when he left. But not everyone felt they could wait. Some people had a friend who was paralyzed. He could not walk. So these friends thought of another plan. They heard that there was not one space left in the house, around the doors, or even in the windows, so they climbed to the roof. After they reached the top of the roof, they took part of it off, and then, holding ropes on both ends of the stretcher, they let their friend down through the hole in the roof until he was right in front of Jesus. How Jesus must have laughed at the sight of seeing this man coming to him out of the sky! Of course he healed him and told the men thanks for thinking so much of him and of their friend. Isn't that a good story?

If you see a sold out, standing room only, or full sign someday, I hope you will remember the time the room was packed when Jesus was preaching and how he healed the man who came to him out of the sky. Amen.—Wesley T. Runk[8]

---

[7]*Let's Share Jesus Together* (Lima, Ohio: C.S.S. Publishing, 1982), pp. 9–10.
[8]*Let's Share Jesus Together* (Lima, Ohio: C.S.S. Publishing, 1982), pp. 13–14.

October 31: Why Do Bad Things Happen to Good People?
TEXT: Hab. 1:13c
Object: Three posters of punctuation marks

I have three punctuation marks on these charts. A period follows a simple declaration, such as, "I'm going home." An exclamation point follows a bold expression, such as, "I'm going home!" A question mark follows a question such as, "When are we going home?"

Questions are very important. We learn by asking, and no doubt you are asking many questions now. Sometimes people question God. A prophet named Habakkuk asked questions because he couldn't understand the ways of God. Listen to this verse.

One question that many ask is, "Why do bad things happen to good people?" Not long ago a church group was going to church camp when their bus was wrecked. Four teenagers were killed, along with the adult driver. Our question could be, "Why didn't God prevent that wreck?" After all, those were good kids on their way to learn about God.

Any answer to this difficult question sounds bad. For instance, we could say, "God wanted those people to be in heaven with him." That doesn't sound right, because their parents and friends wanted them on Earth.

We may have questions for God, too. When we are asked questions that we can't answer, it is better simply to admit, "I don't know." Anything we say will probably make the situation worse, or indicate something about God that is not true.

To deal with hard questions, we must look at what we already know for sure. We say, "I know God is very wise and loves me," or "I know Jesus came to save us and that God is with us now." In this way, what we believe sustains us. We pray about the things we don't understand and we leave them in God's hand. We trust God and he may answer our question when the time is right.

It's okay to say, "I don't know." In most cases it is best to say that, and in the meantime we simply trust God.—Kenneth Cox

November 7: It's Guaranteed
TEXT: 1 Cor. 1:4–9, esp. v. 8
Object: Some form of guarantee cut from a newspaper or magazine

Good morning, boys and girls. How many of you have ever heard the saying, "This is guaranteed or your money back"? Do you know what that means? [*Let them answer.*] That's right. It means that whatever you buy that has a guarantee will do what it is supposed to do or you can get all your money back. I know a lot of people who will buy only certain kinds of clothes because they know that the clothes are guaranteed. There are a lot of things that are guaranteed, and when you buy these things you need not worry. Most of the time the thing you buy with a guarantee works just as the people who sold it to you said it would. But if for some reason there is something wrong with it, they will always give you your money back no matter how long you have used it or worn it. That is a guarantee.

There is another guarantee that I want to talk about this morning that is just as good as any you have ever heard of or seen. There is the guarantee that when Jesus comes back to Earth he will accept you as part of his group of believers and as members of God's world forever. For everyone who believes today and tomorrow has all of the good things that Jesus gives to us in this life; but they will also have all of the good things in the life to come. That is a guarantee. Jesus promised it and we know that his guarantee is true. We don't have to wait until the new world to be happy, to have love, to be without fear. We can have those things today when we believe in Jesus. But I want to tell you that the guarantee is that they will not stop here but will go on and on forever.

Some people wonder if God can keep such wonderful promises. They wonder if heaven can be such a good place for just believing that Jesus is the Son of God. The answer to that question is, don't wait until then to find out. If you want to see if God's guarantee is good, then try him out now. See if what he promises you comes true today. That is the guarantee of God. He will not only take care of you today but he will also take care of you in heaven. The other way is true also. God does not only guarantee you that you will find happiness in heaven, he also guarantees it to all of his believers here on Earth. The next time that you hear someone make you a guarantee about something you want to buy, I want you to think about the guarantee that God makes to all believers.—Wesley T. Runk[9]

November 14: We (and Angels) Must Make Choices
TEXT: Jude 6
Object: A Christmas angel

We think about angels more around Christmas because they are part of the account of the birth of Jesus. Humans have a lot in common with angels. We, like angels, are created to serve and worship God. Another common characteristic is that both angels and humans must choose between right and wrong.

After God created the angels, an angel named Satan chose to rebel against God. A group of angels followed Satan by making the same decision to disobey God. Listen to this verse.

Other angels did not take part in this rebellion but chose to remain obedient to God. These are the angels we hear of in the Bible who appeared to Mary and Joseph and helped God's chosen people. They are still with us today and might even be in this sanctuary right now.

We, like angels, must make a decision between following God or rebelling against him. This decision is made at a point when we accept or reject Jesus as our savior. Similar decisions must be made every day. Even though we are Christians, we must still decide between right and wrong. We must decide whether we will be selfish or unselfish. Selfish people care only about themselves and about whether they are getting what they want. If we are waiting in line at the water fountain and let someone get a drink of water first, we have made a choice to be unselfish. If a playmate tempts us to steal a piece of candy from the story, we are confronted with a decision. We can steal and become a thief or we can be courageous, say no, and remain honest.

We and angels must make choices. We must choose to be obedient every day. Then we are like the good angels that appeared to the shepherds announcing the birth of Jesus. We are like them when we decide to do unselfish, kind, and honest acts every day.—Kenneth Cox

---

[9]*Pass It On* (Lima, Ohio: C.S.S. Publishing, 1977), pp. 89–90.

November 21: Winter Wonders

TEXT: Gen. 1:1

Object: Bare tree branch or twigs

Song: "This Is My Father's World"

Hello, boys and girls. I'm glad to see you today. Now, I know you're asking yourself why I'm holding a dead branch in my hand, right? But this branch isn't really dead; it's dormant. Some might say this branch is asleep. During the winter, many trees become dormant and lose their leaves. One would think there is no life in this branch. But just wait! Come spring, what will happen? [*Wait for response.*] After the temperature begins to rise, warm rains will descend on the Earth and there will be more daylight hours, and tiny new leaves will appear on the branches.

Can you name some other signs of winter we see in the natural world? Yes, frost on your car windows, frozen ponds, snow and ice. What about longer hours of darkness and shorter hours of daylight? Many animals sleep or hibernate during the long, cold winter. Before winter begins they must eat lots of food, which provides nourishment during their time of sleep. Some animals grow warmer winter fur for protection. Some types of birds migrate or move to a warmer climate to survive the winter. There are many wonders during this season.

God had a plan when he created the Earth. He planned for the seasons and he planned for all the animals. But most important, God has a plan for you and for me. Listen as I read Genesis 1:1: "In the beginning God created the heavens and the Earth." We know that God is in control of the universe.

[*Pray that each child will realize the plans that God has for their lives. Lead them in singing one stanza of "This Is My Father's World" before they go to their seats.*]

November 28: Believers Are Like Sponges

TEXT: John 7:38

Object: Two small buckets, two different-sized sponges

Believers in the Lord Jesus Christ are like sponges. Sponges soak up water like this. By dipping this sponge in the water in this bucket we can transfer some liquid to this empty bucket. To get the water out of the sponge, we must squeeze it, like this.

When believers pray to God and receive abundant blessings, we are like sponges filled with water. We may pray for more blessings and be disturbed when those good things are not received. When this happens we are like a saturated sponge that cannot hold any more water. We are at out limit of being able to receive.

When we share the blessings of God, like squeezing a sponge, we are able to receive more blessings. God desires for us to be like channels of blessings, not filled sponges. He is willing to bless us and allow his goodness to flow into other people's lives all over the world. Those blessings are called "living water." Listen to this verse.

The Bible teaches that we can grow in grace. As we share the blessings of God we are like trees that are growing and able to bear larger quantities of fruit. So we are like larger sponges, like this. Instead of being small, we have grown, and look at the larger quantity of water that this big sponge can hold!

What are we to share? We are to share our money with those who have needs. We are to share our food with the hungry. We are to give our love to the lonely. We are to share our knowledge of Jesus with those who have never heard his name. In the process, the world is blessed because of the living water that is flowing through our lives. We are blessed too as we grow in grace. The more we grow, the more we understand how much God loves us and the world, and how he is willing to help those who need his care.

This week, pray and ask for God's blessings, but don't forget to squeeze yourself out. This way, the goodness of Jesus Christ can flow through your life to a thirsty world.—Kenneth Cox

December 5: The Difference Between Needs and Wants
TEXT: Ps. 40:1
Object: Mission picture of poverty groups
Song: "People Need the Lord"

Good morning, boys and girls. I'm glad to see you today. [*Show mission picture.*] I'm holding a picture of people who have many needs. These people need health care, their children need education, they need food for healthy bodies, they need safe drinking water, and they need homes that protect them from the old winds and heat of summer. The parents of these children need jobs to support their families. Some of these children may live in an orphanage because their parents have died from disease, or from war, or their parents may not be able to care for them at home.

I would say that for most of you these needs have already been met. You have families who provide nutritious food, comfortable homes, and safe water. You attend school and you see a doctor when you become ill. These are basic human requirements. Of course, we all also have *wants,* or things we think we need. Can you list some things that are outside the needs list? [*Wait for response.*] What about a new bicycle, a new dress, or brand-name athletic shoes advertised by a popular sports figure. Parents may want a new car, a new house, or an expensive vacation.

Now, let me ask you this: Which is more important to survival, a *want* or a *need?* A need, of course. That brings me to the focus of this children's sermon. All people need the Lord. Our missionaries go into foreign countries to tell people about Jesus. But we have people living in our own community who do not attend church or maybe have never been to church. They need to know Jesus, too.

Listen as I read from Psalm 40:17: "Yet I am poor and needy; may the Lord think of me. You are my help and my deliverer; O my God, do not delay." [*Pray, asking God to make the children aware that they need the Lord in all things. Ask a soloist to sing both stanzas of "People Need the Lord" before the children return to their seats.*]—Carolyn Tomlin

December 12: The First Christmas
TEXT: Luke 2:7
Object: Small nativity scene
Song: "Silent Night, Holy Night"

Hello, boys and girls. I'm happy to see you. Today we are talking about a special holiday that is coming up in which we give and receive presents. Does anyone know which holiday I'm thinking of? [*Wait for response.*] Of course, it's Christmas. Listen as I tell you about the first Christmas. As I mention each person, I'll place them in the nativity scene.

Mary and Joseph had to travel to the town of David, which was Bethlehem, to register, as was demanded by Caesar Augustus. While they were there, Mary's baby was born. But there were no hotels for the travelers to stay in. Joseph found a stable where animals lived and some fresh hay. He filled a small wooden box with hay and Mary wrapped the baby in soft cloths and placed him in the manger.

In a nearby field, shepherds watched their flocks that same night. An angel of the Lord appeared to them, and the angel said, "Do not be afraid. I bring you good news of great joy that will be for all the people. A Savior has been born to you; he is Christ the Lord. Go to Bethlehem and you will find the baby wrapped in cloths and lying in a manger." When the angels left, the shepherds hurried to Bethlehem and found Mary, Joseph, and the baby. They bowed and worshiped the new king.

The shepherds left and spread the word about what had been told to them about this child. Everyone who heard it was amazed at what the shepherds said to them. This was the first Christmas, and it's the real reason we celebrate Christmas today—to honor the birthday of the Christ child.

We've already used Scripture in today's sermon, but let me read to you Luke 2:7: "And she gave birth to her firstborn, a son. She wrapped him in cloths and placed him in a manger, because there was no room for them in the inn." [*Lead the children and congregation in singing "Silent Night, Holy Night." Close in prayer, asking God to bless each child during this holy season.*]

December 19: A Gift for Jesus
TEXT: 2 Cor. 8:3
Object: Several coins
Song: "What Can I Give Him"

Hello, boys and girls. I'm glad to see you today. [*Reach into pocket and remove some coins, such as pennies, nickels, and dimes. Look at the money. Count the amount.*] You know, I was thinking about what this money would buy. If this were your money, how would you spend it? [*Wait for response.*] Yes, you could buy some candy, a soft drink, perhaps an ice cream cone. Or you might buy someone in your family a small present. Do you have other suggestions as to how this money could be spent? [*Wait for response.*]

Did anyone think about giving this to God? You might think that this amount of money wouldn't go very far in supporting our church, or that it wouldn't make much difference when the church budget is large. But when we all give the resources that God has allowed us to earn, we can do great things for Christ. Let's talk a minute about where the money we give to our local church goes. First, we give a percentage to our convention. Some of the money stays in our local association and Christian agencies. Our money also pays the salaries of the church staff. Missionaries around the world depend on our offerings, and we must pay for utilities and for the maintenance of our buildings. So you see, it is very important that we all do our part in supporting the Kingdom of God.

We read in 2 Corinthians 8:3, "For I testify that they gave us much as they were able, and ever beyond their ability." [*Lead the children in singing "What Can I Give Him." Pray, thank-*

ing God for our church and for the people who support his kingdom. Ask the pianist to continue playing as the children return to their seats.]—Carolyn Tomlin

December 26: A Gift for Jesus
TEXT: 2 Cor. 8:5
Object: An attractively wrapped present with a red paper heart inside
Song: "What Can I Give Him?"

Hello, boys and girls. I'm glad to see you today. You must be wondering what I have wrapped as a present. Let's see what happens if I shake it. Nothing. Does it have an odor? No. There is nothing about this present that tells you what it is—until it is opened. Well, why don't we open it? [*Make sure that all of the children can see as you open the present and remove the heart.*] Now, why would I wrap a red paper heart? Can anyone tell me? [*Wait for response.*]

In the 1800s, Christina G. Rossetti wrote a simple poem entitled "What Can I Give Him?" The poem was about a child wanting to give the Baby Jesus a gift, but the child was so poor she could not afford a present. If she were a shepherd she would bring him a lamb. If she were a Wise Man she could do her part. At the end, she decides that giving Jesus her heart would be the best present she could give.

And you know something? When you give Jesus your heart and live for him, that makes him very happy. In fact, that's the best present you could give. So the next time you see a heart like this, remember that your best gift is to give yourself.

Read 2 Corinthians 8:5: "They gave themselves first to the Lord." [*Lead the children in singing "What Can I Give Him?" Close in prayer, asking each child to give Jesus their best gift, their heart.*]—Carolyn Tomlin

CONTRIBUTORS AND ACKNOWLEDGMENTS

CONTRIBUTORS

Block, Daniel I. Sampey Professor of Old Testament Interpretation, Southern Baptist Theological Seminary, Louisville, Kentucky

Bramlett, Perry C. Minister, author and lecturer, C. S. Lewis for the Local Church Interstate Ministries, Louisville, Kentucky

Brand, Rick. Pastor, First Presbyterian Church, Henderson, North Carolina

Caldwell, Chris. Pastor, Broadway Baptist Church, Louisville, Kentucky

Cox, Ken. Pastor, First Baptist Church, New Barton, Texas

Dipboye, Larry. Pastor, First Baptist Church, Oak Ridge, Tennessee

Dockery, David S. President, Union University, Jackson, Tennessee

Durst, Rodrick K. Dean, Golden Gate Baptist Theological Seminary, Mill Valley, California

Farmer, David Albert. Pastor, Silverside Church, Wilmington, Delaware

Feddes, David. Preacher on The Radio Pulpit of "The Back to God Hour," Palos Heights, Illinois

Ferguson, Robert U. Pastor, Emerywood Baptist Church, High Point, North Carolina

Ferris, Theodore Parker. Former rector, Trinity Church, Boston, Massachusetts

Fields, Henry. Pastor, First Baptist Church, Toccoa, Georgia

Green, Cheryl L. Associate pastor, Ebenezer A.M.E. Church, Evanston, Illinois

Hammer, Randy. Pastor, First Congregationalist Church, Albany, New York

Harding, Joe A. Retired United Methodist minister, Nashville, Tennessee

Holladay, Jim. Pastor, Lyndon Baptist Church, Louisville, Kentucky

Huffman, John C. Retired Baptist minister, Louisville, Kentucky

406

Hull, David W. Pastor, First Baptist Church, Huntsville, Alabama

Hull, William E. Professor and former administrator, Samford University, Birmingham, Alabama

Killinger, John. President, Mission for Biblical Literacy, Warrenton, Virginia

Lacy, Donald Charles. United Methodist minister and author, Yorktown, Indiana

Landrum, Eli, Jr. Baptist pastor and editor

Langwig, Robert. Retired Presbyterian minister, Tucson, Arizona

Lloyd, Samuel T., III. Rector, Trinity (Episcopal) Church, Boston, Massachusetts

Lytch, Stephens G. Pastor, Second Presbyterian Church, Louisville, Kentucky

Massey, James Earl. Dean Emeritus and professor at Anderson University School of Theology and former Dean of the Chapel and professor at Tuskegee University

Matthews, C. David. Baptist pastor

McEachern, Alton H. Retired pastor, Sharpsburg, Georgia

Moore, William G. Pastor, Cornerstone Baptist Church, Clinton, South Carolina

Murphy, Lael P. Associate minister at The Old South Church, Boston, Massachusetts

Norén, Carol M. Author and professor of preaching, North Park Theological Seminary, Chicago, Illinois

Phillips, E. Lee. Minister and freelance writer, Norcross, Georgia

Pratt, Lucy. Candidate for Holy Orders, Church of the Epiphany (Episcopal), Chicago, Illinois

Proper, Heather. Candidate for ministry in the Evangelical Covenant Church, Chicago, Illinois

Richardson, Paul A. Professor of music, Beeson Divinity School, Samford University, Birmingham, Alabama

Runk, Wesley T. Lutheran minister and owner of the C.S.S. Publishing Company, Lima, Ohio

Schweizer, Eduard. Author, retired professor, and rektor (president), University of Zurich, Switzerland

Shields, Bruce E. Professor of preaching, Emmanuel School of Religion, Johnson City, Tennessee

Skinner, Craig. Author, retired professor of practical theology, and native of Australia recently residing in Hiram, Georgia

Standiford, Jim. Pastor, First United Methodist Church, San Diego, California

Stout, Kenneth B. Professor of preaching and Christian ministry, Andrews University, Barrien Springs, Michigan

Strand, Tyler A. Dean, Cathedral of the Holy Trinity (Episcopal), Makati City, Metro Manila, Republic of the Philippines

Stratman, Gary D. Pastor, First and Calvary Presbyterian Church, Springfield, Missouri

Tate, Marvin. Senior professor of old testament interpretation, Southern Baptist Theological Seminary, Louisville, Kentucky

Thomas, Christy. United Methodist minister, Wichita Falls, Texas

Thompson, John. Minster of pastoral care, Venice Presbyterian Church, Venice, Florida

Tomlin, Carolyn. Writer for a variety of publications, specializing in church curriculum materials, Jackson, Tennessee

Tomlin, W. Matt. Pastor, Ward's Grove Baptist Church, Jackson, Tennessee

Tuck, William Powell. Retired Baptist minister, Richmond, Virginia
Turner, William, L. Teacher of preaching and retired pastor, South Main Baptist Church, Houston, Texas
Vinson, Richard B. Dean, Baptist Theological Seminary at Richmond, Richmond, Virginia
Walsh, Albert J. D. Pastor, Heidelberg United Church of Christ, Heidelberg, Pennsylvania
Warner, Laceye. Professor of evangelism, Duke University Divinity School, Durham, North Carolina

ACKNOWLEDGMENTS

All of the following are used by permission:
Excerpts from C. David Matthews in *Award Winning Sermons,* Vol. 2, ed. by James C. Barry, (Nashville: Broadman Press, 1978), pp. 47–53.
Excerpts from Eli Landrum Jr., *More Than Symbol* (Nashville: Broadman Press, 1983), pp. 96–98.
Excerpts from David Feddes, "Healing Broken Hearts" (Ps. 147:3), *The Back to God Hour,* Vol. 45, No. 6.

INDEX OF CONTRIBUTORS

SERMON TITLE INDEX

Children's sermons are marked as (cs); sermon suggestions as (ss)

SCRIPTURAL INDEX

INDEX OF PRAYERS

INDEX OF MATERIALS
USEFUL AS CHILDREN'S STORIES AND
SERMONS NOT INCLUDED IN SECTION XI

INDEX OF MATERIALS USEFUL
FOR SMALL GROUPS

TOPICAL INDEX

426

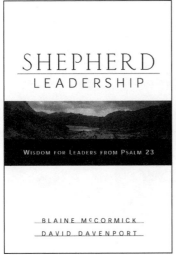

Shepherd Leadership:
Wisdom for Leaders from Psalm 23

Blaine McCormick
David Davenport
Foreword by Ken Blanchard
$21.95 Hardcover
ISBN: 0-7879-6633-9

"What a joy to learn that David Davenport has placed his thoughts on paper! He has touched thousands with his teaching—may he and Blaine touch even more through this book."

—Max Lucado, best-selling author and pulpit minister,
Oak Hills Church of Christ

"Providing fresh insight into one of the most cherished texts in the Bible, David Davenport and Blaine McCormick walk with us beside the 'quiet waters' of our contemplation and embolden us for ethical, fearless, and transformational leadership. The truth of the Psalmist's verse never changes, only our needs and willingness to listen to Shepherd's voice. This book enables, ennobles, and encourages the Christian leader for even greater service."

—Andrew K. Benton, president, Pepperdine University

Psalm 23, the Shepherd's Psalm, provides us with ancient wisdom for today's business leadership challenges—and a lens through which to consider our own leadership as well as the leadership of those around us. It teaches that we can be vigilant without being adversarial, that we can serve without being passive, and that we can guide without commanding. *Shepherd Leadership* offers a visionary new model for transforming leadership practices in business, nonprofit, and religious settings. McCormick and Davenport inspire leaders with a fresh interpretation of this familiar biblical passage, helping all to integrate their spiritual life with their working life through a unique blend of spiritual wisdom and business leadership strategy.

BLAINE McCORMICK (Waco, TX) is assistant professor of business management at Hankamer School of Business, Baylor University. He is a business consultant, speaker, and the author of two previous books.

DAVID DAVENPORT (Danville, CA) is Distinguished Professor of Public Policy and Law at Pepperdine University. He also serves on a number of corporate and nonprofit boards. He was formerly president of Pepperdine University and president of Starwire, Inc.

[Price subject to change]

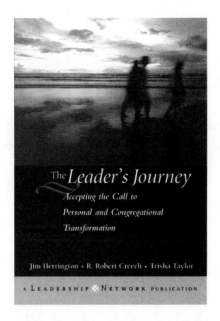

The Leader's Journey: Accepting the Call to Personal and Congregational Transformation

Jim Herrington
R. Robert Creech
Trisha Taylor
$23.95 Paperback
ISBN: 0-7879-6266-X

"*The Leader's Journey* is a gift that issues from the authors' unflagging commitment to the ministry of the church and a love for the church's leaders who labor faithfully for the church."
—J. Bradley Creed, provost and professor of religion, Samford University, Birmingham, Alabama

"*The Leader's Journey* made my brain sweat (fresh ways to think) and filled my heart with hope (the possibility of transformation). This is not a quick-fix disappointment. Enjoy the pathway it's transforming."
—Jared Roth, vice-president and COO, International Church of the Foursquare Gospel

Many books describe elements of church leadership—what it is and how to do it—but very few focus on the process of personal transformation that is central to being able to lead well. Based on sound psychological research and theory and the Leader's Edge seminars, *The Leader's Journey* provides pragmatic steps for engaging in the personal transformation journey as part of effective congregational leadership. The book builds on Jim Herrington's earlier *Leading Congregational Change* to combine the best of two views of leadership—leadership as organizational development and leadership as personal transformation—and gives readers a practical, programmatic process to help them grow as leaders.

JIM HERRINGTON (Bellaire, TX) is executive director of Mission Houston, an interdenominational, multicultural group of churches in the greater Houston, Texas, area.

R. ROBERT CREECH (Houston, TX) has been senior pastor of the 3,000-member University Baptist Church in Houston, Texas, since 1987.

TRISHA TAYLOR (Houston, TX) is a fellow in the American Association of Pastoral Counselors and serves on the staff of the Union Baptist Association Center for Counseling in Houston, Texas.

[Price subject to change]

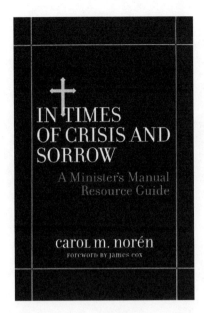

In Times of Crisis and Sorrow: A Minister's Manual Resource Guide

Carol M. Norén
Foreword by James Cox
$24.95 Hardcover
ISBN: 0-7879-5420-9

"One of the finest contributions to pastoral publishing this year . . ."
—Preachings, 1/02

"A practical, thoughtful (and exceedingly thorough) resource no pastor should be without! Norén offers the kind of help many (new) pastors have longed for."
—Jana Childers, professor of homiletics, San Francisco Theological Seminary

"A remarkably thorough and helpful resource. Norén offers valuable theological reflection, contextual analysis, and pastoral guidance for ministry in times of crisis and sorrow. I wish I had had this book when I was a pastor."
—Charles L. Campbell, associate professor of homiletics, Columbia Theological Seminary, Decatur, Georgia

In a single volume, *In Times of Crisis and Sorrow: A Minister's Manual Resource Guide* offers a practical and professional guide for dealing with grief, sorrow, crises, and other difficult situations in the life of a congregation. In addition to containing a wealth of new material, the book also draws from the best of *The Minister's Manual*, which has served as a well-thumbed resource and a source of inspiration for more than seventy-five years. *In Times of Crisis and Sorrow* is a much-needed desk reference that takes an ecumenical approach and includes a wealth of illustrative examples and valuable material, such as scripture readings, prayers, eulogies, sermons, and testimonials.

CAROL M. NORÉN (Chicago, IL) is on the faculty of North Park Theological Seminary. She is an ordained minister and has been a hospital chaplain. She has taught at Princeton Theological Seminary and Duke Divinity School and has also been a guest lecturer at seminaries in Europe, Australia, and across the United States.

[Price subject to change]